BRITAIN

**FODOR'S
TRAVEL PUBLICATIONS**

NEW YORK • TORONTO
LONDON • SYDNEY • AUCKLAND

WWW.FODORS.COM

CONTENTS

KEY TO SYMBOLS

- Map reference
- Address
- Telephone number
- Opening times
- Admission prices
- Underground station
- Bus number
- Train station
- Ferry/boat
- Driving directions
- Tourist office
- Tours
- Guidebook
- Restaurant
- Café
- Bar
- Shop
- Number of rooms
- Air conditioning
- Swimming pool
- Gym
- Other useful information
- ▷ Cross reference
- ★ Walk/drive start point

Understanding Britain	**5**
Living Britain	13
The Story of Britain	27
On the Move	**43**
Arriving	44
Getting Around	46
Visitors with a Disability	62
Regions	**63**
London	**64**
Sights	72
Walks	92
What to Do	100
Eating	108
Staying	114
The West Country	**118**
Sights	120
Walks and Drives	146
What to Do	154
Eating	160
Staying	166
The South East and East Anglia	**170**
Sights	172
Walks and Drives	202
What to Do	206
Eating	212
Staying	218

Wales   **222**
     Sights   224
     Walks and Drives   240
     What to Do   252
     Eating   256
     Staying   260

The Midlands   **264**
     Sights   266
     Walks and Drives   282
     What to Do   286
     Eating   292
     Staying   296

The North   **300**
     Sights   302
     Walks and Drives   326
     What to Do   342
     Eating   348
     Staying   354

Scotland   **358**
     Sights   360
     Walks and Drives   386
     What to Do   394
     Eating   400
     Staying   406

Practicalities   **411**

Maps   **454**

Index   **475**

175

120

322

366

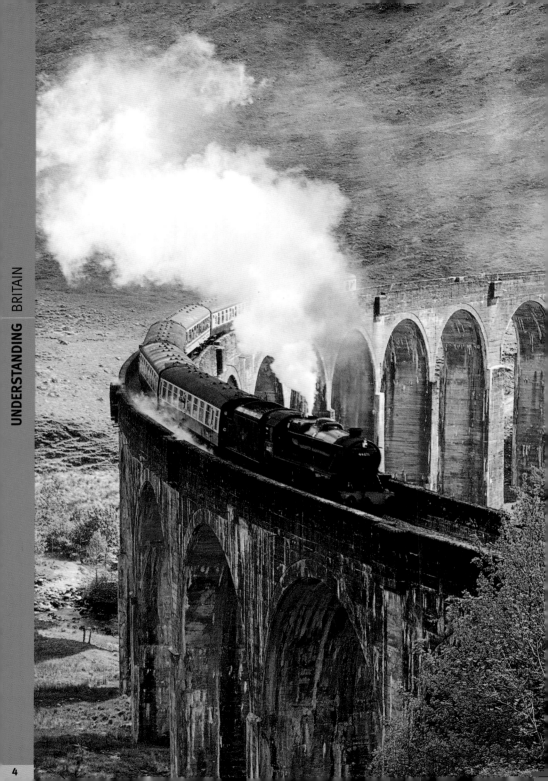

UNDERSTANDING BRITAIN

Understanding Britain is an introduction to the country, its geography, economy, history and its people, giving a real insight into the nation. Living Britain gets under the skin of Britain today, while The Story of Britain takes you through the country's past.

Understanding Britain   6
    The Best of Britain   10

Living Britain   13

The Story of Britain   27

On a map of the world Britain looks surprisingly small. But don't assume that you can see the whole country in just a week or two. Unrivalled variety, from world-class culture in dynamic cities to a beautiful, subtle patchwork of landscapes shaped by thousands of years of history, is concentrated in this densely populated island. Britain's inhabitants can be contradictory. They can prize both order and individuality, and value tradition but look forward rather than back. They've made their mark on their island with prehistoric monuments, castles, stately homes and elegant abbeys, all playing a part in Britain's dramatic history. And they've changed the world with the English language, the Industrial Revolution…and the gin and tonic.

WHAT IS BRITAIN?

Even to those who live there, the word 'Britain' is a source of confusion. It covers England, Wales and Scotland. Britain plus Northern Ireland equals the United Kingdom, the political entity that is governed from the capital city, London. The Republic of Ireland is a separate country, but the islands of Ireland and Britain plus the Channel Islands make up the British Isles. A government survey in 2001 found that fewer than half of Britons thought of themselves as British; they much preferred to describe themselves as English, Welsh or Scottish.

Covering 130,357sq km (50,318sq miles) England is the largest nation in Britain, followed by Scotland at 77,080sq km (29,753sq miles), then Wales at 20,758sq km (8,012sq miles).

In a country where every hillside and woodland is named, it is not surprising that Britain's regions have a proliferation of names. England, Wales and Scotland consist of areas of local government known as counties. Most counties have very long histories, distinct characters and attract fierce loyalties. We've divided Britain into seven regions, based on county boundaries and London, see the map on page 9.

THE ECONOMY

In the 19th century Britain was the world's superpower and its empire stretched across one quarter of the world's surface. Two world wars diminished the country's strength and influence considerably. Today the UK is one of the top three European economies and a member of the G8 group of leading industrialized nations. Services and the financial sector are superseding manufacturing and industry as the basis of the economy. Unemployment is low compared to some European countries, but there are pockets of deprivation in most cities, and rural economies are increasingly threadbare as the younger generation relocate to the cities to find work.

POLITICS

Despite being one of the first countries to develop a parliamentary democracy, Britain retains a monarch, currently Queen Elizabeth II. Decisions are made in two debating chambers: the House of Lords and the House of Commons. The Commons, where ultimate legislative power rests, consists of 646 Members of Parliament (MPs) who each represent a constituency in the UK. There are three main political parties: Labour,

Liberal Democrat and Conservative. Britain's 'first past the post' electoral system, in which the MP who wins the most votes in their constituency then represents their party in Parliament, generally means that one party is in overall control and forms the government. Since 1997 the official Opposition has been the Conservatives (the Tories), with the Liberal Democrats also wielding considerable influence. The current Labour government is led by Prime Minister Gordon Brown. One of the first policies to be put into effect by the Labour government, in the last ten years, was to devolve power to Scotland, Wales and Northern Ireland. The Welsh Assembly in Cardiff has 60 members and Scotland's Parliament has 129 MSPs (Members of the Scottish Parliament). These bodies make decisions about their respective countries' domestic issues such as health and education.

Britain is a member of the European Union (EU) and the North Atlantic Treaty Organization (NATO), and is one of the five permanent members of the United Nations Security Council. Relations with other European nations are usually good, if complex, and Britain often acts as a transatlantic intermediary between the United States and the rest of Europe.

HERITAGE

Look beyond the modern veneer of Britain and you find links to the past everywhere. Many British cities and towns have Roman origins: place names ending with 'caster' or 'chester', for example, come from the Roman word *castrum*, meaning a military base. So unruly were the locals that Britain was the only province in the Roman Empire to have a permanent garrison of soldiers. Medieval walls remain intact around York, Chester and Conwy, with substantial remains elsewhere.

By early medieval times most of today's settlements were already on the map. Their names are not far removed from the originals. The suffixes -ham, -ton and

-ing suggest Saxon origins; Vikings from Scandinavia settled in eastern England in places that carry the suffix -by (such as Whitby).

For many centuries, Britain's most impressive buildings were castles, stately homes and places of worship. Castles were erected to defend coasts, towns and borders. Many were deliberately 'slighted' (rendered unusable) by opponents—

notably during the Civil War in the 17th century—and now stand as jagged ruins. Kenilworth Castle is one of the finest of these. The opulent stately homes of Britain's landed gentry can also be hugely impressive, and today many are open to the public.

Religious buildings provide another key to the country's past. While Saxon church architecture is rare, the Normans introduced a huge scheme of church building. Their rounded arches gave way in turn to elaborate Gothic flourishes. Meanwhile, monasteries were among the richest landowners of medieval Britain. Their dissolution in the 1530s by Henry VIII ended a centuries-old way of life. Most became roofless ruins; many stand today as poignant landmarks.

Britain's countryside has been shaped by its people. Throughout the centuries, settlers have largely removed Britain's ancient forests, leaving tracts of moorland on higher ground, full of heather, bogs and bracken; at lower levels, fields are bounded by hedges and dry-stone walls.

Pre-Roman settlers left numerous reminders of their existence. The early farming communities of the Neolithic period and Bronze Age erected ceremonial sites, such as stone circles and burial mounds. You can find some of Britain's richest concentrations of such prehistoric sites in western Cornwall, Dartmoor (in Devon), Wiltshire and even as far north as the Orkney Islands in Scotland.

LANGUAGE

English owes its roots to a mixture of Teutonic and Latin languages, reflecting waves of invasion during the early medieval period. Through Britain's vast colonial expansion it has become the first language of approximately 375 million people, and is understood by many more.

Traditional English dialects have been steadily eroded over the past century. Where there are differences, they tend to be minor. But somehow accents have survived to a surprising degree. The Scottish accent is unmistakable; the West Coast accent (especially around Glasgow) can be incomprehensible to outsiders. Speakers in Yorkshire and Lancashire tend to use broad vowel sounds with subtle local variations. Liverpudlian has been immortalized by the Beatles, Brummy is the key signature of the West Midlands, South Wales has a singsong quality and the West Country has a distinct burr. In the South East the differences have blurred, with 'Estuary English' gaining ground over the crisp Home Counties accent.

Welsh, an old Celtic language that was used by the Iron Age peoples before the Romans arrived, is still spoken by around a quarter of the population of Wales. Banned by Henry VIII when Wales was officially united with England in 1535, it survived and is now taught in schools, and appears on bilingual signs. In Scotland, Gaelic is another ancient Celtic language, but it is less widely spoken than Welsh.

Opposite *Sunrise at Stonehenge, a 5,000 year old monument*
Left *Scottish clans were identified by their different tartans*

BRITAIN'S REGIONS AT A GLANCE

THE WEST COUNTRY

Cornwall, Devon, Dorset, Wiltshire, Somerset and Gloucestershire. *Main cities: Bristol, Plymouth.* The West Country has beautiful, long beaches along an extraordinarily varied coastline. Prehistoric sites punctuate the rural landscape.

THE SOUTH EAST AND EAST ANGLIA

Counties surrounding London—Hertfordshire, Essex, Buckinghamshire, Surrey—are known as the Home Counties. Sussex (West and East), Berkshire, the Isle of Wight and Hampshire don't neighbour London but are considered part of the South East. *Main city: London.* The South East is densely populated, yet has large areas of countryside—much of it a prosperous commuterdom known as the 'stockbroker belt', with property prices to match. East Anglia comprises Norfolk, Suffolk, Cambridgeshire and northern Essex. *Main cities: Cambridge, Peterborough, Norwich.* Mainly flat, fertile farmland towards England's east coast, East Anglia is dominated by fields of crops, watery landscapes of reedy marshes and coastal dunes (including some important bird reserves), country estates and historic villages and small towns, many with imposing churches and varied architecture.

LONDON

Greater London includes vast suburbs that stretch out to the M25 motorway. Inner, or central, London is the political and economic heart of Britain.

THE MIDLANDS

Ill-defined, but includes the central English 'shires', including Warwickshire, Shropshire, Herefordshire, Staffordshire, Derbyshire, Leicestershire, Rutland, Worcestershire, Nottinghamshire and Northamptonshire—and arguably Lincolnshire. *Main cities: Birmingham, Coventry, Nottingham, Derby, Leicester.* Britain's industrial heartland is in the Midlands, notably around Birmingham and the surrounding 'Black Country', with some of the world's earliest Industrial Revolution sites. Here, the Peak District, with its spectacular scenery, is among the most prized landscapes.

WALES

Main cities: Cardiff, Swansea. Wales is an ancient kingdom, separate from England until 1535, and with its own Assembly since 1999. It's largely rural, with most of the population living in the south. The Marches share the borderland with England. South Wales includes the industrial valleys north of Cardiff—now economic backwaters since coal mining has virtually halted. In mid-Wales sheep outnumber people. North Wales includes Snowdonia, the highest mountain area in Wales and England, and the low-lying Isle of Anglesey. Pembrokeshire, in the west, is known for its unspoiled coast.

THE NORTH

Yorkshire, Lancashire, Cumbria, Durham and Northumberland. *Main cities: Leeds, Bradford, Manchester, Liverpool, Sheffield, Newcastle.* England's highest land, including the Pennine Hills that divide the region in two, the North spans the mountains of the Lake District and the heathery plateaux of the North York Moors. It is densely populated in the south, but much emptier farther north, beyond York and west of Newcastle, and towards central and northern Northumberland.

SCOTLAND

Main cities: Glasgow, Edinburgh, Aberdeen. Natural features divide Scotland more clearly than its administrative districts. The mountainous Western Highlands feature the Trossachs; Wester Ross, among the most spectacular of all highland scenery, in the far northwest; the Cairngorm Mountains; the islands and archipelagos, including the Western Isles or Outer Hebrides (Lewis and Harris, North Uist, South Uist and Barra), the Inner Hebrides (Skye, Arran, Mull, Bute and smaller islands), and the isles of Orkney and Shetland. Lowlands flow south of the Highland Fault, including Glasgow and Edinburgh, the Southern Uplands and the green hills and ruined abbeys of the Borders.

Below *Fishing boats still ply the waters back to Whitby harbour*
Right *The Jaws of Borrowdale, Lake District*

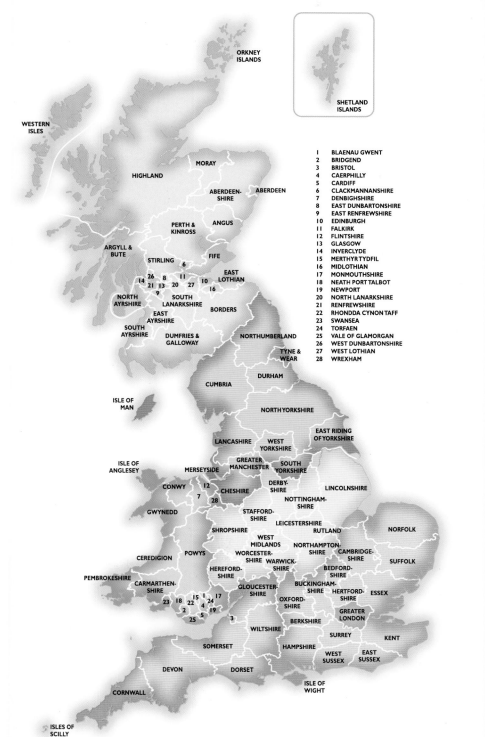

ORKNEY
ISLANDS

SHETLAND
ISLANDS

WESTERN
ISLES

MORAY

HIGHLAND

ABERDEEN-
SHIRE   ABERDEEN

PERTH &
KINROSS   ANGUS

ARGYLL &
BUTE

STIRLING   FIFE
6
14 26 8 11   EAST
21 13 20 27 10   LOTHIAN
9   16
NORTH
AYRSHIRE   SOUTH
LANARKSHIRE
EAST   BORDERS
AYRSHIRE
SOUTH
AYRSHIRE   DUMFRIES &
GALLOWAY   NORTHUMBERLAND

TYNE &
WEAR

DURHAM

ISLE OF
MAN   CUMBRIA

NORTH YORKSHIRE

EAST RIDING
OF YORKSHIRE
LANCASHIRE   WEST
YORKSHIRE
ISLE OF   GREATER   SOUTH
ANGLESEY   MERSEYSIDE   MANCHESTER   YORKSHIRE
CONWY   DERBY-   LINCOLNSHIRE
12   CHESHIRE   SHIRE
7   NOTTINGHAM-
GWYNEDD   28   SHIRE
STAFFORD-
SHIRE   LEICESTERSHIRE
SHROPSHIRE   RUTLAND   NORFOLK
WEST
CEREDIGION   POWYS   MIDLANDS   NORTHAMPTON-
WORCESTER-   SHIRE   CAMBRIDGE-
SHIRE   WARWICK-   SHIRE   SUFFOLK
PEMBROKESHIRE   HEREFORD-   SHIRE   BEDFORD-
SHIRE   SHIRE
CARMARTHEN-   BUCKINGHAM-   HERTFORD-
SHIRE   GLOUCESTER-   SHIM   SHIRE   ESSEX
23 18   15 17   SHIRE   OXFORD-
2 22 4 24   SHIRE   GREATER
5 19   LONDON
25   3   BERKSHIRE   KENT
WILTSHIRE   SURREY
SOMERSET   HAMPSHIRE   EAST
WEST   SUSSEX
SUSSEX
DEVON   DORSET
ISLE OF
WIGHT
CORNWALL

ISLES OF
SCILLY

1	BLAENAU GWENT
2	BRIDGEND
3	BRISTOL
4	CAERPHILLY
5	CARDIFF
6	CLACKMANNANSHIRE
7	DENBIGHSHIRE
8	EAST DUNBARTONSHIRE
9	EAST RENFREWSHIRE
10	EDINBURGH
11	FALKIRK
12	FLINTSHIRE
13	GLASGOW
14	INVERCLYDE
15	MERTHYR TYDFIL
16	MIDLOTHIAN
17	MONMOUTHSHIRE
18	NEATH PORT TALBOT
19	NEWPORT
20	NORTH LANARKSHIRE
21	RENFREWSHIRE
22	RHONDDA CYNON TAFF
23	SWANSEA
24	TORFAEN
25	VALE OF GLAMORGAN
26	WEST DUNBARTONSHIRE
27	WEST LOTHIAN
28	WREXHAM

LONDON

British Museum, London (▷ 74) Nothing less than an anthology of civilization; highlights include the Egyptian Room and the treasures from Sutton Hoo in Suffolk.

Royal Botanic Gardens, Kew, Surrey (▷ 81) Awarded World Heritage status in 2003, Kew's Royal Botanic Gardens have an unparalleled collection of plants.

St. Paul's Cathedral (▷ 86) Sir Christopher Wren's masterpiece is a dramatic combination of vast, airy spaces and elaborate decoration.

Tate Modern, London (▷ 89) You'll either love the art or not, but there's no disputing the triumphant building.

Tower of London (▷ 90) Prison, palace, home to the Crown Jewels and symbol of 1,000 years of Britain's royal history.

THE WEST COUNTRY

Avebury, Wiltshire (▷ 121) Avebury is home to Britain's largest stone circle.

Bath, Somerset (▷ 122) Britian's most elegant and most complete Georgian city and home to the country's only hot spring.

Lost Gardens of Heligan, Cornwall (▷ 135) Thankfully found and being restored, there are exotic plants, summer houses, pools and a grotto to discover at this fantastic estate.

Westonbirt Arboretum, Gloucestershire (▷ 145) 18,000 trees, including many rare species, in one of Europe's most diverse collections.

THE SOUTH EAST AND EAST ANGLIA

Bignor Roman Villa, West Sussex (▷ 174) Bignor's second-century owners commissioned breathtaking mosaics for their house, which survive today.

Weald and Downland Open Air Museum, West Sussex (▷ 197) More than 40 historic buildings, from medieval homes to a Victorian school, all in the fresh air.

Dover Castle, Kent (▷ 181) From the Iron Age to the Cold War, this fortress has defended Britain's shores; exhibitions and reconstructions tell its story.

Windsor Castle (▷ 200) Admire the Queen's principal residence and the largest occupied castle in the world.

Hampton Court Palace, Surrey (▷ 183) Once a home to British monarchs, this Tudor palace on the Thames has magnificent interiors, gardens and a tricky maze.

Royal Pavilion, Brighton (▷ 175) An Indian-style stone-built palace constructed in the early 19th century for the Prince Regent, King George IV.

WALES

Caernarfon Castle, Gwynedd (▷ 227) Dwarfing the town, this harbourside castle was built by Edward I in 1283.

Bodnant Garden, Conwy (▷ 227) With blazing flower displays in a gorgeous location in Wales, Bodnant is one of Britain's most popular gardens.

Snowdonia National Park (▷ 248) Wales's largest and most dramatic national park draws walkers and outdoor enthusiasts from around the world.

MIDLANDS

Chatsworth House, Derbyshire (▷ 269) A palatial 17th-century house in the country with plenty of stories to tell.

Ironbridge Gorge Museums, Staffordshire (▷ 272 Several fascinating museums stand in the true birthplace of the Industrial Revolution.

Peak District National Park (▷ 275) The caverns and crags of the Peak District are a perennial draw to walkers and outdoor enthusiasts.

Stratford-upon-Avon, Warwickshire (▷ 276) The home of Britain's greatest playwright and a wealth of Tudor architecture.

Warwick Castle, Warwickshire (▷ 281) A slickly run showpiece castle, with lots of holiday events.

THE NORTH

Baltic Centre for Contemporary Art, Newcastle upon Tyne (▷ 316) An art gallery leading the way in a city's regeneration.

Castle Howard, Yorkshire (▷ 306) The drive through the estate is a dramatic prelude to this grand 18th-century house, still the home of the Howard family.

Castlerigg Stone Circle, Cumbria (▷ 328) At the heart of the Lake District, this megalithic monument has a more scenic location than Stonehenge (▷ 143).

Hadrian's Wall, Northumberland (▷ 308) One Roman emperor's attempt to keep northern barbarians out is now Britain's most spectacular Roman ruin.

Hazelwood, York (▷ 357) An elegant and useful bed-and-breakfast in the heart of York.

Lindisfarne Priory, Northumberland (▷ 312) Founded in AD635, Lindisfarne was an early crucible of English Christianity and remains a place of pilgrimage.

Linthwaite House, Windermere (▷ 357) A delightful hilltop hotel in the Lake District with a fishing lake.

Rievaulx Abbey, Yorkshire (▷ 318) Perhaps the most beautiful and moving of England's ruined monasteries.

SCOTLAND

Burrell Collection, Glasgow (▷ 372) An outstanding collection of art, textiles and objects from around the world.

Calanais Standing Stones, Isle of Lewis (▷ 380) Pre-dating Egypt's pyramids by a millennium, there's mystery and beauty in these standing stones.

Eilean Donan Castle, Highlands (▷ 370) Imagine a classic Scottish castle beside a misty loch, it's probably Eilean Donan that you're thinking of.

Gleneagles, Auchterarder (▷ 401) Two convincing reasons to stay at Scotland's top hotel: the golf and Andrew Fairlie's sublime cooking in the restaurant.

Inverewe Gardens, Highlands (▷ 376) Plants from the Himalayas, the Antipodes and South America flourish in this remote Scottish garden.

Maes Howe, Orkney (▷ 381) This burial chamber dates from 2800BC and may be the only World Heritage Site with Viking graffiti.

Clockwise left to right *The Davies Alpine House at Kew Gardens, Surrey; Majestic Warwick Castle, Warwickshire; Anne Hathaway's pretty cottage in Stratford-upon-Avon*

TOP EXPERIENCES

Step back 800 years and walk around York's medieval walls, then explore the narrow lanes inside (▷ 323).

Take a trip on a steam train. The North Yorkshire Moors Railway is one of the most scenic (▷ 317).

Visit Harrods in London, and if you miss the sales (in January and July), content yourself with a tour of the amazing food halls (▷ 101).

Have a cream tea, a refreshing afternoon tradition at any time of the year (▷ 442).

Go clubbing at Fabric in London, where Britain's best DJs play cutting-edge dance music (▷ 103).

Rent a bicycle and explore some of England's lanes or go mountain biking in Wales (▷ 254).

Take a ride on the London Eye for a bird's-eye view of the capital (right and ▷ 81). Try to pick a clear day for far-reaching views.

Relax at a restored spa. Harrogate (▷ 343) and Bath (▷ 155) have stunning new spas, based on the Roman originals.

People-watch at a Season event such as Royal Ascot (▷ 85) or the Royal Academy's Summer Exhibition (▷ 102) each year in June.

See a Shakespeare play in Stratford-upon-Avon (▷ 276) or at the Globe Theatre (▷ 87) in London, a striking re-creation of a 16th-century theatre.

Go punting in Oxford to see the spires of this university city from its waterways (▷ 190).

Watch the sun set from a Pembrokeshire beach (▷ 236), but bring a warm sweater.

Sing along at a rugby match in Wales, especially if the national side is playing (▷ 253).

Climb a Munro in Scotland Buachaille Etive Beag, in the middle of Glen Coe, is a relatively easy and accessible introduction to the delights of the Scottish hills (▷ 371).

Sample a pint or two of real ale, but choose your pub carefully: free houses often stock interesting beers from independent local breweries.

Pack a picnic for a day out in the Lake District (▷ 312).

See a city from the top deck of a double-decker bus. London has red double-deckers as part of the public transport system; the cities of London, Oxford, Cambridge, Bath and York have special sightseeing tours by double-decker bus (▷ 55).

Party at a festival for free at raucous Hogmanay in Edinburgh (▷ 399) or the colourful Notting Hill Carnival in London (▷ 107).

Put on a pair of walking boots and explore a national park on foot.

Watch a traditional ceremony. Changing the Guard is the most famous daily event in London (▷ 107).

Opposite Weymouth beach is great place for families in the summer

LIVING BRITAIN

Society and Royalty   14
Politics and Economy   16
The British   18
Urban and Rural   20
Sport and Leisure   22
Arts, Media and Culture   24
Science and Technology   26

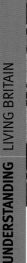

Is Britain a classless society? True, the country is more meritocratic than it used to be; high-profile jobs are no longer awarded on the basis of your lineage or alma mater, and celebrities are replacing high society. But the Establishment is alive and well, if slightly less obvious. You won't find it at the traditional gatherings—Royal Ascot horse racing in June, Cowes Week yachting in August—which now attract corporate guests, nor between the pages of the society bible, *Tatler* magazine. Instead think of grouse shoots on Scottish estates and magazines like *Country Life* and *The Field*. But for those who still cherish manners, Debrett's etiquette guides continue to be required reading. The monarchy may be a limited and expensive institution, but many believe that it still has a role in modern society, not least to attract people to Britain with wonderful spectacles such as Trooping the Colour in June and royal properties such as Windsor Castle and Buckingham Palace.

PICTURE THIS

Lucian Freud's portrait of Queen Elizabeth II was unveiled in 2002. Considered unflattering by some, including, the newspapers say, the subject herself, it testifies to the importance of the portrait in British society. It is difficult to tour a stately home without the great and the good looking down upon you. The tradition follows the fashion for genealogy among the aristocracy, and the Reformation in the 16th century, when religious imagery was proscribed. The best assortment of famous faces is in the National Portrait Gallery in London, where the marvellous collection ranges from a 1505 painting of Henry VII by an unknown artist, right up to a contemporary work of Sir Richard Branson in mixed-media by Scottish artist David Mach.

Above clockwise from left to right *The annual Trooping the Colour ceremony marks the Queen's birthday; Georgian Ashcombe House in Wiltshire belongs to pop icon Madonna; the royal wedding of Prince Charles to Camilla Parker Bowles, April 2005; jewellers G Collins and Sons Ltd proudly display their royal warrant, awarded July 2007*

SEASON HAMPER

Britain's social elite once laid out rugs and prepared picnics at the summer events, such as race meetings and open-air operas, that made up 'The Season'. Today you're more likely to find corporate hospitality tents. But that doesn't mean that the picnic-goer shouldn't make an effort for the sake of tradition. Since the picnic hamper sends out subtle signals to others, there are certain things you should specify. Smoked salmon, for example, should be wild not farmed. And strawberries should be English rather than Spanish. Scots may prefer to include some specialities from north of the border such as cullen skink soup or oatcakes. There are simple rules for drinks too. Cans must be avoided. Pimms—a sweet, alcoholic drink created in 1823—is traditional, but chilled champagne is preferred.

ROCK'S SQUIREARCHY

In the 1990s the pop group Blur satirized the British aspiration to buy 'a very big house in the country'. In spite of their lyrics, country homes are now the choice of celebrity 'new money'. Wiltshire is popular with a number of showbiz musical types: Nick Mason of Pink Floyd lives in Middlewick House in Wiltshire, while the singer Madonna owns Ashcombe House and estate, not too far from Sting at Lake House, near Amesbury. Elsewhere, Jamiroquai's flamboyant Jay Kay resides at Horsenden Manor, Buckinghamshire, close to Oasis' Noel Gallagher in Chalfont St. Giles. And so it goes on. In rural Britain celebrities try to blend into the background. There are no Hollywood-style 'Homes of the Stars' tours, but that magnificent stately home you see from the car is more likely to house a collection of guitars than the family silver.

BY APPOINTMENT TO
HER MAJESTY THE QUEEN
JEWELLER
G. COLLINS & SONS LIMITED
ROYAL TUNBRIDGE WELLS

ROYAL WARRANT

Keep your eyes open and you'll spot royal warrants everywhere in Britain. Companies as well as individuals appointed to provide goods and services to the royal family can display a royal coat of arms for five years. The practice, which began in the 15th century, gives an insight into the royal lifestyle—look no further than a royal mole controller and a chimney sweep. Some six champagne houses have royal warrants, and several chocolatiers—including Cadburys for the staff, and Prestat or Bendicks for the royals. The monarchy, enthusiasts of outdoor pursuits, has four official gunmakers, providers of riding breeches and fishing tackle, and a royal taxidermist.

MARRIAGE OF THE DECADE

It's a sign of how times have changed in Britain over the last 20 years that one of the first big marriages of the 21st century was not even a marriage in the traditional sense of the word. Rock legend Elton John and his partner David Furnish celebrated their civil partnership in December 2005, the first time such relationships have been recognized in the UK. The venue was Windsor's venerable old Guildhall, where Prince Charles and Camilla Parker-Bowles had also tied the knot just six months previously. Guests at the party that followed John's formal ceremony included Sarah Ferguson, Hugh Grant, Rod Stewart and Victoria Beckham.

Tony Blair ended 10 years in office as Prime Minister in June 2007. He handed over power to his former Chancellor of the Exchequer (the UK's Finance Minister, usually considered the second most powerful British official), Gordon Brown. By 2008 there were many other new brooms in the corridors of power. In Scotland the nationalists won power in Holyrood for the first time, and promised a referendum on secession from the Union with England. In Wales Labour was forced into a coalition with the Nationalists. The third strand of Labour's devolved government, the Mayor of London, also experienced radical change with Londoners selecting the colourful Conservative Boris Johnson to replace socialist Ken Livingstone.

General elections are held every four to five years in the UK (the term is not fixed). Candidates fight to represent one of 646 constituencies in the House of Commons as Members of Pariament (MPs). Although Britain has a ruling monarch, the Queen's role is considered by many to be largely symbolic.

Above clockwise from left to right *The State Opening of Parliament taking place in the House of Lords, 2004; architect Richard Rogers designed the sleek Lloyd's headquarters in London; a Morgan sports car—much desired by classic car enthusiasts; the housing market is a strong economic force in 21st-century Britain*

HOUSE OF LORDS

Historically, the most reliable way of gaining a seat in the House of Lords was to inherit it. But in 1999 Labour government reforms threw out all but 92 of the hereditary peers. So how can you join the Lords today? You should be British—some aspiring members have had to renounce their birth citizenship to qualify. Senior figures in the military and the judiciary have an advantage, and the Church of England's 24 bishops are guaranteed a seat for now. Former politicians, including former prime minister Baroness Thatcher, and businessmen, such as Lord Sainsbury, aren't uncommon. And you needn't be old: Baroness Warsi is the youngest of the present House—born in 1971. Or you can just be nominated as a People's Peer (42 have joined the House since 2000). But, with eminent scientist Dr. Susan Greenfield among them, they're hardly average either.

A POLITICIAN'S WORD

As if being part of the world's oldest parliamentary democracy doesn't keep them busy enough, dozens of members of parliament (MPs) supplement their £61,820 salaries with second jobs. Many are directors of companies, or highly paid consultants, some pulling in several hundred thousand pounds a year. The most intriguing moonlighters are the novelists. In the 1990s the Conservative MP Edwina Currie began writing racy novels—with titles such as *A Parliamentary Affair*—in her spare time, while fellow Conservative Ann Widdecombe was advanced £100,000 for two novels of her own. Not surprisingly, a recent analysis of MPs' attendance records revealed that on average those with second jobs turned up to 30 per cent fewer Commons votes than those without.

CLASSIC CARS

Almost 100 years ago the son of a clergyman started a company in Malvern, Worcestershire. He called it Morgan, and despite the decline of Britain's manufacturing industries, which saw the demise of many glamorous names in motoring, it still builds elegant sports cars today. Esteemed by Prince Charles, Aston Martin is owned by Kuwaiti investors and Jaguar is now owned by Indian giant Tata. BMW and Volkswagen took over Rolls-Royce and Bentley. Britain's car firms of the future will probably be, like their cars, small but tenacious. Morgan now employs 160 people, producing some 14 cars per week. Waiting time has slipped below one year. Surrey-based Caterham has been making speedy Caterham 7s for almost 50 years.

PROPERTY BOOM OR BUST

No longer is the weather the chief British talking point: It is now house prices. Since the property booms of the 1980s and 1990s, housing 'equity' is the nation's biggest source of inherited wealth. Britain has long had higher rates of home ownership than the rest of Europe. Margaret Thatcher's government promoted home ownership in the 1980s, chiefly by selling local government-owned social housing stock. House prices spiralled upwards again in the late 1990s, this time under a Labour government. But not everyone rejoiced. The average price of a London property is now over £350,000, 13 times the average national salary. In contrast, the average price in Wales is just £154,000. The market that has benefited many is pitiless to first-time buyers, who have little chance of affording their own home.

IT'S A LOTTERY

The launch of the National Lottery in 1994 gripped the nation. It created a fund to benefit charitable and cultural projects—and offered a great opportunity to gamble. Since then, lottery money has helped fund a great variety of projects, some renowned—Tate Modern, the Eden Project—others less so. But one lasting effect has been to stimulate cultural tourism in deprived areas. The Lowry Centre in Manchester's Salford Quays is typical. Celebrating the life and work of local artist L. S. Lowry, it attracts thousands of visitors a year, most of whom would never have come to Manchester before. The lottery now sells fewer tickets, despite huge advertising campaigns and a relaunch as Lotto. The museum-building boom has slowed down, but the fun of a wager has bequeathed Britain many new visitor attractions and created many new millionaires.

The 57.1 million inhabitants of mainland Britain (a further 1.7 million live in Northern Ireland) represent one of the most ethnically diverse and vibrant cultures in the world. Besides the Scots, English and Welsh, 270 ethnic groups call Britain home. Britain has long been an immigrant nation, colonized by Angles and Saxons from northern Europe, Celts from Ireland and Vikings from Scandinavia. In recent centuries the British Empire opened the way for people to arrive from Africa, Asia and the Caribbean, with many new migrants coming from Eastern Europe. But if there is no such thing as a typical Briton, national characteristics do exist. Some say the British are reserved, although this is less true the farther north you travel. Others think the British are belligerent, defining themselves by battles won—from Waterloo in 1815 against the French to the World Cup in 1966 when the English soccer team beat the Germans. Any so-called 'bulldog spirit', however, is balanced by a self-deprecating sense of humour and an instinct for compromise.

Above clockwise from left to right *The Last Night of the Proms at the Royal Albert Hall, South Kensington, London; Musicians at Spitalfields Market perform during a Japanese festival; Lord Bath of Longleat at his Elizabethan mansion in Wiltshire*

PEOPLE ARE STRANGE

The British have long tolerated eccentrics. Cambridge University's Trinity College, for example, once permitted one of its students, the poet Lord Byron (1788–1824), to keep a bear in his rooms. That tradition of cherishing individuality is embodied today by the occupant of the vast Longleat estate, Alexander Thynne, the seventh Marquess of Bath. His spectacular Elizabethan mansion, set within park-land landscaped by Capability Brown and open to the public since 1949, has latterly been accompanied by a safari park. Lord Bath has painted vivid murals of his mistresses (he prefers the term 'wifelet') and of his 150 noble ancestors, and hung them throughout the west wing of the house.

GOOD SENSE OF HUMOUR?

The Edinburgh Fringe Festival is the world's largest open arts festival, attracting a million people to 20,000 individual performances. This gives the festival's most prestigious award, the Perrier Award for the best comedy act, the stamp of authority. The list of nominees reads like a who's who of the British comedy scene. The first winners were the Cambridge Footlights in 1981, including Stephen Fry and Emma Thompson. Al Murray, Dave Gorman, Johnny Vegas, the League of Gentlemen, Dylan Moran, Bill Bailey, Alan Davies, Steve Coogan, Frank Skinner, Eddie Izzard, Jack Dee—these past winners are British TV regulars. And typically white males, fuelling critics' claims that the award is now more mainstream than fringe.

RISE AND FALL

Unbelievably, at the beginning of the 20th century the British Empire comprised a quarter of the world's land surface and over a quarter of its population. It was the largest empire in the world's history. This colonial heritage can now be appreciated at the British Empire and Commonwealth Museum in Bristol (www.empiremuseum.co.uk). Housed in engineer Isambard Kingdom Brunel's Temple Meads train terminus, the BECM embodies the grandeur (and, some would argue, vanity) of the British Empire. Having started with a trading outpost in Newfoundland in 1497, the empire withered after World War II when many colonies gained independence in the 1950s and 1960s and the Commonwealth of Nations was formed. Several former colonies will soon celebrate a half-century of self-rule—Ghana was one of the first in 2007.

FLYING THE FLAG

Each year the Proms—the annual series of classical music concerts sponsored by the BBC—heralds much singing of patriotic hymns and flying of flags: both the red, white and blue Union Flag of the United Kingdom and the red-on-white St. George's Cross of England. A few years ago this patriotic display was criticized within the BBC, on the grounds that these flags are often employed by right-wing political groups like the National Front. Now ordinary people have reclaimed the flag, particularly the St. George's Cross, first flown in 1189. The watershed was 2002, when the soccer World Cup and the Queen's Golden Jubilee carpeted England with flags, particularly the St. George's Cross, given a new lease of life by the devolution of Scotland and Wales. Some may find it vulgar, but flying the flag is no longer the mark of a bigot.

SIKH HERITAGE

The largest Sikh temple outside India is in Havelock Road, Southall—a London suburb with a predominantly Asian population. Second in size only to the Golden Temple at Amritsar, in northern India, the London temple opened in 2003. It cost £17 million to construct, a sum raised by the local community. They hope that the building—which has capacity for 3,000 worshippers and can provide 20,000 meals over a festival weekend—will become a tourist attraction. However, some are less happy about an unfortunate coincidence: Havelock Road is named after Major-General Sir Henry Havelock. Sir Henry earned his knighthood crushing the Indian Mutiny of 1857, which challenged British rule in India. But, in a final twist, Sikhs remained loyal to the British colonialists in 1857 and many served in Havelock's forces.

One of the most densely populated countries in Europe, Britain's population of about 57.1 million is spread across 228,800sq km (88,375sq miles) with 660 people per square mile. France, with a similar population, has just 285 people per square kilometre. Yet despite the claustrophobic statistics, breathing space is easily found, and often surprisingly close to Britain's cities, such as in the Peak District National Park between urban giants Manchester and Sheffield. Britain has been inhabited for thousands of years, and even on the remote Scottish islands you cannot escape evidence of the generations that have shaped the landscape. The lot of the rural dweller includes a number of grievances, from restrictions on hunting to rural poverty, and an often crisis-hit farming industry. A central complaint is that decisions that affect farming communities are made by urbanites with little understanding of the countryside. Meanwhile Britain's cities thrive, with exciting new arts venues, retail districts and nightlife. Revitalized Birmingham, Cardiff, Manchester and Newcastle upon Tyne are on the up, with the caveat of a changing job market and uncertain property prices.

ORGANIC FARMING
Whether due to an awakening of environmental awareness, an increased interest in personal health, or canny marketing, demand for organically produced food is booming in Britain. One of the people meeting this demand is the Prince of Wales. In 1990 Prince Charles formed Duchy Originals, a company producing organic foods, from biscuits to bacon to beer. The project germinated at the Prince's Highgrove home in Gloucestershire and now extends across his estates, from the Duchy of Cornwall—allocated to each heir to the throne since the 14th century—to land in Lincolnshire. Duchy Originals is a successful and profitable enterprise (the profits go to the Prince's charities), and the amount of land converted to organic production doubles every year.

Above clockwise from left to right *Harvest time in the intensively farmed British countryside; a plaque commemorates the Doughty Street home of Charles Dickens; the Lowry Centre at regenerated Salford Quays, Manchester; organic produce is for sale all over Britain, here at Southwark market*

THE NATIONAL TRUST

In 2002 Tyntesfield—a Victorian Gothic Revival mansion near Bristol—was put up for sale. Mercifully, because the house retained many of its original contents, the National Trust stepped in to save it for the nation, and it is now open to the public on a limited basis. This is a time of confidence for the NT. Founded in 1895 by Victorian philanthropists, it aims 'to preserve places of historic interest or natural beauty permanently for the nation to enjoy'. In response, membership has hit three million, more than all the political parties together. Stately homes are the Trust's most visible assets, though the NT has also rescued industrial and 20th-century buildings, including the childhood homes of former Beatles John Lennon and Sir Paul McCartney in Liverpool. Heritage is no longer stuck in the past.

THRILL OF THE CHASE

Hunting foxes with hounds has been part of British country life for generations and is synonymous with the sight of scarlet-clad horseback riders. Some people think it was the stereotype of fox hunting as a sport for the priviledged that led first the Scottish (in 2002) and then the Westminster parliament (in 2005) to make hunting foxes with dogs illegal. The decision was unpopular with the hunting fraternity, and many saw it as an unjust swipe at a country-dwelling minority by city-based liberals. But has the ban made a difference? Many hunts continue to meet, to exercise their horses and their dogs. Fox numbers appear unchanged—they are mostly controlled by rifles and roadkill anyway. Governments north and south of the border have suggested enforcement of the ban is not a priority. Perhaps only a handful of foxes can tell the difference.

REBIRTH OF A CITY

To the buzzing guitars of rock band Oasis, the city of Manchester redefined itself at the end of the nineties. Always famous for music (it boasts the superb Hallé Orchestra), the city found a new cultural dynamism with several new museums and regenerated urban areas such as the Northern Quarter. Warehouses were converted to loft apartments, attracting new city-centre residents, essential for urban vitality. But despite the investment, Manchester remains a community of independents and individuals: bars, record labels, shops and the Mancunians themselves. Nowhere is this better demonstrated than by the rise and rise of FC United. This new football team was formed by disaffected fans of the city's biggest club, Manchester United. Now they are climbing through the divisions and already attracting crowds that would do justice to any League Two outfit.

BLUE PLAQUES

Imagine the talented rock guitarist Jimi Hendrix (1942–70) and the popular classical composer George Frideric Handel (1685–1759) discussing chords, tough crowds and flammable instruments. Apart from a mismatch in time (the small matter of over 200 years), this unlikely pair did have a brick wall in common. Hendrix stayed at No. 23 Brook Street in London's Mayfair from 1968 to 1969, entertaining, among others, The Beatles. George Friederic lived next door at No. 25 (now the Handel House Museum) for much of his life. This coincidence is commemorated by a Blue Plaque, one of 800 dished out by English Heritage to mark the homes of notable former residents. Look hard enough and you'll spot one almost anywhere in London, especially in Bloomsbury and the Royal Borough of Kensington and Chelsea. The scheme has been gradually extended across the country.

SPORT AND LEISURE

It doesn't take a genius to guess Britain's national sport. Even during the summer months when the football (soccer) season is over, newspapers speculate about player transfers. Most interest is in the English Premier League, but football is taken equally seriously in the provincial towns and local parks. England's rugby team has enjoyed more success in recent years, but it often struggles to outshine its neighbours in Wales, France, Ireland and Scotland. However, matches between them are eagerly anticipated. If you cannot get a ticket, then watch the big TV screen with a pint of beer in the local pub. Others prefer the peace of the British countryside, usually explored on foot, but also by mountain bike or on horseback. Public footpaths and bridleways lace the country, linking towns and villages, although most of the land in Britain is privately owned. Meanwhile, two out of three people are gardeners, a group that spends £3.5 billion a year on the hobby. But the number-one leisure activity—in the country with the longest working hours in Europe—is shopping.

Above clockwise from left to right *England's Premiership football league attracts footballers from around the globe; a fan at a national game displays his patriotism; National Trust properties and gardens around the country feature a wealth of flowers and exotic plants; Lords in London is the home of England's national cricket team*

SHOP TILL YOU DROP

'The English are a nation of shopkeepers': Napoleon's famous jibe (originally coined in 1775 by economist Adam Smith) is no longer very apt. Nowadays, the British are a nation of shoppers. Every month shoppers spend at least £20 billion— approximately the annual gross domestic product of Morocco—at the stores on Britain's preferred leisure activity. And not just in city streets. Since Britain's first out-of-town shopping mall opened in 1976, more than 500 'retail parks' have mush- roomed. Every week 500,000 consumers visit Lakeside in Essex or lose themselves among the 330 shops of Bluewater in Kent. Besides identical selections, these places provide important jobs behind the tills.

THE FUTURE IS ROSY

The most-visited National Trust property in Britain is Wakehurst Place, an Elizabethan house in Sussex. This outpost of the Royal Botanical Society, which also runs world-renowned Kew Gardens in London, is famous for its extensive gardens. But while most of Britain's army of avid gardeners are content to nurture their prize rose bushes, the Royal Botanical Society has grander ambitions. Housed next door to Wakehurst is the Millennium Seed Bank. This international project aims to collect and conserve the seeds of 24,000 (or 10 per cent) of the world's plants, safeguarding species that may be at risk of extinction. Already the seeds of 97 per cent of Britain's native flora have been collected in a unique act of preservation. Interactive exhibitions in the Millennium Seed Bank building are open to the public.

PLUCKY LOSERS?

The loyal British sports fan has become increasingly accustomed to tearful failure. Despite creating many of the world's sports, the country sometimes seems to have forgotten how to win them. England's 1966 victory in the soccer World Cup has assumed a hallowed status in English sporting folklore. On the cricket pitch, England's celebrated victory over Australia to win the Ashes trophy in 2005 felt like the exception that proves the rule and they rather limply conceded the prize again in Australia two years later. The Wimbledon tennis tournament each June brings an outpouring of patriotism shortly followed by resigned expectations of doing better next time. The British still excel at snooker and darts—perhaps because they're pub games.

IT'S NOT CRICKET

English cricket is going through a radical change. Where once you might have found only the gentlemen of the Marylebone Cricket Club politely applauding, you may now find international matches supported by a much more vocal crowd of all ages and gender. Much of this new-found fervour stems from 2005, when England finally wrested the Ashes trophy off the previously all-conquering Australians. But some is due in part to the enthusiasm for the game spreading from Britain's ethnically diverse urban communities, from Pakistan, India, Bangladesh and the West Indies. Cricket can still be found on village greens, but is also strong on urban playing fields, and innovations like floodlit 20-20 games, where each side bats for only 20 overs, have dramatically altered the previously plodding nature of the sport.

TIME GENTLEMEN, PLEASE!

British bars and pubs continue to seem very restricted in their opening hours. You will still hear the traditional landlord's cry of "Time, please!" as he announces that the bar is closing and you have 15 minutes to finish your drinks and leave, but this no longer has to be at 11pm. In Scotland the system of extending licensing hours had been commonplace, so in 2005 England and Wales adopted a more flexible approach, allowing bars to apply for 24-hour opening. Many pubs, however, opted to retain their 11–11 hours, while others chose later closing times, especially on the weekend. Scottish laws are now changing to coincide with those south of the border, but with each pub licensed for different hours, but it's best to check your closing times before you get the drinks in.

Britain's journalists and paparazzi work hard to feed a media industry desperate for stories. There are more than 20 national newspapers, from brash, populist tabloids to stimulating broadsheets. Governments are anxious to maintain positive relations with the more influential papers. There is also an immense appetite for magazines, unaffected by high levels of internet access; newsagents can cater to the most obscure interests. Broadcasting is less partisan than the papers, with the BBC indebted to television viewers who pay a compulsory annual fee. Britain's film industry is erratic but theatre is in better shape, with a hit-packed West End, and the government-funded Royal Shakespeare Company and the National Theatre. Lower ticket prices for concerts, ballets and operas aim to increase accessibility.

GLOBAL ARCHITECTURE

You have to travel a long way to escape the work of Norman Foster, born in 1935. Farther than Bilbao in Spain, where the British architect has redesigned much of the metro system; and past Berlin, where his renovation of the Reichstag won the Pritzker Architecture Prize. Across the world in Hong Kong, you pass through Lord Foster's Chep Lap Kok international airport, built on a man-made island. Back home, London's Canary Wharf tube station and the Great Court in the British Museum are among the distinctive buildings designed by the ubiquitous Foster and Associates. One of the newest additions to London's skyline is the environmentally friendly and self-ventilating Swiss Re headquarters, known locally as 'the Gherkin' (pickle).

Above clockwise from left to right *The Queen Elizabeth II Great Court in the British Museum, London; Shoreditch street art by Banksey, a Bristol-based graffiti artist; the* Angel of the North *stands proud on a hilltop above Gateshead; audiences pack the stalls at the Globe Theatre, London*

FASHION

The Alexander McQueen success story goes from the East End of London to the fashion houses of Paris. Born in 1969, the son of a London taxi driver, McQueen left school at 16 more interested in couture than cab driving. Following his apprenticeship on Savile Row, London, he completed an MA at St. Martin's School of Art. After a celebrated collection for his final exams, fashion's *enfant terrible* left London for Paris, working for Givenchy then Gucci. By 2001 the three-time British Designer of the Year had a reputation for being brilliant but difficult, once declining an invitation from the Queen. During the biannual London Fashion Week (February and September), alumni of Britain's art colleges aspire to follow in his footsteps.

POTTER POWER

J. K. Rowling (born 1965) is a publishing sensation. The author of the Harry Potter series of children's books is the latest in a tradition of British writers—among them Roald Dahl (1916–90) and C. S. Lewis (1898–1963)—whose work appeals to both adults and children. Yet Rowling's success is unparalleled. Although paid an advance of just £2,500 for the first book, *Harry Potter and the Philosopher's Stone* (2000), her earnings exploded to about £28 million per year, making her one of the richest (and most charitable) women in the country. The films of the Potter books have been shot at various historic locations around the country, including the Bodleian Library and Christ Church college in Oxford, Alnwick Castle in Northumberland and Gloucester Cathedral.

A MATTER OF TASTE

Since the 1990s one man has dominated the British art scene. Charles Saatchi (born 1948) made his fortune founding two advertising agencies with his brother Maurice, and invests it in contemporary British art. Having bankrolled the Brit Art movement, in April 2003 he moved his Saatchi Gallery to County Hall, on London's South Bank. Legal wrangling surrounded the gallery's withdrawal in 2005, but a new venue in a former army barracks in Chelsea opened in 2008. Not everyone is impressed by the young British artists. Saatchi took his Sensation exhibition, including *The Holy Virgin Mary* by Chris Ofili—which featured his trademark use of elephant dung—to New York's Brooklyn Museum of Art in 1999. Then-mayor Rudy Giuliani was so outraged he threatened to cut the museum's subsidy.

BRITISH POP

The fame of British pop music is due to a formula that took an established sound—typically American—and put a fresh spin on it. In the early 1960s the Beatles and the Rolling Stones updated R&B and sold it back to the States. Punk, reggae and electronic dance music were equally invigorated in the 1970s and 1980s. This talent for reinvention, if a little threadbare during the Britpop years in the 1990s, is still strong. A homespun variation is the work of Eliza Carthy, daughter of Norma Waterson and Martin Carthy—key figures in centuries-old British folk music. While her body piercings and vividly dyed hair are anything but conventional, the accomplished singer and fiddler takes traditional British folk songs and forms such as reels, jigs and square dances, and subtly modernizes them with electronic flourishes.

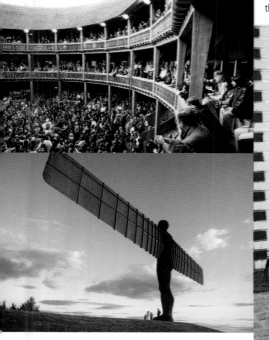

JOHNSON AND MACARTHUR

Seldom has second place meant so much. In 2001 Ellen MacArthur sailed *Kingfisher,* a state-of-the-art yacht, solo around the world in the Vendée Globe 2000 race. She didn't win, but the 25-year-old completed the fastest solo circumnavigation by a woman. In 2005 she then broke the record for the fastest solo effort by anyone. McArthur's record-breaking achievement mirrors those of another famous British woman, Amy Johnson. In 1930, at the age of 26, Johnson became the first woman to fly solo from Britain to Darwin, Australia; the 16,000km (10,000-mile) route took 20 days, three days short of the record. Born in Hull in 1903, Johnson took up flying in 1928. She went on to achieve many record flights in the 1930s. Her plane, a de Havilland Gypsy Moth named Jason, is displayed in the Science Museum in London.

Since the 1970s Britain has developed from a manufacturing-based economy to a high-tech, knowledge-based economy. Scientific research is concentrated in areas such as the 'Silicon Fen' around Cambridge. Probably the most ground-breaking research programme is the Human Genome Project, which aims to decode the human genome; it is hoped the information will contribute to the cure of many illnesses. High levels of personal computer ownership, internet access and the numerous websites hosted in the country reflect the new skill trends. Hardly surprising when you consider that the inventor of the World Wide Web is a Briton, Tim Berners-Lee.

DOLLY THE SHEEP

Dead sheep rarely get pride of place in a national museum. But Dolly wasn't just any sheep. Produced in 1996 by scientists at the Roslin Institute in Scotland, Dolly was the world's first animal to be cloned from an adult cell, and was hailed as a scientific sensation. The subsequent debate about cloning was fuelled by her premature death. After the post-mortem Dolly (named after country singer Dolly Parton) was stuffed, and she is now on display in Edinburgh's National Museum of Scotland.

THE CLOCKWORK WIRELESS

Having come up with a number of the world's most useful inventions, including the train, the television and the gin and tonic, Britons seemed to have run out of steam. But inventors, such as Trevor Baylis, onetime escapologist with the Berlin State Circus, continue to tinker in garden sheds. Watching a documentary about AIDS in Africa, he realized that advice about the disease could be communicated more widely if radios were more readily obtainable.

His solution was the wind-up radio—batteries not required—which was both cheap and practical in areas with patchy electricity. After a battle to get his invention produced, Trevor's radios are now distributed in the world's poorest countries and are a trendy accessory in the West.

Above clockwise from left to right *British inventor Trevor Baylis with his clockwork radio; the world's first cloned sheep with her naturally conceived lamb, named Bonnie*

HIC WILLELM·DVX ALLOQVITVR·SV

THE STORY OF BRITAIN

Prehistory–1066: The Beginnings   28
1066–1399: Medieval Britain   30
1399–1603: Tudor Britain   32
1603–1714: Turbulent Britain   34
1714–1815: Engineering Britain   36
1815–1901: Victorian Britain   38
1901–1999: 20th-Century Britain   40
2000–present: 21st-Century Britain   42

Stone monuments, earth mounds, shattered pottery, tools and the occasional skeleton provide scattered clues to prehistoric life in Britain—tribal societies that had developed over millennia before work began on Stonehenge in the third millennium BC. From about 600BC Celtic influences with strong traditions in art, music and war arrived from central Europe. The Druidic elite that oversaw spiritual life confronted Julius Caesar's troops during the first Roman invasion in 55–54BC.

A century later, in AD43, Emperor Claudius started the job of conquest proper, and for 400 years southern Britain was a Roman province, adopting its gods, fashions, laws and language. Saxon raids tested an overstretched empire in the fifth century, and in AD410 the Romans pulled out, leaving southern Britain to split into petty kingdoms.

The Pope sent missionaries from Rome in AD597 to bring the kingdoms into the Catholic faith. By the eighth century pagan Vikings were raiding the eastern coast, soon settling in northern England. The treaty of AD871 between the Danes and Alfred, king of Wessex, was the basis of the kingdom of England. When Edward the Confessor, died in 1066, a power struggle ensued between his successor Harold Godwinson, William, Duke of Normandy and King Harald of Norway.

Above clockwise from left to right *Medusa features on a floor mosaic at the Roman Villa, Bignor; an excerpt from the Lindisfarne Gospels (710–721) showing St. Luke; Chysauster Iron Age Fort, Cornwall; a Celtic cross at St. Mary's Abbey on the island of Iona, Inner Hebrides; Vortigern, prince of southeast Britain, makes a treaty with the Saxons*

THE LAST HOURS OF PETE MARSH

One day in the first century BC a man now nicknamed Pete Marsh marvelled at visions induced by his final meal of mistletoe and herbs. Behind him a Druid raised his club. Having smashed Pete's skull the priest garrotted him and then threw him into the sacred bog water of Lindow Moss, gateway to the gods. The remarkably preserved corpse was recovered from the Cheshire peat bog in 1984. According to archaeologists, Pete was one more victim of the Druidic human sacrifices described by Roman historians. The theory fits his bodily injuries and the mistletoe grains found in his stomach. Alternatively, this may just have been a pre-historic mugging. Whatever the case, Pete Marsh—now a permanent resident of the British Museum—and other similarly mutilated 'bog bodies' provide testimony to the grim but common social rituals of their age.

ST. AUGUSTINE'S MISSION

In AD597 Abbot Augustine and a group of nervous monks from Rome landed in Thanet, Kent. They were greeted by the equally wary King Aethelbert of Kent, who cautiously met them out in the open. But the meeting was no accident: The delegation had been sent by Pope Gregory to spread the Christian word in a land of many tribes and beliefs; and Aethelbert's Christian wife had probably paved their way. Sixth-century Britain was an uneasy, often violent place and en route the reluctant missionaries sent Augustine back to talk the Pope out of the whole idea—to no avail. In the event, Aethelbert was converted and, with his support, Augustine established an episcopal base in Canterbury. The kingdom of Kent now had the backing of Rome.

ESCAPE FROM LINDISFARNE

The east coast of Britain was a dangerous place in the eighth and ninth centuries. Plagued by Scandinavian raids, monasteries with their religious bullion were especially hard hit. After Danish attacks in 875, the monks of Lindisfarne island fled, taking the holy, illuminated Lindisfarne Gospels with them. The Latin text had been produced in about 720; an Anglo-Saxon translation was added in about 960. The Gospel Book was probably produced to highlight the cult of former bishop-monk St. Cuthbert (634–87). His relics too were carried to safety: By 995 they were enshrined in Durham. When the cathedral was pillaged during the 16th-century Reformation the Gospels were taken to London, eventually to be housed in the British Library.

A STAND AGAINST ROME

When Emperor Claudius decided to finish his predecessor Julius Caesar's job and conquer Britain in AD43, he faced stiff opposition from King Caratacus (Caradoc) who, along with his brother Togodumnus, ruled the very powerful Catuvellauni tribe. They met the Romans in force at the River Thames, but Togodumnus was cut down and Caratacus fled to the west. Five years later he was back, turning the tide of invaders from the western part of Britain now called Wales. His success was short-lived and he escaped again, only to be betrayed by Cartimandua, queen of the Brigantes. Taken to Rome in chains, Caratacus so impressed Emperor Claudius that he and his family were pardoned, and lived the rest of their days in Italy.

VORTIGERN'S LEAP

Deserted by Rome, fifth-century Britain descended into civil war. Vortigern (Gwrtheyrn), king of Powys in Wales, was in dispute with the Picts of Scotland, and invited Saxon mercenaries from Germany to strengthen his position; in return for their help the Saxons received land. But having established a foothold, they wanted more. Hundreds of their fellow countrymen poured in, expanding their territories while (according to sixth-century historian Gildas) massacring the British and destroying their towns. According to a later legend, Vortigern, reviled by his people for letting in the enemy, escaped to the Lleyn Peninsula in northern Wales. Here he leaped—or perhaps was pushed—from a clifftop called Nant Gwrtheyrn (Vortigern's Stream), and died on the rocks below.

After King Harold's defeat at Hastings in 1066 the Norman conquest began in earnest. William I's followers bought land and built castles and new cathedrals; in 1086 England was surveyed in the Domesday Book. The main Norman dynasty itself died out after the civil war of King Stephen's reign (1135–54). Rule passed to a grandson, Henry II, who inherited an 'empire' that extended from central France to northern England. His son, Richard I, neglected the English kingdom, preferring the glory of the Third Crusade. His successor, brother John, lost the French lands and battled with his English barons. The authority of the English Crown was further challenged in the 13th century by Simon de Montfort, whose rebellion was crushed at Evesham in 1265. Welsh defiance in the 1270s was met with full-scale invasion by Edward I. His intervention in the Scottish power struggle between King John de Balliol and Robert the Bruce backfired in Edward II's reign with the rout of the English at Bannockburn. Edward III then reclaimed French territories and triggered the Hundred Years War.

THE FATAL ARROW?
Arrows fly across the Hastings battle scene on the 11th-century Bayeux Tapestry; corpses litter the ground. Above the confusion are embroidered the words: 'Harold Rex Interfectus Est'; King Harold is dead. William, Duke of Normandy won the day at the Battle of Hastings on 14 October 1066. But is it King Harold shown gripping an arrow in his eye? Eyewitness William of Poitiers notes that Harold's face was unrecognizable after the battle, and he was identified by marks on his body. In order to give her son a decent burial, Harold's mother, Gytha, offered the Normans his body's weight in gold. William refused, adding that too many lay unburied due to Harold's greed for power. But one legend claims the body was found and buried at Waltham, Essex.

Above clockwise from left to right *Richard I got to within 19km (12 miles) of Jerusalem on the Third Crusade (1191); looking over All Souls College from the top of St. Mary's Tower in Oxford; in 1348 the Black Death killed a third of the population; a bronze statue of Robert the Bruce on the site of the Battle of Bannockburn, 1314; King John reluctantly signs the Magna Carta in 1215 on the Thames island of Runnymede*

FOUNDING OF OXFORD UNIVERSITY

A royal quarrel led to the foundation of the world's first English-speaking university. Henry II was at loggerheads with Philip Augustus of France, and in 1167 banned English students from attending Paris University. Some teaching had taken place in Oxford since the late 11th century, but now the scholars moved in. In 1188 the historian and cleric Gerald of Wales (Giraldus Cambrensis) lectured to a gathering of dons, and in 1190 the first foreign student, Emo of Friesland, was admitted. As student numbers grew, so did friction with the townspeople—in 1209 the first of many 'town versus gown' riots broke out. After this a group of disgruntled clerks packed their bags and headed east to establish Cambridge University.

MAGNA CARTA

On 15 June 1215 peace negotiations at Runnymede between King John and his rebel barons were concluded with the sealing of the Magna Carta—the Great Charter. This charter of 'rights' was a significant development in the English constitution, setting limits on royal authority within the rule of law (typically set by the Crown): 'No free man shall be arrested or imprisoned…or victimized in any other way…except by the lawful judgement of his peers or by the law of the land' (Article 39). In the 13th century 'free man' applied to a powerful minority. John, however, was merely playing for time—civil war broke out within months. Nevertheless, a principle of law was established that would, over the centuries, be regarded as the bedrock of democracy.

THE TURBULENT PRIEST

Thomas Becket (1118–70), son of a Norman merchant, rose from banker's clerk to royal chancellor. He won Henry II's confidence and was appointed Archbishop of Canterbury in 1162. At once, Becket opposed the king on matters of Church rights. Angry and betrayed, Henry ordered his arrest and Becket fled to France. Attempts at reconciliation failed. Events came to a head when Becket returned to suspend the Archbishop of York for usurping his archiepiscopal rights. His rival complained to the king, whose irritated response— 'will no one rid me of this turbulent priest?'—was unfortunately overheard by four knights. They murdered Becket inside Canterbury Cathedral—an act greeted with disgust. Becket was canonized two years later; Henry did public penance.

THE IRON RING

Edward I consolidated his conquest of Wales with an iron ring of fortresses. Work began on his castle-palace at Caernarfon in 1283, as building got under way in Harlech and Conwy. The chief mason in charge of all these schemes—as well as several other sites—was Master James of St. George (c1235–1308), from Savoy. An army of craftsmen and workers came from all over England to realize his figure-of-eight design at Caernarfon, where the walls incorporated different-coloured stone, symbolic of Constantinople's imperial defences. Practical features included a gatehouse with six fortified portcullises, massive towers and a town wall punctuated with eight watchtowers and two gateways. The ring of Edwardian castles is now a UNESCO World Heritage Site.

When Welsh landowner Owain Glyndwr took up arms against Henry IV, his countrymen readily followed. Welsh independence came within reach, but superior royal forces crushed the campaign in 1413. The Hundred Years War rumbled on in France, with a major English triumph at Agincourt, but at home conflict over the throne plunged the country into 30 years of civil war. The rival houses of Lancaster and York were reconciled only when Lancastrian Henry VII married Elizabeth of York in 1485 and established the Tudor dynasty.

The Tudor age brought religious upheaval, overseas exploration and invasion threats. Henry VIII married six times in his bid to secure the dynasty, rejecting papal authority in the process. After Henry's only son's brief, staunchly Protestant reign, Mary Tudor failed to force a return to Catholicism. Her half-sister Elizabeth attempted a middle way, but incurred the wrath of Catholic Spain with the execution of Mary, Queen of Scots for conspiracy. The failure of Spain's subsequent invasion attempt sealed Elizabeth's popularity. During her long reign composers such as William Byrd and writers such as William Shakespeare led a cultural renaissance; and Sir Francis Drake and Sir Walter Raleigh sailed to a New World.

BREAKING WITH ROME

After more than 20 years of marriage to Catherine of Aragon, Henry VIII had no male heir. His eye was caught by lady-in-waiting Anne Boleyn, whom he determined to marry. In 1527 Cardinal Wolsey, his Lord Chancellor and, as the head of the English Church, the next most powerful man in Britain, tried to persuade the Pope to annul the marriage—without success. Wolsey was dismissed by the frustrated king in 1529 and he turned instead to theologian Thomas Cranmer, who engineered the 1534 Act of Supremacy, acknowledging Henry as head of the Church of England and severing the link with Rome. Having married his mistress, Henry then plundered church funds by dissolving and looting the country's monasteries.

UNCLE JASPER'S RISKY CAREER

Jasper Tudor (1431–95) was a key player during the Wars of the Roses. The Tudor family had married into the Lancastrian dynasty. Jasper's royal cause was stalled in 1461, when Lancastrian Henry VI was deposed by the Yorkist Edward IV. But Jasper had high hopes for his nephew Henry, Earl of Richmond, who had a claim to the throne. Slipping in and out of the country, Jasper maintained the rebels' momentum, before smuggling Henry to safety in Brittany in 1471. Fourteen years later the Tudors landed at Milford Haven and marched to Bosworth, where Richard III and the Yorkist cause were defeated. As king, Henry VII made his uncle Duke of Bedford and Lieutenant of Wales and the Marches in gratitude.

SHIPSHAPE

From the day of her accession in 1558, Elizabeth I faced a constant threat of war from Catholic Spain. In 1588, provoked by the execution of Mary, Queen of Scots, and by raids on Spanish treasure ships, Philip II of Spain finally despatched an invasion armada. Elizabeth had inherited a poorly funded and depleted navy, and in 1569 persuaded explorer John Hawkins to restore it. Hawkins was determined to replace unwieldy 'floating fortresses' with faster, more flexible galleons that relied on broadside guns. Overcoming naval opposition, he designed *The Revenge*, which served as Sir Francis Drake's flagship against the Spanish. By 1588 a new, manoeuvrable and well-run fleet was ready to repel the Spanish Armada—with a little help from the weather.

THE PRINTING PRESS

Thirty years after Johannes Gutenberg's invention of movable type in 1440, the printing industry had yet to take off in Britain. A leading Kent merchant, William Caxton (1422–91), who learned the skill in Cologne, anticipated the demand for printed books. He tested the waters by producing the first printed book in English—Caxton's own translation of a history of Troy—from Bruges in about 1474. The book was a great success. Three years later he and his apprentice Wynkyn de Worde had a press in Westminster, printing works by writers such as Chaucer, the poet and monk John Lydgate, and Sir Thomas Malory, as well as translations of works about religion, ethics and chivalry. The press quickly gained in influence, helping to create the early flowering of English literature.

SLASHES AND RUFFS

The wedding of Henry VII's sister to the king of France was an opportunity for English aristocrats to note the latest fashions of the French court. Strangest of these was a style copied from German and Swiss troops and dating from the Battle of Grandson in 1476—when soldiers had plundered supplies of silk and cut it up to patch their clothes. Soon every Tudor trend-follower was ordering 'slashed' doublets, breeches and sleeves, with outer materials cut into slits and the lining—in contrasting textures and colours—pulled through. Meanwhile, necklines plunged, leaving undershirts (or chemises) showing. The chemise was drawn together at the neck with a string, producing a concertina effect that over the years evolved into the full-blown, chin-tickling ruff.

Opposite and above clockwise from left to right Henry VIII; *William* Shakespeare; *15th-century Little Moreton Hall; The* Golden Hind *circumnavigated the world in 1577–80 with Sir Francis Drake at the helm*

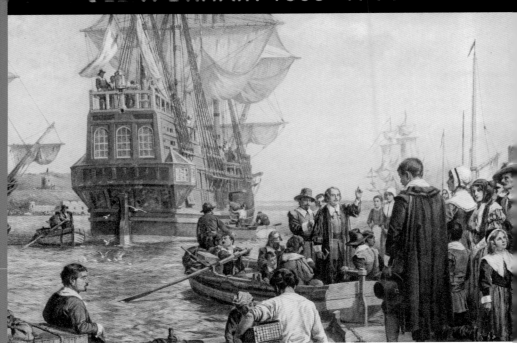

Elizabeth I died unmarried and heirless. James VI of Scotland, son of Mary, Queen of Scots, acceded to the English throne as James I in 1603. Within two years he was nearly blown away when Guy Fawkes attempted to blow up the Houses of Parliament in protest at anti-Catholic measures. Money was another worry: James spent extravagantly on the arts and on buildings such as the Banqueting House in Whitehall, architect Inigo Jones' Renaissance showpiece. Costly foreign wars lingered into the reign of Charles I, provoking complaints from the English Parliament, already suspicious of royal 'papist' tendencies. Mutual distrust escalated into civil war, which ended with the king's execution. Radicals looked to the victorious Puritan general Oliver Cromwell for far-reaching reforms, but without success; Parliament was dismissed again, and Cromwell ruled as Lord Protector until his death in 1658. The monarchy was restored in 1660 upon Charles II's return from exile. Smouldering religious enmities found expression through a burgeoning party political system. From the ashes of the 1666 Great Fire of London emerged Sir Christopher Wren's new capital. By the time Scotland was incorporated within the union in 1707, a constitutional, Protestant royal succession had been established.

Above clockwise from left to right *The Pilgrim Fathers prepare for the New World; the Gunpowder Plotters, 1605; English physicist Sir Isaac Newton conducts an experiment on light; a spark from the house of the king's baker started the Great Fire of London in 1666*

THE *MAYFLOWER* PILGRIMS

Suspicious of James I and his tolerance of Catholicism, some Protestants broke away from the Church altogether. Unable to practise their faith openly, about 125 Puritans from Scrooby in Nottinghamshire emigrated to the tolerant Netherlands. Fearing the advance of Catholic Spain, the community then accepted an offer of land in the New World colony of Virginia. Lacking adequate funds, about 50 'Pilgrims' struck a deal with other emigrants and investors, and in September 1620 set sail from Plymouth in the *Mayflower*. After a stormy voyage the ship reached Cape Cod Bay, America. Several weeks on, the Puritans founded the New Plymouth settlement.

THE CAREER OF APHRA BEHN

With the return of the monarchy in 1660 theatres reopened their doors and enjoyed a boom in 'Restoration' plays by a new generation of dramatists. Most remarkable among them was Aphra Behn (1640–89), the first female professional writer. She gained access to Charles II's court through her husband, a Dutch merchant. When he died Behn was sent to the Netherlands as a royal spy. Of her plays the most popular was *The Rover* (1678), tracing a cavalier's adventures. She also wrote poetry and novels, including *Oroonoko* (1688), an indictment of slavery based on her travels to Surinam. Behn often published anonymously to conceal her sex, but was admired by her contemporaries. She is buried in Westminster Abbey.

DRAWING A BLANK

John Poyer, mayor of Pembroke, entered the Civil War as a staunch Parliamentarian. But he and his comrades, Colonel Powell and Rowland Laugharne—impatient with their meagre pay and obliged to fund their soldiers with their own money—threw in their lot with the Royalists. When Oliver Cromwell (1599–1658) arrived with an army in 1648, demanding Pembroke Castle, Poyer opened fire, killing 16 men. The turncoats held their ground firmly for six weeks but eventually surrendered and were convicted of treason. Cromwell decided to spare two of them, and sent three pieces of paper to their cell: one was blank, the others read 'Life granted by God'. Poyer drew the blank, and was duly shot in 1649.

SIR ISAAC NEWTON

The 17th century was a time of renewed intellectual activity, called by some a 'scientific revolution'. Among the greatest thinkers of the age was Sir Isaac Newton (1642–1727). As a student he was sent home from Cambridge in 1665 to escape the plague, and spent his unexpected leisure time figuring out differential calculus and gravity. Among other interests he also studied alchemy, and used astronomy to interpret the chronology of the Bible. His ground-breaking work on optics showed that light is composed of all colours; in the same vein he invented a reflecting telescope in 1668. Today, though, his best-known work is *Principia* (1687), setting out the theory of space, time and planetary motion that revolutionized our understanding of the universe.

THE ACT OF UNION

Although Scotland and England shared a monarch from 1603, they were still independent states at the beginning of the 18th century. In 1688 the Catholic James II was removed from the throne and replaced by Protestant William of Orange. The new king was keen to unite the two nations and end the enmity; James and his heirs, however, had strong Scottish support. Met with hostility or indifference, William's attempt failed—as did another in 1702 when Anne, James' daughter, came to the throne. In 1705 the Scottish Parliament alarmed Westminster by claiming the right to choose its own monarch after Anne's death. Negotiations were stepped up: On 12 May 1707 the Scottish Parliament was abolished and its MPs and peers moved to London.

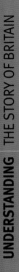

George, Elector of Hanover, was invited to take the British crown in 1714—the Georgian period was under way. It began inauspiciously with a Jacobite uprising and ran into financial scandal with the collapse in 1720 of the South Sea Company, whose investors ranged from ministers to maids.

This was a century of naval triumphs and territorial acquisition, of innovation and revolution. Agriculture produced new breeding and planting techniques, and land tenants were obliged to make way for cattle and crops. Inventions such as Sir Richard Arkwright's spinning jenny, a yarn-spinning machine, threatened jobs and provoked riots. In 1769 James Watt patented the steam engine while new smelting methods made iron production easier. Britain earned from her colonies and spent on wars, but in the 1760s American colonists began to protest against 'taxation without representation'. Concepts of rights framed during their successful independence struggle influenced radicals at home and revolutionary thinkers in France; as French heads fell, Britain's government clamped down on any suspected dissidence. Napoleon's march through Europe made popular heroes of his adversaries Nelson and Wellington. Pressure for reform continued, finally rewarded with a partial extension of the vote in 1832.

JOSIAH WEDGWOOD

Wedgwood (1730–95) was a true person of his times—the Industrial Revolution. Born into a family of Staffordshire potters, he developed a distinctive style of fine blue china with white cameo designs, which flourished in the 1760s. This was also the age of the canal, and the Trent and Mersey Canal linked the Wedgwood works to the international market. An active reformer, in 1769 Wedgwood designed Etruria, a new pottery works that included a factory village for the workers, and also lobbied hard for road improvement. In 1785 he formed the General Chamber of Manufacturers of Great Britain, bringing industrialists together as a single, increasingly powerful voice in British politics.

THE PEELERS

It was Sir Robert Peel (1788–1850) who created Britain's first effective police force. The first 'peelers' or 'bobbies' were nicknamed after the Tory home secretary (later prime minister) and in 1829 stepped on to London's streets in blue uniforms and top hats. Their Whitehall headquarters was off Scotland Yard. Many of them were ex-soldiers—'blue devils' was another nickname for them. Londoners prized their freedom and at first the badly paid constables faced suspicion and hostility. They were attacked, beaten up, and even stoned. When a constable was killed by rioters in 1831, the coroner's jury recorded a verdict of justifiable homicide. Gradually, however, under their Irish chief Richard 'King' Mayne, who ran the force until his death in 1868, they won public trust and affection.

EDINBURGH'S NEW TOWN

Advances in medical science were partly responsible for the huge growth in Britain's population during the late 18th century. In Scotland alone the population trebled between 1750 and 1800. Edinburgh, the medieval capital, was bursting at the seams. In 1767 James Craig (d 1795) was given permission to design an area of neoclassical buildings set on a grid of wide streets to the north of the city. The town council decreed that each pavement should be 3m (10ft) wide and no more than 0.3m (1ft) above the street. Also, tenants of the new houses should be allowed to set up links to the common sewer, thereby improving general hygiene and ending the practice of emptying chamber pots out of the window.

MAD KING GEORGE

In 1788 Britain had lost all control of the American colonies and trouble was brewing across the English Channel. King George III (1738–1820) had appointed William Pitt as his prime minister in the face of political hostility. At this uneasy time the king began to show signs of bizarre behaviour, attacking his son and talking incessant gibberish. Dr. Francis Willis was summoned and prescribed a harsh regime involving straitjackets and fierce poultices. The king recovered—probably in spite of this treatment—though the condition re-emerged in 1810, when he declined into mental instability, made worse by deafness and blindness. Prince George, then the heir to the throne, was established as Prince Regent. It's now believed that George suffered from porphyria, a metabolic disorder.

THE BATTLE OF WATERLOO

In 1815, back from exile on Elba, the French emperor Napoleon Bonaparte (1769–1821) advanced into Belgium. After fending him off at Quatre Bras, the Duke of Wellington's army sheltered behind a ridge near Waterloo. His Prussian allies had retreated, chased by the French, who fought them at Wavre and turned back—convinced that they had seen them off. Back at Waterloo on 18 June, wave after wave of Napoleon's troops was repelled, but eventually a farmhouse guarding the ridge was taken—Wellington's position looked bleak. Then the Prussians reappeared. Napoleon dithered over his next move and the French were routed. Surveying the carnage, Wellington remarked that the worst sight apart from a battle lost was a battle won.

Opposite and above clockwise from left to right *Ironbridge Gorge; Dividend Hall of the South Sea Company, c1808; a row of smartly dressed Victorian policemen; French Emperor Napoleon Bonaparte*

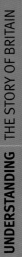

Victorian Britain was confident and ambitious. Its empire spread across the globe, and industries led the way to a modern, machine age. Mass production and mass communication changed lives and expectations; steam power and the telegraph reduced time and travel, and towns sprang up as people flocked to work in factories, mines and mills. Money was being made, and industry created a new high society.

At the same time, those left at the bottom of the heap faced poverty and squalor; disease was rife in the overcrowded city slums. Calls for reform gathered pace, and by the end of the 19th century a string of new laws had been passed to meet the needs of industrial society, with attempts to tackle the worst abuses of child exploitation and an emphasis on wider education. Public lending libraries appeared, housed in typically grand civic buildings, as did public baths and a network of schools. Funds from the 1851 Great Exhibition were used to set up the Victoria & Albert Museum, to inspire and educate with the best of British design. By the turn of the 20th century consumers were being tempted by the media of photography, recorded music and moving pictures, and a different kind of horsepower made its debut on the road.

ISAMBARD KINGDOM BRUNEL

As a young man Isambard Kingdom Brunel (1806–59) nearly drowned when water flooded into his father's pioneering project, the Thames Tunnel. Brunel recovered in Bristol, where he designed the Clifton Suspension Bridge in 1831—the city's most famous landmark—and was engineer to the Great Western Railway. He was also responsible for three innovative transatlantic ships: the *Great Western,* the *Great Eastern,* and the first large screw-propelled iron ship, the *Great Britain,* now moored at Bristol. Unusually, Brunel received an academic education rather than training as an apprentice, and retained his faith in scientific principles. His excessive workload probably contributed to his early death.

BACK TO BASICS

By the mid-19th century Britain was an industrial nation. As work became more mechanized, some mourned the loss of craftsmanship and individual dignity. Artist and socialist William Morris (1834–96) was among those who tried to redress the balance. As a leading light of the Arts and Crafts Movement, Morris harked back to the Middle Ages, as a time when art and life were inextricably linked, and sought to restore beauty to manufactured goods. His firm produced romanticized medieval designs for wallpaper, fabrics, tapestries and stained glass; the Kelmscott Press, which he founded in 1896, printed exquisitely decorated books. The Arts and Crafts style was showcased by his own home near London, Red House, designed by his partner Philip Webb.

HARD TIMES

Victorians loved the railways—none more so than Charles Dickens (1812–70), who wrote a breathless account of the speedy journey to the south coast. Making the most of the new express trains, he took his mistress, actress Ellen Ternan, and her mother to France in 1865. But on the way back disaster struck. The train from Folkestone to London was derailed on a viaduct at Staplehurst: Some carriages fell on the bridge and many people were killed or injured. One, containing Dickens and his companions, was left balancing on the edge. Having climbed free, Dickens rescued his companions and retrieved the final instalment of his last novel, *Our Mutual Friend*. The author never recovered from the shock of the incident, and his health declined until his death in 1870.

THE WILDERNESS YEARS

When her husband Prince Albert died of typhoid fever in 1861, Queen Victoria wrote that 'the world is gone for me'. She duly retreated into seclusion. Despite continuing to work at her house at Balmoral, Victoria refused to appear in public. Her prolonged absence from the public led to mockery by some, who nicknamed her 'Mrs Brown' for her dependence on Scottish manservant John Brown. Benjamin Disraeli (1804–81), who took over as prime minister in 1874, set about winning her over with flattery and gestures, such as the title Empress of India in 1876. Gradually Victoria re-emerged: During her Golden Jubilee of 1887 and Diamond Jubilee of 1897 she was greatly cheered by a public whose suspicion had given way to affection and respect.

DOCTORS AS HEROES

In the 19th century the Scottish universities gave Britain its medical elite, notably the chief medical officers of health in the 1850s. Edinburgh's Henry Littlejohn and Glasgow's William Russell ensured the cities were adequately drained and supplied with clean water, in projects such as Glasgow's Loch Katrine pipeline (1859). Medical missionaries such as David Livingstone (1813–73) and researchers such as Ronald Ross (1857–1932), who conquered the malaria-bearing mosquito, and Sir Robert Philip (1857– 1939), who did the same for tuberculosis, became role models. Robert Knox, who employed bodysnatchers Burke and Hare in the 1820s to supply corpses for his Edinburgh dissection room, did not. Author Arthur Conan Doyle (1859–1930) studied medicine at Edinburgh University. He modelled Sherlock Holmes on his professor, Joseph Bell, who could deduce a scenario from the tiniest details.

Opposite and above clockwise from left to right *Isambard Kingdom Brunel's rail bridge spans the River Tamar; Queen Victoria, Queen of England and Empress of India; King Arthur and Sir Lancelot captured in stained glass by William Morris*

In 1903 the American Wright brothers, Orville and Wilbur, completed the first successful powered flight. Several years later air forces took to the sky as the world went to war. Many of those who survived the horrors of World War I returned to unemployment or meagre pay. Wage disputes almost paralyzed Britain during the General Strike of 1926, and depression hit hard after the Wall Street Crash in 1929. In 1936 shipbuilders marched from Jarrow in the northeast to London to voice their desperation.

Television first appeared in the 1930s, but it was the wireless radio that dominated interwar entertainment. Millions tuned in to hear war declared on Nazi Germany in 1939. World War II left Britain weary and ready for change: A new welfare state promised health, education and security for all. Even as the empire was dissolving, its colonies demanding independence, immigration was encouraged to make up the workforce.

The first motorway, bypassing Preston, was opened in 1958. A year later the Mini was introduced. In the 1960s designer Mary Quant and The Beatles set the pace in fashion and pop. Heavy industry declined in the 1970s and 1980s amid conflict and strikes. By the century's end power had devolved from Westminster to Scotland and Wales, and peace in Northern Ireland inched closer.

THE FRONTLINE SUFFRAGETTE

Emmeline Pankhurst (1858–1928) was the leading light of the campaign for women's suffrage—the right to vote. With her daughter Christabel (1880–1958), she founded the Women's Social and Political Union in 1903, promoting militant tactics. In 1908 she received the first of a series of prison sentences, including one for a bomb attack on a property belonging to the Chancellor of the Exchequer. Under the 'Cat and Mouse Act' she was released to regain her health and then re-arrested 12 times. With the outbreak of war in 1914, Emmeline turned her campaigning energies to recruiting troops to fight Germany. Women over 30 finally got to vote in 1918, with equal voting rights following on some 10 years later.

EUROTUNNEL

Plans for an underwater tunnel to be built beneath the English Channel to link Britain with the European continent were first mooted in 1802, envisaging horse-drawn transport and even stables. In the 1880s work began on early train tunnels on each side of the English Channel, only to be halted by Queen Victoria amid fears that British security would be breached. In the 1960s, and with Britain's entry into the European Economic Community in 1973, further plans were made but then abandoned due to government crises and the rise in world oil prices. Digging finally began again in 1987 and, after many years of delays and funding problems, the French and British tunnels were joined up in December 1990. In November 1994 trains carried their first passengers along the 50km (31 miles) of the Channel Tunnel.

CASTAWAY CHOICE

Like all the best ideas, the longest-running radio show in the world is exceptionally simple. It is the British Broadcasting Corporation's (BBC) *Desert Island Discs*. The programme was first aired in 1942 and continues to be broadcast on the Radio 4 channel. Each week a guest is 'stranded' on an imaginary desert island: They are permitted to take eight favourite pieces of music, one book and a luxury item. A copy of The Bible and Shakespeare's complete works are already on the island. Castaways have included royalty and five prime ministers. Musical trends have fluctuated but the most recent lists show that Beethoven's *Symphony No. 9* is the most requested piece of classical music, followed by Schubert's *Quintet in C* and *Soave sia il vento* from Mozart's *Cosi Fan Tutte*. The Beatles dominate the pop chart.

THE BLITZ

In September 1940 Germany began a series of night bombardments, described by the British press as Blitz (German for lightning) attacks. Between 7 September and 2 November, London suffered nightly raids. Later the focus shifted to other British cities and ports, and heavy strikes on Birmingham continued until 16 May 1941; intermittent air attacks continued through the remainder of the war. Over 3.5 million houses were destroyed and about 30,000 people killed—just over half were Londoners. There were 57 bombing raids on the capital alone, using 13,561 tonnes of explosive. By the war's end Allied pilots flying over Germany would drop more bombs in a single week than the total tonnage of bombs that hit London during the darkness of 1940–41.

THE WELFARE STATE

A month after the end of the war in Europe Britain went to the polls. Having led the country to victory, Conservative leader Sir Winston Churchill (1874–1965) hoped to take the helm in peacetime, but the electorate was hungry for change. Labour gained power with a landslide vote, promising to provide basic care for everyone, from cradle to grave: the Welfare State. Three years of legislation introduced an extended National Insurance scheme which was to fund pensions and pay during illness and unemployment, and free health care for all with the founding of the National Health Service in 1946. The school-leaving age was raised to 15 and free secondary education was ensured. Homelessness, exacerbated by the war, was tackled with a massive state house-building programme.

Opposite and above clockwise from left to right *The suffragette movement resulted in women gaining the right to vote in 1918; Winston Churchill led Britons through the horrors of the blitz 1940–41; Mary Quant was a leading designer during the swinging sixties*

Above *European tastes are catered to in shops across Britain*

Britain entered the new millennium with not so much a bang as a fizzle when a fireworks show failed to turn the Thames into a spectacular 'river of fire'. Things picked up with a successful, if rain-sodden, Commonwealth Games hosted by Manchester in 2002. The monarchy recovered from a few rocky years after the death of Princess Diana, with the Queen celebrating her Golden Jubilee in 2002. As well as the consequences of European Union expansion, Britain now faces the same issues as other countries around the world—a volatile global economy and threats to national security and to the environment.

QUIDS IN

In the 1990s the euro, the single European currency, was at the root of a serious dissent within the ruling Conservative Party. In the early 2000s the Labour government struggled to sell the idea to a sceptical Britain. By 2008 the wrangling over a new EU treaty rumbled on and the prospect of Britain ever joining the eurozone seemed encreasingly dim. Despite the growing strength of the euro, it may be some years still before Britain sees the end of the quid (pound).

NEW BRITONS

The expansions to the European Union since 2004 has resulted in an influx of workers from Eastern Europe. The popular press characterised the newcomers as Polish plumbers and Hungarian nannies. In reality, workers have come from all over the new European Union to fill a vast range of vacancies in the UK workplace, and with them has come a new chapter in the cultural diversity of Britain. And it hasn't just been the cities where the new arrivals have settled. You're as likely to find a Polish food shop, or overhear conversations in Lithuanian in a small town in the Lake District as you are in the urban centres. How long this boom will last is hard to say, but as the economies of the new Europe grow, some of the traffic has started to go back the other way, with Polish companies recruiting in the British regions to fill the vacancies left at home.

GOODBYE, HELLO

Half a million people waited for up to 12 hours to file past the Queen Mother's coffin in Westminster Hall before her funeral in 2002. Westminster Abbey's tenor bell tolled for 101 minutes, one for each year of her life. Born Elizabeth Bowes-Lyon, she married the Duke of York in 1923 and he became King George VI in 1936. An estimated 300 million people watched on television as a carriage carried her coffin to the abbey, followed by the solemn entourage of royals and political leaders. In contrast, the marriage of her grandson, Charles, to Camilla Parker-Bowles on 9 April 2005 was a rather subdued affair. The Prince, who divorced Diana, Princess of Wales nine years before, and the newly created Duchess of Cornwall, took their vows in a small civil ceremony at the Guildhall in Windsor.

ON THE MOVE

On the Move gives you detailed advice and information about the various options for travelling to Britain before explaining the best ways to get around the country once you are there. Handy tips help you with everything from buying tickets to renting a car.

Arriving	44
Getting Around	46
Driving	48
Trains	52
Coaches	54
Buses	55
Ferries	56
Domestic Flights	57
Cycling in Britain	59
Taxis	60
Visitors with Children	61
Visitors with a Disability	62

ARRIVING BY AIR

This is the most common method of entering the UK, and London, Britain's principal gateway, has air connections to all major world cities. Most long-haul flights arrive at Heathrow or Gatwick, while the capital's three other airports—Stansted, Luton and London City—serve mainly short-haul destinations.

All airports have information desks, shops, banks, restaurants, car-rental companies, hotel reservation desks and left-luggage facilities. If departing from Heathrow or Gatwick make sure you know which terminal you need. Taxis are usually available outside the terminals.

A number of airports in other parts of the country also accept international flights. These include Birmingham International, Leeds-Bradford, Edinburgh, Glasgow (International and Prestwick), Manchester and Southampton. **See also** Some Low-cost and Domestic Airlines (▷ 57).

LONDON HEATHROW (LHR)

The world's busiest airport lies 19km (12 miles) west of central London. It has five terminals:
1, 2 and 3 in the main complex, 4 on the south side of the airport and 5 on the west. All terminals are linked to the London Underground (one station serves Terminals 1, 2 and 3, another serves Terminal 4 and a third serves Terminal 5), reached by moving walkways and elevators.

For general information about Heathrow tel 0870 000 0123 or visit www.heathrowairport.com.

LONDON GATWICK (LGW)

Britain's second-largest airport is 48km (30 miles) south of central London. Its two terminals, North and South, are linked by Gatwick Transit, an efficient, free monorail. Trains run every 3–4 minutes from each terminal, with a journey time of just under 2 minutes. South Terminal handles much of Gatwick's traffic—domestic, international and charter flights. For more information tel 0870 000 2468 or visit www.gatwickairport.com.

LONDON STANSTED (STN)

Stansted, in Essex, is 56km (35 miles) northeast of London, not far from Cambridge. Its large, modern terminal (1991) was designed by Norman Foster. Rapid transit trains shuttle between this and the airport's two other buildings. London's fastest-growing airport is a base for low-cost airlines such as Ryanair and easyJet. There are no black taxis at Stansted. Tel: 0870 000 0303 or visit www.stanstedairport.com.

LONDON LUTON (LTN)

Luton airport occupies an ugly array of buildings 52km (32 miles) north of central London. A new passenger terminal opened in 1999, along with Luton Parkway train station, from where there are frequent trains to King's Cross. Luton caters mainly to low-cost charter flights, plus scheduled easyJet services. Tel 01582 405100 or check www.london-luton.co.uk for information.

LONDON CITY (LCA)

The capital's smallest (and newest) airport, set in the regenerated Docklands area 10km (6 miles) from central London, is especially popular with visitors on business. Flights operate to more than 20 European destinations and British towns and cities. Tel 020 7646 0088 or visit www.londoncityairport.com.

GLASGOW AIRPORT (GLA)

Glasgow Airport, located 13km (8 miles) west of the city is the busiest of Scotland's three international airports. It receives flights from 35 destinations in Britain, Europe and North America. Tel 08700 400008 or visit www.glasgowairport.com.

MANCHESTER AIRPORT (MAN)

Manchester Airport is the principal airport in the north of England and operates flights to every continent from its three terminals. The airport is situated 16km (10 miles) south of the city. Tel 09010 101000 or visit www.manchesterairport.co.uk.

ARRIVING BY RAIL

Eurostar trains from France (Paris, Avignon and Lille) and Belgium (Brussels) speed to St. Pancras International Station in under three hours. Passports are required for travel and, on arrival, you must also clear customs. There are escalators and elevators to the main Waterloo complex and signs to the Under-

FROM	TAXI
Heathrow	1 hr, £40–70. Terminal 1: 020 8745 7487 Terminal 2: 020 8745 5408 Terminal 3: 020 8745 4655 Terminal 4: 020 8745 7302 Terminal 5: N/A
Gatwick	60–75 min, £93.50 Checker Cars: 01293 568800
Stansted	1–2 hours, £98. Checker Cars: 01279 662444
Luton	45 min–1hr, £63. Cabco: 01582 736666, Alpha taxis: 01582 595555
London City	20–30 min, £35. Taxi rank outside terminal.

ground (Northern, Bakerloo, Jubilee, and Waterloo and City lines) and buses. A taxi stand is outside the station on the left.

Trains from other parts of Britain arrive at one of London's main terminals, all of which have Underground and bus links (▷ 52–55).

ARRIVING BY COACH

If you travel to Britain by coach (long-distance bus) you will probably arrive at London's Victoria Coach Station (VCS).

» Victoria Coach Station 164 Buckingham Palace Road, London SW1W 9TPTel: 020 7222 1234

» National Express Tel: 08705 808080; www.nationalexpress.com

» Greenline 4a Fountain Square, 123–151 Buckingham Palace Road, London SW1W 0SR; tel: 0870 608 7261; www.greenline.co.uk

ARRIVING BY CAR

Eurotunnel operates the train service for cars, caravans and motorcycles through the Channel Tunnel. The journey from Calais to Folkestone takes 20 minutes; drivers and passengers remain in their vehicles. At Folkestone, the terminal joins the M20 north (junction 11a). The drive to London takes 1 hour 30 minutes.

ARRIVING BY FERRY

Ferries now face stiff competition from Eurostar and Eurotunnel, so they can be a relatively inexpensive way of crossing the Channel. Various companies operate passenger and vehicle services between Britain and Europe. Trains run from ports on the south coast—Dover, Folkestone, Ramsgate and Newhaven—to London Victoria. The train operator National Express East Anglia runs a

service from Harwich to Liverpool Street. Along with regular ferry services, certain ports, such as Calais, operate faster high speed crafts.

CITY LINKS FROM FERRY PORTS

» Dover Shuttle bus to Dover Priory Station, then train to London Charing Cross, 1 hour 45 min–2 hours

» Fishguard Train to Swansea, 3 hours 30 min

» Folkestone M20 to London, 1 hour 30 min–2 hours

» Harwich Train to London Liverpool Street, 1 hour 30 min

» Holyhead Train to Crewe (2 hours) via Chester (1 hour 40 min)

» Newcastle Bus to city centre and train station (20 min)

» Newhaven Train to London Victoria, from 1 hour 15 min

» Portsmouth Train to London Waterloo, 1 hour 35 min

GETTING TO CENTRAL LONDON FROM THE AIRPORT

TRAIN	UNDERGROUND	BUS	CAR
Heathrow Express to Paddington, 15–20 min. Daily 5.10am–11.47pm, £14.50 (one way). Heathrow Connect to Paddington, 1 hr 22 min, 4.42am–11.54pm, £6.90 (one way).	Piccadilly Line takes 1 hr. Mon–Sat 5.10am–11.50pm, Sun 5.57am–11.30pm, £4.	National Express to Victoria Coach Station, 45 min. Every 5–40 min, £8 (return).	East along M4 from junction 3 or 4. For Terminal 5 use junction 14 on M25.
Gatwick Express to Victoria, 30 min. 4.35am–1.35am, every 15 mins 5.50am–12.35am, £16.90 (one way) First Capital Connect to King's Cross, City, Farringdon, Blackfriars and London Bridge, 40 min, from £8.90.	N/A	National Express to Victoria Coach Station, 1 hr 20 min. Every hour, £12.20 (return).	North along M23 from junction 9.
Stansted Express to Liverpool Street, 40 min. Mon–Sat 5.30am–1.30am, £24 (return).	N/A	National Express to Victoria Coach Station, 90 min. Every 30 min, £17 (return). Terravision 1–2 per hour to Liverpool Street Station or Victoria Coach Station (£13 return).	South along M11 from junction 8.
Shuttle bus £1 to Luton Airport Parkway Station for First Capital Connect to King's Cross, Farringdon, City, Blackfriars and London Bridge, 35 min. Daily 7am–10pm, £12. Some night services.	N/A	Greenline Bus No. 757 to Victoria Coach Station, 90 min. Every 12–15 min, £13 (return). easyBus runs minibuses to Baker Street in central London every hour. From £2	South along M1 from junction 10A.
N/A	DLR takes 22 mins. Mon–Sat 5.30am–12.30am Sun 7am–11.20pm every 10–16 min, £4.	N/A	N/A

You'll need to tackle the public transport system to cross London. The Underground train network (known as the Tube), the world's oldest, is quicker than taking a bus, but it can be hot and stuffy. Buses can be a pleasant alternative, offering views from the top deck. Riverboats run from quays along the River Thames to certain attractions, while taxis are a convenient but expensive option. Or you could walk—many Tube stations are actually close to each other.

MAKING IT EASY—TICKETS

You can buy tickets for all forms of public transport at most Underground stations, train stations, information offices and many other outlets. Carry small change so you can use ticket machines instead of queuing at a ticket office. You can buy individual tickets for all types of transport, but the best option is a Travelcard. These are valid for the entire network in selected zones and give unlimited travel in the paid-for zone.

Central London occupies Zone 1, with Zones 2–9 following in progressively wider concentric rings, which are colour-coded on Tube maps. It is sensible to pay a little extra to allow travel in more zones.

One-Day Travelcard
Zones 1 and 2: adult £6.80/5.30 (peak/off-peak), child £3.40
Zones 1–4, adult £9.40/5.90, child £4.70

Three-Day Travelcard
Zones 1 and 2: adult £17.40, child £8.70

Family Travel
Up to four children pay £1 each when accompanied by an adult-rate Travelcard holder.

Watch out for pickpockets. Ensure that your bags are closed and avoid carrying valuables in back pockets or rucksacks. Mobile phones won't work underground. Download Tube information in French, German, Spanish, Italian or Portuguese from www.tfl.gov.uk/ Check that trains are running in the update section or use the journey planner.

For up-to-date news and more information tel 020 7222 1234, or go to www.tfl.gov.uk.

THE UNDERGROUND

London Underground operates some 500 trains between 260 stations. Twelve colour-coded lines make up the Greater London Underground system, each with its own name. Trains run Mon–Sat 4.40am–12.45am (Sun 6.45am–12.20am), but try to avoid the rush hours (7–9.30am, 4.30–7pm). It is cheaper to travel after 9.30am and on weekends.

Space is limited so don't take too much luggage; fold buggies (strollers) when you get on the train.

If you cannot produce a valid ticket you will be liable for a £20 fine.

Most stations have electronic ticket gates. If your ticket does not work, find a staff member. You will need your ticket to leave the station; don't discard it.

BUSES

London's iconic red double-decker buses are a good way to make short journeys. Main bus stops (red circle on a white background) have timetables and route information. Buses stop automatically. At request stops (white circle on a red background) you must hail buses. At night treat all stops as request stops. Night buses (number preceded by 'wN') run 11pm–6am on main routes. Each route is identified by a number on the front of the bus. In central London you must buy a ticket from a roadside machine before boarding.

The Riverside service links the South Bank to the West End, with 40 attractions along the route.

A single adult fare on most routes within Greater London is £2. Children under 14 travel free. 14- to 15-year olds may travel free if they have photo ID.

RIVERBOATS

Most riverboat services start from Westminster or Embankment piers and run 6.30am–9.30pm. The routes run as far as Hampton Court Palace to the west and on to the Thames Barrier to the east.

Left *Tower Bridge and HMS* Belfast

TRAINS AND TRAMS

London is not the only British city to have an underground train system. Several other cities throughout the country have an alternative public network to the busy road systems. Glasgow's is called the Subway and it runs daily to 15 stations on a circular route around the city. A single adult fare starts at £1.10 and a one-day pass costs £2.50. Trains run at intervals of 5 to 8 minutes.

Newcastle upon Tyne has called its underground the Metro, and it runs daily to 60 stations throughout Tyne and Wear. A single adult fare costs between £1.30 and £2.80.

Birmingham's tram network is also known as the Metro. It connects Wolverhampton with Birmingham via 23 stops. A single fare costs from £1.10. And Manchester's tram service is the Metrolink, running to 37 stops with single fares costing from 70p.

HOW TO USE THE UNDERGROUND

» Stand on the right on escalators so that people in a hurry can pass by you on the left.

» If you have bulky items, buggies or folding bicycles you can go through the special wide gates. A staff member will let you through.

» Stand clear of the train's closing doors. Obstructing them causes delays.

» Mind the gap between the platform and the train.

» Let passengers off the train before you get on.

» Note that there is no air-conditioning on the Underground and delays are not uncommon so it can get very hot, especially in summer.

» Stand behind the yellow line on the platform when waiting for a train.

» Threats and violent behaviour should be reported to members of staff.

UNDERSTANDING THE UNDERGROUND MAP

TUBE STATION

A simple dash indicates a station with no interchanges.

MAIN LINE STATION

This symbol indicates a connection with a main line station.

You will see a map like the section below in the train. Follow your journey, count the stops and watch for the names of stations so you know where to get off.

COLOUR-CODED LINES

Each line is colour-coded to make navigation easy.

STATION WITH INTERCHANGE

Interchanges with other Underground lines and with suburban rail are marked with a white circle. Two white circles show more than one line interchange.

INTERCHANGING LINES

These symbols (left) show stations with connecting lines and their relevant colours.

© Transport for London   Reg. user No. 02/3702

DRIVING

One of the best ways of getting around the country and of seeing Britain is by car. On the whole, motorists drive safely, roads are good, if busy, and signposting is efficient. In some parts of Britain, driving is the only way of getting around, as local transport can be limited. The network of narrow, crooked lanes between small towns and villages makes a delightful opportunity to see the country, while the fast motorways link major towns and cities. Note that you must drive on the left-hand side of the road.

CAR RENTAL

Arranging to rent a car through your travel agent before arriving can save money and allows you to find out about deposits, drop-off charges, cancellation penalties and insurance costs in advance. However, the usual established car rental companies have offices throughout Britain. Smaller, local companies and online agents may offer better deals; check the *Yellow Pages*.

You must have a valid driver's licence. An International Driving Permit may be useful if your licence is not in English.

Most rental firms require the driver to be at least 23 years old and have at least 12 months' driving experience.

Rental rates usually include free unlimited mileage.

It is important to ensure that you have some form of personal insurance along with Collision Damage Waiver (CDW). Many companies also offer Damage Excess Reduction (DER) and Theft Protection for an additional premium. You will also have to pay more for additional drivers.

Find out what equipment comes as standard: air-conditioning is not always available.

Most cars use unleaded fuel; make sure you know what's required (unleaded or diesel) before filling up the tank.

Although reputable companies operate new fleets and service them to a high standard, it is advisable to make your own checks before accepting a rental car, including checking for tyre wear. Insist on a different vehicle if you are unhappy with this. Check that rear seat belts are fitted and arrange for child car seats if you have small children.

FUEL

All large garages (gas stations) are self-service and sell higher- octane unleaded petrol (gas), unleaded 95 octane fuel and diesel. Note that leaded four-star fuel has been phased out. Higher octane is the most expensive. Prices vary slightly across the country.

CONGESTION CHARGE

A congestion charge operates in central London. It costs £8 per car per day Monday to Friday 7am–6-.30pm, excluding public holidays. You can pay online (www.tfl.gov.uk), by phone 24 hours a day (tel 0845 900 1234), in person at outlets such as petrol stations and shops, or by credit or debit card at self-service machines at parking areas inside the zone and at other locations. You need to pay in advance or on the day, prior to 10pm. The charge rises to £10 if you pay after 10pm.

Digital cameras check number plates; those in breach of regulations are fined £120.

THE LAW

Drive on the left.
» The wearing of seat belts is obligatory, including in the back.
» Motorcyclists must wear helmets at all times.
» The speed limit in built-up areas is 30mph (48kph); outside built-up areas the speed limit is 60mph (97kph) on single carriageways and 70mph (113kph) on dual carriageways and motorways (highways), unless a sign indicates otherwise.
» There are tough laws against drinking and driving. The best advice is not to drink alcohol at all if you are going to driving.
» Red routes are priority routes controlled by the police where no stopping is allowed at any time.
» Cars are banned from using bus lanes—look for signs.
» Give way to traffic coming from the right at roundabouts (▷ left).

MAKING IT EASY AT ROUNDABOUTS (TRAFFIC CIRCLES)

 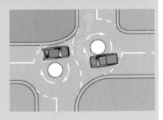

When approaching a roundabout, give priority to traffic on your right, unless directed otherwise by signs, road markings or traffic lights. Look forward before moving off to make sure traffic in front has moved. Watch out for vehicles already on the roundabout; be aware that they may not be signalling correctly, or at all.

Give way to traffic on your right. Use the left-hand lane (if there is one) to turn left. Use mini roundabouts in the same way.

PARKING

Street parking in major cities is limited and for short periods.

Check for restrictions to certain vehicles or at certain time periods. NOTE: Do not park on a pedestrian crossing or area marked with zigzags; at the side of a road that has a central double white line; on a clearway (marked by a red cross) during operational times; on a cycle or bus lane or a tramway; in bays reserved for doctors, ambulances or disabled drivers.

METERS

Meter parking is charged by the hour or minute and charges vary.

The maximum stay at a meter is generally two hours and usually you cannot return to the same parking spot within an hour.

In general, meter parking is free Monday to Friday after 6.30pm, Saturday from 1.30pm and Sunday all day, but there are some exceptions.

CAR RENTAL FIRMS

NAME	TELEPHONE	WEBSITE
Alamo	0870 599 3000	www.alamo.co.uk
Avis	0870 010 0287	www.avis.co.uk
Budget	01344 484100	www.budget.com
Easycar	0906 33 33 33 3	www.easycar.com
Europcar	0870 607 5000	www.europcar.com
Hertz	0870 599 6699	www.hertz.co.uk
National	0870 400 4579	www.nationalcar.co.uk
Practical	01217 728599	www.practical.co.uk
Sixt Kenning	01246 506218	www.e-sixt.com
Thrifty	01494 751 500	www.thrifty.co.uk

ROAD SIGNS AND DRIVING TIPS

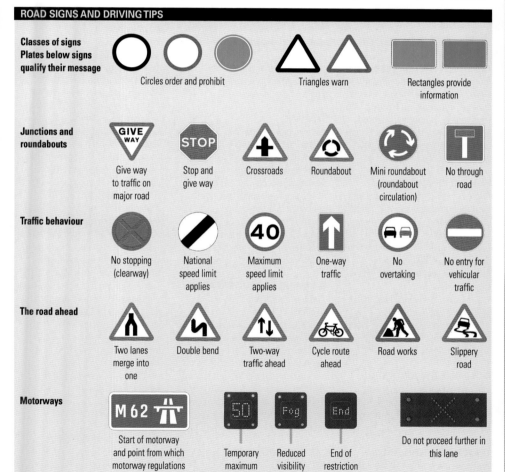

Classes of signs
Plates below signs
qualify their message

Circles order and prohibit

Triangles warn

Rectangles provide information

Junctions and roundabouts

Give way to traffic on major road

Stop and give way

Crossroads

Roundabout

Mini roundabout (roundabout circulation)

No through road

Traffic behaviour

No stopping (clearway)

National speed limit applies

Maximum speed limit applies

One-way traffic

No overtaking

No entry for vehicular traffic

The road ahead

Two lanes merge into one

Double bend

Two-way traffic ahead

Cycle route ahead

Road works

Slippery road

Motorways

Start of motorway and point from which motorway regulations apply

Temporary maximum speed limit

Reduced visibility ahead

End of restriction

Do not proceed further in this lane

ON-STREET PAY AND DISPLAY

If you park in a 'pay and display' area you must buy a ticket from the machine and display it clearly inside your vehicle as it will be checked. Some machines require you to type in the first three numbers of your vehicle number plate.

PARKING RESTRICTIONS

A single yellow line indicates that parking restrictions apply; a notice should explain exactly what these restrictions are.

No parking is allowed at any time on a double yellow line.

A broken yellow line indicates limited restrictions.

A single red line indicates that stopping is not permitted.

Many residential streets in urban centres are reserved for permit-holding residents only.

CAR PARKS (PARKING LOTS)

The biggest car park operator in Britain is National Car Parks (NCP, tel 0845 050 7080, www.ncp.co.uk). Rates are high.

TRAFFIC WARDENS/FINES

Traffic wardens patrol streets in all major cities. The Fixed Penalty Notice for parking offences is £60–120.

If you get a parking ticket, don't ignore it. Many fines carry a discount if paid within 14 days.

STOPPING

You may pick up and drop off passengers in restricted areas but not on clearways—red routes in London.

Continuous loading/unloading is permitted except where kerb markings indicate a loading ban, or on clearways (marked by a red cross) or other restrictions.

Check for official notices on posts or walls nearby to see when restricted hours apply.

CLAMPING AND TOWING AWAY

If your car is parked illegally it may be clamped; the notice posted on your windscreen explains how to get it released. Vehicles are usually released within one hour of payment. If your vehicle is removed it will cost at least £125 to get it back. Vehicles must be collected in person and you must produce at least one form of identification, such as your driver's licence.

CAR BREAKDOWN AND ACCIDENTS

Several organizations in the UK can assist you in the event of breakdown. Check whether membership in your home country entitles you to reciprocal assistance from one of the British organizations.

AT THE SCENE OF AN ACCIDENT

If, as a driver, you are involved in a road traffic accident, stop and remain at the scene and give your vehicle registration number, your name and address, and that of the vehicle owner, to anyone with reasonable grounds for asking for those details. If you do not exchange those details at the scene, you must report the accident at a police station or to a police officer within 24 hours.

MOTORWAYS

Britain has a vast network of motorways serving all parts of the country. The major arteries are the M1 north, M2 to the southeast, M3 south, M4 west, M5 southwest, the M6/M74 to Scotland, the M62 across the Pennines and the M8 across Scotland's central belt. The M6 has an alternative toll section that avoids a notorious congested area, between junctions 4 and 11 around Birmingham. Cars pay £4.50 (or £3.50 between 11pm and 6am).

Many motorways are fitted with electronic information panels that can be clearly seen from a distance and inform motorists of situations ahead on the road, such as accidents, fog or other problems.

When joining the motorway from a slip road (ramp), give priority to traffic already on the motorway. Do not overtake on the inside—this is against the law—except where traffic is stationary and the lane you are in is moving faster than the outer lanes, or where a slip road is indicated off the motorway by a short dotted line.

Keep a safe distance from the vehicle in front.

Do not exceed the 70mph (113kph) speed limit.

Do not drive on the hard shoulder except in an emergency or if you are directed to do so.

The above chart lists major points on Britain's road network. Use the chart to gauge the distance in miles (green) and duration in hours and minutes (blue) of a car journey.

BREAKDOWN ORGANIZATIONS

The Automobile Association (AA)
Lambert House, Stockport Road, Cheadle SK8 2DY, tel 0870 600 0371 (information) or 0800 444999 (new members), www.theaa.com; open daily 24 hours. You can become a member on the spot but it will cost you more than if you join beforehand.

The AA website (www.theaa. com) provides advice on what to do in the event of breakdown; a 'Route Planner', with maps and directions; traffic news and online road status reports. AA Roadwatch, tel 0870 600 0371, has the latest on traffic jams.

Calls cost up to 75p per minute from landlines. Mobile costs may vary.

The Environmental Transport Association (ETA)
68 High Street, Weybridge, Surrey KT13 8RS, tel 0845 389 1010. The breakdown number is supplied on joining and the service operates 24 hours (www.eta.co.uk).

The Royal Automobile Club (RAC)
RAC Motoring Services, Great Park Road, Bradley Stoke, Bristol BS32 4QN, tel 0870 572 2722 for membership enquiries. For breakdown assistance tel 0800 828282 24 hours (www.rac.co.uk).

TRAINS

The railway is a British invention and, unfortunately for passengers, much of the 19th-century network is still in operation. However, the services generally work fairly efficiently and are not oppressively crowded outside peak periods. Following denationalization and the breakup of the British Rail network, over 20 different companies now operate the trains. This can lead to differing facilities and some curious price anomalies as each company determines its own fare structure. In some cases it is worth checking whether another company serving the same region can offer an alternative route or lower price.

Train services can be notoriously unreliable in hot weather (warped tracks), cold weather (icy tracks) and in autumn (leaves on the line), so always leave plenty of time for your journey, especially if you have to change trains.

Essential engineering work, usually carried out on weekends and public holidays, can severely disrupt services, with buses sometimes replacing trains in certain areas. Details are displayed at relevant stations, or check in advance with National Rail Enquiries (www.nationalrail.co.uk).

TRAIN INFORMATION

Detailed information for the whole network—including operating companies, timetables, fares and restrictions—is available from National Rail Enquiries. Tel: 08457 484950; minicom: 0845 605 0600; www.nationalrail.co.uk. Their useful free map and guide to using the national rail network is available at stations. Staffed stations usually have free timetables of local services, and almost all stations display timetables. Note that weekend service is more limited.

There are two classes of train travel: first and standard. First class is much more expensive but does guarantee you a seat on trains as well as complimentary drinks and newspapers. Standard class is acceptable and you can reserve a seat for longer journeys if you book your ticket in advance.

Sleeping compartments can be reserved with First Scotrail on some overnight services to and from Scotland (tel 0845 755 0033, www.firstscotrail.com).

OTHER USEFUL CONTACTS

Eurostar Tel 08705 186186 (UK), 0033 8 92 35 35 39 (France), 0032 25 28 28 28 (Belgium); www.eurostar.com.
Eurotunnel Tel 08705 35 35 35; www.eurotunnel.com.

HOW TO BUY TICKETS

You must always buy a valid ticket for your journey before you board the train or you may be liable for a fine. You can buy a ticket in person for any destination served by any company from any rail station, from the ticket office. Many stations have automated machines selling tickets for shorter journeys. Most London Underground stations also sell rail tickets, as do travel agents. Credit and debit cards are accepted. Station staff are obliged to inform you of the cheapest available fare.

Standard ticket machines accept larger-denomination coins and £5 and £10 notes (not too crumpled) and will give change unless they indicate otherwise. An increasing number of automated ticket machines, especially on commuter routes, also accept debit and credit cards.

You can also buy tickets online through www.thetrainline.com or www.qjump.co.uk, both of which give prices and fast booking for different types of tickets for any journey. You can also book through a train operating company's website.

Smaller, unstaffed stations often have ticket machines or machines that issue a 'permit to travel': insert any amount of money and this will be deducted from the fare when a member of staff issues your ticket later in the journey. If there is no

means of buying a ticket in advance, you will be sold one on the train.

Seat reservations are usually necessary for long-distance routes, and are advisable at peak times. They are compulsory for certain services, in which case there is no extra charge.

TYPES OF TICKET

Rail travel is expensive and with so many different ticket options available, it pays to do some research in advance to find the best bargains. For some discounted fares you will need to buy tickets a week or more in advance. Unless you ask for first class, tickets issued will usually be for standard class travel.

A cheap day return (round trip) is the best option for a day out, but you can buy and use it only after 9.30am. Day return tickets usually consist of two separate tickets ('out' and 'return'), so make sure you keep both and use the correct one.

Except for certain 'rover' or 'open' tickets, your journey(s) must be on the date(s) shown on the ticket and you cannot break the journey. This means you cannot get off en route and join a later train—if you get off before your original destination, you must then buy another ticket. At staffed stations you can buy tickets for travel on a specific date. If you change your plans you can get a refund, provided you have not started your journey.

Tickets for journeys between London terminus stations will normally include travel on the Underground, but check your ticket before you set out.

Other Tickets

Apex This term refers to options for certain long-distance journeys,

TYPES OF RAILCARD

RAILCARD	ELIGIBILITY	PRICE	INFORMATION
Disabled Person's	Holder plus adult companion	£18	www.railcard.co.uk
Family	Up to 4 adults and 4 children	£24	www.railcard.co.uk
Network	Over 16s for travel in London, South East	£20	www.railcard.co.uk
Senior	Ages 60 and over	£24	www.railcard.co.uk
Young Person's	Ages 16–25, and full-time students of any age	£24	www.railcard.co.uk

bought three or more days in advance. The earlier you reserve, the more you save on the normal fare.

Plusbus A rail ticket with one day's unlimited bus travel on services at either end of the journey. Available for participating stations only (www.plusbus.info).

CONCESSIONS AND PASSES

Children under 5 travel free and 5- to 15-year-olds pay half price for most tickets, but check as there are some exceptions.

Britrail Pass This gives unlimited rail travel in Britain and Northern Ireland for non-UK residents only, but can only be purchased abroad. The BritRail Consecutive Pass gives freedom of travel over 4, 8, 15 or 22 consecutive days or a calendar month, and the BritRail FlexiPass covers any 4, 8 or 15 days of travel in a two-month period. Also available are Party Passes (50 per cent discount for third and fourth passengers); Family Passes (free travel for an accompanying child aged 5–15) and regional passes (days out from London, Scotland and Wales). For information visit www.britrail.com.

Regional passes For Scotland, Wales and regions of England.

Railcards For extensive use of services in southeast England it may be worth buying a railcard, valid for a year. It costs £20 and gives 33 per cent off fares to stations in the region. A Young Person's Railcard (16–25 year olds and mature students in full-time education) costs £24 and is valid across the country. You'll need a passport-size photograph and proof of eligibility to buy one railcard.

AT THE STATION

Most train stations have electronic information displays showing departure times, station stops, platform numbers and estimated time of arrival. Larger stations are more like airport terminals, showing departures and arrivals for each platform. Information for visitors with a disability or with children is given later in this chapter (▷ 61–62).

London has 10 main termini, each serving a different region of the country, as well as providing cross-city services (see also Arriving, ▷ 44). Services from London can reach most parts of Britain in a day—Intercity trains on major routes travel at 140mph (225kph), so journeys from one end of the country to the other can take just a few hours. Conversely, some trains stop at every station, and going even a relatively short distance can seem interminable.

Keep your ticket with you at all times, or you may be liable to a penalty fare (£20, or the single fare to the next scheduled stop, whichever is the greater) and have to buy a ticket at the full fare.

Most urban stations have automatic barriers. Put your ticket into the slot on one side. If you have a return ticket it then pops back out at the top: remember to collect it. The barrier will then open for you to pass. If you have a disability, luggage, children, or just need help, go instead to the staffed gate at the side of the barrier. The barriers retain used tickets at the end of a journey.

Check the displays and listen to announcements to find out which platform (track) you need.

Changing trains can be tricky if your connection time is tight. So, if in doubt, ask the station staff. It is worth checking the train's destination with a guard as you board the train, especially if you are in a hurry or if services are experiencing problems, as platforms can be changed at short notice.

Avoid weekday rush hours (7–9.30am and 4.30–7pm) if possible. Note that the evening rush hour often starts earlier on Friday, especially before public holidays.

Allow plenty of time, especially to make connections.

Few stations have left-luggage facilities, for security reasons, but King's Cross Station in London provides a good, facility.

MAIN TICKET OPTIONS

TICKET TYPE	RESTRICTIONS	VALIDITY
Open single (one way)	None	On the date shown, or on either of the two following days
Day single/day return	None	Date shown; return same day
Saver return	Peak travel restrictions	Return within one calendar month
SuperSaver return	Not available for travel before 9.30am,	Return within one calendar month on Fri, summer Sat and peak holidays
Network AwayBreak	Not before 9.30am	London and South East only; return within five days
Cheap day return	Not before 9.30am	Return the same day
In approximately descending order of price.		

COACHES

Coaches (long-distance buses) run from London's Victoria Coach Station (VCS) to all parts of the country and are a slow but much less expensive alternative to train travel. The main operator in Britain is National Express, whose routes cover the whole country. Journey times can be long (with some changes necessary), but coaches are comfortable, with air conditioning, toilets and sometimes refreshments. At Victoria Coach Station you can buy or reserve airport coach tickets, tours and excursions, London travelcards, theatre and concert tickets, domestic and European rail tickets, ferry and hovercraft tickets, hotel accommodation and travel insurance.

TIPS

» It is cheaper to reserve in advance and travel midweek.
» You can get advance purchase coach tickets until two hours before departure. For some journeys, tickets are also available from the driver.
» You can reserve by phone, online at sites such as www.nationalexpress.com, at travel agents and at coach stations.
» Victoria Coach Station ticket hall is open daily 6am–11.30pm for tickets.
» Ticket types include standard single (one way) or return (round trip), plus various saver tickets that acan be booked in advance.

» Luggage allowances are two medium-size suitcases and one item of hand luggage per person, with no guarantee that any excess will be carried. Properly folded and covered bicycles are acceptable, as are assistance dogs.

USEFUL CONTACTS

Victoria Coach Station 164 Buckingham Palace Road, London SW1W 9TP. The Ticket Hall is open daily 7am–10pm. The Travel Counter is open Mon–Fri 8–6, Sat 8–4.
National Express Tel 08705 808080 (bookings, daily 8am–10pm); www.nationalexpress.com. For detailed information, routes, timetables and bookings.

Other booking services include www.travelocity.co.uk and Traveline (tel 0871 200 2233; www.traveline.org.uk) or www.coachtourismcouncil.co.uk.

Scottish **Citylink** connects 200 towns and cities in Scotland and beyond. Tel 08705 505050; www.citylink.co.uk.
Green Line Travel Office 4a Fountain Square, 123–151 Buckingham Palace Road, London SW1W 0SR; tel 0870 608 7261; www.greenline.co.uk. Services between London, local cities and airports.

COMPARATIVE JOURNEYS AND FARES BY TRAIN AND COACH		
DESTINATION	BY TRAIN	BY COACH (FROM VICTORIA COACH STATION)
Bath	1 hour 25 min (Paddington), £23.50	3 hours 30 min, £16.50
Cambridge	46 min (King's Cross), £14	2 hours, £14
Oxford	1 hour (Paddington), £18	1 hour 40 min, £16
Stratford-upon-Avon	2 hours 14 min (Paddington), £29.50	3 hours 25 min, £17.50
Windsor	50 min (Waterloo), £14.20; 35 min (Paddington, change at Slough), £10.20	1 hour 13 min, £10
York	2 hours (King's Cross), £41	5 hours 45 min, £25.70
Prices are based on cheapest available day return/two singles from London booked 5 days in advance.		

BUSES

Local buses often make a pleasant alternative to trains. Major towns and cities usually have frequent buses, but services can be erratic elsewhere, especially in rural areas. Some night services (buses have an 'N' prefix) are available in major towns and cities. Tourist information offices can provide information and timetables, but these can be complicated, so check carefully for services that run only on certain days or are otherwise restricted. In rural areas such as much of Wales and Scotland, the Lake District and Cornwall, the Royal Mail Postbus (tel: 0845 774 0740) also carries passengers. Several competing bus companies may operate in urban areas. In some cases the services may overlap, but tickets are not valid on rival company buses.

BUYING TICKETS
Tickets are usually bought from the driver as you board.

Children under 5 travel free, and those aged 5–15 travel for half fare. Card concessions for students and seniors are also available.

Except within London, you can usually buy single (one-way) or return tickets. There are also a number of saver tickets available, especially in tourist areas, often in the form of 'rover' tickets that allow unlimited travel for set periods, usually ranging from one day to a week. Where there are competing bus companies, your ticket will not be valid on services run by a rival operator.

If you are using the London Underground as well, it's best to buy a Travelcard (▷ 46).

BUS STOPS
Bus stops are usually a sign on a pole giving the number(s) of the buses serving that stop, its location and the destination (direction of travel), sometimes accompanied by sheltered seats. Newer stops in towns and cities often have displays showing the destinations and expected times of the buses. In contrast, rural bus stops may be difficult to spot and won't have much information.

Buses will stop at main bus stops if passengers are waiting to get on or off. At a 'request stop' (usually intermediate stops and rural stops), stick out your arm to hail the bus. Check the number and destination on the front of the bus before you get on, as the stop may serve different routes.

ON BOARD
Driver-only buses often have two doors: one at the front, where you board, and one midway, where you get off.

Show your pass or have change ready to pay the driver when you board. Drivers and conductors prefer the exact fare and in many cities no change is given.

On all buses, press the red button once to get off and the bus will stop at the next stop.

Keep your ticket until the end of the journey as inspectors may board buses to check tickets.

AIRPORT BUSES
These useful services run to Heathrow, Stansted, Luton, East Midlands, Birmingham and Manchester airports as well as many smaller regional airports. Tell the driver which terminal you require when stowing your bags. Booking is not necessary, and timetables and tickets are available from relevant stations and on board. Stations with coach links to Heathrow include Feltham, Oxford, Reading, Swindon, Watford and Woking.

SIGHTSEEING TOURS
Major towns and cities can offer sightseeing tours on open-top buses. There may also be a commentary as you explore the place. Contact City Sightseeing Tours (tel 01708 866000; www.city-sightseeing.com).

TOP 10 SIGHTSEEING TOURS			
CITY	PRICE	TIMES/FREQUENCY	START POINT
Bath	£10	Every 15 min (peak), hourly (off peak)	Bath Abbey station
Cambridge	£10	Every 20–40 min	Silver Street
Edinburgh	£10	Every 15–30 min	Waverley Bridge
Glasgow	£9	Every 15–30 min	George Square
London	£21	Every 10–20 min	Haymarket, Whitcomb Street, Woburn Place
Manchester	£7	Every 45 min	St Peter's Square
Oxford	£11.50	Every 10–30 min	Oxford train station
Stratford-upon-Avon	£11	Every 20–60 min	Pen and Parchment Inn, Bridgefoot
Windsor	£7	Every 20–60 min	Castle Hill
York	£9	Every 15–30 min	Exhibition Square

peak holiday times, if you require a specific crossing time or if you have a vehicle. Those on foot can usually just turn up and pay, as there is a wide choice of frequent passenger services. On vehicle ferries, the price will include the vehicle and a number of passengers (usually up to five).

So many factors affect the ticket price—such as the length of stay, size and type of vehicle—that it is best to browse the websites or discuss your needs with the operator before booking.

FERRIES

In addition to the main ferry ports such as Dover or Folkestone for overseas arrivals and departures, there are also several dedicated domestic ferry terminals serving the various otherwise inaccessible parts of Britain, including the Scottish Islands and a number of tourist attractions just off the mainland. Vessels range from large vehicle ferries to smaller and faster catamarans and hovercrafts.

Some services are seasonal and also may be badly disrupted by tidal and weather conditions, so always check sailings in advance, especially for longer journeys. Some vessels may be affected more than others, for example hovercraft crossings may be suspended while catamaran services are still running.

BUYING TICKETS

Information about timetables and fares is available direct from the ferry companies. Tickets can be reserved in advance from the ferry operator by phone or online, through travel agents and tourist information offices, and also from train stations as part of a train journey—for example to the Isle of Wight from Portsmouth or Lymington. Advance reservation is advised and may be compulsory at

ON BOARD

Ferries are generally comfortable, with refreshments, toilets and TVs. Foot passengers should turn up at least 10 minutes before departure time. Boarding could involve steep ramps, so take care with buggies (strollers). On passenger ferries, buggies and larger items of luggage may be stored out on the deck to leave the inside clear. Otherwise, there are luggage storage areas inside. Staff will be on hand to help. Once on board there should be plenty of seats and you can explore the vessel. Smoking is not allowed except in designated outdoor areas.

Drive your vehicle on board the ferry through the back of larger ferries where you will be directed to a parking space. Passengers can then go up to the decks. An announcement is made when it is time to return to the car.

MAJOR DOMESTIC FERRY ROUTES		
ROUTE	OPERATOR	BOOKINGS
Aberdeen–Orkney and Shetland	Northlink Ferries, Kirkwall, Orkney KW15 1QX	0845 6000 449; www.northlinkferries.co.uk
Liverpool–Isle of Man	Isle of Man Steam Packet Company Limited, Sea Terminal, Douglas IM1 2RF	0870 552 3523; www.steam-packet.com
Lymington–Yarmouth Portsmouth–Ryde and Fishbourne	Wightlink Ferries, Portsmouth PO1 2XB	0870 582 7744; www.wightlink.co.uk
Penzance–St. Mary's, Isles of Scilly	Isles of Scilly Steamship Company, Quay Street,	0845 710 5555; www.islesofscilly-travel.co.uk Penzance TR18 4BZ
Southampton–Cowes	Red Funnel Ferries, 12 Bugle Street Southampton SO14 2JY	0870 444 8898; www.redfunnel.co.uk
Southsea–Ryde	Hovertravel Ltd, Quay Road, Ryde, Isle of Wight PO33 2HB	01983 811000; www.hovertravel.co.uk
Western Isles, Skye, Arran and small islands west of Scotland	Caledonian MacBrayne (CalMac) Ltd, The Ferry Terminal, Gourock PA19 1QP	0870 565 0000; www.calmac.co.uk

DOMESTIC FLIGHTS

Generally speaking, domestic air travel is a relatively expensive option in Britain but, thanks to often ruthless competition from an increasing number of low-cost airlines, airfares in Britain are coming down. In addition, new routes are being established all the time. These include Luton to Aberdeen, which offers an inexpensive and convenient service compared to the arduous road or rail options from the south. Note that routes can close without much advance notice, so keep an eye on the airlines' websites.

Advertisements for fantastic offers often appear in newspapers but, even if you act immediately, it is almost impossible to reserve tickets at the advertised prices. But if you are flexible about departure dates and times, some real bargains can be had. Check carefully what the price includes, such as taxes and other charges, credit-card booking fees and so on. Be aware that some advertised fares are one-way only. All domestic flights and those to destinations within the European Union (EU) carry a £10 departure tax (usually included in the price).

SOME LOW-COST AND DOMESTIC AIRLINES

AIRLINE	CONTACT	FLY FROM
Air Southwest	0870 241 8202 www.airsouthwest.com	Plymouth, Newquay, London Gatwick, Leeds, Bradford, Bristol, Newcastle, Glasgow, Manchester
bmi baby	0870 264 2229 www.bmibaby.com	Aberdeen, Birmingham, Cardiff, Durham Tees Valley, East Midlands, Edinburgh, Glasgow International, Inverness, Jersey, Leeds-Bradford, London Gatwick, London Heathrow, Manchester, Newquay, Norwich, Stornoway
easyJet	0905 560 7777 www.easyjet.com	Aberdeen, Belfast, Bournemouth, Bristol, Doncaster, East Midlands, Edinburgh, Glasgow International, Inverness, Liverpool, London Gatwick, London Luton, London Stansted, Newcastle
Euromanx	0870 787 7879 www.euromanx.com	Bristol, East Midlands, Edinburgh, Glasgow International, Liverpool, London City, London Stansted, Manchester, Ronaldsway (Isle of Man), Southampton
Flybe	0870 567 6676 www.flybe.com	Aberdeeen, Birmingham, Bristol, Edinburgh, Exeter, Glasgow International, Leeds-Bradford, Liverpool, London Gatwick, London Luton, Manchester, Newcastle, Norwich, Ronaldsway (Isle of Man), Southampton, Southend
Ryanair	0906 270 5656 www.ryanair.com	Aberdeen, Birmingham, Blackpool, Bournemouth, Bristol, Cardiff, Doncaster, Durham Tees Valley, East Midlands, Edinburgh, Glasgow Prestwick, Leeds-Bradford, Liverpool, London Gatwick, London Luton, London Stansted, Manchester, Newcastle, Newquay
Isles of Scilly Travel Skybus	0845 7105 555 www.islesofscilly-travel.co.uk	Bristol, Land's End, Newquay, Southampton, St. Mary's (Isles of Scilly)
Loganair	0870 850 9850 or 01856 872494 (Orkney services) www.scotairways.co.uk	Sumburgh, Kirkwall, Wick, Aberdeen, Inverness, Edinburgh, Glasgow, Ronaldsway (Isle of Man), Campbeltown, Islay, Tiree, Barra, Benbecula, Stornoway
Jet2.com	0871 226 1737 www.jet2.com	Bournemouth, Leeds-Bradford, London Gatwick, Manchester, Newcastle

For flights to other destinations the charge is £40. These taxes are doubled for business and first class. Also take into consideration the cost and inconvenience of having to get to, and away from, a local airport.

BUYING A TICKET

You can reserve tickets direct from the airlines by phone or online, or through travel agents. If you reserve online the tickets will be mailed to you. If time is short you can collect them at the airport, but some companies may charge for this.

If you have reserved far enough in advance you may be able to amend or cancel tickets for a charge. Online travel agents include:
www.cheapflights.co.uk
www.ebookers.com
www.expedia.co.uk
www.lastminute.com
www.opodo.co.uk
www.travelbag.com
www.travelocity.com

ON BOARD

For security reasons no sharp objects (including scissors and cutlery) are allowed in hand luggage. Lists of prohibited items are displayed at airports. Any items found will be confiscated. Domestic flights are relatively short, with few frills (depending on your class of ticket), but simple refreshments will be available on the longer journeys.

Smoking is prohibited on board and in airports.

REGIONAL AIRPORTS

Aberdeen Dyce, Aberdeen AB21 7DU, tel 0870 040 0006; www.baa.com

Birmingham International Birmingham B26 3QJ, tel 0870 733 5511; www.bhx.co.uk

Blackpool Squires Gate Lane FY4 2QY, tel 01253 343434

Bournemouth Cavendish Road BH1 1RA, tel 01202 364000

Bristol International Bristol BS48 3DY, tel 0871 334 4444; www.bristolairport.co.uk

Cardiff International Vale of Glamorgan CF62 3BD, tel 01446 711111; www.cwfly.com

Doncaster Sheffield Robin Hood Doncaster DN9 3RH, tel 0870 833 2210

Dundee Riverside DD2 1UH, tel 01382 662200

Durham Tees Valley Darlington DL2 1LU, tel 01325 332811

Edinburgh Edinburgh EH12 9DN, tel 0870 040 0007; www.edinburghairport.com

Exeter Exeter EX5 2BD, tel 01392 367433; www.exeter-airport.co.uk

Glasgow Paisley PA3 2SW, tel 0870 040 0008; www.glasgowairport.com

Leeds Bradford Leeds LS19 7TU, tel 0113 250 9696; www.lbia.co.uk

Liverpool Liverpool L24 1YD, tel 0870 750 8484; www.liverpoolairport.com

Manchester Manchester M90 1QX, tel 09010 101000; www.manchesterairport.co.uk

Newcastle Woolsington, Newcastle upon Tyne NE13 8BZ, tel 0871 882 1121; www.newcastleairport.co.uk

Newquay St. Mawgan TR8 4HP, tel 01637 860600; www.newquay-cornwallairport.com

East Midlands Castle Donington DE74 2SA, tel 01332 852852; www.eastmidlandsairport.com

Prestwick Aviation House, Prestwick KA9 2PC, tel 01292 511000; www.gpia.co.uk

Southampton Wide Lane, Southampton SO18 2NL, tel 0870 040 0009; www.southamptonairport.com

CYCLING IN BRITAIN

Thanks to organizations such as Sustrans (Sustainable Transport), Britain's network of cycle routes now covers more than 16,093km (10,000 miles). Routes are suitable for a range of journeys and include off-road sections, such as canal towpaths, holiday routes for experienced riders, and urban routes for commuters, school runs or shopping trips. There are also countless outlets all over the country offering bicycle and equipment rental and practical advice. Local tourist information offices should have details.

ON THE ROAD

In urban areas some parts of the road network have designated cycle lanes, denoted by painted white lines, signposts and/or painted illustrations of a bicycle on the road or footpath. Many stretch for a distance, running along footpaths (some of which have separate sections for cyclists and pedestrians), while others cover just a few paces. With the exception of small children, cycling is not allowed on the pavement and cyclists must obey the general rules of the road, such as traffic lights and one-way streets. Where cycle lanes run along main roads, they may have their own dedicated traffic lights. Bicycles are not allowed on motorways. Cycling among traffic and pedestrians can be dangerous, so care and vigilance is needed at all times.

SAFE CYCLING

» Wear bright clothing and at night wear fluorescent clothing. Use your lights at night. Helmets are not compulsory, but are advisable. Many Londoners wear masks to protect against pollution.
» Make other road-users aware of your movements. Indicate clearly and in advance.
» Watch out for car doors opening without warning.
» Avoid cycling along the inside of traffic when there is a left turn ahead.
» Always lock your bicycle to a fixed object.

BICYCLES ON PUBLIC TRANSPORT

Although most rail operators will carry bicycles on board, individual company regulations differ, so con- tact National Rail Enquiries or check with the train company in advance. Space for bicycles is very limited, so reserve as far ahead as possible, especially at peak times. A reserva- tion charge may apply. Outside peak times there may be space in the guard's van (luggage car) if you arrive with a bicycle, but there is no guarantee. Folding bicycles are usu- ally carried free on most trains and other forms of public transport, but it may be wise to check with the relevant company.

In London you can take your bicycle on the surface lines of the Underground network—District, Circle, East London, Hammersmith and City and Metropolitan lines—but not on the deeper lines that have elevators and escalators. A map showing which parts of the network you can use is available from any Underground station.

Some passenger ferries have limited space for bicycles so, again, check in advance. Coaches (long-dis- tance buses) accept folding bicycles carried in a protective case.

USEFUL CONTACTS

National Rail Enquiries Tel 0845 748 4950; www.nationalrail.co.uk
CTC Parklands, Railton Road, Guild- ford GU2 9JX; tel 0870 873 0060; www.ctc.org.uk. National cycling organization.
A to B Magazine 40 Manor Road, Dorchester DT1 2AX; tel 01305 259998; www.atob.org.uk
Spokes.org.uk Scottish-based cycling organization with information on bicycles north of the border.
Sustrans 2 Cathedral Square, Bristol BS1 5DD (head office); tel 0845 113 0065; www.sustrans.org.uk
Transport for London Tel 020 7222 1234; www.tfl.gov.uk. Publishes a series of 14 free cycling maps covering ` the whole of the London area.

TAXIS

Taxis are a relatively expensive way of getting around, but are useful in certain circumstances, such as airport trips for groups. There are essentially two types of taxi: licensed taxis, such as the traditional black London cab (not confined to the capital), which display a licence on the rear of the vehicle and the private hire operator or minicab. Like its red buses, London's black cabs are world famous and the design remains distinctive. You can still rely on a London cabby to know where he's going; drivers must pass exams, called 'The Knowledge', to demonstrate that they know the city well enough to take passengers anywhere in London by the most direct route. Fares in London taxis are set by the regulatory Public Carriage Office; licensed taxis inside and outside London should all be fitted with a meter.

IN LONDON

London's cabs are metered and fairly expensive, but are a quick and safe way to get about.

You'll find designated taxi stands outside train stations and large hotels, and at numerous points throughout the city.

To hail a cab in the street look for an illuminated orange 'TAXI' light on top of the cab and stick out your arm. Tell the driver your destination through the open window, then get in the back seat.

You can also book through Black Cab London (tel: 0871 871 8710), but you may be charged extra. For more information on London taxis and charges, visit www.tfl.gov.uk.

OUTSIDE THE CAPITAL

Elsewhere in Britain you will find private taxi firms, including some using traditional black cabs. Ranks (taxi stands) are usually found outside stations and at other points around larger towns and cities, such as shopping malls. All private taxis are licensed and regulated and should have meters. Vehicles can range from ordinary saloon (sedan) and estate cars (station wagons) to seven-seaters.

If you are going a long way or are unsure of the distance, ask for a price quote before you set off.

Unlike black cabs, it is acceptable to sit in the front passenger seat of ordinary taxis.

Private taxis can also be booked by phone; look in the *Yellow Pages* for local firms.

MINICABS

Minicabs are saloon cars that should be reserved only by telephone or from a minicab company's office. It is not advisable to hail one in the street, and solo women should be wary. Although licensing has been introduced, some claiming to be minicab drivers may be untrained or uninsured, and vehicles may be substandard.

Avoid minicabs touting at airports and stations as they overcharge and are even more likely to be unlicensed or uninsured. You can take licensed cabs from taxi stands or book with a recommended minicab firm in advance.

TIPS

» Taxis become scarce at busy times, especially on Friday and Saturday nights after 10pm, so it may be wise to reserve a ride home in advance if you are going out in the town.

» A tip of 10–15 per cent of the total fare is expected (especially in major cities like London), but not compulsory.

VISITORS WITH CHILDREN

The British can be intolerant of children in public places, and this is often most obvious on public transport. However, if you simply avoid using trains (especially on commuter routes) and the London Underground at peak times, your journey will be much less stressful.

TRAINS
Telephone 08457 484950 or visit www.nationalrail.co.uk to check for any possible problems regarding your journey.

Avoid the rush hour—before 9.30am or between 4.30 and 7pm—as commuter trains can be extremely crowded and, on the busiest routes to and from London, it is often impossible to get a seat. Large stations will have lifts (elevators), but these can be unreliable. Don't try to push a buggy (stroller) through the ticket barrier unless it is open. Instead, show your ticket at one of the staffed gates to be let through. Newer trains with sliding doors should pose few problems for buggies or pushchairs, but beware of large or high gaps between the platform and the train.

Many train companies have a family carriage, with extra room for buggies and larger tables. Some companies also offer special travel packs for children, including simple games and crayons. First Great Western (www.firstgreatwestern. co.uk), runs routes west from London and has good facilities. Baby-changing facilities are generally only available on trains with toilets for passengers with disabilities.

THE UNDERGROUND
The London Underground is also best avoided during rush hours.

Most Underground stations do not have elevators. Stairs and escalators are often steep and long so you may need to rely on help from fellow passengers. Take particular care with the gap between the platform and the train, and with childrwen near to sliding doors.

AIRLINES
When checking in always explain that you are travelling with small children. You may get an empty seat beside you, or one close to the front of the plane where the movement will be less extreme.

Children under two usually travel for a nominal fare and are not usually allocated a separate seat. If a child is sitting on your lap you will be given a special seat belt that attaches to your own.

Most airlines provide children's travel entertainment packs, and may have other facilities. Children's meals are provided on all carriers.

FERRIES
Motion sickness can affect small children on ferries, so invest in some travel sickness wristbands, which are safe and surprisingly effective.

A night crossing can be a good family choice if you reserve a cabin in advance.

Above *Hastings*

While the majority of Britain's tourist attractions are geared to visitors with disabilities, public transport still lags behind. Avoid peak times if possible. Guide dogs are welcome on all forms of public transport and staff are generally very helpful. Whichever form of transport you intend to use, it is best to phone in advance if you need special help or services. Shopping malls and main streets in major towns sometimes have motorized buggies on loan (often free) to those with disabilities. There are also a number of free 'land train' vehicles for transport around shopping areas. All London black taxis have wheelchair access, as have an increasing number of modern cabs in larger towns and cities.

The Royal Association for Disability and Rehabilitation (RADAR, tel 020 7250 3222; www.radar.org.uk) has two publications: *If only I'd known that a year ago* has transport information and *Holidays in Britain and Ireland–A Guide for Disabled People* covers 1,500 places to stay.

TRAINS

With the exception of the old 'slam-door' types, trains usually have wheelchair access.

Arrange for assistance at least 24 hours in advance by contacting the station you are departing from. Information is available from National Rail Enquiries (tel 0845 748 4950; minicom: 0845 605 0600; www.nationalrail.co.uk).

Portable ramps are available at most stations, and some trains carry lightweight versions for use at unstaffed stations.

There are usually accessible toilets on long-distance trains and many regional services.

Eurostar trains are fully wheelchair-accessible.

LONDON UNDERGROUND AND DOCKLANDS LIGHT RAILWAY (DLR)

Each Underground station has a wide access gate, so you can avoid the ticket barrier. A map detailing accessibility is available from www.tfl.gov.uk.

To check that elevators are operating at stations you are visiting call 020 7308 2800 (office hours) or 020 7222 1234 (other times).

Most DLR stations are accessible by elevator or ramp. Call Customer Services on 020 7363 9700 during office hours.

There are elevators, escalators and/or ramps on every DLR platform, and tactile edges for those with visual impairments. Each train has a designated wheelchair bay.

BUSES AND COACHES

While a number of urban single-deck buses are accessible for wheelchairs, double-decker buses and coaches are not.

Manual wheelchairs can be carried on board, but only if folded and if there is room. Powered vehicles or wheelchairs are not permitted on board coaches.

Low-floor accessible buses are being introduced in London and in many other urban areas. www.nationalexpress.com/coach/ourservice/disabled.cfm This site gives details of wheelchair accessibility on National Express long-distance buses.

FERRIES

Improvements have been made to UK ports to cater for those with disabilities, but contact the port in advance. It may be necessary to reserve a cabin with accessible facilities, particularly on longer crossings.

AIR TRAVEL

Most airlines can help passengers with special requirements. There are designated parking spaces for visitors with disabilities in BAA-run airports. Telephone 0800 844844 to book a parking place.

Heathrow For information on Heathrow's facilities for disabled people, go to the Special Needs section of their website—www.heathrowairport.com. All Heathrow Express trains (tel 0845 600 1515) are wheelchair-accessible.

Gatwick Tel 0870 000 2468.

Stansted The Stansted Express train is wheelchair-accessible. Tel 0870 574 7777.

Luton The shuttle bus is wheelchair-accessible and there are elevators at Luton Parkway station (tel 01582 405 100).

USEFUL WEBSITES

www.tourismforall.org.uk
Dedicated to promoting awareness of the needs of mobility-impaired tourists, this site has advice for travellers, including visitors to Britain.

www.radar.org.uk
Go to the online shop to buy guides specifically for disabled travellers, including places to stay and travel advice. You can also get a guide to (and a key for) some 7,000 dedicated, locked toilet facilities specifically for disabled people.

www.rnib.org.uk
The Royal National Institute for the Blind website has all kinds of information for the visually impaired, including a guide to hotels that cater for this specialist need, places of interest and entertainment venues as well as links to useful companies.

REGIONS

This chapter is divided ino the seven regions of Britain (see pages 8–9).
Places of interest are listed alphabetically in each region.

Britain's Regions 64–410

London	64
The West Country	118
The South East and East Anglia	170
Wales	222
The Midlands	264
The North	300
Scotland	358

SIGHTS 72
WALKS 92
WHAT TO DO 100
EATING 108
STAYING 114

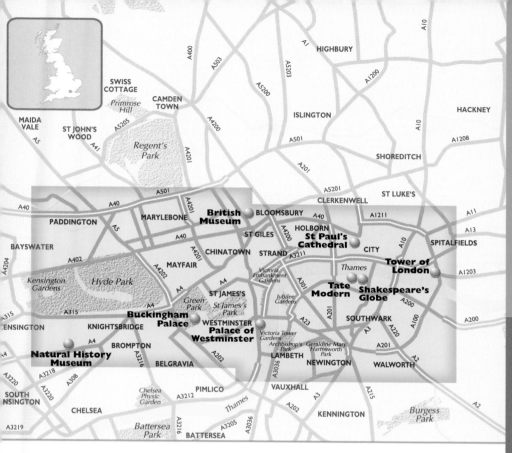

LONDON

Not so much a single city as a vast and sprawling metropolis, held together by the sparkling thread of the River Thames, London is a captivating, noisy and confident world capital. All Britain's road numbers radiate from Trafalgar Square, and that's a good place to start.

Nelson's Column towers above a fine array of state buildings, churches and galleries. To the south, Whitehall leads to Westminster, with its Gothic cathedral and the distinctive frontage of the Palace, overlooking the river. This is home of the United Kingdom's parliament and at one end Big Ben's tower is a traditional symbol of British democracy. Another road from Trafalgar Square leads to Buckingham Palace, London home of the Queen and another iconic symbol of the state. North of Trafalgar Square, Charing Cross Road runs up to the shopping mecca of Oxford Street, and demarcates the edge of Soho, still a Bohemian and exciting quarter. Not far away is the West End and Piccadilly Circus, a byword for bustle and hubbub. East of Trafalgar Square, the Strand and Fleet Street lead into the original heart of London, still known simply as the City. The Tower of London and St. Paul's Cathedral are probably the best-known sights here, along with the unmistakable turrets of Tower Bridge.

The size of London can be intimidating. Happily its transport infrastructure is quite robust. Get a Travelcard and spend the day on the Tube, red buses or the Docklands Light Railway. From Kew Gardens in the west, to Highgate and Hampstead in the north, the Imperial War Museum in the south or Greenwich in the east, London can fill as much time as you can spare.

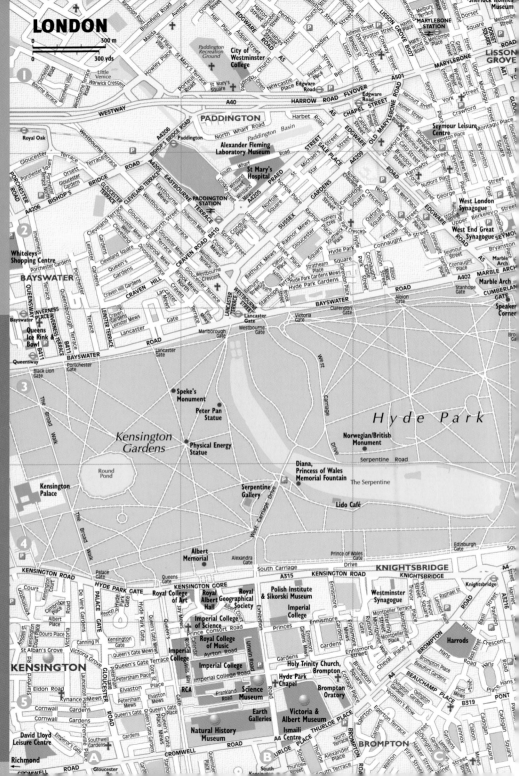

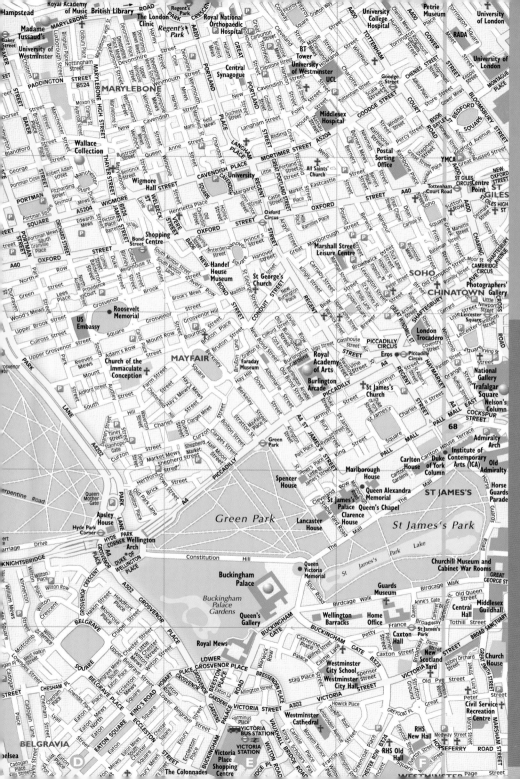

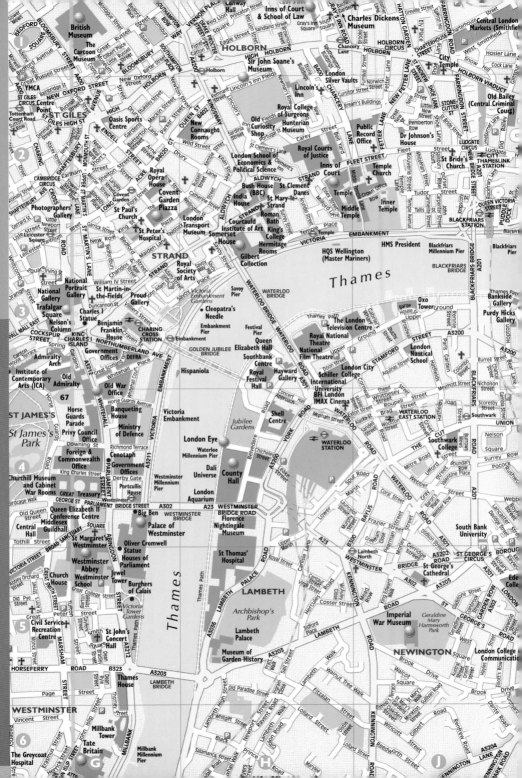

Street	Page	Grid
Abbey Orchard Street	67	F5
Abingdon Street	68	G4
Albemarle Street	67	E3
Aberdour Street	69	L5
Albert Court	66	B4
Albert Place	66	A4
Albion Mews	66	C2
Albion Street	66	C2
Albion Way	69	K1
Aldersgate Street	69	K1
Aldgate High Street	69	M2
Baker Street	67	D1
Bankside	69	K3
Bayswater Road	66	B3
Beauchamp Place	66	C5
Bedford Square	67	F1
Bedford Street	68	G2
Belgrave Place	67	D5
Belgrave Square	67	D4
Berkeley Square	67	E3
Berkeley Street	67	E3
Bermondsey Street	69	L4
Berners Place	67	F2
Berwick Street	67	F2
Bevis Marks	69	M2
Birdcage Walk	67	E4
Bishop's Bridge Road	66	A2
Bishopsgate	69	L1
Blackfriars Bridge	68	J3
Blackfriars Lane	68	J2
Blackfriars Road	68	J3
Black Prince Road	68	H6
Blandford Street	67	D1
Blomfield Road	66	A1
Blomfield Street	69	L1
Bloomsbury Street	67	F1
Bloomsbury Way	68	G2
Borough High Street	69	K4
Borough Road	68	J5
Boscobel Street	66	B1
Bow Street	68	G2
Brick Lane	69	M1
Broad Sanctuary	67	F5
Brompton Road	66	B5
Buckingham Gate	67	E4
Buckingham Palace Road	67	E5
Burlington Arcade	67	E3
Burlington Arcade	67	E3
Byward Street	69	M3
Cadogan Square	66	C5
Camomile Street	69	L2
Cannon Street	69	K2
Carnaby Street	67	E2
Cavendish Square	67	E2
Chancery Lane	68	H1
Charing Cross Road	67	F2
Cheapside	69	K2
Chesham Place	67	D5
City Walk	69	L4
Clabon Mews	66	C5
Cleveland Terrace	66	A2
Clifton Place	66	B2
Cockspur Street	67	F3
Commercial Street	69	M1
Conduit Street	67	E2
Connaught Street	66	C2
Constitution Hill	67	E4
Cornhill	69	L2
Craven Hill	66	A2
Craven Road	66	A2
Cromwell Road	66	A5
Cumberland Gate	66	C2
Curzon Street	67	D3
Downing Street	68	G4
Druid Street	69	M4
Drury Lane	68	G2
Duke of Wellington Place	67	D4
Duke Street Hill	69	L3
Eastbourne Terrace	66	A2
Eaton Square	67	D5
Eccleston Street	67	D5
Edgware Road	66	B1
Endell Street	68	G2
Exhibition Road	66	B4
Farringdon Road	68	J1
Farringdon Street	68	J1
Fenchurch Street	69	L2
Fetter Lane	68	J1
Finsbury Circus	69	L1
Fitzroy Sqare	67	E1
Fleet Street	68	H2
Garden Row	68	J5
Gloucester Place	66	C1
Gloucester Road	66	A5
Goodge Street	67	F1
Grafton Street	67	E3
Grange Road	69	L5
Gray's Inn Square	68	H1
Great Dover Street	69	K4
Great Portland Street	67	E1
Grosvenor Crescent	67	D4
Grosvenor Gardens	67	E5
Grosvenor Place	67	D4
Grosvenor Square	67	D2
Hanover Square	67	E2
Harley Street	67	D1
Harper Road	69	K4
Hatton Garden	68	J1
Haymarket	67	F3
Hay's Mews	67	E3
Headfort Place	67	D4
Hendre Road	69	M6
Heneage Street	69	M1
Henley Drive	69	M5
High Holborn	68	H1
Hobart Place	67	D5
Holborn	68	J1
Holborn Viaduct	68	J1
Horseferry Road	67	F5
Houndsditch	69	L1
Hyde Park Corner	67	D4
Hyde Park Gate	66	A4
Jamaica Road	69	M4
James Street	67	D2
Jay Mews	66	A4
Jermyn Street	67	E3
Joan Street	68	J4
John Adam Street	68	G3
John Carpenter Street	68	J2
John Islip Street	68	G6
John Maurice Close	69	L5
John Prince's Street	67	E2
Kennington Road	68	H5
Kensington Gore	66	A4
Kensington Road	66	A4
Kensington Court	66	A4
Kensington Court Place	66	A5
Kensington Gate	66	A5
Kensington Gore	66	A4
Kensington Road	66	A4
Keppel Street	67	F1
Keyse Road	69	M5
Keyworth Street	68	J5
King Edward Street	69	K2
King William Street	69	L2
Knightsbridge	66	C4
Lambeth Palace Road	68	H5
Lambeth Road	68	H5
Langham Place	67	E1
Leadenhall Street	69	L2
Leicester Square	67	F3
Leinster Terrace	66	A2
Lennox Garden Mews	66	C5
Lennox Gardens	66	C5
Leroy Street	69	L5
Lexington Street	67	F2
Leyden Street	69	M1
Lincoln's Inn Fields	68	H2
Lombard Street	69	L2
London Bridge	69	L3
London Wall	69	K1
Long Acre	68	G2
Long Lane	68	J1
Lower Grosvenor Place	67	E5
Lower Thames Street	69	L3
Ludgate Hill	68	J2
Maida Avenue	66	A1
Manchester Square	67	D2
Manchester Street	67	D1
Mansell Street	69	M2
Marble Arch	66	C2
Marshalsea Road	69	K4
Marsham Street	67	F5
Marylebone High Street	67	D1
Marylebone Road	66	C1
Mermaid Court	69	K4
Merrick Square	69	K5
Meymott Street	68	J3
Middlesex Street	69	M1
Middle Street	69	K1
Millbank	68	G6
Minories	69	M2
Montague Place	67	F1
Moorgate	69	L1
Mortimer Street	67	E2
New Bond Street	67	E3
New Bridge Street	68	J2
New Burlington Place	67	E2
Newcastle Place	66	B1
New Cavendish Street	67	D1
New Fetter Lane	68	J2
New Kent Road	69	K5
New Oxford Street	67	F2
Newport Street	68	H6
Northumberland Avenue	68	G3
Old Bond Street	67	E3
Old Kent Road	69	L5
Old Marylebone Road	66	C1
Old Paradise Street	68	H5
Old Park Lane	67	D4
Old Pye Street	67	F5
Oxford Street	67	D2
Paddington Street	67	D1
Palace Gate	66	A4
Pall Mall	67	F3
Park Crescent	67	D1
Park Lane	67	D3
Parliament Square	68	G4
Parliament Street	68	G4
Piazza	68	G2
Piccadilly	67	E3
Piccadilly Circus	67	F3
Pont Street	66	C5
Porchester Road	66	A2
Portland Place	67	E1
Portman Square	67	D2
Praed Street	66	B2
Queen Anne's Gate	67	F4
Queen Elizabeth Street	69	M4
Queenhithe	69	K3
Queensberry Place	66	B5
Queensborough Terrace	66	A2
Queen's Gardens	66	A2
Queen's Gate	66	A4
Queensway	66	A2
Queen Victoria	68	J2
Regent Street	67	E2
Richmond Mews	67	F2
Rothsay Street	69	L5
Russell Street	68	H2
St Botolph Street	69	M2
St George's Road	68	J5
St Giles High Street	68	G2
St James's Street	67	E3
St Martin's Lane	68	G2
St Martin's Le Grand	69	K2
St Paul's Churchyard	69	K2
St Thomas Street	69	L3
Savile Row	67	E3
Seymour Street	66	C2
Shaftesbury Avenue	67	F2
Shoe Lane	68	J2
Sloane Street	66	C4
Soho Square	67	F2
Southampton Row	68	G1
Southwark Bridge	69	K3
Southwark Bridge Road	69	K3
Southwark Street	68	J3
Stamford Street	68	H4
Strand	68	H2
Sussex Gardens	66	B2
Tavistock Street	68	G3
Thayer Street	67	D1
Threadneedle Street	69	L2
Thurloe Place	66	B5
Thurloe Square	66	B5
Tooley Street	69	L3
Tower Bridge	69	M3
Tower Bridge Approach	69	M3
Tower Bridge Road	69	L5
Tower Hill	69	M3
Union Street	68	J4
Upper Thames Street	69	K2
Vauxhall Bridge Road	67	E5
Vernon Place	68	H1
Victoria Embankment	68	H3
Victoria Street	67	E5
Walworth Road	69	K6
Wardour Street	67	F2
Waterloo Bridge	68	H3
Waterloo Road	68	H3
Westbourne Street	66	B2
Westminster Bridge	68	H4
Westway	66	A1
Whitehall	68	G3
Wigmore Street	67	D2
Wilton Road	67	E5
Wormwood Street	69	L2
York Road	68	H4

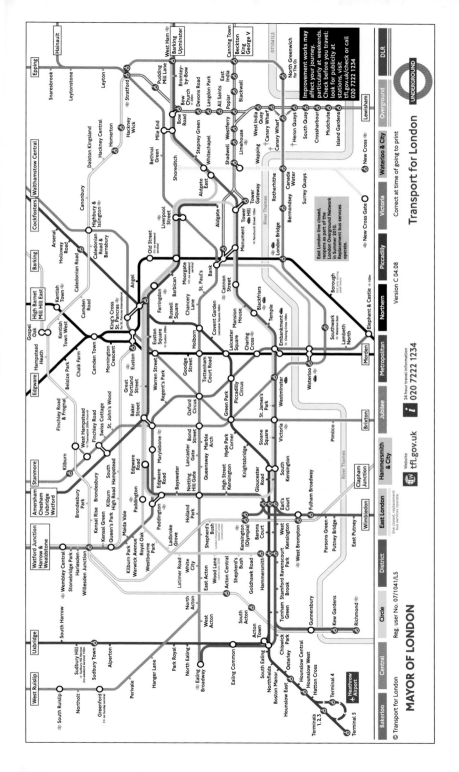

71

Above *Canary Wharf at Docklands, London*

BRITISH LIBRARY

www.bl.uk

Britain's national library, once housed in the British Museum (▷ 74–75), got its very own building in 1998. The collection includes every book published in the UK since 1911. There are currently about 150 million items in more than 400 languages, including Leonardo da Vinci's notebook and the earliest printed book, the *Diamond Sutra*. Enter via the information desk and walk round the floor-to-ceiling glass shaft to see some of the beautiful bindings of the King's Library, consisting of 60,000 volumes that once belonged to George III (1738–1820) and that were donated by his son George IV (1762–1830) in 1823. The outer walls store the British Library's stamp collection—the world's finest.

The John Ritblat Gallery displays more treasures, including editions of the *Magna Carta*, the 13th-century charter of rights (▷ 31), and a surviving manuscript in Shakespeare's own hand. The Workshop of Words, Sounds and Images explains how books and newspapers are created, and how sound is recorded. ✚ 67 off D1 ✉ 96 Euston Road NW1 2DB ☎ 020 7412 7332 🕐 Public areas, exhibitions and bookshop: Mon, Wed–Fri 9.30–6, Tue 9.30–8, Sat 9.30–5, Sun 11–5. Reading rooms open to readers only ♿ Free

🚇 King's Cross, St. Pancras International, Euston, Euston Square 🖵 🍴 🏧

BRITISH MUSEUM

▷ 74–75.

BUCKINGHAM PALACE

▷ 76.

CANARY WHARF

www.museumindocklands.org.uk

The Docklands area has suffered many ups and downs over the years. By the 15th century, the docks were key to London's growth. And by 1930 there were 100,000 workers employed in the area. The Museum in Docklands, which opened in a 19th-century warehouse in 2003, tells the story of the port, its people and the passing cargoes.

After the massive redundancies of the 1960s and 1970s, the regeneration of Docklands began. The aim was to create a business district, and the area has certainly become busier with each passing decade. Britain's tallest building, Canary Wharf Tower, stands at 244m (800ft) and is the only skyscraper in the world to be clad in stainless steel. Unless you work here, access is not permitted.

Instead of the dockers, there are now 55,000 office workers based in Docklands. You can travel past the skyscrapers on the Docklands Light Railway (DLR) route to Greenwich and beyond–the monorail is raised above the ground.
Museum in Docklands ✚ 69 off M2 ✉ No. 1 Warehouse, West India Quay E14 4AL ☎ 0870 444 3857 🕐 Daily 10–6 ♿ Adult £5, child (under 16) free; valid 1 year 🚇 Canary Wharf, West India Quay DLR 🍴 🖵 🍷

CHARLES DICKENS MUSEUM

www.dickensmuseum.com

Charles Dickens (1812–70), the prolific novelist and commentator on Victorian society, lived at this Georgian terraced house in Bloomsbury from 1837 to 1839. It's been dedicated to his life and work, displaying original manuscripts, first editions, letters, personal effects and 19th-century paintings. Perhaps the most interesting room is the study where he completed his first full-length novel, *The Pickwick Papers*, while only in his 20s, and where he later wrote *Oliver Twist* and *Nicholas Nickleby*.
✚ 68 off H1 ✉ 48 Doughty Street WC1N 2LX ☎ 020 7405 2127 🕐 Mon–Sat 10–5, Sun 11–5 ♿ Adult £5, child (under 16) £3, family £14 🚇 Russell Square, King's Cross, Chancery Lane 🏧

Opposite page *British Library gates*
Below *Charles Dickens' former home*

INFORMATION

www.thebritishmuseum.org

➕ 68 G1 ✉ Great Russell Street WC1B 3DG ☎ 020 7323 8299 ⏰ Sat–Wed 10–5.30, Thu–Fri 10–8.30. Great Court: Sun–Wed 9–6, Thu–Sat 9am–11pm. Check times for temporary exhibitions. ✋ Free; charges for some temporary exhibitions ⊖ Holborn, Tottenham Court Road, Russell Square, Goodge Street 📷 90-min tours of highlights: daily 10.30, 1, 3, adult £8, child (under 11) £5. 'eyeOpener' 30- to 40-min introductory tours: daily every 15 min, 11–3.45, free. Audiotours in several languages, £3.50. Foreign language tours: 020 7323 8181 📖 £8 (English) and from £3 (in several languages) 🍴 Court Restaurant, Great Court: Sat–Wed 11–5 (last orders), Thu–Fri 11–10. Reservations, 020 7323 8990 ☕ Court Café (Great Court): Sun–Wed 9–5.30, Thu–Sat 10–9. Gallery Café, next to Room 12: daily 10–5 🛍 Bookshop, children's shop and guide shop

Above *The Great Court Glass Canopy at the British Museum, designed by Norman Foster*

INTRODUCTION

Britain's largest museum, covering 33ha (81.5 acres), has more than four million objects on display in around 90 galleries, the result of more than 200 years of collecting, excavation and unashamed looting.

Wealthy physician Sir Hans Sloane (1660–1753) spent his life collecting assorted coins, books and natural history specimens that, on his death, amounted to 80,000 items. The government bought the collection and put it on display as the British Museum in 1759.

WHAT TO SEE

There are two entrances, both leading into the covered Great Court, the hub of the museum and the main information office. The collections are arranged by geography, culture and theme, but the size of the place can be bewildering. Collections from the same culture are not always on the same floor.

GREAT COURT AND READING ROOM

Sir Robert Smirke's imposing, neoclassical building is entered via the Great Court, added in 2000 and designed by Norman Foster. The curved glass canopy has created a huge, light space and it's worth lingering here to enjoy the sculpture displays.

At the heart of the court is the circular Reading Room, completed in 1857 to the design of Smirke's brother, Sydney. Karl Marx and other intellectuals once beavered away here, and today you can see the domed ceiling and floor-to-ceiling bookcases from a viewing area.

MAIN FLOOR

ROSETTA STONE (ROOM 4)

The Rosetta Stone was instrumental in solving puzzles of the ancient Egyptian world. The black basalt slab, discovered by Napoleon's army in the Nile Delta in 1799, reproduces the same text in three languages: Greek, Demotic and Egyptian. This offered the first opportunity for modern scholars to crack the code of Egyptian hieroglyphics by comparing them with known scripts.

ELGIN MARBLES (ROOM 18)

The question of where the Elgin Marbles should be kept—in Greece or in Britain—still causes debate. These frieze reliefs, carved between 447 and 431BC, were taken by Lord Elgin, then British ambassador in Constantinople, from the Parthenon in Athens. Elgin obtained a licence from the Turkish Sultan to remove the stones, which had suffered severe damage in 1687 and, arguing that they would not survive if they remained in Greece, brought them to Britain.

ASSYRIAN RELIEFS (ROOM 9)

Vivid carved figures carrying pots and weapons, taking part in daily activities or military campaigns, were cut into panels for the Assyrian kings' palaces and temples, and have survived from 880–612BC. Like comic strips, they relate their stories from one end of a wall to the other. Some of the most striking friezes come from the great palace of King Sennacherib, who came to the throne of Assyria in 704BC.

UPPER FLOORS

PORTLAND VASE (ROOM 70)

This ancient cameo-glass vase was probably made in Rome between AD5 and 25. It eventually reached the hands of the third Duke of Portland in 1786, who lent it to potter Josiah Wedgwood (▷ 36), who copied its cameo design and made it famous.

SUTTON HOO SHIP BURIAL (ROOM 41)

These treasures are from an Anglo-Saxon royal burial ship that survived intact in Suffolk (▷ 197) and was excavated in 1939. The ship was probably a monument to Raedwald, the last pagan king of East Anglia, who died in about 625. Besides fine gold jewels, the boat contained silver bowls and plates, silver drinking horns, a shield, a sword with jewelled gold hilt and an iron helmet with bronze and silver fittings.

LEWIS CHESSMEN (ROOM 42)

Carved from the tusks of walruses, these squat figures were discovered on the island of Lewis in the Outer Hebrides of Scotland in 1831 by a crofter. Scandinavian in origin, they depict the figures used on a chess board and are believed to date from the 12th century.

EGYPTIAN MUMMIES (ROOMS 61–66)

Rows of preserved bodies wrapped in bandages and surrounded by their prized possessions and preferred foods have a gruesome fascination. The craftsmanship and elegance of the items are breathtaking.

LINDOW MAN (ROOM 37)

Nicknamed 'Pete Marsh' by the archaeologists who found him in a peat bog in Cheshire (▷ 28), Lindow Man is a well-preserved 2,000-year-old corpse. Among the theories that abound is one that he was sacrificed during a Druid ceremony, and he was beaten to death. There are signs of a blow to his head and a wound to his throat, and mistletoe grains were found in his gut, suggesting that he was fed a hallucinatory meal before being knocked out, strangled and drowned.

LOWER FLOORS

THE SAINSBURY AFRICA GALLERIES (ROOM 25)

Bringing together the museum's vast collection of African artefacts into one series of rooms, the highlights here are the remarkable brass head of an Obas (king) of Benin from the 18th century and the Tree of Life, a contemporary work from Mozambique made entirely of decommissioned weapons from the country's civil war (1976–1992).

TIPS

›› Get your bearings in the Great Court, where you can pick up detailed floor plans and information.

›› Don't expect to see everything in a day; focus on what interests you the most and make for one or two galleries, or choose one or two collections.

›› Visit in the evening, when the Great Court's restaurants and shops are open. On Thursdays and Fridays the major galleries stay open late.

Below *Detail of the ceiling in the Reading Room at the British Museum*

INFORMATION

www.royal.gov.uk
www.royalcollection.org.uk
✚ 67 E4 ✚ Buckingham Gate SW1A
1AA ☎ 020 7766 7300 ⊘ Late Jul–late
Sep (precise dates vary) daily 9.45–6
(last admission 3.45); timed ticket system
with admission every 15 min ✋ State
Rooms: adult £15.50, child (5–16) £8.75,
family £39.75; joint tickets are available
for the State Rooms, Royal Mews and
Queen's Gallery ⊜ Victoria, Green
Park, Hyde Park Corner ◀ Self-guiding
tours 📖 Official guidebook £4.95 in
English, Chinese, French, German, Italian,
Japanese, Russian and Spanish 📸

BUCKINGHAM PALACE

Buckingham Palace is a world-famous symbol of monarchy and focus for ceremonial occasions as well as one of Queen Elizabeth II's residences.

The palace so familiar to millions from newsreels and postcards has had centuries of piecemeal architectural changes. Originally plain Buckingham House, it was built in 1702 as the Duke of Buckingham's city mansion. King George III snapped it up as a private residence in 1761 and work began on embellishments and additions. When Queen Victoria and Prince Albert moved into the palace in 1837, a whole new wing was added to accommodate their fast-growing family, closing off the three-sided quadrangle and removing the Marble Arch that provided its grand entrance. The present forecourt, where the Changing the Guard ceremony (▷ 107) takes place, was formed in 1911, as part of the Victoria Memorial scheme.

THE STATE ROOMS

Of the palace's 660 rooms, visitors can see about 20. Enter the palace through the Ambassadors' Court and go through John Nash's Grand Hall to climb the curving marble of the Grand Staircase to the first-floor State Rooms. Beyond the small Guard Room, hung with Gobelin tapestries, is the Green Drawing Room where official visitors gather before being presented to the Queen. Some of George IV's fine Sèvres porcelain can be seen here. Ahead is the Throne Room, a theatrical 20m (65ft) space leading up to the chairs of state. This leads into the 47m (155ft) Picture Gallery, displaying works by Peter Paul Rubens, Rembrandt van Rijn and Anthony van Dyck. The Silk Tapestry Room links the Picture Gallery with the East Gallery, leading into the Ball Supper Room and the vast Ballroom, used for investitures and state banquets.

The West Gallery leads to the State Dining Room, in white and gold with deep-red walls. Next is the sumptuous Blue Drawing Room, with a dazzling Nash ceiling and huge Corinthian columns. The opulence continues in the Music Room, with its domed ceiling and columns of lapis lazuli.

A blaze of white and gold greets you in the White Drawing Room, where there is more wonderful French furniture. The intricately designed Minister's Staircase leads to the ground floor and the Marble Hall, displaying statues of nymphs. Other attractions are the Queen's Gallery and the nearby Royal Mews.

Above *The Queen's London residence, Buckingham Palace*

CHELSEA

www.chelseaphysicgarden.co.uk
Britain's second-oldest botanical garden (Oxford's is older) was founded in 1673 by the Society of Apothecaries of London to study plants for medical purposes, which is still the case.

The 2ha (5-acre) walled plot has some 5,000 species, rare trees and a rock garden (1772) with basaltic lava brought back from Iceland by English botanist Sir Joseph Banks (1743–1820), who accompanied Captain James Cook (1728–79) on his first voyage to the Pacific.

On display are flowering shrubs and rare peonies, as well as culinary herbs, edible flowers, poisonous plants and plants used to make dyes and fibres.

At the behest of Charles II (1630–85), the Royal Hospital Chelsea (Mon–Sat 10–12, 2–4, Sun 2–4; closed Oct–end Apr Sun) was built by Sir Christopher Wren (1632–1723) in the late 17th century as almshouses for veteran soldiers. It still serves that purpose today, and the Chelsea Pensioners, as the residents are known, are a familiar sight. Their dress uniform is a scarlet tunic and a tricorn hat. The hospital has a small museum with uniforms and medals, and the panelled Great Hall. Outside, you can wander in the south grounds, the site of the annual Chelsea Flower Show since 1913 (▷ 107).

Chelsea Physic Garden ✚ 67 off D5
✉ 66 Royal Hospital Road SW3 4HS
☎ 020 7352 5646 ◷ Early Apr–late Oct Wed 12–5, Sun 2–6 ✋ Adult £5, child (5–15) £3.50 Ⓜ Sloane Square 🖥 🏛 ▯

COUNTY HALL

www.countyhallgallery.com
www.londonaquarium.co.uk
www.namcostation.co.uk
The former headquarters of the Greater London Council house two major attractions.

Dalí Universe is dedicated to surrealist artist Salvador Dalí (1904–89). It features a permanent exhibition of more than 500 works, including the red Mae West Lips sofa. The Dalí collection is complemented also by a regularly changing programme of blockbuster art exhibitions.

One of Europe's largest aquariums, the London Aquarium occupies three floors and represents a variety of environments. The highlight is the three-level Atlantic and Pacific exhibit, where large sharks and stingrays glide menacingly about. There are brightly patterned fish to enjoy in the coral reef and Indian Ocean exhibitions, and you can stroke a stingray on the simulated beach.

County Hall is also home to Namco Station, a huge leisure complex.

✚ 68 H4 ✉ County Hall, Westminster Bridge Road SE1 7PB
Dalí Universe ☎ 020 7620 2720 ◷ Daily 10–6.30 (last admission 5.30pm) ✋ Adult £12, child (over 12) £8, under 12s free, family £30; audio guide £2.50
London Aquarium ☎ 020 7967 8010 ◷ Daily 10–6 ✋ Adult £13.25, child (3–14) £9.75, family £44
Namco Station ◷ Daily 10am–midnight Ⓜ Waterloo, Westminster 🖥 🏛

COVENT GARDEN

www.coventgardenmarket.co.uk (market)
www.coventgardenlife.com (general)
Covent Garden became the site of a fruit and vegetable market in the 19th century, but when market traders moved out in 1974 it was turned into the present Piazza, with shops, stalls, eating places and street entertainers (who have to prove their worth by audition), such as the gold-painted man (pictured right).

There's still a daily market held here (Mon–Sat 10–7, Sun 11–6), with a wonderful range of crafts, jewellery, clothing and accessories (Tue–Sun) and antiques (Mon).

To the northwest of the Piazza is the magnificently refurbished Royal Opera House (▷ 104). On the opposite side of the Piazza you'll find the former Flower Market, now London's Transport Museum (Sat–Thu 10–6, Fri 11–9), with enough red buses and Tube iconography to please any enthusiast. Nearby are two of the area's famous theatres, the elegant Theatre Royal Drury Lane and the Lyceum (▷ 103), on Shaftesbury Avenue.

✚ 68 G2 ✉ Covent Garden Market WC2E 8RF ☎ 020 7836 9136 ◷ Open access ✋ Free Ⓜ Covent Garden
🍴 🖥 ▯ 🏛

DESIGN MUSEUM

www.designmuseum.org
In 1989 a 1950s warehouse on Butler's Wharf was converted into the Design Museum, the first in the world to be dedicated to 20th- and 21st-century design. One of London's most inspiring attractions, it has an evolving permanent collection of design classics, while temporary exhibitions range from retrospectives of the works of great designers to thematic shows.

✚ 69 M4 ✉ 28 Shad Thames SE1 2YD ☎ 0870 833 9955 ◷ Daily 10–5.45 ✋ Adult £8.50, child (over 12) £6.50, under 12s free Ⓜ London Bridge, Tower Hill (or Tower Gateway for DLR) 🚢 St. Katharine's Pier 🖥 ▯ 🏛

Below *Street performers thrill the crowds in Covent Garden*

Left *A compass on the dome of the Old Royal Naval College at Greenwich*
Above HMS Belfast *is moored on the Thames close to Tower Bridge*

GREENWICH

www.cuttysark.org.uk
www.oldroyalnavalcollege.org
www.nmm.ac.uk

Approach Greenwich by river for views of some of London's finest architecture. Historic buildings and the museums are the big draw, but it's also worth browsing the craft stalls at the weekend market.

The sleek tea clipper *Cutty Sark,* by Greenwich Pier, was built in 1869 to carry cargo between Britain and the Orient. The ship was badly damaged by fire in 2007, but you can see it's restoration in progress at the visitor centre.

The Old Royal Naval College was created by Sir Christopher Wren (1632–1723) in 1664 as a hospital for sailors. Two areas are open to the public: the Painted Hall and the chapel.

The National Maritime Museum tells the story of Britain's maritime history, from the failed 16th-century invasion of the Spanish Armada to the 20th century. Among the collection of ships, paintings, navigational instruments and explorers' relics is the jacket Nelson was wearing when he was fatally wounded at the Battle of Trafalgar in 1805.

The Royal Observatory was founded by Charles II in 1675 to tackle the problem of finding longitude at sea. The Gate Clock measures Greenwich Mean Time, the standard by which time is set around the world. Stand astride the Greenwich Meridian, marked by a brass strip, and you'll have one foot in the eastern hemisphere and the other in the western.

➕ 459 K18 ✉ Cutty Sark and Old Royal Naval College, King William Walk SE10 9HT. National Maritime Museum and Royal Observatory: Greenwich Park SE10 9NF ☎ Cutty Sark: 020 8858 2698. Old Royal Naval College: 020 8269 4747. National Maritime Museum and Royal Observatory: 020 8858 4422 🕐 Cutty Sark Conservation Project: Sun–Tue 11–5. Old Royal Naval College: daily 10–5; grounds: daily 8–6. National Maritime Museum and Royal Observatory: daily 10–5 💷 *Cutty Sark*: free, no access to the ship. Old Royal Naval College: free. National Maritime Museum: free, charge for special exhibitions 🚇 Cutty Sark DLR 🚈 Greenwich 🚢 Riverboat from Westminster Millennium Pier (1hr) 📷 Cutty Sark and National Maritime Museum 🖥 (National Maritime Museum)

HAMPSTEAD

www.cityoflondon.gov.uk/openspaces

Hampstead Heath is a wonderfully diverse public open space of 320ha (790 acres). Londoners come here to exercise and picnic and swim in the three ponds (Kenwood Pond for women, Highgate Pond for men and Hampstead Pond for mixed bathing). South of the ponds is Parliament Hill, from the top of which are extensive views over central London.

At the northern end of the heath is Kenwood House (Apr–end Oct daily 11–5; rest of year daily 11–4), built in 1616 and remodelled by Robert Adam in 1764 for the Earl of Mansfield. It was left to the nation in 1927 by the first Earl of Iveagh, along with its outstanding collection of paintings. Here you will find Rembrandt's brooding *Portrait of the Artist* (c1665) and Vermeer's *The Guitar Player* (c1676), among other important works by English and Dutch masters.

The English poet John Keats (1795–1821) came to reside in Hampstead in 1818, fell in love with his next-door neighbour, Fanny Brawne, and became engaged to her in 1819. During his brief time at Keats House (re-opens 2009 after refurbishment) in Keats Grove he wrote some of his best-loved poems.

Built in 1695, red-brick Fenton House (Mar Sat–Sun 2–5; Apr–end Oct Sat–Sun 11–5, Wed–Fri 2–5) on Windmill Hill, off Hampstead Grove, is one of the best of its period still surviving in London. Period furnishings are complemented by a lovely collection of ceramics and 17th-century needlework and the Benton Fletcher Collection of 17th- and 18th-century instruments.

Sigmund Freud (1856–1939), the founder of psychoanalysis, lived at 20 Maresfield Gardens, in south Hampstead, from 1938, after escaping Nazi-occupied Vienna. The Freud Museum (Wed–Sun 12–5) is devoted to his life and work and includes his famous analysis couch.

➕ 459 K18 ☎ Hampstead Heath Information Centre 020 7482 7073

⊙ Open access ✋ Free ⓔ Hampstead
ⓔ Hampstead Heath

IMPERIAL WAR MUSEUM
www.iwm.org.uk
An imposing pair of naval guns guards the entrance to this fascinating but sobering museum, and provides a taster of the collection, which covers wars involving Britain or the Commonwealth since 1914. The museum's real emphasis and strengths are in its focus on the effects of war in the 20th century on the lives of soldiers and civilians alike. It leaves you with no doubt as to what war is really like.

Military equipment is on show in the Large Exhibits Gallery, where tanks, artillery, submarines and planes are parked, or suspended. Other displays include a recreation of World War I trench warfare and the World War II Blitz, accompanied by sounds and smells. The Secret War exhibition features one of the remaining German Enigma machines, used to encode messages. The art galleries give an impressive insight into war; the centrepiece is *Gassed* by John Singer Sargent (1856–1925).

The Holocaust Exhibition (not for children under 14) examines the Nazi persecution of Europe's Jewish communities and other groups from 1933 to 1945.

HMS Belfast (Mar–end Oct daily 10–6; rest of year daily 10–5) is moored near Tower Bridge. The only surviving armoured warship to be built in the first half of the 20th century, it had an active career during World War II.
✚ 68 J5 ✉ Lambeth Road SE1 6HZ ☎ 020 7416 5320 ⊙ Daily 10–6 ✋ Free (except for some special exhibitions) ⓔ Lambeth North, Elephant and Castle, Southwark, Waterloo ◀ Audio guides £3.50 📖 £3.50 ▢ 🏛

INNS OF COURT
www.lincolnsinn.org.uk; www.graysinn.org.uk; www.innertemple.org.uk; www.middletemple.org.uk
Four Inns of Court were created in the 14th century to provide accommodation for lawyers and their pupils: Gray's Inn, Lincoln's Inn and two inns at Temple. They are the home of London's legal profession, and every barrister (higher court advocate) must be a member of an Inn.

Lincoln's Inn (Mon–Fri 9–5.30) spans 400 years; 15th-century Old Hall is the setting for the Jarndyce v. Jarndyce case in Dickens' novel *Bleak House,* while gas lamps light New Square's 17th-century houses.

Blitz bombing destroyed much of Gray's Inn (gardens only Mon–Fri 12–2.30), but the most important buildings have been restored. These include the 17th-century gateway into the gardens, first laid out in 1606 by English philosopher and statesman Sir Francis Bacon (1561–1626).

Two Inns of Court make up the Temple (Inner Temple gardens Mon–Fri 12.30–3. Middle Temple Hall Sep–end Jul Mon–Fri 10–12, 3–4; closed Aug. Middle Temple gardens May–end Jul, Sep Mon–Fri 12–3). The 12th-century Temple Church still stands at the heart of this network of alleys, gardens and courtyards, where the first recorded performance of Shakespeare's *Twelfth Night* took place.
Lincoln's Inn ✚ 68 H2 ✉ WC2A 3TL ☎ 020 7405 1393; *Gray's Inn* ✚ 426 H1 ✉ 8 South Square WC1R 5ET ☎ 020 7458 7800; Inner Temple/Middle Temple ✚ 426 J2–J3 ✉ King's Bench Walk EC4Y 7HL/ Middle Temple Lane EC4Y 9BT ☎ Inner Temple 020 7797 8250; Middle Temple 020 7427 4830 ✋ Free ⓔ Chancery Lane (closed Sun), Blackfriars, Holborn, Temple

KENSINGTON
www.hrp.org.uk
A royal home for more than 300 years, Kensington Palace is probably most famous as the home of Diana, Princess of Wales. 'Diana: a Princess Remembered' includes some of her most famous dresses.

The Queen's Apartments, including Queen Mary's Bedchamber, and King's Apartments, with ceiling paintings by William Kent (c1685–1748), are of interest for their opulence.

Hyde Park was opened to the public by James I in the 17th century. Members of the Household Cavalry exercise their horses along Rotten Row and at 10.30am and 12pm you can watch them riding to and from the Changing the Guard ceremony at Buckingham Palace (▷ 107).

The city's greenery extends west into Kensington Gardens, the grounds of Kensington Palace. The Serpentine Gallery hosts changing exhibitions of contemporary art (daily 10–6 during exhibitions, free). North of here are two sculptures: *Physical Energy* (1904), by George Frederick Watts (1817–1904), and *Peter Pan* (1912) by Sir George Frampton (1860–1928), commemorating the hero of J. M. Barrie's story. Close by, the Diana, Princess of Wales Memorial Playground opened in 2000. Queen Victoria's beloved husband, Prince Albert, who died of typhoid, is commemorated in the dazzling Albert Memorial.
Kensington Palace ✚ 66 A5 ✉ Kensington Gardens W8 4PX ☎ 0870 751 5170 ⊙ Mar–end Oct daily 10–6; rest of year 10–5 ✋ Adult £12.30, child (5–15) £6.15, family £34 ⓔ High Street Kensington, Queensway, Notting Hill Gate 📖 Sound guide included in price; guidebook in several languages £3.95 🍴 Orangery Restaurant 🏛

Below *The statue of Prince Albert on the Albert Memorial in Kensington Gardens*

LONDON EYE

www.londoneye.com

Europe's largest observation wheel offers the best overview of London from 135m (443ft) above the Thames. The capsules have clear views from large windows and the wheel is in constant motion. Reservations recommended.

🕂 68 H4 ✉ Westminster Bridge Road SE1 7PB ☎ 0870 500 0600 (reservations) 🕙 Jul–end Aug daily 10am–9.30pm; Jun, Sep daily 10–9; rest of year daily 10–8 💷 Adult £15, child (5–15) £7.50 🚇 Waterloo, Westminster, Embankment, Charing Cross 🚢 Riverboat to Waterloo Millennium Pier ❓ Arrive 30 min before the flight 📖 Souvenir book and guide £5, in English, French, German, Spanish and braille 🍴 In the Flight Zone, County Hall, and outside in Jubilee Gardens 🏛 Jubilee Gardens

MADAME TUSSAUD'S

www.madame-tussauds.com

Madame Tussaud's waxworks collection changes all the time—celebrities know they've made it when their waxwork appears here. One of the highlights is the Chamber of Horrors. Next door, the Stardome—formerly known as the London Planetarium—opened in 1958 and is one of the largest in the world. Its centrepiece is an eight-minute audio-visual star show.

🕂 67 D1 ✉ Marylebone Road NW1 5LR ☎ 0870 999 0293 (reservations only; fee applies) 🕙 Mon–Fri 9.30–5.30, Sat–Sun 9–6 (extended hours peak times). Stardome shows every 20 min daily 10.30–closing (peak times), Mon–Fri 12.30–closing, Sat–Sun 10.30–closing (off-peak times) (not recommended for under 5s) 💷 Adult £22.50, child (5–16) £18.50, family (must reserve ahead) £74 (includes Stardome); call ahead to check 🚇 Baker Street ❓ Reserve a timed ticket in advance to avoid a long wait 📖 Guidebook £4.50 🍴 🏛

NATURAL HISTORY MUSEUM

▷ 82–83.

PALACE OF WESTMINSTER

▷ 84.

Opposite *The London Eye at dusk*

Above *Richmond Park is home to several herds of deer*

RICHMOND

www.visitrichmond.co.uk

Several important attractions make Richmond-upon-Thames an excellent day trip. Ham House (Apr–end Oct Sat–Wed 12–4; closed Thu, Fri), in Ham Street, is one of the most beautiful and well-preserved Stuart houses in Britain, filled with rare furniture, paintings and textiles. Built in 1610, it was the home of the Tollemache family, who were deeply involved in the Civil War and Restoration court politics (▷ 34).

Enclosed as a hunting ground by Charles I in 1637, Richmond Park (open access during daylight hours) is the largest open space in London. Herds of graceful deer still graze here. In springtime, the Isabella Plantation is a particularly beautiful area of the park.

There's something to see all year round at Kew's Royal Botanic Gardens near Richmond (Apr–end Aug Mon–Fri 9.30– 6.30, Sat–Sun 9.30–7.30; Sep–end Oct daily 9.30–6; Nov–end Jan daily 9.30–4.15; Feb–end Mar daily 9.30–5.30). The gardens were created during the reign of George III and developed into one of the world's foremost facilities for horticultural research.

The Temperate House, once the world's largest greenhouse, has an elevated gallery from where to view the plants, including the Chilean wine palm, planted in 1846.

The Princess of Wales Conservatory opened in 1987: Arid desert moves gradually to orchid-filled tropics. British native wild flowers are the theme at Queen Charlotte's Cottage and Gardens.

🕂 459 K18 ℹ Tourist Information Centre, Old Town Hall, Whittaker Avenue, Richmond, Surrey TW9 1TP, ☎ 020 8940 9125 🚇 Richmond 🚉 Richmond

NATURAL HISTORY MUSEUM

One of Britain's most exciting and imaginative museums, the Natural History Museum explores all aspects of the world in which we live and the creatures that share it. Its vast collections, numbering more than 70 million items (not all on display) range from massive dinosaur skeletons to tiny insects and from glittering gemstones to fossils of long-dead creatures. There are specimens collected by famous botanist-explorers, including Captain Cooke and Charles Darwin himself. Best of all, there are state-of-the-art displays that grab the imagination, put everything into context and bring to life the past, present and future of our world.

The galleries are organised in colour-coded zones, each presenting particular aspects of natural history. The focus of the Red Zone is on the planet itself, the forces that have shaped it, its continuing evolution and the impact humans have had on it. An amazing sculpture of the earth gives perspective to the planet itself. The Green Zone begins with the cathedral-like Central Hall and its Diplodocus skeleton, and continues to explore the path of evolution from marine fossils to primates—and how we, as its inhabitants, fit into it. Along the way there's the enticing (to some) creepy crawlies area and displays dealing with ecological issues.

Many visitors head straight for the Blue Zone, a perennially popular part of the museum. This is where you will find the spectacular array of dinosaurs skeletons and mammal specimens, including some of the world's biggest creatures. There are fascinating facts to learn about all of these, and about the way our own bodies work in the human biology section. Finally, for the Orange Zone you need to head outside (summer only), to a wonderful wildlife garden conserving thousands of native British plants and animals. This is where you will also find the Darwin Centre, a place of important scientific research.

In addition to all this, there are lots of special activities and informative tours to add even more to the enjoyment of this incredible place, which has enthralled generations of children and inspired them to one day bring their own children here.

INFORMATION

www.nhm.ac.uk

66 B5 Cromwell Road SW7 5BD
020 7942 5000 Daily 10–5.50.
Wildlife Garden: Apr–end Oct daily 12–5 (except during bad weather) Free.
Special exhibitions fee varies, child (5–16) £3 South Kensington Tours of Darwin Centre (over 10s only), free, reservations required £4.50 in several languages

Above The buildings of the Natural History Museum in South Kensington.
Opposite People and a dinosaur skeleton in the Natural History Museum.

INFORMATION

www.parliament.uk

🗺 68 G4 ✉ Parliament Square SW1A 0AA ☎ 020 7219 4272 (House of Commons Information Office), 0870 906 3773 (summer tours tickets) 🕐 Tours during summer recess, Aug, Mon, Tue, Fri, Sat 9.15–4.30, Wed, Thu 1.15–4.30; Sep–early Oct Mon, Fri, Sat 9.15–4.30, Tue–Thu 1.15–4.30 ✋ Public Gallery (House of Commons) and Visitors Gallery (House of Lords) free; tours see below
🚇 Westminster 🚢 Westminster Millennium Pier 🎫 Tour during summer recess: adult £12, child (4–16) £5, family £30 📖 Free 💻 🏛

Below *The seat of government in Britain, the Houses of Parliament at the Palace of Westminster*

PALACE OF WESTMINSTER

Despite their appearance, the Houses of Parliament, which form the main part of the Palace of Westminster, are 19th-century buildings. The original medieval palace was virtually destroyed by fire in 1834 and the competition to design a replacement in Elizabethan style was won by architect Charles Barry (1795–1860) and his assistant, Augustus Pugin (1812–52). The famous clock tower housing Big Ben (the hour bell), was completed in 1858.

Westminster Hall remains from an earlier age. The walls date from the late 11th century, while the magnificent hammerbeam roof was installed in the 14th century, removing the need for supporting pillars. This huge hall witnessed many significant events in history, including the trial of Charles I (he stepped through a window of the hall out onto the scaffold for his execution), the trial of the Gunpowder Plot conspirators, and countless royal speaches and international government conferences. The hall has also been used for the lyings-in-state of George VI, Queen Mary, Winston Churchill and the late Queen Mother.

The Jewel Tower (Apr–end Oct daily 10–5; rest of year daily 10–4) was used to store Edward III's treasures. An exhibition in the tower explains the history of Parliament.

For a guided tour of the Houses of Parliament, UK residents should contact their Member of Parliament. Visitors from overseas are not admitted during session but may enter during the summer recess on a pre-reserved tour. Anyone is able to attend debates in both the House of Commons and the House of Lords (join the queue outside St. Stephen's Entrance and expect to wait one to two hours during the afternoon). The tower is off limits to visitors from outside the UK. UK residents can arange a visit through their local MP.

ROYAL ACADEMY OF ARTS

www.royalacademy.org.uk

Burlington House was built as a Palladian mansion for the Earl of Burlington in around 1720. Since 1768 it has been the Royal Academy of Arts, England's first formal art school. English portrait painter Sir Joshua Reynolds (1723–92) was the first president, and painter John Constable (1776–1837)was among its students. The Royal Academy hosts the Royal Academy Summer Exhibition (Jun to mid-Aug).

➕ 67 F3 ✉ Burlington House, Piccadilly W1J 0BD ☎ 020 7300 8000 (general), 020 7300 5760 (recording) 🕐 Exhibitions: Sat–Thu 10–6, Fri 10–10. Fine Rooms: Tue–Fri 1–4.30, Sat–Sun 10–6 ✋ Adult £8–£11, child (12–18) £3–£4, child (8–11) £2.Booking essential either through website or ticket office: tickets available 48hrs in advance from ticket office 🎫 Tours of Fine Rooms Tue–Fri 1pm, free 🚇 Green Park, Piccadilly Circus 🍴 🛒 ♿ 📷

ST. PAUL'S CATHEDRAL

▷ 86.

SCIENCE MUSEUM

www.sciencemuseum.org.uk

The Science Museum celebrates humankind's greatest inventions and scientific achievements.

Most people start in the popular Launchpad, a hands-on gallery for children. The ground floor focuses on power and space; main attractions include the *Apollo 10* command module and the 1829 rail locomotive *Rocket*. The Flight gallery exhibits the *Gypsy Moth* plane *Jason*, flown from Britain to Australia by aviator Amy Johnson (1903–41) in 1930. Galleries on the upper floors tell the story of the science and art of medicine and the Wellcome Wing has iexhibitions about medical science.

➕ 66 B5 ✉ Exhibition Road SW7 2DD ☎ 0870 870 4868 🕐 Daily 10–6 ✋ Main museum free (charges for some special exhibitions); IMAX: adult £7.50, child (16 and under) £6; SimEx Simulator: adult £4, child (16 and under) £3; Motionride Simulator: adult £2.50, child (16 and under) £1.50 🚇 South Kensington 📖 £2 🛒 📷

SHAKESPEARE'S GLOBE

▷ 87.

SIR JOHN SOANE'S MUSEUM

www.soane.org

From the moment you knock to be allowed in, it's clear that this is a museum unlike any other. Sir John Soane (1753–1837) was Professor of Architecture at the Royal Academy of Arts and arranged his eccentric and eclectic collection of art and objects for the benefit of his students, filling every inch of space in his house. You'll find yourself wandering among Classical and Renaissance statues and busts, marbles and bronzes, urns, altars, antique gems, odd bits of demolished London buildings, Indian ivory-inlaid furniture, Peruvian ceramics, cork models of Greek temples, Napoleonic medals, thousands of architectural drawings, and a couple of mummified cats. The Picture Room is a highlight: The ingenious use of hinged screens instead of walls allowed Soane to fit more than 100 works into this small room, including William Hogarth's celebrated *A Rake's Progress* (1733). Just enjoy the experience: A floorplan suggests the route Soane himself recommended.

➕ 68 H1 ✉ 13 Lincoln's Inn Fields WC2A 3BP ☎ 020 7405 2107 🕐 Tue–Sat 10–5; first Tue each month also 6–9pm ✋ Free; donations box provided 🎫 Guided tour Sat 11 (tickets sold from 10.30) £5 🚇 Chancery Lane (closed Sun), Holborn 📷

Below *Sir John Soane's Museum, housing paintings, sculptures, architectural models and drawings created and collected by the 19th-century architect*

INFORMATION

www.stpauls.co.uk

✚ 69 K2 ✉ St. Paul's Churchyard EC4M
8AD ☎ 020 7246 8348 ◷ Mon–Sat
8.30–4.30. Daily for services. Triforium
tours (Library, West End Gallery, Trophy
Room and Wren's Great Model); advance
reservation required, tel: 020 7246
8357 (Mon–Fri 9–2); £12 ♿ Cathedral,
Crypt and Galleries: adult £10, child
(6–16) £3.50, family £23.50 ◉ St.
Paul's, Blackfriars 🚇 Blackfriars 🚌 £4
🚍 Guided tours (in English only) Mon–Sat
11, 11.30, 1.30 and 2. Adult £3, under 16s
£1. Audio tours (9.30–4): £3.50 in various
languages 🍴 Refectory restaurant
▢ Crypt Café ♿

TIP

» There are free organ recitals at 5pm
every Sunday, but bring some loose
change for the collection at the end.

Below *Inside St Paul's Cathedral,*
completed in 1711

ST. PAUL'S CATHEDRAL

Britain's only domed cathedral, St. Paul's is second only in size to St. Peter's in
Rome. Sir Christopher Wren's masterpiece is a dramatic combination of vast,
airy spaces and elaborate decoration. A wide flight of steps leads up to the
west front entrance, flanked by two clock towers.

THE DOME AND GALLERIES

Eight pillars support the huge dome, 111m (364ft) high and weighing about
65,000 tonnes. The acoustics are such that someone standing on the opposite
side of the gallery will hear your whispers clearly after several seconds' delay.
The frescoes on the dome depict scenes from the life of St. Paul and were
painted by Sir James Thornhill between 1716 and 1719. The Golden Gallery runs
around the outer dome, a breathtaking 85m (280ft) from the cathedral floor. A
hole in the floor gives a dizzying view down.

THE CHANCEL

This part of the cathedral is a riot of 19th-century Byzantine-style gilding. In
the north choir aisle is a marble sculpture, *Mother and Child*, by Henry Moore
(1898–1986). A marble effigy of poet John Donne (1572–1631) stands in the
south choir aisle. This is one of the few effigies that survived the Great Fire of
London in 1666, and you can make out scorch marks on its base.

The Duke of Wellington (1769–1852), hero of the Napoleonic Wars and prime
minister from 1828 to 1830, lies in a simple Cornish granite casket. Admiral
Nelson (1758–1805), who died in action at the Battle of Trafalgar, lies in the
middle of the crypt. Nelson's coffin went with him into battle, and after his
death he was preserved in it in French brandy for the journey home. At Gibraltar
the coffin was put into a lead-lined casket and steeped in distilled wine. Finally
his remains were encased in two more coffins before being buried under
Cardinal Wolsey's 16th-century sarcophagus.

THE CATHEDRAL'S HISTORY

The first St. Paul's was built in AD604, rebuilt 300 years later after a Viking
attack and replaced by a Norman cathedral, Old St. Paul's, in 1087. After its
destruction in the Great Fire of 1666, Sir Christopher Wren (1632–1723) was
commissioned to build a new one. It was finally completed in 1710.

SHAKESPEARE'S GLOBE

The original Globe was one of Britain's first purpose-built theatres, erected by a company that included Shakespeare in 1599. It was destroyed by fire during a production of *Hamlet* in 1613. A project began in 1969 to create an accurate, functioning reconstruction, using materials, tools and techniques closely matching those of Elizabethan times, but it was 1997 before it was finished.

The theatre is built of unseasoned oak and held together with 6,000 oak pegs. It is crowned with the first thatched roof to be built in the city (understandably) since the Great Fire in 1666. In the middle, an elevated stage and an open-air yard are surrounded on three sides by covered tiers of benches that seat 1,500. Productions are held in the afternoon (May–end Sep only), much as in Shakespeare's day, subject to fine weather.

If you can't get to see a performance, it's worth taking a guided tour. This enables you to see the remarkable building up close and in detail, in the company of a knowledgeable guide who will bring the project and its history to life. It also includes a visit to the excellent exhibition, where various aspects of the theatre are illustrated. One area deals with the rebuilding of the Globe, from the vision and determination that made it possible to the skilled craftspeople who carried out the task. There's also a collection of costumes (you can even try on a suit of armour) and fascinating information about the particular skills of designing clothing for the stage. Music was always an important part of theatrical performances, and a display case holds early instruments of the kind played in Shakespeare's day. Elsewhere, there's a recreation of an early printing press and touch screens that tell how special effects were created.

INFORMATION

www.shakespeares-globe.org
✚ 69 K3 ✉ 21 New Globe Walk, Bankside SE1 9DT ☎ 020 7902 1400, 020 7401 9919 (box office) 🕐 Oct–Mar daily 10–5; mid-Mar to Apr 9–5, 23 Apr–early Oct Mon–Sat 9–12.30, 1–5, Sun 9–11.30, 12–5. Theatrical performances late Apr–early Oct daily 🎟 Exhibition and theatre tour: adult £9, child (5–15) £6.50, family £25. Theatre performance: adult £15–£33, child (under 16) £11–£27, plus (600) £5 standing only tickets ⓔ Blackfriars, Cannon Street, London Bridge, St. Paul's, Southwark 📖 £3 🍴 Daily 12–2.30 💻 🖥 10–10 🏛

Above *The new Globe Theatre on Bankside, a replica of Shakespeare's original of 1599*

SOMERSET HOUSE

www.somersethouse.org.uk
The rejuvenation of this great riverside landmark has given London a new arts complex in a splendid 18th-century setting.

The Courtauld Institute of Art Gallery houses a stunning assembly of six private collections, featuring Old Masters, Impressionist and post-Impressionist paintings, sculpture and applied arts. A suite of softly top-lit rooms displays works by Paul Cézanne, Vincent Van Gogh, Paul Gauguin and Edouard Manet.

The Hermitage Museum in St. Petersburg lends a changing display of objects to the Hermitage Rooms at Somerset Houser.

The Gilbert Collection has closed to visitors and is moving to its new home in a suite of rooms at the Victoria and Albert Museum which are due to open in 2009.
✚ 68 H3 ✉ Strand WC2R 0RN ☎ 020 7845 4600 🕐 Daily 10–6; extended hours for Courtyard, River Terrace Café and Admiralty Restaurant 🎫 Somerset House: free. Courtauld Institute of Art Gallery: adult £5–£6, child (under 16) free; free Mon 10–2 🚇 Temple (closed Sun), Covent Garden, Charing Cross, Embankment 🚢 Riverboat to Embankment Pier 📖 £4.95 🍴 Admiralty Restaurant 🍽 River Terrace Café ♿

TATE BRITAIN

www.tate.org.uk/britain/
The Tate Gallery, now Tate Britain, transferred its international collection to Tate Modern (▷ opposite) in 2000, allowing its British collection from 1500 to the present day (the world's largest) to spread out considerably. Despite this, the gallery still owns far more than it can display, and the paintings on show, presented chronologically, are changed every year. All the great names of British art are represented, from Nicholas Hilliard's 16th-century portrait of Queen Elizabeth I and fashionable 17th-century portraits by Sir Peter Lely and Sir Godfrey Kneller, through the work of major 18th-century figures such as William Hogarth, Joshua Reynolds and Thomas Gainsborough, and progressing into

innovative 19th-century paintings by William Blake, John Constable and J. M. W. Turner, who is especially well represented. The Pre-Raphaelites are represented in force, and the collection moves into the 20th century with work by L. S. Lowry, Henry Moore, Barbara Hepworth, Francis Bacon, David Hockney and Lucian Freud. A boat service links the gallery with Tate Modern.
✚ 68 G6 ✉ Millbank SW1P 4RG ☎ 020 7887 8008 (recording), 020 7887 8000 🕐 Daily 10–5.50 🎫 Free, donations welcome. Charge for special exhibitions 🚇 Pimlico, Vauxhall, Westminster 🚢 From Tate Modern (every 40 min) 🚌 Mon–Fri 11, 12, 1.15, 2, 3; Sat–Sun 12, 3. Free. Audiotours free, English, French, German, Italian, Spanish 📖 £4.99 🍴 🍽 ♿

TATE MODERN

▷ 89.

TOWER BRIDGE

www.towerbridge.org.uk
London's best-known bridge links the Tower of London and the south bank of the River Thames. It opened to the public in 1982. The hydraulically operated bascules are the main draw, designed to allow tall ships to sail through and is still lifted more than 900 times a year.

The neo-Gothic towers are also an attraction. Climb to the upper walkways and engine rooms, where an exhibition details the controversies that preceded the construction of the bridge, opened in 1894.
✚ 69 M3 ✉ SE1 2UP ☎ 020 7403 3761 🕐 Apr–end Sep daily 10–6.30; rest of year daily 9.30–6 🎫 Adult £6, child (5–15) £3, family £10–£14 🚇 Tower Hill, London Bridge, Tower Gateway DLR 🚢 Riverboat to Tower Millennium Pier 📖 £2.50 ♿

TOWER OF LONDON

▷ 90.

TRAFALGAR SQUARE

New Year's Eve, pigeons, Admiral Lord Nelson and two national galleries on London's central square. One of the world's most famous squares sits at the northern end of Whitehall (▷ 91), commemorating

Admiral Lord Nelson's victory against Napoleon and the French at the 1805 Battle of Trafalgar. Nelson towers on his 56m (184ft) column in the square, guarded by four bronze lions.

Steps lead up to the Corinthian portico of the church of St. Martin-in-the-Fields (Mon–Wed 10–7, Thu–Sat 10–10, Sun 12–7), at the northeastern corner of the square. Officially the parish church of Buckingham Palace, St. Martin's has strong royal connections.

The National Gallery's (daily 10–6, Wed to 9pm) collection of Western European art, dating from 1250 to about 1900, is arranged by period. Paintings from 1500 to 1600 are displayed in the West Wing. In the North Wing are painters from the Dutch School including Peter Paul Rubens, Rembrandt van Rijn and Jan Vermeer—and Impressionists. One highlight of the Sainsbury Wing, which focuses on the early Renaissance, is Sandro Botticelli's (c1445–1510) Venus and Mars.

Tucked away at the back of the National Gallery, the National Portrait Gallery (Sat–Wed 10–5.50, Thu–Fri 10–8.50) is a Who's Who of the key players in British history, science and the arts. Founded in 1856, the collection consists of more than 7,000 paintings, drawings, sculptures and photographs, arranged chronologically over three floors. Dominating the second floor's Tudor Galleries is the magnificent portrait of Elizabeth I (1592) by Marcus Gheeraerts the Younger (1561–1635), a tour de force of political propaganda. Rooms 4–8 are devoted to the Stuarts, while other rooms focus on the 18th century, and include a unique, unfinished sketch (c1810) of Jane Austen by her sister. Victorians fill most of the first-floor rooms. Britain since 1990 occupies the ground floor and includes Bryan Organ's famous 1981 painting of Princess Diana sitting cross-legged, contrasting with the formality of earlier royal portraits.
Britain and London Visitor Centre ✚ 67 F3 ✉ 1 Lower Regent Street SW1Y 4XT (call in person only) 🕐 Open access 🎫 Free 🚇 Charing Cross, Leicester

TATE MODERN

Tate Modern, housed in the spectacularly restored Bankside Power Station, is one of the world's leading museums of modern art, and even approaching the gallery is stimulating, especially if you cross the Millennium Bridge, with its wonderful river views, from St. Paul's Cathedral.

Though the building is huge, its popularity—more than 5 million visitors a year—and the importance of its growing collections soon made it clear that it just wasn't big enough. In 2006, just six years after it opened, plans were submitted (and subsequently approved) for a stunning extension by architects Herzog & de Meuron, which will not only provide Southwark with an exciting new landmark, but also enable the museum to fulfil its remit to become the finest showcase of contemporary art in the world.

The permanent collection represents one of the finest collections of international modern art in the world, and covers all of the major movements and the most influential artists from the beginning of the 20th century on. Whatever your preferences—Fauvism, Expressionism, Surrealism, Abstract, Pop art, installation works, video, sculpture—there is so much to discover here that a single visit will need careful planning to include just some of the many highlights. Masterpieces are too numerous to mention, and include works by Picasso, Matisse, Dalí, Magritte, Pollock, Naum Gabo, Giacometti, Lichtenstein and Warhol. The collection of Conceptual Art includes some of the most challenging works of the most recent decades.

The galleries are organized so that each gives an immediate overview of key periods in modern art in its central area, with the opportunity to delve deeper into the subject in the surrounding displays. This provides the visitor with an excellent perspective of the development of contemporary art. In addition there are always temporary exhibitions that warrant a special visit on their own. Recent highlights have include Cy Twombly's Cycles and Seasons, Street Art, and An Urban History of Photography.

INFORMATION

www.tate.org.uk/modern/
🕂 69 K3 ✉ Bankside SE1 9TG ☎ 020 7887 8008 (recording), 020 7887 8000 🕓 Sun–Thu 10–6, Fri–Sat 10–10 ✋ Free, donations welcome. Charge for special exhibitions 🚇 Southwark, Blackfriars, St. Paul's 🚢 From Tate Britain (every 40 min) 🚌 Daily 11, 12, 2, 3, free. Audiotours £2, English, French, German, Italian, Spanish 📖 £4.99, in several languages 🍴 🛍 🏛

Above *Tate Modern art gallery opened in May 2000 in a converted power station on London's South Bank*

INFORMATION

www.hrp.org.uk

⊞ 69 M3 ✉ Tower of London EC3N 4AB ☎ 0844 482 7777 (recording), 0844 482 7799 (tickets) 🕐 Mar–end Oct Tue–Sat 9–5.30, Sun–Mon 10–5.30; rest of year Tue–Sat 9–4.30, Sun–Mon 10–4.30. Last admission 1 hr before closing. All internal buildings close 30 min after last admission; Tower closes 1 hr after last admission. To watch the Ceremony of the Keys (▷ 107) apply in writing at least 6–8 weeks in advance for free tickets to The Ceremony of the Keys Office, HM Tower of London, London EC3N 4AB 🎫 Adult £16.50, child (5–15) £9.50, family £46 🚇 Tower Hill, Tower Gateway DLR 🚢 Tower Millennium Pier 📷 £4.95, English, French, Russian, Italian, Japanese 🎧 Audioguide, £3.50, in English, French, German, Italian, Japanese, Russian, Spanish, Korean and Chinese 🍴 🛍 🏛

TIPS

» Crowds can be a problem in the summer. To save waiting, buy tickets in advance by telephoning 0844 482 7799 or online at www.hrp.org.uk.

» There are free daily guided tours by yeoman warders; times are posted at the entrance.

Above *Nighttime at the Tower of London, seen from across the River Thames*

TOWER OF LONDON

Prison, palace, home to the stunning Crown Jewels and an enduring symbol of 1,000 years of Britain's royal history. In previous centuries, prisoners accused of treason would enter the Tower of London by boat through Traitors' Gate— some, such as Henry VIII's second wife, Anne Boleyn, taking their final journey. Today the visitors' entrance is through the Middle Tower and you'll probably get out alive.

THE WHITE TOWER

At the heart of the Tower is its oldest medieval building, the White Tower, thought to date from 1078 and built to serve as a fortress and a royal residence. There's an exhibition about small arms, from the Royal Armouries collection, and spiral stairs lead to the gloriously simple Chapel of St. John the Evangelist. John Flamsteed (1646–1719), Charles II's astronomer, observed the stars from the turrets before moving to a new headquarters located at Greenwich (▷ 78).

THE CROWN JEWELS

First stop for many visitors is the Jewel House, where displays tell the history of the Coronation Regalia (Crown Jewels) before reaching the treasury, where the jewels are kept. An excellent visual story of the jewels entertains those waiting to view the exhibits, and it is possible to repeat the circuit round the jewels immediately for a second look.

The jewels date mainly from the restoration of the monarchy in 1660 (▷ 34). Among the priceless stones in the collection is the world's biggest cut diamond, the 530-carat First Star of Africa.

TOWER GREEN

The famous prisoners incarcerated and executed here over the years provide the human interest. The Bloody Tower gets its name from the supposed murder of the two princes, Edward and Richard, sons of Edward IV and allegedly the victims of their ambitious uncle, Richard III. The Queen's House, a black-and-white building next to the Bloody Tower, was the scene of Guy Fawkes' interrogation in 1605 (▷ 34) and of a daring escape when the Earl of Nithsdale, imprisoned after the 1715 Jacobite rebellion, made his getaway dressed as a woman. The high-ranking prisoners were kept in the 13th-century Beauchamp Tower. Tower Green was the main focus for suffering and heroics, and was where Anne Boleyn, among others, was beheaded.

VICTORIA AND ALBERT MUSEUM

www.vam.ac.uk

In 1852, the aim in creating the V&A (as it is known) was to give everyone access to great art and to provide a source of inspiration for British manufacturers and designers. Tens of thousands of items are on show, including fashion and textiles, furniture and paintings, jewellery, ceramics, glass, silver and ironwork.

The national collection of photography treats you to more than 300,000 photos, displayed in an elegant gallery that showcases key photographers from all over the world, including William Henry Fox Talbot and Henri Cartier-Bresson.

✚ 66 B5 ✉ Cromwell Road SW7 2RL ☎ 020 7942 2000 🕐 Daily 10–5.45 (Fri to 10pm), 👋 Free, except for some special exhibitions and events 🚇 South Kensington 📖 £4.99 🕐 Free introductory tours daily (1 hr) on the half-hour 10.30–3.30; meet in the Grand Entrance 🍴 💻 🏛

WALLACE COLLECTION

www.wallacecollection.org

The Hertford family began this world-class collection of art when the fourth Marquess of Hertford, living in Paris during the French Revolution, bought 18th-century paintings, porcelain and furniture. His son, Sir Richard Wallace, added Renaissance ceramics, bronzes and jewellery, and his widow left the collection to the nation in 1897.

✚ 67 D2 ✉ Hertford House, Manchester Square W1V 3BN ☎ 020 7563 9500 🕐 Daily 10–5 👋 Free 🚇 Bond Street, Baker Street 🕐 Free guided tours Mon–Fri 1, also Wed, Sat 11.30, Sun 3 📖 £7 💻 🏛

WESTMINSTER ABBEY

www.westminster-abbey.org

The largest surviving medieval church in London has been the setting for all royal coronations since 1066, and its mausoleum commemorates 3,300 of the nation's most famous historical figures. You enter by the north transept, then turn left to take a one-way, clockwise tour of the church and cloisters. North of the sanctuary is the Lady Chapel, where you can view the white-marble effigy of Elizabeth I, who died in 1603. The main part of the chapel, with its fan-vaulted ceiling, is an impressive setting for the royal tombs arranged around the altar and aisles.

The south transept, also known as Poets' Corner, is where great poets, authors, artists and actors are honoured with memorials. Nearby, the Abbey Museum has macabre wax effigies of Queen Elizabeth I, Charles II and Lord Nelson.

✚ 68 G5 ✉ Parliament Square SW1P 3PA ☎ 020 7654 4900 🕐 Mon–Tue, Thu–Fri 9.30–4.45 (last admission 3.45), Wed 9.30–7, Sat 9.30–2.45 (last admission 1.45). Sun worship only. Times vary; check before visit. College Garden: Apr–end Sep Tue–Thu 10–6; rest of year Tue–Thu 10–4 👋 Adult £10, child (under 16) £7, family £24 🚇 St. James's Park, Westminster 🕐 90-min tours, £5 per person. Audioguides £4 📖 £3–£8 💻 🏛

WHITEHALL

Whitehall is the broad avenue connecting Trafalgar Square (▷ 88) with Parliament Square. Heading south, the navy was run from the first building on the right, the Admiralty, when the British fleet was considered the most powerful in the world.

Next is Horse Guards Parade, where two members of the Household Cavalry mount guard on horseback daily between 10am and 4pm. Beyond Horse Guards is the gated entrance to Downing Street, where the prime minister and chancellor have their official residences.

At the heart of Whitehall is the Cenotaph, designed by Sir Edwin Lutyens in 1920 to commemorate the victims of World War I.

The Churchill Museum and Cabinet War Rooms (daily 9.30–6), reached by turning right on to King Charles Street, were the secret underground rooms where Sir Winston Churchill oversaw his World War II plans.

✚ 68 G4 🛈 Britain and London Visitor Centre, 1 Lower Regent Street SW1Y 4XT (call in person only) 🕐 Open access 👋 Free 🚇 Charing Cross, Westminster

Left *Exhibits in the Victoria and Albert Museum*
Below *Gargoyles decorate the exterior stonework of Westminster Abbey*

BRIDGING THE GAP

A walk along the South Bank, tracing the history of its bridges and highlighting the buildings in between.

THE WALK
Distance: 2.75 miles (4.4km)
Allow: 1hr 15min
Start/end: Westminster tube station
AA Street by Street London

★ This is a well-trodden route and a favourite for many people as it exudes a sense of space in an otherwise highly populated city. Long before the Romans arrived, the river was used as a highway by sea-faring traders. The Italians, delighted by its potential, built the first timber bridge in AD50. By the Middle Ages the river had become so polluted that it constituted a serious hygiene problem—it's no surprise that conditions provided the breeding ground for the Black Death, which arrived in 1348 carried by rats on ships from Europe. With such a colourful history, no wonder it's endearingly called Old Father Thames.

Leave Westminster tube station by Exit 1 to follow signs to Westminster Pier. Walk up the steps to your right and cross Westminster Bridge (initially built from stone in the 1740s, its opening was delayed by sabotage from ferrymen and the death of its sponsor. The Gothic patterns seen on the decorative wrought-iron bridge today are the work of Charles Barry, the Parliament architect, when rebuilding commenced in 1854). Turn left along the riverfront.

❶ Ahead are the 32 transparent pods of the 2,100-ton London Eye, a huge modern Ferris wheel.

Walk past Jubilee Gardens; on the right, is the next bridge, Hungerford, sandwiched between two newer pedestrian bridges called the Golden Jubilee Bridges.

❷ In contrast, Hungerford, the only combined rail and foot crossing over the Thames, was built as a suspension bridge and bought in 1859 to extend the railway line to Charing Cross station. Its legacy lives on in the West Country, for the Clifton Bridge in Bristol was constructed from the recycled, original Hungerford Bridge.

Continue ahead past the Royal Festival Hall and look to the opposite bank of the Thames for Cleopatra's Needle. After the National Film Theatre and its outdoor café is Waterloo Bridge.

❸ When work began to replace the original Waterloo Bridge in 1939, World War II was looming on the horizon. The new bridge eventually opened six years later, having been built mainly by women. Its architect, Sir Giles Gilbert Scott, was also the designer behind the popular red telephone kiosk and Bankside power station, now the impressive Tate Modern.

The path bends to the right, past the Royal National Theatre and the Hayward Gallery, before reaching Gabriel's Wharf.

④ Busy with shops and restaurants, Gabriel's Wharf was once the site of the Eldorado Ice Cream Company. Some 5.3ha (13 acres) in the area were saved from development into office buildings by the Coin Street Community Builders, an association formed in 1984 to create a better community environment. Here you can see some of the 160 box-style houses built in Upper Ground.

Turn right at the Riviera restaurant and walk through the central path lined on either side with a series of wooden sculptures. Turn left at the end into Stamford Street and 91m (100yds) further on take another left turn into Barge House Street. Ahead, the brown brickwork of the Oxo Wharf somewhat shrouds the entrance to the Oxo Tower.

⑤ This is another building with power station roots is the Oxo Wharf, which was acquired in the 1920s by the Meat Extract Company that made the Oxo cubes still available from supermarkets today. The art deco Oxo Tower has 3m (10ft) windows, which, at night, are illuminated in such a way as to spell out the distinctive 'noughts and crosses' in red neon lights to all four corners of London.

Enter the glass doors to your left and catch the escalator to the eighth floor for a view of the skyline, then descend again and continue along the ground floor to the riverside exit. Turn right and then turn left to cross Blackfriars Bridge.

⑥ Blackfriars, the final bridge along this stretch known as the South Bank, opened in 1769 and was originally named after the Tory Prime Minister, William Pitt—it didn't take long to change the name, though. The present construction has five cast-iron arches. The remains of the rail bridge that once ran parallel look almost surreal, like the posts of a scarlet-tinted wedding cake rising out of the water—well, we did say it was surreal.

At the end of the bridge, turn left to follow the Thames Path along the wide pavement adjacent to the river. The first boat you will pass on your left is HMS *President*. The next set of buildings to your right after Temple tube station belong to the University of London. Immediately after these comes majestic Somerset House (▷ 88).

A further 183m (200yds) ahead the path passes Cleopatra's Needle before reaching Embankment tube. Northumberland Avenue is the next road to appear on your right. About 183m (200yds) further on is Horse Guards Avenue, which is sandwiched between the formidable buildings of the Old War Office and the Ministry of Defence. You are now almost parallel with the London Eye (▷ 81), on the opposite bank of the River Thames. When you reach Westminster Bridge turn right into Bridge Street, to Westminster tube and the start.

PLACE TO VISIT
HAYWARD GALLERY
✉ Belvedere Road, London SE1 8XX
☎ 0871 663 2500

WHERE TO EAT AND DRINK
Sarni's in Gabriel's Wharf serves good hot chocolate, coffee and sandwiches. There's outside seating only, so if you're after somewhere warmer try EAT on the ground floor of the Oxo Tower. Just before Cannon Street Rail Bridge is The Anchor, a 17th-century inn. It's thought that Samuel Pepys watched the Fire of London in 1666 from here. A spit-and-sawdust sort of place with creaking floors, it has a wide range of dishes including a good value, pre-theatre menu.

WHEN TO GO
Go early morning or evening when the glass and gilt on the buildings literally sparkles in the sunlight.

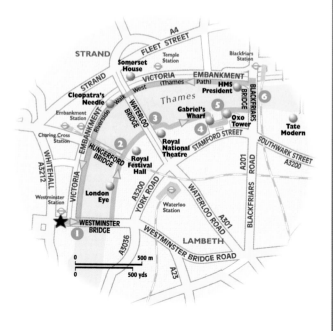

Opposite *The London Eye and County Hall can be seen from Westminster Bridge*

CORRIDORS OF POWER

A look at some of the city's landmarks, from Whitehall through to Smithfield.

THE WALK
Distance: 4 miles (6.4km)
Allow: 2hrs 30min
Start: Westminster tube station
End: Farringdon tube station
AA Street by Street London

★ This walk starts across the road from the Houses of Parliament at Westminster Abbey. It's easy to take sights for granted in a city with another symbol of its historic importance around every bend.

Leave Westminster tube following signs to the Houses of Parliament. Cross St. Margaret Street to Westminster Abbey and the adjacent St. Margaret's Church (▷ 81).

❶ Westminster Abbey is where every English king and queen since 1066 has been crowned and where many are buried. On a corner opposite Horse Guards Parade is one of the best places to stand for a grandstand view of the Queen's

carriage as it heads up Whitehall for the State Opening of Parliament. Turn back along St. Margaret Street and continue ahead as the road becomes Parliament Street, and then Whitehall. Follow it along past the Cenotaph.

❷ The Cenotaph is a simple memorial to those people who died in World War I and World War II, all the way to Trafalgar Square.

Turn right here and cross onto Northumberland Avenue. Turn right into the Strand, which links the City of London with Westminster.

❸ The Strand was once one of the most influential thoroughfares in Britain, with many fine mansions, some of which you can still see. The street names from here on give a clue to the past inhabitants. Think of dukes and earls—Arundel, Surrey and Essex—as the Strand enters Aldwych (a name that derives from 'Old Wic' meaning old settlement).

The grand buildings in this area are symbols of the architectural legacy of the Empire. If you're after proof, notice how Canada House, the South African Embassy and the Australian High Commission each take pride of place in Trafalgar Square, the Strand and Aldwych respectively.

Turn right at Savoy Street to see the Queen's Chapel of the Savoy or continue along the Strand, past Somerset House (▷ 88).

❹ The magnificent Somerset House has awesome grounds for central London and is a much-favoured location for film companies setting scenes against the building's grandeur and seclusion.

Turn right into Surrey Street, past the Roman Baths, left into Temple Place and left again along Arundel Street. The two churches in the middle of

Above *Water fountains at Somerset House*

the road are St. Mary-le-Strand and St. Clement Danes. After these the road becomes Fleet Street.

5 Where the Strand ends and Fleet Street begins are a number of banks. These serviced those working at the Inns of Court, including Lloyds Bank and Child & Co Bankers. The latter has a display of guns in a cabinet that the partners of the bank acquired during the Gordon Riots of 1780 'for the defence of the building'. Here too is one of the first cheques ever written—made out in 1705.

After the banks of Lloyds and Child & Co turn right into Whitefriars Street. At the end turn left and left again into Dorset Rise. Take the next right into Dorset Buildings, past the Bridewell Theatre and along Bride Lane to St Bride's Church. Cross New Bridge Street. You are now in Ludgate Hill. Turn left into the street called Old Bailey and continue to the Central Criminal Court.

6 This court is known as 'The Old Bailey' and lies on the site of the notorious former Newgate Prison.

Cross Newgate Street and follow Giltspur Street until you reach St. Bartholomew's Hospital.

7 Walk under the archway to the hospital, with the only remaining sculpture of Henry VIII, to visit St. Bartholomew-the-Less, the parish church of the hospital where Stuart architect Inigo Jones was baptised.

Otherwise continue past the central square opposite Smithfield Market, and notice the marks on the stone wall left by a Zeppelin raid during World War I, to St Bartholomew-the-Great.

8 This is another great church, which dates from 1123 and is still surrounded by small streets as it was in the Middle Ages. Nearby is Smithfield, the scene of jousting, tournaments and fairs and the set of executions where criminals were

not just hanged but boiled, roasted or burned. During the Peasants' Revolt of 1381 the rebel leader Wat Tyler was stabbed by the Lord Mayor William Walworth and taken to St Bartholomew's Hospital, but he was dragged out and decapitated.

Turn left on West Smithfield, right on Long Lane and left into Hayne Street, then turn left again into Charterhouse Street. At St. John Street turn right and then bear left into St. John's Lane. A few paces on is St. John's Gate. Keep going and cross Clerkenwell Road to reach Grand Priory Church, bear left ahead to Jerusalem Passage, then turn left at the end, on to Aylesbury Street. Cross Clerkenwell Road and walk along Britton Street, turning right into Benjamin Street and left at the end to reach Farringdon tube where the walk ends.

WHERE TO EAT AND DRINK

The Black Friar in Queen Victoria Street is a special pub and has a bronze art nouveau/Edwardian interior. There are bar snacks, ales on tap and gallons of atmosphere. The cavernous, highly attractive Jerusalem Tavern in Britton Street was an old sstyle coffee house and now it serves an interesting selection of beers, including organic wheat beer.

PLACES TO VISIT
SOMERSET HOUSE

✉ The Strand, London WC2R 0RN
☎ 020 7845 4600
📖 Guidebook £4.95

WHEN TO GO

Go early in the morning to steer clear of the crowds at Westminster Abbey; avoid this walk on Mondays when some of the places are closed.

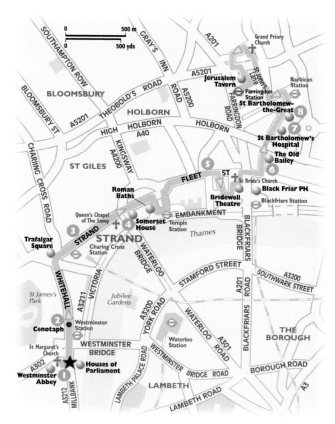

THE FLAMING CITY

A linear walk tracing the route of the Great Fire of 1666, an event that created a demand for new furniture.

LONDON • WALK

REGIONS

THE WALK

Distance: 2.25 miles (3.6km)
Allow: 2hrs
Start: Monument tube station
End: Farringdon tube station
AA Street by Street London

★ This walk, through some of the better-known parts, will sharpen your senses and alert you to some of the buildings and streets you may be familiar with, and others that you have yet to notice.

Take the Fish Street Hill exit from the tube station and bear right towards the Monument. Follow the cobbled street for 18m (20yds) to see the plaque that marks the spot on the corner of Pudding Lane where the ill-fated bakery once stood.

❶ Londoners in the 17th century must have wondered what had hit them when, within months of fighting off the Great Plague, a fire

of monumental proportions began at a bakery in Pudding Lane. It was 2 in the morning on 2 September 1666 when the baker discovered the fire. He escaped to safety along a roof, but his young assistant was not so lucky, nor were the 13,000 houses, 87 churches and 40 livery halls that perished in the flames. Incredibly, only eight people lost their lives, although how many later died after being left homeless is unknown. It took five days to contain the fire, partly because of the high number of houses with timber roofs and the rudimentary fire-fighting equipment available at the time.

Bear right, then cross Lower Thames Street at the pedestrian crossing to reach St. Magnus the Martyr Church. A few paces further to the right of the church, climb a set of steps and, ignoring the first exit, continue to arrive on the west side of London Bridge. Continue ahead, away from the river, along King

William Street and shortly turn left along Arthur Street and then sharp right into Martin Lane, past the Olde Wine Shades. At the end turn left into Cannon Street. (For a detour to see the red-brick houses that survived the fire, turn next left into Laurence Poultney Hill.)

Cross the road and turn right into Abchurch Lane. At the end bear left along King William Street towards Bank tube station. Keep to the left, past the front of Mansion House.

❷ Notice the street on the left, Walbrook: this is the site of one of Wren's finest churches, St. Stephen Walbrook Church.

Turn left into Queen Victoria Street. Continue ahead, then turn right into Bow Lane, past St. Mary Aldermary and a row of shops, to St. Mary-le-Bow at the end. Turn

Above *Even the walls of Ludgate Prison collapsed during the Great Fire of 1666*

96

left into Cheapside which, despite being the widest road in the City, also went up in flames. Cross this road, turn right into Wood Street. On your right was the site of one of London's debtors' prisons. Turn left into Goldsmith Street and, at the Saddlers Hall opposite, turn left and rejoin Cheapside. Turn right and cross the pedestrian crossing to St. Paul's Cathedral. Walk through the churchyard, bear left to reach Ludgate Hill and the City.

③ Within six years the City had been rebuilt, its boundaries extended and London was in the midst of an economic boom. By 1700 the population had increased five-fold to 500,000 inhabitants. Prosperity offered an opportunity to give the City a facelift but, due to the sheer cost and to property rights, most of the rebuilding followed the original street lines. It did, however, create

a safer, more sanitary capital than before, and with the new houses came a demand for new furniture, which was excellent news for cabinetmakers. To meet heavy demands furniture was, for the first time, offered across a range of quality and price.

Turn right and right again into Avenue Maria Lane, which becomes Warwick Lane. At the end turn left along Newgate Street. At the traffic lights turn right along Giltspur Street, then left into Cock Lane.

④ The statue on the building at the corner of Cock Lane of the 'Golden Boy' marks the spot where the fire is thought to have ended. On this site, until 1910, stood a pub called The Fortune of War, where body-snatchers would leave bodies on benches and wait to hear from the surgeons of the nearby hospital.

Where a road meets Cock Lane, turn right on Snow Hill, past an angular building, and right at Farringdon Street (which becomes Farringdon Road). At the second set of traffic lights turn right for Farringdon tube, where the walk ends.

WHERE TO EAT AND DRINK
The culinary highlight of this walk has to be the Place Below, a restaurant in the crypt of St Mary-le-Bow Church. It's very popular with discerning City workers for its mouth-watering vegetarian menu. If you arrive before midday, not only do you avoid the rush but the food is cheaper too.

PLACES TO VISIT
MUSEUM OF LONDON
✉ 150 London Wall, London EC2Y 5HH
☎ 0870 444 3852
🕐 Daily 10–6
✋ FREE

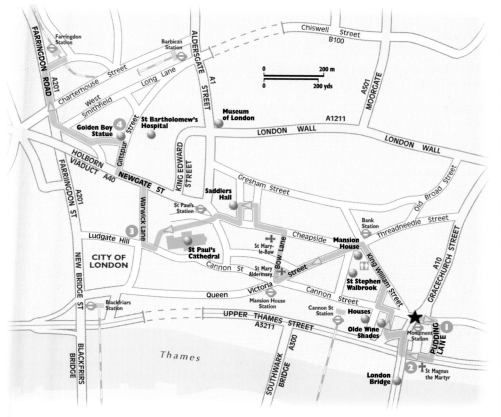

ROSES AND ROMANCE AROUND REGENT'S PARK

Rose gardens, an open-air theatre, panoramic views from Primrose Hill, birdsong along the Regent's Canal, and Little Venice.

THE WALK

Distance: 3.25 miles (5.3km)
Allow: 1hr 30min
Start: Baker Street tube station
End: Warwick Avenue tube station
AA Street by Street London

★ Along these canals you will see barges rather than gondolas, but on a fine, balmy day you can return to Regent's Park in the evening for a performance at the magical open-air theatre. You never know, this walk could well turn out to be a recurring midsummer night's dream. Arrive early to enjoy a leisurely picnic and drink champagne on the lawn, and afterwards take a stroll to Primrose Hill to see London's carpet of tiny flickering lights below.

Take the north exit from Baker Street tube and turn right, along Baker Street. Cross the road via two sets of pedestrian lights and enter Regent's Park. Turn right. Cross the bridge over the lake and then continue on left, passing the pretty bandstand.

❶ Take a wander through the circular Queen Mary's Gardens (no dogs) inside the Inner Circle of Regent's Park. You can reach them by taking the path ahead instead of turning left after the bandstand. Enclosed by hedges, the rose gardens are quiet, yet vibrant and include a fountain.

Turn left when you reach the Inner Circle road and the open-air theatre is on your right.

❷ Regent's Park's Open Air Theatre was founded in 1932 and is the premier professional outdoor theatre in Britain. Many well-known artists have appeared here during the summer season including Deborah Kerr, Vivian Leigh, Felicity Kendal, Jeremy Irons and Maria Aitken. With seating for well over 1,000, the theatre is larger than the Barbican and the Olivier Theatre.

Beyond The Holme turn left, through the metal gates, and over Long Bridge. When the paths fork ahead, take the right-hand one and continue straight ahead at the next crossing of paths.

Continue on through the gate, cross the Outer Circle road and then follow the path opposite to cross Primrose Hill Bridge. Turn left along a path leading down to the Regent's Canal, then take a sharp left. Continue along this path—which initially leads underneath the bridge and then past ZSL London Zoo's aviary—for approximately 400m (0.25 miles).

❸ ZSL London Zoo is the world's oldest scientific zoo and was established in 1828. You will also pass under four bridges (some with ornate ironwork) and see some colourful canal boats.

At the fourth bridge turn left up the path, signed 'London Zoo, Regent's Park' leading to St Mark's Church. At the gate turn left along Prince Albert Road and past an entrance to London Zoo. Continue for 91m (100yds) then, at the pedestrian lights, cross the road to enter Primrose Hill. Take the right-hand path and follow it uphill to the viewpoint.

❹ The views over London from Primrose Hill are exhilarating. In many ways this walk was John Nash's dream; in 1820 when he designed the area, it was the grandest planning scheme ever devised for central London and has not been matched since. Sprinkle on to this some grand terraces and the result is idyllic Regent's Park and its little sister, Primrose Hill.
 The banks of the canal are ivy-clad with weeping willows, and palatial homes line this stretch of the walk. Nash's scheme was based on a park peppered with large villas that looked like separate mansions but which actually consisted of more than 20 houses.

Follow the path that bears left, leading downhill, to join a straight path that leads to Prince Albert Road. Cross at the zebra crossing and turn right. In about 14m (15yds) turn left.
 Don't cross the bridge but turn right along a hedge-lined path that bends sharply to the left on to the tow path. Turn right and follow the towpath for 800m (0.5 miles). Continue ahead under the railway bridges—less enchanting, but rest assured that better things lie ahead—and, after a few paces,

you'll pass the houseboats moored at Lisson Green before a towpath tunnel. As the canal disappears under another tunnel, walk up the steps on the right and continue along Aberdeen Place. At the end cross a road and follow Blomfield Road into Little Venice.
 Cross Warwick Avenue and follow the road as it bends to the right, past the footbridge. Turn right into Warwick Place and left with Warwick Avenue tube 91m (100yds) ahead.

WHERE TO EAT AND DRINK
Try Amoul on nearby Formosa Street, with a Lebanese-inspired menu. Alternatively, try The Waterside Café in Little Venice.

PLACES TO VISIT
ZSL LONDON ZOO
✉ Regent's Park, London NW1 4R9
☎ 020 7722 3333
🕐 Daily 10–5.30
💳 Adult £15.40, Child £11.90, Family £49.10

WHEN TO GO
Try this walk on the weekend, when the route is quieter and you can enjoy a peaceful stroll by the water.

Below Regent's Park is the perfect place to get away from the busy city streets

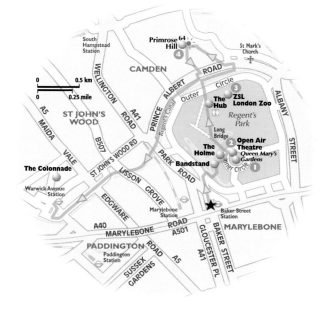

Above *The Lido Café beside the Serpentine in Regents Park*

SHOPPING

AGENT PROVOCATEUR

www.agentprovocateur.com

Seductive underwear sold in a boudoir-style shop by the son and daughter-in-law of Vivienne Westwood, famous for her punk designs in the 1970s.

✉ 16 Pont Street SW1X 9EN ☎ 020 7235 0229 ⏰ Mon–Sat 11–7 🚇 Knightsbridge, Sloane Square

ANDERSON & SHEPPARD

Considered to be the best tailor's shop around 'The Row', Anderson's was established in 1906. Expect to pay £2,000 for a classic English gentleman's suit at this traditional shop.

✉ 32 Old Burlington Street W1 ☎ 020 7734 1420 ⏰ Mon–Fri 8.30–5 🚇 Piccadilly Circus, Oxford Circus

BERWICK STREET

This is a gem of an old-fashioned fruit and vegetable market tucked away in busy Soho. As well as fresh veg there is a selection of cheeses, bread, herbs and spices on sale. Loud stallholders, media and fashion folk plus a few shady characters from the nearby red-light area set a unique scene.

⏰ Mon–Fri 8–6 🚇 Piccadilly Circus

BRICK LANE

Buzzing multi-ethnic East End street market, selling clothes and food, but specializing in Asian goods.

⏰ Sun 8–3 🚇 Liverpool Street, Aldgate East

CHOCOLATE

www.artisanduchocolat.com

Styling themselves as partners in life and in chocolate, Gerard Coleman and Anne Weyns began selling chocolate in Borough Market at the end of the 1990s. Their sought-after produce accompanied the last flight of Concord and is served at many of London's top restaurants. Here you can buy them by the bar, or try their signature Os.

✉ 89 Lower Sloane Street SW1W 8DA ☎ 020 7824 8365 ⏰ Mon–Sat 10–7, daily in Dec 🚇 Sloane Square

CHRISTIE'S

www.christies.com

James Christie conducted his first sale in 1766, and went on to hold the greatest auctions of his time. Christie's salerooms are now world famous, auctioning major artworks. Most auctions are free and public; some require a ticket, which should be reserved in advance.

✉ 85 Old Brompton Road SW7 3LD ☎ 020 7930 6074 ⏰ Variable 🚇 South Kensington

THE CONRAN SHOP

www.conran.com

Designer Terence Conran's glorious emporium is filled with super-stylish household items. This is a 'must see' shop for fans of modern interiors—stocking classics, such as Eames chairs—and prices are not as high as you might imagine.

✉ Michelin House, 81 Fulham Road SW3 6RD ☎ 020 7589 7401 ⏰ Mon, Tue, Fri 10–6, Wed, Thu 10–7, Sat 10–6.30, Sun 12–6 🚇 South Kensington

COVENT GARDEN

▷ 77.

FORTNUM AND MASON

www.fortnumandmason.co.uk

Founded in 1707 as a grocery shop, this famous store is wood-panelled and lit with chandeliers. The ground-floor food hall is fantastic.

✉ 181 Piccadilly W1A 1ER ☎ 020 7734 8040 ⏰ Mon–Sat 10–8, Sun 12–6 🚇 Green Park, Piccadilly Circus

GUINEVERE

www.guinevere.co.uk

The original antiques emporium on the King's Road, and probably the best. The eclectic selection of fine antiques ranges as much in price as in age and origin.

574–580 King's Road SW6 2DY ☎ 020 7736 2917 ◷ Mon–Fri 9.30–6, Sat 10–5.30 Ⓤ Fulham Broadway

HAMLEYS
www.hamleys.co.uk
The 'World's Finest Toyshop' and certainly one of the biggest. Five large floors full of toys. Staff demonstrate the latest gadgets. Great fun for all ages.

✉ 188–196 Regent Street W1B 5BT ☎ 0800 2802 444 ◷ Mon–Fri 10–8, Sat 9–8, Sun 12–6 Ⓤ Oxford Circus

HARRODS
www.harrods.com
Harrods' vast, terracotta building belies its origins as a small grocer's shop in 1849. There are 330-plus departments. The ground-floor food halls are a highlight.

✉ 87–135 Brompton Road SW1 7XL ☎ 020 7730 1234 ◷ Mon–Sat 10–8, Sun 12–6 Ⓤ Knightsbridge

HARVEY NICHOLS
www.harveynichols.com
Shopoholics and fashionistas make a beeline for Harvey Nichols. This chic department store has marvellous window displays and an ultra-trendy beauty bar. There are six floors of clothing and housewares, and a food market on the fifth floor, as well as a stylish café, restaurant and popular sushi bar.

✉ 109–125 Knightsbridge SW1X 7RJ ☎ 020 7235 5000 (recorded information) ◷ Mon–Fri 10–8, Sat 10–8, Sun 12–6 Ⓤ Knightsbridge

LIBERTY
www.liberty.co.uk
The mock-Tudor building was actually built in the 1920s. The interior contains a varied stock ranging from ornaments and rugs that seem to have been gathered on an explorer's travels to up-to-the-minute fashion designer apparel.

✉ 210–220 Regent Street W1B 5AH ☎ 020 7734 1234 ◷ Mon–Thu 10–9, Sat 10–8, Sun 12–6 Ⓤ Oxford Circus

LILLYWHITE'S
A large department store dedicated entirely to sport, Lillywhite's can kit you out for most mainstream sporting activities.

✉ 24–36 Lower Regent Street SW1Y 4QF ☎ 0870 333 9600 ◷ Mon–Sat 10–9, Sun 12–6 Ⓤ Piccadilly Circus

MULBERRY
www.mulberry.com
Ready-to-wear fashions for men and women, plus accessories, bags, luggage and smaller items, all in top-quality leather.

✉ 41–42 New Bond Street W1S 2RY ☎ 020 7491 3900 ◷ Mon–Sat 10–6, Thu 10–7 Ⓤ Bond Street

NEAL'S YARD REMEDIES
www.nealsyardremedies.com
They may have branches all over the capital and wider afield now, but this is where the wholesome skincare and therapy business began in 1981. A great range of soaps, scrubs and benign smelly things to go in the bath or shower.creams, scented candles and perfumery, now owned by Estée Lauder.

✉ 15 Neal's Yard WC2H 9DP ☎ 020 7379 7222 ◷ Mon 10–7, Tue–Fri 10.30–7, Sat 9.30–7, Sun 11.30–6 Ⓤ Covent Garden

PETTICOAT LANE
London's most famous market was originally named after the garments sold by French immigrants in the 1700s. It now has a Cockney feel and sells cheap clothing. Around 1,000 stalls; busiest on Sunday.

✉ Middlesex Street and Wentworth Street ◷ Mon–Fri 8–3, Sun 9–3 Ⓤ Liverpool Street, Aldgate

PORTOBELLO ROAD
One of London's famous established markets, Portobello Road market has hundreds of stalls selling antiques, vintage clothing, and objets d'art. Not cheap and there is a lot of junk, but fun to catch the 'Notting Hill' vibe. Runs from Pembridge Road (Notting Hill Gate Underground) north up to Westbourne Park Road (Ladbroke Grove Undergound).

◷ Mon–Wed 8–6.30, Thu 8–1, Fri–Sat 7–6.30 Ⓤ Notting Hill Gate, Ladbroke Grove

SELFRIDGES
www.selfridges.com
A Victorian facade hides this popular store, now a modern emporium filled with designer clothes, accessories and a huge beauty hall. There is also an eclectically stocked food hall and 18 places to eat and drink.

✉ 400 Oxford Street W1A 1AB ☎ 0800 123400 ◷ Mon–Sat 9.30–8 (to 9pm Thu), Sun 12–6 Ⓤ Marble Arch, Bond Street

W & G FOYLE LTD
www.foyles.co.uk
Not the eccentrically shambolic place its reputation was founded on, but this one-time largest bookshop in the world is still a must for booklovers. Proximity to thriving Soho ensures the film and music departments are outstanding and there are often literary events to tie in with book launches.

✉ 113–119 Charing Cross Road WC2H 0EB ☎ 020 7437 5660 ◷ Mon–Sat 9.30–9, Sun 12–6, public holidays 11–8 Ⓤ Tottenham Court Road 🍴

YOUNG ENGLAND
www.youngengland.com
Traditional children's clothing including pinafore dresses, kilts, romper suits, baby bootees and velvet-trimmed woollen coats are on offer here. This is the place to come for a high-quality, classic look. Elizabeth Street is a Pimlico jewel—while you're here look for other outstanding shops such as Philip Treacy hats, Chatsworth Farm Shop and Jeroboam for delicious food.

✉ 47 Elizabeth Street SW1W 9PP ☎ 020 7259 9003 ◷ Mon–Fri 10–5.30, Sat 10–3 Ⓤ Sloane Square, Victoria

ZAVVI
www.zavvi.co.uk
This megastore sells everything from chart hits to specialist stock, as well as computer games.

✉ 1 Piccadilly Circus W1J 0TR ☎ 020 7439 2500 ◷ Mon–Sat 9am–11pm, Sun 12–6 Ⓤ Piccadilly Circus

ENTERTAINMENT AND NIGHTLIFE

333
www.333mother.com
Excellent club with a music policy that embraces breaks and beats, soul, funk, reggae, drum 'n' bass and hip-hop. Eclectic Sundays include house and disco.
✉ 333 Old Street EC1V 9LE ☎ 020 7739 5949 🕐 Bar: daily 8pm–3am. Club: Fri–Sat 10pm–5am 🖐 £5–£10 🚇 Old Street

ALDWYCH THEATRE
www.aldwychtheatre.com
Completed in 1905, during a build-ing boom after the demolition of London's old 'theatreland'. Stages drama, dance and musicals.
✉ Aldwych WC2B 4DF ☎ 08704 000805 🖐 £15–£39.50 🚇 Covent Garden

ALMEIDA THEATRE
www.almeida.co.uk
Housed in a building dating from 1837. Renowned for premiering exciting new plays.
✉ Almeida Street, Islington N1 1TA ☎ 020 7359 4404 🖐 £6–£30 🚇 Angel

BAR RUMBA
www.barrumba.co.uk
Established basement club with great dancing and regular theme nights including eclectic dance and salsa every Tuesday. Music also includes drum and bass, house and hip-hop.
✉ 36 Shaftesbury Avenue WC1D 7ER ☎ 020 7287 6933 🕐 Mon, Thu–Fri 8pm–3am, Tue 6pm–3am, Sat 9pm–3am, Sun 8pm–1.30am 🖐 £3–£12; free before 9pm 🚇 Piccadilly Circus

BUSH HALL
www.bushhallmusic.co.uk
Formerly a ballroom, Bush Hall reopened in 2000 as a small concert hall staging classical concerts, recit-als, jazz and rock concerts.
✉ 310 Uxbridge Road, Shepherd's Bush W12 7LJ ☎ 020 8222 6955 🖐 £6–£35 🚇 Shepherd's Bush

CARLING ACADEMY BRIXTON
www.brixton-academy.co.uk
Large auditorium where you can catch touring rock/pop acts.
✉ 211 Stockwell Road, Brixton SW9 9SL ☎ 08707 712000, box office 020 7771 3000 🖐 Varies 🚇 Brixton

CARLING APOLLO HAMMERSMITH
www.hammersmithapollo.net
Large mainstream rock and pop venue on a busy roundabout in the heart of Hammersmith, near to a selection of pubs and restaurants. Good sound and sightlines.
✉ Queen Caroline Street W6 9QH ☎ 08706 063400 🖐 £10–£75 🚇 Hammersmith

CHUCKLE CLUB
www.chuckleclub.com
Students' union bar offering cheap drinks and an established comedy club which pulls in some of the best comics in the business.
✉ Three Tuns Bar, London School of Economics, Houghton Street WC2A 2AE ☎ 020 7476 1672 🕐 Sat 7.45pm–11pm 🖐 £8–£10 🚇 Holborn

COMEDY STORE
www.thecomedystore.co.uk
The best in stand-up comedy with improvisation ('improv') from the Comedy Store Players and big British TV and radio names.
✉ 1a Oxendon Street SW1Y 4EE ☎ 08700 602340 🕐 Tue–Thu, Sun 8pm–10.15pm, Fri–Sat 8pm–10.15pm, midnight–2.15am; over 18s only 🖐 £12–£15 🚇 Piccadilly Circus, Leicester Square

CURZON MAYFAIR
www.curzoncinemas.com
This well-known art-house cinema first opened in 1934.
✉ 38 Curzon Street, Mayfair W1Y 7TY ☎ 020 7495 0500 🚇 Green Park

DUKE OF YORK'S THEATRE
www.theambassadors.com/dukeofyorks
Hosts acclaimed drama tested else-where, perhaps the Young Vic, on the Edinburgh Fringe or at the Royal Court Theatre.
✉ St. Martin's Lane WC2N 4BG ☎ 08700 606623 🖐 £10–£45 🚇 Leicester Square

Below The club scene is vibrant in Britain's capital

EAST VILLAGE

www.eastvillageclub.com

Styling itself as a small club with big ideas, East Village is a bar/club between trendy Hoxton and the City. An ambitious roster of DJs includes some big names, so keep an eye on the listings.
✉ 89 Great Eastern Street EC2A 3HX
☎ 020 7739 5173 🕐 Thu–Sun 9pm–4am
🚇 Old Street

ELECTRIC CINEMA

www.the-electric.co.uk

Originally opened in 1910, the Electric later turned to repertory cinema—classics and independent films—and now has a brasserie.
✉ 191 Portobello Road W11 2ED ☎ 020 7908 9696 🚇 Ladbroke Grove, Notting Hill Gate

FABRIC

www.fabric-london.com

Fabulously cool Fabric is one of London's superclubs and a cutting-edge venue, playing eclectic dance music for an easy-going, mixed crowd. Next to Spitalfields market in Farringdon.
✉ 77A Charterhouse Street EC1M 3HN
☎ 020 7336 8898 🕐 Fri 10pm–6am, Sat 10pm–8am, some Sun from 10pm
✋ £5–£16 🚇 Farringdon

HEAVEN

www.heaven-london.com

London's most famous gay and mixed club. Popcorn on Monday, playing commercial and funky house; Work! on Wednesdays lets you show off your dance moves. Saturdays are Heaven nights with house, pop, r'n'b and cabaret.
✉ The Arches, Villiers Street WC2N 6NG
☎ 020 7930 2020 🕐 Mon, Wed, Sat (some Thu and Fri) 10pm–6am ✋ £5–£12
🚇 Embankment, Charing Cross

HOME BAR

A large basement where you can chill out on tatty furniture, sip drinks without interruption and enjoy laid-back grooves and upbeat tunes (retro, hip-hop). The crowd is relaxed and the ambience friendly.
✉ 100–106 Leonard Street EC2A 4RH

☎ 020 7684 8618 🕐 Mon–Thu 5pm–1am, Fri 5pm–2.30am, Sat 5pm–6am ✋ Mon–Fri free, Sat £5 🚇 Old Street

IMAX CINEMA

www.bfi.org.uk/imax

A 485-seat cinema housed in a space-age structure, with the biggest film screen in Britain. Visually overwhelming but limited number of films.
✉ 1 Charlie Chaplin Walk, South Bank SE1 8XR ☎ 08707 872525 🚇 Embankment, Waterloo

JAZZ CAFÉ

www.meanfiddler.com

Live jazz, soul, world music, hip-hop, R&B—it's all here.
✉ 5 Parkway, Camden Town NW1 7PG ☎ 0870 060 3777 ✋ £10–£20
🚇 Camden Town

JONGLEURS COMEDY CLUB, BATTERSEA

www.jongleurs.com

Part of a countrywide chain of comedy clubs with consistently high-quality stand-up performers. This was the first, opened in 1983. Originally a 1920s ballroom, it now has bar, grill and late-night venue.
✉ Bar Risa, 49 Lavender Gardens SW11 1DJ ☎ 0870 787 0707 🕐 Thu–Sat from 8.30pm ✋ £9–£15 🚂 Clapham Junction

LONDON COLISEUM

www.eno.org

Home to English National Opera (who always sing in English) with regular visits from Welsh National Opera, Opera North and the Royal Festival Ballet. ENO is known for some innovative productions.
✉ St. Martin's Lane WC2N 4ES ☎ 020 7632 8300 ✋ £10–£83 🚇 Charing Cross, Leicester Square

LONDON PALLADIUM

www.rutheatres.co.uk

A 2,300-seat theatre built in 1910.
✉ Argyll Street W1V 1AD ☎ 0870 890 1108 ✋ £25–£55 🚇 Oxford Circus

LYCEUM THEATRE

The Lyceum Theatre is built on a site that was once occupied by David

Garrick's 1771 excellent concert and exhibition hall.
✉ Wellington Street WC2E 7DA ☎ 0870 243 9000 ✋ £22.50–£75 🚇 Charing Cross

LYRIC THEATRE

www.nimaxtheatres.com

A friendly theatre, the oldest on Shaftesbury Avenue.
✉ Shaftesbury Avenue W1V 7HA ☎ 0870 890 1107 ✋ £20–£55 🚇 Piccadilly Circus

MARKET PLACE

www.marketplace-london.com

Market Place is a classic London DJ bar with panelled walls and very good food. Downstairs is larger, with room to dance and alcove tables.
✉ 11 Market Place W1W 8AH ☎ 020 7079 2020 🕐 Mon–Fri 11am–1am, Sst noon–1am, Sun 1pm–11pm ✋ Free–£7
🚇 Oxford Circus

MINISTRY OF SOUND

www.ministryofsound.com

Perhaps London's most famous club, the Ministry is a huge place where you can experience world-class DJs. Never mind the unfriendly bouncers, long queues and high admission prices and party past dawn.
✉ 103 Gaunt Street SE1 6DP ☎ 0870 060 2666 🕐 Fri 10.30pm–5.30am, Sat 11pm–7am ✋ £15–£20 🚇 Elephant and Castle

NATIONAL THEATRE

www.nationaltheatre.org.uk

The National Theatre Company's base. Three auditoriums: the Cottesloe, with no fixed seats or staging; the Lyttelton; and the Olivier, named after Sir Laurence Olivier, the NT's first director.
✉ South Bank SE1 9PX ☎ 020 7452 3000
✋ £12.50–£47.50 🚇 Waterloo

NOTTING HILL ARTS CLUB

www.nottinghillartsclub.com

Set in a basement, with projector images on the whitewashed walls and fabrics. Reasonably priced drinks include great cocktails and Champagne. Frequent live bands.
✉ 21 Notting Hill Gate W11 3JQ ☎ 020 7460 4459 🕐 Mon–Wed 6pm–1am, Thu–Fri 6pm–2am, Sat 4pm–2am, Sun

4pm–1am. Last entry 1 hour before closing
✉ £5–£8 Ⓜ Notting Hill Gate

ODEON LEICESTER SQUARE
www.odeon.co.uk
Famous West End showpiece in the heart of London's 'movieland' used for many film premieres.
✉ 22–24 Leicester Square WC2H 7LQ
☎ 0871 2244007 Ⓜ Leicester Square, Piccadilly Circus

OLD VIC
www.oldvictheatre.com
Historic building (1818) where Britain's National Theatre began before transferring to the South Bank in the 1970s. Most theatre greats of the 20th century have appeared here.
✉ The Cut, Waterloo Road SE1 8NB
☎ 0870 060 6628 ✋ £7.50–£47.50
Ⓜ Waterloo, Southwark

PIZZA EXPRESS JAZZ CLUB
www.pizzaexpresslive.com
All kinds of modern and contemporary jazz performed in the basement area under the main Pizza Express restaurant in Soho (reserve ahead).
✉ 10 Dean Street W1D 3RW ☎ Jazz Club 020 7439 8722, restaurant 020 7437 9595
✋ £17.50–£22 Ⓜ Tottenham Court Road

PRINCE CHARLES
www.princecharlescinema.com
Central independent cinema offering seats at lower than usual West End prices. Foreign-language films shown with English subtitles.
✉ 7 Leicester Place WC2H 7BP
☎ Information: 0901 272 7007 (25p per min); reservations: 0870 811 2559
Ⓜ Leicester Square, Piccadilly Circus

RONNIE SCOTT'S
www.ronniescotts.co.uk
Britain's top jazz venue and one of the world's most famous jazz clubs, where the best players perform.
✉ 47 Frith Street W1D 4HT ☎ 020 7439 0747 ✋ £20–£36; more for special gigs
Ⓜ Tottenham Court Road

ROYAL ACADEMY OF MUSIC
www.ram.ac.uk
Free lunchtime recitals at one of London's four music colleges.

Reasonably priced evening chamber and orchestral performances.
✉ Marylebone Road NW1 5HT ☎ 020 7873 7373 ✋ £4–£20 Ⓜ Regent's Park

ROYAL ALBERT HALL
www.royalalberthall.com
Renowned venue for major concerts and the Proms; cheap tickets are sold on a first-come, first-served basis.
✉ Kensington Gore SW7 2AP ☎ 020 7589 3203 (info), 020 7589 8212 (reservations)
Ⓜ South Kensington

ROYAL OPERA HOUSE
www.royaloperahouse.org
Principal venue for world-class classical music, opera and ballet. Home to the Royal Ballet.
✉ Bow Street WC2E 9DD ☎ 020 7304 4000 ✋ Varies Ⓜ Covent Garden

SADLER'S WELLS THEATRE
www.sadlerswells.com
Europe's finest dance venue, offering classical ballet, modern dance and opera.
✉ Rosebery Avenue EC1R 4TN ☎ 020 7863 8000 ✋ £10–£38 Ⓜ Angel

THE SCALA
www.scala-london.co.uk
Former cinema turned clubbing venue with three floors and several bars. The Scala hosts house and breakbeat nights.
✉ 275 Pentonville Road N1 9NL ☎ 020 7833 2022 🕐 Fri–Sat 10pm–6am
✋ £8–£15 Ⓜ King's Cross

SHEPHERD'S BUSH EMPIRE
www.shepherds-bush-empire.co.uk
Friendly mid-sized venue with good acoustics, a balcony and bar.
✉ Shepherd's Bush Green W12 8TT ☎ 08707 712000 ✋ £10–£30
Ⓜ Shepherd's Bush

SOUTH BANK CENTRE
www.southbankcentre.org.uk
Arts complex comprising the Royal Festival Hall for large-scale classical music performances, the mid-sized Queen Elizabeth Hall for small orchestral concerts and the Purcell Room for chamber music, accompa-

nied singers and solo musicians.
✉ South Bank Centre SE1 8XX ☎ 0871 663 2501 ✋ Varies Ⓜ Embankment, Waterloo

THEATRE ROYAL HAYMARKET
www.trh.co.uk
As famed for its beautiful 18th-century pillared façade and the mirrors and gilding in the Grand Saloon bar as for its productions.
✉ Haymarket SW1Y 4HT ☎ 0870 901 3356 ✋ £12.50–£60 Ⓜ Piccadilly Circus

TURNMILLS
www.turnmills.co.uk
Highly regarded club playing house music in a maze-like layout. Friday and Saturday are theme nights and there's a gay evening once a month on a Saturday.
✉ 63b Clerkenwell Road EC1M 5PT
☎ 020 7250 3409 🕐 Fri 10.30pm–7.30am, Sat 10pm–late ✋ £10–£15 Ⓜ Farringdon

WIGMORE HALL
www.wigmore-hall.org.uk
London's favourite intimate concert and recital venue, with acoustics of legendary perfection. The architectural elegance, all marble and plaster with cupola, matches the peerless quality of the great classic performances.
✉ 36 Wigmore Street W1U 2BP ☎ 020 7935 2141 ✋ Varies Ⓜ Bond Street

ZOO BAR
www.zoobar.co.uk
Central London bar popular with Londoners after work and buzzing with a party atmosphere. Features a comprehensive cocktail list with a happy hour until 7.30pm.
✉ 13–17 Bear Street WC2H 7AS ☎ 020 7839 4188 🕐 Daily 4pm–3am (Sun closes 2am) ✋ £5–£10 Ⓜ Leicester Square

SPORTS AND ACTIVITIES
ALL ENGLAND LAWN TENNIS AND CROQUET CLUB
www.wimbledon.com
Private club founded in 1868. Centre and No. 1 courts used only for the Championships; others used all year by club members and also by LTA-sponsored players.

✉ PO Box 98, Church Road, Wimbledon SW19 5AE ☎ 020 8944 1066 Ⓔ Southfields 🚉 Wimbledon

ARSENAL

www.arsenal.com

Famous north London club, usually near the top of the Premiership. Moved from their historic Highbury home to a new 60,000-seater stadium in 2007.

✉ Emirates Stadium, Highbury House, 75 Drayton park N5 1BU ☎ 020 7704 4000 Ⓔ Arsenal

CENTRAL LONDON GOLF CENTRE

www.clgc.co.uk

Golf tends to be rather exclusive in the capital, but this small course and driving range is one of the few where you can turn up and play, and probably the closest to central London. Come for the convenience rather than the quality of the 9-hole course. Equipment hire available.

✉ Burntwood Lane, Wandsworth W17 0AT ☎ 020 8871 2468 🕐 Course daily daylight hours, Driving range: Mon–Fri 8am–10pm, Fri 8–8, Sat–Sun 7–6 💰 £11–£27. Driving range £4–£6 Ⓔ Earlsfield

CHELSEA

www.chelseafc.co.uk

A wealthy team, owned by a Russian billionaire, that has played since 1905, Chelsea established themselves in the 'big four' winning the Premier League twice in the mid-noughties.

✉ Stamford Bridge, Fulham Road, Chelsea SW6 1HS ☎ 08719 841905 Ⓔ Fulham Broadway

HYDE PARK

www.royalparks.gov.uk

The Serpentine, an 11ha (27-acre) lake, has facilities for rowing, canoeing and paddle boats.

✉ Bluebird Boats, The Boathouse, Serpentine Road, Hyde Park W2 2UH ☎ 0207 262 1330 Ⓔ Hyde Park Corner, Marble Arch, Knightsbridge

A free two-hour Friday Night Skate (www.thefns.com) starts at 8pm from the Duke of Wellington Arch, in Hyde Park. You must be good at braking and turning at speed and fast enough to keep up with the marshals. Skaters are advised to wear body armour, a helmet and reflective clothing. The Rollerstroll (www.rollerstroll.com) is a less taxing skate in the summer. Meet at 2pm on Serpentine Road, Hyde Park.

✉ Slick Willies, 12 Gloucester Road (☎ 020 7225 0004) rent out skates. 💰 Rental £10 a day Ⓔ High Street Kensington

LONDON WETLAND CENTRE

www.wwt.org.uk

Excellent hides and over 130 species of birds annually on a 43ha (106-acre) site. Special events include walks, talks, craft demonstrations and workshops.

✉ Queen Elizabeth's Walk, Barnes SW13 9WT ☎ 020 8409 4400 🕐 Late Mar–late Oct daily 9.30–6; rest of year daily 9.30–5 💰 Adult £8.13, child (4–16) £4.50, family £27.73 Ⓔ Hammersmith 🚉 Barnes

LORD'S

www.lords.org.uk

Historic home of cricket, hosting internationals, one-day games, cup finals and semi-finals.

✉ St. John's Wood Road NW8 8QN ☎ MCC info: 020 7289 1611; tickets: 020 7432 1000 Ⓔ St. John's Wood

QUEEN'S CLUB

www.queensclub.co.uk

International tennis stars warm up for Wimbledon in the Stella Artois tournament, held here in June.

✉ Palliser Road, West Kensington W14 9EQ ☎ 020 7385 3421 Ⓔ Barons Court

REGENT'S PARK LAKE

www.royalparks.gov.uk

Boating facilities on the park's lake, which also has islands, a heronry and waterfowl.

✉ Boathouse Café, Hanover Gate, Outer Circle NW1 4RL ☎ 020 7486 7905 Ⓔ Baker Street, Marylebone, Regent's Park, Great Portland Street, Camden Town

Above *Centre Court at the All England Lawn Tennis and Croquet Club, Wimbledon*

SERPENTINE LIDO
www.serpentinelido.com
Hyde Park's Lido has been in existence for more than 100 years. You can swim in the Serpentine or sunbathe in a deckchair. Also a small pool for children.
✉ Hyde Park W1J 7NT ☎ 020 7706 3422 🕐 Early Jun to mid-Sep daily 10–6 👆 Adult £3.50, child (3–15) 80p, family £8 Ⓜ Hyde Park Corner

TOTTENHAM HOTSPUR
www.tottenhmhotspurs.co.uk
Universally known as Spurs, Tottenham have played at their White Hart Lane stadium since renting it from brewers in 1899.
✉ White Hart Lane, Bill Nicholson Way, High Road, Tottenham N17 0AP ☎ 0870 420 5000 🚃 White Hart Lane

TWICKENHAM STADIUM
www.rfu.com
Rugby union's major venue also has a Museum of Rugby, and there are tours of the stadium.
✉ Rugby House, 21 Rugby Road, Twickenham TW1 1DZ ☎ 020 8892 2000; tours: 020 8892 8877 🕐 Museum: Tue–Sat 10–5, Sun 11–5. Closed post-match Sun. Matchdays: no tours and museum open for match ticket holders only 👆 Tours/museum: adult £10, child £7 🚃 Twickenham

HEALTH AND BEAUTY
GEO. F. TRUMPER
www.trumpers.com
One of London's first barber shops, Geo. F. Trumper opened in 1875 and still offers wet shaves and haircuts as well as colognes.
✉ 20 Jermyn Street SW1Y 6HP ☎ 020 7734 1370 🕐 Mon–Fri 9–5.30, Sat 9–5; reservation essential 👆 Wet shave £30 Ⓜ Green Park, Piccadilly Circus

PORCHESTER SPA
Good-value spa in west London. Three Turkish hot rooms, two Russian steam rooms, a cold plunge pool, a whirlpool bath and an art deco swimming pool, all for less than £20.
✉ Porchester Centre, Queensway W2 5HS ☎ 020 7792 3980 🕐 Daily 10–10. Women

only: Tue, Thu–Fri, Sun (10–4). Men only: Mon, Wed, Sat. Mixed couples: Sun 4–10 👆 Adult £19.45. Mixed couples ticket: £27.50 Ⓜ Bayswater

TRIYOGA
www.triyoga.co.uk
Europe's top spot for yoga, packed with celebrity clients. Also offers treatments such as massage, shiatsu and acupuncture.
✉ 6 Erskine Road NW3 3AJ ☎ 020 7483 3344 🕐 Mon–Fri 6am–9.30pm, Sat 8–7.30, Sun 9–9 👆 Classes from £11 Ⓜ Chalk Farm

FOR CHILDREN
MADAME TUSSAUD'S
▷ 81.

NAMCO STATION
Three levels of entertainment with bowling, video games and rides.
✉ County Hall, Riverside Building, South Bank SE1 7PB ☎ 020 7967 1066 🕐 Daily 10am–midnight 👆 Free Ⓜ Waterloo, Westminster

NATURAL HISTORY MUSEUM
▷ 82–83.

SCIENCE MUSEUM
▷ 85.

V & A MUSEUM OF CHILDHOOD
www.vam.ac.uk/moc
A museum specific to children and toys. Children can play with some of the 6,000 exhibits in this collection.
✉ Cambridge Heath Road E2 9PA ☎ 020 8980 2415 🕐 Daily 10–5.45 👆 Free Ⓜ Bethnal Green

ZSL LONDON ZOO
www.zsl.org/zsl-london-zoo/
London Zoo opened in 1828 and is now an internationally important conservation centre. Check the events schedule for feeding times, when the modernist Penguin Pool becomes crowded.
✉ Regent's Park NW1 4RY ☎ 020 7722 3333 🕐 Early Mar–late Oct daily 10–5.30; rest of year daily 10–6.30 👆 Adult £13, child (3–15) £10, family £41 Ⓜ Camden Town

Above *A meerkat in ZSL London Zoo*

DAILY CEREMONIES

CEREMONY OF THE KEYS
www.hrp.org.uk
Every evening at 9.50pm the ceremony of locking up the Tower of London begins. Assemble at the West Gate at 9.15pm. Apply in writing for free tickets to The Ceremony of the Keys Office, HM Tower of London, London EC3N 4AB (▷ 90) at least 6 weeks in advance.
✉ Tower of London EC3N 4AB ☎ 0870 756 7070 ⊕ Nightly ✋ Free ⊜ Tower Hill

CHANGING THE GUARD
www.royal.gov.uk
Footguards in full dress uniform of red tunics and bearskin hats change shifts in the Guard Mounting ceremony.
✉ Buckingham Palace SW1A 1AA, Horse Guards SW1A 2AX ☎ 020 7930 4832 ⊕ Buckingham Palace: Early April– end July daily 11.30; rest of year alternate days. Horse Guards Arch: Monday–Saturday 11am, Sunday 10am ⊜ Buckingham Palace: St. James's Park; Horse Guards: Charing Cross

APRIL

FLORA LONDON MARATHON
www.london-marathon.co.uk
Some 46,500 runners start the world's biggest road race. Apply from August to late October for the following April.
✉ From Greenwich SE10 to The Mall SW1 ☎ 020 7902 0200 ⊕ Third Sunday in April ✋ Free ⊜ Start: North Greenwich. Finish: Green Park, St. James's Park

MAY

CHELSEA FLOWER SHOW
www.rhs.org.uk
Premier flower show held in the grounds of Chelsea Royal Hospital, usually attended by the Queen.
✉ Royal Hospital, Royal Hospital Road SW3 4SL ☎ 020 7649 1885 ⊕ Late May ⊜ Sloane Square

JUNE

TROOPING THE COLOUR
On the Queen's official birthday the 'colour' (flag) of one of the Household Cavalry's seven regiments is 'trooped' in her presence at this ceremony.
✉ Horse Guards Parade, Whitehall SW1A 2ax ☎ 020 7414 2479 ⊕ Third Saturday of June ✋ Free ⊜ Westminster, Charing Cross

WIMBLEDON LAWN TENNIS CHAMPIONSHIPS
www.wimbledon.com
International tennis championships held over two weeks.
✉ The All England Lawn Tennis and Croquet Club, Church Road, Wimbledon SW19 5AE ☎ 020 8944 1066 ⊕ Last week June, first week July ✋ £5–£91 ⊜ Southfields ⊜ Wimbledon

AUGUST

NOTTING HILL CARNIVAL
www.nottinghillcarnival.biz
Join a million people at one of Europe's biggest street parties. Fabulous costumes, steel drums and sound systems.
✉ Notting Hill W10/W11 ☎ 020 7727 0072 ⊕ Sunday, Monday; August Bank Holiday weekend ✋ Free ⊜ Ladbroke Grove

OCTOBER/NOVEMBER

STATE OPENING OF PARLIAMENT
www.parliament.uk
See the Queen arrive in a State coach attended by the Household Cavalry to reopen Parliament following its summer recess.
✉ House of Lords, Parliament Square SW1A 0PW ☎ 020 7219 4272 ⊕ Date varies, phone to confirm ⊜ Westminster

Right *A Yeoman at the Tower of London*

EATING

PRICES AND SYMBOLS

The prices are for a two-course lunch (L) and a three-course à la carte dinner (D). Prices in pubs are for a two-course lunchtime bar meal and a two-course dinner in the restaurant, unless specified otherwise. The price for wine is for the least expensive bottle sold.

For a key to the symbols, ▷ 2.

ABANNACH

www.albannach.co.uk
Scottish fine dining in central London comes with a generous helping of Scottish art nouveau style, à la Charles Rennie Mackintosh. Choco-late tones, leather chairs and clean lines set the scene for classic dishes based on seasonal Scottish ingredi-ents. You could start the meal with a trio of cured fish, or lightly smoked wood pigeon with Scottish cherry wine sauce, then move on to a loin of Highland venison with thyme potato cake and parsnip purée, or perhaps the rib eye of Buccleuch

beef with cavalo nero and wild mushrooms. Yes, there is haggis, neeps and tatties on the menu too, with the option of vegetarian haggis. Desserts include a traditional Cranachan with shortbread and a Border tart with whisky cream, and there is, of course, a comprehensive range of whiskies. The Theatre Menu and Buffet Menu offer good value.
✉ 66 Trafalgar Square, London WC2N 5DS
☎ 020 7930 0066 🕐 Mon–Sat noon–1am
✋ L £30, D £45, Wine £16.50 🚇 Charing Cross

ALASTAIR LITTLE RESTAURANT

The fixed-price menu runs on Mediterranean lines with a nod to Italy. Superb breads precede a starter of, say, pappardelle with game sauce or potato pancake with smoked eel. Follow up with bacon braised in red wine. Finally don't miss roasted black figs with honey and mascarpone.
✉ 49 Frith Street W1V 5TE ☎ 020 7734 5183 🕐 12–3, 5.30–11.30; closed Sun, L

Above *Lively Covent Garden has a great atmosphere*

Sat, Christmas, public holidays ✋ L £38, D £40, Wine £20 🚇 Tottenham Court Road

AL DUCA

www.alduca-restaurant.co.uk
Reasonably priced but classy restau-rant. First-rate fish (char-grilled tuna with barlotti beans) and pasta dishes (such as ricotta and spinach ravioli). The 130 or so Italian wines are evenly spread in terms of price.
✉ 4–5 Duke of York Street SW1Y 6LA
☎ 020 7839 3090 🕐 12–2.30, 6–11; closed Sun, Christmas, New Year, public holidays ✋ L £22.50, D £27.50, Wine £16
🚇 Piccadilly

ASSAGGI

A relaxed Italian restaurant with bare floorboards, wooden tables and plenty of yellow and terracotta. The cooking is traditional Italian, with an emphasis on fine flavours and quality ingredients. Starters may include *fregola con arselle* (fregula pasta with clams) or *calamari ripieni* (stuffed squid). Main courses include pasta and dishes such as *quaglia ripiena* (stuffed roasted quail) or *filetto di vitello al rosmarino* (pan-roasted fillet of white veal, rosemary and glazed baby onions).

✉ 39 Chepstow Place W2 4TS ☎ 020 7792 5501 🕐 12.30–2.30, 7.30–11; closed Sun, two weeks at Christmas, public holidays 🖐 L £28, D £35, Wine £21.95 💳 🚇 Notting Hill Gate, Bayswater

BARRAFINA
www.barrafina.co.uk

This is a stylish tapas bar in the heart of the West End, offering an excellent range of expertly prepared sharing plates, including authentic Spanish cold meats, tortillas, seafood and hot meat dishes such as grilled quail with al-i-oli and grilled chicken with Romesco sauce.

✉ 54 Frith Street, London W1D 4SL ☎ 020 7813 8016 🕐 Mon–Sat noon–3, 5–11, Sun 12.30–3.30, 5.30–10.30 🖐 L £25, D £40, Wine £15.50 🚇 Tottenham Court Road

BLUEPRINT CAFÉ
www.danddlondon.com

A bustling, stylish restaurant on the first floor of the Design Museum with views to die for. The menu is sophisticated yet simple. Changed twice daily, Modern British dishes with Middle Eastern and Asian influences, such as rabbit cooked with peppers and black olives, are presented in a straightforward manner.

✉ The Design Museum, 28 Shad Thames SE1 2YD ☎ 020 7378 7031 🕐 12–3, 6–11, closed D Sun, 25–28 Dec, 1 Jan 🖐 L £18, D £23, Wine £15 🚇 Tower Hill, London Bridge

BOUNTIFUL COW

For beef lovers—this place specializes in succulent aged steaks and gourmet homemade burgers, all cooked to perfection on the grill. Other dishes on the menu include lighter choices such as sandwiches or an omelette with chips. The pub has been redesigned in chic bistro style, with touches of the Wild West in period posters on the walls.

✉ 51 Eagle Street, Holborn, London WC1R 4AP ☎ 020 7404 0200 🕐 Daily noon–11.30 (food served noon–3 and 5–10.30) 🖐 L £25, D £35, Wine £12 🚇 Holborn

LE CAPRICE RESTAURANT
www.le-caprice.co.uk

The menu at this unashamedly glamorous, retro-chic restaurant offers a tireless repertoire of uncomplicated, well-presented staples: eggs Benedict, deep-fried haddock with minted pea purée and chips, and a selection of traditional comfort desserts like treacle sponge pudding. Reserve in advance.

✉ Arlington House, Arlington Street SW1A 1RT ☎ 020 7629 2239 🕐 12–3, 5.30–12; closed 1 Jan, Aug public holiday, D 24 Dec, 25–26 Dec, L 27 Dec 🖐 L £21, D £27.50, Wine £18.50 🚇 Green Park

CHAMPOR CHAMPOR
www.champor-champor.com

A small, South East Asian restaurant. Roughly translated, champor champor means 'mix and match' in Malay, and this is reflected in the fusion of Asian cuisines with its roots in Malaysia. A two-course fixed-price meal might include ostrich sausages in Szechuan pepper and Japanese miso followed by duck confit in a green curry sauce.

✉ 62 Weston Street SE1 3QJ ☎ 020 7403 4600 🕐 6.15–10.15 (times may vary—check); closed Sun, five days at Easter, seven days Christmas–New Year 🖐 L £19.90 D £27.90, Wine £14 🚇 London Bridge

CHRISTOPHER'S
www.christophersgrill.com

At the heart of Covent Garden and Theatreland, this is an American-themed establishment, with a martini bar and private rooms downstairs and a large restaurant upstairs. There's a huge menu, big on steaks, fish and a healthy intake of seasonal produce. Tuck into Maryland crabcake for starters, or try the blackened salmon with jambalaya risotto. Get a window seat for epic metropolitan views. Pre- and post theatre menus are very popular.

✉ 18 Wellington Street, Covent Garden

WC2E 7DD ☎ 020 7240 4222 🕐 Mon–Fri 12–3, 5–11.30, Sat 11.30–3.30 (brunch), 5–11.30, Sun 11.30–3.30 (brunch), 5–10.30 🖐 L £16.25, D £19.50, Wine £17 💳 🚇 Covent Garden, Temple, Embankment

CHUTNEY MARY
www.chutneymary.com

This popular Indian restaurant has acquired a menu that combines old favourites with exciting new specialities, such as the buttered crab popular in Bombay's seafood restaurants or Chutney Mary's own creation, an Indian foie gras dish with seared mango and mild chilli marsala jelly.

✉ 535 King's Road, Chelsea SW10 0SZ ☎ 020 7351 3113 🕐 12.30–3, 6.30–11.30; closed L Mon–Fri, D Christmas 🖐 L £20, D £27, Wine £17.50 💳 🚇 Fulham Broadway

THE DUKE OF CAMBRIDGE

This was one of London's first pubs to specialize in organic food, wines and beers. Blackboard menus feature seasonal Modern European dishes and change twice a day. Dishes might include pumpkin and sage soup, grilled asparagus with anchovies, capers and poached egg, pan-fried sea trout, slow roast pork belly and baked aubergine with tomato, onion and parsley. Leave space for rhubarb fool with shortbread. All dishes are available as children's portions. There is a garden and a patio.

✉ 30 St. Peter's Street N1 8JT ☎ 020 7359 3066 🕐 12–11 (Sun 12–10.30). Restaurant: 12.30–3, 6.30–10.30 (Sun 12.30–3, 7–10); closed 25–26 Dec, 1 Jan 🖐 L £13.50, D £19, Wine £13.50 🚇 Angel

THE EAGLE

The Eagle helped create the gastro pub. Expect big flavours. The straightforward, rustic blackboard-driven menu leans towards southern Europe and the Pacific Rim.

✉ 159 Farringdon Road, Clerkenwell EC1R 3AL ☎ 020 7837 1353 🕐 12–11; closed D Sun 🖐 Bar meals from £5, Wine £11.85 🚇 Angel, Farringdon

FIFTEEN LONDON

www.fifteenrestaurant.com

This venture from celebrity chef Jamie Oliver can be reserved for months in advance. But don't let that put you off—Fifteen offers simple but creative cooking. The general theme is Italian with a British flavour—tagliatelle of Snowdonia lamb being a good example.

✉ 13 Westland Place N1 7LP T ☎ 0871 330 1515 ⏰ 12–2.15, 6.30–9.30; closed D Sun, public holidays ✋ L £22, D (6 courses) £60, Wine £16 Ⓜ Old Street

THE FLASK

In one of the loveliest corners of 'village London', the Flask can boast poets and highwaymen among its famous and not-so-famous former clientele. T.S. Elliot and Sir John Betjeman both enjoyed the odd sip here and Dick Turpin once hid in the cellar. There's a good range of hot and cold food on a twice daily changing menu, from sandwiches to full-on char-grilled affairs and an excellent array of puddings. The real ales and bottled beers are very popular and there's an extensive wine list.

✉ Highgate West Hill N6 6BU 3AL ☎ 020 8348 7346 ⏰ 12–11, L served 12–3, D 6–10 (Sun 6–9.30) ✋ L £10.20, D £14, Wine £10 Ⓜ Highgate

FRENCH HOUSE

The weekly changing menus at this small bar might feature a delicious navarin of lamb, roast monkfish with Parma ham, confit of duck with braised lentils and red cabbage, or for a vegetarian option, try the risotto of roast pumpkin.

✉ 49 Dean Street, Soho W1D 5BG ☎ 020 7437 2799 ⏰ 12–12 (Sun 12–10.30). Restaurant: Mon–Sat 12–3, 5.30–11 ✋ L (3 courses) £30, D £30, Wine £15 Ⓜ Leicester Square

THE GLASSHOUSE

www.glasshouserestaurant.com

This chic restaurant is modern and airy, with extremely hospitable and knowledgeable service. Uncomplicated dishes—perhaps an assiette of duck or a warm salad of woodpigeon—are accompanied by something from the extensive and globally diverse wine list. Reservations are advised.

✉ 14 Station Road, Kew TW9 3PZ ☎ 020 8940 6777 ⏰ 12–2.30, 7–10.30; closed Christmas, 1 Jan ✋ L £18.50, D £35, Wine £15 ♿ Ⓜ Kew Gardens

HUSH

www.strictlyhush.com

Even in Mayfair, this place stands out as particularly chic, with its long curvy bar, limestone floors and elegant simplicity. As a bonus, there's outdoor seating on a peaceful cobbled terrace deceptively close to the bustle of Bond Street (a great spot for breakfast). Chef David Rood produces modern eclectic cuisine, offering such combinations as confit of duck with Szechuan vegetables and sesame dressing, or rare seared tuna with soy and ginger. There are also such bistro classics as moules marinière with crusty bread and steak tartare with pommes allumettes, alongside British favourites like steak and ale pie and grilled calf's liver with bubble and squeak and crispy bacon. A couple of good-value set menus are offered. There's also a cocktail lounge.

✉ 8 Lancashire Court, Brook Street, London W1S 1EY ☎ 020 7659 1500 ⏰ Call for times or check on the website ✋ L £35, D £50, Wine £16.50 ♿ Ⓜ Bond Street

INN THE PARK

www.innthepark.co.uk

Open all day, and spilling out onto decks overlooking Duck Island, Inn the Park serves up good value British food. There's good use of fish and meat from small suppliers all over Britain—Cumbrian and Scottish beef, Welsh lamb, Bideford Bay oysters—served without fuss, with the freshest accompanying vegetables. High Tea is a favourite with parkgoers—finger sandwiches, scones with clotted cream and an excellent selection of preserves. If you want to enjoy the park to its full on a summer's day you can order a picnic from a menu that begins with children's portions and ends with the champagne accompanying £45 per head variety.

✉ St. James's Park SW1A 1AA ☎ 020 7451 9999 ⏰ 8am–10.45pm (9am–10.45 Sat–Sun) ✋ L £21, D £27.50, Wine £14.50 ♿ Ⓜ St. James's Park

J SHEEKEY

This much-loved seafood establishment is in a class of its own when it comes to fish dishes. Menus can include seared tuna with fennel and Sicilian tomato salad, along with a smoked anchovy dish with slow-baked beetroot and horseradish cream. Reserving is essential.

✉ 28–32 St. Martin's Court WC2N 4AL ☎ 020 7240 2565 ⏰ 12–3, 5.30–midnight; closed 24 Dec, public holidays ✋ L £19.50, D £26, Wine £17.75 ♿ Ⓜ Leicester Square

LAMB AND FLAG

This is an atmospheric Covent Garden pub, dating back to Elizabethan times, with low ceilings and high-backed settles. Traditional English pub food is on the menu, including Toad in the Hole, beef and onion pie and lamb hotpot, and there's a good range of beers.

✉ 33 Rose Street, Covent Garden, London, WC2E 9EB ☎ 020 7497 9504 ⏰ 11–11; food noon–3.30 (Sat–Sun 3–5) ✋ Bar L £10 Ⓜ Covent Garden, Leicester Square

THE LANSDOWNE

One of the earlier dining pubs in Primrose Hill, The Lansdowne blends an airy bar and outdoor seating with a slightly more formal upper dining toom. Here you'll find waiter service, and it's worth reserving your table. All food is freshly prepared on the premises, using organic or free-range ingredients wherever possible. The seasonal menu offers such dishes as home-made pizzas and sausages, chicken and chorizo stew and grilled sea bass with purple-sprouting broccoli. Children welcome.

✉ 90 Gloucester Avenue, Primrose Hill NW1 8HX ☎ 020 7483 0409 ⏰ 12–11 (Sat–Sun 9.30am–11pm). Restaurant Tue–Sat 7–10, Sun 1–3; closed 26 Dec ✋ Bar L £8, D £28, Wine £13.90 Ⓜ Chalk Farm

LINDSAY HOUSE RESTAURANT

www.lindsayhouse.co.uk

Ring the bell for admission to this quirky Soho success story and succumb to the twin temptations of cutting-edge cooking and sheer indulgence. Chef Richard Corrigan and his team rarely put a foot wrong. Expect the likes of red leg partridge with bread pudding, game pie or monkfish with octopus daube and monkfish cheeks. Jacket and tie preferred; children welcome.

✉ 21 Romilly Street W1V 5AF ☎ 020 7439 0450 🕐 12–2.30, 6–11; closed Sun, L Sat, one week Christmas, one week Easter ✋ L £22, D £30, Wine £29 🚇 Leicester Square

MAISON BERTAUX

Everyone knows about the sumptuous afternoon teas served in London's top hotels, but if you're in the Soho area it's worth stopping in at this authentic French patisserie. Now in its third generation of the same family, it is one of London's best-loved tea shops, and offers seven kinds of tea to accompany the mouthwatering cakes and pastries. Light lunches are also served.

✉ 28 Greek Street, Soho, London W1D 5DD ☎ 020 7437 6007 🕐 Mon–Sat 9–7, Sun 9.30–8 ✋ L £10 🚇 Picadilly Circus or Leicester Square

MORO

www.moro.co.uk

Packed Spanish/North African eatery with good-value meals. Many dishes are inspired by the wood-fired oven, and range from simple grilled chicory with jamon and sherry vinegar to more complex wood-roasted turbot with roast beetroot lentils. Desserts are equally Moorish in their origins—yoghurt cake with pistachios, malaga raisin ice cream. The wine list is biased towards Spain and reasonably priced.

✉ 34–36 Exmouth Market, Clerkenwell EC1R 4QE ☎ 020 7833 8336 🕐 12.30–2.30, 7–10.30; closed Sun, Christmas, New Year, public holidays ✋ L £21, D £27, Wine £12.80 🚇 Farringdon Road, Angel

OLD BANK OF ENGLAND

www.moro.co.uk

Delicious traditional pies are served here. Alternatively, there's a good range of soups, sandwiches, burgers and meals such as bangers and mash. The building alone is worth a visit, a magnificent structure that used to house a branch of the Bank of England.

✉ 194 Fleet Street, London EC4A 2LT ☎ 020 7430 2255 🕐 Mon–Fri 11–11; food served noon–9 (8 on Fri) ✋ L £15, D £25, Wine £12.50 🚇 Temple

THE ONLY RUNNING FOOTMAN

www.themeredithgroup.co.uk/Only/theOnly.html

This Mayfair eatery has a smart pub with an all-day menu on the ground floor and fine dining upstairs —there's also a private dining room and a small cookery school on higher floors. The pub menu includes several breakfast choices and a

Above *The capital's restaurants cater to a global palate*

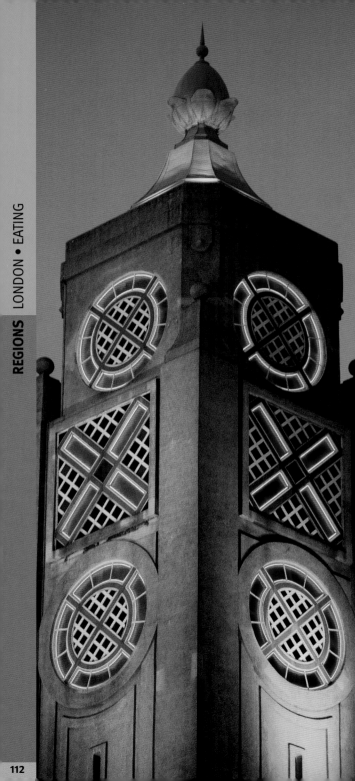

tempting range of good-value meals, such as fish pie, beef lasagne and a 'pie of the day'. Upstairs, you could begin with a terrine of foie gras and green peppercorns, sweet wine jelly and toasted brioche, then tuck in to lobster and clam spaghettini with slow-roasted tomato, or perhaps a slow roast of Gloucester Old Spot pork with apple sauce and marjoram jus. Many items carry the provenance of the main ingredients. ✉ 5 Charles Street, London W1J 5DE ☎ 020 7499 2988 ◷ Mon–Fri 7.30am–10pm, Sat–Sun 9.30am–10pm ✋ 3rd floor L £22, D £45, Wine £13.50 ♿ Ⓜ Green Park

THE OXO TOWER RESTAURANT

www.harveynichols.co.uk

With its amazing view through floor-to-ceiling windows overlooking the river and City beyond, this cubed tower cannot fail to impress. Cooking is modern in style but not outlandish, in dishes such as lobster, tomato and basil jelly with Sevruga caviar and pan-fried veal sweetbreads with a sauce of ceps, parsley and lemon oil. Desserts might include coconut rice pudding with spiced ice cream. ✉ 8th Floor, Oxo Tower Wharf, Barge House Street SE1 9PH ☎ 020 7803 3888 ◷ 12–2.30, 6–11 (bar 11–11); closed 25–26 Dec ✋ L (3 courses) £33, D £36, Wine £16.50 Ⓜ Blackfriars

THE REAL GREEK

www.therealgreek.co.uk

This characterful Victorian pub has been transformed into an urban-fashionable bistro. You enter The Real Greek via the adjoining sister venture, Mezedopolio, a wine and medezes bar. Look for salt cod in batter or salad of lump-fish roe to start with followed by lamb kebab served with sweetbreads and rice, or pan-fried fish with macaroni. Reservation advised. ✉ 15 Hoxton Market N1 6HG ☎ 020 7739 8212 ◷ 12–11; closed Sun, 24–26 Dec, public holidays ✋ L £12, D £18, Wine £12 Ⓜ Old Street

Left *The Oxo Tower at dusk*

THE RED FORT

www.redfort.co.uk

This long-established Indian consists of a busy basement bar and a more formal ground-floor restaurant. The latter specializes in cuisine from the New Delhi region and offers diners both an à la carte and a two-course set menu. You might start with monkfish tikka and follow with anaari champ—lamb chop in star anise and pomegranate jus. Children welcome. ✉ 77 Dean Street W1D 3SH ☎ 020 7437 2525 ⏰ 12–2.15, 5.45–11.15; closed L Sat, Sun, 25 Dec 🍴 L £12, D £16, Wine £19 💳 🚇 Leicester Square

RESTAURANT GORDON RAMSAY

www.gordonramsay.com

Gordon Ramsay is probably the most acclaimed chef in Britain today and Royal Hospital Road is the foundation of his empire. For somewhere with such a huge reputation, it is surprisingly intimate. Service is as good as it gets, with every dish accurately explained and plenty of help when navigating the wine list. Simplicity, integrity and lightness of touch are Ramsay hallmarks, along with determination and consistency. The quality of ingredients is irreproachable in, for example, roasted fillet of halibut with carrot and coriander papardelle, baby navet and passionfruit butter sauce, while timing is dead-on. Desserts are a delight. Prices are reasonable. ✉ 68 Royal Hospital Road SW3 4HP ☎ 020 7352 4441 ⏰ 12–2.30, 6.45–11; closed Sat–Sun, two weeks Christmas, public holidays 🍴 L £40, D £70, Wine £21 💳 🚇 Sloane Square

THE RIVER CAFÉ

www.rivercafe.co.uk

The River Café is still serving some of the best Italian food around. The emphasis is on the finest raw materials lovingly prepared. The twice-daily-changing menu might include plump whole pigeon roasted in the wood oven, tender to the bone and accompanied by mouthwatering roasted pumpkin, fennel, celeriac and carrots. Desserts are typically Italian and fairly simple.

✉ Thames Wharf, Rainville Road W6 9HA ☎ 020 7386 4200 ⏰ 12.30–3, 7–11; closed D Sun, Easter, 24 Dec–1 Jan, public holidays 🍴 L £36, D £41, Wine £12.50 💳 🚇 Hammersmith

ROYAL CHINA

If you are in the docklands, this is a terrific spot to sample some traditional Cantonese cuisine while enjoying superb views of the river. There's an excellent range of dim sum and a variety of hot and cold appetizers, while the seafood menu features lots of prawn, squid and oyster dishes alongside sea bass, sole and cod. Meat dishes include crispy shredded beef in a bird's nest and double cooked Szechuan roast pork. The set meal options are always good value and include carefully chosen dishes, including a vegetarian meal. ✉ Canary Wharf Riverside, 30 Westferry Circus, London E14 8RR ☎ 020 7719 0888 ⏰ Daily; call for times 🍴 L £30, D £45 🚇 Canary Wharf

ST. JOHN

www.stjohnrestaurant.co.uk

This restaurant has a menu that nods at traditional British cooking. There's plenty of offal—salted kid's liver, pressed pork and gizzard, tiny, tender rabbit's heart, kidneys and liver—and unusal ingredients such as smoked eel with bacon and mash, roast bone marrow and tripe, sausage and chick peas. More cautious diners might opt for langoustine with mayonnaise or cod and chips. ✉ 26 St. John Street EC1M 4AY ☎ 020 7251 0848 ⏰ 12–3, 6–11; closed Sun, L Sat, Easter, Christmas, New Year 🍴 L £19, D £25, Wine £17 🚇 Farringdon

SAGAR

Vegetarians will find the trip to Hammersmith well worthwhile for this upmarket and highly rated vegetarian restaurant with a long menu of meat-free dishes, largely based on the cuisine of the Udipi region of India. With exceptionally reasonable prices, it's usually very busy, but there's a great atmosphere. Freshly made breads are great for dipping in

the sambar, and the thalis selections are interesting and expertly prepared. Spicing places the emphasis on maintaining distinct flavours rather than going for the burn. ✉ 157 King Street, Hammersmith W6 9JT ☎ 020 8741 8563 ⏰ 12–2.45, 5.30–10.45 (11.30 on Fri), Sat noon–11/30, Sun noon–10.45 🍴 L £12, D £20, Wine £12.95 🚇 Hammersmith

SANTINI

www.santini-restaurant.com

This elegantly modern family-run restaurant in Belgravia is a favourite for those seeking authentic Italian cuisine in a sophisticated setting, with outside dining available in summer. Service is good and there is an excellent wine list. ✉ 20 Ebury Street, London SW1W 0NZ ☎ 020 7730 4094 ⏰ 12–3, 6–11.30; closed L Sat–Sun, 25–26 Dec, 1 Jan, Easter Sun 🍴 L £20, D £30, Wine £27 🚇 Victoria

SMITHS OF SMITHFIELD

www.smithsofsmithfield.co.uk

The top floor of this ever trendy restaurant complex boasts views over the City and St. Paul's Cathedral. Each floor is aimed at a different clientele, so there is something for most tastes and pockets, from bar food to fine dining. Look for the rare breed steaks—all from named suppliers. ✉ Top Floor, 66–67 Charterhouse Street EC1M 6HJ ☎ 020 7251 7950 ⏰ 12–3.30, 6.30–12; closed L Sat, 25–26 Dec, 1 Jan 🍴 3rd floor L £22, D £29, Wine £16.50 💳 🚇 Farringdon, Barbican, Chancery Lane

TAMARIND

www.tamarindrestaurant.com

With a cuisine that has been called nouvelle Indian, the Tamarind is a sophisticated contemporary basement curry house in Mayfair. The flavours are subtle—expect to taste the lamb in the Rogan Josh—and the desserts are restrained by Indian standards. ✉ 20 Queen Street, Mayfair W1J 5PR ☎ 020 7629 3561 ⏰ 12–2.45, 6–11.15; closed L Sat, 25–26 Dec, 1 Jan, public holidays 🍴 L £16.95, D £49.50, Wine £22 💳 🚇 Green Park

PRICES AND SYMBOLS

Prices are the starting price for a double room for one night, unless otherwise stated. Breakfast is included unless noted otherwise. All the hotels listed accept credit cards unless otherwise stated. Note that rates vary widely throughout the year.

For a key to the symbols, ▷ 2.

BENTLEY KEMPINSKI

www.thebentley-hotel.com
Tucked away in a residential area of Kensington, this exclusive hotel has lavish public areas and luxurious bedrooms and suites. Total indulgence, fine shopping in Kensington and Chelsea, and the proximity of the Royal Albert Hall and the South Kensington museums are the main attraction. Rooms are well-equipped with state-of-the-art entertainment systems, telephones and Internet access as well as personal luxuries, and hotel services. Fine dining, based on international cuisines is offered in the 1880 restaurant, perhaps after cocktails in the swish Malachite piano bar,

and there's also a brasserie-style restaurant for breakfast, lunch and afternoon tea. The fabulous Kalon Spa includes the only authentic Turkish Bath in a London hotel, along with a full range of relaxing and rejuvenating treatments in a soothing atmosphere.

✉ 27–33 Harrington Gardens, London SW7 4JX ☎ 020 7244 5555 🖐 Telephone for prices ⓘ 64 🔲 🔽 🚇 Gloucester Road

THE BERKELEY

www.the-berkeley.com
The Berkeley never fails to impress. Having undergone refurbishment there is an excellent range of bedrooms, each one furnished with care and attention to detail. The striking Blue Bar enhances the reception rooms. The health spa offers a range of treatment rooms and includes an open-air rooftop pool. Two restaurants provide a contrast of style: modern snack-style at the Boxwood Café and French cuisine at Pétrus. There is a sauna and spa.

✉ Wilton Place, Knightsbridge SW1X 7RL ☎ 020 7235 6000 🖐 £369 ⓘ 214 🔲 🏊 🔽 🚇 Knightsbridge

BYRON HOTEL

www.capricornhotels.co.uk
This terraced house retains a number of original features. Bedrooms vary in size but all are well furnished and equipped with modern facilities. There's a dining room, for breakfast, and a guest lounge.

✉ 36–38 Queensborough Terrace W2 3SH ☎ 020 7243 0987 🖐 £85 ⓘ 45 🚇 Bayswater

CAVENDISH

www.thecavendish-london.co.uk
Anyone who remembers the TV series, *The Duchess of Duke Street*, will be interested to learn that it was based on this hotel and its Edwardian supremo, Rosa Lewis. Times have changed, and the hotel is now in chic modern style, but the famously high standards live on, and it's location, off Piccadilly, is perfect for theatreland and some of London's best shopping streets. Sumptuous bedrooms come in a variety of styles and sizes, from the Classic, with a queen-size bed,

Above *Black cabs are synonymous with busy London streets*

to a Penthouse suite with separate bedroom, but all have sharp and uncluttered decor, subtle lighting and great views of the surrounding St. James's area. The restaurant serves British cuisine with traditional and creative influences, all based on fresh, seasonal produce.

✉ 81 Jermyn Street, London W1Y 6JF ☎ 020 7930 2111 ⚐ £175–£440 ① 230 ⊕ 🚇 Piccadilly Circus or Green Park

CLARIDGE'S
www.claridges.co.uk

Impressive standards of luxury, style and service are upheld at this iconic bastion of British hospitality. Sumptuously decorated, air-conditioned bedrooms have Victorian or art deco themes to reflect the architecture of the building. Excellent service and dishes at the restaurant, Gordon Ramsay at Claridge's, run by Mark Sargeant, a protégé of Gordon Ramsay. Reservations are advised.

✉ Brook Street W1A 2JQ ☎ 020 7629 8860 ⚐ £306 ① 203 ⊕ 🏊 Use of sister hotel's pool 🛎 🚇 Bond Street

CROWN MORAN
www.crownmoranhotel.co.uk

If a central location is not a top priority, this striking Irish-owned hotel in Cricklewood has much to recommend, not least the warmth of the Irish hospitality. There are two underground stations within a 10-minute walk for speedy access to the city. The bedrooms are modern and particularly spacious, and have high-speed Internet access and a work desk, as well as multi-channel TV and tea- and coffee-making facilities. The King Sitric Bar and Grill is under the direction of award-winning chef Stephen Scuffell, and the speciality of the house is 28-day aged Irish steaks. There's also good food in The Crown pub, a lively venue for live bands and DJs, sport TV and quiz nights. An excellent leisure centre, for residents only, has personal trainers and spa treatments.

✉ 142–152 Cricklewood Broadway, Cricklewood, London NW2 3ED ☎ 020 8452 4175 ⚐ £125–£190 ① 116 ⊕ 🏊 🛎 🚇 Kilburn or Willesden Green

DELMERE
www.delmerehotel.co.uk

A central location just north of Hyde Park and affordable prices would be enough of an attraction, but here you can add the friendly welcome of a privately owned hotel and an appealing range of facilities. The bedrooms are smart and stylish, and have orthopaedic mattresses, wireless Internet, beverage-making equipment and other thoughtful amenities. La Perla Restaurant serves good continental cuisine and there's a relaxing bar.

✉ 130 Sussex Gardens, Hyde Park, London W2 1UB ☎ 020 7706 3344 ⚐ £69–£149 ① 36 🚇 Paddington

THE DORCHESTER
www.dorchesterhotel.com

One of London's finest hotels, The Dorchester is sumptuously decorated. Bedrooms are beautifully furnished and have huge, luxurious baths. The Promenade is ideal for afternoon tea or drinks. In the evenings you can relax to the sound of live jazz in the bar, and enjoy a cocktail or an Italian meal. Other dining options include the traditional The Grill and The Oriental. There is a spa, gym, sauna, solarium and Jacuzzi.

✉ Park Lane W1A 2HJ ☎ 020 7629 8888 ⚐ £417 ① 250 ⊕ 🛎 🚇 Hyde Park Corner

EURO HOTEL
www.eurohotel.co.uk

This friendly bed-and-breakfast enjoys an ideal location in a leafy Georgian crescent. Many of the bedrooms have private bathrooms.

✉ 51–53 Cartwright Gardens, Russell Square WC1H 9EL ☎ 020 7387 4321 ⚐ £75 ① 34 🚇 Russell Square

FOUR SEASONS HOTEL LONDON
www.fourseasons.com

This long-established hotel is in the heart of Mayfair. Service is superlative. The large bedrooms are elegant and the conservatory rooms are particularly special.

✉ Hamilton Place, Park Lane W1A 1AZ ☎ 020 7499 0888 ⚐ £423 ① 220 ⊕ 🛎 🚇 Hyde Park Corner

THE GAINSBOROUGH
www.eeh.co.uk

This smart mid-Georgian town house is located in a quiet street near the Natural History Museum. Bedrooms are individually designed and decorated in fine fabrics, with quality furnishings. There is a small lounge and 24-hour room service.

✉ 7–11 Queensberry Place, South Kensington SW7 2DL ☎ 020 7957 0000 ⚐ £182 ① 49 🚇 South Kensington

GALLERY
www.eeh.co.uk

This stylish property offers friendly hospitality, attentive service and sumptuously furnished bedrooms, some with a private terrace. Public areas include a choice of lounges (one with Internet access) and an elegant bar. Room service is available 24 hours a day.

✉ 8–10 Queensberry Place, South Kensington SW7 2EA ☎ 020 7915 0000 ⚐ £188 ① 36 🚇 South Kensington

GRANGE BLOOMS
www.bloomshotel.com

Part of an 18th-century terrace, this elegant town house is just around the corner from the British Museum. Bedrooms are furnished in Regency style and day rooms consist of a lobby lounge, a garden terrace, a breakfast room and cocktail bar, all graced with antique pieces, paintings and flowers. There is 24-hour room service.

✉ 7 Montague Street WC1B 5BP ☎ 020 7323 1717 ⚐ £195 ① 26 🚇 Russell Square

GREAT EASTERN HOTEL
www.great-eastern-hotel.co.uk

A modern minimalist hotel with a prime location in the heart of the City. Air-conditioned bedrooms are simple yet stylish, and equipped with DVD and CD players. The impressive array of restaurants includes the elegant Aurora, offering fine dining, Fishmarket, a fish restaurant with champagne bar, Terminus serving all day meals and snacks and Miyabi, a Japanese restaurant. There is a gym complete with treatment rooms, a steam room and personal trainers.

✉ Liverpool Street EC2M 7QN
☎ 020 7618 5000 💷 £311 🛏 267
♿ 🍴 🚇 Liverpool Street

THE HALKIN HOTEL
www.halkin.como.bz

Contemporary in design, this individual hotel is in a peaceful area just a stroll away from Hyde Park. The stylish, fully air-conditioned bedrooms combine comfort with practicality and many include state-of-the-art facilities. You'd expect impressive food from this chic hotel, and it delivers. The restaurant, Nahm, is run by chef David Thompson, an expert on Thai cuisine.

✉ Halkin Street, Belgravia SW1X 7DJ
☎ 020 7333 1000 💷 £175 🛏 41 ♿
🚇 Hyde Park Corner

HART HOUSE HOTEL
www.harthouse.co.uk

This elegant Georgian house enjoys a prime location. Both bedrooms and public areas are smartly furnished and stylishly decorated and retain much of the original character of the house.

✉ 51 Gloucester Place, Portman Square W1U 8JF ☎ 020 7935 2288 💷 £105
🛏 16 🚇 Baker Street, Marble Arch

HOTEL LONDON KENSINGTON
www.millenniumhotels.com/gloucester

Air-conditioned bedrooms are furnished in a variety of contemporary styles. Additional amenities are provided in club rooms, which have a dedicated lounge. Eating options include Singaporean cuisine and more formal Italian food.

✉ 4–18 Harrington Gardens SW7 4LH
☎ 020 7373 6030 💷 £250 🛏 610 ♿
🍴 🚇 Gloucester Road

LANDMARK
www.landmarklondon.co.uk

You might expect the classic Victorian opulence of a London hotel built in 1899, but the Thai influences are a delightful surprise, drawn from the Landmark's sister hotel in Bangkok. Guests here want for nothing, and the bedrooms are some of the largest in London, luxuriously furnished and with marble bathrooms. The hotel has several places to eat and drink, but the eight-storey glass atrium of the Winter Garden, open all day, has the most memorable setting, complete with lofty palm trees. The Cellars, once a billiards room, is more clubby, with a huge fireplace and wood-panelled walls, while the Mirror Bar is a modern space for cocktails. The Landmark Spa and Health Club offers a reduced-price day membership to guests and a range of facilities.

✉ 222 Marylebone Road, London NW1 6JQ
☎ 020 7631 8000 💷 £255–£395 🛏 299
♿ 🏊 🍴 🚇 Marylebone

LANGORF HOTEL
www.langorfhotel.com

This elegant Edwardian building has been tastefully furnished throughout. The bedrooms are smartly presented. Public areas include a small lounge and a dining room.

✉ 20 Frognal, Hampstead NW3 6AG
☎ 020 7794 4483 💷 £85 🛏 31
🚇 Finchley Road

LINCOLN HOUSE HOTEL
www.lincoln-house-hotel.co.uk

Friendly, family-run Georgian town house which has been impressively renovated.

✉ 33 Gloucester Place W1U 8HY ☎ 020
7486 7630 💷 £69 🛏 23 🚇 Marble Arch

LONDON BRIDGE
www.londonbridgehotel.com

In the heart of vibrant Southwark and just across the river from the Financial District, this is a fine independent hotel that stylishly blends classical features with a chic modern décor of pale cream and restful earth tones, highlighted in leather and suede furniture, polished wood and woven fabrics. Bedrooms are equally stylish, roomy and relaxing. Careful lighting enhances the ambience, but there are fibre-optic reading lights too, and equally thoughtful facilities include large flat-screen TV, radio, high-speed Internet and voicemail, mini-bar, trouser press and a large safe.
Executive rooms, designed for business guests, and luxury apartments are also available. Modern British cuisine is served in the Londinium restaurant (named after the Roman remains unearthed during the building of the hotel), with Malaysian food in the Georgetown restaurant and simple dishes available in the Borough Bar.

✉ 8–18 London Bridge Street, London SE1 9SG ☎ 020 7855 2200 💷 £188–£264
🛏 138 ♿ 🍴 🚇 London Bridge

MANDARIN ORIENTAL HYDE PARK
www.mandarinoriental.com

Bedrooms and suites are decorated to a high standard in this stylish hotel, and many have superb views. There's a choice of dining options: The Park Restaurant, offering light brasserie-style dishes; the sophisticated Foliage, serving the highest standard of cuisine; and the fashionable Mandarin Bar serving light snacks and exotic cocktails.

✉ 66 Knightsbridge SW1X 7LA ☎ 020
7235 2000 💷 £425 🛏 200 ♿ 🍴
🚇 Knightsbridge

MAYFLOWER
www.mayflowerhotel.co.uk

Stylish and modern, this elegant guest house has some inspired touches, including hand-carved wooden beds and mellow colour combinations, set off by lofty ceilings and plenty of natural light. Each of the bedrooms has individual decor, and facilities include a private marbled bathroom, individual climate control, a hi-fi system, satellite TV, electronic safe and complimentary wireless Internet. The hotel has an equally stylish lounge, with leather sofas and original art, and a juice bar. Breakfast is served either in the bright breakfast room or in the pretty garden.

✉ 26–28 Trebovir Road, London SW5 9NJ
☎ 020 7370 0991 💷 £99–£219 🛏 47
♿ 🚇 Earl's Court

MENTONE HOTEL
www.mentonehotel.com

This bed-and-breakfast in a Victorian

terrace overlooking pleasant gardens is close to many of central London attractions. Bedrooms have private bathrooms. Tennis courts.

✉ 54–56 Cartwright Gardens, Bloomsbury WC1H 9EL ☎ 020 7387 3927 🖐 £75 ⓘ 43 Ⓜ King's Cross, Russell Square, Euston

MILLENNIUM GLOUCESTER MILESTONE HOTEL AND APARTMENTS

www.milestonehotel.com

This town house has been carefully restored and the bedrooms are of a very high standard; facilities include DVD players in each. There are superb suites and some duplexes. A snug bar has a conservatory and there is also a luxurious lounge.

✉ 1 Kensington Court W8 5DL ☎ 020 7917 1000 🖐 £305 ⓘ 57 Ⓢ 🅢 Ⓜ High Street Kensington

ST. GEORGE HOTEL

www.stgeorge-hotel.net

A Grade II listed (landmark) house in the West End. Bedrooms are well furnished. Breakfast is served in a smart breakfast room and the staff offer a warm welcome.

✉ 9 Gloucester Place W1U 3JH ☎ 020 7486 8586 🖐 £75 ⓘ 19 Ⓜ Baker Street

THE SAVOY

www.the-savoy.co.uk

Service is impeccable at this renowned hotel (pictured below) and bedrooms and suites offer excellent levels of comfort. The choice of dining areas presents a predicament; whether to opt for the Grill run by chef Marcus Wareing, an alumnus of Gordon Ramsay's restaurant, the River Restaurant or La Banquette. Jackets and ties are preferred. No visit would be complete without afternoon tea in the Thames Foyer, perhaps enjoying the regular Sunday afternoon tea dance.

✉ Strand WC2R 0EU ☎ 020 7836 4343 🖐 £395 ⓘ 263 Ⓢ 🅢 ➤ Indoor Ⓜ Charing Cross

WASHINGTON MAYFAIR

www.washington-mayfair.co.uk

Perfectly placed for the high-end shopping of Bond Street and Regent Street, this is an art-deco gem with all its elegant 1913 style preserved and the addition of the latest conveniences, including mobile phone hire, computer-coded security systems, and your own personal telephone number, with voice mail and Internet connection. Spacious rooms are chic and comfortable,

Master Suites have sitting and dining areas, and Executive Studio Suites have the biggest bathrooms. Service is friendly and helpful, and includes full concierge service, and 24-hour porterage and room service. Madison's Restaurant serves creative international cuisine (as well as pre-theatre meals).

✉ 5 Curzon Street, Mayfair, London W1J 5HE ☎ 020 7499 7000 🖐 £294–£382 ⓘ 171 Ⓢ 🅢 Ⓜ Green Park or Bond Street

WINDERMERE

www.windermere-hotel.co.uk

Convenient for Buckingham Palace, Westminster and the Tate Gallery, this charming little hotel is friendly and welcoming, with a good range of facilities. Each of the bedrooms is individually styled and amenities include a hospitality tray, satellite TV, in-room safe, telephone with modem point and ISDN 2 for video conferencing, and free wireless Internet access. The restaurant offers delicious modern British and European cuisine as well as a hearty English breakfast.

✉ 142–144 Warwick Way, Victoria, London SW1V 4JE ☎ 020 7834 5163 🖐 £119–£159 ⓘ 20 Ⓜ Victoria

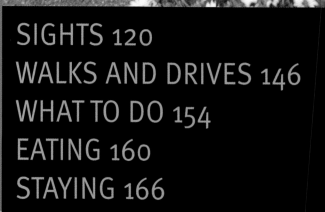

SIGHTS 120

WALKS AND DRIVES 146

WHAT TO DO 154

EATING 160

STAYING 166

THE WEST COUNTRY

England's West Country stretches for 200 miles (323km) from the rolling chalk downlands of Dorset and Wilt-shire to the dramatic granite cliffs of Land's End, sticking a famous rocky finger into the Atlantic Ocean. The vast Neolithic landscape centred around Stonehenge and Avebury is a big draw, but there are hundreds of historic sights throughout the region. On the shores of the English Channel, breathtaking Lulworth Cove features a rare geological phenomenon: this 'Jurassic Coast' is a UNESCO World Heritage Site for its proliferation of dinosaur fossils. Farther west, a historic mining landscape has taken on a surprising new lease of life—the Eden Project, near St. Austell in Cornwall, is a unique series of vast geodesic domes, filling former quarry workings with sustainable eco-systems from around the world.

Of the region's towns and cities, the Georgian spa town of Bath is probably best known. It preserves its Roman baths and medieval cathedral amid grandiose streets and crescents. Novelist Jane Austen lived here for a while, but preferred nearby Bristol, which was built on maritime trade and retains a worldly feel through its diverse communi-ties and impressive buildings. The Clifton Suspension Bridge, designed by Isambard Kingdom Brunel in the 1830s and spanning the Avon Gorge, is a symbol of the city's wealthy past.

North of Bristol and Bath, the Cotswolds are a modest line of limestone hills, but their rich farmland left a fantastic legacy in the district's many stone-built towns and villages. This is an England close to the postcard idyll. Fortunately, all the way west into Cornwall there are pretty little villages, hidden coves and wooded valleys to explore, with excellent beaches and a pair of upland National Parks to complete the picture.

ABBOTSBURY

www.abbotsbury-tourism.co.uk

Thatched ironstone cottages line the streets of this village while beyond a huge 15th-century tithe barn and the hilltop St. Catherine's Chapel of *c*1400 there are tangible reminders of the Benedictine abbey, founded in 1026, that gave the village its name. Built to store a tenth of all local produce that was harvested, the tithe barn is now a themed play area. Abbotsbury Swannery (mid-Mar to end Oct daily 10–6; closing time varies in Oct, last admission 1 hour before closing), set up by monks in the 14th century, gives unrivalled opportunities to see swans close up. There are feeding sessions daily at 12 and 4. The swans build their nests between March and the end of April. Hatching is from mid-May to the end of June, and cygnets gain their wings in September and October. West of the village, the Sub Tropical Gardens (Mar–end Oct daily 10–6; rest of year daily 10–4) are awash with colour as late spring brings camellias, rhododendrons and perfumed magnolias.

➕ 430 G20 ℹ The Esplanade, Weymouth DT4 7AN, tel 01305 785747

ANTONY HOUSE

www.nationaltrust.org.uk

Cornwall's finest Georgian mansion is very much a family house, the seat of the Carews. Built by Sir William Carew between 1711 and 1721, and replacing a Tudor house, the building is made of silver-grey Pentewan stone, with two colonnaded wings of red brick. Inside it retains its original oak panelling, single four-poster beds, portraits by Sir Joshua Reynolds (1723–92) and a portrait of Charles I (1600–49) at his trial. The formal gardens contain the national collection of day lilies and summer border plants, as well as azaleas, rhododendrons and magnolias. The grounds also feature an 18th-century dovecote.

Left *Swans at Abbotsbury, Dorset*
Right *The sun rises over Avebury stone circle at dawn*

➕ 428 D21 ✉ Torpoint, Plymouth PL11 2QA ☎ 01752 812191 🕐 Apr–end May, Sep–end Oct (also Sun, Jun–end Aug public holidays) Tue–Thu 1.30–5.30 (last admission 4.45) ✋ House and garden: adult £6, child (5–16) £3, family £15. Woodland garden: £5.20

AVEBURY

www.nationaltrust.org.uk

Set in chalk downlands and now a World Heritage Site, the village of Avebury is enclosed by the largest prehistoric stone circle in the British Isles. Built of local stone between 2600BC and 2100BC, it consists of two circles surrounded by a larger henge (a banked circular enclosure) along which are 200 huge standing stones. A wide processional avenue of megaliths once led 2.5km (1.5 miles) beyond West Kennet to the site of the Sanctuary, a temple complex from around 3000BC. Fyfield Down, a National Trust nature reserve east of the village, is littered with natural sarsen stones. A 15-minute walk to the south is Silbury Hill, Europe's largest artificial mound (2700BC), which allegedly took around 80 million man hours to construct. Its original purpose is a mystery, but it is thought to have ritual significance. Across the road, a path climbs to West Kennet Long Barrow, a huge stone-chambered tomb built around 3700–3500BC. The Alexander Keiller Museum (Feb–end Oct daily 10–5; rest of year daily 10–4), by Avebury Manor, explains the history of the Avebury landscape.

➕ 430 H18 ℹ Avebury Chapel Centre, Green Street, Avebury SN8 1RE, tel 01672 539425

BATH

▷ 122–125.

BEDRUTHAN STEPS

According to legend, a giant called Bedruthan used these great coastal rock stacks as stepping stones. They can be seen from the clifftop coast path and a viewpoint near the parking area. The National Trust has built a secure stairway to the beach from the clifftop at Carnewas. Be warned, though, as it is unsafe to swim here and there is a risk of being cut off by the tide.

➕ 428 C20 ℹ Red Brick Building, North Quay, Padstow PL28 8AF, tel 01841 533449

BERKELEY CASTLE

www.berkeley-castle.com

Dominating the village of Berkeley and home of the Berkeleys for more than 850 years, this 12th- and 14th-century castle is a rambling fortress surrounded by walls 3m (14ft) thick and graced by Elizabethan terraced gardens and a vast park. The Great Hall, with its original timber roof, marks where the rebel barons of the West Country met in 1215 before going on to Runnymede to force King John to seal the Magna Carta (▷ 31). In the keep are the dungeons, including the cell where Edward II was murdered in a most brutal manner in 1327 after his deposition.

➕ 430 G18 ✉ Berkeley GL13 9BQ ☎ 01453 810332 🕐 Apr–end Sep Tue–Sat 11–4, Sun 2–5; Oct Sun 2–5. Butterfly House closed Oct ✋ Castle and gardens: adult £7.50, child £4.50, family £21. Gardens only: adult £4, child £2. Butterfly House: adult £2, child £1 🚻 📷

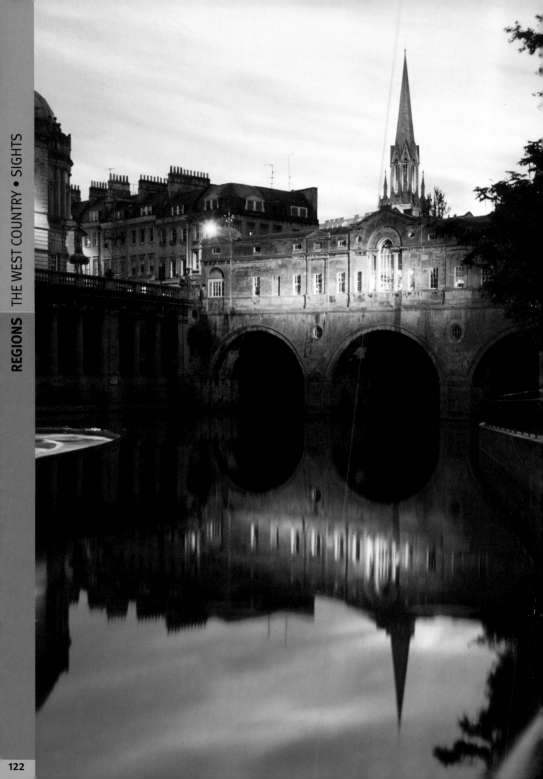

INTRODUCTION

The city is built from eye-pleasing, honey-coloured limestone, and has a striking setting amid seven hills, where the Cotswolds meet the Mendip Hills, and on the banks of the River Avon and the Kennet and Avon Canal. The hills can make walking tiring, but you are compensated by the wonderful views. With more than 20 museums and historic sites, a huge choice of accommodation and plenty of specialist shops—including a daily antiques market in Bartlett Street—there is definitely something for everyone. In between sightseeing, you can take in vibrant streetlife from any number of cafés in the form of street entertainment. If you're based in London, Bath makes a great day out, as it's only about two hours by fast train from London Paddington.

Roman Bath was founded in AD44 as the settlement of Aquae Sulis. Bath prospered through the wool trade in medieval times, but its modern importance dates from the 18th century, after its Roman hot springs were rediscovered in 1755. They were made fashionable by the dandy Richard 'Beau' Nash (1674–1762), who was paramount in attracting London's high society to the baths and springs, as well as to the grand balls and assemblies. Today, Bath is the country's only hot spring.

WHAT TO SEE

THE PUMP ROOM

www.romanbaths.co.uk

The high-ceilinged, chandelier-lit Georgian Pump Room (1796) is a great Bath institution, where a chamber trio provides accompaniment to afternoon tea within sight of the King's Bath. This room was originally built for a serious purpose. A group of doctors, led by William Oliver (inventor of the Bath Oliver biscuit), felt that invalids should be able to come together to drink Bath's mineral waters. But Richard 'Beau' Nash, the city's Master of Ceremonies, had greater ambitions. Realizing that a Pump Room could be useful as a meeting place, he hired musicians to play and fashionable visitors flocked in.

➕ 124 B2 ☎ Stall Street BA1 1LZ ☎ 01225 477785 ⏰ Mar–end Jun, Sep–end Oct daily 9–5; Jul–end Aug daily 9–9; rest of year daily 9.30–4.30

ROMAN BATHS

www.romanbaths.co.uk

From the genteel elegance of the Georgian Pump Room you suddenly walk into Roman times in the finest bathhouse site in Britain. A self-guiding tour leads past displays of finds from the site down to the waters. The highlights of the visit are the pool and the Roman Bath (the Great Bath). The spring, still bubbling up at a constant 46°C (116°F), was sacred to the goddess Sulis, who was thought to possess curative powers. The Romans made a sanctuary around the spring, and both Celts and Romans bathed and made offerings.

➕ 124 B2 ☎ Stall Street BA1 1LZ ☎ 01225 477785 ⏰ Jan, Feb, Nov, Dec daily 9.30–5.30; Mar–end Jun, Sep, Oct daily 9–6; Jul, Aug daily 9am–10pm, last admission 1 hour before closing

BATH ABBEY

www.bathabbey.org

Not in fact an abbey but a church, this building (begun in 1499) represents one of the crowning examples of the Perpendicular style. Legend has it that the shape of the church was dictated to its founder, Bishop Oliver King, in a dream by angels. This story is immortalized on the west front, which shows the carved angels ascending and descending on ladders, and the founder's

INFORMATION

www.visitbath.co.uk

➕ 457 G18 ℹ Abbey Chambers, Abbey Church Yard, Bath BA1 1LY, tel 0906 711 2000 (50p a minute) ⏰ Jun–end Sep Mon–Sat 9.30–6, Sun 10–4; rest of year Mon–Sat 9.30–5, Sun 10–4 ❓ The Bath Pass (available for 1, 4, 7 or 15 days) gives free entry to more than 30 attractions in the Bath and Bristol area; details from the tourist information office. The Bath Visitor Card gives exclusive discounts on a range of attractions and restaurants around the city for 21 days. You can buy on-line, call 0870 420 1278, or from the tourist information office. There are also a number of free guided walking tours of the city. Details from the tourist information office

🚉 Bath Spa, 0.25 miles (400m) from central Bath

Opposite page *Bath is Britain's most complete Georgian city and one of the most elegant—World Heritage Site status has ensured its preservation*

Above *Water of the Sacred Spring flows under an arch at the Roman Baths*

TIPS

» Bath is ideal for a weekend break, with a huge choice of accommodation at all prices.
» Try to go early to the Pump Room and Roman Baths to avoid the crowds.
» Parking in the city is a real problem, so either come by public transport or use the park-and-ride service.

signature—a carving of olive trees surmounted by crowns. The airy interior is most notable for the size of its windows and the delicate fan vaulting, completed by George Gilbert Scott in the late 19th century. The huge east window depicts 56 scenes from Christ's life, while the floor and walls, crammed with elaborate memorials and Georgian inscriptions, make fascinating reading. The Norman Chapel (also known as the Gethsemane Chapel) has clear traces of the older, Norman chapel on this site.

✚ 124 C2 ✉ Abbey Churchyard BA1 1LY ☎ 01225 422462 ⏰ Easter–late Oct Mon–Sat 9–6, Sun 1–2.30, 4.30–5.30; rest of year Mon–Sat 9–4.30, Sun 1–2.30, 4.30–5.30

FASHION MUSEUM AND ASSEMBLY ROOMS

www.fashionmuseum.co.uk

This large and prestigious collection, once known as the Museum of Costume, displays fashionable dress for men and women dating from the late 16th century to the present. The star attraction is the silver tissue dress dating from the 1660s, although many visitors are interested in the early 19th-century clothes, familiar to many from film adaptations of Jane Austen's novels. The collection is held at the Assembly Rooms, also familiar to those who know their Austen.

✚ 124 B1 ✉ Bennett Street BA1 2QH ☎ 01225 477789 ⏰ Mar–end Oct daily 10.30–6; rest of year daily 11–5

NO. 1 ROYAL CRESCENT

www.bath-preservation-trust.org.uk

This house was designed by John Wood the Younger (1767–74) and offers a chance to see inside one of the town houses in Bath's most celebrated architectural set piece, the Royal Crescent. It has been restored to its appearance of 200 years ago, with pictures, china and furniture of the period and a kitchen with a dog-powered spit used to roast meat in front of the fire. The first-floor windows are the only ones of the original height—all the others

Below *A red Victorian post box standing on Argyle Street*

were lengthened in the 19th century. Wood's father (also John) was the architect of The Circus (1754–70), a circular piazza close by.

➕ 124 A1 ✉ 1 Royal Crescent BA1 2LR ☎ 01225 428126 🕓 Mid-Feb to late Oct Tue–Sun 10.30–5; late Oct–early Nov Tue–Sun 10.30–4; early Dec Sat–Sun 10.30–4, last entry 30 mins before closing

MORE TO SEE

BUILDING OF BATH MUSEUM
www.bathmuseum.co.uk
This highly informative museum explains how Bath developed into the city you see before you. Housed in a little chapel, the museum tells how the former wool trading town of Bath was transformed into the most chic resort in England.

➕ 124 B1 ✉ Countess of Huntingdon's Chapel, The Vineyards, The Paragon BA1 5NA
☎ 01225 333895 🕓 Mid-Feb to end Nov Tue–Sun, public holidays 10.30–5

JANE AUSTEN CENTRE
www.janeausten.co.uk
An exhibition charts the life and works of the great novelist (1775–1817) who made two long visits to Bath in the 18th century, and also lived here from 1801 to 1806. The city features in *Persuasion* (published posthumously in 1817) and *Northanger Abbey* (1818).

➕ 124 B1 ✉ 40 Gay Street BA1 2NT ☎ 01225 443000 🕓 Nov–end Mar Sat 10–5.30, Sun–Fri 11–4.30; Apr, Jun, Sep, Oct 9.45–5.30; Jul, Aug Thu–Sat 9.45–7, Sun–Mon 9.45–5.30

AMERICAN MUSEUM IN BRITAIN
www.americanmuseum.org
The gracious 19th-century Claverton Manor house has recreations of American homes from different states from the 17th to 19th centuries, as well as folk art and exhibits about Native Americans and the Shakers.

➕ 124 off C1 ✉ Claverton Manor BA2 7BD ☎ 01225 460503 🕓 Late Mar–end Oct Tue–Sun 12–5 (daily Aug); last entry 4

Top *St. John's Bridge, Trim Street at dusk*
Above *The Sun God from the Temple of Sulis Minerva*
Below *A reminder of Bath's former residents outside the Roman Baths*

BODMIN MOOR
www.bodminmoor.com

Best seen from the A30 road west of Launceston (▷ 135), Bodmin Moor is a rather bleak, wild terrain punctuated by gnarled granite 'tors' (outcrops), and home to rare plants such as bog orchids, as well as birds such as lapwings and snipe. On the moorland fringes, the De Lank and Fowey rivers are important territories for otters.

There are no major settlements, but some of the village churches have fine features, including whimsical carved 16th-century pew ends at Altarnun, and 15th- and 16th-century stained glass, some of the finest in Cornwall, at St. Neots.

The Cheesewring, a strangely shaped rock outcrop, is close by near Minions, with a Bronze Age stone circle.

✚ 456 D20 🛈 The Shire Hall, Mount Folly Square, Bodmin PL31 2DQ, tel 01208 76616

BOURNEMOUTH
www.bournemouth.co.uk

The glory of this large Victorian seaside resort is its 7 miles (11km) of golden sands, offering safe, clean bathing beneath sandstone cliffs. In

Below *Bournemouth's sandy beach is popular in the summer*

Lower Gardens is the helium-filled, tethered Bournemouth Eye Balloon (Mar–end Sep daily 7.30am–11pm) giving a bird's-eye view of the town from 150m (500ft). The Bournemouth Symphony Orchestra, based in Poole, has an international reputation. The Russell-Cotes Art Gallery and Museum (Tue–Sun 10–5), on the cliffs, has a rich Victorian art collection.

Hengistbury Head, just east of town, is good for fine harbour views.

✚ 458 H20 🛈 Westover Road, Bournemouth BH1 2BU, tel 08450 511700 🅱 Bournemouth

BOWOOD HOUSE AND GARDENS
www.bowood.org

The family home of the Marquis and Marchioness of Lansdowne since 1754 stands in parkland created by the 18th-century landscape gardener Capability Brown. Built in 1624, the house was finished by the architect Robert Adam (among others) in the 18th century. The main draws of Bowood, however, are the gardens and grounds, featuring terraced rose gardens, Arboretum, Doric Temple, cascade waterfall, Hermit's Cave and woodland walks. The Rhododendron Walks, a woodland garden, is ablaze with rhododendrons and azaleas (late Apr–early Jun). For children, there is a playground and the Soft Play Palace.

✚ 458 G18 ✉ Calne SN11 0LZ ☎ 01249 812102 🕓 End Mar–early Nov daily 11–5.30 (grounds 11–6) 🎫 Adult £8, child (5–15) £6.50, child (2–4) £4.50; season tickets available. Rhododendron Walks: adult £5.75, child (under 16) free, or £24.75 if combined with house 🍴 🏛

BRADFORD-ON-AVON
www.bradfordonavon.co.uk

Almost every route into this hillside town is down a steep incline lined with mellow Bath-stone weavers' cottages, old inns and flower-decked shops. The tall but tiny Saxon Church of St. Laurence is one of the most complete examples from that time, while The Hall (1610) is a fine example of Jacobean architecture. By the River Avon and the Kennet and Avon Canal, Barton Farm Country

Park has a well-preserved 14th-century stone tithe barn with a massive timbered roof.

✚ 457 G18 🛈 50 St. Margaret's Street, Bradford-on-Avon BA15 1DE, tel 01225 865797 🅱 Bradford-on-Avon

BRISTOL
▷ 127.

BRIXHAM
www.theenglishriviera.co.uk

Perhaps when you think of Brixham, you think of boats. It is one of the few thriving fishing ports left in the region from where you can sail or take a pleasure cruise to surrounding resorts. It has a working atmosphere in its narrow streets and Victorian cottages rising above the quayside where a full-scale replica of Sir Francis Drake's ship of 1577, the *Golden Hind,* is moored.

There is also a strong tradition of local art here, on show by the harbour at the Strand Art Gallery, with local artists' work on sale.

The clifftop walks to the east along Berry Head, offer fine views.

✚ 457 E21 🛈 The Old Market House, The Quay, Brixham TQ5 8AW, tel 0906 6801268

BROWNSEA ISLAND
www.nationaltrust.org.uk/brownsea

This tranquil 200ha (500-acre) island is reached by boat from Poole Quay and Sandbanks (on the edge of Bournemouth). Its woodlands, marshland and wild heath are a haven for many forms of wildlife, including wading birds, herons, sand lizards, red squirrels, mink and other animals. The visitor office has an exhibition about the island, and there are marked nature trails.

In 1907 Lord Baden-Powell (1857–1941) took 20 boys to camp here, and in so doing established the Boy Scout movement.

✚ 458H20 ✉ Poole Harbour BH13 7EE ☎ 01202 707744 🕓 Oct daily 10–4; mid-Mar to mid-Jul and Sep daily 10–5; mid-Jul to end Aug daily 10–6; check time of last boat 🎫 Landing fee: adult £4.20, child (5–16) £2, family £10.40; additional ferry charge ❓ Guided nature tours (tel 01202 709445) 🏛

BRISTOL

A strong sense of maritime past pervades the premier city in southwest England, where a huge millennium facelift has created tree-lined avenues and turned Queen Square into a traffic-free haven.

Bristol was a leading port and commercial hub from the 12th century, and from the 15th to 18th centuries it was England's second city after London. Maritime wealth endowed it with imposing churches, notably the late 13th-century St. Mary Redcliffe (Redcliffe Hill) and the eclectic cathedral, with a Norman chapter house.

The former docks (most of the business has moved to Avonmouth) are now busy with places to eat and family attractions, including museums and boat trips. In the Harbourside area are At-Bristol (daily 10–5, and until 6 at weekends and on public holidays), covering a state-of-the art planetarium and the science and technology museum, Explore. In Great Western Dock is the SS *Great Britain* (Apr–end Oct daily 10–5.30 (10–6 Aug); rest of year daily 10–4.30), the world's first steam-powered ocean liner, built by the English engineer and inventor Isambard Kingdom Brunel (1806–59) and launched in 1843. In the original Temple Meads station, built by Brunel, the British Empire and Commonwealth Museum evokes Britain's Empire days, with the story of exploration, trade and conquest, and the legacy on life today.

The Old City, with its Georgian merchants' buildings, is now home to banks and restaurants, while East Side presents a scene of international influence with foods and goods from Asia and the Caribbean; meanwhile the West End around Park Street is the hip area, with funky shops selling the latest fashions and gifts.

The elegant Georgian suburb of Clifton has honey-coloured stone terraces, crescents and squares similar to those found in Bath (▷ 122–125). There are modern malls such as Broadmead and the traditional covered market at St. Nicholas, a market site since 1743.

Clifton Suspension Bridge (in Clifton) is the symbol of the city and probably Brunel's best-known design. It is a delicate engineering miracle spanning the Avon Gorge. Begun in 1836, it was finally opened in 1864, and its 214m (702ft) span was, at the time, the world's greatest. By the bridge are fine views from a camera obscura tower, best seen on a bright day. Close by is the visitor information point, where tours of the bridge can be arranged for groups.

INFORMATION

www.visitbristol.co.uk

✚ 457 G18 ❶ Centre Harbourside, Explore At-Bristol, Anchor Road, Bristol BS1 5DB, tel 0906 711 2191 (50p a minute) 🚉 Bristol Temple Meads

Above *Clifton Suspension Bridge, Bristol*

BUCKFASTLEIGH

www.buckfastleigh.org

This southern gateway town to Dartmoor is home to the South Devon Valley Railway (Easter–early Nov, www.southdevonrailway.org), a nostalgic steam line which runs along a 7-mile (11km) stretch of the River Dart as far as Totnes (▷ 142).

The station site is shared by the Buckfast Butterfly Farm (Easter–end Oct daily) and Dartmoor Otter Sanctuary (Easter–end Oct and Mar daily, Sat, Sun only at other times), and combined tickets are available. You can watch butterflies from all over the world fly free here.

The Otter Sanctuary is a refuge for this endangered species, with an underwater viewing area for observing these normally elusive animals.

To the north, off the A38 road, is Buckfast Abbey, home to a community of around 40 monks with an audio-visual presentation, interesting exhibition and tea rooms. ✚ 456 E20 ⛹ Leonards Road, Ivybridge PL21 0SL, tel 01752 897035

BUCKLAND ABBEY

www.nationaltrust.org.uk

This medieval monastery was converted into an imposing Elizabethan mansion after the Dissolution of the Monasteries in the mid-16th century (▷ 32). It is best known for its connection with Sir Francis Drake (c1540–96), who moved into Buckland Abbey in 1582 and stayed for 13 years. The house remained the property of the Drake family until 1794, and it passed into the care of the National Trust in 1938. ✚ 456 D20 ✉ Yelverton PL20 6EY ☎ 01822 853607 🕐 Abbey and grounds: Easter–end Oct Fri–Wed 10.30–5.30; Nov–end Dec 12–4; mid-Feb to Easter Sat–Sun 2–5 ♿ Abbey and grounds: adult £7.09, child (5–16) £3.54, family £17.72. Grounds only: adult £3.63, child £1.81; free Nov–end Mar 🍴 🏛

CERNE ABBAS

www.cerneabbas.org

Carved into the chalk hillside northeast of the village is the Cerne Abbas Giant, a 55m (180ft) figure of a

Above *Detail of St. Paul's Chamber in Gough's Cave, Cheddar Gorge*

naked man holding a club. The figure may be associated with fertility rites and possibly dates from before the Roman occupation, or could be (according to a recent theory) a 17th-century caricature of Oliver Cromwell, but his origins remain a mix of fact and speculation. There is a viewing point by the A352 road.

Cerne Abbas itself derives its name from a Benedictine abbey founded here in AD987. Only the abbey guest house and 15th-century gatehouse remain. ✚ 457 G20 ⛹ 11 Antelope Walk, Dorchester DT1 1BE, tel 01305 267992

CHEDDAR GORGE

www.cheddarsomerset.co.uk

www.cheddarcaves.co.uk

This dramatic natural spectacle can be enjoyed either by a drive along the road, a walk along the top or a tour of the adjoining limestone caves. Cheddar Gorge cuts dramatically beneath towering limestone cliffs, through the Mendip Hills for nearly 3km (2 miles). It is thought to have been formed by meltwater during various ice ages over the past two million years. The B3135 road winds along the bottom of the gorge, with numerous stopping places from where you can admire

the scene. Cave systems riddle the gorge: The Cheddar Caves (Jul–end Aug daily 10–5; rest of year daily 10.30–4) have two show caves— Gough's Cave and Cox's Cave—with tinted rock formations, stalagmites and stalactites.

In centuries past the caves formed the ideal conditions for maturing cheese, and while most cheddar cheese is now manufactured elsewhere (and not just in Britain), you can still see it being made at the Cheddar Cheese Dairy and Craft Village.

About 9.5km (6 miles) south are the Wookey Hole Caves (Apr–end Oct daily 10–5; rest of year daily 10–4), where you take a 40-minute guided tour. The first cave dive was made in the Witch's Parlour in 1935, and 25 caverns have since been discovered. Part of the Wookey Hole Caves complex are the River Axe ravine and the Victorian papermill (handmade paper), a mirror maze and old-fashioned pier amusements. ✚ 457 F19 ⛹ The Gorge, Cheddar BS27 3QE (closed in winter), tel 01934 742343

CHELTENHAM

www.visitcheltenham.com

This Regency town (it received the royal approval of George III) is renowned for its terraces, wrought-iron balconies, leafy thoroughfares, parks, floral displays, horse racing, music festival in July and literature festival in October.

The town spreads south along the Promenade, a wide, leafy street with pavement cafés and elegant shops. The Art Gallery and Museum (Mon–Sat 10–5.20, closed public holidays) in Clarence Street has an excellent section about the Arts and Crafts movement. Close by is the Holst Birthplace Museum (Feb–end Nov Tue–Sat 10–4; plus some public holidays), dedicated to Gustav Holst (1874–1934), composer of *The Planets*.

Pittville Park has lakes and a show-piece Pump Room, built in the Greek Revival style in 1825. A mineral spring was discovered here in 1715. You can still take the salty waters.
✛ 430 G17 ℹ 77 Promenade, Cheltenham GL50 1PJ, tel 01242 522878 🚆 Cheltenham

CHESIL BEACH
This huge wall of shingle, 18 miles (30km) long, up to 50ft (15m) high and more than 525ft (160m) wide—is one of the south coast's most pronounced natural features, and is famous for its colony of terns. The beach is separated from the mainland by a channel and tidal lagoon called The Fleet, and joins the mainland at Abbotsbury (▷ 121). Swimming at any time is extremely unsafe.
✛ 430 G20 ℹ The Esplanade, Weymouth DT4 7AN, tel 01305 785747

CIRENCESTER
www.cotswold.gov.uk
During the Roman occupation, Cirencester was *Corinium*, England's second most important city after London. Now it is a sedate market town, focusing around its Market Place (markets Mon and Fri), which in turn is dominated by St. John the Baptist Church, one of the grandest Cotswold 'wool churches', built when the wool trade brought great prosperity during the 15th century.

The town's attractive Cecily Hill, leads into Cirencester Park, laid out

geometrically in the 18th century. The Corinium Museum (daily 10–5, Sun 2–5) celebrates the city's Roman heritage. The Brewery Arts Centre (Mon–Sat 9.30–5.50, Sun 10–4) has craft workshops.
✛ 458 H18 ℹ The Corn Hall, Market Place, Cirencester GL7 2NW, tel 01285 654180

CLOVELLY
www.clovelly.co.uk
Of all Devon's picture-postcard villages, this is one of the most visited. It can be overcrowded in peak season. A visit requires stamina and suitable footwear, as all visitors (and residents) must walk down to it; but a Land Rover service takes you back up to the parking area (Easter–end Oct). Its single cobbled street, known as Up-Along and Down-Along, is lined with colour-washed cottages (some 16th-century), and slopes steeply 120m (400ft) to the harbour.
✛ 456 D19 ℹ Clovelly, near Bideford, EX39 5TA, tel 01237 431781 🖐 Entrance to village: adult £5.50, child (7–16) £3.50, family £15

CORFE CASTLE
www.nationaltrust.org.uk
Reduced to a jagged ruin after a long siege during the English Civil War (1642–48), but still dominating the view from miles around, Corfe Castle stands on a steep mound at a breach in the Purbeck Hills. It was built in Norman times and added to by King John. At the time of its demise the castle was the family seat of royalist Sir John Bankes, Attorney General under Charles I.

Much of the grey stone used to build the village of Corfe was quarried from the castle itself. The village has several good tea rooms, shops, restaurants and pubs.

Take a steam-train ride on the Swanage Railway from Swanage to Corfe (Easter–end Oct daily, most days Feb and Mar; some days rest of year; www.swanagerailway.co.uk).
✛ 458 G20 ✉ Near Wareham BH20 5EZ ☎ 01929 481294 🕐 Mar, Oct daily 10–5; Apr–end Sep daily 10–6; rest of year daily

10–4 🖐 Adult £5.09, child (5–16) £2.54, family £12.72 🍴 ☐ ♿

CORSHAM COURT
www.corsham-court.co.uk
Set in the small Cotswold town of Corsham is this Elizabethan manor of 1582, altered over the centuries and largely the work of architects John Nash and Thomas Bellamy.

The current owners, the Methuen family, bought the manor in 1745. The State Rooms and Picture Gallery display works by Reynolds, Rubens and Van Dyck. Landscaped by Capability Brown, the grounds feature formal lawns, flowering shrubs and herbaceous borders, avenues of mature trees, a lake and a Gothic bathhouse.
✛ 457 G18 ✉ Corsham SN13 0BZ ☎ 01249 712214 🕐 Mid-Mar to end Sep Tue–Thu, Sat, Sun 2–5.30 (last entry 30 min before closing time); rest of year Sat, Sun 2–4.30 🖐 House and gardens: adult £6.50, child £3. Gardens only: adult £2.50, child £1.50 ☐ ♿

COTEHELE
www.nationaltrust.org.uk
In a secluded position above the River Tamar, Cotehele is a remarkable Tudor survival. Built between 1485 and 1627 by the Edgcumbe family, it became their second home when they moved to Plymouth Sound in 1533, although relatives continued to live there. Still unlit by electric light, the house is filled with collections of furnishings, tapestries and armour.

There is much to see in the grounds, with a medieval dovecote, an 18th-century tower and craft workshops. There are also woodland and riverside walks.

The restored sailing barge *Shamrock*, at Cotehele Quay, is an outstation of the National Maritime Museum in Greenwich (▷ 78).
✛ 456 D20 ✉ St. Dominick, near Saltash PL12 6TA ☎ 01579 351346 🕐 House: mid-Mar to early Nov Sat–Thu 11–4.30. Gardens: daily 10–dusk 🖐 Adult £8, child (5–16) £4, family £22. Garden and mill only: adult £4.72, child (5–16) £2.36, family £11.81 ☐ ♿

DARTMOOR NATIONAL PARK

www.dartmoor-npa.gov.uk

The highest land in southern England, filling most of the space between Exeter (▷ 132) and Plymouth (▷ 138), is a granite plateau of rugged, desolate beauty. The heathery moors are speckled with the remains of prehistoric settlements and punctuated by streams and tors (jagged outcrops), such as the outstanding viewpoints of Hound Tor and Hay Tor. Walkers should be competent navigators, as even the shortest distance can be confusing. There are signs and painted stones as guides, but it's best to buy a map from one of the visitor offices in any main town.

Beneath the tors are cob-and-thatch villages such as Lustleigh and North Bovey. The verdant east side includes the Teign Valley and dramatic Becky Falls.

Castle Drogo (Easter–end Oct daily 11–5, close Tue some weeks), near Drewsteignton, is architect Sir Edwin Lutyens' 20th-century masterpiece, a blend of Arts and Crafts and medievalism.

✚ 456 E20 ℹ Tavistock Road, Princetown, Yelverton PL20 6QF, tel 01822 890414

DARTMOUTH

www.discoverdartmouth.com

A web of criss-crossing cobbled streets and narrow alleyways gives the ancient town and deep-water port of Dartmouth an unrivalled setting at the mouth of the River Dart. The steep green hills on either side flank a yacht-filled estuary. Enjoy the scene by taking a boat trip or climb to the roof of the small 14th-century fortification of Dartmouth Castle (Apr–end Jun and Sep daily 10–5; Jul–end Aug daily 10–6; rest of year Sat–Sun 10–4), guarding the mouth of the river.

The Paignton and Dartmouth Steam Railway reaches the river from the east side, ending at Kingswear on the opposite bank.

✚ 457 E21 ℹ The Engine House, Mayor's Avenue, Dartmouth TQ6 9YY, tel 01803 834224

DORCHESTER

www.westdorset.com

This county town features as Casterbridge in *The Mayor of Casterbridge* (1886) by West Country author Thomas Hardy (1840–1928).

East of town, the National Trust maintains two of his houses: Max Gate (Apr–end Sep Mon, Wed, Sun 2–5), which he designed and lived in from 1885 until his death; and his birthplace, Hardy's Cottage (mid-Mar to end Oct Sun–Thu 11–5), near Higher Bockhampton, an isolated thatched cottage in the forest. His heart is buried nearby in Stinsford churchyard. Hardy's study is recreated in the Dorset County Museum (Jul–end Sep daily 10–5; rest of year, Mon–Sat 10–5) in the town centre; where on show are items from Maiden Castle, Europe's largest Iron Age hillfort (south of town), finally abandoned during the Roman occupation after AD43.

✚ 457 G20 ℹ 11 Antelope Walk, Dorchester DT1 1BE, tel 01305 665700 🚉 Dorchester

DUNSTER

www.visitdunster.co.uk

Outstanding in an area known for the beauty of its villages, Dunster has a broad High Street, lined with cottages and former merchants' houses, which leads from the unusual 17th-century octagonal Yarn Market towards the entrance of Dunster Castle (mid-Mar to late Jul, Sep, Oct Fri–Wed 11–4.30; late Jul–early Sep Fri–Wed 11–5).

The castle has been the home of the Luttrell family for 600 years. Between 1868 and 1872 the architect Anthony Salvin attuned the castle for comfortable living, but retained the 17th-century plasterwork and oak staircase. St. George's Church, once both a Benedictine priory and parish church, is the largest in Exmoor and dates mainly from the 15th century.

✚ 457 E19 ℹ Exmoor National Park Centre, Dunster Steep TA24 6SE, tel 01643 821835

Above left *Sunrise from Cockern Tor near Two Bridges in Dartmoor National Park*
Above right *A view from Kingswear, up the River Dart and across to Dartmouth*

EDEN PROJECT

Unique in Britain, this is one of its most visited creations, examining our relationship with the natural world. Constructed in a disused china clay mine near St. Austell, the Eden Project is a 15ha (37-acre) floral and rainforest gateway into the world of plants. Two gigantic framed structures dubbed 'biomes' house a diverse range of wild and cultivated plants. A third structure, The Core, houses classrooms and exhibition space.

Each biome contains areas representing the vegetation of a number of countries: The humid tropics biome has plants and products from Amazonia, West Africa, Malaysia and Oceania; humidity and temperature are controlled to recreate rainforest conditions. A waterfall also cascades from high above the plants. The warm temperate biome focuses on Southern Africa, the Mediterranean and California, and has a magical array of Californian wild flowers. A fascinating video of the construction can be viewed in a small building next door. The grounds outside Eden make up the roofless biome—plants from Britain's own temperate climate, including native Cornish flora.

The story of the development of Eden is short but impressive. Conceived in 1994, it wasn't until May 1997 that the Millennium Commission granted the first £37.5 million. It took six months to clear the site of 1.8 million tonnes of soil. Future plans include a fourth biome known as The Edge, housing a desert landscape.

During the summer there are animated displays, performance artists, storytelling and workshops throughout the day.

INFORMATION

www.edenproject.com

✚ 456D21 ✉ Bodelva, St. Austell PL24 2SG ☎ 01726 811911 🕐 Late Mar–end Oct daily 10–6 (last admission 4.30); Nov–late Mar daily 10–4.30 (last admission 3) 💷 Adult £14, child (5–18) £5, family £35 🚇 St. Austell 🚌 Shuttle from St. Austell every 30–60 min

🍴 ☕ ♿

TIPS

» Come by bus or coach to avoid a long wait to get in.
» If you walk or cycle you get a £4 discount.

Below *Biomes, Eden Project, Mid Cornwall*

Left *The north side of Exeter Cathedral, Exeter*

EXETER
www.exeter.gov.uk
During World War II, Exeter was subject to a massive bombing raid that all but destroyed the historic town. It continues as a regional and shopping hub, although the city's core is a mixture of ancient buildings, such as the Guildhall in the High Street, scattered among bland postwar redevelopments.

The best-preserved streets include Southernhay, Stepcote Hill and the gracious close around the miraculously intact cathedral, considered the finest specimen of the decorated Gothic style in the country. It has the largest expanse of continuous vaulting in the world, as well as an ornate west facade and 13th-century misericords (carved benches). The old quayside area is lively with places to eat, bars and craft shops, and there are boat tours and walkways.

✚ 457 E20 🚹 Civic Centre, Dix's Field, Exeter EX1 1RQ, tel 01392 665700 🚇 Exeter St. Davids/Exeter Central

EXMOOR NATIONAL PARK
www.exmoor-nationalpark.gov.uk
High moors look out over rolling pastures and wooded river valleys to some of Britain's highest cliffs. The coast path makes the most of the views, but drives along the A39 and along lonely roads over the moor are exhilarating too. Virtually together are the resorts of Lynton, up on the hill,

and Lynmouth, down by the sea—the two are joined by a cliff railway; close by are the dramatic Valley of Rocks, with jagged outcrops and feral goats, and Watersmeet, where two rivers join in a wooded valley. Farther east, Selworthy has an array of thatched cottages, while inland Dunkery Beacon commands a colossal view over Exmoor, Devon and South Wales. The area around Malmsmead was immortalized in R.D. Blackmore's novel *Lorna Doone* (1869), based on a real Exmoor family of outlaws.

✚ 457 E19 🚹 Fore Street, Dulverton TA22 9EX, tel 01398 323841

FALMOUTH
www.acornishriver.co.uk
This port and resort faces the Fal estuary (also known as Carrick Roads), a vast natural harbour filled with boats of all sizes. Numerous pleasure craft ply the harbour and the River Fal to Truro. Guarding each side of the estuary are two perfect examples of 16th-century military architecture, built during the reign of Henry VIII (1491–1547): St. Mawes Castle (Jul–end Aug Sun–Fri 10–6; Apr–end Jun and Sep Sun–Fri 10–5; Oct daily 10–4; rest of year Fri–Mon 10–4), reached by ferry; and the larger Pendennis Castle (Jul–end Aug daily 10–6; Apr–end Jun and Sep daily 10–5; Apr–end Sep closes Sat at 4; Oct–end Mar, daily 10–4), on the town side. In Discovery Quay,

the National Maritime Museum Cornwall (daily 10–5) is Cornwall's prime attraction of its kind, chronicling the county's maritime heritage and showing 120 craft from the National Small Boat Collection.
✚ 456 C21 🚹 11 Market Strand, Prince of Wales Pier, Falmouth TR11 3DF, tel 01326 312300 🚇 Falmouth

FLEET AIR ARM MUSEUM
www.fleetairarm.com
Housed in a huge hangar, this major aviation museum tells the story of the men and women of the flying navy. Highlights include the chance to experience life aboard an aircraft carrier, and the interactive Leading Edge exhibition, with dramatic lighting and engine sounds. Or you can become a virtual pilot in the Lockheed Martin Merlin Experience. There is also the opportunity to climb inside a Concorde as the test flight craft is housed here. You'll be surprised at just how small it is.

Permanent displays include a wide collection of models, photographs, uniforms and equipment.
✚ 457 G19 ✉ RNAS Yeovilton, Ilchester BA22 8HT ☎ 01935 840565 🕐 Apr–end Oct daily 10–5.30; Nov–end Mar 10–4.30 (last admission 90 min before closing) 💷 Adult £10.50, child (5–16) £7.50, family £32 ▯ ▦

FOWEY
www.fowey.co.uk
Pronounced foy, this particularly appealing Cornish port rises steeply beside its estuarine harbour, with a jumble of narrow streets and crooked alleys peeking between rooftops to the water. The town stages a highly popular Regatta and Carnival week in mid-August, and there is a lively boating scene at the harbourside, with several choices of boat trips. The ferries extend the scope for walks: You can take the ferry to Polruan and walk along the wooded riverbank to Bodinnick, where another ferry brings you back to Fowey. In high season, the town

gets very busy so it's best to park at the top and walk down.

⊞ 456 D21 🔢 5 South Street, Fowey PL23 1AR, tel 01726 833616

GLASTONBURY

www.glastonburytic.co.uk

Modern Glastonbury retains a sense of the past; people of all faiths and New Age culture adherents congregate here. Many legends surround this town. One claims that King Arthur is buried in Glastonbury Abbey (Apr–end Sep daily 9.30–6; rest of year 10–4.30; opening times extended slightly in some months), which is on the site of a fourth-century monastery. Another legend claims that Joseph of Arimathea came here with the Holy Grail, and buried it in the Chalice Well. Glastonbury Tor offers spectacular views from the 15th-century tower on its summit.

The famous festival site is at the nearby village of Pilton.

⊞ 457 F19 🔢 9 High Street, Glastonbury BA6 9DP, tel 01458 832954

GLOUCESTER

www.gloucester.gov.uk

The jewel of Gloucester's compact historic heart is the cathedral (daily 7.30–6), housing the tomb of Edward II (1284–1327), magnificent medieval stained glass in its east window, and 14th-century fan vaulting in its cloisters—little wonder then that it was used for the filming of the first, second and sixth Harry Potter stories.

Cathedral Green is fringed by buildings from the 15th to 18th centuries and the transformed Victorian docks have shops, bars, restaurants and cafés in the preserved warehouses.

Among the city's museums is the National Waterways Museum (daily 10–5; last admission 4), which charts the story of Britain's waterways.

Take a trip along the historic canal within the docks aboard the *Queen Boadicea II*.

⊞ 457 G17 🔢 28 Southgate Street, Gloucester GL1 2DP, tel 01452 396572
🚉 Gloucester

HIDCOTE MANOR GARDEN

www.nationaltrust.org.uk

Hidcote, north of Chipping Campden, represents one of the great innovative garden designs, the creation of horticulturist Major Lawrence Johnston between 1907 and 1948. The gardens are made up of a series of structured outdoor 'rooms', each with its own character and separated by walls and hedges of copper and green beech, box, holly, hornbeam and yew. There are outstanding herbaceous borders, old roses and rare or unique plants and trees from all over the world.

The varied styles of the garden rooms peak at different times of year, making Hidcote impressive and colourful during any season. It can get overcrowded on public holidays and Sundays.

⊞ 458 H17 ✉ Hidcote Bartrim, near Chipping Campden GL55 6LR ☎ 01386 438333 🕐 Mid-Mar to end Jun, Sep Sat–Wed 10–6, Jul, Aug Fri–Wed 10–6; Oct Sat–Wed 10–5, last admission 1 hour before closing 💷 Adult £7.72, child (over 5) £3.86, family £19.27 🍴 🛍 ♿

ISLES OF SCILLY

www.simplyscilly.co.uk

Lying 28 miles (45km) off Land's End, this archipelago of 100 isles and islets (only five of which are inhabited) offers an idyllic retreat. Attractions are distinctly low-key: wild flowers, birdwatching, tiny villages, walking, boating, beaches, cycling and snorkelling.

St. Mary's, where the ferry and helicopter arrive from Penzance, is the biggest island, and has enough of interest to fill a day, with a concentration of prehistoric sites and a coastal path circling the island.

On car-free Tresco, the subtropical gardens of Tresco Abbey (daily 10–4), created by Augustus Smith are the major attraction.

The other inhabited Scillies are windswept Bryher, St. Agnes with its old lighthouse and St. Martin's—the latter with some of the best beaches in southwest England.

⊞ 456 C19 🔢 High Street, Hugh Town, St. Mary's TR21 0LL, tel 01720 422536

Above *A red-brick path and green hedges form just one of the small gardens at the National Trust Hidcote Manor Gardens, Hidcote Bartrim.*

KINGSTON LACY

www.nationaltrust.org.uk

For more than 300 years Kingston Lacy was the home of the Bankes family after they were ousted from Corfe Castle (▷ 129) by the Roundheads in the Civil War. The 17th-century house was designed by Sir Roger Pratt and radically altered during the 19th century by Sir Charles Barry, the architect of the Houses of Parliament. The lavish interior has intricate marble and woodcarving, paintings by Peter Paul Rubens, Anthony van Dyck and Peter Lely, and a Spanish Room with walls of gilded leather.

The park features shady walks, azaleas, camellias, formal lawns, a Victorian fernery and a sunken garden planted with hyacinths, begonias and heliotropes.

⊞ 458 G20 ✉ Wimborne BH21 4EA ☎ 01202 883402 🕐 House: Easter–end Oct Wed–Sun 11–4. Garden and park: Easter–end Oct daily 10.30–6; Nov–late Dec Fri–Sun 10.30–4; Feb to mid-Mar Sat–Sun 10.30–4 💷 Adult £10, child (5–16) £5, family £25. Park and garden only: adult £5, child £2.50, family £12.50 🍴 ♿

LACOCK ABBEY

www.nationaltrust.org.uk

Lacock Abbey was founded in 1232 and retains much of its medieval fabric, including the cloisters, sacristy and nuns' chapter house. After the Dissolution of the Monasteries in the mid-16th century, it became a family home, and later acquired an octagonal Tudor tower and brewery. Owned largely by the National Trust, the village of Lacock is mostly grey-stone houses and thatched cottages dating from medieval times to the 19th century. The Fox Talbot Museum commemorates abbey resident and photographer William Fox Talbot (1800–77), who invented the positive/negative process that eventually led to the development of modern photography.

✚ 457 G18 ✉ Lacock, near Chippenham SN15 2LG ☎ 01249 730459 ⊙ Mid-Mar to end Nov Wed–Mon 1–5.30 (closed Good Fri). Grounds and cloisters: Mar–end Nov daily 11–5.30 (closed Good Fri). Museum: mid-Feb to end Oct daily 11–5.30; Nov–21 Dec, Jan Sat–Sun 11–4 (closed Good Fri)

✋ Abbey, grounds, cloisters and museum: adult £9, child (5–16) £4.50, family £23.10. Museum, grounds and cloisters: adult £5.40, child £2.70, family £13.90. Abbey, grounds and cloisters: adult £7.20, child £3.60, family £18.50 🍴 🖥 🎫

LAND'S END

www.visitcornwall.com

Mainland Britain culminates in spectacular fashion at its south-west tip, with jagged granite cliffs plunging into the Atlantic. Land's End has been commercialized since Victorian days when Grace Thomas set up her First and Last House and sold refreshments to visitors. Today it has expanded to include restaurants, animal attractions, craft and gift shops and exhibitions. Once on the cliff path, however, you can soon leave the crowds behind. One of the most dramatically remote and rugged sections of the Cornish cliffs extends southeast to Porthcurno and Treen.

✚ 456 B21 🚉 Station Road, Penzance TR18 2NF, tel 01736 362207

LANHYDROCK HOUSE

www.nationaltrust.org.uk

Only the gatehouse, entrance porch and north wing remain of the original house, which was built in 1642 but nearly completely destroyed by a fire in 1881. It belonged to the Robartes family until 1953 when it was donated to the National Trust. Around 50 display rooms reflect the life of a wealthy Victorian household. This archetypal masters/servants life ranges from the state rooms and the children's nursery wing to the warren of kitchens, larders and sculleries below stairs. However, most people visit the house for the exceptional grounds, which are filled with magnolias, rhododendrons and camellias. Adjoining the house are the formal gardens with clipped yews and bronze urns.

✚ 456 D20 ✉ Lanhydrock, near Bodmin PL30 5AD ☎ 01208 265950 ⊙ House: Easter–end Sep Tue–Sun 11–5.30; Oct Tue–Sun 11–5. Gardens: daily 10–6 ✋ Adult £9, child (5–16) £4.50, family £22.50. Gardens and grounds: adult £5.10, child £2.55

LAUNCESTON

www.visitcornwall.com

Once a walled town (one gateway survives), a hub of straw hat-making and the capital of Cornwall, this small town clusters around a hilltop Norman castle (Apr–end Jun, Sep daily 10–5; Jul–end Aug daily 10–6; Oct daily 10–4), where you can climb to the top of the keep. Despite increasing decay over the centuries and a battering in the Civil War (▷ 34) (when it was taken by marauders four times), an impressive amount survives. Elsewhere in the town are pleasant Georgian and earlier facades, some of the finest can be found around Castle Street, where the Lawrence House Museum (Apr–end Sep Mon–Fri 10.30–4.30) records local history.
✚ 456 D20 ℹ Market House Arcade, Market Street, Launceston PL15 8EP, tel 01566 772321

THE LIZARD

www.visitcornwall.com

The Lizard peninsula stretches from Helston in the north to Lizard Point, the most southerly point of the British mainland. This is an area of contrasts, with rugged cliffs and open flat moorland on the west side, and softer verdant landscapes around the Helford River to the east. Especially attractive are the thatched waterside cottages at Cadgwith and Helford 16km (10 miles) northeast. Inland, the Goonhilly Earth Station (mid-Mar to end Jun, Sep daily 11–5; Jul, Aug daily 10–6; Oct–23 Dec daily 11–4) is the futuristic receiving station for satellite-relayed phone calls and has tours from its visitor centre. Kynance Cove is 3km (2 miles) north of Lizard Point. This white-sand beach is beneath cliffs of serpentine rock, so named because it resembles snake skin.
✚ 456 C21 ℹ 79 Customer Services Office, Isaac House, Tyacke Road, Helston TR13 8RR, tel 01209 614000

LONGLEAT

www.longleat.co.uk

Britain's first safari park lies beside a sumptuous Elizabethan mansion (completed 1580), with formal gardens and parkland landscaped by Capability Brown in the 18th century. The drive-through reserve gives an opportunity to encounter hundreds of exotic animals roaming free, including white tigers, lions and gorillas. You can drive your own car or take the safari bus. Visit the world's longest hedge maze (2.7km/ 1.7 miles) or take a trip on a safari boat on the huge lake. Among some of the treasures inside the house are hunting scenes by John Wootton and 17th-century Flemish tapestries.
✚ 457 G19 ✉ Near Warminster BA12 7NW ☎ 01985 844400 🕐 House: daily 11–3.30 except mid Feb, Easter daily 10–4.30; Apr–Oct Mon–Fri, 10–5, Sat, Sun and school holidays 10–5.30. Safari Park: mid Feb, Easter Mon–Fri 10–3.30, Sat, Sun and school holidays 10–4; Apr–Oct Mon–Fri 10–4, Sat, Sun and school holidays 10–5. Other attractions Apr–Oct daily 10–5. Timed tickets (house): guided tours only Oct–Easter 11–3 🖐 House: adult £10, child (3–14) £6. Safari park: adult £11, child £8; additional charges for some attractions. Passport ticket (all attractions and unlimited access): adult £22, child (3–14) £16 🍴 ♿ ⛪

LOST GARDENS OF HELIGAN

www.heligan.com

The largest garden reclamation project in Europe has revealed a series of magnificent gardens that fell into neglect in the years during and after World War I, as the estate gardeners were enlisted and Heligan became forgotten. Restoration began in 1990 when the new owners discovered

the old garden scheme buried within seemingly impenetrable thicket. It has now been restored to its fomer glory. The Jungle features giant Australian tree ferns, palms and bamboo; the Productive Gardens have more than 300 varieties of fruits and vegetables, including pineapples grown in specially heated glasshouses; the Pleasure Grounds reveal gardens of many countries, summerhouses and pools, and a crystal grotto; and the Lost Valley is an area of woodlands and wetlands.
✚ 456 D21 ✉ Pentewan, St. Austell PL26 6EN ☎ 01726 845100 🕐 Mar–end Oct daily 10–6 (last admission 4.30); rest of year daily 10–5, (last admission 3.30) 🖐 Adult £8.50, child (5–16) £5, family £23.50
🍴 ♿ ⛪

LULWORTH COVE

▷ 136.

LUNDY ISLAND

www.lundyisland.co.uk

Although two hours' journey on the MS *Oldenburg* from either Bideford or Ilfracombe, this remote island in the Bristol Channel is worth the trip. Measuring about 3 miles (5km) long and about 0.5 miles (1km) across, it has granite cliffs rising to 400ft (130m) and is the haunt of basking sharks, naturalized Asian sika deer, mountain goats and its very own Lundy ponies. The hub of island life is the Marisco Tavern, a very friendly pub that brews its own beer. Accommodation, ranging from a lighthouse to a 13th-century castle, is limited on Lundy although in great demand, and is run by the Landmark Trust.
✚ 456 D19 ℹ Lundy Shore Office, The Quay, Bideford EX39 2LY, tel 01271 863636

Left *Cliffs at Lands End*
Right *The Lost Gardens of Heligan are a must-see for any budding horticulturalist*

INFORMATION
www.weymouth.gov.uk
⊞ 457 G20 ⓘ The Esplanade,
Weymouth DT4 7AN, tel 01305 785747

TIPS
» To explore another part of the Army Ranges, start farther east from Tyneham (an abandoned village used for military exercises), and head out to the clifftops. To check public access times to the Lulworth Army Ranges ☎ 01929 404819 (extension 4819).
» Boat trips give dramatic views of the coastline.

LULWORTH COVE

On the Purbeck Heritage Coast between Swanage and Weymouth, Lulworth Cove is an oval bay with cross-sections of spectacularly folded rock strata. A 1.5km (1-mile) walk west along the well worn (and steep) track from the parking area leads to the natural limestone arch of Durdle Door, above a long, clean and (mostly) pebbly beach. Close to the west side of the Cove, the waves foam into Stair Hole, another natural sculpture. Here the earth's forces have lifted, twisted and folded the rock strata over 90 degrees. The cliffs present a risk of falling rocks, so take great care when walking beneath them; public notices warn of the dangers of climbing on the rocks.

PLANTS AND WILDLIFE
The wide range of habitats resulting from this geological diversity supports a variety of birdlife: kittiwakes, shags, cormorants and fulmars on the cliffs, along with buzzards, kestrels and occasional peregrines. Lulworth has its own butterfly, the Lulworth Skipper, first discovered in 1832. This small brown-and-black species is seen in July and August and is very rare outside Dorset. Among the variety of vibrant wild flowers found here are five rare species of orchid.

At Easter, most weekends, in August and at certain other times you are allowed into the Lulworth Army Ranges. This coastal strip extends east to Kimmeridge over some of the wildest scenery on the south coast. The presence of the army has saved this landscape from modern intrusions, and the area is a stronghold for plants such as Adonis blue, early spider orchid and wild camomile. Walking is tough going, with steep gradients and dizzying drops. You must keep to the paths at all times as there are unexploded munitions lying around. You can enter from the east side of Lulworth Cove through a gate.

Just below the cliffs are the remains of a fossil forest. Trees from the Jurassic period became submerged in a swamp, allowing algae to grow around them, and sediments trapped by the algae hardened into the round limestone 'burrs' seen today. To find out more about the area, visit the Rock Gallery which tells the story of Lulworth from 150 million years ago to the present day.

Above *Horse-shoe shaped Lulworth Cove forms part of an astounding coastline that is rich in geological oddities and strange natural geometry*

LYDFORD GORGE

www.nationaltrust.org.uk

Outside the village of Lydford and on the western edge of Dartmoor, this secretive wooded gorge stretches for 1.5 miles (2.5km). The path leading down to it passes the 90ft (30m) White Lady waterfall on its way through the deep ravine where the river has formed a series of potholes, including the thundering Devil's Cauldron. You'll need stout footwear as the paths are narrow and can be slippery. Lydford itself has a ruined castle, the 16th-century oak-timbered Castle Inn and the 15th-century Church of St. Petrock.
✚ 456 E20 ✉ The Stables, Lydford, Okehampton EX20 4BH ☎ 01822 820320 ◷ Easter–end Sep daily 10–5; Oct 10–4; rest of year, waterfall only, daily 11–3 ✋ Adult £4.85, child (5–16) £2.40 ▢ ▦

LYME REGIS

www.lymeregistourism.co.uk

On a coastline renowned for its Jurassic fossils—snail-like ammonites can even be seen embedded in garden walls—is this old port and sedate Regency seaside resort. It has a tangle of narrow streets, with galleries, cafés, craft and antiques shops, set above a gently shelving beach. The favourite place of Jane Austen (1775–1817), she set part of her novel *Persuasion* (1817) here. The snaking breakwater known as The Cobb was where a cloaked Meryl Streep stood in the British movie of *The French Lieutenant's Woman* (1981), based on John Fowles's novel of 1969.
✚ 457 F20 ℹ Guildhall Cottage, Church Street, Lyme Regis DT7 3BS, tel 01297 442138

MILTON ABBAS

www.ruraldorset.com

Milton Abbas has a single street with thatched white cottages set back from neatly trimmed grass verges. It was created between 1771 and 1790 by the owner of Milton Abbey, Joseph Damer, later Earl of Dorchester. He found that the village of Middleton spoiled the view from his house, so he demolished it, replaced it with an artificial lake and built this new model village for his tenants, out of sight. With the exception of the Abbey Church and Abbot's Hall, the ruined abbey buildings were removed to make way for a Gothic mansion set in parkland landscaped by Capability Brown.
✚ 457 G20 ℹ 1 Greyhound Yard, Blandford Forum DT11 7EB, tel 01258 454770

MORWENSTOW

www.visitcornwall.com

In 1834 the eccentric Celtic poet and cleric Reverend Robert Hawker (1803–75) arrived in this parish. He adorned the three chimneys on the vicarage: One is based on the towers of favourite churches; another on the tower of an Oxford college; and the kitchen chimney was a model of his mother's tomb. He was devoted to giving church burials to drowned sailors who had been washed ashore. The small driftwood hut on the cliffs was where he wrote his poetry.
✚ 456 D19 ℹ The Crescent, Bude EX23 8LE, tel 01288 354240

NETHER STOWEY

www.visitsomerset.co.uk

At the heart of this village at the foot of the Quantock Hills is the conservation area of Castle, St. Mary and Lime streets, with architecture dating from medieval times. In Lime Street you will come across Coleridge Cottage. Nether Stowey's most famous inhabitant, the poet Samuel Taylor Coleridge (1772–1834), lived here with his family from 1796 until 1800, while he wrote works including *Kubla Khan* (1797) and *The Rime of the Ancient Mariner* (1798). The cottage is owned by the National Trust, which has preserved the great poet's reading room, bedroom and various memorabilia.
✚ 457 F19 ℹ Bridgwater House, King Square, Bridgwater TA6 3AR, tel 01278 436438 ◷ Mon–Fri (closed public holidays)

Left *The Cobb, a long winding brickwork pier on the edge of Lyme Regis Harbour*
Below *Tregonwell Almshouses, Milton Abbas*

PADSTOW

www.visitcornwall.com

Overlooking the Camel Estuary, Padstow is the quintessential Cornish fishing port and well known for its seafood restaurants. Life revolves around the busy harbour (boat trips available), from which a tight maze of narrow streets and alleys leads off. A passenger ferry runs to Rock, where there are walks to Pentire Head, while on the Padstow side you can walk north to Stepper Point for views along the coast.

For cyclists, the Camel Trail is a scenic 17-mile (28km) traffic-free route along an old rail track partly following the estuary. Bicycles can be hired locally.

✚ 456 C20 ℹ Red Brick Building, North Quay, Padstow PL28 8AF, tel 01841 533449

PAINSWICK

www.painswick-pc.gov.uk
www.visitthecotswolds.org.uk

This little Cotswold-stone town slopes to the Painswick Brook, where several former textile mills can be seen. Ninety-nine 200-year-old yews clipped into arches and geometric shapes punctuate the almost surreal churchyard, along with an array of 17th- and 18th-century

tombstones in a range of shapes and styles—some hexagonal, others triangular or adorned with scrolls. On the edge of town, Painswick Rococo Garden (mid-Jan to end Oct) is a careful recreation of an exuberant 18th-century design using a painting by Thomas Robins in 1748.

✚ 457 G18 ℹ Subscription Rooms, Kendrick Street, Stroud GL5 1AE, tel 01453 760960

PLYMOUTH

www.visitplymouth.co.uk

The maritime past is writ large over this major naval port. Although badly damaged during World War II, it has managed to retain historic areas. Notable are the Barbican, on the west side of Sutton Harbour (including New Street), Prysten House and the grassy Hoe, where the lighthouse known as Smeaton's Tower looks over Plymouth Sound. It was from Plymouth in 1588 that the navigator Sir Francis Drake (c1540–96) sailed out to crush the Spanish Armada, though he did have time to finish his game of bowls first, or so the story goes. In 1620 a more peaceable crew, the Pilgrim Fathers, set off from Plymouth aboard the *Mayflower* to start a new life in North America.

The Plymouth *Mayflower* Museum (daily 10–4), in Barbican Quay, provides a vivid journey through Plymouth's past; opposite is the National Marine Aquarium (summer daily 10–6; rest of year daily 10–5), Britain's biggest and Europe's deepest aquarium, with stunning exhibits.

✚ 456 D21 ℹ Plymouth Mayflower, 3–5 The Barbican, Plymouth PL1 2LR, tel 01752 266030/306330 ▣ Plymouth

POLPERRO

www.visitcornwall.com

Perhaps the most engaging of Cornish fishing villages, Polperro has colour-washed houses set around a small harbour sheltered by two sea walls at the mouth of a steep valley. Craft shops, galleries, pubs and restaurants are in plentiful supply, although this is still a working fishing port.

Cars are banned from the narrow streets, and access is on foot—or by horse-drawn carriage—from the parking area above the main village, or you can walk in from Talland Bay, 1.5km (1 mile) east along the scenic coast path.

✚ 456 D21 ℹ The Guildhall, Fore Street, East Looe PL13 1AA, tel 01503 262072; ⊙ Easter–end Oct

PORT ISAAC

www.visitcornwall.com

A fishing village since medieval times, Port Isaac has clung to its Cornish character despite the steady flow of tourists. Narrow, twisting streets, fish cellars and 'drangs' (geranium-filled alleys) are particular features. The narrowest of all is Squeezebelly Alley. Boat trips are available at the harbour. The fishing fleet still sails at dawn and the day's catch will end up on the menus of many local restaurants, so it's worth visiting one of them.

✚ 4565 C20 🛈 Red Brick Building, North Quay, Padstow PL28 8AF, tel 01841 533449

POWDERHAM CASTLE

www.powderham.co.uk

This archetypal English castle is steeped in history, having belonged to the earls of Devon since 1391. Overlooking the Exe Estuary, it is set in fine natural parkland, grazed by a herd of deer, and also has a heronry and hosts jousting tournaments in the summer. The house, which was much modified during the 19th and 20th centuries, has a banqueting hall, music room and a chapel once a medieval barn. There's also a resident ghost—reportedly a grey lady haunting the area around the staircase.

✚ 457 E20 ✚ Kenton, Exeter EX6 8JQ ☎ 01626 890243 🕐 Mid-Mar to end Oct Sun–Fri 10–5.30, 45-min tours every 30–45 min; last tour 4.30 💷 Adult £8.50, child (5–14) £6.50, family £24 🍴 🛒 ♿

RESTORMEL CASTLE

www.englishheritage.org.uk

Norman castle sites are often reduced to a few grassy humps, but this is an exception, occupying a high mound defended by a deep moat, above the Fowey Valley. The considerable 12th- and 13th-century remains include the gate, keep, kitchens and private rooms, with the walls standing almost at their original height. The castle was a symbol of power and wealth and was once home to Edward the Black Prince (1330–76), heir to the English throne. It was abandoned long before the Civil War, but briefly held a Parliamentarian garrison before falling to the Royalists in 1644.

✚ 456 D20 ✉ Near Lostwithiel PL22 0BD ☎ 01208 872687 🕐 Easter–end Jun, Sep daily 10–5; Jul–end Aug daily 10–6; Oct daily 10–4 💷 Adult £2.40, child (5–16) £1.20 🍴 Snack kiosk ♿

SALISBURY

www.visitwiltshire.co.uk

England's tallest spire (123m/ 404ft) announces Salisbury Cathedral from miles around. Started in 1220 and completed in only 38 years, it is uniformly Early English (the first period of Gothic architecture before it evolved into Decorated and then Perpendicular styles). In the north aisle a dialless clock dates from 1386 and is probably the oldest mechanism in working order in the world. The miniature fan-vaulted roof in the grilled Audley Chantry is adorned with ancient roundels (decorative medallions), while the cloisters are the largest of any English cathedral. The library over the East Walk contains one of the four original copies of the Magna Carta—England's first bill of rights, imposed on King John by rebel barons in 1215 (▷ 31).

Outstanding in a city that is already well endowed with fine streets is Cathedral Close—England's largest—whose houses date from the 14th to 18th centuries. Among them is Mompesson House (mid-Mar to end Oct Sat–Wed 11–5), a fine example of Queen Anne-style architecture. Another house contains the Salisbury and South Wiltshire Museum (all year Mon–Sat 10–5; Jul–end Aug Sun 2–5), with archaeology galleries presenting the area's rich prehistoric heritage, including Stonehenge (▷ 143).

Alongside the impressive architecture are huge green swathes of parkland, where you can walk, take a picnic, play tennis and rent a rowing boat on the river, or listen to live music outdoors in summer. The spacious Market Square has a lively market on Tuesday and Saturday.

Old Sarum (Apr–end Jun and Sep daily 10–5; Jul–end Aug daily 9–6; Oct and Mar daily 10–4; rest of year daily 11–3), about 2 miles (3km) north of the city centre, is the dramatic remains of the settlement that preceded modern Salisbury. It was inhabited from the Iron Age until Norman times. Now deserted, it retains huge Iron Age earthworks, and the scant remains of a Norman palace, castle and cathedral.

✚ 458 H19 🛈 Fish Row, Salisbury SP1 1EJ, tel 01722 334956 🚉 Salisbury

Oppostie page *Boats crowd the harbour at Padstow on the Camel estuary*
Below *Salisbury Cathedral lit at night*

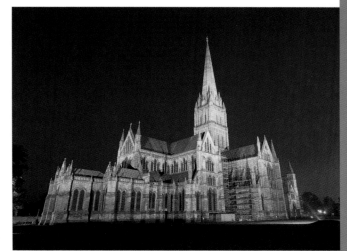

INFORMATION
www.visitcornwall.com

🕀 456 C21 🅸 The Guildhall, Street-an-Pol, St. Ives TR26 2DS, tel 01736 796297

🚉 St. Ives

TIP
» The town gets crowded. Use the park-and-ride at Trenwith, by the leisure centre (then a short bus ride or 10-minute walk downhill via steps); or park at Lelant Saltings Station, eight minutes by train.

ST. IVES

St. Ives is renowned for its modern art gallery, and arty fishing port brimming with character. Other highlights are excellent surfing and bathing beaches. St. Ives began life as a small fishing community that built its wealth on pilchards. During the 20th century, tourism, surfing and the town's reputation as a centre of art made it a magnet for holidaymakers. The hub of the old fishing quarter is Downlong, a maze of tiny stepped streets and alleys with names like Salubrious Place and Teetotal Street.

Mediterranean light qualities and the magnificent coastal scenery have attracted painters and sculptors to St. Ives since the 1880s, including the potter Bernard Leach (1887–1979), the painter Ben Nicholson (1894–1982) and his sculptor wife Dame Barbara Hepworth (1903–75). Her studio and house in Barnoon Hill is now the Barbara Hepworth Museum and Sculpture Gallery (Mar–end Oct daily 10–5.20; rest of year Tue–Sun 10–4.20), where everything is much as she left it when she died.

Housed in a stylish, modern building with views out to sea, the Tate St. Ives gallery (Mar–end Oct daily 10–5.20; rest of year Tue–Sun 10–4.20) has an international reputation due to the work of the St. Ives School. The curved atrium allows light to flood into the gallery, which has innovative and sometimes controversial exhibitions of modern art to rival its namesakes in London (▷ 89).

The Penwith Gallery (Tue–Sat 10–1, 2.30–4.30) and St. Ives Society of Artists Gallery (Mar–early Jan Mon–Sat 10–5.30, Aug Sun 2.30–5.30) showcase good local art. An arts festival in September offers a music and literature, while shopping tends naturally towards art, clothes (lots of surfing gear) and gift shops.

The Penwith peninsula has cliff scenery, old tin mines and prehistoric sites, while Iron Age Chysauster Ancient Village (5 miles/ 8km southwest) has the oldest identifiable village street in Britain.

Opposite *The sweeping sands of St. Ives Bay, Lands End Peninsula, Cornwall*

ST. JUST-IN-ROSELAND

www.visitcornwall.com

This heavily restored church sits tranquilly by the Fal Estuary, but it is the churchyard rather than the building that draws thousands of visitors each year. It slopes down from the lychgate and is a riot of subtropical and flowering shrubs alongside indigenous broad-leafed species. In the early 20th century, the Reverend Humfrey Davis endowed its many paths with granite steps, each carved with words of wisdom—'God is Love', 'O sweet St. Just in Roseland, thy name forever dear'—some from the scriptures or hymns, others that he devised himself.

✚ 456 C21 ℹ Millennium Rooms, The Square, St. Mawes TR2 5AG, tel 01326 270440

ST. MICHAEL'S MOUNT

www.nationaltrust.org.uk

The great granite crag of St. Michael's Mount rises dramatically out of Mounts Bay near Penzance. It mirrors Mont St-Michel in Normandy, as French monks arrived here in the 11th century and established a priory. Over the centuries it was a castle, and then a private house, owned by the St. Aubyn family since 1660. The warren of rooms leads up to the 14th-century church at the highest point, for sweeping views towards Land's End (▷ 134) and the Lizard peninsula (▷ 135).

The mount is connected to the mainland by a causeway that appears at low tide; at other times take the little ferry.

St. Michael's Mount is also the legendary home of the giant Cormoran, who was killed by Kack the Giant Killer.

✚ 456 C21 ✉ Marazion, near Penzance TR17 0EF ☎ 01736 710265 ⏰ Easter–end Jun, Sep, Oct Sun–Fri 10.30–5; Jul–end Aug Sun–Fri 10.30–5.30, last admission 45 mins before closing. Private gardens: Apr, May Mon–Fri; Jul–end Oct Thu–Fri ✋ Mon–Fri (except gardens); adult £6.60, child (5–16) £3.30, family £16.50. Ferry: adult £1.50, child (under 15) £1 🍽 🖥 🖼 Easter–end Oct ❓ Phone ahead in bad weather to check ferry is operating

SLIMBRIDGE

www.wwt.org.uk

The Wildfowl and Wetlands Trust —the inspiration of the English artist and naturalist Sir Peter Scott (1909–89)—was established on the saltmarshes at Slimbridge in 1946.

Equipped with an observation tower and state-of-the art visitor centre, Slimbridge is the winter home of species such as white-fronted geese and Bewick's swans that migrate every year from Siberia—they pair for life and some pairs have been coming here for over 20 years.

The reserve is home to the largest and most varied collection of wildfowl in the world, including rare and endangered swans, geese, ducks and pink flamingos.

✚ 457 G18 ✉ Slimbridge GL2 7BT ☎ 01453 890333 ⏰ Apr–end Oct daily 9.30–5.30; rest of year daily 9.30–5 ✋ Adult £7.22, child (4–16) £3.95, family £20.11 🖥 🖼

SNOWSHILL MANOR

www.nationaltrust.org.uk

From the outside, Snowshill Manor appears to be a traditional Tudor manor house, built of golden yellow Cotswold stone, set in walled gardens. Within it reveals the hand of the eccentric sugar plantation owner and architect Charles Paget Wade, who acquired the house in 1919 and gave it to the National Trust in 1951. His fascination with craftsmanship extended to collecting a vast range of seemingly unrelated objects such as bicycles, clocks, toys, Japanese samurai armour and such curios as a Georgian iron-toothed man trap. His living quarters, in the smaller cottage on the far side of the garden, were equipped in an equally inventive manner.

✚ 457 H17 ✉ Snowshill, Broadway WR12 7JU ☎ 01386 852410 ⏰ House: Easter–end Oct Wed–Sun 12–5. Garden: Easter–end Oct Wed–Sun 11–5.30. Shop and restaurant: Easter–end Oct Wed–Sun 11–5.30; Nov–early Dec Sat–Sun 12–4 ✋ Adult £7.30, child (5–16) £3.70, family £18.60. Garden, shop and restaurant: adult £4, child £2, family £10 ❓ Entrance to manor by timed ticket only (every 10 min) at busy times 🍽 🖼

STONEHENGE

▷ 143.

Below St. Michael's Mount

STOURHEAD

www.nationaltrust.org.uk

The estate surrounds a Palladian-style mansion built between 1721 and 1725 by the Scottish architect Colen Campbell (1679–1726). It is crammed with treasures that include the Regency library, paintings by Canaletto (1697–1768) and Sir Joshua Reynolds (1723–92), and furniture designed by Thomas Chippendale (1718–79).

Henry Hoare II, son of a wealthy banker, laid out pleasure gardens between 1741 and 1780, inspired by his tour of Europe. They are a stunning attraction in their own right and feature the Pantheon and Temple of Apollo, a grotto, and a temple to Flora, all set around a central lake.

There are beautiful walks on the estate, especially to King Alfred's Tower, a triangular folly made of red brick, from where there are great views.

✚ 457 G19 ✉ Stourton, Warminster BA12 6QD ☎ 01747 841152 Ⓒ Garden: daily 9–7 (or dusk, last admission 30 min before closing). House: Easter–end Oct Fri–Tue 11.30–4.30 (or dusk), (last admission 4). Tower: Easter–end Oct daily 11.30–4.30 ✋ Garden and house: adult £10.50, child (5–16) £5.20, family £25. Garden or house: adult £6.30, child £3.40, family £15. Tower: adult £2.20, child £1.40, family £5.40 🍴 ☕ 🏧

TINTAGEL CASTLE

www.englishheritage.org.uk

Fact mingles with legend at this spectacularly sited 13th-century clifftop ruin. The site has attracted competing claims for its origins: an Iron Age enclosure, a Celtic monastery, a Roman signal station and (perhaps spuriously) as the court of King Arthur. Legend has it that Arthur was born here in the late 5th century to Queen Igraine.

Access is up a long, steep flight of steps. Cars must be left at the village of Tintagel next to the castle, where the National Trust maintains a small 14th-century manor house known as the Old Post Office (Easter–end Sep daily 11–5.30; Oct daily 11–4), whose central hall rises the full height of the building.

✚ 456 D20 ✉ Tintagel PL34 0HE ☎ 01840 770328 Ⓒ Easter–end Sep daily 10–6; Oct daily 10–5; Nov–Easter daily 10–4. Closed 24–26 Dec, 1 Jan and on other occasions, especially due to severe weather conditions ✋ Adult £4.50, child (5–15) £2.30 🏧

TORQUAY

www.englishriviera.co.uk

Torquay is the major town of the English Riviera. It is part of an area known as Torbay, which also includes Paignton and Brixham (▷ 126). Its almost balmy climate and safe beaches make it the country's second most visited seaside resort after Blackpool (▷ 304).

One feature of the town is its well-kept municipal parks. The Rock Walk, also known as Royal Terrace Gardens, features exotic shrubs and trees, and it is enchantingly lit at night.

Bygones Lifesize Victorian Street (Nov–end Mar daily 10–5; Apr, Jun, Sep, Oct daily 10–6; Jul, Aug Fri–Tue 10–6, Wed, Thu 10–9.30), in St. Mary-church, is a recreation of a Victorian shopping street giving a flavour of a bygone age.

On the east side of town, Kent's Cavern (Mar–end Jun and Sep–end Oct daily 10–4; Jul–end Aug daily 10–4.30; Nov–end Feb daily 10–3.30) reveals evidence of Palaeolithic inhabitants.

The Model Village (daily from 10; for closing and illumination times tel: 01803 315315), near the cliff railway leading to Babbacombe Beach, is a masterpiece of miniature landscape gardening.

✚ 457 E20 ℹ Vaughan Parade, Torquay TQ2 5JG, tel 09066 801268 🚆 Torquay

TOTNES

www.totnesinformation.co.uk

Totnes has a pervasive sense of the past. On a mound above the River Dart are the Norman remains of Totnes Castle (Apr–end Jun and Sep daily 10–5; Jul–end Aug daily 10–6; Oct daily 10–4), while in the town's compact centre are 15th-century St. Mary's Church and the fine 16th-century Guildhall. The Butterwalk hosts a costumed Elizabethan charity market on Tuesday in summer and a general market on Friday and Saturday. In Fore Street, the Elizabethan Museum (Easter–end Oct Mon–Fri 10.30–5) features displays on local history.

Take the 12-mile (20km) trip along the River Dart to Dartmouth (▷ 130), or the steam-train ride on the South Devon Railway to Buckfastleigh (▷ 128).

✚ 457E20 ℹ The Town Mill, Coronation Road, Totnes TQ9 5DF, tel 01803 863168 🚆 Totnes

STONEHENGE

This immensely significant site, Europe's most famous prehistoric wonder, stands at the core of a ceremonial landscape containing 450 protected ancient monuments of national importance. Stonehenge retains a powerful atmosphere of mystery and awe because very little is known about the site. Was it a temple or a huge astronomical calendar? Why did people build it and how was this great engineering feat achieved?

What you see are the remains of a sequence of monuments erected in three phases between around 3050BC to around 1600BC. The outer circular bank and ditch are the oldest parts, probably constructed over 5,000 years ago. About 475 years later a double circle of 80 bluestones (so called because of their natural colour) was erected. These stones weighed up to four tonnes each and were brought more than 200 miles (320km) from the Preseli Hills in southwest Wales (▷ 236). It is believed that they were floated on rafts across the Bristol Channel, then dragged over tracks of logs.

In 1650BC the bluestones were taken down and two rings of sarsen stones, brought from the nearby Marlborough Downs, were erected as an outer ring of standing stones, with lintels across the top of them, and an inner horseshoe of five pairs of uprights with lintels. Later still, some of the bluestones were lined up between the two rings of sarsens and in an inner horseshoe.

The largest bluestone—the so-called Altar Stone—was set at the mid point, where it still lies. The Altar Stone draws the eye towards the Heelstone, over the peak of which the sun rises on 21 June, the longest day of the year. This occurrence has led many to believe that the site had a connection with sun worship, and there are many visitors around this time.

English Heritage has for many years been investigating ways to improve facilities and restore a degree of calm around the stones, plagued by the proximity of the busy A303. Thwarted by lack of government funding for road works, that project is on hold, but meantime new excavations have been under way, with findings soon to be published.

INFORMATION

www.english-heritage.org.uk

✚ 458 H19 ✉ Stonehenge, SP4 7DE

☎ 0870 333 1181 🕐 Mid-Mar to end May daily 9.30–6; Jun–end Aug 9–7; Sep to mid-Oct 9.30–6; mid-Oct to mid-Mar 9.30–4; closed 24–26 Dec 🚻 Adult £6.30, child (5–15) £3.20, family £15.80 ❓ Admission includes audio tour 🔲 🏛

Above *The mystical stone circle of Stonehenge, erected between 3000 and 1600BC, Wiltshire, England now a World Heritage Site*
Opposite *An archway at Tintagel Castle, North Cornwall*

TRELISSICK GARDEN

www.nationaltrust.org.uk

Endowed with panoramic views along the Fal Estuary, Trelissick is a garden and extensive woodland park with walks that are accessible all year. At the heart of the estate is the garden, where tender and exotic plants thrive in the sheltered conditions. The magnolias, camellias and rhododendrons produce magnificent spring blossoms, and there are more than 100 species of hydrangea. There is also a walled garden with fig trees and climbers, a shrub garden and the Cornish Apple Orchard.

Try to time your visit to see one of the musical or theatrical events that are occasionally staged here.
✚ 456 C21 ✉ Feock, Truro TR3 6QL
☎ 01872 862090 ❸ Feb–end Oct daily 10.30–5.30 (or dusk); rest of year daily 11–4
✋ Adult £6.60, child (5–16) £3.30, family £16.50 🍴 ☐ 🏛

TRURO

www.visitcornwall.com

Tin and copper mining made Truro prosperous in the 18th and 19th centuries, and evidence of that heyday survives in Lemon Street, with its Georgian houses of Bath stone, and in the elegantly curved Walsingham Place. Truro's triple-spired cathedral—the first to be erected on a new site since Salisbury Cathedral in 1220—was built between 1880 and 1910 to the design of John Pearson, who showed ingenuity in creating a soaring structure within the cramped site of the former parish church. In River Street, the Royal Cornwall Museum (Mon–Sat 10–5) chronicles the county's history, and displays portraits by the 18th-century Cornish artist John Opie.
✚ 456 C21 ℹ Boscawen Street, Truro TR1 2NE, tel 01872 274555 🚉 Truro

TYNTESFIELD HOUSE

www.nationaltrust.org.uk

For an insider's view of the conservation work that restores and maintains Britain's stately homes, visit Tyntesfield House, near Bristol. The house was built for a wealthy merchant, William Gibbs, in 1864, and remained in the Gibbs family until 2002, when it was acquired by the National Trust. Although the Victorian interiors survive intact, an extensive, costly and fascinating programme of restoration is under way. The house itself is an arresting Gothic Revival masterpiece, with pinnacles, turrets and a sumptuous chapel that has few peers in Britain. Tours are by timed ticket only, and there is limited parking on the site; it's best to use the bus service from Nailsea or Bristol.
✚ 457 G18 ✉ Wraxall, North Somerset BS48 1NT ☎ 0870 458 4500 (information); 0844 800 4986 (bookings) ❸ Mid-Mar to end Oct Sat–Wed 11–5 ✋ Adult £9.45, child (5–16) £4.75, family £23.65 ☐

WELLS

www.visitsomerset.co.uk

The limestone city of Wells, stood beneath the southern slopes of the Mendip Hills, displays the unspoiled perfection of an entire range of ecclesiastical buildings set around a green at the top of the main street. Relatively small crowds make the city a prime base for exploring Somerset's sights, such as Cheddar Gorge (▷ 128), Exmoor (▷ 132) and Bath (▷ 122–125).

The glories of the cathedral begin with its extraordinarily ornate west front (mid-13th century) adorned with more than 400 separate statues, originally in vivid hues and gold. The severe Early English nave is dominated by two unique curving scissor arches, boldly crossing it and interrupting the view. These were added in the 14th century to strengthen the base of the sinking central tower. Leading off the north transept is a well-worn flight of stone steps to the impressive octagonal chapterhouse.

Next to the cathedral, the 13th-century Bishop's Palace (Apr–end Oct daily 10.30–5.30, last admission 5) is still the private residence of the Bishop of Bath and Wells and has imposing state rooms. Surr-ounded by a moat with swans and set in landscaped gardens (which include the ruins of the Great Hall), it is entered by the drawbridge and gatehouse.

The 14th-century Vicar's Close, said to be the oldest complete medieval street in Europe, now accommodates staff of the cathedral and school; the fine 14th-century Astronomical Clock in the north transept has mounted knights emerging on the hour.

Other attractions are comparatively low key, with everything within a few minutes' walk. Close to the cathedral is the marketplace (market Wednesday and Saturday), and the Wells and Mendip Museum (Easter–end Oct daily 11–5; rest of year Wed–Mon 11–4), in a Tudor building, records the area's history.
✚ 457 G19 ℹ Town Hall, Market Place, Wells BA5 2RB, tel 01749 672552

WESTBURY WHITE HORSE

www.visitwiltshire.co.uk

This huge, ungainly depiction of a horse carved on a chalk hillside is the oldest of its kind in Wiltshire. The original Saxon horse—said to have commemorated King Alfred's victory over the Danes at the Battle of Ethandun (Edington) in AD878—was remodelled in 1778 and altered from cart breed to blood breed by a presumptuous Mr. Gee. At the top of the hill is Bratton Castle, a large prehistoric earthwork with a long barrow. Superb views extend far across Wiltshire and Somerset.

⊞ 457 G19 🛈 Central Car Park, Warminster BA12 9BT, tel 01985 218548

WESTONBIRT ARBORETUM

www.forestry.gov.uk/westonbirt

Worth visiting at any time of year but especially magnificent in autumn, this is among the largest and most diverse collections of trees and shrubs in Europe. The 18,000 trees, set in 240ha (600 acres) of landscaped, wooded grounds criss-crossed with trails (many suitable for visitors in wheelchairs), were planted from 1829 to the present day and come from all over the world. There is a visitor office with an exhibition and video. Various events are held throughout the year, from concerts to open-air plays in summer to autumn.

⊞ 457 G18 ✉ Near Tetbury GL8 8QS
☎ 01666 880220 🕐 Mon–Fri 9–8 (or dusk if earlier), Sat, Sun 8–8 (or dusk if earlier); Dec–end Mar closes at dusk or 5pm 🖐 Oct–end Nov: adult £8, child (under 18) £2; Mar–end Sep: adult £7, child £2; Jan–end Feb: adult £5, child £2 🖵 🏧

WEYMOUTH

www.weymouth.gov.uk

Once King George III (1738–1820) began visiting this Dorset seaside town in 1789, it soon became a fashionable holiday place. Much of the original character of the town has been retained in its Georgian facades, ironwork balconies and bow windows that characterize the wide Esplanade.

The long arc of golden sand, which offers safe bathing in the sheltered bay, hosts numerous traditional attractions such as Punch and Judy puppet shows. The harbour is a starting point for boat trips and ferries to the Channel Islands, and is overlooked by Brewers Quay, a brewery converted into courtyards and cobbled alleys with attractions and specialist shops. In Barrack Road, Nothe Fort (May–end Sep daily 10.30–5.30; rest of year Sun and public holidays 11–5.30) is a huge Victorian fort with coastal views and 70 rooms to explore.

A 15-minute walk (or a train ride from the Esplanade) east along the seafront leads to Lodmoor Country Park (open at all times). These 142ha (350 acres) of parkland include an RSPB (Royal Society for the Protection of Birds) nature reserve and the popular Sea Life aquarium (daily from 10, closing time varies throughout the year).

⊞ 457 G20 ✉ The Esplanade, Weymouth DT4 7AN, tel 01305 785747 🚉 Weymouth

Opposite *Gardens at Tyntesfield House*
Below *The Westbury White Horse on Salisbury Plain is one of several chalk horses on the Wiltshire hillside*

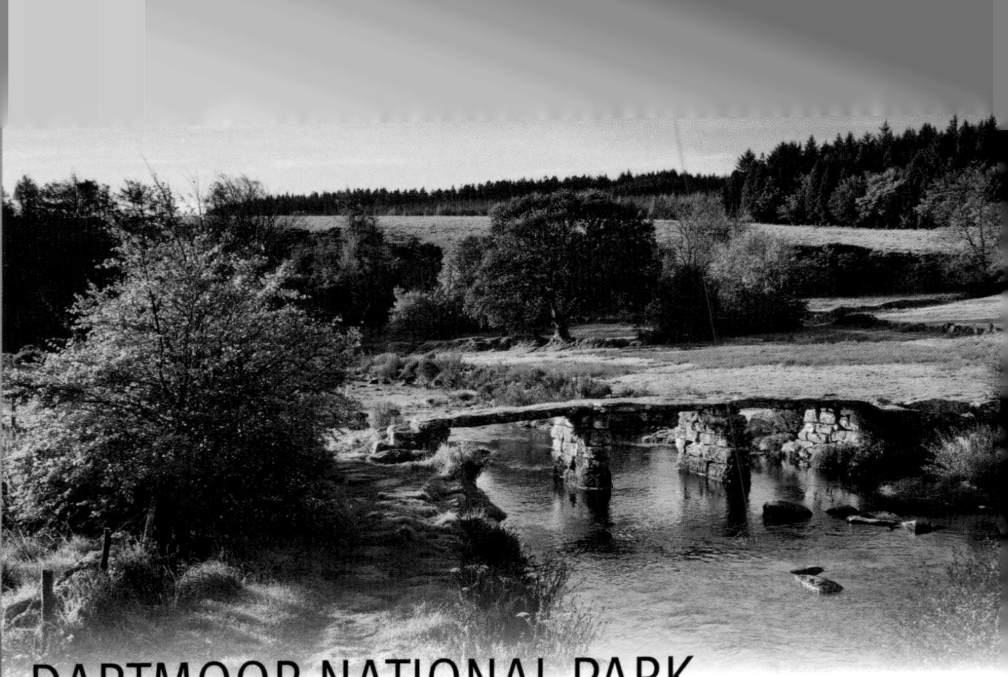

DARTMOOR NATIONAL PARK

Winding, narrow roads traverse valleys where ponies, cattle and sheep roam free. Dartmoor (▷ 130) is a diverse area of wilderness, with rugged hills and moorland carpeted with colourful heather, tempered by wooded river valleys and ancient villages.

THE DRIVE

Distance: 65 miles (105km)
Allow: 3–4 hours, plus time for wandering
Start/end: Tavistock

★ Leave Tavistock on the B3357 that heads eastwards to the moors and climbs on to Dartmoor.

❶ You'll soon see Vixen Tor away to the right; this is the largest of Dartmoor's many tors—outcrops of weathered granite.

Soon after you come to the crossroads at Two Bridges. Turn left and shortly left again to follow the B3212 to continue northeast (signposted Moretonhampstead).

❷ On the way you pass through Postbridge, where the largest and best-preserved of Dartmoor's clapper bridges—planks or stone slabs laid across stones—crosses the East Dart River. The bridge has been used by tin miners and farmers since medieval times.

The next right turning (towards Widecombe in the Moor) is a diversion to Grimspound, a 3,000-year-old Bronze Age settlement. To reach it follow the lane for 1 mile (1.5km) and park at the steps on the left by a bend in the road.

❸ Grimspound consists of the faint, circular outlines of 24 huts, which probably had roofs of timber and turf.

❹ Farther along the B3212 is the Miniature Pony Centre (mid-Mar to end Oct daily 10.30–4.30).

Continue on the B3212 to Moretonhampstead.

❺ A series of fires in the 19th century destroyed many of Moretonhampstead's buildings, but a fine row of 17th-century almshouses survives in Cross Street.

❻ The architect Sir Edwin Lutyens' early 20th-century Arts and Crafts masterpiece Castle Drogo is just to the north.

At Moretonhampstead turn right on the A382 (signposted Bovey Tracey). Turn right on to the B3387 for Haytor Vale and the descent to Widecombe in the Moor.

❼ Widecombe in the Moor is a candidate for the most popular Dartmoor village, set neatly in a hollow among granite ridges. The roof of the surprisingly grand late 14th-century church—'the cathedral on the moor'—has a whimsical set of bosses featuring a pelican, a scapegoat and three interlocking rabbits forming the special sign of the tin miners—who paid for the majestic church tower.

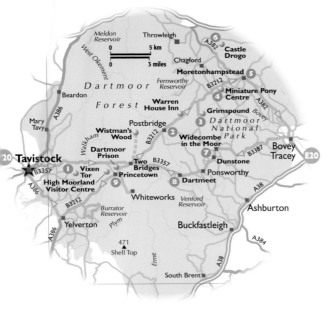

From Widecombe follow tiny winding lanes to Dunstone and to Ponsworthy. The road climbs to Dartmeet, where the East and West Dart rivers converge near another old clapper bridge.

8 The area around Dartmeet is lush and green, and only a few minutes' strolling is needed to escape the bustle of this very popular place.

From Dartmeet continue on the B3357 back to Two Bridges, but this time head southwest to Princetown.

9 At 427m (1,400ft) above sea level, Princetown is one of England's highest villages. It is also among the bleakest, inhabited mostly by staff of the high-security Dartmoor Prison, a grey edifice built originally for prisoners of the Napoleonic Wars (1800–15). The village is also home to the High Moorland Visitor Centre. South of the village, a dead-end road to Whiteworks reaches perhaps the loneliest settlement in Dartmoor,

a row of cottages looking out over empty moor.

From Princetown continue west on the B3212, from which you can divert to Burrator Reservoir. Carry on along the B3212 to Yelverton and the A386, which returns you to Tavistock.

WHERE TO EAT
Warren House Inn, in a high position with excellent views over the moor (1 mile/1.6km) east of Postbridge on the B3212 (tel: 01822 880208), serves sandwiches, hot meals and cream teas. Badger's Holt at Dartmeet (tel: 01364 631213) is a picturesque restaurant and gift shop.

PLACES TO VISIT
CASTLE DROGO
✉ Moretonhampstead EX6 6PB
☎ 01647 433306
🕐 Late Mar to early Nov Wed–Mon
💷 Adult £7.09, child £3.54, family £17.72. Gardens only: adult £4.54, child £2.50

HIGH MOORLAND VISITOR CENTRE
✉ Princetown PL20 6QF
☎ 01822 890414
🕐 Easter–end Oct daily 10–5; Nov–Easter daily 10–4

WHEN TO GO
Dartmoor is a delight on clear days but beware the moorland mists.

Opposite *Clapper Bridge, Dartmoor National Park.*
Below left and right *Rock formations on Dartmoor National Park*

HAYTOR

Haytor is one of the most prominent of all Dartmoor's many tors, or granite outcroppings. A magnificent viewpoint in itself, it is also surrounded by disused quarries, where the trackbeds of long-vanished tramways make useful routes for walkers.

THE WALK

Length: 4 miles (6.5km) or 5 miles (8km) including Saddle Tor
Allow: 2.5–3 hours
Start/end: Parking area at Haytor map ref 429 E20
OS Landranger map: 191
OS Explorer map: OL28

★ This walk over western Dartmoor is one of the most accessible sections of the open moor.

Leave the parking area and cross the road to take the wide grassy path up to the rocky summit of Haytor. You can also climb to the top of the tor by a flight of steps carved into the rock; walk around the left side of the rock mass.

❶ The view ahead shows the prominent Hound Tor, slightly to the left, with Greator Rocks to its right. Straight ahead is Haytor Down, and beyond is the wooded valley of the River Bovey. To the northeast (right) are the remains of Haytor Quarry.

Continue around the rock mass and take the first path to the right of the quarry. Walk towards the perimeter fence of the quarry and join a track on the right. The route skirts the right-hand edge of the quarry. Beyond the quarry, bear left to follow the granite tramway. You pass the entrance to the quarry, and then the tramway bears right over a stone embankment to reach a T-junction. Turn left and continue to follow the tramway, bearing to the left. You will eventually see Smallacombe Rocks on the right. Take any of the paths that lead off to the right across the open moor towards these rocks.

❷ Smallacombe Rocks gives an extensive view of the surrounding moor. You can extend the walk northeast from here, via a demanding route heading down the valley to the east and up to the summit of Hound Tor, named after a hound who, according to legend, was turned to stone for disturbing a witches' coven. Beneath this tor are the excavated remains of a medieval village, where you can see the layout of several houses, complete with fireplaces.

Turn around to face Haytor, and locate a quarry behind Holwell Tor farther down the slope and to the right. Take the path leading from Smallacombe Rocks to the point just to the left of this quarry. This leads back to the tramway. Turn right along the tramway, walking past a ruined building and the quarry itself. Continue around the back of the quarry and cross over the remains of a bridge (the path is narrow and not particularly well defined, so you will need to clamber over a few rocks). After crossing the bridge, bear left up to the top of Holwell Tor. From Holwell Tor walk directly across the moor on a narrow and ill-defined path that heads to Low Man, a cliff to the right of Haytor. At Haytor, re-trace your steps to the parking area.

❸ From the top of Holwell Tor you can extend the walk by continuing southwards across the moor to Saddle Tor, where you turn left across the low and wide ridge leading back to Haytor. This extension gives far-ranging views.

TIPS
» Be aware that Dartmoor can be a disorienting place, and paths shown on OS (Ordnance Survey) maps are not necessarily visible on the ground.
» This route relies on landmarks for navigation, so it should not be attempted in poor visibility. A compass may be useful in case of mist.
» The walk can be extended in various directions, but for walks across the open moor you will need a good map and a compass.

WHERE TO EAT
There's usually an ice-cream van in the parking area, otherwise drive to Widecombe in the Moor (about 2 miles/3.5km off the route) for cafés and a pub.

PLACE TO VISIT
GRIMSPOUND
✉ Challacombe, Moretonhampstead, Dartmoor (6 miles (9.6km) southwest of Moretonhampstead of the B3212)
🎫 Free (English Heritage)

WHEN TO GO
It is advisable to choose a clear, dry day for walking on the moor; you will also see the views at their best.

Opposite *Haytor, Dartmoor National Park*
Above *Bluebells blanket Dartmoor in spring*

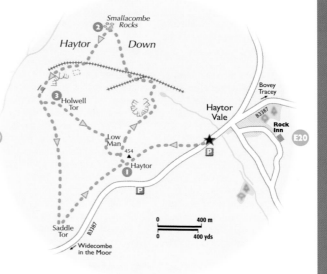

EXMOOR NATIONAL PARK

Starting from the pleasant resort of Lynton, this tour of Exmoor (▷ 132) follows the scenic A39 coast road before heading inland to the heart of Somerset.

THE DRIVE

Distance: 65 miles (105km)
Allow: 3 hours plus stops
Start/end: Town Hall, Lee Road, Lynton EX35 6BT, tel: 01598 752225

★ Leave Lynton town hall and follow signs for the Valley of Rocks, to the west of town.

❶ This beautiful moorland valley strongly appealed to the 18th- and 19th-century Romantic poets— William Wordsworth (1770–1850), Samuel Taylor Coleridge (1772–1834) and Robert Southey (1774–1843).The Valley of the Rocks runs parallel to the sea and has rock formations jutting out of its slopes. The finest view is from Castle Rock, which drops 120m (400ft) to the sea but can be climbed easily from its landward side. There is a picnic area to the left of the entrance to the valley.

From the valley entrance the road passes the Lee Valley estate and continues past the Lee Abbey

Christian Community. It then climbs steeply. At the next fork bear right (signposted Woody Bay). Pass the Woody Bay Hotel and then, at a T-junction, turn right and just past a telephone box fork right downhill, signed Hunter's Inn.

❷ Make a detour to visit Trentishoe, where the tiny church has an unusual musicians' gallery. Note the notch cut out of the railings to allow the movement of the double bass player's bow. Hunter's Inn is a starting point for walks along the Heddon Valley to the sea at Heddon's Mouth, where there are remains of a small port, including the ruins of a lime kiln; fertilizer was shipped to Wales from here.

Bear left towards Killington, and turn right on the A39 towards Barnstaple. At Parracombe, leave the A39 and branch right through the village.

❸ Parracombe Old Church (open, but no longer in use) is a remarkable specimen of medieval architecture.

It is essentially unrestored, and narrowly escaped demolition in the 19th century thanks to a spirited campaign led by the author and art critic John Ruskin in 1879. It has box pews, a simple screen, a flagstone floor and an ancient roof, but no stained glass or organ.

Return to the A39 to Blackmoor Gate and turn left on the A339 towards South Molton.

Detour to visit Arlington Court by turning right, then left towards Barnstaple. After 3 miles (5km) turn left, signposted Arlington Court.

❹ Arlington Court is an early 19th-century house crammed with eclectic bits and pieces gathered by Rosalie Chichester (step-aunt of yachtsman Sir Francis Chichester) up to her death in 1949. There are model ships, tapestries, stuffed birds, paperweights and other unrelated items. From May to the end of August you can also watch, via CCTV, the largest colony of lesser horseshoe bats in Devon. The stable block has a collection of 19th-century horse-drawn vehicles, some of which are used to take visitors around the grounds of the estate, which includes an ornamental Victorian garden and a lake with a bird hide.

Return to the A399, turn right towards South Molton, then left on the B3358 to Simonsbath.

❺ Simonsbath is the westernmost settlement in Somerset. Although barely a hamlet, it does have an important place in the history of Exmoor, for it was the first farming estate carved out of the great royal hunting forest from the 17th century onwards. The Boevey family carried out stock-rearing experiments, improved many of the roads, enclosed land and introduced Cheviot sheep to the area.

From Simonsbath keep forward on the B3223, then fork right, keeping to the B3223 at the junction with the B3224. At a crossroads turn right to detour to Tarr Steps (signposted).

❻ Spanning the River Barle, Tarr Steps is an ancient stone clapper bridge of 17 large granite slabs. It has certainly existed since medieval times (although the river has demolished it on many occasions), but its origins may be even earlier.

Return to the B3224 and take the lane opposite to descend to Winsford.

❼ Winsford is a village of many thatched roofs—the Royal Oak Inn has the most elaborate—as well as no fewer than eight bridges across the rivers Winn and Exe.

Turn left at Winsford and keep left at subsequent junctions to reach the B3224. Turn left to Exford.

❽ Exford village, with its large green overlooked by cottages and hotels, has been a crossing-point over the

Exe since prehistoric times, although the opening of roads in the 19th century really put Exford on the map. Its church, up the hill, has an exceptional screen dating from the 15th century. Turn right in Exford and fork right again on the road that leads northeast and over the west shoulder of Dunkery Hill towards Luccombe. After you cross over the ridge at Dunkery Hill, a right turn gives access to the main parking area leading along the ridge to Dunkery Beacon.

❾ The summit at Dunkery Beacon offers one of the best views in the West Country: South Wales is visible on a clear day, including two summits of the Brecon Beacons (▷ 240–241).

Continue through Luccombe to reach the A39. Turn left towards Lynton. A dead-end road on the right from the A39 leads to the National Trust village Selworthy.

❿ Selworthy's church is adorned with symbols of the Passion and angels. Continue on the A39 up Porlock Hill to return to Lynton.

PLACE TO VISIT
ARLINGTON COURT
✉ Barnstaple EX31 4LP
☎ 01271 850296
🕐 Easter–end Oct Sun–Fri 11–5. House and carriage collection from 10.30. Grounds: Nov–end Mar daily dawn–dusk
Adult £7.09, child £3.54, family £17.72

WHERE TO EAT
The Royal Oak (tel 01643 851 455), a thatched inn in Winsford. Watersmeet House in Lynmouth (▷ 153).

Opposite *Castle Rock at sunset*
Below *Flowering heather, Dunkery Beacon*

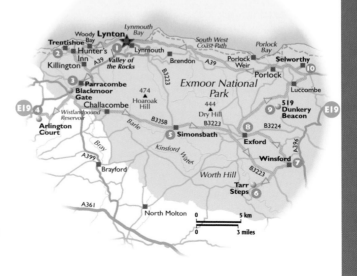

WATERSMEET AND THE LYNMOUTH FLOODS

The tranquil waters of Hoaroak Water and the East Lyn River once swelled up to biblical proportions in a catastrophic flood. They gouged out spectacularly deep ravines some 180m (600ft) beneath the moorland plateau, running closely parallel to the coast.

THE WALK

Length: 3 miles (4.5km)
Allow: At least 90 min
Start/end: National Trust parking area at Combe Park, Hillsford Bridge 1.5 miles (2.5km) south of Lynmouth map ref 429 E19
OS Landranger map: 180
OS Explorer map: OL9

★ Watersmeet, where the Hoar Oak Water and East Lyn River converge, is a popular spot for visitors to this part of the Exmoor National Park.

Turn left out of the parking area, and then right to go over Hilsford Bridge. Immediately pass through a gate on the left and proceed along the right bank of Hoaroak Water (signposted Watersmeet), descending slightly through a steep-sided, wooded valley, with the river rushing through the rocky ravine below. The route passes a waterfall and a viewing point on the left, and then reaches a flight of steps leading to the left to Watersmeet.

Continuing along the path bearing to the right, the route proceeds up the right bank of the East Lyn River, past a junction with another path leading to Watersmeet and the remains of a lime kiln.

❶ The lime kiln was used to burn limestone shipped from South Wales and used as fertilizer. The view ahead extends to Countisbury Common, which rises to 343m (1,125ft). In the early 18th century the English writer and adventurer Daniel Defoe (1660–1731) described Exmoor as a 'filthie barren waste', at a time when wild landscapes were perhaps not appreciated as they are today.

The route then leads through semi-natural oak woodland. At a junction, take the footpath ahead (signposted Rockford); the path drops through a beech glade to reach the riverbank. Carry on, and then cross Ash Bridge and turn left on the other side (signposted Watersmeet).

❷ Red and roe deer frequent the moorlands and woodlands in this area. The smaller roe deer are shy creatures, but they may be glimpsed occasionally at dawn or dusk. When a roe deer is startled and runs off at speed, you may see the prominent white patch on its rump; the bucks have small antlers with short branches. The red deer is the largest native land animal in Britain. The fully grown stag is a formidable sight, standing as tall as 1.2m (4ft) at the shoulder, with antlers up

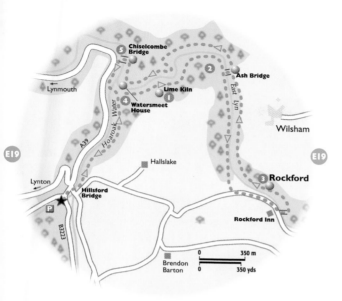

Chiselcombe
Bridge

Ash Bridge

Lime Kiln

Watersmeet
House

Lynmouth

Wilsham

Hallslake

Lynton

Hillsford
Bridge

Rockford

Rockford Inn

Brendon
Barton

0   350 m
0   350 yds

to 70cm (28in) long. Their main habitats are Exmoor and the Scottish highlands.

3 For an optional detour you can continue for 1 mile (1.5km) along the right bank to the hamlet of Rockford, where the Rockford Inn is a useful refreshment stop; you can then return via the path on the opposite bank.

To continue, carry on past Crook Pool, then along the narrow path that undulates above the river. Keep along the river bank to pass Watersmeet House and bear right around the garden fence.

4 A huge Monterey pine once shaded Watersmeet House itself, but it was taken down in 2007; a younger replacement has since been planted. During the late 18th century such landscapes found favour with the Romantic movement. The Reverend W. S. Halliday purchased this site in 1829 and built Watersmeet as a hunting lodge and retreat. Today it is owned by the National Trust and has a café.

Carry on for a short distance along the right bank of the river and go over stone Chiselcombe Bridge.

5 Chiselcombe Bridge was paid for by members of the public after an ancient bridge on the site was swept away in the notorious floods of 15 August 1952, when a 12m (40ft) wall of water rushed down into Lynmouth, killing 34 people and destroying several houses and bridges. The flood came after

228mm (9in) of rain fell within 24 hours—one of three heaviest periods of rainfall yet recorded in the British Isles. It is estimated that more than 13.6 billion litres (3 billion gallons) of water fell on the area that is drained by the two Lyn rivers.

On the other side of the bridge turn left and continue back up the riverbank. Turn left down some steps to cross back over Hoaroak Water by a wooden footbridge just above Watersmeet. Take the steps on the right, following signs to Hillsford Bridge, then bear right to retrace your steps upriver to the bridge and the parking area in Combe Park.

WHERE TO EAT

Watersmeet House offers a selection of food and drink in a riverside setting. The Rockford Inn in Brendon, near Lynton (tel: 01598 741214) is a traditional country pub serving hot and cold meals, real ales and Devon cream teas.

PLACE TO VISIT
WATERSMEET HOUSE

✉ Watersmeet Road, Lynmouth EX35 6NT ☎ 01598 753348 🕐 Easter–end Sep daily 10.30–5.30, Oct 10.30–4.30 💷 Free. Pay-and-display parking

Opposite and below *Waterfalls at Watersmeet, near Lynmouth*

Above *Torquay's busy harbour*

BABBACOMBE DOWNS
BABBACOMBE THEATRE
www.babbacombe-theatre.com
This is a place to visit for
old-fashioned seaside variety
shows and comedy, as well as
musicals and touring bands.
✉ Cary Point, Babbacombe Downs,
Torquay TQ1 3LU ☎ 01803 328385
🕐 Box office: mid-Feb to end Dec
Fri–Mon 10–5, Tue–Thu 10–9 (5 when no
performance) 🎫 Adult £15, child (under 16)
£8 🚌 🚉 Torquay

BARNSTAPLE
THE TARKA TRAIL
www.biketrail.co.uk
Try the 180-mile (290km) Tarka Trail,
through the area described in author
Henry Williamson's 1927 book *Tarka
the Otter.* Bicycles can be hired from
the Biketrail shop at Fremington
Quay. You need National Cycle
Network Map No.27. See Sustrans,
▷ 59.
✉ The Stone Barn, Fremington Quay,
Barnstaple EX31 2NH ☎ 01271 372586
🚲 Bicycle rental from £5.50 per hour (£10
per day) 🚌 Fremington Quay
Heritage Centre 🚉 Barnstaple

BATH
GEORGE BAYNTUN
www.georgebayntun.com
A bookshop engaged in buying,
selling, binding and restoring
old and rare books since 1829.
Specializes in English literature,
particularly classics and modern
first editions, plus antique prints
(including views of Bath). The shop
has retained much of its 19th-
century character.
✉ Manvers Street, Bath BA1 1JW
☎ 01225 466000 🕐 Mon–Fri 9–1, 2–5.30,
Sat 9.30–1 🚉 Bath Spa

THE GLASS HOUSE
www.bathaquaglass.com
Decorative glass in many forms, including jewellery and stained glass.
Also Bath Aqua Glass, a hand-blown
and attractively tinted glass (inspired
by Roman and Georgian glass),
Bristol Blue Glass, made since the
1780s, and lesser-known Exmoor
Cranberry Glass from Porlock Weir in
Somerset.
✉ 1–2 Orange Grove, Bath BA1 1LP
☎ 01225 311183 🕐 Mon–Sat 9.30–6,
Sun 12–6 🚉 Bath Spa

GUILDHALL MARKET
A traditional market experience in
an 18th-century building—a market
has existed on this site since its
Royal Charter of 1284. The huge
range of stalls sell jewellery, coffee
beans, haberdashery, hardware,
delicatessen and French groceries.
✉ High Street, Bath BA2 4AW
☎ 01225 477945 🕐 Mon–Sat (also Sun
in Dec) 9–5 (times for individual traders vary)
🚌 🚉 Bath Spa

HOUSE OF BEARS
From cuddly friends by mainstream
manufacturers to the idiosyncratic
and downright peculiar output of
artisan bear makers, this shop on
one of Bath's main thoroughfares is
a bear lover's heaven.

22A Broad Street, Bath BA1 5LN
☎ 01225 443091 ⏰ Mon–Sat 10–5
🚇 Bath Spa

THEATRE ROYAL BATH
www.theatreroyal.org.uk
Opened in 1805, and steeped in history, the Theatre Royal has drama, opera, ballet; plus fringe productions and jazz in the Ustinov Studio and children's works in The Egg.
✉ Sawclose, Bath BA1 1ET
☎ 01225 448844 ⏰ Box office: Mon–Sat 10–8, Sun and public holidays 12–8
✋ £10–£30, 40 standby tickets costing £5 available from noon on day of performance
🍴 🖥 🚇 Bath Spa

THERMAE BATH SPA
www.thermaebathspa.com
Reconnecting Bath with its origins, this spa draws on natural thermal springs. Bathers can enjoy an open-air roof-top pool, steam rooms, massage and treatments.
✉ Hetling Pump Room, Hot Bath Street, Bath BA1 1SJ ☎ Reservations: 0844 888 0844 ⏰ Daily 9am–10pm (last entry 8pm)
✋ Two hours £22, 4 hours £32, all day £45 (not including treatments) 🍴 🖥 🏛
🚇 Bath Spa

WOODS
Stylish bar in a Georgian building. Popular with visiting actors and a glitzy crowd.
✉ 9–13 Alfred Street, Bath BA1 2QX
☎ 01225 314812 ⏰ Closed Sun evening
🚇 Bath Spa

BISHOPS LYDEARD
CEDAR FALLS
www.cedarfalls.co.uk
Health farm offering short breaks, treatments and alternative therapies plus a golf course, tennis courts and outdoor pool.
✉ Bishops Lydeard, Taunton TA4 3HR
☎ 01823 433233 ⏰ Call for details
✋ Full day from £83; individual treatments from £9.50 🍴 🖥

BOURNEMOUTH
BOURNEMOUTH INTERNATIONAL CENTRE (BIC)
www.bic.co.uk
Arts and leisure complex hosting theatre, music, ballet and even darts. Concerts by the Bournemouth Symphony Orchestra.
✉ Exeter Road, Bournemouth BH2 5BH
☎ 01202 456400; box office: 08701 113000 ⏰ Box office: daily 10–5.30 (or until 30 min after performance starts). By phone: Mon–Sat 9.30–8.30, Sun 9.30–5.30 (8.30 if there is a show) ✋ Various
🍴 🖥 🚇 Bournemouth

THE OPERA HOUSE
www.operahouse.co.uk
A huge venue that gave the south coast's clubbers an alternative to Brighton, where guest and resident DJs play house, trance and drum and bass.
✉ 570 Christchurch Road, Boscombe, Bournemouth BH1 4BH ☎ 08701 989877, 08701 989898 (ticketline) ⏰ Varies, see website for listings ✋ £10–£50
🚇 Bournemouth

BRISTOL
ARNE HERBS
www.arneherbs.co.uk
Herbs, both rare and household, but all pesticide-free, are sold at Anthony Lyman-Dixon's nurseries.
✉ Limeburn Nurseries, Limeburn Hill, Chew Magna, Bristol BS40 8QW
☎ 01275 333399 ⏰ Daily 10–4

BOOKBARN
www.bookbarn.co.uk
In an old government warehouse by the A39 at White Cross, this is the largest second-hand bookshop in the country with more than 5 million titles. The shelves stretch on and up, with 200 or so different categories. If you're a collector, or just love books, you may wish to allocate several hours to your visit.
✉ Unit 1–2, Hallatrow Business Park, Wells Road, Hallatrow, Bristol BS39 6EX 🚗 Off A39, by junction with A37 from Bristol, between Temple Cloud and Farrington Gurney

BROADMEAD
www.bristolbroadmead.co.uk
One of the region's leading shopping districts. Department stores, major chains and specialist shops, some concentrated in the Mall Galleries Cabot Square and Quakers Friars developments. There is also a range of markets.
✉ Broadmead Shopping Centre, Bristol BS1 3DX ☎ 0117 925 7053
⏰ Mon–Sat 9–6 (8 Thu), Sun 11–5; individual stores may differ 🍴 🖥
🚇 Bristol Temple Meads

COLSTON HALL
www.colstonhall.org
Concert hall presenting major artists in pop music, classical music and opera, as well as regular stand-up comedy performances. Reservations are advised.
✉ Colston Street, Bristol BS1 5AR
☎ 0117 922 3686 (bookings) ⏰ Mon–Sat 10–8.30 (Sun from 5pm if performance)
✋ Various 🖥 🍴 🚇 Bristol Temple Meads

GLOUCESTERSHIRE COUNTY CRICKET CLUB
www.gloscricket.co.uk
There's an Edwardian pavilion at this tree-fringed cricket club.
✉ County Ground, Nevil Road, Bishopston, Bristol BS7 9EJ ☎ 0117 910 8000; box office: 0117 910 8010 ⏰ Box office: Apr–end Sep Mon–Fri 9.30–4
✋ Adult £11–£18, child (5–15) £5–£8
🍴 🖥 🚇 Bristol Temple Meads (2 miles/3km)

JESTERS COMEDY CLUB
www.jesterscomedyclub.co.uk
This venerable Bristol comedy club moved into an Edwardian cinema on Cheltenham Road in 2008. Many of the building's original features have been restored, making it an elegant backdrop for new and touring comedians.
✉ 135–137 Cheltenham Road Bristol BS6 5RR ☎ 0117 909 6655 ⏰ Thu–Sat from 7.30 🚇 Montpelier

THE OLD DUKE
Said to be the oldest- established jazz venue in the country. Live music every night, including trad, blues and jazz-funk. Three-day jazz festival over August public holiday.
✉ 45 King Street, Bristol BS1 4ER
☎ 0117 927 7137 ⏰ Daily 12–12
🍴 🚇 Bristol Temple Meads

ST. NICHOLAS MARKET

The antithesis of Bristol's modern shopping areas, this 18th-century open-air and covered market has been the traditional focal point for shopping in the city since 1743. Organic fruit and vegetables, and exotic delicacies. Great for olives and local honey, second-hand books and trendy clothing (modern fashion and retro).

✉ Corn Exchange, Bristol BS1 1JQ
☎ 0117 922 4017 🕐 Mon–Sat 9.30–5 (extended in Dec) 🍴 🖳 🚉 Bristol Temple Meads

WATERSHED

www.watershed.co.uk

With three cinema screens, art spaces and a relaxing, laid-back bar and café, the Watershed Media Centre makes good use of its quay-side location in two large, former Victorian warehouses. Art-house movies as well as mainstream, and some interesting exhibitions and installations.

✉ 1 Canon's Road, Harbourside BS1 5TX
☎ 0117 927 6444 🕐 Box office: Mon–Fri from 9am (Sat–Sun 10am) until 15 mins after last performance begins 🍴 🚉 Bristol Temple Meads

BURTON BRADSTOCK

FLYING FRENZY

www.flyingfrenzy.com

Paragliding over Dorset, with taster days that guarantee solo flying, and four-day courses.

✉ The Old Dairy, Manor Farm, Burton Bradstock, Bridport DT6 9PW ☎ 01308 398777 🕐 All year (subject to weather). Advisable to reserve at least one month in advance 🖐 Taster day £120. Includes equipment 🖳

CHEDDAR GORGE

CHEDDAR GORGE CHEESE COMPANY

www.cheddargorgecheeseco.co.uk

This is more than a shop selling cheese; watch many varieties of Cheddar cheese being made and taste them.

✉ The Cliffs, Cheddar Gorge BS27 3QA
☎ 01934 742810 🕐 Daily 10–4.30
🖐 Adults £1.95, children free 🍴

CHELTENHAM

CHELTENHAM RACECOURSE

www.cheltenham.co.uk

Home of National Hunt racing. The annual highlight is March's The Festival and the Cheltenham Gold Cup race. Reserve tickets in advance.

✉ Prestbury Park, Cheltenham GL50 4SH
☎ 01242 537642 (24 hours) 🕐 8 meetings Oct–end May; call for dates. Advance reservations required for special events
🖐 £7.65–£30 🍴 🖳 🚉 Cheltenham Spa

THE COURTYARD

www.visitcheltenham.gov.uk

Escape the chain stores on two levels of chic boutiques and specialist shops around a sunken piazza and elevated walkway.

✉ Montpellier Street, Cheltenham GL50 1SR 🕐 Generally Mon–Sat 9–5.30
🖳 🍴 🚉 Cheltenham Spa

EVERYMAN THEATRE

www.everymantheatre.org.uk

An attractive and decorative venue staging drama, musicals, opera and ballet. Also runs a large educational department with numerous workshops.

✉ Regent Street, Cheltenham GL50 1HQ
☎ 01242 572573 🕐 Box office: Mon–Sat 9.30–8.30 (6 in Aug), Sun from 2 hours before a performance 🖐 £6–£25 🍴 🖳
🚉 Cheltenham Spa

CIRENCESTER

COTSWOLD WATER PARK

www.waterpark.org

Britain's largest lakeland park with 133 lakes for watersports. Equipment can be rented.

✉ Keynes Country Park, Spratsgate Lane, Shorncote, Cirencester GL7 6DF ☎ 01285 861459 🕐 Open access 🖐 Free admission to park, but individual charges for activities
🖳 🏛

EXETER

COOLINGS WINE BAR

On medieval Gandy Street, this is a popular place to enjoy a drink.

✉ 11 Gandy Street, Exeter EX4 3LS
☎ 01392 434184 🕐 Daily 10am–midnight
🚉 Exeter Central

EXETER PHOENIX

www.exeterphoenix.org.uk

An impressive cultural centre offering exhibitions, art-house films, music gigs and workshops.

✉ Bradninch Place, Gandy Street, Exeter EX4 3LS ☎ 01392 667080 🕐 Box office: Mon–Sat 10–8 🖐 £4.50–£16
🖳 🖥 🚉 Exeter Central

NORTHCOTT THEATRE

www.exeternorthcott.co.uk

Unusual because it has its own in-house professional theatre company, it also stages touring shows, opera and ballet.

✉ Stocker Road, Exeter EX4 4QB
☎ 01392 493493 🕐 Box office: Mon–Sat 10–8 (6 on non-performance days)
🖐 £10–£17 🖳 🖥 🚉 Exeter Central

THE ORANGE ELEPHANT FARM SHOP AND ICE CREAM PARLOUR

www.tavernersfarm.co.uk

The orange elephants in question are pedigree South Devon cattle, with their distinctive long faces and golden colour. This is the last milking herd in the country and the milk is used to make a rich ice cream. You can also buy organic meats and visit the organic vegetable garden.

✉ Taverner's Farm, Lower Brenton, Kennford, Exeter, Devon EX6 7YL ☎ 01392 833 876 🕐 Tue-Sat 10–5, Sun 11–4
🖳 Café 🚗 Off A38 southwest of Exeter

FALMOUTH

THE POLY

www.thepoly.org

More than your average arts centre, the Poly is the home of the Royal Cornwall Polytechnic Society. As well as a 200-seat theatre and cinema, exhibition spaces and café, there are science events and design shows.

✉ Church Street, Falmouth TR11 3EG ☎ 01326 212300 ⏰ Box office: Mon–Sat 10–5 ✋ Various 🖥 🚆 Falmouth

GLOUCESTER
GLOUCESTER ANTIQUE CENTRE
Britain's largest provincial antiques market in a converted Victorian warehouse in the revamped historic dockland area of the city, and with 140 dealers represented.

✉ 1 Severn Road, Gloucester GL1 2LE ☎ 01452 529716 ⏰ Mon–Sat 10–5, Sun 11.30–4.30 ✋ Free 🖥 🚆 Gloucester

GLOUCESTER RFC
www.gloucesterrugbyclub.com
Home to a leading rugby union club, Gloucester's Kingsholm is a notoriously raucous ground.

✉ Kingsholm Road, Gloucester GL1 3AX ☎ 0871 871 8781 ⏰ Sep–end May ✋ Adults £20–£42, child (under 16) £10–£14 🚆 🚆 Gloucester

HOUSE OF THE TAILOR OF GLOUCESTER
www.tailor-of-gloucester.org.uk
A tiny shop and the location of *The Tailor of Gloucester*, which Beatrix Potter sketched while visiting the city. Books, toys and ornaments, plus merchandise from other children's classics such as *Winnie the Pooh*. Small museum.

✉ 9 College Court, Gloucester GL1 2NJ ☎ 01452 422856 ⏰ Mon–Sat 10–4, Sun 12–4 ✋ Free 🚆 Gloucester

GREAT TORRINGTON
DARTINGTON CRYSTAL
www.dartington.co.uk
Known worldwide for its fine crystal. Visitors' centre, factory tours, factory seconds shop, plus bargains from other brands such as Denby and Portmeirion pottery and knitwear from the Edinburgh Woollen Mill.

✉ Great Torrington EX38 7AN ☎ 01805 626242 ⏰ Mon–Fri 9.30–5, Sat 10–5, Sun 10–4. Tours: Mon–Fri only. ✋ Shop: free. Tour: adult £5, child (under 16) free. Visitors' centre: adult £2.50, child (under 16) free 🍴

HAYLE
SHORE SURF SCHOOL
www.shoresurf.com
A safe introduction to surfing at beaches in the St. Ives Bay area. Lessons for all abilities and age groups (over-8s).

✉ 46 Mount Pleasant, St. Ives Bay, Hayle TR27 4LE ☎ 01736 755556 ⏰ Daily 10.15–12.45, 2.15–4.45 ✋ Half-day £25, full day £40. Equipment included

HELSTON
THE FLAMBARDS EXPERIENCE
www.flambards.co.uk
Several all-weather attractions: a recreated Victorian village, a life-size street during the World War II Blitz, a Science Centre and rides.

✉ Clodgey Lane, Helston TR13 0QA ☎ 01326 573404; recorded information: 08456 018684 (24 hours) ⏰ Easter–end Oct daily 10.30–5. Other times vary ✋ Adult £5.95, child (3–10) £3.50–5 🍴 🖥 ♿

LAUNCESTON
JAMAICA INN
www.jamaicainn.co.uk
A coaching inn immortalized by Daphne du Maurier, who stayed here in 1930. The setting, legends and atmosphere of Bodmin Moor inspired her novel *Jamaica Inn* (1936). The Smugglers Museum features smuggling memorabilia and contains The Daphne du Maurier Room.

✉ Bolventor, near Launceston PL15 7TS ☎ 01566 86250 ⏰ Daily 11–11. Museum: Easter–end Oct daily 10–5; Nov–end Dec and Feb–Easter daily 11–4 ✋ Museum: adult £3.95, child (4–16) £3.25, family £9.95

LISKEARD
TRAGO MILLS
www.tragomills.co.uk
A regional institution, selling thousands of cut-price items from DIY goods to Oriental carpets, all displayed in warehouses. Lower end of the market. Also in Falmouth and Newton Abbot.

✉ Twowatersfoot, Liskeard PL14 6HY ☎ 01579 348877 ⏰ Mon–Sat 9–5.30, Sun 10–4 (viewing from 9.30). Extra 30 min shopping before closing 🖥 🚆 Liskeard

LIZARD
THE LIZARD PASTY SHOP
www.connections.co.uk/lizardpastyshop
Ann Muller's small shop sells arguably some of Cornwall's finest pasties. They are handmade with local ingredients and make a good snack on a trip to The Lizard.

✉ Beacon Terrace, The Lizard, Helston TR12 7PB ☎ 01326 290889 ⏰ Easter–end Oct Mon–Sat 9.30–2.30; rest of year Tue–Sat 9.30–2.30

Opposite and left *The west has something for everybody to enjoy, from outdoor pursuits to cultural events*

LOOE

PURELY CORNISH

www.purelycornish.co.uk
Locally produced food and crafts from a converted 16th-century bakehouse. They will also make up hampers of Cornish goodies for shipping.

✉ Buller Street, East Looe, Looe, Cornwall PL13 1AR ☎ 01503 262696 ⊕ Daily 10–5

LOSTWITHIEL

HAYE FARM CIDER

Haye Farm's orchards have been producing traditional Cornish cider since 1200.

✉ Haye Farm, St. Veep, Lerryn, Lostwithiel PL22 0PB ☎ 01208 872250 ⊕ Daily 8am–late

NEWQUAY

NATIONAL SURFING CENTRE

www.nationalsurfingcentre.co.uk
The British Surfing Association holds major surfing championships at their facility on Fistral Beach. Tuition for all levels for ages eight upwards, from half-days to one-week courses.

✉ Fistral Beach, Newquay TR7 1HW ☎ 01637 850737 ⊕ Easter–end Oct daily; advance reservation recommended 🖐 From half a day: £30. Price includes equipment 🚉 Newquay

NEWTON ABBOT

SHILSTONE ROCKS RIDING AND TREKKING CENTRE

www.dartmoorstables.com
Half- and full-day escorted rides or treks over Dartmoor on well-trained horses. Hard hats provided.

✉ Widecombe in the Moor, Newton Abbot TQ13 7TF ☎ 01364 621281 ⊕ Rides at 10 and 2 🖐 £30 for 1 hour

PAIGNTON

QUAYWEST WATERPARK

www.quaywest.co.uk
Eight flumes and slides—including the Devil's Drop, a 20m (65ft) free fall. Inner tubes, mats supplied.

✉ Goodrington Sands, Paignton TQ4 6LN ☎ 01803 555550 ⊕ Late May–early Sep daily 10–6 🖐 All-day ticket: adult £10.95, child (under 3ft 6in/1.06m) £3.95 🍴 ☐ 🚉 Paignton

Above *Watergate Bay, Cornwall*

PENRYN

CORNISH CUISINE

www.smokedsalmon-ltd.com
An appetizing selection of smoked Cornish produce: local organic cheeses, mackerel and game.

✉ The Smokehouse, Islington Wharf, Penryn TR10 8AT ☎ 01326 376244 ⊕ Mon–Fri 9–4.30 🚉 Penryn

MENALLACK CORNISH FARMHOUSE CHEESES

A must for cheese aficionados, Menallack uses unpasteurized milk from local animals to handmake 19 specialist cheeses. Over 50 varieties of Cornish cheese are sold in the shop.

✉ Menallack Farm, Treverva, Penryn TR10 9BP ☎ 01326 340333 ⊕ Mon–Fri 9–5, Sat 9–12.30 🚉 Penryn

PORTHCURNO

THE MINACK THEATRE

www.minack.com
Open-air theatre cut into the Cornish cliffs with the Atlantic as a backdrop. Plays, musicals and opera in the 24-week summer season.

✉ Porthcurno, near Penzance TR19 6JU ☎ 01736 810694; box office: 01736 810181 ⊕ Box office: (pre-season) Easter to mid-May Mon–Fri 9.30–5.30; mid-May to mid-Sep (season) Mon–Fri 9.30–8, Sat– 9.30–5.30. Visitor centre: Apr–end Sep daily 9.30–5.30; rest of year 10–4 🖐 Visitor centre: £3, child (12–15) £1.20. Performances: adult £7–£8.50, child (under 16) £3.50–£4.50 ☐ 🚉 Penzance (10 miles/16km)

ST. IVES

ISOBAR

www.theisobar.com
St. Ives' hippest bar. There are live music nights throughout the year. Tapas and snacks are available.

✉ Street-An-Pol, St. Ives TR26 2DS ☎ 01736 799199 ⊕ Club: July–end Aug Mon–Sat; rest of year Wed–Sat 🖐 Club: free before 9.30pm or 10.30pm, £5 or £6 after 🚉 St. Ives

SALCOMBE

SALCOMBE DINGHY SAILING

www.salcombedinghysailing.co.uk
Hire a Wayfarer or a Laser Pico sailing dinghy to scoot around the sheltered Salcombe estuary. Beginners and those who are a bit rusty will find the tuition sessions a great starting point.

✉ 1 Seaview, East Prawle, Kingsbridge, Devon TQ7 2BZ ☎ 01548 843927 (Book through Salcombe Tourist Information Centre) ⊕ Apr–end Oct 10–5.30 reservations advised 🖐 Individual Tuition 1.5 hour £45, half day £85, full day £130, rental only from £45 per day

SALISBURY

CHARTER MARKET
www.salisbury.gov.uk
A centuries-old outdoor market with a huge range of reasonably priced fresh farm produce.
✉ Market Square, Salisbury
☎ 01722 434652 🕐 Tue and Sat (except third Tue in Oct) 8–4 🚌 🚉 Salisbury

SALISBURY PLAYHOUSE
www.salisburyplayhouse.com
Stages Shakespeare, modern drama and annual pantomime.
✉ Malthouse Lane, Salisbury SP2 7RA
☎ 01722 320333 🕐 Box office: Mon–Sat 10–8 (or 6 if no performance) 🎫 £10–£19
🚌 🚗 🚉 Salisbury

SALTASH

ST. MELLION GOLF COURSE
www.st-mellion.co.uk
The West Country's top golf venue with two championship golf courses. There is also a beauty salon and health spa on site.
✉ St. Mellion, Saltash PL12 6SD
☎ 01579 352002 🕐 All year, open to non-members 🎫 Nicklaus Course £60 per round; Old Course £40 per round 🍴 🚌
🚉 Bere Alston (3 miles/5km)

STREET

CLARKS VILLAGE
www.clarksvillage.co.uk
Over 90 outlets, including Marks & Spencer, Royal Worcester, Dartington Crystal and many shoe shops, with up to 60 per cent discounts.
✉ Farm Road, Street BA16 0BB
☎ 01458 840064 🕐 Mon–Wed, Fri–Sat 9–5.50, Thu 9–8, Sun 10–5 (some stores 11–5) 🍴 🚌

TRURO

HALL FOR CORNWALL
www.hallforcornwall.co.uk
First-rate arts centre, hosting ballet, theatre, bands and operas.
✉ Back Quay, Truro TR1 2LL
☎ 01872 262466 🕐 Box office: Mon–Sat 9–6 (later on performance night) 🎫 £5–£30
🍴 🚉 Truro

FEBRUARY/MARCH

BATH LITERATURE FESTIVAL
www.bathlitfest.org.uk
Started in 1995, this is now a well-established event with readings and presentations by leading authors in some of the most historic buildings in Bath.
✉ 2 Church Street, Abbey Green, Bath BA1 1NL ☎ 01225 463362 🕐 1 week, late February–early March 🚉 Bath Spa

MAY

BATH INTERNATIONAL MUSIC FESTIVAL
www.bathmusicfest.org.uk
Classical music, jazz, contemporary music and world music in various locations in Bath.
✉ 2 Church Street, Abbey Green, Bath BA1 1NL ☎ 01225 463362 🕐 Late May–early June, two weeks 🚉 Bath Spa

JUNE

ROYAL BATH AND WEST SHOW
www.bathandwest.co.uk
Get a taste of rural life at the west's best agricultural show, including rare breeds of British farm animals.
✉ Royal Bath and West Showground, Shepton Mallet BA4 6QN ☎ 01749 822200 🕐 Four days early June

GLASTONBURY FESTIVAL
www.glastonburyfestivals.co.uk
The largest open-air music and performing arts festival in the world. Also theatre, circus, cabaret and children's activities. Tickets sell out in days.
✉ Pilton, 6 miles (9km) east of Glastonbury ☎ 0115 912 9129 🕐 Late June 🚉 Glastonbury

ROYAL CORNWALL SHOW
www.royalcornwallshow.org
This three-day annual country show (first held in 1793) includes an agricultural display, Cornish food and drink, a flower show and a steam fair with traction engines and a traditional fairground.
✉ Royal Cornwall Showground, Wadebridge PL27 7JE ☎ 01208 812183 🕐 Mid-June three days 🎫 Adults £6.50–£13, child £3.20–£6.50

JULY

CHELTENHAM INTERNATIONAL FESTIVAL OF MUSIC
www.cheltenhamfestivals.co.uk
Among the top British classical music events, with a reputation for a contemporary bias. The Fringe Festival runs alongside, with jazz, dance, theatre, children's events, street entertainers and fireworks.
✉ Various locations ☎ 01242 227979 🕐 Early July, two weeks 🚉 Cheltenham

AUGUST

BRISTOL INTERNATIONAL BALLOON FIESTA
www.bristolfiesta.co.uk
With 120 hot-air balloons, half a million visitors, and a glow-in-the-dark night flight finale, this is a spectacular, family-friendly annual summer event.
✉ Ashton Court Estate, Long Ashton, Bristol BS41 9JN ☎ 0117 953 5884 🕐 Thursday–Sunday, mid-August 🚉 Bristol Temple Meads

NOVEMBER

BURNING BARRELS
www.tarbarrels.co.uk
On Guy Fawkes Night the residents of Ottery St. Mary shoulder flaming, tar-soaked barrels and run through the village in a 17th-century tradition. The streets get crowded and chaotic, so this event may not be suitable for children.
✉ Ottery St. Mary ☎ 01404 813964 🕐 5 November

PRICES AND SYMBOLS

The restaurants are listed alphabetically within each town. The prices are the average price for a two-course lunch (L) and a three-course à la carte dinner (D) for one person. The wine price is for the least expensive bottle.
For a key to the symbols, ▷ 2.

BATH
CAVENDISH RESTAURANT

www.dukesbath.co.uk

The Cavendish Restaurant is just a few minutes' walk from Pulteney Bridge and the centre of this historic city, and is located at the heart of the Dukes Hotel, set in an elegant Georgian town house. There are two dining rooms and a secluded patio garden for summer dining. The Modern British food is rooted in the freshest locally sourced West Country ingredients, with organic and free-range produce used wherever possible. Choices on the refreshingly simple à la carte menu might include Mendip venison with a pear and celeriac bake, or breast of black leg chicken with a jambonette of the leg and a white bean and truffle purée.

✉ Dukes Hotel, Great Pulteney Street BA2 4DN ☎ 01225 787960 ⏰ 12–2.30, 6.30–10 🍷 L £12.95, D £29.50, Wine £16
🚗 M4 J18 take A46 to Bath. At lights turn left towards A36, at next lights turn right and right again into Great Pulteney Street
🚆 Bath Spa

WOODS RESTAURANT

www.woods.co.uk

John Wood was the architect and builder of much of Georgian Bath and the restaurant bearing his name occupies the ground floor of five of his town houses. Just a short walk from the historic town centre, a small reception area leads into the large brasserie-style dining room, which has a wooden floor and walls decorated with horse-racing prints. The cooking style is simple and uncluttered, making good use of well-sourced produce in starters like guinea fowl and prune rillette with honey-pickled vegetables and red pepper syrup. Follow with a properly cooked calves' liver with a balsamic reduction adding a touch of sharpness, and finish with a well-made dessert such as maple and coffee parfait served with a sticky espresso and whisky syrup.

✉ 9–3 Alfred Street, Bath BA1 2QX ☎ 01225 314812 D12–2.30, 6–10; closed Sun (open for special request), 25–26 Dec, 1 Jan 🍷 L £12.95, D £31 🚆 Telephone for directions

BOURNEMOUTH
BISTRO ON THE BEACH
www.bistroonthebeach.co.uk
This colourful, buzzing bistro offers great sea views, plenty of friendly spirit and good-value, no-nonsense cooking. The food is Modern British, with a comprehensive selection of specials.

✉ Solent Promenade, Southbourne Coast Road, Southbourne, Bournemouth BH6 4BE ☎ 01202 431473 ⏰ Daily 6.30–12 🍽 D £18.95, Wine £12.50 🚗 From Bournemouth take coast road to East Cliff. At lights turn right then right again to join overcliff. In 1 mile (1.5km) at mini roundabout take second exit; 400m (440 yds) to parking area. Path leads to bistro 🚉 Bournemouth

BRADFORD-ON-AVON
THE KINGS ARMS
www.kingsarms-bath.co.uk
Originally a monks' retreat, this 11th-century Bath stone building with a pantiled roof was converted into a pub in the 17th century. The bar food includes game casserole and a goats' cheese crostini salad.

✉ Monkton Farleigh BA15 2QH ☎ 01225 858705 ⏰ Mon–Fri 12–3, 6–10; Sat–Sun 12–11 🍽 L £13.90, D £18.85, Wine £12.50 🚗 Follow A4 from Bath to Bradford-on-Avon. At Bathford join A363, turning left to Monkton Farleigh

BRIDPORT
RIVERSIDE RESTAURANT
www.thefishrestaurant-westbay.co.uk
In 1976 the well-known architect Piers Gough reconstructed this restaurant which is located on an 'island' overlooking the West Bay fishing port. A recent extension has provided a further dining area. The business has been in the same family for some 44 years, with the emphasis today based around fresh fish and shellfish—mostly from local waters—alongside an intelligent, simply-cooked approach. There is shellfish (when available) such as crab salad (whole or dressed), or local Channel lobster served in a number of ways. The daily specials are worth checking out, such as fillet of sea bass with slow-roasted belly of pork. Meat and vegetarian options are also offered on the daily specials list.

✉ West Bay DT6 4EZ ☎ 01308 422011 ⏰ 12–2.30, 6.30–9; closed Mon (excluding public holidays), D Sun; 30 Nov–14 Feb 🍽 L £16.50, D £27, Wine £15 🚗 A35 Bridport ring road, turn to West Bay at Crown roundabout

BRISTOL
CULINARIA
www.culinariabristol.co.uk
This suburban bistro has made a virtue out of its simply constructed menu—it's a takeaway too. The food is mostly on the Mediterranean side, but makes good use of local sources as well—you might find the roast guinea fowl is served in a Somerset brandy with apples, and the rump of lamb, served with haricot beans and a red wine sauce, comes from the nearby Mendip Hills.

✉ 1 Chandos Road, Redland, Bristol BS6 6PG ☎ 0117 973 7999 ⏰ Thu–Sat 12–2, 6.30–9.30 🍽 L £15, D £24.75, Wine £12 🚗 Call for directions 🚉 Bristol Temple Meads

CHELTENHAM
CAFÉ PARADISO
www.aliashotels.com
Café Paradiso in Alias Hotel Kandinsky (▷ 167) is bright and welcoming. Very much in the Italian mould but with modern European influences. Try the 'Paradiso Pronto' menu for quick lunches or linger over Sunday lunch.

✉ Bayshill Road, Montpellier, Cheltenham GL50 3AS ☎ 01242 527788 ⏰ Mon–Sat 12–2.30, 6.30–10, Sun 7–9 🍽 L £10.95, D £25, Wine £15.50 🚗 From junction 11 of M5 take A40 to town centre. Right at second roundabout, second exit at third roundabout into Bayshill Road. Hotel on corner of Bayshill and Parabola roads 🚉 Cheltenham Spa

LE CHAMPIGNON SAUVAGE
www.lechampignonsauvage.co.uk
The understated exterior of Le Champignon Sauvage belies the excitement to be found within. David Everitt-Matthias' cooking style is often startling, earning him a peer-less reputation for hard work and dedication. Pressed skate, potato and leek terrine, with oyster and leek emulsion is a technical *tour de force*, exquisitely layered, and subtly flavoured. Equally impressive desserts include a hot fig tart with a honey spice bread ice cream. Vegetarian options are by request only.

✉ 24–28 Suffolk Road, Cheltenham GL50 2AQ ☎ 01242 573449 ⏰ Tue–Sat 12.30–1.30, 7.30–9. Closed Easter, three weeks in Jun and 10 days at Christmas 🍽 L £23, D £28, Wine £11 🚗 South of town centre near Boys' College on A40 (Oxford). Call for exact details 🚉 Cheltenham Spa

DARTMOUTH
JAN AND FREDDIES BRASSERIE
www.janandfreddiesbrasserie.co.uk
Located in the heart of Dartmouth, this stylish brasserie with contemporary yet comfortable decor, polished wood tables, smart lighting and lots of mirrors is just a stone's throw from the River Dart. The informal atmosphere is complemented by relaxed and friendly service, and there's a lively bar area at the rear. Unfussy modern British dishes are prepared with an emphasis on top-quality local ingredients and a focus on flavour. Begin with a light bavarois with Devon blue cheese and pear and walnut salad, or perhaps a fresh bisque of local crab with saffron oil, followed by halibut poached in red wine with roasted beetroot, cauliflower puree and a light fish sauce. Desserts include a superb hot chocolate fondant accompanied by vanilla parfait, roasted hazelnuts and an espresso caramel.

✉ 10 Fairfax Place, Dartmouth TQ6 9AD ☎ 01803 832491 ⏰ 12.30–2, 6.30–9; closed Sun, Christmas, L Mon 🍽 Telephone for prices 🚗 Fairfax Place runs parallel to South Embankment. Restaurant faces Hawley Road

Above left *Mackerel in the pretty, coastal village of Flushing, Cornwall*

THE NEW ANGEL

www.thenewangel.co.uk

Even if proprieter and chef John Burton Race hadn't splashed himself all over the tabloids and TV by appearing in ITV's 'I'm a celebrity get me out of here', you would probably want to seek out his busy quayside restaurant. The modern French cuisine has survived the chef's turbulent private life to emerge both highly regarded and respectful of its origins. Stars from the fixed-price lunch menu might be a starting carpaccio of Dexter Beef with horseradish cream and rocket salad, while the à la carte makes good use of the restaurant's location with something like half a steamed Dartmouth lobster with truffle cream, new potatoes and fresh salad shoots.

✉ 2 South Embankment, Dartmouth TQ6 9BH ☎ 01803 839425 ◷ 12–2.30, 6.30–10. Closed 25 Dec 🍴 L £24.50, D £33, Wine £16 🚌 In the Centre of Dartmouth by the waterfront, opposite the passenger ferry

Below *Pretty Mousehole harbour*

DORCHESTER

YALBURY COTTAGE & RESTAURANT

www.yalburycottage.com

Local ingredients, in season, are the key to this idyllic rural retreat. With a daily changing menu, often depending on the catch of local fishermen, you might start with a Portland shellfish ragout followed by roast loin of Tolpuddle lamb. The Taste of Dorset cheeseboard is a particular source of pride and all the puds are freshly cooked.

✉ Lower Bockhampton DT2 8PZ ☎ 01305 262382 ◷ Daily 7–9, also Sun 12–2.30 🍴 L £26, D £34, Wine £12.95 🚌 3km (2 miles) east of Dorchester. From B3150 roundabout, take second exit. Through Hollow Hill and after 600yds (550m) turn right into Bockhampton Lane then 400yds (365m) on left. 🚉 Dorchester South

EXETER

MICHAEL CAINES AT ABODE EXETER

www.michaelcaines.com

The old Royal Clarence Hotel emerged from a makeover as ABode Exeter. Stylish with darkwood floors and trendy artwork on the walls,

Caines is committed to local produce and seasonal ingredients, so look for the roasted Cornish sea bass with a cauliflower purée, or Gressingham duckling with baby turnips. Reserve a table for weekends.

✉ Cathedral Yard, Exeter EX1 1HD ☎ 01392 223638 ◷ Mon–Sat 12–2.30, 7–10 🍴 L £13, D £26, Wine £18.25 🚌 From junction 30 of the M5, towards the A379. Follow signs to the city centre and the hotel is opposite the cathedral behind High Street 🚉 Exeter Central

FALMOUTH

FALMOUTH HOTEL

www.falmouthhotel.com

From its spectacular beachfront location, this graceful Victorian hotel ticks all the boxes, with its wonderful sea views, inviting lounges, leafy grounds, impressive leisure facilities and choice of dining options. The Trelawney Restaurant is full of period grandeur, complete with chandeliers. Appealing fixed-price menus make intelligent use of the abundant Cornish larder. Dishes are fresh, simply prepared and clean flavoured. Recommendations include pan-fried Gressingham duck

breast with potato dauphinoise and lightly spiced black cherry sauce; and grilled fillet of salmon with crushed new potato salad, baby spinach and white wine and dill velouté.

✉ Castle Beach, Falmouth TR11 4NZ ☎ 01326 312671 🕐 12.30–2, 7–9.30; closed L Sat ✋ L £12.50, D 25 🚗 A39, Western Terrace, over roundabout onto Melvill Road. Continue to next roundabout and hotel is on right

FOWEY
FOWEY HALL
www.foweyhall.com
The dining room at this fine hotel (▷ 168) offers a dazzling Modern British menu packed with luxury local produce. Stick to the simple dishes and you'll be blown away.

✉ Hanson Drive, Fowey PL23 1ET ☎ 01726 833866 🕐 Daily 12–2.15, 7–10 ✋ L £12, D £32.50, Wine £10.25
🚗 Arriving in Fowey cross mini roundabout into town centre. Pass school on right after 400m (440 yards) and turn right into Hanson Drive 🚉 Par

HANSONS
www.foweyhallhotel.co.uk
Mussels from the estuary in front of this elegant hotel, along with locally caught lobster, fish and shellfish, form the core of the daily changing, 'modern country-house' style menu. Children are also well-catered for in this family-focused restaurant.

✉ Fowey Hall, Hanson Drive, Fowey PL23 1ET ☎ 01726 833866 🕐 12–2, 7–10 ✋ L £15.95, D £35, Wine £17 ☎ Arriving in Fowey cross mini roundabout into town centre. Pass school on right after 400m (440yds) turn right into Hanson Drive 🚉 Par

ISLES OF SCILLY
THE ISLAND
www.islandhotel.co.uk
The dining room of this hotel (▷ 168) offers Modern British food with the emphasis on excellent fish and seafood. You may wish to finish off a meal with the excellent selection of Cornish cheeses.

✉ Tresco TR24 0PU ☎ 01720 422883 🕐 Daily 12–2.30, 7–9 ✋ L £10, D £38, Wine £15 🚁 Helicopter service from Penzance to Tresco; hotel in northeast of island

LYME REGIS
ALEXANDRA
www.hotelalexandra.co.uk
This elegant restaurant in the welcoming Alexandra hotel (▷ 168) serves up imaginative dishes including pan-fried crab cakes with saffron sauce and horseradish potato cake, with locally made ice cream for dessert. Sophisticated tastes cater to older palettes. No children under 10.

✉ Pound Street, Lyme Regis DT7 3HZ ☎ 01297 442010 🕐 Daily 12.30–1.30, 7–8.30; closed Jan ✋ L £17.95, D £29.95, Wine £14.95 🚆 🚗 From A30 turn on to A35, A358, then take the A3052 onwards to Lyme Regis

MARAZION
GODOLPHIN ARMS
www.godolpinarms.co.uk
Family-run, with a friendly welcome and good service, the restaurant in this hotel (▷ 168) offers plenty of seafood, including *moules marinière*, alongside pub favourites such as chargrilled steaks. Less familiar options might include roasted avocado and goats' cheese served with apple and a tomato and basil sauce. There's a family room and garden terrace.

✉ Marazion, near Penzance TR17 0EN ☎ 01736 710202 🕐 Mon–Sat 10.30am–11pm, Sun 12–10.30 ✋ Bar L £12, D £25, Wine £11 🚗 From A30 follow the signs for Marazion for 1.6km (1 mile) until you reach the hotel/pub; at the end of the causeway continue to St. Michael's Mount

Left *Michael Caines at Abode, Exeter*

MIDSOMER NORTON
THE MOODY GOOSE AT THE OLD PRIORY
www.moodygoose.co.uk
With its origins in the 12th century, the Old Priory Hotel can claim to be one of the oldest buildings in Somerset. The Moody Goose restaurant moved here from Bath in 2005 and has continued to impress diners with its innovative modern British food. It makes good use of the kitchen garden for herbs and vegetables in season; look for characterful dishes such as roasted quail with a spinach and ricotta cake and a sage cream, or poached rabbit saddle, confit leg with tarragon sauce and herb gnocchi.

✉ Church Square, Midsomer Norton BA3 2HX ☎ 01761 416784 🕐 12–1.30, 7–9.30. Closed Sun ✋ L £16, D £25, Wine £16.95 ☎ Down Midsomer Norton High Street, right at lights, then right at roundabout in front of church

MOUSEHOLE
OLD COASTGUARD HOTEL
www.oldcoastguardhotel.co.uk
Those in the know come to this hotel (▷ 168) to enjoy fresh regional produce, meats and cheeses prepared and presented in a variety of contemporary and traditional ways, with plenty of vegetarian and seafood options. Expect terrine of guinea fowl and ham, followed perhaps by wild sea bass, grilled salmon, rib-eye steak or pan-fried duck. Round off your meal with Cornish ices.

✉ The Parade, Mousehole TR19 6PR ☎ 01736 731222 🕐 Daily 12–2.30, 6–9.30 ✋ L £14, D £30, Wine £14 🚗 A30 to Penzance, take coast road through Newlyn to Mousehole, inn is first building on left

NETTLECOMBE
MARQUIS OF LORNE
www.marquisoflorne.com
This cosy inn provides an ideal setting in which to enjoy home-cooked food and real ales. The daily changing blackboard menus offer tasty dishes based on fresh local produce, whether you choose a light snack or à la carte dinner in

the separate dining room—but be warned, the portions are generous. The proprietors have joined the Campaign for Real Food, and even the children's menu provides wholesome cooking.

✉ Nettlecombe DT6 3SY ☎ 01308 485236 ◷ Mon–Sat 12–3, 6.30–11, Sun all day 🖐 L £14, D £18.50, Wine £13.95 🚗 North from Bridport on A3066, after 2.5km (1.5 miles) after mini roundabout turn right, through West Milton, straight over junction (signposted Powerstock), pub is 500m (550 yds) on left

PADSTOW
THE SEAFOOD RESTAURANT
www.rickstein.com

The success of chef/proprietor Rick Stein's TV programmes and books might be relied upon to fill the tables here, but this restaurant is rightly popular on its own merits. Passion, care and attention to detail are apparent throughout. Main courses such as sea bass with tomato, butter and vanilla vinaigrette rely on the exemplary quality of the fish and accurate cooking. Children under three are not welcome. Accommodation is also available (▷ 169).

✉ Riverside, Padstow PL28 8BY ☎ 01841 532700 ◷ Daily 12–2, 7–10; closed 1 May and one week at Christmas 🖐 L £27, D £36, Wine £19 🚗 Take A389 towards Padstow, after 5km (3 miles) turn right at T-junction. At signs for Padstow town centre turn right to centre; restaurant on riverside

ST. PETROC'S HOTEL AND BISTRO
www.rickstein.com

St. Petroc's Hotel (▷ 169) has an unpretentious eatery. A European menu strong on Mediterranean flavours specializes in sea-fresh fish. Reservations are essential in summer.

✉ 4 New Street, Padstow PL28 8EA ☎ 01841 532700 ◷ Daily 12–2, 7–10; closed 1 May and one week at Christmas 🖐 L £18.50, D £24.50, Wine £17 ◷ 🚗 Take A30, A38 and A389 towards Padstow. Continue 5km (3 miles), turn right at T-junction and follow signs to Padstow town centre

PENZANCE
THE SUMMER HOUSE
www.summerhouse-cornwall.com

The food here is Mediterranean using the freshest of local and Cornish produce. The tropical walled garden is perfect for summer drinks and dining. Children under eight are not welcome.

✉ Cornwall Terrace, Penzance TR18 4HL ☎ 01736 363744 ◷ 7–9.30; closed Nov–end Feb Mon–Wed 🖐 D £29.50, Wine £14 🚗 Enter Penzance on A30 and drive along harbour past open-air bathing pool. Follow promenade and turn right immediately after Queen's Hotel; Summerhouse 30m (33 yds) on left 🚉 Penzance

PLYMOUTH
TANNERS RESTAURANT
www.tannersrestaurant.co.uk

Tanners is housed in one of Plymouth's oldest domestic buildings, the 15th-century house where the Pilgrim Fathers ate their final meal in England. The restaurant offers a modern menu with daily specials acknowledging French, British and American influences—butternut squash linguine, seafood stew, and maple pecan bread and butter pudding.

✉ Prysten House, Finewell Street, Plymouth PL1 2AE ☎ 01752 252001 ◷ Tue–Sat 12–2.30, 7–9.30; closed first week in Jan 🖐 L £13.50, D £31, Wine £12.95 🚗 Town centre, behind St. Andrews Church, on Royal Parade 🚉 Plymouth

PORLOCK
ANDREWS ON THE WEIR
www.andrewsontheweir.co.uk

A fine example of the 'restaurant with rooms' concept, Andrews is a delightful Georgian house set back from the water's edge. The modern European cooking style delivers balanced combinations of ingredients, such as slow roasted Somerset tenderloin pork, perhaps with a confit of onions and squash risotto, or pan-roasted skate wing, caught locally of course, with brown butter, capers and parsley. The two-course fixed-price lunch is particularly good value.

✉ Porlock Weir TA24 8PB ☎ 01643 863300 ◷ 12–3, 6.30–10. Closed Jan,

Mon, Tue 🖐 L £10, D £38.50, Wine £14 🚗 From M5 J 25 follow A358 towards Williton, then A39 through Porlock, turning right, down to Porlock Weir.

THE OAKS HOTEL
www.oakshotel.co.uk

The use of superior ingredients is evident in the traditional British cuisine at this hotel's (▷ 169) restaurant. The appealing four-course dinner menu ends with home-made chocolates. The vegetarian menu is by request only. Children under eight are not welcome.

✉ Porlock TA24 8ES ☎ 01643 862265 ◷ 7–8.30, closed Nov–end Mar 🖐 D £30, Wine £12.50 🚗 At bottom of Dunstersteepe Road, on left after entering Porlock from Minehead

ST. IVES
PORTHMINSTER BEACH RESTAURANT
www.porthminstercafe.co.uk

The large but intriguing menu of predominantly Mediterranean-style dishes has a dash of the Orient, but you can still get tasty Helford River oysters and Cornish crabs. Reserve a window table.

✉ Porthminster, St. Ives TR26 2EB ☎ 01736 795352 ◷ Daily 12–3.30, 6.30–10; closed early Nov– end Mar 🖐 L £23, D £27.50, Wine £11.95 🚗 On Porthminster Beach, behind St. Ives train station 🚉 St. Ives

ST. MAWES
HOTEL TRESANTON
www.tresanton.com

The restaurant acknowledges the great French brasseries and ocean-going liners of the 1930s. The food is simple; fish and meat is either pan-fried, seared or roasted.

✉ 27 Lower Castle Road, St. Mawes TR2 5DR ☎ 01326 270055 ◷ Daily 12–2.30, 7–9.30 🖐 L £21, D £39, Wine £13.50 🚗 From St. Austell take A390 towards Truro. After 6.5km (4 miles) turn on to B3287 to St. Mawes. Hotel is in the town centre, on the waterfront

Right *A dusk view of the harbour bridge, Torquay*

SHERBORNE
THE GREEN
www.thegreensherborne.co.uk
This attractive old stone, Grade II-listed property is easy to spot with its distinctive, smart green-painted woodwork. Inside, the period character of the old building is retained in the exposed beams, wooden floor and antique wooden tables and chairs, complemented by a further dining room upstairs for private parties. Relaxed, friendly service and atmosphere establishes this as a popular venue. The cooking is modern with simple but stylish presentation from a talented team. You might start with carpaccio of yellowfin tuna loin with pickled ginger, coriander, guacamole, lime and soy, and go on to fillet of Cornish brill with new potatoes, ratatouille, broccoli, courgettes and cherry tomato dressing. Lemon crème brûlée with a compote of blueberries and shortbread makes the perfect finish.
✉ 3 The Green, DT9 3HY ☎ 01935 813821 🕐 12–2, 7–9; closed Sun, Mon, 2 weeks Jan, 1 week Jun, 1 week Sep, public holidays, Christmas 🍴 L £18.95, D £30, Wine £14

TORQUAY
ORESTONE MANOR HOTEL RESTAURANT
www.orestonemanor.co.uk
The highly regarded, contemporary English cuisine makes use of locally landed seafood. The friendly and intelligent service is a strength.
✉ Rockhouse Lane, Maidencombe TQ1 4SX ☎ 01803 328098 🕐 Daily 12–2.30, 7–9 🍴 L £15, D £39, Wine £14.95 🚗 From Teignmouth take A379, through Shaldon towards Torquay. In 5km (3 miles) take sharp left into Rockhouse Lane. Hotel is signed

WATERGATE BAY
FIFTEEN CORNWALL
www.fifteencornwall.co.uk
This much-heralded restaurant translates the original Fifteen urban look into something more relevant to its coastal location. Accessed via a decked area, the contemporary new-build beachside restaurant is a relaxed open-plan affair with wood floors and stylish decor. At first-floor level above the 2-mile (3km) beach, window tables enjoy superb views across the bay. Like Jamie Oliver's blueprint London outlet, Fifteen Cornwall supports disadvantaged youngsters as they build a career in the industry. The sunny Mediterranean-style cooking rooted in Italy, is driven by simplicity and quality seasonal produce. Cornish fillet of John Dory with Charlotte potatoes, cockles, and rock samphire in a crab brodo show the style.
✉ On The Beach, Watergate Bay TR8 4AA ☎ 01637 861000 🕐 12–2.30, 6.15–9.15 🍴 Telephone for prices 🚗 M5 to Exeter and join A30 westbound. Exit Highgate Hill junction, following signs to airport and at T-junction after airport, turn left and follow road to Watergate Bay

WELLS
GOODFELLOWS
www.goodfellowswells.co.uk
The mulberry-coloured shopfront of this establishment houses an informal patisserie and coffee shop. Downstairs provides a modern, bright main restaurant with an open-plan kitchen and there's further restaurant space upstairs with a glass atrium, and an adjoining courtyard. The technically accomplished and skilled modern European cooking offers top-notch fish and seafood with Mediterranean influences—a light style with intense flavours from oils and vinaigrettes using the likes of black olives, capers and anchovy or truffle oil. A six-course tasting menu is also available, and typical dishes might include local purple potato and Chew Valley smoked eel terrine with caper vinaigrette to start, followed by roast cod and sea bass with squid ink linguine and bouillabaisse sauce, with excellent patisserie, perhaps a summer fruit tart, to finish.
✉ 5 Sadler Street, BA5 2RR ☎ 01749 673866 🕐 12–2, 6.30–9.30; closed Sun, Mon, D Tue, 25–27 Dec, 1 Jan 🍴 L £17, D £36, Wine £15

ZENNOR
THE GURNARD'S HEAD
www.gurnardshead.co.uk
Located on the winding coast road and close to the cliffs, this substantial inn combines a country atmosphere—log fires, solid wood floors and tables—with modern cooking. Service is suitably relaxed and friendly, while the kitchen makes good use of the abundant local produce on a sensibly compact daily-changing menu. Traditional British classics sit comfortably alongside ideas from the European mainland, mostly France and Spain. Expect simply presented, clean and vibrant cooking in dishes like jellied pork and sage terrine or shin of beef braised in ale with mashed potato and thyme dumplings. Lemon posset is a typical dessert, or finish with a plate of three West Country cheeses served with soda bread and apple jelly.
✉ Treen TR26 3DE ☎ 01736 796928 🕐 12–2.30, 6.30–9.30; closed 24–25 Dec 🍴 L £XX, D £25, Wine £XX 🚗 6 miles (10km) west of St. Ives by B3306

PRICES AND SYMBOLS

Prices are the starting price for a double room for one night, unless otherwise stated. Breakfast is included unless noted otherwise. All the hotels listed accept credit cards unless otherwise stated. Note that rates vary widely throughout the year.

For a key to the symbols, ▷ 2.

BATH
APSLEY HOUSE HOTEL

www.apsley-house.co.uk

Apsley House bed-and-breakfast is conveniently located within walking distance of the heart of the city. The house is extremely stylish and elegant, and the spacious bedrooms (three with a four-poster bed) have fine views. There's also a bar, lounge and garden. No dogs.

✉ Newbridge Hill, Bath BA1 3PT
☎ 01225 336966 ⊗ Closed one week at Christmas ✋ £75 ⓘ 13 ⊟ On A431, 1 mile (1.6km) west of city ⊠ Bath Spa

THE QUEENSBERRY HOTEL

www.thequeensberry.co.uk

This delightful hotel in four town houses is on a quiet street near the city centre. Spacious bedrooms are tastefully furnished, and deep armchairs, fresh flowers and marble bathrooms add to their appeal. There are comfortable lounges, a small bar and a courtyard garden. The Olive Tree restaurant offers rustic but modern food. Valet parking service. No dogs.

✉ Russel Street, Bath BA1 2QF ☎ 01225 447928 ✋ £120 ⓘ 29 ⊠ Bath Spa

THE WINDSOR HOTEL

www.bathwindsorguesthouse.com

This Georgian town house is a short, level walk from the heart of town. The historic terraced house is tastefully furnished with 10 individually styled rooms. There's broadband access throughout and on-street parking. No children under 12. No dogs.

✉ 69 Great Pulteney Street, Bath BA2 4DL
☎ 01225 422100 ⊗ Closed one week at Christmas ✋ £85 ⓘ 10 ⊟ M4 junction 18 on to A4, turn left on to A36, then turn right at next mini roundabout and take second turning on left for Great Pulteney Street ⊠ Bath Spa

BOURNEMOUTH
HOTEL MIRAMAR

www.miramar-bournemouth.com

This Edwardian hotel has superb views of the sea and was once as favourite of author J. R. R. Tolkien. Friendly staff provide a relaxing environment. The public areas offer a choice of lounges and there's a croquet lawn.

✉ East Overcliff Drive, East Cliff, Bournemouth BH1 3AL ☎ 01202 556581 ✋ £120 ⓘ 43 ⊟ At Wessex Way roundabout turn into St. Pauls Road. Turn right at next roundabout, take third exit at the next, and 2nd exit at next roundabout into Grove Road. Hotel parking 50m (165ft) on right ⊠ Bournemouth

Left The quay, Clovelly

BRADFORD-ON-AVON
BRADFORD OLD WINDMILL
www.bradfordoldwindmill.co.uk
A unique bed-and-breakfast property, sympathetically restored to retain many original features. Bedrooms are individually decorated and include a number of interesting choices such as a suite with a minstrels' gallery. There's also a comfortable lounge. No children under six, or dogs.
✉ 4 Masons Lane, Bradford-on-Avon BA15 1QN ☎ 01225 866842 🕐 Closed Jan–end Feb and Christmas ✋ £59 🚻 3 🚗 Enter Bradford on A363; at mini roundabout at Castle pub turn towards town centre. After 50m (55 yards) turn left into private drive immediately beside first roadside house (no sign or number)

BRISTOL
HOTEL DU VIN & BISTRO
www.hotelduvin.com
Among the 11 properties in one of Britain's most innovative hotel groups, the Hotel du Vin extends the high standards for which the chain is renowned. The hotel is housed in a converted 18th-century sugar refinery. Bedrooms are exceptionally well designed and the hotel provides great facilities with a modern minimalist feel.
✉ The Sugar House, Narrow Lewins Mead, Bristol BS1 2NU ☎ 0117 925 5577 ✋ £140 🚻 40 🚗 From A4 follow signs for city centre. After 400m (450 yards) pass Rupert Street parking (NCP) on right. Hotel on opposite side of road 🚉 Bristol Temple Meads

CALNE
CHILVESTER HILL HOUSE
www.chilvesterhillhouse.co.uk
This elegant Victorian house stands in well-kept grounds. Dr. and Mrs. Dilley ensure a warm welcome to their bed-and-breakfast, where bedrooms are spacious and comfortable. A set dinner is available by arrangement. Stables and golf course available locally. No children under 12. No dogs.
✉ Calne SN11 0LP ☎ 01249 813981 ✋ £90 🚻 3 🚗 A4 from Calne towards Chippenham; after 0.5 miles (1km) turn right, marked Bremhill. House immediately on right 🚉 Chippenham

CHELTENHAM
ALIAS HOTEL KANDINSKY
www.aliashotels.com
A large, white, Regency villa that blends modern comfort with quirky eclectic decoration. Stylish bedrooms vary in size and have additional facilities such as CD and video players. There are various lounges, a conservatory and the bright Café Paradiso restaurant (▷ 161). Hidden in the cellars is U-bahn, a wonderful 1950s-style cocktail bar.
✉ Bayshill Road, Montpellier, Cheltenham GL50 3AS ☎ 01242 527788 ✋ £150 🚻 48 🚗 From junction 11 of M5 take A40 to town centre. Right at second roundabout, second exit at third roundabout into Bayshill Road. Hotel on corner of Bayshill and Parabola roads 🚉 Cheltenham Spa

CLOVELLY
RED LION HOTEL
www.clovelly.co.uk
A charming 18th-century inn enjoying an idyllic location in this historic fishing village. Bedrooms are sizeable and stylish with spectacular views. Fresh local fish, landed alongside the hotel, features on the daily changing menu. The friendly and attentive service contributes to a relaxing and memorable stay.
✉ The Quay, Clovelly EX39 5TF ☎ 01237 431237 ✋ £112 🚻 11 🚗 Turn off A39 at Clovelly Cross on to B3237. Proceed to bottom of hill, take first turn on left by white rails to harbour

DORCHESTER
YALBURY COTTAGE & RESTAURANT
www.yalburycottage.com
In pretty Lower Bockhampton, this delightfully attractive 300-year-old thatched property is a charming bed-and-breakfast. Oak-beam ceilings, inglenook fireplaces and stone walls are features of the lounge and restaurant (▷ 162). Comfortable, well-equipped bedrooms overlook either the lovely and vivid gardens or adjacent fields.
✉ Lower Bockhampton DT2 8PZ ☎ 01305 262382 ✋ £110 🚻 8 🚗 2 miles (3km) east of Dorchester off A35, past Hardy's Cottage, straight over crossroads, then 400m (450 yards) on left, past red telephone box, opposite village pump 🚉 Dorchester South

EXETER
ABODE HOTEL EXTER
www.abodehotels.co.uk
This much-loved Exeter landmark has been stylishly made over in contemporary style. The Michael Caines restaurant is a draw in itself, but there is less formal dining in the café bar.
✉ Cathedral Yard, Exeter EX1 1HD ☎ 01392 319955 ✋ £125 🚻 53 🚗 From junction 30 of the M5, towards the A379. Follow signs to the city centre and the hotel is opposite the cathedral behind High Street 🚉 Exeter Central

HOTEL BARCELONA
www.aliashotels.com
Within walking distance of the city centre, the Barcelona provides stylish accommodation with a glamorous atmosphere. Public areas include Café Paradiso, an informal eatery with a varied menu, a cocktail bar, a range of meeting rooms and a pretty garden terrace ideal for alfresco dining.
✉ Magdalen Street, Exeter EX2 4HY ☎ 01392 281000 ✋ £125 🚻 46 🚗 From A30 Okehampton follow city centre signs. At Exe Bridges roundabout turn right for city centre up hill over traffic lights. Parking and hotel on right 🚉 Exeter St. David's

FALMOUTH
DOLVEAN HOTEL
www.dolvean.co.uk
The attractive bedrooms of this bed-and-breakfast are individually decorated, with comfortable beds. There is an inviting lounge, and delicious home-cooked breakfasts are served at individual tables in the dining room. No children under 12. No dogs.
✉ 50 Melvill Road, Falmouth TR11 4DQ ☎ 01326 313658 ✋ £70 🚻 10 🚗 On

main road to Pendennis Castle and National Maritime Museum

FOWEY
FOWEY HALL
www.vonessenhotels.com

This mansion looks out on to the English Channel from its wonderful setting high above the estuary. The imaginatively designed bedrooms offer charm, individuality and sumptuous comfort, while beautifully appointed public rooms include the wood-panelled dining room where accomplished cuisine is served (▷ 163). Families are very much a priority here with a range of facilities to entertain children of all ages. Enjoying glorious views, the well-kept grounds have a covered pool and sunbathing area. There's a wooden play area, garden games and indoor area with computer games, mpvies and table tennis. ✉ Hanson Drive, Fowey PL23 1ET ☎ 01726 833866 ✋ £175 (half board) ⓘ 36 ⛴ 🚌 Arriving in Fowey cross mini roundabout into town centre. Pass school on right after 400m (450 yds) turn right into Hanson Drive 🚗 Par

FROME
THE TALBOT 15TH-CENTURY COACHING INN
www.talbotinn.com

Located in the peaceful village of Mells near Bath, this 15th-century inn retains many original features. Careful renovation has resulted in well equipped bedrooms (all with private bathroom) and the rustic public areas are full of character and offer a relaxed, informal setting for the enjoyment of good food and real ales. ✉ Selwood Street, Mells BA11 3PN ☎ 01373 812254 ✋ £95 ⓘ 8 🚗 A36 Bath to Warminster road, right into Frome, A362 to Radstock and follow signs for Mells 🚗 Frome

ISLES OF SCILLY
THE ISLAND
www.tresco.co.uk/holidays/island_hotel.asp

Staff provide a warm welcome and attentive service at this hotel with sea views from most bedrooms and public areas. Bedrooms, some in separate buildings in the grounds, are brightly furnished and many have a private balcony. There's a fine restaurant (▷ 163), heated outdoor pool, tennis courts, croquet and sea fishing. No dogs. ✉ Tresco TR24 0PU ☎ 01720 422883 🕙 Closed Nov–end Feb ✋ £135 including breakfast and dinner ⓘ 47 ⛴ 🚁 Helicopter service from Penzance to Tresco; hotel in northeast of island

LANLIVERY
CROWN INN
www.wagtailinns.com

With worn stone flags and rustic beams, this is a popular Cornish dining pub with a pair of en-suite bedrooms in the main building. Further accommodation is found in a converted outbuilding and a new block overlooking the garden. While the pub is traditional in character the rooms are far more contemporary in their styling without being out of place. ✉ PL30 5BT ☎ 01208 872707 ✋ £40 ⓘ 9 🚗 Signed off A390 2 miles (3km) west of Lostwithiel. Pub is 800yds (730m) down lane into village, opposite church.

LYME REGIS
ALEXANDRA
www.hotelalexandra.co.uk

This welcoming, family-run hotel dates back to 1735. Public areas have ample sitting areas to relax, unwind and enjoy the magnificent views. Imaginative, innovative dishes are served in the elegant restaurant (▷ 163). Bedrooms, which vary in size, have attractive furniture. ✉ Pound Street, Lyme Regis DT7 3HZ ☎ 01297 442010 🕙 Closed Jan and Christmas ✋ £105 ⓘ 26 🚗 From A30 turn on to A35, A358, then take A3052 to Lyme Regis

LYNMOUTH
RISING SUN HOTEL
www.risingsunlynmouth.co.uk

Impossibly romantic smugglers inn. The building is all you'd expect of a 14th-century construction—thatched roof, panelled walls and oak floors–and the location, overlooking the harbour and East Lyn River, is charming. The individually designed bedrooms are located within the inn or in adjoining cottages and have modern facilities. No children under eight. No dogs. ✉ Harbourside EX35 6EG ☎ 01598 753223 ✋ £120 ⓘ 16 🚗 Leave M5 at junction 23, take A39 to Lynmouth, hotel opposite harbour

MARAZION
GODOLPHIN ARMS
www.godolphinarms.co.uk

This 170-year-old hotel is right on the water's edge opposite St. Michael's Mount. Stunning views of the Mount are on offer from most of the bedrooms, which themselves are colourful, comfortable and spacious. There is a good restaurant (▷ 163), and even direct access to a large beach. ✉ Marazion, near Penzance TR17 0EN ☎ 01736 710202 🕙 Closed 23–27 Dec ✋ £85 ⓘ 10 🚗 From A30 follow signs for Marazion for 1 mile (1.6km) to the hotel, at the end of the causeway to St. Michael's Mount

MOUSEHOLE
OLD COASTGUARD HOTEL
www.oldcoastguardhotel.co.uk

With its stylish bar, brasserie (▷ 163) and sun lounge, this is the perfect base to explore this part of west Cornwall. Above the village, the hotel is set in subtropical gardens leading down to the sea, and most of the bedrooms (21 in all) enjoys spectacular views over Mounts Bay. No dogs. ✉ The Parade TR19 6PR ☎ 01736 731222 🕙 Closed 25 Dec ✋ £90 ⓘ 21 🚭 In restaurant 🚗 A30 to Penzance, take coast road through Newlyn to Mousehole; hotel is first building on left

MULLION
POLURRIAN
www.polurrianhotel.com

This long-established hotel is set in landscaped gardens, 100m (300ft) above the sea. Public areas are spacious and comfortable, and the bedrooms are individually styled. There are well-equipped leisure facilities with sauna, solarium,

Above *Mousehole, Cornwall*

Jacuzzi, gym, squash and tennis courts, cricket net, and two heated pools (one outdoors). Use of the croquet lawn, putting green, mountain bikes, surf and body boards is welcomed.

✉ Mullion TR12 7EN ☎ 01326 240421 ✋ £124 (includes breakfast and dinner) ① 39 🚗 🎾 🚗 From A30 take A3076 to Truro. Follow signs for Helston on A39 then A394 to The Lizard and Mullion

NETHER STOWEY
APPLE TREE
www.appletreehotel.com

This is a convenient and popular place. Bedrooms have plenty of character, with several situated in an adjoining wing, overlooking the garden. The friendly owners make every effort to ensure that guests have an enjoyable stay. No dogs.

✉ Keenthorne, Nether Stowey, Bridgwater TA5 1HZ ☎ 01278 733238 ✋ £80 ① 15 🚗 From Bridgwater follow A39 towards Minehead; hotel on left 2 miles (3km) past Cannington 🚊 Bridgwater

PADSTOW
THE SEAFOOD RESTAURANT
www.rickstein.com

Rick Stein's Seafood Restaurant (▷ 163) enjoys an enviable reputation, and it is no surprise to discover that high standards are maintained in the accommodation here. Bedrooms are spacious and comfortable with fine-quality fixtures and fittings.

Additional rooms are housed close by in St. Edmunds, where refurbishment has resulted in luxurious standards with much style.

✉ Riverside, Padstow PL28 8BY ☎ 01841 532700 ③ Closed 1 May and 24–26 Dec ✋ £125 ① 20 🚗 Take A389 towards Padstow, after 3 miles (5km) turn right at T-junction. At signs for Padstow town centre turn right to centre; restaurant on riverside

ST. PETROC'S HOTEL AND BISTRO
www.rickstein.com

One of the oldest buildings in town, this lovely bed-and-breakfast establishment is located just up the hill from the picturesque harbour. Style, comfort and individuality are all great strengths here. The bistro (▷ 164) is very popular.

✉ 4 New Street, Padstow PL28 8EA ☎ 01841 532700 ③ Closed 1 May and 24–26 Dec ✋ £115 ① 10 🚗 Take A30, A38 and A389 towards Padstow. Continue 3 miles (5km), turn right at T-junction and follow signs to Padstow town centre

PORLOCK
THE OAKS HOTEL
www.oakshotel.co.uk

A charming Edwardian house, located and in attractive grounds, with elevated views across the village towards the sea. Bedrooms are thoughtfully furnished and comfortable, and the public rooms include a charming bar and peaceful drawing room. The dining room (▷ 164)

features a daily changing menu. No children under eight.

✉ Porlock TA24 8ES ☎ 01643 862265 ③ Closed Nov–end Mar (except Christmas and New Year) ✋ £145 ① 8 🚗 At bottom of Dunstersteepe Road, on left after entering Porlock from Minehead

POWERSTOCK
THREE HORSESHOES INN
www.threehorseshoesinn.co.uk

A Victorian inn at the centre of a quiet West Dorset village, the Three Horseshoes has three comfortable, en-suite guest rooms, two with views down the valley. There's an unpretentious bar serving local beers, and a diminutive dining room for eating the freshest local produce, including vegetables and herbs from the pub's own garden.

✉ Powerstock, Bridport DT6 3TF ☎ 01308 483328 ✋ £80 ① 3 🚗 3 miles (5km) from Bridport, Powerstock is signed off the A3066, Bridport to Beaminster road.

ST. MAWES
IDLE ROCKS
www.idlerock.co.uk

Superbly situated on the waterside overlooking the attractive fishing port with excellent sea views and an outdoor terrace for use in the summer. Bedrooms are individually styled and furnished to a high standard.

✉ Harbour Side, St. Mawes TR2 5AN ☎ 01326 270771 ✋ £156 (including breakfasat and dinner) ① 27 🚗 Off A390, onto A3078, and 14 miles (22.5km) to St. Mawes. Hotel on left

TORQUAY
COLINDALE HOTEL
www.colindalehotel.co.uk

This friendly bed-and-breakfast, set in attractive gardens, is stylish and elegant, and service is attentive. Guest rooms, some of which have views over Torbay, are well appointed. Excellent, freshly cooked dinner (by prior arrangement, high season only) and breakfast feature interesting dishes. No children under 11. No dogs.

✉ 20 Rathmore Road, Chelston, Torquay TQ2 6NY ☎ 01803 293947 ✋ £60 ① 8 🚊 Torquay

SIGHTS 172

WALKS AND DRIVES 202

WHAT TO DO 206

EATING 212

STAYING 218

SOUTH EAST AND EAST ANGLIA

It would be easy to overlook the counties that surround the English capital as a metropolitan hinterland. But what a mistake that would be! Leaving aside the lovely university cities of Oxford and Cambridge, which should be on any visitor's itinerary, this is a region of market towns and typically English villages, many complete with thatched roofs and village greens.

To the north of London, the landscape flattens into the wide open skies of East Anglia. Beyond Cambridge's venerable academic institutions, Ely's magnificent cathedral tower rises high above the Fenland. Norwich, too, is a treasure trove of medieval buildings and at its feet lie the Norfolk Broads, a web of lakes and rivers and a magnet for wildlife.

To the south of the capital, Kent is still a county of orchards and hop fields, though perhaps less idyllic than it once was. Its southern tip is guarded by the castle at Dover. Here, where continental Europe is barely 20 miles (32km) away across the sea, over 1,000 years of fascinating defence history can be traced through the tunnels and fortifications hollowed out of the famous white cliffs.

Defence is very much the theme of another south coast city—Portsmouth. This is the home of the Royal Navy, an appropriate place to find the salvaged hulk of the *Mary Rose*, Henry VIII's flagship. The rolling hill country of the North and South Downs and the Chilterns is where the rich and famous have always sought a refuge from the bustle of city life. There are several historic homes and palaces. and at Windsor the castle is the greatest of all the Royal residences. Upstream from here, the River Thames meanders through Oxford, where the students ply their punts and the tourists gape at the 'dreaming spires' of the magnificent university colleges.

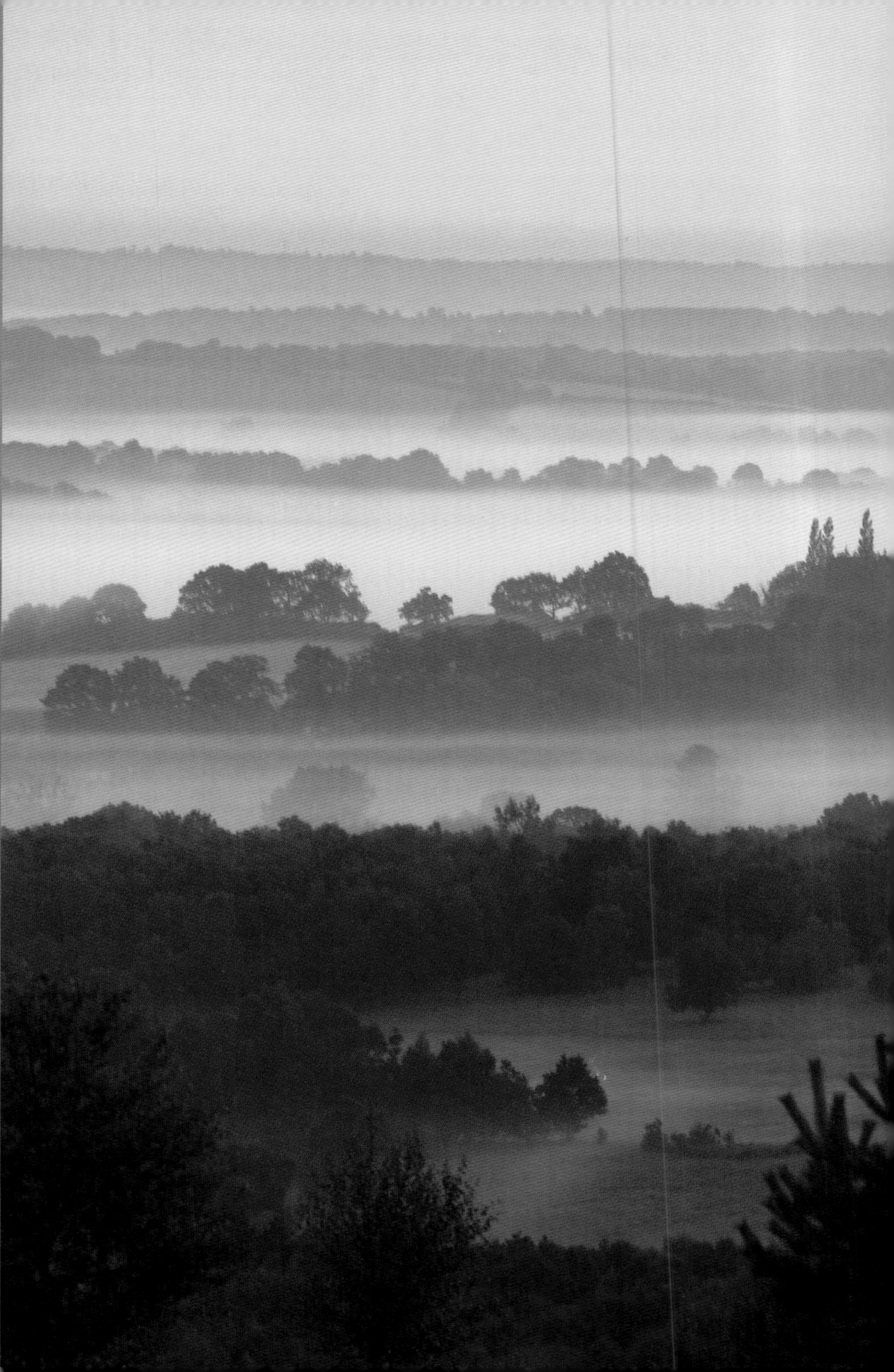

ALDEBURGH

www.suffolkcoastal.gov.uk

Fishermen still launch their boats here from the shingle beach and sell the day's catch from their huts. The 14th-century Church of St. Peter and St. Paul has a stained-glass window commemorating the composer Benjamin Britten (1913–76), who lived in Aldeburgh from 1947 to 1957. He is buried in the churchyard beside the English tenor Sir Peter Pears (1910–86), his partner and a co-founder of the internationally renowned annual music festival based around Snape Maltings, inland at Snape, each June.

Britten's famous opera, *Peter Grimes,* is based on *The Borough* by the 18th-century Aldeburgh poet George Crabbe (1754–1832) and which was thought to have been set here.

✚ 459 M17 ▐ 152 High Street, Aldeburgh IP15 5AQ, tel 01728 453637

ALFRISTON

www.visitsussex.org

Alfriston's high street is a wonderful example of an old Sussex village, with many fine medieval, tile-hung and timber buildings, antiques shops, inns and tea shops. By the church and The Tye (village green) is the first property acquired by the National Trust, the 14th-century thatched Clergy House (Good Fri to mid-Dec Sat–Mon, Wed, Thu; Mar Sat–Sun), purchased in 1896 for the sum of £10.

Carved on the South Downs, 2 miles (3.5km) northeast of Alfriston, is the Long Man of Wilmington, an enigmatic figure and Europe's largest known representation of the human form. Of unknown date or purpose, the figure stands 70m (230ft) tall.

✚ 459 L20 ▐ 37 Church Street, Seaford BN25 1HG, tel 01323 897426

AMBERLEY WORKING MUSEUM

www.amberleymuseum.co.uk

There's a little bit of everything at this open-air industrial history museum on the site of a former limeworks in the South Downs, covering 150 years of working life in southeast England. On display are a 1920s bus garage, a rural telephone exchange from the 1930s, the Connected Earth exhibition of telecommunications down the ages and the EDF Electricity Hall, showing a range of domestic appliances from the past. Among the many craftspeople at work are a blacksmith and a walking-stick maker.

A narrow-gauge railway and vintage buses travel the length of the museum.

✚ 458 K19 ✉ Amberley, near Arundel BN18 9LT ☎ 01798 831370 🕐 Mid-Feb to end Oct Wed–Sun, public hols and local school hols 10–5.30 (last admission 4.30) 💷 Adult £9.30, child (5–15) £5.80, family £26.50 🚉 Amberley ▢ 🎫

ARUNDEL

www.sussexbythesea.com

From a distance, the handsome town of Arundel looks rather French, with its castle and spiky Gothic Revival cathedral on a hilltop. The compact, hilly core takes only a few minutes to walk through, but has plenty of brick, flint and timbered architecture to enjoy and antiques shops in which to browse. Arundel Castle (end Mar–end Oct Tue–Sun, also Mon in Aug and public hols) has been home to the dukes of Norfolk and their ancestors for more than 850 years. Largely rebuilt in Gothic style in the 19th century, it is rich in furnishings and art treasures. Close by is the Roman Catholic Cathedral of Our Lady, completed in 1873.

To the north, the River Arun flows through the Wildfowl and Wetland Trust (WWT) Arundel nature reserve (daily), where hundreds of swans, geese and ducks can be observed at close quarters.

✚ 458 K20 ▐ 13 Crown Yard Mews, Arundel BN18 9AJ, tel 01903 882268 🚉 Arundel

ASHDOWN FOREST

www.ashdownforest.co.uk

This former royal hunting ground is the single largest tract of open land in southeast England, and one of the last surviving areas of lowland heath in Europe. The whole area is open to walkers, although the maze of paths can be disorienting. A number of parking areas along the B2026 make good starting points. This was the landscape that inspired the *Winnie the Pooh* stories; the author A. A. Milne (1882–1956) lived nearby, and the sandy tracks, Scots pines and Poohsticks Bridge still closely resemble E. H. Shepherd's (1879–1976) illustrations in the books.

✚ 459 K19 ▐ Ashdown Forest Centre, Wych Cross, Forest Row RH18 5JP, tel 01342 823583

Opposite *The early morning mist in Ashdown Forest*
Below *Battlements of Arundel Castle with boats on the River Arun*

AUDLEY END HOUSE AND GARDENS

www.english-heritage.org.uk

One of England's greatest Jacobean country houses lies just west of Saffron Walden. Built between 1605 and 1614 by Thomas Howard, first Earl of Suffolk, on the scale of a great royal palace, it was reduced in size over the next century, with modifications by architects Sir John Vanbrugh (1664–1726) and Robert Adam (1728–92). James I decided it was 'too large for a king'.

The interior is largely the influence of the third Baron Braybrooke, who inherited the house in 1825 and filled the many rooms (30 are now open to the public) with furnishings and works of art. The gardens and parkland that surround the house were landscaped by Capability Brown (1715–83), with Palladian bridges and temples.

The busy medieval market town of Saffron Walden (1 mile/1.5km east), named after the saffron crocuses growing in the surrounding fields, makes a good detour for its timber-framed buildings, turf maze and its grand flint church which is 300 feet (61m) long and almost as high.

➕ 459 L17 ✉ Audley End, Saffron Walden CB11 4JF ☎ 01799 522399 🕐 House: Mar Sat–Sun10–4; Apr–end Sep Wed–Sun 11–5 (Sat 11–3); Oct, mid Nov to mid Dec Sat 10–3, Sun 10–4. Apr–end Jun, Sep–end Dec by tour only. Garden: end Feb Sat–Sun 11–4; Mar, Oct Sat–Sun 10–5; Apr–end Sep Wed–Sun and public hols 10–6; mid-Nov to mid-Dec Sat–Sun 10–4. Last admission 1 hour before closing 🚻 Audley End, 1 mile (1.5km) ✋ House and grounds: adult £9.20, child (5–16) £4.60, family £23. Grounds only: adult £5, child £3,80, family £12.50 🖥 ⌨

BATEMAN'S

www.nationaltrust.org.uk

The English writer Rudyard Kipling (1865–1936), probably most famous as the author of the two *Jungle Books* (1894–95), made this small Jacobean house his home from 1902 until his death. It remains much as it was when he lived here and is filled with traces of his extraordinary life

and work. The magnificent book-lined study is where he wrote *Puck of Pook's Hill* (1906) and *Rewards and Fairies* (1910).

The grounds include a mulberry garden, rose garden and a wild garden where a watermill grinds corn into flour most Saturday afternoons.

The 1928 Rolls-Royce Phantom, in which Kipling loved to explore the Sussex countryside, is still in the garage.

➕ 459 L19 ✉ Burwash, Etchingham TN19 7DS ☎ 01435 882302 🕐 Late Mar–end Oct Sat–Wed, Good Fri 11–5 ✋ Adult £6.50, child (5–16) £3.25, family £16.25 🖥 ⌨

BEACHY HEAD AND THE SEVEN SISTERS

www.sevensisters.org.uk

The high chalk ridge of the South Downs ends at the south coast in spectacular style with a range of dazzling white cliffs at Beachy Head and the Seven Sisters. Useful starting points are from the visitor office: You can walk out to Cuckmere Haven, the village green at East Dean and Birling Gap, where steps lead to a pebble beach. A path heads along the clifftops, but keep away from the sheer edge, as the cliff can crumble away without warning.

➕ 459 L20 ℹ Seven Sisters Country Park Visitor Centre, Exceat BN25 4AD (just off A259 between Eastbourne and Seaford), tel 01323 870280

BEAULIEU

www.beaulieu.co.uk

Ancestral home of the Montagu family, 16th-century Beaulieu Palace House is best known as the site of the National Motor Museum, where 250 vintage vehicles and the Motorsport Gallery celebrate Britain's achievements in the sport.

Beaulieu Palace House contains furniture, paintings, portraits and family memorabilia, and staff in Victorian costume explain domestic life. The estate also includes the remains of a 13th-century Cistercian abbey, housing an exhibition of monastic life.

A high-level monorail transports visitors through the grounds and gardens, or you can explore Beaulieu at ground level by following the Mill Pond Walk.

➕ 458 H20 ✉ Beaulieu, Brockenhurst SO42 7ZN ☎ 01590 612345 🕐 May–end Sep daily 10–6; rest of year daily 10–5 ✋ All sights: adult £15.25, child (5–12) £8, youth (13–17) £9, family £45 🖥 🍽 ⌨

BIGNOR ROMAN VILLA

Set beneath the South Downs near Pulborough, Bignor is one of the grandest Roman houses in Britain and one of the largest outside Italy. Occupied between the second and fourth centuries, it was rediscovered in 1811 when a farmer was ploughing his field. Within the thatched structures that preserve the villa are spectacular mosaics of the Venus and Cupid Gladiators, the Gorgon Medusa and Zeus's cupbearer, Ganymede. The 25m (80ft) mosaic pavement on the north corridor is the longest on display in Britain. A hole in the floor reveals the hypocaust (underfloor heating system), and the results of other excavations are exhibited.

➕ 458 J19 ✉ Bignor RH20 1PH ☎ 01798 869259 🕐 Mar–end Apr Tue–Sun, public holidays 10–5; Jun–end Sep daily 10–6; May and Oct daily 10–5 ✋ Adult £4.60, child (5–15) £2 🖥 ⌨

BRIGHTON

Brighton is probably Britain's liveliest seaside resort, raucous but Bohemian, with top arts and clubbing venues and some fanciful Regency architecture.

Brighton's reputation for glamour and flamboyance began in the late 18th century when the Prince Regent, later King George IV (1762–1830), first visited and followed his father in starting a trend for seaside holidays and sea bathing. The Royal Pavilion (daily), the king's astonishing palace (1815–23) in the centre of town, is an oriental extravaganza bristling with Indian-style minarets and onion domes. Its carefully restored interior, famous for its sumptuous decor and elaborate chinoiserie, makes it one of the most extraordinary palaces in Europe. Across the gardens is the former royal stable block, similarly exotic, now housing the Dome concert hall and the Brighton Museum and Art Gallery (closed Mon, except public holidays), with lively exhibits on Brighton's social history, and collections of art nouveau furniture and 20th-century fashion.

CENTRAL HIGHLIGHTS

Brighton had humble beginnings as a fishing village. Behind the elegant sweep of Regency seafront terraces you'll find The Lanes, a warren of narrow streets and alleys with smart antiques, gifts and designer clothing shops, cafés, restaurants and galleries. North Laine, tucked between The Lanes and the station, is crammed with more than 320 shops—selling everything from 1950s kitsch to funky fashions—plus cafés and pubs. And by the train station there's a huge Sunday market with antiques and collectables.

THE SEAFRONT

White stucco buildings create a wonderfully elegant seafront: Lewes Crescent, at the west end, is its grandest moment. Brighton Pier pulsates with seaside amusements. Near the pier are artsy shops, and at weekends during the summer it's a lively area, with street entertainers and beach volleyball. Brighton Sea Life Centre (daily) has an underwater tunnel that allows close viewing of sharks and other marine life.

INFORMATION

www.visitbrighton.com
✚ 459 K20 ℹ The Royal Pavilion Shop, 45 Pavilion Buildings, Brighton BN1 1EE, tel 0906 7112255 (recording) 🚃 Brighton

TIP

» There is plenty of parking on Madeira Drive, below the esplanade, but otherwise parking in town can be tricky.

Above *A view of Brighton pier through deckchairs on the beach*
Left *Looking over Beaulieu River towards Palace House at Beaulieu, a mix of 19th-century additions with sections of the original 14th-century abbey gatehouse*

INFORMATION

www.broads-authority.gov.uk

🚩 463 M16 ℹ️ 18 Colegate, Norwich NR3 1BQ, tel 01603 610734

THE BROADS

Between Norwich and the North Sea coast lie the Broads, a complex of six slow-moving rivers and 41 broads (shallow lakes), providing 122 miles (196km) of navigable waterways. Formed by peat digging in medieval times, this is Britain's largest protected wetland, and the natural habitat of many rare plants and animals.

Hiking, angling and birdwatching are all popular activities in the area, but the best way to see the Broads is by boat. The focus of activity is the small town of Wroxham, 8 miles (13km) northeast of Norwich, where boats can be hired. If you don't want to pilot your own boat, various boat trips are available from Wroxham, Potter Heigham and Thorpe St. Andrew, including sightseeing with a commentary, dinner cruises and evening trips with live music. At Horning you can even get a trip on a Mississippi-style paddle boat (no gambling though).

The Broads are rich in wildlife, and the best place to experience its diversity is at one of the Norfolk Wildlife Trust's reserves. The one at Ranworth Broad (accessible all year) has interpretive boardwalks and the floating Broads Wildlife Centre (Apr–end Oct daily), with interactive displays and wonderful views. Binoculars and telescopes are provided at the upstairs windows. The Hickling Broad reserve (accessible all year) has boardwalks with informative display panels, plus a summertime boat trip, and is also home to the Raptor Roost, at the end of a walk from the car park. Visitors can see the raptors coming and going from a viewing area.

Other Norfolk Broads attractions include Fairhaven Woodland and Water Garden (all year, daily), with 131 acres (53ha) of beautiful ancient woodland and glorious water gardens around a private 'broad' with boat trips in an Edwardian-style launch, *Primrose*, in summer. Various special events are held here throughout the year.

Above *The sun sets over boats moored at Horsey, Norfolk Broads National Park*

BLENHEIM PALACE

www.blenheimpalace.com

One of the largest private houses in Britain and the ultimate in English baroque was designed by Sir John Vanbrugh (1664–1726) and Nicholas Hawksmoor (1661–1736) and was given by Queen Anne to John Churchill, first Duke of Marlborough (1650–1722), in recognition of his crushing victory over the French at the Battle of Blenheim in 1704. It is still the home of the Churchill family, now occupied by the 11th Duke and his family.

The Churchill Exhibition, a major highlight, is the room where Sir Winston Churchill (1874–1965), Britain's prime minister during World War II, was born on 30 November. He is buried, with his wife, in the village of Bladon nearby. The gilded state rooms overlook lawns and formal gardens laid out by Capability Brown (1715–83).

Beautiful Blenheim Lake, spanned by Vanbrugh's Grand Bridge (and it is grand), forms the focal point of the grounds. From the house, look along past the lake to a massive column at the top of which the first duke stands surveying his empire. Also in the grounds are a butterfly house, maze, people-sized games of chess and draughts, and a wooden playground area. A fun miniature railway takes you in brightly painted carriages from the house to the maze and games area.

🚩 458 H17 ✉ Woodstock OX20 1PX ☎ 01993 811325 (recording), 01993 811091 🕓 Palace and gardens: mid-Feb to mid-Dec daily 10.30–5.30 (last admission 4.45). Park: daily 9–4.45 🚻 House and gardens peak season: adult £16.50, child £10, family £44. Park and gardens: adult £9.50, child £4.80, family £24.50 🍴 🖵 🏧

BODIAM CASTLE

www.nationaltrust.org.uk

With its tall drum towers at each corner and walls rising virtually to their original height over a wide, waterlily-filled moat, this substantial ruin recalls a fairytale castle. Bodiam was built by Sir Edward Dalnygrigge in 1385, both as a defence and a comfortable home. There is also a small museum of castle finds with a scale model of Bodiam Castle as it was in 1385.

🚩 59 L19 ✉ Bodiam, near Robertsbridge TN32 5UA ☎ 01580 830436 🕓 Daily 10.30–6 (last admission 5), mid-Feb to end Oct; Sat–Sun 10.30–4 or dusk (last admission 3), rest of year 🚻 Adult £4.60, child (5–16) £2.30, family £11.50 🖵 🏧

BROADSTAIRS

www.thanet.co.uk

With its seven sandy bays, Broadstairs is a mixture of a sedate, old-fashioned resort and a fishing port with winding streets and ancient fishermen's cottages. Writer Charles Dickens (1812–70) was a regular visitor from 1837. Dickens House Museum (Easter–end Jun daily 2–5; Jul–end Sep daily 10–5; Oct–Easter Thu–Sun 2–5), on Victoria Parade, was once the home of Mary Pearson Strong, on whom Dickens based the character of Miss Nancy Trotwood for his novel *David Copperfield*. The parlour re-creates the scenes of the book, much as in the original illustrations by H. K. Browne ('Phiz'). The novel was written nearby at Dickens' seafront home, which is now called Bleak House.

🚩 459 M18 ℹ 2 Victoria Parade, Broadstairs CT10 1QL, tel 01843 861232 🚉 Broadstairs

THE BURNHAMS

www.northnorfolk.org/tourism

This scattering of villages with the prefix Burnham lies along the coast of north Norfolk, an area of lonely salt marshes, vast sandy beaches and flint church towers. Burnham Market has a wide village green surrounded by mostly 17th- and 18th-century houses. Burnham Thorpe is famous as the birthplace of Admiral Lord Nelson (1758–1805), the hero of the Battle of Trafalgar. The house was demolished in 1803 and replaced by the present rectory, but All Saints' Church has a marble bust of Nelson. Burnham Overy Staithe is a pleasant former port overlooking salt marshes, with a tower windmill beyond.

🚩 463 L15 ℹ Staithe Street, Wells-next-the-Sea NR23 1AN, tel 01328 710885

CANTERBURY

www.canterbury.co.uk

Much remains of the medieval city that grew up catering to millions of pilgrims who journeyed each year to the shrine of the English saint, Thomas Becket (▷ 31). Becket was murdered in Canterbury Cathedral (where he was Archbishop) in order to please King Henry II, in 1170. The pilgrims' journey was immortalized in *The Canterbury Tales*, by Geoffrey Chaucer. The cathedral, approached via the ornate 16th-century Christ Church Gate, dates from around 1070. Its main glory is the 12th- and 13th-century stained glass featuring pilgrim scenes. In the northwest transept a stone marks the spot where Becket died.

Several charitable hospitals founded in medieval times to accommodate pilgrims include Eastbridge Hospital (Mon–Sat; closed Christmas week and Good Fri), 35 High Street. Another example is the Poor Priests' Hospital in Stour Street, within which is the Museum of Canterbury (Jun–end Sep daily; Oct–end May Mon–Sat), charting 2,000 years of the city's history.

Medieval city walls enclose three sides of Canterbury and its narrow, crooked alleys (notably Mercery Lane) lined with timbered leaning buildings. One of the original 14th-century gates, West Gate (closed Sun, Christmas week and Good Fri), on St. Peter's Street, still survives. The underground Roman Museum (closed Sun during Nov–end May), in Longmarket, houses the remains of a Roman house and re-created interiors.

Outside the city are the ruins of St. Augustine's Abbey (daily; Apr–end Jun Wed–Sun; Oct–end Mar Wed–Sun), founded in AD597, and burial place of the missionary who brought Christianity to Britain.

🚩 459 M19 ℹ 12–13 Sun Street, The Buttermarket, Canterbury CT1 2HX, tel 01227 378100 🚉 Canterbury East, Canterbury West

INFORMATION

www.visitcambridge.org

✚ 459 K17 ℹ The Old Library, Wheeler Street, Cambridge CB2 3QB, tel 0871 226 8006 ❓ Walking tours daily, call 01233 457574 for details 🚂 Cambridge

Above The Bridge of Sighs, so called because it resembled the Venetian bridge, was built in 1831 by Henry Hutchinson

INTRODUCTION

One of the best and most well-known university towns in England covers more than 700 years of academic history, and is packed with ancient colleges and other architectural landmarks.

Examples of modern industry may be the first sight of Cambridge as you enter from the flat countryside that surrounds it, so the dense and incongruously beautiful core of this historic city may be a very nice surprise. About half of the university's 30 or so colleges have medieval origins, and are mainly within 10 minutes' walk of each other. You can visit most of them, although some charge an entrance fee, and many are closed while exams are being held.

WHAT TO SEE

THE COLLEGES

The obvious starting point is King's Parade; climb the tower of the University church (also known as Great St. Mary's) for a rare high-level view. On one side is the classical Senate House, where university students receive their degrees, next to Gonville and Caius College (pronounced keys—and everyone drops the Gonville part). In the other direction, Market Hill hosts a bustling market (Mon–Sat).

King's College Chapel, known throughout Britain for its Chapel Choir, has an annual Christmas Eve carol service that attracts crowds who start waiting outside at dawn. It's well worth catching a choral evensong. The chapel was built between 1446 and 1515 under kings Henry VI (1421–71), Henry VII (1457–1509) and Henry VIII (1491–1547). It is perhaps the greatest example of the uniquely English late Gothic Perpendicular style, typified by its magnificent stained glass and the wedding-cake fan vaulting that made it the largest single-span vaulted roof of its time. By the altar is Peter Paul Rubens' masterpiece The

Adoration of the Magi, originally painted for a convent in Louvain, Belgium, and donated by Major A. E. Allnatt in 1961.

Trinity is the largest college in Cambridge, founded in 1546 by Henry VIII, and its Great Court is the largest of the courtyards at both Cambridge and Oxford universities. One of Trinity's other major features is the Wren Library—designed by Sir Christopher Wren (1632–1723) and completed in 1695—which houses almost 60,000 historic books and manuscripts, including the original manuscript of *Winnie the Pooh* by A. A. Milne (a Trinity student). Trinity's neighbour, and the second-largest college, is St. John's, founded in 1511. Its notable features include the elegant turreted gatehouse, the Bridge of Sighs and the 13th-century School of Pythagoras.

The best of the rest include: Queens', with its half-timbered Cloister Court and matchstick-like Mathematical Bridge; Emmanuel's garden; Jesus, with cloister-like seclusion and an impressive chapel; and Clare, an elegant Renaissance creation with a stone bridge.

THE CITY

Among the large stretches of greenery spread around the city are The Backs (the area along the river that gives classic back-door views of Queens', King's, Trinity, Clare and St. John's colleges, and glimpses into their gardens), where you can go punting, Jesus Green and Parker's Piece. Around Jesus Lock are the college boathouses, where you can watch crews rowing on the river, possibly in training for the Oxford v. Cambridge boat race (Mar). Farther away from the city centre, the University Botanic Garden (daily) has mature trees, a scented garden, rockeries and several national collections of species.

Two of Cambridge's best museums are free: The Fitzwilliam Museum (Tue–Sun and some public holiday Mon), in Trumpington Street, has a collection of fine jewellery, porcelain, furniture and glass, paintings by Paul Cézanne, Picasso, Peter Paul Rubens, John Constable and William Blake, watercolours by J. M. W. Turner and prints by Rembrandt. In contrast, intimate little Kettle's Yard (Tue–Sun and public holiday Mon) is a stylish gallery offering a marriage of 18th-century furnishings, antique Oriental rugs and avant-garde art.

MORE TO SEE

Out of town, but served by regular buses from Cambridge rail station, the Imperial War Museum Duxford (daily) occupies a former military airbase. It has Europe's main collection of military and civil aircraft, plus vehicles, submarines and helicopters. The Normandy Experience recreates what it was like for an infantryman landing on D-Day, while an innovative building houses the American Air Museum.

TIPS

›› Parking is a real problem in the city, so use public transport; or if you come by car, use the park-and-ride service.

›› Punting is definitely harder than it looks, and punting traffic jams are a common sight on the River Cam in summer. You can rent a chauffeur at any of the rental places; details from the tourist office.

Left *King's College, Cambridge, renowned for its chapel and choir*

CASTLE RISING

www.english-heritage.org.uk

When it was built in the 12th century, Castle Rising was the largest castle in the country. The roof has gone now, but the staircase approach survives in good condition and the keep walls stand at their original height. One of its more famous inhabitants was Isabella of France (1292–1358), the queen of England whose son, Edward III (1312–77), locked her up here in 1330 following her part in the murder of his father, her husband Edward II. She is said to still haunt the castle.

✚ 463 L15 ✉ Castle Rising PE31 6AH ☎ 01553 631330 🕐 Apr–end Oct daily 10–6; rest of year Wed–Sun 10–4 ✋ Adult £3.85, child (5–15) £2.20, family £11.50 ♿

CHARTWELL

www.nationaltrust.org.uk

This Victorian house was the country home of Britain's prime minister during World War II, Sir Winston Churchill (1874–1965), from 1924 until his death. The rooms look as if he has just stepped outside: there are books, maps, pictures, photographs and personal belongings, including hats, uniforms and Churchill's famous cigars. He and his wife, Lady Clementine Spencer-Churchill, added several features to the grounds, including a small lake and Churchill's studio, where he loved to paint. The studio is still full of his works, some of which display a definite talent. He said he gained great strength from painting and it helped to combat his 'Black Dog' depressions.

The playhouse in the garden, created by Churchill for his children, shows the delight he took in his family; Lady Churchill's Rose Garden and the Golden Rose Walk are both a treat for rose lovers.

✚ 459 K19 ✉ Mapleton Road, Westerham TN16 1PS ☎ 01732 868368 (recording), 01732 868381 🕐 Jul–end Aug Tue–Sun and public holidays 11–5 (last admission 4.15); late Mar–end Jun, Sep–end Oct Wed–Sun and public holidays 11–5 (last admission 4.15) ✋ House, garden and studio: adult £10.10, child (5–16) £5.05, family £25.25. Garden and studio: adult £5.05, child £2.50, family £12.60 🍴 ♿

CHATHAM HISTORIC DOCKYARD

www.thedockyard.co.uk

Chatham is the world's most complete dockyard to survive from the age of sail and was once England's most important naval dock. It closed in 1984 to become a working museum. In dry dock are three battleships, while the Wooden Walls exhibition recreates the sights, sounds and smells of the Royal Dockyard from 1758. Inside the working Ropery, traditional techniques are used to make rope to rig the world's greatest sailing ships. The Museum of the Royal Dockyard celebrates 400 years of the history of Chatham and the Royal Navy.

Take a cruise on the paddle-steamer *Kingswear Castle* (Jul–end Sep).

✚ 459 L18 ✉ Dock Road, Chatham ME4 4TZ ☎ 01634 823807 (recording), 01634 823800 🕐 Mid-Feb to end Oct 10–6; Nov–early Feb 10–4, last entry 45 min before closing ✋ Adult £13.50, child (5–15) £9, family £38 🚉 Chatham, 1 mile (1.5km) 🍴 🛍 📷

CHICHESTER

www.visitchichester.org

This small, pleasant city still has its original Roman street plan, with two main routes crossing west to east and north to south, enclosed by remains of the city wall (itself partly rebuilt in medieval times). A 16th-century market cross marks the central point. Close by, the *cathedral*, smaller than most, is early Norman in style, with Early English additions, and has an unusual detached belfry, a tapestry by English artist John Piper (1903–92) and stained glass by the French painter Marc Chagall (1887–1985).

During the 18th century, Chichester was enhanced by such buildings as Pallant House (closed Mon except public holidays), now a museum with an outstanding

collection of British modern art. A short distance to the west of the city is Fishbourne Roman Palace (Feb to mid-Dec daily; rest of year Sat–Sun), the largest known Roman residence in Britain, built around AD75. Much of the villa has been excavated and several rooms have been constructed over the museum to protect the delicate remains from the British weather. The palace has the largest collection of in-situ mosaics in Britain and a Roman garden replanted to the original first-century plan.

✚ 458 J20 🛈 29A South Street, Chichester PO19 1AH, tel 01243 775888 🚉 Chichester

CHILTERN OPEN AIR MUSEUM

www.coam.org.uk

More than 30 historic buildings dating from around 1500 to the 1950s have been rescued from demolition and re-erected here on the outskirts of Chalfont St. Giles. There are houses, barns, granaries, an apple store, forge, factory, toll house, sports pavilion, an Edwardian cast-iron public toilet and a mission hall, each appropriately furnished. Hands-on activities include brickmaking, straw plaiting and rag rugmaking.

High Wycombe Toll House, a three-roomed house built in 1826 for the collector of tolls on the London to Oxford road at High Wycombe, is 9 miles (14km) east of Chalfont St. Giles.

✚ 458 J18 ✉ Newland Park, Gorelands Lane, Chalfont St. Giles HP8 4AB ☎ 01494 872163 (recording), 01494 871117 🕓 Late Mar–end Oct daily 10–5 (last admission 3.30) 🏛 Adult £7.50, child (5–16) £5, family £22 ▯ ⌨

DOWN HOUSE

www.english-heritage.org.uk

Charles Darwin (1809–82), one of the most influential scientists of

the 19th century, occupied Down House from 1842 until his death. On the ground floor, the drawing room, dining room, billiard room and study have been furnished and decorated to portray the domestic daily life of his family. In the study are his writing desk and chair, where he wrote the ground-breaking *On the Origin of Species by means of Natural Selection* (published in 1859), along with some of the 5,000 objects associated with his research. On the first floor is an exhibition covering Darwin's life and work.

✚ 459 K18 ✉ Luxted Road, Downe BR6 7JT ☎ 01689 859119 🕓 Mar, Nov to mid-Dec Wed–Sun 11–4; Apr, Jun, Sep, Oct Wed–Sun 11–5; Jul, Aug daily 11–5 🏛 Adult £7.20, child (5–16) £3.60, family £18 ▯ ⌨

DOVER CASTLE

www.english-heritage.org.uk

On clear days you can see the coast of France from this giant fortress, perched on the famous White Cliffs and commanding the shortest sea crossing between England and the Continent. The castle's maze of tunnels, many created for defence during the Napoleonic Wars (1800–15), reveal a fascinating secret world from the darkest days of World War II.

No fortress in England can claim a longer continuous history than Dover Castle. Within the ramparts of an Iron Age fort, the Romans built a lighthouse, which still stands, while in the Saxon period the earthworks were re-used for a town. The Church of St. Mary in Castro within the castle walls is one of the most complete Saxon churches in southern England.

The Norman keep, built in the 1180s, houses two exhibitions that highlight the castle's key role when the country was under threat of invasion. The 1216 Siege Experience retraces how a group of rebel barons invited Prince Louis of France to invade England and take the throne from King John. A Castle Fit for a King covers preparations for Henry VIII's visit to Dover in 1539.

The castle saw dramatic action during World War II. In 1940 it was from the underground tunnels here that Vice Admiral Ramsay and Prime Minister Sir Winston Churchill masterminded the evacuation from Dunkirk of 388,000 troops in Operation Dynamo. The tour of the Secret Wartime Tunnels re-creates Britain at war through sounds, smells and archive film clips. The lights dim, the drone of bombers can be heard overhead and the sound of people at work fills the Anti-Aircraft Operations Room, the Telephone Exchange and Repeater Station.

✚ 459 M19 ✉ Dover CT16 1HU ☎ 01304 211067 🕓 Apr–end Jul daily 10–6; Aug daily 9.30–6; Nov–end Jan Thu–Mon 10–4; Feb to mid-Mar daily 10–4. Closed 24–26 Dec, 1 Jan 🏛 Including Secret Wartime Tunnels: adult £9.80, child (5–16) £4.90, family £24.50 🚉 Dover Priory, 1.5 miles (2.5km) ❓ Tours of Secret Wartime Tunnels last about 50 min (last tour 1 hour before closing) for up to 30 people; first-come, first-served 🍴 ▯ ⌨

ELY

www.ely.org.uk

Dwarfing the old-fashioned town that huddles on a rise in the flat farmlands of the Fens, is Ely cathedral, which dates from the 11th century. The east end was rebuilt in Purbeck marble around 1250, while the collapse of the tower in 1322 necessitated the erection of the breathtakingly delicate lantern tower, lodged on eight oak pillars. In the cathedral precinct is the prestigious King's School, founded by Henry VIII. Combined tickets are available for the cathedral, the attached Stained Glass Museum (daily) and Ely Museum (daily), an absorbing local collection in the Old Gaol in Market Street. Also included is Oliver Cormwell's House (daily), the former home in St. Mary's Street of the man who defeated Charles I and became leader of the country as Lord Protector in 1653 (▷ 34).

✚ 459 L16 🛈 Oliver Cromwell's House, 29 St. Mary's Street, Ely CB7 4HF, tel 01353 662062 🚉 Ely

Far left *Dover Castle was known as the Key to England under Henry VIII*
Left *Chichester Cathedral's spire can be seen from many miles around*

EXBURY GARDENS AND STEAM RAILWAY

www.exbury.co.uk

One of the world's finest displays of rhododendrons, azaleas and camellias lies within this wonderful 80ha (200-acre) landscaped woodland garden on the east bank of the Beaulieu River. Created by the English collector and taxonomist Lionel de Rothschild (1882–1942) in the 1920s, this is a garden for all seasons. Come in early spring to see magnolias and camellias in bloom and the daffodil meadow a carpet of shimmering gold. Mid-spring brings rhododendrons and vibrant azaleas. The rose garden and herbaceous gardens are at their best in the summer, while autumn features displays of colour from Japanese maples, deciduous azaleas and flourishing dogwoods.

The gardens are wonderful for strolling, with excellent pathways, but tired feet and anyone with mobility difficulties will appreciate the little steam railway that follows a 1.2 mile (2km) circuit through themed gardens and woodland and past lakes and ponds. There's a stop in the American Garden so you can get off to explore on foot, then return later by train or walk back.

The famous Domesday Yew is an ancient tree said to have been itemised in the Domesday Book, the detailed survey of England that was commissioned in 1086 by William the Conqueror.

✚ 448 H20 ✉ Exbury SO45 1AZ ☎ 023 8089 9422 (recording), 023 8089 1203 🕐 Daily 10–5.30, early Mar–early Nov ✋ Mid-Mar to mid-Jun (depending on flowering season): adult £7.50, child (3–15) £1.50; train £3. Rest of year: adult £5, child £1; train £2.50 🍴 🏛

FELBRIGG HALL

www.nationaltrust.org.uk

In the tranquil countryside of Norfolk is one of the great 17th-century houses of East Anglia. It was begun in the 1620s by a lawyer, Frances Windham, whose grandson William made modifications and filled the rooms with pictures (including many seascapes) he had acquired on a Grand Tour of Italy. Intricate plaster ceilings and a fine library are further high notes of the interior. Less grand, perhaps, but equally fascinating is the kitchen, with its array of household implements, utensils and gleaming copper pots and pans.

Outside, the walled garden contains a fully functioning dovecote and the National Collection of Colchicums. There is free access to the large estate, where waymarked trails thread their way past venerable trees.

The nearby 15th-century parish church, standing all alone, has box pews, memorial brasses and interesting family monuments.

✚ 463 M15 ✉ Felbrigg, near Norwich NR11 8PR ☎ 01263 837444 🕐 House: late Mar–end Oct Sat–Wed 11–5. Garden: IMar–end Oct Sat–Wed 11–5, also Thu Fri

end May, mid-Jul to Aug and Oct ✋ Adult £7.15, child (5–16) £3.30, family £17.70 🍴 💻 🏛

GREAT DIXTER

www.greatdixter.co.uk

The highly respected gardening author Christopher Lloyd (1922–2006) created one of the most experimental, exciting and constantly evolving gardens of our time at Great Dixter. Yew topiary, riotous mixed borders, an exuberant Exotic Garden, carpets of meadow flowers, formal pool and natural ponds contribute to the overall effect. The house, Lloyd's birthplace and home, dates from around 1450, but was restored and enlarged by architect Sir Edwin Lutyens (1869–1944) in 1912.

✚ 459 L19 ✉ Northiam TN31 6PH ☎ 01797 252878 🕐 House and gardens: Easter–end Oct Tue–Sun, plus bank-holiday Mon, 2–5. Gardens: 11–5 ✋ House and gardens: adult £8, child £3.50. Gardens only: adult £6.50, child £3 🏛 Garden centre

Above *A delightful cottage garden in Great Dixter*
Above left *Brightly coloured flowers and trees reflected in the lake in Exbury Gardens*

HAMPTON COURT PALACE

This magnificent Tudor palace on the banks of the River Thames was begun in 1514 as a country residence for Thomas Wolsey (c1475–1530), Lord Chancellor and cardinal to Henry VIII. Fourteen years later, Wolsey presented it to the king, and for centuries it was home to British monarchs. The palace is a mix of styles—extensive Tudor buildings have late 17th-century baroque additions by Sir Christopher Wren. One of the main highlights is the Great Hall, a stunning example of a grand medieval hall, with an ornate hammerbeam roof. The walls are lined with wonderful Gobelins tapestries depicting the Story of Abraham, which were commissioned by Henry VIII. In the time of James I, the hall witnessed a performance by Shakespeare's own theatre company. The Chapel Royal, splendidly ornate, is also redolent with the history of one of England's most notorious monarchs, and another important treasure is the series of paintings, *The Triumphs of Caesar* by Mantegna. Considered one of the most important representations of European art of the 15th century, they were brought here by Charles 1 in 1629. Costumed guides and audio tours lead the way through corridors, grand apartments, lavish bedrooms and vast kitchens that remain much as they were when in use. Be sure to allow time for the riverside gardens, 60 acres (24ha) of formal and informal plantings and 750 acres (303ha) of parkland. The Maze, planted in 1690, is fiendishly frustrating.

In summer you can arrive by riverboat from Westminster (tel 020 7930 2062), Richmond or Kingston-upon-Thames (tel 020 8546 2434).

INFORMATION

www.hrp.org.uk

✚ 459 K18 ✉ Hampton Court, East Molesey KT8 9AU ☎ 0870 752 7777 🕐 Late Mar–late Oct daily 10–6; rest of year daily 10–4.30. Last admission 1 hr before closing. Informal Gardens: 7am–8pm or dusk 👋 Adult £13, child (5–16) £6.50, family £36; tickets cheaper if booked online 🚉 Hampton Court

🍴 ▢ 🏛

Above *The landscaped flower gardens at Hampton Court*

HASTINGS

www.visit1066country.com

Forever associated with the Norman invasion, Hastings is a mix of faded seaside resort and attractive fishing port. The old town, a labyrinth of narrow streets, lies east of the centre. The Victorian East Hill Cliff Railway (summer daily 10–5.30; rest of year daily 11–4) climbs to the sandstone cliffs for coastal walks to Fairlight Cove. Across the valley, the Norman ruins of Hastings Castle (daily) crown West Hill.

Don't miss the site of the 1066 Battle of Hastings, at Battle, where Battle Abbey (daily) marks the spot of the Norman victory (▷ 30). ✚ 459 L20 🚹 Queens Square, Priory Meadow, Hastings TN34 1TL, tel 0845 274 1001 🚉 Hastings

HATFIELD HOUSE

www.hatfield-house.co.uk

A sumptuous 1611 Jacobean house, Hatfield was the childhood home of Queen Elizabeth I (▷ 32). It stands on the site of the Royal Palace of Hatfield, of which a wing survives. Inside are magnificent state rooms, furniture, tapestries and paintings. Historic mementoes collected over the years by the Cecils, residents for 400 years, include the national collection of model soldiers. Look for the Grand Staircase, a superb example of Jacobean craftsmanship. ✚ 459 K18 ✉ Hatfield AL9 5NQ ☎ 01707 287010 🕓 House: Easter Sat–end Sep Wed–Sat 12–5 (guided tours

only on weekdays except public holidays and Aug). Park and West Gardens: daily 11–5.30. East Gardens: Mon 11–5.30 👐 House, park and West Gardens: adult £10, child (5–15) £4.50, family £26. Park and West Gardens: adult £6.50, child £4. Park only: adult £2.50, child £1.50 🚉 Hatfield 🍴 🏛 Garden centre and shop

HEVER CASTLE AND GARDENS

www.hevercastle.co.uk

A part doubled-moated 13th-century castle and part Tudor manor house, Hever Castle was the childhood home of Henry VIII's second wife, Anne Boleyn (1501–36). She lived here with her family until she married the king in 1533 (▷ 32).

The castle owes much of its present appearance to lavish early 20th-century renovations by American-born millionaire William Waldorf Astor (1848–1919), who bought the castle and added mock medieval features and a neo-Tudor village behind it for servants and guests. In the gatehouse is an alarming array of instruments of discipline, torture and execution. The Astor family adorned the grounds with formal Tudor, rose and Italian gardens, yew topiary in the form of chessmen, a yew maze and a water maze.

Hever's fine church has a memorial to Sir Thomas Bullen, Anne's father, who is buried here. ✚ 459 K19 ✉ Hever, near Edenbridge TN8 7NG ☎ 01732 865224 🕓 Castle: Mar–Easter Wed–Sun 12–5; Easter–end Oct

daily 12–6; Nov to mid-Dec Thu–Sun 12–4. Gardens: daily 10.45. Last admission 1 hr before closing 👐 Castle and gardens: adult £11.50, child (5–15) £6.30, family £29.30. Gardens only: adult £9.30, child £6, family £24.60 🚉 Hever 🍴 ☕ 🏛

HIGHCLERE CASTLE

www.highclerecastle.co.uk

This great 19th-century house was designed in the 1830s by Sir Charles Barry (1795–1860), one of the architects of the Houses of Parliament in London. The interiors, a heady blend of Gothic, Moorish and rococo influences, are filled with treasures that include items of Tutankhamun's treasure, found in 1922 by the fifth Earl of Carnarvon and Egyptologist Howard Carter when they discovered his tomb. The present (eighth) earl is the Queen's horseracing manager, and the Horseracing Exhibition celebrates Highclere's 100-year association with the sport. Within the grounds are walled gardens and an orangery. ✚ 458 H19 ✉ Near Newbury RG20 9RN ☎ 01635 253204 (recording), 01635 253210 🕓 Easter, Jul–end Aug Sun–Thu 11–4.30, also public holidays 👐 Castle and gardens: adult £8.50, child (4–15) £4, family £20. Gardens and grounds only: free 🍴 ☕ 🏛

HOLKHAM HALL

www.holkham.co.uk

Built between 1734 and 1764 by the agriculturalist Thomas Coke (1697–1759), first Earl of Leicester, and home to seven generations of his family, this is regarded as one of the greatest examples of the English Palladian style. Beyond its austere, grey facade lies a treasure house of ancient statues, furnishings and paintings by Peter Paul Rubens, Anthony Van Dyck, Thomas Gainsborough and others.

The Bygones Museum (Easter, early May–end Oct Sun–Thu), housed in the stable block, is packed with more than 4,000 domestic and agricultural objects, ranging from Victorian money boxes to vintage cars.

➕ 463 L15 ✉ Holkham, near Wells-next-the-Sea NR23 1AB ☎ 01328 710227 🕐 Jun–end Sep Sun–Thu 1–5 (last admission 4.30); Easter and public holidays in May and Aug Sun–Mon 12–5 (last admission 4.30). Park: all year ✋ Hall: adult £6.50, child £3.25. Bygones Museum: adult £5, child £2.50. Hall and Bygones Museum: adult £10, child £5, combined family ticket £25. Park: free 🍴 🏛

HOUGHTON HALL

www.houghtonhall.com

Britain's first prime minister, Sir Robert Walpole (1676–1745), had this Palladian mansion built in the 1720s. The work of architects James Gibb, Colen Campbell and others is complemented by the elaborate interior decoration of William Kent. Bedrooms are decorated in the style of ancient Rome, while the magnificent two-storey hall was inspired by the hall in the Queen's House in Greenwich. In the north office wing the Cholmondeley Soldier Museum has about 20,000 models.

➕ 463 L15 ✉ Houghton, near King's Lynn PE31 6UE ☎ 01485 528569 🕐 Park, grounds, soldier museum and walled garden: Wed, Thu, Sun and public holidays 11–5.30. House: late Mar–late Sep Wed, Thu, Sun and public holidays 1.30–5 (last admission 4.30) ✋ Adult £8, child (5–16) £3, family £20. Excluding house: adult £5, child £2 🖥 🏛

IGHTHAM MOTE

www.nationaltrust.org.uk

Part of the pleasure of visiting this moated manor house is touring through the woods of the Weald of Kent. The half-timbered building dates from 1330 but its main features span many centuries. The Great Hall is the oldest room in the house, while the chapel is Tudor, the drawing room has a Jacobean fireplace and the billiard room is unmistakably Victorian.

In fine weather there is access to the tower for views of the estate that offers secluded walks through woodland and farmland.

➕ 459 L19 ✉ Ightham, Ivy Hatch, Sevenoaks TN15 0NT ☎ 01732 811145 🕐 House and gardens: mid-Mar to end Oct Thu–Mon 11–5; Nov to mid-Dec Sat–Sun 11–3. Estate: dawn–dusk ✋ Adult £8.95, child (5–16) £4.50, family £22.40 🍴 🖥 🏛

ISLE OF WIGHT

▷ 186.

JANE AUSTEN'S HOUSE

www.jane-austens-house-museum.org.uk

In the middle of the village of Chawton is the red-brick 17th-century house in which novelist Jane Austen (1775–1817) lived with her mother and sister Cassandra during her most prolific writing years, from 1807 to 1817. Here she revised *Sense and Sensibility*, *Pride and Prejudice* and *Northanger Abbey*, and wrote *Mansfield Park*, *Emma* and *Persuasion*. The house, which has been restored to its appearance in the early 1800s, is full of family belongings, including manuscripts, Jane's writing table and her comb.

➕ 458 J19 ✉ Chawton, Alton GU34 1SD ☎ 01420 83262 🕐 Jun–end Aug daily 10–5; May–end May, Sep–end Dec daily 10.30–4.30; Jan–end Feb Sat–Sun 10.30–4.30 ✋ Adult £6, child (8–18) £2 🏛

KNEBWORTH HOUSE

www.knebworthhouse.com

The country park has a maze, state-of-the-art adventure playground, deer park, gardens designed by Sir Edwin Lutyens (1869–1944) and a herb garden designed by Gertrude Jekyll (1843–1932). The house dates from Tudor times but was embellished in 1843 by Victorian novelist Sir Edward Bulwer Lytton into the high Gothic fantasy seen today.

➕ 459 K17 ✉ Knebworth SG3 6PY ☎ 01438 812661 🕐 Times vary widely and are subject to change during special events—call for details ✋ All attractions: adult £9.50, child (4–16) £9, family £33. Gardens and park: adult and child £7.50, family £26, season ticket £34 🚉 Knebworth 🖥 🏛

Opposite left *Hever Castle, the childhood home of Anne Boleyn*
Opposite right *Hastings' funicular railway*
Below *Stately Knebworth House*

INFORMATION

www.wightlink.co.uk
www.hovertravel. co.uk
www.redfunnel.co.uk
www.islandbreaks.co.u
✚ 458 H20 🛈 81–83 Union Street,
Ryde PO33 2LW, tel 01983 813818
🚢 (to catch ferry) Portsmouth
Harbour, Southampton, Lymington Pier
📷 Wightlink ☎ 0871 376 1000;
Hovertravel ☎ 01983 811000;
Red Funnel Ferries ☎ 0870 444 8898

ISLE OF WIGHT

A spectacular coastline, a wide range of family attractions and a mild climate make the Isle of Wight a popular holiday destination. You can leave your car on the mainland as the island has excellent public transport.

THE WEST

Scenery varies from the lonely marshes of the north coast to the southern landslipped cliffs around St. Catherine's Point. The best viewpoint of all is Tennyson Down, named after the 19th-century poet who lived nearby; a path leads along the ridge to the cliff end above the chalk pinnacles known as The Needles. At Alum Bay a chairlift descends to the beach for close-up views of multihued sand cliffs. On the north coast, Yarmouth is a characterful port with whitewashed cottages and a castle.

THE EAST

This area includes a string of quiet resorts—Ryde, Sandown, Shanklin and Ventnor, with golden sands, calm waters and esplanades. In Ventnor's balmy climate, subtropical species flourish in the Ventnor Botanic Garden (daily; closed Mon, Fri Nov, Dec and weekdays Jan, Feb). Southeast of the yachting resort of Cowes (which hosts a famous regatta each August) is Osborne House (daily; closed Mon, Tue Nov–end Mar), Queen Victoria's Italianate seaside retreat, which she had built between 1845 and 1851. Outside the island's capital, Newport, Carisbrooke Castle (daily) is an impressive Norman ruin, where you can still see the treadwheel that prisoners were forced to walk to draw water from the well; donkey power was later used.

Below *Sailing boats in Cowes harbour, Isle of Wight*

KNOLE

www.nationaltrust.org.uk

England's largest country house has several curious vital statistics: 365 rooms (one for each day of the year), 52 corridors (one for each week) and seven courtyards (one for each day of the week).

The original 15th-century house was extended and remodelled by the first Earl of Dorset in 1603 with trademark Jacobean curly gables and tall chimneys. It has been the family home of the Sackvilles since 1603 and was the birthplace of author Vita Sackville-West (1892–1962) and the setting of Virginia Woolf's (1882–1941) novel *Orlando* (1928). Its 13 sumptuous state rooms, decorated in the early 17th century, have furniture, tapestries and paintings, and even an early royal toilet.

Take a walk around the huge free deer park to see these elegant animals.

459 L19 Sevenoaks TN15 0RP 01732 450608 (recording), 01732 462100 House: late Mar–end Oct Wed–Sun and public holidays 12–4. Garden: late Mar–late Oct Wed 11–4. Park: daily House: adult £8.10, child (5–16) £4, family £20.20. Garden: adult £2, child £1 Sevenoaks, 1.5 miles (2.5km)

LAYER MARNEY TOWER

www.layermarneytower.co.uk

Layer Marney Tower, an astonishing sight in the quiet Essex countryside, is the tallest Tudor gatehouse in the country, built by Henry, first Lord Marney, in the early 16th century. Unfortunately the grand architectural scheme, including a courtyard that would have rivalled Hampton Court Palace (▷ 183), was never completed, as the first lord's son died leaving no male heirs to continue the work, and all that stands is one of four sides. Within the grounds are the parish church and a medieval barn where farm animals roam.

459 L17 Layer Marney CO5 9US 01206 330784 Easter–end Sep Sun–Thu 12–5 Adult £4.25, child (3–16) £2.75, family £13 Colchester

Above Leeds Castle stands on two islands in a lake formed by the River Len

LEEDS CASTLE

www.leeds-castle.com

Set on two islands in the middle of a lake and rising dreamlike above its own watery reflection, Leeds Castle was originally a Norman stronghold and was a royal residence from 1278 to 1552, for no fewer than six medieval queens. It was fortified and enlarged by a series of royal incumbents and became a firm favourite of Henry VIII and his first queen, Catherine of Aragon (1485–1536). The landscaped grounds consist of formal gardens, including the English-cottage-style Culpeper Garden and Mediterranean-style Lady Baillie Garden, a maze leading to a secret grotto, a vineyard and an aviary.

The unusual Dog Collar Museum (same hours as castle) has a collection dating back more than 400 years.

459 L19 near Maidstone ME17 1PL 0870 600 8880 (recording), 01622 765400 Apr–end Sep daily 10–7 (last entry 5pm); Oct–end Mar daily 10–5 (last entry 3pm) Adult £14, child (4–15) £8.50 Bearsted Shop, garden centre

LULLINGSTONE ROMAN VILLA

www.english-heritage.org.uk

Possibly the luxury summer house of an important Roman official, the villa's mostly fourth-century remains include painted walls and fine mosaic floors. In around AD390, Lullingstone's occupiers converted to Christianity and installed a chapel in one of the rooms. This is one of the first surviving Christian chapels in England. Combine this with a visit to Lullingstone Castle close by (Fri–Sun and public holidays, Mar–end Sep), a Tudor and Queen Anne family mansion with a unique 'World Garden'.

459 L18 Lullingstone Lane, Eynsford, Dartford DA4 0JA 01322 863467 Apr–end Sep daily 10–6; Oct–end Nov, Feb–end Mar daily 10–4; Dec–end Jan Wed–Sun 10–4 Adult £4, child (5–16) £2 Eynsford, 0.75 miles (1km)

MARWELL ZOOLOGICAL PARK

www.marwell.org.uk

Marwell is a conservation and breeding centre for endangered species. In the parkland live over 250 species of animals and birds including rhinos, pygmy hippos, giraffes, zebras, tigers, lemurs, cheetahs and monkeys. Tropical World, World of Lemurs and the Australian Bush Walk are popular exhibits. Attractions for children include a miniature railway, adventure playground, and Encounter village, where you can get close to some of the residents.

You can use the frequent road train for larger distances.

458 H19 Colden Common, near Winchester SO21 1JH 01962 777407 late Mar–late Oct daily 10–6; rest of year 10–4 Adult £12.04, child (3–14) £8.40, family £39.54 Winchester

187

OXFORD

INTRODUCTION

Oxford rivals Cambridge as one of the world's foremost university cities. The campus is home to 39 colleges and to Britain's oldest library. It is also a hotbed of interesting buildings, historically and architecturally, and has some pretty riverside walks.

Enclosed by the rivers Cherwell and Thames, Oxford is a beautiful city of honey-coloured Cotswold stone. This world-famous seat of learning is a compact historic city and easily explored on foot. The university's colleges stand in cloistered seclusion and can be hard to identify as they are not clearly signed, but between them display a wonderful array of ancient, Classical and modern architecture. You can go into many of them, but respect 'Private' notices. Don't miss the back lanes and alleys, particularly Merton Street/Oriel Street, and Queen's Lane/New College Lane (leading beneath the Bridge of Sighs; just off here the Turf Tavern is a popular students' pub). The high street, known as The High, runs from Carfax Tower east to Magdalen Bridge over the River Cherwell, dividing the city into north and south.

Everywhere in this city of spires and greenery you sense learning has been going on a long time: since 1167 in fact, when a number of English scholars, expelled from the Paris Sorbonne, settled here to found the university. As with its ancient rival, Cambridge (▷ 178–179), students are attached to individual colleges, mostly set around quadrangles (or quads), each with a chapel and dining hall. Most of the central colleges have medieval origins and display a mix of architectural styles, from Renaissance to modern. The colleges originated in the 13th century, when a series of town-versus-gown (townspeople against students) confrontations hastened the establishment of halls of residence. These were succeeded by the first colleges. Since 1974, all but one of them has admitted both men and women—St. Hilda's remains the sole women-only college.

WHAT TO SEE

VIEWS OVER THE CITY

At the beginning of a visit to Oxford, it's a good idea to get your bearings from the rooftops. You can climb the tower of St. Michael's Church in Cornmarket Street, the city's oldest building. Or survey the city from Carfax Tower, a remnant of the 14th-century St. Martin's Church, at the busy crossroads known as Carfax, the city's focal point. Another excellent vantage point is the University Church of St. Mary the Virgin, High Street, dating from 1280. This parish church also serves the university and for a time was the university's reference library and venue for degree ceremonies. Climb the 27m (90ft) tower to the external viewing gallery. It also served as a courtroom for the trials of bishops Latimer, Ridley and Cranmer between 1555 and 1556. They were found guilty of heresy and were burned at the stake in Broad Street: 100m (110yd) away you will find the Martyrs' Memorial commemorating the event.

CHRIST CHURCH

Founded in 1524, Oxford's largest and most visited college has the biggest quadrangle, and its chapel, Christ Church Cathedral (predating the college), is England's smallest cathedral. Within the Great Hall you will find features from the *Alice in Wonderland* stories written by former don Charles Dodgson, better known as Lewis Carroll (1832–98), while Ante Hall became Hogwarts Hall in the *Harry Potter* movies.

Christ Church Picture Gallery is the only public gallery in any college in either Oxford or Cambridge, and has a collection of 300 paintings, with Italian

INFORMATION

www.visitoxford.org
The official tourism site for the city and the surrounding area. It has a useful search facility as well as a guide to the colleges and a booking service online
✚ 458 J18 🏠 15–16 Broad Street OX1 3AS, tel 01865 252200 ❓ Guided walking tours of the city and colleges from the tourist information centre (first-come, first-served). Punts and rowing boats available from Magdalen Bridge or the Cherwell Boathouse, Bardwell Road.
🚃 Oxford 🚌 From London services run every 10–20 min from Victoria Coach Station via Marble Arch (pay on board), then hourly throughout the night.

Opposite *The Oxford University Museum of Natural History contains dinosaurs and other exhibits of interest*

Old Masters—among them Tintoretto, Leonardo da Vinci, Michelangelo and Carracci—being well represented.

✚ 191 B3 ✉ St. Aldates OX1 1DP ☎ 01865 276492 ◉ College: Mon–Sat 9–5, Sun 1–5, last entry 4.30. Picture Gallery: Apr–end Sep Mon–Sat 10.30–5, Sun 2–5; Oct–end Mar Mon–Sat 10.30–1, 2–4.30

THE RIVERS THAMES AND CHERWELL
These waterways slice through remarkably verdant land close to central Oxford. The tree-lined Cherwell (pronounced charwell) is the place for punting and provides almost rural views of Magdalen College (pronounced mordlin), one of the richest and most spacious colleges, founded in 1458 and set in its own deer park—walks through here are really stunning. University rowing crews train on the Thames (also known here as the Isis). Stroll through the Oxford Botanic Garden, founded in 1621 and the oldest of its kind in Britain, to Christchurch Meadow and the confluence of the rivers, or rent a punt or rowing boat from Magdalen Bridge or the Cherwell Boathouse in Bardwell Road.

✚ 191 B3, C3

RADCLIFFE SQUARE
This is an eye-catching architectural group belonging to the university. The Sheldonian Theatre (built between 1664 and 1668) was the first major architectural work by architect Sir Christopher Wren, who was Professor of Astronomy at the time. The interior assumes the shape of a Roman theatre and its grand ceremonial hall is used for university functions and concerts. High above, the cupola is an excellent viewpoint.

Close by, the Bodleian Library is one of six copyright libraries in the UK, entitled to receive a copy of every book published in the country. The circular domed Radcliffe Camera of 1737–49, designed by James Gibbs, is a reading room for the library.

✚ 191 C2 ✉ Between Broad Street and High Street ☎ Sheldonian Theatre: 01865 277299. Bodleian Library: 01865 277000 ◉ Sheldonian Theatre: daily 10–12.30, 2–4.30 (times may vary). Bodleian Library: audio tours Mon–Fri 9–4.15; guided tours Mon–Sat 10.30, 11.30, 2, 3

ASHMOLEAN MUSEUM
Britain's oldest public museum (opened in 1683) and currently undergoing an ambitious new development, the Ashmolean houses Oxford University's priceless collections from the time of early man to the 20th century. Come here to see material about early cultures in Europe, Egypt and the Near East, and an antiquities department covering everything from the Stone Age to Victorian times. Linked to the museum by the new development, the Cast Gallery has a staggering 100,000 casts (not all on show at one time), which together give a privileged overview of Classical sculpture. The museum is named after Elias Ashmole, who bestowed his collection upon the University of Oxford in 1683. The University Museum nearby has fascinating collections on natural history.

✚ 191 B2 ✉ Beaumont Street ☎ 01865 278000 ◉ Tue–Sat 10–5 and public holidays, Sun 12–5 (except Cast Gallery); closed during St. Giles' Fair early Sep

Below *The circular dome and drum of the Radcliffe Camera*

OTHER HISTORIC COLLEGES
Merton College (founded 1264) has peaceful gardens and the 14th-century Mob Quad, Oxford's oldest quadrangle, while New College (founded in 1379 despite its name) is famous for its hall, cloister, chapel and gardens enclosed by the old city wall. Peep into St. John's College, founded 1555, with its arcaded Canterbury Quad, and Queens College (founded 1341) for buildings by Sir Christopher Wren and Nicholas Hawksmoor. Farther out in Parks Road is Keble College (1870), a relative newcomer whose elaborate red-brick buildings are a Victorian tour de force.

MORE TO SEE

PITT-RIVERS MUSEUM AND UNIVERSITY MUSEUM

www.prm.ox.ac.uk

This cavernously old-fashioned museum is an anthropology collection of more than 250,000 objects—among them masks and shrunken heads. Or just admire the Victorian Gothic architecture.

⊞ 191 B1 ⊠ Parks Road OX1 3PP ☎ 01865 270927 🕓 Mon 12–4.30, Tue–Sun 10–4.30

MUSEUM OF OXFORD

www.museumofoxford.org.uk

This museum gives a succinct survey of the city from prehistoric times to the present, from mammoths to Morris Motors. It has archaeological finds, including a Roman pottery kiln, paintings and furniture from houses in Oxford.

⊞ 191 B2 ⊠ Town Hall Building, St. Aldates OX1 1DZ ☎ 01865 252761 🕓 Tue–Fri 10–5, Sat–Sun 12–4

OXFORD CASTLE

Tracing its origins back to the 1071, Oxford's forbidding castle spent most of the last hundred years as a prison. Since 1996, it has been converted into a luxury hotel and restaurant complex. The core of the ancient structure, including the St George's Tower is now the 'Unlocked: Oxford Castle' visitor attraction.

⊞ 191 A2 ⊠ 44–46 Oxford Castle, Oxford OX1 1AY ☎ 01865 260666 🕓 Daily 10–5 (last tour 4.10)

MODERN ART OXFORD

www.modernartoxford.org.uk

This stylish gallery occupies a former brewery. It has changing exhibitions of contemporary art from Britain and beyond, as well as talks, live music and children's activities, plus a café selling very good cakes, and a shop.

⊞ 191 B2 ⊠ 30 Pembroke Street OX1 1BP ☎ 01865 722733 🕓 Tue–Sat 10–5, Sun 12–5

TIPS

» Visit in term-time for the real student atmosphere.

» Come by public transport or use the park-and-ride services from the outer ring roads.

» They may look private, but you can visit many colleges; some have a small admission charge.

» City Sightseeing hop-on, hop-off open-top buses give a useful overview with live commentary.

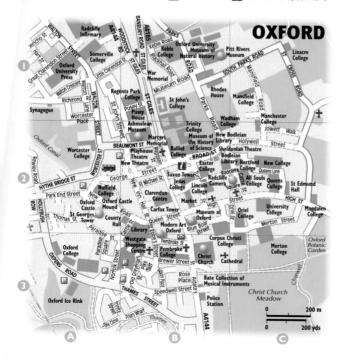

OXFORD

NEW FOREST

www.thenewforest.co.uk

Strikingly remote, grazed by free-ranging ponies and cattle, and one of England's largest stretches of open, undeveloped country, the New Forest is excellent for walking, camping and picnicking (▷ 202–205). Established in 1079 as a hunting forest for Norman royalty, it has remained largely intact. At Lyndhurst, the New Forest Centre (daily) has an exhibition on the area. Some of the most popular attractions lie in the southeastern corner, including Beaulieu (▷ 174), Exbury Gardens (▷ 182) and Bucklers Hard, a hamlet with a nautical air, and the launching point of several ships from the fleet of Admiral Lord Nelson (1758–1805).

The pretty Bolderwood and Rhinefield ornamental drives are roads planted with giant fir, redwood and cypress trees.

458 H20 Lyndhurst Visitor Information Centre, The Main Car Park, Lyndhurst SO43 7NY, tel 023 8023 2269 Brockenhurst

Below *Norwich Cathedral has the largest cloisters of any English cathedral*

NORWICH

www.visitnorwich.co.uk

Norwich is one of Britain's most complete medieval cities. Among the old streets is cobbled Elm Hill, full of antiques, crafts and specialist shops. Northeast in the city is the cathedral, founded in 1096 and with a 15th-century spire rising to 96m (315ft). It has a magnificent stone-vaulted roof with 1,106 carved stone bosses depicting the Bible story.

Southwest of the cathedral is the marketplace, a maze of narrow alleyways with stalls that operate six days a week. Norwich's newest public building is the architecturally acclaimed Forum, home to several specialist shops and the 2nd Air Division Memorial Library, which recalls the role of US airmen in East Anglia. The Royal Arcade is where you'll find Colman's Mustard Shop and Museum (Mon–Sat 9.30–5), and can buy tiny tins of Norwich's most famous product. In Bridewell Alley, the Bridewell Museum (Apr–end Oct) chronicles local trades and industries.

Looking onto the marketplace, 12th-century Norwich Castle (daily) has a fine museum and art gallery, where there is a huge collection of ceramic teapots and works by the early 19th-century Norwich School of landscape painters.

Dragon Hall (daily) is a 15th-century merchants' hall; The Sainsbury Centre for the Visual Arts (closed Mon), is an outstanding art collection in a modern building by architect Norman Foster, at the University of East Anglia, 3 miles (5km) west of Norwich.

463 M16 The Forum, Millennium Plain, Norwich NR2 1TF, tel 01603 727927 Norwich

ORFORD

www.orford.org.uk

Orford, with its brick-and-timber cottages, was a thriving port when Henry II (1133–89) built Orford Castle (daily) here as a coastal defence in 1165. Its unique polygonal keep survives almost intact with a spiral staircase inside each of the three immense towers.

Orford is now separated from the sea by 10-mile (17km) Orford Ness (ferries Jul–end Sep Tue–Sat; Apr–end Jun, Oct Sat only), the largest vegetated shingle spit in Europe. Formerly a top-secret military site, it is now an important location for breeding and passage birds and has rare shingle flora species.

459 M17 Station Building, Woodbridge IP12 4AJ, tel 01394 382240

OXFORD

▷ 188–191.

PARHAM HOUSE AND GARDENS

www.parhaminsussex.co.uk

Built in 1577, the house contains a variety of furniture and textiles, and a collection of needlework. The 18th-century Pleasure Grounds include a lake, trees and bulbs, and a maze. Descendants of the original 17th-century deer herd roam the park.

458 K19 Near Pulborough RH20 4HS 01903 744888 (recording), 01903 742021 House: Easter–late Sep Wed, Thu, Sun and public holidays 2–5, plus Tue and Fri, Aug. Gardens: 12–5 House and gardens: adult £7.50, child (5–15) £3.50, family £20. Gardens: adult £5.50, child £2.50, family £14

PORTSMOUTH

At first sight Portsmouth, the home of Britain's naval heritage, may not seem a great place for a day out, but it has pockets of huge historic interest, mostly concentrated around the waterfront. It has been a naval base since the 12th century and the hub of one of the most powerful seaborne fighting forces in history. The city is the home port of the Royal Navy and consequently was heavily bombed during World War II.

A couple of minutes' walk from Portsmouth Harbour station is the Historic Dockyard (daily) with its celebrated warships. Naval officers guide you around Nelson's flagship HMS *Victory* to recall the appalling conditions on board and see the spot where Nelson died in battle in 1805 (▷ 37). Close by is the world's first iron-clad battleship, HMS *Warrior*, launched in 1860. Rescued in 1982 after sinking in 1545, Henry VIII's warship *Mary Rose* features a rich array of finds that provides an unrivalled time capsule of Tudor life. Also in the dockyard, the Royal Naval Museum (daily) charts the history of British maritime defence.

TOWN HIGHLIGHTS

Soaring high over the shops and restaurants of the Gunwharf Quays development, the 170m (558ft) Spinnaker Tower (daily) opened in 2005 to give the best viewing platform on the south coast. The glass floor on one level gives a dizzying sense of being on top of things, while from the top level you are exposed to the bracing fresh air. At the end of the High Street lies Old Portsmouth, an area of cobbled streets lined with Tudor and Georgian houses and pubs. These streets were once full of press gangs seeking new naval recruits, whom they forced to join a leaving ship.

OTHER SIGHTS

Over the water at Gosport (reached by ferry), Explosion! Museum of Naval Firepower (Sat–Sun) displays hardware from the Battle of Trafalgar to the present day.

Southsea Castle (Apr–end Sep daily), on Clarence Esplanade, was built in 1595 to protect Portsmouth against French invasion. Next door, the D-Day Museum and Overlord Embroidery (daily) records the largest invasion force ever gathered: for D-Day (6 June 1944). Its embroidery measures 83m (272ft).

INFORMATION
www.visitportsmouth.co.uk
✚ 458 J20 ⚑ Clarence Esplanade, Southsea PO5 3PB, tel 023 9282 6722
⚑ Portsmouth Harbour

Above *Lord Nelson spent his last hours on board HMS* Victory

PENSHURST PLACE AND GARDENS

www.penshurstplace.com

Begun in 1340 for London merchant Sir John de Pulteney, this fortified manor house contains extensive collections of furniture, tapestries, paintings, porcelain and armour acquired by the Sidney family. The famous Elizabethan poet, Sir Philip Sidney, was born here in 1554. The lofty chestnut-beamed Baron's Hall, dating from 1341, is among the outstanding original features. For younger visitors there is an adventure playground and a woodland trail.

The Tudor walled garden has more than 1 mile (1.5km) of yew hedging dividing it into self-contained rooms. ✚ 459 L19 ✉ Penshurst, Tonbridge TN11 8DG ☎ 01892 870307 🕐 House: late Mar–end Oct daily 12–4. Gardens: late Mar–end Oct daily 10.30–6 🖐 House and grounds: adult £8.50, child (5–16) £5.50, family £23. Grounds only: adult £7, child £5, family £20 🍴 🏛

PETWORTH HOUSE AND PARK

www.nationaltrust.org.uk

No other National Trust property can rival Petworth for its art collection. The 300 oil paintings include 20 by Anthony Van Dyck, 20 by J. M. W. Turner and work by Joseph Reynolds and Titian, as well as ancient and neoclassical sculpture. The deer park has been captured on canvas by Turner. The Red Room and the Carved Room of the late 17th-century mansion contain English sculptor Grinling Gibbons' (1648–1721) finest limewood carvings, while the kitchens incorporate Victorian technology.

✚ 458 J19 ✉ Petworth GU28 0AE ☎ 01798 343929 🕐 House and Servants' Quarters: mid-Mar to early Nov Sat–Wed 11–5 (extra rooms shown Mon–Wed, except public holidays). Pleasure Ground: early Mar Sat–Wed 11–4; late Mar–early Nov Sat–Wed 11–5; early Dec Thu–Sun 10–3.30; late Nov Wed–Sat 10–3.30. Park: daily 8–dusk 🖐 House, Servants' Quarters and Pleasure Ground: adult £8.60, child (5–16) £4.30, family £21.50. Pleasure Ground: adult £3.40, child £1.70. Park: free 🚉 Petworth 🍴 🖥 🏛

Above *Rye's half-timbered, red-roofed houses make an attractive picture*

PEVENSEY CASTLE

www.english-heritage.org.uk

William the Conqueror (1027–87) landed at Pevensey for his invasion of England in 1066, and occupied the remains of this Roman fort. What survives today is the Roman outer wall and towers, standing almost to their full height, and the partially subsided Norman castle. In World War II the fortifications, gun emplacements and a blockhouse for anti-tank weapons were added.

✚ 459 L20 ✉ Pevensey BN24 5LE ☎ 01323 762604 🕐 Apr–end Sep daily 10–6; Oct daily 10–4; Nov–end Mar Sat–Sun 10–4 🖐 Adult £4, child (5–16) £2 🚉 Pevensey & Westham 🍴 🏛

POLESDEN LACEY

www.nationaltrust.org.uk

In the early 20th century, this 1824 Regency house was home to society hostess Mrs. Ronald Greville. King George VI and Queen Elizabeth spent part of their honeymoon here in 1923. The house is much as it was at the time of Mrs. Greville's celebrated parties.

✚ 458 K19 ✉ Great Bookham RH5 6BD ☎ 01372 458203 (recording), 01372 452048 🕐 House: mid Mar to end Oct, Wed–Sun 11–5; late Oct Wed–Sun 11–4. Gardens: early Feb, late Oct–23 Dec, Jan daily 11–4; mid-Feb to late Oct daily 11–5 🖐 House and gardens: adult £9.50, child £5, family £24. Gardens only: adult £5.90, child £3.10, family £15. £1 voucher for tea room available if arriving by public transport (please present valid ticket) 🚉 Boxhill & Westhumble, 2 miles (3km) 🍴 🖥 🏛

PORTSMOUTH

▷ 193.

ROLLRIGHT STONES

www.english-heritage.org.uk
www.rollrightstones.co.uk

Three groups of stones—The King's Men, The King Stone and The Whispering Knights—together span nearly 2,000 years of the Neolithic and Bronze Ages. The King's Men is a large circle of about 70 stones, while The King Stone is a prominent outlier stone. A little more difficult to find are The Whispering Knights, a short walk east from the main layby.

✚ 458 H17 ✉ near Chipping Norton 🕐 Open access 🖐 Nominal charge for King's Men

Right *Autumn colours are reflected in Middle Lake at Sheffield Park Garden*

RYE AND WINCHELSEA

www.visitrye.co.uk

Rye and Winchelsea are two small historic towns. Just 2 miles (3km) apart, they were two of the five medieval Cinque Ports, part of a confederation that supplied ships to the navy in return for privileges from the king. The sea has receded, leaving shingle beaches and the two towns seemingly suspended in time.

The larger of the two, Rye, is a huddle of cobbled streets, medieval half-timbered, red-tiled houses and elegant Georgian buildings, with the most photogenic spots along Mermaid Street. Parts of the 14th-century defences still remain, such as Landgate Arch and Ypres Tower, a 13th-century lookout that houses the Rye Castle Museum (Apr–end Oct Thu–Mon; rest of year Sat–Sun).

Facing the church, in West Street, is the early 18th-century Lamb House (Apr–end Oct Thu and Sat pm), home of American novelist Henry James (1843–1916) from 1898 until his death. It was later occupied by the author E. F. Benson.

Winchelsea, the smallest town in England (population 400), began life at sea level until its destruction in a storm in 1287. It was rebuilt to a grid pattern (one of the best examples of town planning in medieval England) on the clifftop, fortified with walls and gateways against French invaders. Most buildings have 17th- and 18th-century facades but many are older. Three gates survive of the medieval defences. At the centre,

St. Thomas's Church is a fragment of a once larger building. Medieval Court Hall (May–end Sep Tue–Sun and Mon public holidays), restored in the 16th century, houses the local museum.

➕ 459 L19 ℹ️ The Heritage Centre, Strand Quay, Rye TN31 7AY, tel 01797 226696
🚌 Rye, Winchelsea

ST. ALBANS

www.stalbans.gov.uk

Taking its name from St. Alban, the first English Christian martyr, the town grew up around the abbey that preserved the saint's shrine. Today's cathedral (daily 8.30–5.45) is a mish mash of styles, but nonetheless impressive. The extensive remains of the Roman city of Verulamium can be seen, in open parkland close to the cathedral. The Verulamium Museum (Mon–Sat 10–5, Sun 2–5) exhibits many of the archaeological finds and the hypocaust and theatre are impressively well preserved.

➕ 459 K18 ℹ️ Town Hall, Market Place, St. Albans AL3 5DJ, tel 01727 864511
🚌 St Albans

SANDRINGHAM

www.sandringham-estate.co.uk

Sandringham is the Norfolk country retreat of Queen Elizabeth II. It was built in 1870 for the Prince of Wales (later Edward VII). The main ground-floor rooms are much as they were in Edwardian times, while the old stable, coach houses and power house contain a museum of Royal Family possessions. There is

free access to the many paths in the surrounding country park.

➕ 463 L15 ✉️ The Estate Office, Sandringham PE35 6EN ☎️ 01553 772675
🕐 House: Easter–end Sep daily 11–4.45; Oct daily 11–4. Museum: Easter–end Sep daily 11–5; Oct daily 11–4. Gardens: Easter–end Sep daily 10.30–5; Oct daily 10.30–4. Estate closed for 1 week late Jul–early Aug 🎫 House, museum and gardens: adult £9, child (5–15) £5, family £23. Museum and gardens: adult £6, child £3.50, family £15.50. Garden tours from £1.50 ❓ Guided garden tours: Fri–Sat 11 and 2 🍴 🛍️ 📷

SANDWICH

www.whitecliffscountry.org.uk
www.open-sandwich.co.uk

The sea has receded from what was once England's major port, but Sandwich is still one of the best-preserved medieval towns in Britain. The Guildhall Museum (Apr–end Nov Tue–Sun) covers the history of Sandwich. Walk beside the River Stour to the Old Toll Bridge, from where the Sandwich River Bus takes you to Richborough Roman Fort (Easter–end Sep daily). Dating to the Roman invasion of AD43, the fortified walls and foundations of a triumphal arch remain.

➕ 459 M19 ℹ️ The Guildhall, Sandwich CT13 9AH, tel 01304 613565; Apr–end Oct
🚌 Sandwich

SHEFFIELD PARK GARDEN

www.nationaltrust.org.uk

This garden was laid out in the 18th century by Capability Brown and expanded in the early 20th century. It is best in early summer, when the rhododendrons and azaleas are in bloom, and in autumn when the foliage is a riot of colour. The main features are four lakes on different levels linked by waterfalls.

➕ 459 K19 ✉️ Sheffield Park TN22 3QX ☎️ 01825 790231 🕐 Jan–end Feb Sat–Sun 10.30–4; Mar–end Apr, Jun–early Oct Tue–Sun 10.30–5.30; May, early–late Oct daily 10.30–5.30; Nov–end Dec Tue–Sun 10.30–4 🎫 Adult £6.60, child (5–16) £3.30, family £16.50 🚌 Sheffield Park; Bluebell Railway from Horsted Keynes ❓ Joint ticket with Bluebell Railway available, tel 01825 720800 🛍️ 📷

SHUTTLEWORTH COLLECTION

www.shuttleworth.org

In an all-grass aerodrome, this collection features around 40 aircraft from 1909 to 1955. Many are the last survivors of their type, including a 1909 Bleriot and a 1941 Spitfire, kept in full working order. The exhibition includes vintage cars, motorcycles, bicycles and horse-drawn carriages. Flying displays take place once or twice a month (May–end Oct), when the museum's airworthy exhibits are flown alongside visiting aircraft, and cars from the collection are given a run.

➕ 458 K17 ✉ Shuttleworth Aerodrome, Old Warden Park, Biggleswade SG18 9EA ☎ 01767 627927 🕐 Apr–end Oct daily 10–5; rest of year daily 10–4 💷 Adult £10, accompanied child up to 16 free; flying display £20 ❓ On flying days flights normally begin at 2pm; evening flying displays begin at 5pm (earlier in late Sep) 🚌 Biggleswade 🍴 🛍 🏛

SISSINGHURST CASTLE GARDEN

www.nationaltrust.org.uk

The writer Vita Sackville-West (1892–1962) and her husband, the diplomat and author Sir Harold Nicolson (1886–1968), created this famous Wealden garden in the 1930s around the ruin of a moated Elizabethan mansion. It consists of a series of small, enclosed compartments that between them provide an outstanding display of hues through the seasons. The brick front range (c1490) and the four-storey tower (c1565) are all that survive of the house.

➕ 459 L19 ✉ Sissinghurst, near Cranbrook TN17 2AB ☎ 01580 710701 (recording), 01580 710700 🕐 Late Mar–end Oct Fri–Tue 11–6.30 💷 Adult £8.10, child (5–16) £4, family £22.50 ❓ Timed entry tickets. Library and Vita Sackville-West's study close at 5.30. Tower and library may be restricted early and late season 🍴 🏛

SOUTHAMPTON

www.southampton.gov.uk
www.visit-southampton.co.uk

Between the modern office blocks and shopping streets, fragments of the old town that was largely

Above *Colourful beach huts at Southwold, a delightful old-fashioned resort*

destroyed during World War II can be found, including a large section of the medieval town wall and its 13 remaining towers. A self-guiding walking tour follows its route—look out for Walk the Southampton Walls signposts and plaques.

The Medieval Merchant's House (Easter–end Sep, Fri–Sun and public holidays) has been restored and furnished to look as it might have done in 1290, while Solent Sky (Mon–Sat 10–5, Sun 12–5) in Albert Road South tells the history of aviation in the Solent area, including the achievements of R. J. Mitchell, designer of the Spitfire.

The Titanic—Southampton Remembers Exhibition in the Maritime Museum (Tue–Sun) in Town Quay has some recordings of the crew and passengers of *Titanic*. On its maiden voyage from Southampton in 1912, this ship sank with the loss of more than 1,000 lives.

Town Quay and Shamrock Quay are among the city's liveliest spots.

➕ 458 H19 ℹ 9 Civic Centre Road, Southampton SO14 7FJ, tel 023 8083 3333 🚉 Southampton Central

SOUTHWOLD

www.visit-southwold.co.uk

The allure of this port-turned-resort is its sedate, old-fashioned character. Groups of brick and colour-washed cottages cluster around greens beneath three landmarks: the lighthouse, Adnam's brewery and

the soaring tower of St. Edmund's Church. In the middle of town there are art galleries, antiques shops, tea rooms and pubs. Below the Sailors' Reading Room—a social club for mariners, with a local history display—some 200 brightly painted beach huts dating from the early 1900s line the beach, near the pier.

➕ 459 N16 ℹ 69 High Street, Southwold IP18 6DS, tel 01502 724729

STAMFORD

www.southwestlincs.com

With golden limestone buildings and cobbled streets opening onto spacious squares, this most attractive of towns is a popular film location for period-costume dramas. Barn Hill offers the best overall view of the houses and medieval churches. To the south is Burghley House (Apr–end Oct daily, except during Burghley Horse Trials in early Sep), a 240-room Elizabethan mansion built by William Cecil (1520–98), chief minister to Elizabeth I. The house has a world-famous collection of tapestries, porcelain and paintings and is set in a beautiful deer park.

➕ 462 K16 ℹ Stamford Arts Centre, 27 St. Mary's Street, Stamford PE9 2DL, tel 01780 755611

STANDEN

www.nationaltrust.org.uk

This is a rare opportunity to see inside one of the greatest houses of the 19th-century Arts and Crafts Movement. Standen was built between 1892 and 1894 by Philip Webb as a country home for London solicitor James Beale. The house has been preserved right down to its original electric light fittings; William Morris carpets, textiles and printed wall coverings include many original to the house. The hillside garden looks far over the Sussex Weald countryside.

🕂 459 K19 ✉ West Hoathly Road, East Grinstead RH19 4NE ☎ 01342 323029 ◷ Early Mar Sat, Sun 11–4.30; mid-Mar to mid-Jul, Sep–end Oct Wed–Sun 11–4.30; end Jul–end Aug Wed–Mon 11–4.30 ♿ Adult £7.80, child (5–16) £3.90, family £19.50. Garden only: adult £4.60, child £2.30 🚉 East Grinstead 🍴 ♿

SUTTON HOO

www.nationaltrust.org.uk

In 1939, excavation of an Anglo-Saxon royal burial site led to the discovery of the priceless Sutton Hoo treasure. A warrior's helmet, shield, gold ornaments and Byzantine silver were found close to the sea in the remains of a burial of a 27m (90ft) ship. The exhibition here examines the 50-year excavation of the site, and aspects of Anglo-Saxon life such as craftsmanship, and life and death in seventh-century England. On display are original finds and a full-size reconstruction of King Raedwald's burial chamber.

🕂 459 M17 ✉ Tranmer House, Sutton Hoo, Woodbridge IP12 3DJ ☎ 01394 389700 ◷ Early Feb, late Feb–Easter, Nov–end Jan Sat–Sun 11–4; mid-Feb daily 11–4; Easter–end Oct daily 10.30–5. Closed Mon, Tue oustide school holidays ♿ Adult £5.60, child (5–16) £2.80, family £14.20 🚉 Woodbridge 🍴 ♿

WADDESDON MANOR

www.waddesdon.org.uk

Definitely a chateau in character, Waddesdon was built in the 1870s by Baron Ferdinand de Rothschild, a member of the 19th-century banking dynasty, for his extravagant house parties. Breathtaking for their opulence, the 45 rooms on view contain 18th-century French furniture and one of the world's finest collections of French decorative arts. The grounds are filled with specimen trees, fountains, grottoes and a rococo revival aviary of exotic birds.

🕂 458 J17 ✉ Waddesdon HP18 0JH ☎ 01296 653211 (recording), 01296 653226 ◷ House and cellars: Easter–end Oct Wed–Fri 12–4, Sat, Sun 11–4. Grounds: Easter–end Dec Wed–Sun 10–5; rest of year Sat–Sun 10–5 ♿ House and grounds (peak season): adult £15, child (5–16) £9.35. Bachelors' Wing: £3.50. Grounds only: adult £7, child £3.50. Lower rates apply at different times of the year. National Trust members free ❓ Timed ticket from 10am, first-come, first-served 🍴 ♿

WAKEHURST PLACE

www.kew.org
www.nationaltrust.org.uk

The country offshoot of the Royal Botanic Gardens at Kew (▷ 81) is a beautiful creation in its own right. A picturesque watercourse links lakes and ponds, and the gardens surround an Elizabethan mansion with a rural exhibition.

This is one of the country's most varied gardens, with a worldwide collection, an arboretum, and year-round colour. The Millennium Seed Bank safeguards the world's most endangered plant species in massive underground seed vaults—try the virtual tours with interactive screens. Its aim is to have saved seeds from around 24,000 plants by 2010.

🕂 459 K19 ✉ Ardingly, Haywards Heath RH17 6TN ☎ 01444 894066 ◷ Mar–end Oct daily 10–6; Nov–end Feb daily 10–4.30. Mansion and Seed Bank close 1 hour before gardens ♿ Adult £9.50, under 17s free 🚉 Haywards Heath 🍴 💻 ♿ Garden centre, shop

WEALD AND DOWNLAND OPEN AIR MUSEUM

www.wealddown.co.uk

Set in the South Downs countryside, this is England's leading museum of historic buildings and traditional rural life. Nearly 50 of the region's old buildings have been rescued from destruction, carefully restored and reconstructed. They vividly evoke the homes, domestic gardens and workplaces of the past 500 years. Among them are medieval houses, a Tudor farmstead, a working 17th-century watermill, Victorian workers' cottages, a Victorian school, carpenters' and plumbers' workshops, and seven period gardens dating from 1430 to 1900.

There are also frequent demonstrations of traditional rural crafts and trades.

🕂 458 J19 ✉ Singleton, near Chichester PO18 0EU ☎ 01243 811363 ◷ Mar–end Oct daily 10.30–6; Nov–end Dec, mid-Feb to end Mar daily 10.30–4; Jan to mid-Feb Wed, Sat–Sun 10.30–4 ♿ Adult £8.50, child (5–15) £4.50, family £23.305 🚉 Chichester 💻 ♿

Below *The Millennium Seed Bank at Wakehurst Place*

WINCHESTER

England's ancient capital and seat of the Anglo-Saxon kings, Winchester has a compact historic central area that you can easily explore on foot; antiquarian bookshops are a city speciality; a detailed list is available from the tourist information office.

The city came to prominence under Alfred the Great (AD849–99), who made it the capital of his Wessex kingdom in the ninth century. The highlight of the city is its medieval cathedral, dating from 1079 to 1404, in Norman to Perpendicular styles. The nave was remodelled around 1400, but elsewhere there are many reminders of the building's even greater antiquity, including some original sculptures. The chapels are particularly interesting, recalling former bishops such as St. Swithun and William of Wykeham, the latter twice Chancellor of England and founder of Winchester College and New College, Oxford. The choir stalls are worth close inspection for their elaborate carvings that include monkeys, dragons and owls. Look, too, for interesting monuments and tombs, including the burial places of Izaak Walton and Jane Austen.

Close by are the free City Museum (daily; closed Mon Nov–end Mar) and Winchester College, founded in 1382 and Britain's oldest and one of its most prestigious schools (daily tours). Near Westgate, the Great Hall, built in 1235 (daily), is all that survives of the city's 13th-century Norman castle. You can visit King Arthur's Round Table—a resplendent medieval fake.

The Hospital of St. Cross (daily, closed Sun Nov–end Mar) is a 12th-century almshouse, still home to 25 monks and reached by a tranquil walk across water meadows; by ancient tradition, Wayfarer's Dole (bread and beer) is still given to anyone who asks for it at the porter's lodge.

Winchester also has a strong military heritage. Peninsula Barracks on Romsey Road contains five museums dedicated to individual regiments: the Gurkhas, teh Royal Green Jackets, the King's Royal Hussars, the Light Infantry and the Adjutant General's Corps.

Above *The Round Table in Winchester's Great Hall dates from the 13th century*

Below *Since 1967, 130 cheetahs have been born and bred at ZSL Whipsnade Zoo*

WINDSOR AND ETON
▷ 200–201.

WISLEY, RHS GARDEN
www.rhs.org.uk
The flagship of the Royal Horticultural Society opened as a place of gardening excellence in 1904. Wisley shows British gardening at its best, offering a blend of landscaped gardens and horticultural tips for gardeners. The most important work takes place in trial fields, while elsewhere a series of model gardens serves the needs of a variety of conditions.

The garden's shop boasts the best range of horticultural books in the world.

⊞ 458 K19 ✉ Wisley, Woking GU23 6QB ☎ 01483 224234 ⏰ Mar–end Oct Mon–Fri 10–6, Sat–Sun and public holidays 9–6; rest of year Mon–Fri 10–4.30, Sat–Sun 9–4.30 ♿ Adult £8, child (6–16) £2 🚇 Woking or West Byfleet (then taxi); reduced entry for rail travellers: adult £5.50, child £1.60 ❓ Free to visitors with registered visual impairment and carers of visitors in wheelchairs 🍴 💻 ⊞ Plant sales, shop

WOBURN ABBEY
www.woburnabbey.co.uk
Monastic in name only, Woburn is in fact an 18th-century mansion of Palladian composition, on the site of a Cistercian monastery founded in 1145. It has been home to the dukes of Bedford since 1547 and presently is the home of the 15th Duke. On show here is one of the finest private art collections in Britain, with works by Thomas Gainsborough, Joshua Reynolds and other masters.

In the grounds are a deer park and Woburn Safari Park (mid-Mar to end Oct daily; rest of year Sat–Sun), Britain's largest animal safari park, where you sit in your car and drive around while the animals roam free.

⊞ 458 J17 ✉ Woburn MK17 9WA ☎ 01525 290333 ⏰ Abbey: Easter–end Sep daily 11–5.30 (last entry 4). Park: mid-Mar to end Sep daily 10–5; Oct to mid-Mar daily 10–4.30 ♿ Abbey: adult £10.50, child (3–15) £6. Deer Park: adult £2, child free 🍴 💻 ⊞

ZSL WHIPSNADE ZOO
www.whipsnade.co.uk
Occupying parkland on the Chiltern Hills is one of Europe's largest wildlife conservation centres, home to more than 2,500 creatures, including rare and endangered species. Its herd of eight Asian elephants is the largest breeding group in Britain, and free-roaming animals include Chinese water deer.

Daily demonstrations feature free-flying birds, sea-lion performances and penguin feeding. To get around the park, take the free open-top Safari Bus (a good chance to meet giraffes eye to eye), or alternatively take the Jumbo Express.

The Discovery Centre is a must if you want to encounter crocodiles, snakes, tarantulas and piranhas, in their desert, rainforest and other natural settings.

⊞ 458 K17 ✉ Whipsnade, Dunstable LU6 2LF ☎ 01582 872171 ⏰ Mar–end Sep daily 10–6; Oct daily 10–5; Nov–end Dec daily 10–4 (open until 7 Sun and public holidays Apr–end Oct; last admission 1 hour before close) ♿ Animal Park: adult £17, child £13.50 💻 ⊞

INFORMATION

www.windsor.gov.uk

➕ 458 J18 ℹ 24 High Street, Windsor SL4 1LH, tel 01753 743900 ❓ City Sightseeing Bus tours every 15–60 min from Castle Hill Easter to mid-Nov daily; mid-Nov to Easter Sat–Sun ☎ Book online at www.city-sightseeing. com. Also guided walking tours and boat trips 🚉 Windsor & Eton Riverside (from London Waterloo), Windsor & Eton Central (from London Paddington)

Above *The towers of Windsor Castle are visible for miles around*

INTRODUCTION

The adjoining towns of Windsor and Eton together provide the site of Europe's largest occupied castle and one of Britain's most famous public schools. Both Windsor and Eton are easily explored on foot and have plenty of attractions to fill a day. Less than an hour from London, Windsor's historic grandeur is apparent immediately on arrival. The curving, elevated approach by train from London offers splendid views of the River Thames, Windsor Castle and Eton College, and also crosses Isambard Kingdom Brunel's 1849 wrought-iron bridge.

In addition to the obvious lure of its castle, Windsor has vast open spaces and several other attractions. It is also well stocked with shops, concentrated in a handful of places over a compact area—with everything from main-street names to designer boutiques, antiques, art, gifts and collectables—plus numerous restaurants and cafés, some with outdoor dining.

WHAT TO SEE
WINDSOR CASTLE

www.royal.gov.uk

Windsor Castle towers above the town on a chalk cliff overlooking the River Thames. It is the largest inhabited castle in the world and has been one of the principal residences of the sovereigns of England since William the Conqueror (1027–87) built it. Much of the present-day structure, however, dates from the 19th century.

There are several buildings to visit within the castle complex. St. George's Chapel (worshippers only Sun), begun in 1475 by Edward IV and completed in 1509, is a masterpiece of Perpendicular Gothic architecture. Ten monarchs are buried here. In the northwest chapel the monument to Princess Charlotte (who died in 1817 in childbirth) shows her ascending to heaven with an angel carrying her stillborn child. The chapel's fan-vaulted ceiling is particularly beautiful, as are the elaborate 15th-century choir stalls covered in vignettes and surmounted by banners of the 26 Knights of the Garter, whose installation has taken place here since 1348.

The baroque State Apartments, restored following the fire of 1992, are hung with works from the Royal Collection, the world's finest private art collection, with drawings and paintings by Michelangelo, Canaletto, Peter Paul Rubens and many others. Among the prestigious names who decorated the rooms were the Dutch-born English sculptor and woodcarver Grinling Gibbons (1648–1721) and the Italian interior decorator Antonio Verrio (c1640–1707).

Also on display is Queen Mary's Dolls' House, designed by Sir Edwin Lutyens in 1924. The furnishings are at one-twelfth size, and the plumbing and lighting really work.

Also noteworthy is Prince Albert's marble and mosaic memorial chapel designed by Sir George Gilbert Scott (1811–78). A spectacle not to be missed is the pomp of the Changing of the Guard, which is dependent on the weather (Jul–end Mar alternate days except Sun 11am; rest of year Mon–Sat 11am).
✉ Windsor SL4 1NJ ☎ 020 7766 7304; 01753 831118 (infoline) 🕓 Castle: Mar–end Oct daily 9.45–5.15; rest of year daily 9.45–4.15. Semi-state rooms: Oct–end Mar. Subject to closure on certain days (especially in Jun); call first 💷 Adult: £14.80, child (5–16) £8.50, family £21

WINDSOR TOWN

It is worth exploring Windsor's shops and noteworthy buildings. The Guildhall on the High Street was completed in 1707 by Sir Christopher Wren (1632–1723). Its Tuscan columns on the ground floor do not touch the ceiling; apparently, the town council insisted on having them, but Wren left the gap to prove that they were structurally superfluous.

Farther up the High Street you will pass the 19th-century parish church of St. John the Baptist. From here you can continue up Park Street to the Long Walk, which skirts Windsor Great Park. This 3-mile (5km) avenue was laid out by Charles I and planted with elms. Within the park is the 14ha (35-acre) woodland Savill Garden (daily), which is worth visiting at any time of the year, but is particularly beautiful in spring when the azaleas and camellias are in bloom.

ETON COLLEGE

Across the river from Windsor, over the pedestrian-only Windsor Bridge, is Eton, its appealing main street fronted by Britain's most famous public school. Henry VI (1421–71) founded it in 1440 for 70 King's Scholars or Collegers who lived in the College and were educated free, and for a small number of students who lived in the town of Eton and paid for their education.

Today Eton College is a prestigious boarding school for approximately 1,280 boys between the ages of 13 and 18, distinguished by their traditional 19th-century uniform of black tailcoat, waiscoat and pinstriped trousers. Highlights throughout the visiting season include the School Yard, with its statue of Henry VI, the superb Perpendicular-style College Chapel, the Cloisters and the Museum of Eton Life (late Mar–early Oct daily). Famous old Etonians include the Duke of Wellington (1769–1852) and a number of prime ministers— Sir Robert Walpole (1676–1745), William Gladstone (1809–98) and Harold Macmillan (1894–1986).
✉ Windsor SL4 6DW ☎ 01753 671177 🕓 Easter to mid-Apr, Jul–end Aug daily 10.30–4.30; mid-Apr to end Jun, Sep daily 2–4.30. 1-hour guided tour Mar–end Oct 2.15, 3.15

TIPS

» Tour companies operate a daily service to Windsor, collecting from many London hotels (details from hotels).

» Windsor Castle's State Apartments and Chapel can close at short notice, so call in advance.

» The view of the castle from a riverboat cruiser is very impressive (www.boat-trips.co.uk). French Brothers run cruises from Windsor Promenade.

THE NEW FOREST

Bustling Lyndhurst makes an excellent base for touring the New Forest (▷ 192). This superb area of lowland heath, originally a Norman hunting forest, is renowned for its grazing wild ponies and red deer.

THE DRIVE

Distance: 68 miles (108km)
Allow: 3 hours
Start/end: Lyndhurst, map ref 430 H20
🛈 New Forest Visitor Information Centre, New Street, Lymington SO41 9BH, tel 01590 689000
OS Landranger maps: 184, 195, 196

★ Lyndhurst is the unofficial capital of the New Forest and busy with tourists in summer. In the church-yard is buried Alice Hargreaves (née Liddell), the original Alice of Lewis Carroll's *Alice's Adventures in Wonderland* (1865). The Verderers—the guardians of the forest since Norman times—employ staff called agisters to patrol the forest daily, often on horseback, to supervise the animals grazing on the 36,423ha (90,000-acre) expanse of the forest.

From Lyndhurst take the A337 north. After 2 miles (3.2km) turn left through Minstead, then left, left again and immediately right to cross the A31 to Brook, and follow the B3078 to Fordingbridge.

❶ The little town of Fordingbridge was originally called Forde, but had its name enlarged with the building of the 13th-century bridge, a seven-arched structure that has since been widened. South of the town, 13th-century St. Mary's Church has an imposing 15th-century porch and hammer-beam roof. The Avon is a renowned river for trout and pike. Northwest of town is Rockbourne, a village with an attractive group of Tudor and Georgian cottages alongside a stream, where tiny bridges connect the houses with the road. There's a wide variety of building materials, including tile, timber, flint, brick and thatch. South of the village is the excavated site of Rockbourne Roman Villa, discovered in 1942 by a farmer digging out a ferret; it includes mosaic floors and underfloor heating systems.

Take the A338 south from Fording-bridge. Turn left at Ibsley on a minor road, turn right in half a mile (1km) at Mockbeggar, then turn next left through Linwood, under the A31 and forking right to Bolderwood.

❷ At Bolderwood, in the heart of the forest, the Forestry Commission has created three walks of

Above Ponies congregate to escape the sun

varying lengths through plantations of oak, beech and wellingtonia. The Bolderwood Deer Sanctuary gives the best opportunities for seeing the many deer that inhabit the New Forest, and there is an observation platform (bring binoculars). A memorial is dedicated to Canadian airmen, serving at nearby Stony Cross, who died in World War II. The route also passes the huge Knightwood Oak (▷ 204).

From Bolderwood follow an unclassified road southeast to cross the A35 to Rhinefield.

❸ Some of Britain's tallest trees tower above you on the Rhinefield Ornamental Drive, and include redwoods, spruces and Douglas firs. They were planted in 1859 as an approach to a long-vanished hunting lodge. Beyond the drive are mixed woodlands of beech, oak and pine, and there is also a Tall Trees nature trail. Rhinefield House (a hotel), close by, is an exuberant Victorian building in the style of a castle, and is a good place for refreshment.

Above *Mushrooms growing in the under-growth in the New Forest National Park*
Right *A lone fallow deer stands alert on the plains near Stoney Cross*

Continue from Rhinefield to Brockenhurst.

④ Brockenhurst is a prosperous-looking village and one of the main locations in what was then the 'new' forest. Its church dates from Norman times but the village is predominantly 19th- and 20th-century in character.

From Brockenhurst turn right on to the A337 to Lymington.

⑤ The seaside town of Lymington made much of its money as a spa, salt town and sea port. Lymington's

Georgian and other buildings include Pressgang Cottage—headquarters in 1809 of the local press gang (men who forcibly enlisted others into the army or navy). Also of interest is 18th-century St. Thomas's Church on the High Street. Car ferries make a short crossing to Yarmouth on the Isle of Wight (▷ 186).

Leave Lymington by the B3054 (signposted Beaulieu). After 6 miles (10km) and just before Beaulieu, turn right for Bucklers Hard.

⑥ Remarkably little has changed at the village of Bucklers Hard since

1800, when it was a shipbuilding hub. Three of the ships in Nelson's fleet at the Battle of Trafalgar (1805) were built here. Two rows of 18th-century shipbuilders' cottages slope towards the water. The Bucklers Hard Story reflects on the village's past. Boat trips are available in summer. Return to the B3054 and turn right through Beaulieu. Then take the next right turn for Exbury.

⑦ Late spring—when the rhododendrons and azaleas are out—brings a wealth of colour to Exbury Gardens (▷ 182). Lepe Country Park is a stretch of coast overlooking the Isle of Wight, good for walks.

PLACES TO VISIT
NEW FOREST CENTRE AND MUSEUM
✠ High Street, Lyndhurst SO43 7NY
☎ 02380 283444 🕐 Daily 10–5 💲 Adult £3, child (under 16) free

ROCKBOURNE ROMAN VILLA
✠ Rockbourne SP6 3PG ☎ 0845 603 5635 🕐 Apr–end Oct Mon–Sun 10.30–6 💲 Adult £2.50, child £1.50, family £7

THE BUCKLERS HARD STORY
✠ Beaulieu, Brockenhurst SO42 7XB
☎ 01590 616203 🕐 Easter–end Sep 10.30–5; Oct–Easter 11–4 💲 Adult £4, child £25, family £11

WHERE TO EAT
Stop at Rhinefield House (tel 0845 072 7516, reservations recommended) near Rhinefield, or have a picnic in Lepe Country Park, Exbury. There's also a café and restaurant at Beaulieu.

THE KNIGHTWOOD OAK AND THE PORTUGUESE FIREPLACE

This circuit explores the contrasting landscapes of the New Forest (▷ 192), with its ancient woods of oak and beech typified by Bolderwood.

THE WALK

Distance: 6 miles (9.5km)
Allow: 3 hours
Start/end at: Brock Hill Forestry Commission parking area, off the A35
[map ref] 430 H20
OS Landranger map: 196
OS Explorer map: OL22

★ South of the starting point at Brock Hill is the mid-19th-century conifer plantation of the Rhinefield Ornamental Drive and Blackwater Arboretum, into which the walk can be extended.

Take the gravel path at the southern end of the parking area (beyond the information post), parallel with the road. After 90m (100 yds) turn right just before a bench seat and descend to reach a gravel track. Cross straight over and, where the path curves left, keep straight on to a gate and the A35. Cross over and take the gate opposite. Keep to the path as it leads uphill to a junction, where you turn right and follow the path to Knightwood Oak parking area, then follow the sign to the Knightwood Oak itself.

❶ The Knightwood Oak is the most famous in the forest, thought to be at least 350 years old. It owes its great age to pollarding (pruning its branches) to encourage new growth to provide timber for fuel and charcoal. Its girth is a massive 7m (8 yds).

Return to the parking area, bear right along the road and then right again into mixed woodland. Cross a stream and you'll soon reach a gravel track. Bear right and keep to this trail, passing red marker posts to reach a fork. Keep left until you reach a gate and road. Turn right to view the Portuguese Fireplace.

❷ The Portuguese Fireplace was used in the cookhouse of a Portuguese army unit, deployed in World War I.

Return through Holidays Hill Inclosure to the fork of tracks.

❸ The so-called 'inclosures' are areas of managed woodland where trees are protected from deer and ponies. These 17th-century plantations were used to produce large quantities of timber for the construction and shipbuilding industries. Holidays Hill Inclosure is one of the forest's oldest, and includes 300-year-old oak trees.

Bear left and follow the track to the New Forest Reptile Centre. Walk along the access drive past a cottage dated 1811 then, at a barrier, on your left, drop down on to a path and follow it across a bridge.

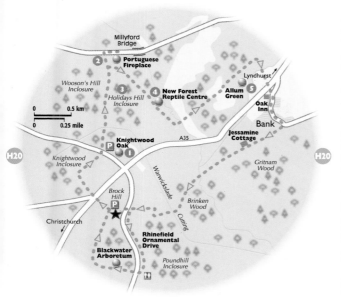

Hursthill Inclosure. Drop down past a turning on the right, then climb again and bear left at a fork. Keep to the marked track as it drops past another turning on the right and leaves Hursthill Inclosure at a gate.

Walk the long straight stretch to the bridge over Highland Water, and follow the track round to the right. A gate leads the waymarked trail into Poundhill Inclosure, and another straight section brings you to a five-way junction at marker post 24.

Turn right here. Now ignore all turnings, and follow the track as it turns sharp right and winds its way to a junction with the Ornamental Drive. Turn left for the last 100 yards (91m) back to the car park.

PLACE TO VISIT
NEW FOREST REPTILE CENTRE
✉ Bournemouth Road, Lyndhurst SO34 7DP
☎ 023 8028 3141 (weekdays only)
🕓 Apr–end Sep daily 10–4.30
✋ Free. Parking £2

WHERE TO EAT
The Oak Inn at Bank (tel 02380 282350) is an 18th-century pub serving local ales and good food. It is just off the A35, southwest of Lyndhurst.

WHEN TO GO
Enjoy drifts of red and gold leaves in autumn or a palette of greens in summer.

Opposite *Blackwater Arboreutm*
Below *Rhinefield Ornamental Drive*

❹ The New Forest Reptile Centre breeds rare species such as the smooth snake and sand lizard for re-release into the wild. On a sunny day you might see adders, grass snakes and rare natterjack toads. Snake-catching was an important trade here in the 19th century. The most celebrated local catcher was Brusher Mills. It is believed he caught around 35,000 snakes, selling them to zoos and for medicine.

Keep to the main path for 0.75 mile (1.2km), skirting the walls to Allum Green and several clearings.

❺ In Allum Green you may see some of the 3,500 New Forest ponies grazing the lawns and trees. They are all owned by local 'commoners' and are descendants of a wild breed peculiar to the area. The owner places a brand mark on each pony, and in autumn they are rounded up and rebranded. It is illegal to feed the ponies. The route climbs gently through the trees to a crossing and then turns right. Shortly, bear half right across the clearing and over a footbridge, then continue through the woodland

edge to a telegraph pole. Bear right for 18m (20 yards), then left through a gate to the A35.

Turn left, then almost immediately right across the road to a gate. Continue to a garden boundary and turn right, along a narrow path leading to a lane in the hamlet of Bank. Turn right, past the Oak Inn and walk through Bank. Just before a cattle grid, turn right through a gate on to a gravelled track towards Brockenhurst. Follow this track for nearly a mile (1.4km) to a junction at a small green.

Fork right towards Brockenhurst, and go through a gate to enter

205

ALDEBURGH

SNAPE MALTINGS CONCERT HALL

www.snapemaltings.co.uk

Home to the International Aldeburgh Festival, plus other events and performances.

✉ Snape, Saxmundham, Aldeburgh IP17 1SR ☎ 01728 687100; box office: 01728 687110 ⏱ Box office: Mon–Sat10–1, 2–4 ✋ Various 🍴 🍷 🏧 🚉 Saxmundham (5.5km/3.5 miles)

ASCOT

ASCOT RACECOURSE

www.ascot.co.uk

Britain's most glamorous racecourse hosts June's Royal Ascot week, noted for visitors' fashions.

✉ Ascot SL5 7JX ☎ 01344 876876 ⏱ Flat racing May–end Oct; National Hunt Nov–end Apr ✋ Adult £10–£63 🍴 🚉 Ascot

ASHFORD

ASHFORD DESIGNER OUTLET

www.ashforddesigneroutlet.com

Outlet with 80 top-name and designer stores offering discounts of up to 50 per cent.

✉ Kimberley Way, Ashford TN24 0SD ☎ 01233 895900 ⏱ Mon–Fri 10–8, Sat 10–7, Sun 11–5 🚉 Ashford International 🚌 Shuttle bus from train station every 15 min 🍴 🛍

BRIGHTON

BRIGHTON DOME

www.brightondome.org

Major complex with three venues hosting music, dance and comedy.

✉ 29 New Road, Brighton BN1 1UG ☎ 01273 709709 ⏱ Box office: Mon–Sat 10–6 ✋ Various 🛍 🍷 🚉 Brighton

BRIGHTON FLEA MARKET

This indoor market has more than 60 stalls selling antiques, furniture and collectables.

✉ 31a Upper St. James's Street, Kemp Town, Brighton BN2 1JN ☎ 01273 624006 ⏱ Mon–Fri 10–5, Sat 10–4.30, Sun 10.30–4.30 🚉 Brighton

CONCORDE 2

www.concorde2.co.uk

Sucessor to the original Concorde club made famous by the likes of Fatboy Slim, C2 is a cosy venue on the famous Brighton seafront for live bands and excellent DJs.

✉ Madeira Shelter Hall, Madeira Drive, Brighton BN2 1EN ☎ 01273 673311 ⏱ Doors open 7pm gig nights, 10pm club nights; check web for details ✋ Price varies 🚉 Brighton

KOMEDIA

www.komedia.co.uk

Theatre and renowned late cabaret bar showcasing comedy, music, cabaret and international theatre.

✉ 44–47 Gardner Street, Brighton BN1 1UN ☎ 01273 647101; box office: 01273 647100 ⏱ Café bar opens daily 10am ✋ Various 🛍 🍷 🚉 Brighton

REVENGE

www.revenge.co.uk

Brighton's biggest gay nightclub, with cabaret and dance music.

✉ 32–34 Old Steine, Brighton BN1 1TR ☎ 01273 606064 ⏱ Daily 10.30pm–3 or 5am (depending on the set) ✋ £1.50–£8.50 🚉 Brighton

RIN-TIN-TIN

Buy original 20th-century nostalgia— old advertising, packaging, labels, posters, magazines, glamour and household items.

✉ 34 North Road, Brighton BN1 1YB ☎ 01273 672424 ⏱ Mon–Sat 11–5.30 🚉 Brighton

Above *Merry-go-round at Brighton*

SALTDEAN LIDO

Classic open-air swimming pool built in 1937 in Hollywood modernist style; worth seeing for the architecture alone.

✉ Saltdean Park Road, Brighton BN2 8SP ☎ 01273 888308 🕐 Late May–end Sep daily 10–6 (weather permitting) 🎫 Adult £4, child (3–16) £3 🚇

CALSHOT
CALSHOT ACTIVITIES CENTRE

www.calshot.com

One of the largest outdoor adventure centres in Britain, with dinghy sailing, windsurfing, kitesurfing, powerboating, canoeing, jet skiing, climbing, skiing, snowboarding, track cycling and archery.

✉ Calshot Spit, Calshot, Fawley, Southampton SO45 1BR ☎ 023 8089 2077 🕐 All year 🎫 Prices vary 🚍

CAMBRIDGE
ALL SAINTS GARDEN ART AND CRAFT MARKET

www.cambridge-art-craft.co.uk

An interesting outdoor market in the heart of the city, which sells all kinds of arts and crafts.

✉ Trinity Street, Cambridge CB2 1TB ☎ 01223 457446 🕐 Sat 10–5; also Fri Jun–end Aug and Wed–Sat in Dec 🚇 Food stalls 🚉 Cambridge

CAMBRIDGE ARTS PICTURE HOUSE

www.picturehouses.co.uk

Cherished Cambridge cinema with three screens showing current and classic films.

✉ 38–39 St. Andrew's Street, Cambridge CB2 3AR ☎ 0871 704 2050 (box office) 🕐 Daily 🎫 Adult £4.40–£7, child (3–14) £5 🚇 🚉 Cambridge

CAMBRIDGE ARTS THEATRE

www.cambridgeartstheatre.com

Small theatre that stages a variety of repertory and other touring productions.

✉ 6 St. Edward's Passage, Cambridge CB2 3PJ ☎ 01223 578933; box office: 01223 503333 🕐 Box office: Mon–Sat 12–8, Sun (performance days only) one hour before curtain up 🎫 Various 🍴 🚇 🚉 Cambridge

CAMBRIDGE CORN EXCHANGE

www.cornex.co.uk

The city's prime concert venue is also used for festivals and shows.

✉ Wheeler Street, Cambridge CB2 3QB ☎ 01223 457555; box office: 01223 357851 🕐 Box office: Mon–Sat 10–6, Sun 6pm or 1 hour before show to 30 min after start of show 🎫 Various 🍴 🚇 🚉 Cambridge

THE EAGLE

Old Cambridge pub—a coaching inn since the 16th century—usually packed with students.

✉ Benet Street, Cambridge CB2 3QN ☎ 01223 505020 🕐 Mon–Sat 11–11, Sun 12–10.30 🚉 Cambridge

CHERTSEY
THORPE PARK

www.thorpepark.com

One of Britain's best theme parks, with thrilling rides, including the world's first 10-looping roller-coaster.

✉ Staines Road, Chertsey KT16 8PN ☎ 0870 444 4466 🕐 Mid-Feb to early Mar times vary; mid-Mar to end Oct daily 🎫 Adult £18–£32, child (4–11) £14–£21, family £54–£88 🍴 🚇 🚉 📯 🚉 Staines, shuttle to Park half hourly

CHICHESTER
CHICHESTER FESTIVAL THEATRE

www.cft.org.uk

This is one of Britain's flagship theatres, with an illustrious reputation. It opened in 1962 with Sir Laurence Olivier as its first director. The smaller, more intimate Minerva theatre was built in 1989.

✉ Oaklands Park, Chichester PO19 6AP ☎ 01243 784437; box office: 01243 781312 🕐 Box office: Mon–Sat 10–8 (6 when no performance), Sun from 2 hours before performance 🎫 Various 🍴 🚇 🚉 🚉 Chichester

CLACTON-ON-SEA
CLACTON FACTORY SHOPPING VILLAGE

www.clactonvillage.co.uk

'Seaside village' factory outlet with 48 stores selling designer and high-street brands at savings of up to 60 per cent, including fashion, confectionery, jewellery and homewares.

✉ Stephenson Road West, Clacton-on-Sea

CO15 4TL ☎ 01255 479595 🕐 Mon–Sat 10–6, Sun 11–5 🍴 🚇 🚉 Clacton

GRAYS
LAKESIDE SHOPPING CENTRE

www.lakeside.uk.com

More than 230 shops, a multiplex cinema and a sports lake with diving school.

✉ West Thurrock Way, Grays RM20 2ZP ☎ 01708 869933 🕐 Mon–Fri 10–10 (10–6 public holidays), Sat 9–9, Sun 11–5 (some larger stores open at 10.30 for viewing). Closed 25 Dec. Individual stores vary 🍴 🚇 🚉 Chafford Hundred (linked by a bridge)

GUILDFORD
YVONNE ARNAUD THEATRE

www.yvonne-arnaud.co.uk

One of the country's leading regional theatres.

✉ Millbrook, Guildford GU1 3UX ☎ 01483 440000 🕐 Box office: Mon–Sat 10–8 (6 non-performance days) 🎫 Adult £13–£26.50, child (under 16) from £7 🍴 🚇 🚉 🚉 Guildford

HEACHAM
NORFOLK LAVENDER

www.norfolk-lavender.co.uk

England's premier lavender farm. Contains the National Collection of Lavenders with over 100 different lavenders to see and smell.

✉ Caley Mill, Heacham PE31 7JE ☎ 01485 570384 🕐 Apr–end Oct daily 9–5; rest of year daily 9–4. Guided tours: May–end Aug up to 4 times a day 🎫 Free. Tours: adult £3, child (11–18) £1.50 🚇 🚉 King's Lynn (12 miles/19km)

HEMEL HEMPSTEAD
THE SNOW CENTRE

www.thesnowcentre.com

With a main slope over 525ft (160m) and a learning slope over 320ft (100m), this indoor complex can sustain subzero temperatures and well-pisted runs even in the heat of summer. Ski, board and boot hire available. Bars and other facilities maintain the authentic après ski feel.

✉ St. Albans Hill, Hemel Hempstead HP3 9NH ☎ 01442 241321 🕐 Daily 🎫 Depends on activity 🚇 🍴 🚉 Hemel Hempstead

LURGASHALL
LURGASHALL WINERY
www.lurgashall.co.uk
This 17th-century farm maintains old English country practices by producing a range of fruit wines, fruit liqueurs and meads.
✉ Dial Green, Lurgashall, Petworth GU28 9HA ☎ 01428 707292 🕐 Mon–Sat 9–5, Sun 11–5 🚉 Haslemere (6 miles/10km)

MIDHURST
COWDRAY PARK POLO CLUB
www.cowdraypolo.co.uk
The home of British polo in beautiful surroundings in the Cowdray Park Estate. The main event is the Gold Cup in July; bring a picnic and enjoy an arena-side view of the action.
✉ Cowdray Park Estate, Midhurst GU29 0AQ ☎ 01730 813257 🕐 Matches: late Apr–early Oct Sat–Sun, public holiday Mon and some weekdays 💷 From £10 per car (including driver and passenger; children under 12 free) 🍴 🚘 ⚐

MILTON KEYNES
XSCAPE
www.xscape.co.uk
An all-in-one giant leisure complex with a huge indoor snowslope, rock climbing, indoor sky-diving, bowling and cinema.
✉ 602 Marlborough Gate, Milton Keynes MK9 3XS ☎ 0871 200 3220 🕐 Daily 9am–11pm 💷 Varies according to activity 🚘 🚉 Milton Keynes

NEWBURY
THE WATERMILL THEATRE
www.watermill.org.uk
Intimate theatre (seating 216 people) within a converted riverside mill, with a superb reputation.
✉ Bagnor, near Newbury RG20 8AE ☎ 01635 45834; box office: 01635 46044 🕐 Box office: Mon–Sat 10–7 (6 non-performance days and last Sat of run) 💷 From £10 🍴 ⚐ 🚉 Newbury

NORWICH
THE ASSEMBLY HOUSE
www.assemblyhousenorwich.co.uk
In a building dating from the 13th century are two concert halls and three galleries with weekly changing exhibitions.

✉ Theatre Street, Norwich NR2 1RQ ☎ 01603 626402 🕐 Box office: as for Norwich Theatre Royal (below) 💷 Various 🍴 🚉 Norwich

BROADS AUTHORITY
www.broads-authority.gov.uk
The wetlands of the Norfolk and Suffolk Broads offer gentle sailing. Yachts and motor cruisers are rented from boatyards. Or book through an agency: Blakes (tel: 08702 202498) or Hoseasons (tel: 01502 500505).
✉ 18 Colegate, Norwich NR3 1BQ ☎ 01603 610734

NORWICH THEATRE ROYAL
www.theatreroyalnorwich.co.uk
This venerable venue is over 250 years old but was completely modernised in 2007. It shows musicals, comedy, drama and touring music.
✉ Theatre Street, Norwich NR2 1RL ☎ 01603 630000 🕐 Box office: Mon–Sat 9.30–8 (9.30–6 on non-performance

days) and for 2 hours before the first performance on Sun 💷 Admission varies 🍴 🚉 Norwich

OXFORD
ALICE'S SHOP
www.sheepshop.com
This is the original Old Sheep Shop (from Lewis Carroll's *Through the Looking-Glass)*, from where the real-life Alice Liddell used to buy her sweets (candy). It stocks a wide range of Alice-themed gifts.
✉ 83 St. Aldate's, Oxford OX1 1RA ☎ 01865 723793 🕐 Daily 11–5 🚘 🚉 Oxford

BLACKWELL'S
www.blackwell.co.uk
Blackwell's Oxford empire spans seven shops, including this renowned academic bookshop, the Art and Poster Shop at No 27 and the Music Shop at Nos 23–25.
✉ 48–51 Broad Street, Oxford OX1 3BQ

☎ 01865 792792 ⏱ Mon–Sat 9–6 (Tue from 9.30), Sun 11–5 🚉 Oxford

THE COVERED MARKET

www.oxford-covered-market.co.uk

Oxford's covered market has been developing since 1773. Today it houses a wide variety of shops, from clothing and footwear to gift shops and jewellers', via butchers' and delicatessens.

✉ The High, Oxford ⏱ Mon–Sat 9–5.30 🚉 Oxford

PHOENIX PICTUREHOUSE

www.picturehouses.co.uk

Opened in 1913, now showing independent and classic films.

✉ 57 Walton Street, Oxford OX2 6AE ☎ Box office: 0871 704 2062 ⏱ Daily ✋ Adults: £4.50–£7, child (3–14) £4.50–5 🍴 🛍 🚉 Oxford

THE RIDGEWAY NATIONAL TRAIL

www.nationaltrail.co.uk/ridgeway

The Ridgeway, which follows a chalk ridge used by prehistoric man, is perhaps Britain's oldest road. It's 85 miles (136km) long and stretches from Overton Hill near Avebury to Ivinghoe Beacon in the Chilterns. There are many places to stop off at along the way.

✉ The National Trails Office, Holton, Oxford OX33 1QQ ☎ 01865 810224

THE UNIVERSITY OF OXFORD SHOP

www.oushop.com

This shop sells official University of Oxford items.

✉ 106 High Street, Oxford OX1 4BW ☎ 01865 247414 ⏱ Mon–Sat 9–5.30 (also Jun–end Aug Sun and public holidays 11–4) 🚉 Oxford

PORTSMOUTH

GUNWHARF QUAYS

www.gunwharf-quays.com

Here there are more than 95 designer outlet stores with up to 70 per cent discounts. Gunwharf Quays is the focus of the redeveloped Portsmouth Harbour.

✉ Gunwharf Quays, Portsmouth PO1 3TZ ☎ 023 9283 6700 ⏱ Mon–Fri 10–6, Sat 9–6, Sun 10–5 🍴 🛍 🚉 Portsmouth Harbour

PORTSMOUTH GUILDHALL

www.portsmouthguildhall.co.uk

Concert hall of 2,000-plus capacity staging rock gigs and classical music events.

✉ Guildhall Square, Portsmouth PO1 2AB ☎ Box office: 023 9282 4355 ⏱ Box office: Mon–Sat 10–6.30 (later on performance days), Sun from 1 hour before performance ✋ Various 🛍 🚉 Portsmouth & Southsea

SOUTHAMPTON

HAMPSHIRE CRICKET CLUB

www.rosebowlplc.com

Hampshire's headquarters has excellent facilities for spectators.

✉ The Rose Bowl, Botley Road, West End, Southampton SO30 3XH ☎ 023 8047 2002; ticket office: 08702 430291 ⏱ Season: Apr–end Sep. Ticket office: Mon–Fri 9–5 ✋ Adult £25–£45, child £15+ 🍴 🛍 🚉 Southampton Parkway and Southampton Hedge End

Opposite *Sailing on Barton Broad in the Norfolk Broads National Park*
Below *Enjoying a game of polo*

SOUTHAMPTON GUILDHALL

www.southampton-guildhall.com

The Southampton Guidlhall is southern England's largest multipurpose entertainment venue, with rock and pop, classical orchestras and comedy.

✉ Civic Centre, Southampton SO14 7LP ☎ 023 8063 2601 ⊕ Box office: Mon–Fri 9–7, Sat 9–5 ✋ Various
▢ 🚹 🚆 Southampton Central

TRING

CHAMPNEYS TRING

www.champneys.com

Based in a private mansion in landscaped parkland, this is one of the world's leading 'destination spas', with over 100 treatments. Over-16s only.

✉ Wigginton, Tring HP23 6HY ☎ 01442 291000; reservations: 08703 300300 ⊕ All year ✋ Day package: 'Relax Day' from £60
🍴 ▢ 🚆 Berkhamsted

VENTNOR

BLACKGANG CHINE

www.blackgangchine.com

Imaginative themed areas plus play areas set on the wooded slopes of Blackgang Chine on the Isle of Wight. Under 14s must be with an adult.

✉ Blackgang, Chale, Ventnor PO38 2HN ☎ 01983 730052 ⊕ Mar–end Oct daily 10–5 (later, floodlit evenings in high season, call for details) ✋ Person (4–60yr) £9.50, family £35. Free return visit within seven days ▢

WINCHESTER

CADOGAN AND JAMES

This deli on a square near the cathedral attracts foodies like moths to a flame. Established by chef James Martin, there's fresh pasta, loads of different cheeses, truffles, preserves and kitchen essentials for aspiring gourmets.

✉ 31a The Square, Winchester SO23 9EX ☎ 01962 840805 ⊕ Mon–Sat 9.30–5.30 (Sun 11–5 in Dec) 🚆 Winchester

WINDSOR

LEGOLAND WINDSOR

www.legoland.co.uk

The ever-popular Lego brick is the theme of this family venue in Windsor Great Park with some 50 interactive rides, live shows, building workshop and other attractions.

✉ Winkfield Road, Windsor SL4 4AY ☎ 08705 040404 ⊕ Mar–end Nov daily 10–5, 6 or 7. Closed Dec–end Feb ✋ 1-day: adult £34, child (3–15) £26
🍴 ▢ 🚆 Windsor & Eton Riverside, Windsor & Eton Central 🚌 Shuttle from both stations; tickets including admission, rail travel and shuttle from most major stations in Britain

Below Cowes Week on the Isle of Wight takes place in August

FESTIVALS AND EVENTS

MAY

NORFOLK AND NORWICH FESTIVAL
www.n-joy.org.uk
Eleven days of classical music, opera, jazz, blues and cabaret.
⊠ Norwich and Norfolk, various venues ☎ 01603 877750 ◉ Early May ✋ Various ⬛ Norwich

BRIGHTON FESTIVAL
www.brightonfestival.org
International performers from the world of theatre, dance, music and literature.
⊠ Brighton, various venues ☎ 01273 700747 ◉ Early to late May ✋ Various ⬛ Brighton

ISLE OF WIGHT WALKING FESTIVAL
www.isleofwightwalkingfestival.co.uk
Two weeks of events and walks at Britain's largest walking festival.
⊠ Isle of Wight, various locations ☎ 01983 813800 ◉ Mid-May

MAY DAY
www.visitoxford.org
Lively all-night parties culminate at Magdalen Bridge, where Magdalen College choir sing in the dawn from the chapel tower to hushed (and tired) crowds.
⊠ Magdalen Bridge, Oxford ☎ 01865 726871 ◉ 30 April to 1 May ⬛ Oxford

JUNE

ALDEBURGH FESTIVAL OF MUSIC AND ART
www.aldeburgh.co.uk
Internationally renowned music and arts festival.
⊠ Snape Maltings, Snape ☎ 01728 687110 ◉ Early to late June ✋ Various ⬛ Saxmundham 3.5 miles (5.5km)

BROADSTAIRS DICKENS FESTIVAL
www.broadstairs.gov.uk/dickensfestival
Week-long celebration of Dickens, including a parade, play, cricket match, Victorian music hall, ball, readings, talks, walks and bathing.
⊠ Broadstairs ☎ 01843 861827 ◉ Mid-June ✋ Free and various ⬛ Broadstairs

CHICHESTER FESTIVITIES
www.chifest.org.uk
An 18-day celebration of music, film, theatre, art and literature.
◉ Chichester, various venues ☎ 01243 785718 ◉ Late June to mid-July ✋ Various ⬛ Chichester

JULY

GOODWOOD FESTIVAL OF SPEED
www.goodwood.co.uk
A high-powered gathering of prestigious motorsport cars and bikes.
◉ Goodwood Estate, Goodwood ☎ 01243 755055 ◉ Last weekend in June ✋ Various ⬛ Chichester

WOMAD FESTIVAL
www.womad.org
This annual celebration of world music is friendly and fun.
◉ Charlton Park, Malmesbury, Wiltshire ☎ 0845 146 1735 ◉ Late July–early August Fri–Sun ✋ £125; day tickets available for Sun only £50 ⬛ Memble

FARNBOROUGH INTERNATIONAL AIRSHOW
www.farnborough.com
An internationally important biennial airshow.
◉ Farnborough, Hampshire ☎ 01252 532800; tickets: 08709 063859 ◉ Mid-July 1 week ✋ £23–£28 ⬛ Farnborough

AUGUST

COWES WEEK
www.cowesweek.co.uk
Yachties and socialites flock to this annual sailing get-together.
◉ Cowes, Isle of Wight ☎ 01983 295744 ◉ From last Saturday of July or first Saturday of August

Right Boats at rest in Rye harbour

ARUNDEL FESTIVAL
www.arundelfestival.co.uk
Ten-day arts festival—drama, concerts and family entertainment—in Arundel Park, Castle and other venues.
◉ Arundel, various venues ☎ 01903 882173 ◉ Last week Aug ✋ Various ⬛ Arundel

SEPTEMBER

RYE FESTIVAL
www.ryeartsfestival.co.uk
A two-week celebration of music, theatre and literature.
◉ Rye, various venues ☎ 01797 224442 ◉ First two weeks September ✋ Various ⬛ Rye

NOVEMBER

LEWES BONFIRE NIGHT
www.lewesbonfirecouncil.org.uk
Largest Guy Fawkes night fireworks event in Britain, with fancy dress parades and marching bands.
◉ Lewes ☎ 01273 483448 ◉ 5 November (except Sunday) ⬛ Lewes

DECEMBER

THE FESTIVAL OF NINE LESSONS AND CAROLS
www.kings.cam.ac.uk/chapel
Carol service broadcast on Radio 4. No advance tickets, start queuing at dawn to get in.
◉ King's College Chapel, Cambridge ☎ 01223 331212 ◉ 24 December 3pm ✋ Free ⬛ Cambridge

EATING

REGIONS SOUTH EAST AND EAST ANGLIA • EATING

PRICES AND SYMBOLS

The restaurants are listed alphabetically within each town. The prices are for a two-course lunch (L) and a three-course à la carte dinner (D). Prices in pubs are for a two-course lunchtime bar meal and a two-course dinner in the restaurant, unless specified otherwise. The wine price is for the least expensive bottle. For a key to the symbols, ▷ 2.

ARUNDEL
GEORGE & DRAGON

Perfectly placed at the end of a lane on the South Downs, this inn is ideal for a walk before or after dinner. Old beams, stone floors and bags of atmosphere draw a crowd, particularly at weekends, so come early for a good table. Expect honest pub grub from a kitchen that does the basics well: a smoked chicken and duck terrine with orange chutney and Melba toast to start perhaps, followed by walnut-crusted cod loin with parsnip purée and minted new potatoes. A short carte is supplemented by a lengthy specials board, with an additional bar selection served at lunchtime.

✉ Burpham BN18 9RR ☎ 01903 883131
🕐 11–2.30, 6–12. Bar meals Mon–Sat 12–2, 7–9, Sun 12–2.30 ✋ D £25, Wine £13.95 🚗 2.5 miles (4km) along no-through road signed Burpham, off A27, 1 mile (1.6km) east of Arundel 🚉 Arundel

BRANCASTER STAITHE
THE WHITE HORSE

www.whitehorsebrancaster.co.uk
The beautiful views from the bistro at this hotel (▷ 218) are complemented by consistently well-prepared, home-cooked, Modern and traditional food, with plenty of fresh fish and vegetarian options. Staff are informal and friendly.
✉ Brancaster Staithe PE31 8BY ☎ 01485 210262 🕐 Daily 12–2, 6.30–9.
✋ L £14.20, D £18.20, Wine £12
🚗 On A149 coast road between Hunstanton and Wells-next-the-Sea

BRAY
THE FAT DUCK

www.fatduck.co.uk
Two small cottages in an English village seem an unlikely location for an international destination restaurant. Chef Heston Blumenthal is the leading exponent in the scientific approach to cuisine. After a palate-cleansing froth of green tea, vodka and lime juice, starters might include quail jelly with pea purée and langoustine cream. The main courses feel more conventional by comparison, but always with a fresh approach. One innovation—Sound of the Sea—is a seafood creation, accompanied by nautical noises on an ipod.
✉ High Street, Bray SL6 2AQ ☎ 01628 580333 🕐 12–1.45, 7–9.45; closed Mon, D Sun, two weeks at Christmas ✋ Fixed price from £95, Wine £30 🚗 From M4 junction 8/9 (Maidenhead) take A308 towards Windsor, turn left into Bray; restaurant in centre of village on right

BRIGHTON
THE GINGERMAN RESTAURANT

www.gingermanrestaurants.com
The Gingerman is a popular place so reserving is essential. There is a two- or three-course fixed-price dinner menu and a simple lunch with two choices at each course. The Modern British menu offers lots of seasonal flavours in food such as English asparagus, summer vegetables and spring lamb.
✉ 21A Norfolk Square, Brighton BN1

2PD ☎ 01273 326688 ⏰ Tue–Sat
12.30–2, 7–10; closed Mon, one week at
Christmas 🖐 L £15, D £30, Wine £13.50
♿ 🅿 Brighton

TERRE À TERRE
www.terreaterre.co.uk
This vegetarian restaurant has a loyal
following. The innovative, flavour-
packed dishes might include arepas
mojo, corn cakes in chermoula
cornmeal, or saltimbocca funghi—a
wild mushroom confit wrapped in
creamed polenta and encased in
sunblushed tomatoes. The wine list
places a strong emphasis on organic
wines with some beers too.
✉ 71 East Street, Brighton BN1 1HQ
☎ 01273 729051 ⏰ Tue–Fri 12–10.30,
Sat 12–11, Sun 12–10. Closed Mon 🖐 L
£19, D £30, Wine £17.10 🅿 Brighton

BROCKENHURST
SIMPLY POUSSIN
www.simplypoussin.co.uk
This conservatory and dining room
is a pillar of quality, offering excellent
and often local ingredients and fine
French technique. Examples from
the Modern menu might include fillet
of sea bass or haunch of venison.
Desserts might include strawberry
pannacotta. No children under seven.
Call ahead to reserve and check
the location.
✉ The Courtyard, Brookley Road,
Brockenhurst SO42 7RB ☎ 01590 623063
⏰ 12–2, 7–10; closed Sun–Mon and 25–26
Dec 🖐 L £10.50, D £15, Wine £14.50
🅿 Village centre through an archway
between two shops

CAMBRIDGE
THE ANCHOR
www.cambridgeanchor.co.uk
Can there be anywhere more
quintessentially Cambridge than
this? Right next to the bridge
over the Cam, with a terrace
overlooking the punt-strewn river,
and surrounded by historic college
buildings, the Anchor is popular with
both students and visitors. The pub
food is hearty and traditional—most
things come with chips, but there
are also blackboards specials
and lighter options such as filled

potatoes available. Excellent real
ales as well as a good wine list.
✉ Silver Street, Cambridge CB3 9EL
☎ 01223 353554 ⏰ 11–11 🖐 L £9,
D £14. Wine £9.95 🅿 Cambridge

MIDSUMMER HOUSE
www.midsummerhouse.co.uk
This large conservatory restaurant
overlooks a pretty walled garden,
and is Cambridge's finest restaurant.
The menu covers much of rural
France, with five choices at each
level à la carte, and a short fixed-
price lunch offering similar dishes.
Deep-fried snails with a lemon,
bacon and artichoke risotto is a typical starter, while sauté salmon with
a white chocolate and caviar sauce
shows some unexpected twists.
Expect well-executed desserts such
as pistachio soufflé, and caramelized
popcorn parfait.
✉ Midsummer Common, Cambridge CB4
1HA ☎ 01223 369299 ⏰ Tue–Sun 12–2,
6–11; closed 20–29 Mar, 14–30 Aug and 18
Dec–3 Jan 🖐 L £26, D £48.50, Wine £20
♿ 🅿 Park in Pretoria Road then cross
footbridge, restaurant on left 🅿 Cambridge

CANTERBURY
AUGUSTINE'S RESTAURANT
www.augustinesrestaurant.co.uk
Fine Georgian town house where
modern European cuisine is the
order of the day. A simple lunch
menu featuring good-value fixed-
price meals aims to please, while
dinner is more daring. Mains might
include roast organic chicken breast
or roasted loin of Moroccan spiced
Kentish lamb.
✉ 1–2 Longport, Canterbury CT1 1PE
☎ 01227 453063 ⏰ 12–2, 6.30–9. Closed
Sun–Mon 🖐 L £15, D £20, Wine £15.95
🅿 Follow signs to St Augustine's Abbey
🅿 Canterbury East or West

DOVE INN
www.shepherdneame.co.uk
This splendid pub offers
astonishingly good food. Blackboard
menus feature fresh fish from
Hythe and local game. Lunchtime
snacks include pan-fried crevettes
with fresh garden herbs and
pickled ginger. Main courses range

from braised shank of lamb and
lemon sole to roast duck. Splendid
sheltered garden for summer meals.
✉ Plumpudding Lane, Dargate ME13 9HB
☎ 01227 751360 ⏰ 11–3, 6–11 🖐 L
£17, D £25, Wine £13 🅿 Off A299, 5 miles
(8km) northwest of Canterbury. Phone for
directions

CHECKENDON
THE HIGHWAYMAN
Hanging baskets on a whitewashed
facade give this country pub a
traditional look on the outside, but
once through the door, although not
modern or overworked, the inside
has a rather stylish look. It is still
countrified—low-beamed ceilings,
open fireplaces, exposed brick
walls—but tastefully appointed.
There are various dining areas and
service throughout is relaxed and
unstuffy. The menus consist of a
set-price and the long carte with around
10 choices per course. The food is
a mix of British and international
ideas with an inevitable twist. Start
with sardines on chargrilled crostini
served with a Bloody Mary ketchup,
followed by very slow cooked (their
words) belly of pork, bacon and egg
risotto and Worcestershire sauce jus.
✉ Exlade Street, Checkendon RG8 0UA
☎ 01491 682020 ⏰ 12–2.30, 6–10;
closed Mon, D Sun; 26 Dec, 1 Jan 🖐 L
£12.95, D £26 🅿 Exlade Street signed off
Reading/Wallingford Road, A4074 0.6km
(0.4 miles)

ELY
THE ANCHOR INN
www.anchor-inn-restaurant.co.uk
Characterized by simple, Modern
British cooking using quality fresh
ingredients, typical dishes at this
inn (▷ 219) might be parma ham-
wrapped pork loin stuffed with
gingercake, or baked fillet of cod
topped with Welsh rarebit.
✉ Sutton Gault, Sutton CB6 2BD ☎ 01353
778537 ⏰ 12–2, 7–9; closed 26 Dec
🖐 L £11.95, D £21, Wine £13.65
🅿 Signposted off B1381 in Sutton village,
7 miles (11km) west of Ely via A142

*Opposite Arundel Cathedral overlooks the
town below from its hilltop*

GORING

THE LEATHERNE BOTTEL

www.leathernebottel.co.uk

With its glorious views over the River Thames and the Berkshire Downs, The Leatherne Bottel enjoys a truly tranquil setting. The addition of a paved terrace and conservatory extension has created a feeling of spaciousness, at the same time extending the wonderful views from the decked alfresco area. Inside, the dining room is no less impressive, combining exposed brickwork and lemon-coloured walls with vibrant artwork and fresh flower displays. Youthful service is enthusiastic and attentive, and there's a small cosy bar. The chef adds Pacific Rim ideas, inspired by her time in New Zealand, to generous-sized modern British and European dishes, handling quality produce with care. Start with steak tartare and horseradish ice cream, and follow with poached monkfish, roast cherry tomatoes and baby leeks, saffron potatoes, lemongrass, ginger and shellfish sauce. ✉ Goring RG8 0HS ☎ 01491 872667 🕐 12–2, 7–9; closed D Sun, Mon (Jan–Apr, Sep–end Nov); 1st 3 weeks Jan 🍽 L £19.95, D £37 🚗 M4 junction 12 or M40 junction 6, signed from B4009 towards Wallingford

GREAT MILTON

LE MANOIR AUX QUAT' SAISONS

www.manoir.com

Little is left to chance at Raymond Blanc's ever-evolving hotel masterpiece (▷ 219). Its vegetable gardens deliver a harvest of organic produce for the kitchen. The dining room is composed of three parts, the most contemporary in style being the conservatory. Service is polished but without pretension. Rooted in French classics, the menu offers à la carte, alongside a list of specialities and a tasting menu for the whole table. Luxurious ingredients abound with foie gras, caviar, oysters and langoustines all featuring in the hors d'oeuvres. Desserts are beautifully crafted and the terrific wine list has an expected French bias; make use of the

excellent half-bottle selection. No jeans, shorts or trainers. ✉ Church Road, Great Milton OX44 7PD ☎ 01844 278881 🕐 Daily 12–2.30, 7–10 🍽 L £45, D £87, Wine £25 🚗 From junction 7 of M40 follow A329 towards Wallingford. After 1 mile (1.6km) turn right, signposted Great Milton Manor

ISLE OF WIGHT

BRASSERIE AT THE GEORGE HOTEL

www.thegeorge.co.uk

The historic, colour-washed George Hotel stands on Yarmouth Square close to the ferry terminal in attractive shoreline grounds abutting the old castle walls. Located at the rear of the 17th-century property, with great views across the Solent, the bright, sunny and informal brasserie has been refurbished in contemporary style, with dark wood and leather seats, to reflect the new style of food on offer. Freshness, simplicity and flavour are the focus of the seasonal Italian-inspired menu. Expect to be wowed, perhaps by crab and scallop lasagne with shellfish cappuccino and basil to start, and a main course of whole Dover sole with rissole potatoes and organic mixed vegetables. Try the honey pannacotta with caramelised fruits for dessert. ✉ The George Hotel, Quay Street, Yarmouth PO41 0PE ☎ 01983 760331 🕐 12.30–3, 7–10 🍽 L £28.95, D £39.50 🚗 Situated between the castle and pier

PRIORY BAY HOTEL

www.priorybay.co.uk

A marine-themed dining room in this peaceful hotel (▷ 219) has beautiful views out to sea (reserve a window table). The seasonally changing menu offers unusual combinations on a classical theme. ✉ Priory Drive, Seaview PO34 5BU ☎ 01983 613146 🕐 Daily 12.30–2.15, 7–9.30 🍽 L £10.40, D £32.50, Wine £14.90 🚗 On B3330 to Nettlestone

THE RED LION

This civilized inn attracts the yachting fraternity, who are drawn by the interesting food as much as the

picturesque setting. Order early to guarantee your chosen dishes from the blackboard as demand is intense. Everything is freshly made from tried and tested recipes, such as lamb tagine or lunchtime favourites such as bangers and mash. Seafood is a big feature. ✉ Church Place, Freshwater PO40 9BP ☎ 01983 754925 🕐 Mon–Sat 11.30–3, 5.30–11, Sun 12–3, 7–10.30 🍽 L £15, D £22, Wine £13 🚗 In Freshwater follow signs for parish church

KING'S LYNN

SPREAD EAGLE INN

A simple Norfolk country inn, with plain tables and wooden floors in the bar area and relaxed service. There's a refreshingly modern approach to food, but still exploiting the excellent supply of local produce. You might find roast monkfish with ham and follow it with a sticky toffee pudding or a deliciously simple apple crumble. Children's portions are available. ✉ Barton Brendish PE33 9GF ☎ 01366 347995 🕐 12.30–2.30, 6.30–11. Closed Mon L Tue–Wed, D Sun 🍽 L £16, D £21, Wine £13.50 🚗 From A1122 take Barton Brendish turning, first left into Church Road, continue past church on left and straight ahead into cul-de-sac. Pub is on left.

LEWES

THE REAL EATING COMPANY

www.real-eating.co.uk

Set in the heart of town, The Real Eating Company is a deli-restaurant outfit, an outpost of the original model in Hove. The classic shop frontage leads into a spacious food/deli shop, leading to the restaurant—a long, oblong room that looks out onto a small-decked alfresco area. The decor is modern, clean and simple, with stripped wood floors, plain walls enlivened by colourful prints and ceiling skylights to add natural light. Tables and chairs are modern wood and service is relaxed, while the cooking's highly assured with chef Darren Velvick's impressive pedigree (ex-head chef at renowned London restaurant Pètrus) to drive things. The cooking is underpinned by a classical repertoire driven by quality local seasonal produce. His modern, simple approach and clean presentation is underscored by fine attention to detail, with lunch a simpler affair. Take herb-crust halibut served with crushed Peruvian potatoes, warm fennel salsa and crayfish tails.

✉ 18 Cliffe High Street, Lewes BN7 2AJ ☎ 01273 402650 🕐 12–3, 6.30–11.30; closed Sun, Mon; 25–26 Dec, 1 Jan ✋ Telephone for prices

LICKFOLD

THE LICKFOLD INN

www.thelickfoldinn.co.uk

Dating back to the 15th century, this charming inn oozes style and sophistication. Built in a herringbone brick pattern, it boasts an abundance of original features, not least a large inglenook fireplace, flagstone floors and sturdy oak beams, and the large terrace is the perfect place for summer dining. Crowd-pleasing menus focus on fish and seafood, and include quality pub food alongside more sophisticated fare. Wok-fried samphire with crayfish tails in a lemon and garlic butter and 8-hour braised shank of South Downs lamb with French beans, roast garlic mash and mint and redcurrant jus are fine examples of the fare on offer.

✉ Lickfold, GU28 9EY ☎ 01798 861285 🕐 12–2.30, 7–9.30; closed, Mon, D Sun, 25–26 Dec ✋ L £12, D £22.50 🚍 signposted from A272, 10km (6 miles) east of Midhurst. From A285 10km (6 miles) south of Haslemere, follow signs for Lurgashall Winery and then continue to Lickfold village

NORWICH

ADLARD'S RESTAURANT

www.adlards.co.uk

Adlard's is a high-class favourite. The short, well-balanced British/French menu might offer a simple seafood theme to start, such as panfried scallops, then progress to roast Gressingham duck with a rhubarb compote. Vegetarian options are available. Desserts might include spiced banana tarte tatin or a lemon

tart. There is an impressive wine list.

✉ 79 Upper St. Giles Street, Norwich NR2 1AB ☎ 01603 633522 🕐 12.30–1.45, 7.30–10.30; closed Sun, L Mon, one week after Christmas ✋ L £13.50, D £20, Wine £18.95 🅿 🚍 In city centre, 200m (220yds) behind City Hall 🚉 Norwich

TATLERS

www.tatlers.com

Brasserie-style restaurant. The atmosphere is friendly and low-key, with relaxed but attentive service. Dishes are Modern British with classical French undertones—black pudding with truffle oil dressing and braised red cabbage and Puy lentils—and local produce features strongly. There's a good wine list too, with half-bottles available.

✉ 21 Tombland, Norwich NR3 1RF ☎ 01603 766670 🕐 12–2, 6.30–10; closed Sun, 24, 26 Dec and public holidays ✋ L £14, D £24, Wine £14.90 🚉 Norwich

OXFORD

BRASSERIE BLANC

www.brasserieblanc.co.uk

At this relaxed French-style brasserie, the food clings to its Gallic roots but substitutes British ingredients where possible, offering satisfying brasserie favourites.

✉ 71–71 Walton Street, Oxford OX2 6AG ☎ 01865 510999 🕐 12–2.45, 6–10.30 ✋ L £12, D £20, Wine £13.25 🅿 🚍 From city centre, north along St. Giles, left into Little Clarendon Street and right at end of Walton Street 🚉 Oxford

QUOD BRASSERIE AND BAR

www.quod.co.uk

In the spacious hall of an old bank, Quod is committed to serving up robust Mediterranean-style food. Expect slow roast lamb shank, duck confit or roast corn-fed chicken alongside pizzas and pasta dishes, good salads and a by-the-glass wine list. The home-made hamburgers shouldn't be overlooked, and everything is served on simple rustic wooden boards. Outside there's an attractive sun deck and, on Sunday evenings, live jazz from 5–7 to help mellow the mood.

✉ Old Bank Hotel, 92–94 High Street, Oxford OX1 4BN ☎ 01865 202505 🕐 7am–11pm ✋ L £9.95, D £14.25, Wine £14.95 🚉 Oxford

ST. ALBANS

ST. MICHAEL'S MANOR

www.stmichaelsmanor.com

A traditional vein runs through a mainly contemporary menu at this hotel (▷ 220), with imaginative touches such as confit of salmon or beetroot and spinach tart.

✉ Fishpool Street, St. Albans AL3 4RY ☎ 01727 864444 🕐 12–2.30, 7–9.30 ✋ L £20, D £24.95, Wine £15.25 🅿 🚍 From St. Albans Abbey follow Fishpool Street towards St. Michael's village. Hotel is 0.5 miles (0.8 km) on left 🚉 St. Albans

Above *The Elm Hill, Norwich*

SISSINGHURST
RANKINS RESTAURANT
www.rankinsrestaurant.com

This intimate restaurant is housed in a timber-framed building dating from 1898, which has in its time been a saddler's and general store. The beamed interior has the feel of a cottage, but with well-spaced tables. The British bistro-style cooking places an emphasis on quality ingredients and simple but attractive presentation. Try Rankins' smokie—a pot of naturally smoked haddock baked in a creamy lemon sauce with cheddar glaze to start—followed by pan-fried lamb noisettes with cauliflower and garlic cream and rosemary gravy. Finish with golden syrup lemon sponge with vanilla ice cream.

✉ The Street, Sissinghurst TN17 2JH ☎ 01580 713964 ⏱ 12.30–2, 7.30–9; closed Mon, Tue, L Wed–Sat, D Sun; public holidays 🍴 L £23.50, D Telephone for prices 🚍 Village centre, on A262

SOUTHWOLD
THE CROWN
www.adnams.co.uk

Both restaurant and bar food at this inn (▷ 221) are of good quality and British in style with European accents. Fresh, local ingredients are prepared and cooked using classical methods. The daily changing fixed-priced menu specializes in local fish. No children under five.

✉ 90 High Street, Southwold IP18 6DP ☎ 01502 722275 ⏱ 12–2, 6–9.30 🍴 L £10, D £21, Wine £15 🚍 Off A12, take A1095 to Southwold and stay on main road into town centre; hotel on left in High Street 🚉 Darsham

STADHAMPTON
THE CRAZY BEAR
www.crazybeargroup.co.uk

A flamboyant refurbishment has resulted in this rural 16th-century hotel (▷ 221) having two separate dining rooms, one embracing fine English dining, the other offering a Thai-style brasserie. Menus from both restaurants are also available in the bar, along with open Swiss sandwiches. Modern dishes in the restaurant might include combinations like Moroccan spiced partridge terrine. The Thai dishes, some of the finest in the country, are best sampled from good-value set menus. No Thai desserts, but classic English offerings might include chocolate marquise.

✉ Bear Lane, Stadhampton OX44 7UR ☎ 01865 890714 ⏱ 12–3, 7–10 🍴 L £15, D £19.50, Wine £14.50 🚗 🚍 From junction 7 of the M40 turn left at end of slip road into Stadhampton village. Over mini roundabout, left at petrol station. Hotel is second on left

WELLS-NEXT-THE-SEA
THE CROWN RESTAURANT
www.thecrownhotelwells.co.uk

Local seafood features on the forward-looking, Pacific Rim-inspired menu—Wells crab with

roasted pepper parfait, for example, while meat dishes are robust but sensitively treated. Finish with almond and apricot tart.

✉ The Buttlands, Wells-Next-The-Sea NR23 1EX ☎ 01328 710209 ⏰ 7–9pm ✋ D £24.95, Wine £13 🚗 9 miles (14km) from Fakenham on B1105. At the top of Buttlands Green

WHITSTABLE
CRAB & WINKLE SEAFOOD RESTAURANT
www.seafood-restaurant-uk.com
This popular modern restaurant has a light-and-airy feel, and is ideally situated above the town's fish market on the quay overlooking the harbour. It's decked out with maritime art, complemented by polished lightwood tables and chairs. In summer the decked balcony is a great place for alfresco dining, while on less clement days the views of the harbour and fishing fleet more than compensate. Not surprisingly given its location, the daily-changing modern menus are awash with fish and seafood, straight from the boats and simply cooked. Take steamed oak-smoked haddock, served with root vegetable rösti, warm leek and wild mushroom salad with grain mustard cream, or shellfish (scallops, mussels, oysters, crevettes and cockles), red onion, fennel and saffron broth with lemon mash.

✉ South Quay, The Harbour, Whitstable CT5 1AB ☎ 01227 779377 ⏰ 11.30–9.30; closed 25 Dec, D 26 Dec, 1 Jan ✋ L £15.50, D Telephone for prices

WINCHESTER
AVENUE RESTAURANT
www.exclusivehotels.co.uk
This fine William and Mary country house sits at the end of a long winding drive, amid 25,5ha (63 acres) of beautifully maintained gardens and majestic Hampshire parkland. Inside, historic charm and contemporary elegance blend seamlessly, with expansive lounges

looking out over a magnificent avenue of lime trees, and a clubby bar made entirely from a single cedar that fell in the grounds in the 1930s. The elegant panelled restaurant (one of two rooms) is reminiscent of an English manor house dining room and is complemented by a terrace for alfresco dining or to enjoy one of the house cocktails. Service is polished and professional, and the cooking in these fine surroundings more than lives up to expectations, offering a classical menu with some tried-and-tested combinations, with great technical skills and a range of modern cooking styles in evidence. Locally sourced produce, flair, imagination and clean flavours all come together in well-executed dishes like Portland crab ravioli with pak choi, grapefruit and vanilla dressing, or Stockbridge organic wild mushroom orzo with winter truffle and cep foam. For dessert, chocolate-lovers will not be able to resist the 'world chocolate compilation' assiette (crème brûlée, ice cream, mousse and hot chocolate shot). Excellent home-made breads and amuse bouche complete the upbeat package, and there's a vegetarian tasting menu with recommended wines.

✉ Lainston House Hotel, Sparsholt SO21 2LT ☎ 01962 776088 ⏰ 12–2, 7–10 ✋ L £21.50, D £48 🚗 4km (2.5 miles) northwest off A272, road to Stockbridge, signed

HOTEL DU VIN & BISTRO
www.hotelduvin.com
The bistro at this branch of the hotel chain harnesses French chic while friendly and knowledgeable staff provide good service. France is the main source of inspiration for the food, but British and Mediterranean influences are welcomed, while the wine list commands respect.

✉ 14 Southgate Street, Winchester SO23 9EF ☎ 01962 841414 ⏰ 12–1.45, 7–9.45 ✋ L £21, D £27, Wine £17 🚌 M3 junction 11 towards Winchester, follow signs. Hotel is 2 miles (3km) from junction 11 on left-hand side just past cinema 🚉 Winchester

WINDSOR
MERCURE CASTLE HOTEL
www.mercure.com
This 16th-century former coaching inn's restaurant creates an intimate atmosphere, while more informal dining is available in the lounge. The two- or three-course menu offers classical French cuisine with game featuring strongly.

✉ 18 High Street, Windsor SL4 1LJ ☎ 01753 851577 ⏰ 12–2, 6.30–9.45 ✋ L £14.50, D £21.50, Wine £15.50 🚗 🚌 From M4 junction 6/M25 junction 15 follow signs to Windsor town centre and Castle. Hotel at top of hill by the castle, opposite Guildhall 🚉 Windsor & Eton Central or Riverside

SIR CHRISTOPHER WREN'S HOUSE HOTEL & SPA
www.sirchristopherwren.co.uk
Formal decor is the setting for accomplished cooking designed to please a classy clientele. Traditional favourites get a modern British twist and fixed-price lunch and children's menus are available.

✉ Thames Street, Windsor ☎ 01753 861354 ⏰ 12.30–2.30, 6.30–10 ✋ L £21.50, D £28.80, Wine £17.50 🚗 🚌 From M4 junction 6 take first exit from the relief road, follow the signs to Windsor, then take the first major exit on left, turn left at lights 🚉 Windsor & Eton Central or Riverside

WOODSTOCK
FEATHERS HOTEL
www.feathers.co.uk
Whether you're looking for something light to eat in the bar, or something a bit more substantial in the interconnecting restaurant, the Feathers Hotel looks to present modern British food at its very best. For a taste of especially good fare look for the Herdwick lamb, or the nut-crusted sea brill and then perhaps follow it with a Cuban chocolate pudding with fresh lime and sorbet.

✉ Market Street, Woodstock OX20 1SX ☎ 01993 812291 ⏰ 12.30–2.30, 7–9.30 ✋ L £19.50, D £37.50, Wine £16.95 🚌 From Oxford take A44 to Woodstock, take first left after lights; hotel on left

Left *Windsor old town has a selection of cafés and pubs*

PRICES AND SYMBOLS

Prices are the starting price for a double room for one night, unless otherwise stated. Breakfast is included unless noted otherwise. All the hotels listed accept credit cards unless otherwise stated. Note that rates vary widely throughout the year.

For a key to the symbols, ▷ 2.

ALBURY
THE DRUMMOND ARMS

The old inn is centrally located in this picturesque village, with attractive gardens running down to a small river. The hotel is well-appointed and has comfortable bedrooms, all of which have private facilities, and one with a sauna and spa bath. The separate restaurant offers an extensive menu where a good selection of traditional pub food is also available in the popular bar. No children under 14 are allowed. No dogs.

✉ The Street, Albury GU5 9AG ☎ 01483 202039 💷 £70 🛈 11 🚗 Off A25 between Guildford and Dorking. Take A248 signed Albury, Godalming; Drummond 1 mile (1.6km) on right

ARUNDEL
NORFOLK ARMS

www.forestdale.com

This Georgian coaching inn enjoys a superb setting beneath the battlements of Arundel Castle. Bedrooms come in a variety of sizes and styles and all are well equipped. Public areas include two bars, a comfortable lounge and a traditional English restaurant.

✉ High Street, Arundel BN18 9AD ☎ 01903 882101 💷 £129 🛈 34 🚉 Arundel

BOSHAM
THE MILLSTREAM HOTEL

www.millstream-hotel.co.uk

Lying in the idyllic village of Bosham, this hotel provides comfortable, well-equipped and tastefully decorated bedrooms. Many guests regularly return here for the relaxed ambience created by the notably efficient and friendly staff. Public rooms include a cocktail bar opening out on to the garden and a pleasant restaurant where freshly prepared food can be enjoyed. The hotel is close to Chichester harbour and sailing trips can be arranged. No dogs.

✉ Bosham Lane, Bosham PO18 8HL ☎ 01243 573234 💷 £138 🛈 35 🚗 4 miles (6km) west of Chichester on A259, left at Bosham roundabout. After 1 mile (1.6km) turn right at T-junction to church and quay, hotel 0.5 miles (800m) on right

BRANCASTER STAITHE
THE WHITE HORSE

www.whitehorsebrancaster.co.uk

Charming hotel on the north Norfolk coast with glorious views over the tidal marshes. Contemporary bedrooms, in two wings, are attractively decorated and thoughtfully equipped. A large bar and lounge area lead to the conservatory restaurant (▷ 212) with its wide-sweeping views.

✉ Brancaster Staithe PE31 8BY ☎ 01485 210262 💷 £100 🛈 15 🚗 On A149 coast road between Hunstanton and Wells-next-the-Sea

BRIGHTON
PASKINS TOWN HOUSE

www.paskins.co.uk

This environmentally friendly town house bed-and-breakfast offers individually designed bedrooms. But breakfast is the speciality and includes home-made vegetarian sausages.

✉ 18–19 Charlotte Street, Brighton BN2 1AG ☎ 01273 601203 🖐 £45 ⓘ 19 🚫 Brighton

CAMBRIDGE
BEST WESTERN GONVILLE HOTEL
www.bwgonvillehotel.co.uk

Well established, with regular guests and very experienced staff, the Gonville is popular for its informality. The air-conditioned public areas are cheerfully furnished, and bedrooms are well appointed.

✉ Gonville Place, Cambridge CB1 1LY ☎ 01223 366611 🖐 £135 ⓘ 73 🚫 From M11 junction 11 take A1309 and follow city centre signs. At second mini roundabout turn right into Lensfield Road over junction with traffic lights; hotel soon on right 🚫 Cambridge

CENTENNIAL HOTEL
www.centennialhotel.co.uk

This friendly hotel has well-present-ed public areas that include a quiet, welcoming lounge and a relaxing bar and restaurant. Bedrooms are generally quite spacious, clean and have a good range of facilities; several rooms are available on the ground floor.

✉ 63–71 Hills Road, Cambridge CB2 1PG ☎ 01223 314652 🕐 Closed 23 Dec–1 Jan 🖐 £88 ⓘ 39 🚫 Cambridge

CANTERBURY
ABODE CANTERBURY
www.abode.co.uk

This historic hotel has cellars that date back to the 12th century. Now it reflects the contemporary stylings of the Abode group—all brown and cream and white. It also means the dining has leapt up to Michael Caines standard.

✉ High Street, Canterbury CT1 2RX ☎ 01227 766266 🖐 £109 ⓘ 72 🚫 From M2 junction 7 follow Canterbury signs on to ring road. At Wincheap roundabout turn into city. Left into Rosemary Lane and into Stour Street; hotel at end 🚫 Canterbury East or West

MAGNOLIA HOUSE
Magnolia House is an attractive guest house, combining a warm welcome with superbly appointed bedrooms. The pleasant lounge looks out over the front garden. Evening meals can be arranged in local restaurants and a wide choice is offered at breakfast. No children under 12. No dogs.

✉ 36 St. Dunstan's Terrace, Canterbury CT2 8AX ☎ 01227 765121 🖐 £95 ⓘ 7 🚫 From A2 take turn for Canterbury, left at first roundabout approaching city (signposted University), then third turn on right

EAST TYTHERLEY
STAR INN
www.starinn.co.uk

A charming 16th-century coaching inn adjoining the village cricket ground in a quiet backwater between Salisbury and Romsey. Accommodation is provided in a purpose-built block separate from the main pub—three spacious bedrooms with high levels of quality and comfort. Award-winning food is a particular attraction. An outdoor children's play area is also available. No dogs.

✉ East Tytherley, near Romsey SO15 0LW ☎ 01794 340225 🕐 Closed Mon (except public holiday Mon) and 25–26 Dec 🖐 £80 ⓘ 3 🚫 5 miles (8km) north of Romsey off A3057, take left turn onto B3084 then left for Awbridge and Lockerley; follow the road past Lockerley for about 1 mile (1.6km)

ELY
THE ANCHOR INN
www.anchor-inn-restaurant.co.uk

With pleasing country views, this 17th-century inn retains many original features and is enhanced by period furniture. Bedrooms are spacious, comfortable and equipped with a host of thoughtful extras. Excellent Modern British cuisine is available (▷ 213). No children and no dogs.

✉ Sutton Gault, Sutton CB6 2BD ☎ 01353 778537 🕐 Closed 26 Dec 🖐 £79.50 ⓘ 4 🚫 Signposted off B1381 in Sutton village, 7 miles (11km) west of Ely via A142 🚫 Ely

FARNINGHAM
BEESFIELD FARM
www.beesfieldfarm.co.uk

This attractive farmhouse bed-and-breakfast is surrounded by open farmland. The individually decorated bedrooms are beautifully appointed and have many thoughtful touches. No children under 12. No dogs. Credit cards are not accepted.

✉ Beesfield Lane, Farningham DA4 0LA ☎ 01322 863900 🕐 Closed 8 Dec–end Jan 🖐 £80 ⓘ 3 🚫 Turn off A20 to A225, then left to Beesfield Lane; farm is 0.5 mile (800m) on left 🚫 Eynsford or Swanley

GREAT MILTON
LE MANOIR AUX QUAT' SAISONS
www.manoir.com

This renowned hotel, set in beautiful grounds and gardens, epitomizes luxury. Bedrooms, either in the main house or the garden courtyard, are individually styled and offer the highest levels of comfort and quality. Stylish public areas feature wonder-ful artwork and include the main reason for any visit to Le Manoir, the conservatory restaurant (▷ 213).

✉ Church Road, Great Milton OX44 7PD ☎ 01844 278881 🖐 £395 ⓘ 32 🚫 From junction 7 of M40 follow A329 towards Wallingford. After 1 mile (1.6km) turn right, signposted Great Milton Manor

ISLE OF WIGHT
AQUA HOTEL
www.aquahotel.co.uk

Public rooms and many of the bedrooms at this friendly, family-run hotel enjoy fine sea views. The bed-rooms are well equipped and some have the added bonus of a balcony. The sea views can also be enjoyed from the gardens. No dogs.

✉ 17 The Esplanade, Shanklin PO37 6BN ☎ 01983 863024 🖐 £60 ⓘ 22 🚫 Off Arthurs Hill/North Road; at Fiveways junction into Hope Road and follow to Esplanade 🚫 Shanklin

PRIORY BAY HOTEL
www.priorybay.co.uk

This peacefully located hotel has its own stretch of sand and a six-hole golf course, tennis, croquet and an outdoor pool. There are also woodland lawns and formal gardens. The well-equipped and mostly spacious bedrooms are very comfortable, and there is a fine dining room (▷ 214).

✉ Priory Drive, Seaview PO34 5BU
☎ 01983 613146 🖐 £90 in cottage, £120 in main building 🛏 31 🚲 🚗 On B3330 to Nettlestone

LAVENHAM
LAVENHAM PRIORY
www.lavenhampriory.co.uk
This superb property dates back to the 13th century. It has been carefully restored, maintaining much of its original character. Breakfast is served in the Merchant's Room or in the sheltered courtyard herb garden. Guests have use of the Great Hall. No children under 10. No dogs.

✉ Water Street, Lavenham CO10 9RW
☎ 01787 247404 🕙 Closed 21 Dec–2 Jan
🖐 £100 🛏 6 🚗 A1141 to Lavenham, turn by side of Swan Hotel into Water Street and then right after 50m (160ft) into private drive

MILFORD-ON-SEA
WESTOVER HALL HOTEL
www.westoverhallhotel.com
This late-Victorian mansion has uninterrupted views across to the Isle of Wight and is just a few moments' walk from the beach. Dramatic stained-glass windows, oak panelling and a galleried entrance hall add to the interior decor, and the bedrooms display panache and originality.

✉ Park Lane, Milford-on-Sea SO41 OPT ☎ 01590 643044 🖐 £206 🛏 12
🚗 Follow M3 and M27 onto A337 to Lymington and signs to Milford-on-Sea on to B3058. Hotel outside village centre, towards cliff

NORWICH
THE OLD RECTORY
www.oldrectorynorwich.com
Just a few minutes from the centre of the city, this fine old Georgian building overlooks landscaped gardens and a swimming pool. The well-appointed rooms are designed individually, in keeping with the proportions of the house; some still

with fireplaces or sloping beams. There's a daily changing menu in the creditable restaurant; room service available Mon–Sat until 9.30pm.

✉ 103 Yarmouth Road, Thorpe St Andrew, Norwich NR7 0HF ☎ 01603 700772
🖐 £115 🛏 8 T 🚗 From A47 on to A1042 towards Norwich north and east. Left at mini roundabout onto A1242. After 0.25 miles (0.4km) through lights, hotel 100yds (90m) on right.

OXFORD
BURLINGTON HOUSE
www.burlington-house.co.uk
A warm welcome is assured at this immaculately maintained Victorian bed-and-breakfast. The attractive furnishing schemes complement the original features, and two of the bedrooms overlook a pretty patio garden. Memorable breakfasts are served in a homey dining room. No children under 12. No dogs.

✉ 374 Banbury Road, Summertown, Oxford OX2 7PP ☎ 01865 513513 🖐 £85 🛏 12
🚗 At Peartree roundabout follow signs to Oxford. At next roundabout take second exit A40. After about 0.5 mile (800m) at next roundabout take third exit. Hotel on corner of fourth road on left
🚉 Oxford

THE OLD BANK HOTEL
www.oldbank-hotel.co.uk
This former bank has been converted into a very stylish and comfortable hotel. Bedrooms are smart and have CD players and air conditioning. Public areas include the vibrant all-day Quod Bar and Restaurant, a separate residents' bar, and an outside courtyard.

✉ 92–94 High Street, Oxford OX1 4BN
☎ 01865 799599 🕙 Closed 25–27 Dec
🖐 £185 🛏 42 🅿 🚉 Oxford

PORTSMOUTH
DE VERE GRAND HARBOUR
www.devere.co.uk
This imposing modern hotel overlooks the Southampton Water from its position by the old town walls. There are leisure facilities in an impressive glass pyramid and the dining options include Allertons Restaurant and No 5 Brasserie, with its

theatre kitchen. Rooms are reliably comfortable and modern, though the furnishing are more traditional than the you might expect in such contemporary surroundings.

✉ West Quay Road, Southampton SO15 1AG ☎ 023 8063 3033 🖐 £109 🛏 173
🚗 M27 Junction 3 follow Waterfront signs. Keep in left lane of dual carriageway then follow Heritage and Waterfront signs into West Quay Road

RYE
JEAKE'S HOUSE
www.jeakeshouse.com
This bed-and-breakfast is in one of the most beautiful parts of town. The individually decorated bedrooms combine traditional elegance and comfort with modern facilities. No children under 12.

✉ Mermaid Street, Rye TN31 7ET
☎ 01797 222828 🖐 £90 🛏 11 🚉 Rye

ST. ALBANS
ST. MICHAEL'S MANOR
www.stmichaelsmanor.com
This hotel, set in extensive grounds, is furnished and decorated to a luxurious standard throughout, and offers excellent dining opportunities (▷ 215). Staff combine warmth with informality.

✉ Fishpool Street, St. Albans AL3 4RY
☎ 01727 864444 🖐 £180 🛏 30
🚗 From St. Albans Abbey follow Fishpool Street towards St. Michael's village. Hotel is 0.5 miles (800m) on left 🚉 St. Albans

SALISBURY
NEWTON FARMHOUSE
www.newtonfarmhouse.co.uk
This farmhouse bed-and-breakfast on the fringe of the New Forest dates from the 16th century. The house has been thoughtfully restored, and five of the eight bedrooms have four-poster beds. Delicious home-cooked breakfasts are served in the charming breakfast room. No dogs. Credit cards not accepted.

✉ Southampton Road, Whiteparish SP5 2QL ☎ 01794 884416 🖐 £80 🛏 8
🚲 🚗 Just south of Salisbury: 6 miles (10km) on A36, 1 mile (1.6km) south of junction with A27 🚉 Salisbury

SEVENOAKS

DONNINGTON MANOR

www.donningtonmanorhotel.co.uk
This extended 15th-century manor
house is on the edge of Sevenoaks.
The original part of the building
boasts public rooms with a wealth of
character including an attractive oak-
beamed restaurant, a comfortable
lounge and an intimate bar.

✉ London Road, Dunton Green, Sevenoaks
TN13 2TD ☎ 01732 462681 ✋ £85
ℹ 59 ⚑ From M25 junction 4 follow
signs for Bromley/Orpington to roundabout.
Turn left on to A224 (Dunton Green), left at
second roundabout, left at Rose and Crown,
hotel is 300m (330 yds) on right

SHERINGHAM

ROMAN CAMP INN

www.romancampinn.co.uk
Ideally placed for touring the north
Norfolk coastline, this hotel provides
spacious bedrooms that are
pleasantly decorated and come with
a good range of useful extras. Public
rooms include a smart conservatory-
style restaurant, comfortable lounge,
smart bar and dining room.

✉ Holt Road, Aylmerton NR11 8QD
☎ 01263 838291 🕐 Closed 25 Dec
✋ £88 ℹ 15 ⚑ On A148 between
Sheringham and Cromer 🚉 Cromer (1.5
miles/2.5km)

SNETTISHAM

ROSE & CROWN

www.roseandcrownsnettisham.co.uk
This 14th-century inn is close to
some of west Norfolk's most beautiful beaches. Public rooms include
a choice of dining areas as well as
a family room and bar. A walled
garden is available on sunny days, as
is a children's play area.

✉ Old Church Road, Snettisham PE31
7LX ☎ 01485 541382 ✋ £110 ℹ 16
⚑ North from King's Lynn on A149 signed
to Hunstanton; hotel in centre of Snettisham
between market square and church
🚉 King's Lynn

SOUTHWOLD

THE CROWN

www.adnams.co.uk/hotels/crown
This old posting inn in the heart of
the town combines a pub, wine bar

Above *Shops at Rye*

and an intimate restaurant (▷ 216)
with superb accommodation. The
bedrooms are tastefully decorated.
Public rooms feature a back-room bar
and an elegant lounge.

✉ 90 High Street, Southwold IP18 6DP
☎ 01502 722275 🕐 Closed first or second
week in Jan ✋ £126 ℹ 14 ⚑ Off A12,
take A1095 to Southwold and stay on main
road into town centre; hotel on left in High
Street 🚉 Darsham

STADHAMPTON

THE CRAZY BEAR

www.crazybearhotel.co.uk
This unusual small hotel combines
modern chic with old-world character. The art deco bedrooms and
extravagant suites are presented and
equipped to a very high standard.
The hotel features two popular and
attractive restaurants (▷ 216).

✉ Bear Lane, Stadhampton OX44 7UR
☎ 01865 890714 ✋ £135 ℹ 17
⚑ From junction 7 of the M40 turn left at
end of slip road into Stadhampton village.
Over mini roundabout, left at petrol station.
Hotel is second on left

WINCHESTER

THE WINCHESTER ROYAL

www.forestdale.com
Situated in the heart of the city, this
friendly hotel can trace its origins
in parts to the 16th century. Many
rooms overlook the landscaped garden and there is a private car park.

✉ Saint Peter Street, Winchester SO23
8BS ☎ 01962 840840 ✋ £149 ℹ 75

⚑ From M3 junction 9 to Winnal Trading
Estate. Follow road to city centre, cross
river, turn left, then first right. On to one-
way system and turn second right. Hotel
immediately on right 🚉 Winchester

WINDSOR

CLARENCE GUEST HOUSE

www.clarence-hotel.co.uk
A Victorian house close to the centre
of this historic Berkshire town, the
Clarence offers excellent value for
money. Although some of the rooms
are on the small side, the facilities
are excellent, including a well-
stocked bar. Breakfasts are taken in
a delightful dining room overlooking
the gardens.

✉ 9 Clarence Road, Windsor SL4 5AE
☎ 01753 864436 ✋ £55 ℹ 20 ⚑ M4
junction 6 dual carriageway to Windsor, left
at 1st roundabout on to Clarence Road

WOODSTOCK

MACDONALD BEAR HOTEL

www.macdonald-hotels.co.uk
This 13th-century coaching inn
exudes charm and comfort. Modern
facilities in the hotel's bedrooms do
nothing to detract from their character. Public rooms include an intimate
bar and restaurant.

✉ Park Street, Woodstock OX20 1SZ
☎ 0870 400 8202 ✋ £80–£230 ℹ 54
⚑ From Oxford, reached from M40 or
A34 to the south of the city, take A44 into
Woodstock and left to town centre; hotel on
left opposite town hall

SIGHTS 224
WALKS AND DRIVES 240
WHAT TO DO 252
EATING 256
STAYING 260

WALES

Another beneficiary of the late 1990s zeal for devolution, Wales is governed by an assembly, and its meeting place in the capital, Cardiff, is now the centrepiece of the city's rejuvenated waterfront. Regeneration is a constant theme, particularly in South Wales, where the ghosts of heavy industry are only just being vanquished. The landscape beneath, of green valleys and broad, sweeping mountains has emerged intact, giving the region an enviable mix of hill country and sea. It's worth visiting the World Heritage Site at Blaenavon to see how important industry was here, but it would be wrong to typecast modern Wales. The far southwest juts into the Irish Sea in a beautiful series of cliffs and headlands. There are hidden coves and sandy beaches to delight any toddler. Pembroke's coast is one of three national parks in the principality. The Brecon Beacons form the higher mountain backdrop to the valleys which descend to the south coast, but in the north, vast Snowdonia protects a highland core of steep and rocky peaks—Snowdon is the highest—which gave birth to much of Britain's mountaineering tradition.

But even amongst the hills you can't escape Wales's industrial heritage. A popular legacy is the network of preserved railways that criss-crosses the country, the trains' whistles echoing round the valleys. Perhaps more so than anywhere else, the north is a land with a different language. You can enjoy getting your tongue round the place names on the island of Anglesey, but in towns like Bangor and Dolgellau, you'll find Welsh is very much the first language. The medieval English tried to suppress this Celtic culture and their fantastic castles at Harlech, Caernarfon and Conwy tell that story effectively, but Wales has clung on to its roots very well and emerged in 21st-century Europe with an enviable indigenous creativity that still finds expression in the many *eisteddfoddau* (Welsh arts festivals) that take place every year across the principality.

ABERDULAIS FALLS

www.nationaltrust.org.uk

The water thunders into a natural amphitheatre of rock in a lovely wooded setting, and has powered industry for more than 400 years. The copper-smelting works founded in 1584 later gave way to flour and grist mills, then tinplate works from 1830 to 1890, and today a hydroelectric plant is installed here. Displays (including letters and engravings) in the information section and turbine house trace the long history of this complicated industrial site.

♦ 457 E18 ✉ Aberdulais, near Neath SA10 8EU ☎ 01639 636674 ◷ Jan–mid Mar Sat–Sun 11–4; Easter–Oct Mon–Fri 10–5, Sat–Sun 11–6; Nov–Dec Fri–Sun 11–4 ✋ Adult £3.63, child (5–16) £1.81, family £9.09 ▯ Sat–Sun and public holidays, in summer

ABERYSTWYTH

www.tourism.ceredigion.gov.uk

Aberystwyth is a lively university town with a strong culture of the Welsh language: Welsh and Celtic manuscripts are displayed in the National Library of Wales on Penglais Hill (Reading Rooms Mon–Fri 9.30–6, Sat 9.30–5; National Screen and Sound Archives Mon–Fri 10–5, Gregynog Exhibition Gallery Mon–Sat 10–5). Bay-windowed Victorian and Edwardian hotels and guest houses line the waterfront, which ends at Constitution Hill, where the electric cliff railway, which opened way back in 1896, climbs for fine views over Cardigan Bay. On top is the world's largest camera obscura.

Watersports enthusiasts can try sailing, kayaking, power boating or windsurfing in Cardigan Bay. From town, steam trains on the Vale of Rheidol Railway (April–end Oct) wind their way through a wooded valley to Devil's Bridge.

♦ 460 E16 🏠 Lisburne House, Terrace Road, Aberystwyth SY23 2AG, tel 01970 612125 🚂 Aberystwyth

Left Aberystwyth's cliff railway gives great views over the city
Above The waters of the River Dulais plunging between rocks at Aberdulais Falls

BLAENAVON WORLD HERITAGE SITE

www.cadw.wales.gov.uk (Ironworks)
www.museumwales.ac.uk (Big Pit)
www.world-heritage-blaenavon.org.uk

Two major sites recall the town's former role as a mainstay of coal and iron production. The Big Pit National Mining Museum gives free underground tours through a coal mine (closed in 1980), with a ride in a miners' cage lift, and with former miners as guides. You can visit the colliery buildings, pithead baths and smithy on the surface, while underground are the coal faces, levels, air doors and pit-pony stables.

Blaenavon Ironworks, dating from 1788, is the best-preserved 18th-century ironworks in Europe. There is also a row of workers' cottages still standing here.

♦ 457 F18 ✉ Blaenavon Iron Works, North Street, Torfaen NP4 9RQ ☎ 01495 792615 ◷ Ironworks: Easter–end Oct Mon–Fri 9.30–4.30, Sat 10–5, Sun 10–4.30.

Big Pit: mid-Feb to end Nov daily 9.30–5 ✋ Big Pit: free. Ironworks: adult £2.70, child (5–16) £2.30, family £7.70 ▯ 🏛

BODELWYDDAN CASTLE

www.bodelwyddan-castle.co.uk

This 19th-century mock castle, complete with turrets and battlements, is now the Welsh headquarters of the National Portrait Gallery, and houses a large collection of Victorian portraits, including Victorian portraiture photographs.

There is plenty here for all ages, with World War I practice trenches, a playground, parkland, walled gardens and a woodland walk.

♦ 460 E14 ✉ Bodelwyddan, near St. Asaph LL18 5YA ☎ 01745 584060 ◷ Nov–end Mar Thu 10.30–5, Sat–Sun 10.30–4; Sep–end Oct, Easter–end Jul Mon–Thu 10.30–5, Sat–Sun 10.30–4; Aug daily 10.30–5 ✋ Adult £5, child (5–16) £2, family £12. Gardens only: adult £3, child £1 🏛

INFORMATION

www.islandofchoice.com

⊞ 460 D14 🛈 Station Site, Llanfair PG LL61 5UJ, tel 01248 713177 🚇 Llanfair PG, Holyhead and intermediate stations

ANGLESEY

Wales' largest island can seem surprisingly flat in comparison to the rugged heights of nearby Snowdonia (▷ 237). Its shores are of the most interest to visitors. On the east and southwest coasts are wide sandy beaches backed by sand dunes, while the north coast is more complicated, with a succession of smaller coves. You can watch puffins, razorbills, fulmars, guillemots and choughs, which all nest on South Stack cliffs, off the northern shore, from the comfort of the RSPB South Stack Cliff Site visitor office.

HISTORIC SIGHTS

The island is linked to the Welsh mainland in spectacular style by Thomas Telford's (1757–1834) seven-arched Menai Suspension Bridge (1826), spanning the Menai Strait. The island's fertile interior is rich in prehistoric sites, including the Bronze Age burial mound at Bryncelli Ddu (east of Llandaniel Fab), with its stone entrance still intact.

　　The coastal town and yachting resort of Beaumaris, on the southeast shore, is the main focus for visitors to the island. A walk past pretty, pastel-painted cottages will take you to Beaumaris Castle, which dates from 1295 (Oct, Apr–end May daily 9.30–5; Jun–end Sep daily 9.30–6; rest of year Mon–Fri 9.30–4, Sat–Sun 11–4), the last of Edward I's (1239–1307) iron ring of fortresses, a chain of castles built to subdue the Welsh. Although unfinished, the castle is regarded as a perfect example of medieval military architecture, with symmetrical concentric walls designed by James of St. George. The 1614 Courthouse (Easter–end Sep daily 10.30–5) is still in use, while Beaumaris Gaol shows how nasty a Victorian prison could really be.

HIKING

For coastal walks, head to the breezy summit of Holyhead Mountain (216m/710ft), which is the highest point in Anglesey and is capped by an Iron Age fort. Although it's on the separate Holy Island, it is still part of Anglesey. Alternatively, you can stroll along the dunes from Newborough Warren, in the southeast of the island, to the peninsula and lighthouse of Llanddwyn Island.

Below *Looking down over South Stack Lighthouse and coastline on Holy Island off the Isle of Anglesey*

Above *The Talybont Reservoir was built in the 1930s to supply water to Newport*

BODNANT GARDEN

Set above the River Conwy, with views across the valley to Snowdonia (▷ 237), Bodnant is one of the most visited of all British gardens.

By turns formal and informal, it was first planted in 1875 by the Aberconway family, whose descendants still run the shop and plant centre. There are Italianate terraces, a huge lily pond and a deep wooded valley known as The Dell. Spring brings shows of daffodils, camellias, magnolias and Japanese-style cherry blossom, while early summer has rich displays of rhododendrons, azaleas and laburnum. Late summer bursts into bloom with roses, clematis and waterlilies.

🖼 460 E14 ✉ Tal-y-Cafn, Colwyn Bay LL28 5RE ☎ 01492 650460 🕐 Mid-Mar to end Nov daily 10–5 💷 Adult £7.20, child (5–16) £3.60 🅿 🏛 Shop and garden centre

BRECON BEACONS NATIONAL PARK

www.breconbeacons.org
While lacking the extreme drama of the very highest peaks of Snowdonia National Park in the north of the country (▷ 237), these highlands of South Wales have exhilarating walks and views, particularly on the precipitous sandstone ridge that rises to Pen y Fan (886m/2,907ft).

The eastern flanks comprise the Black Mountains, a series of ridges and lonely valleys; here a road edges past the ruins of 13th-century Llanthony Priory and over the Gospel Pass to drop steeply to the secondhand bookshop mecca and charming market town of Hay-on-Wye, famous for its literary festival.

The Georgian town of Brecon and its surroundings mark the central ground of the national park and make a good base for visits. To the west is Black Mountain (confusing, since there are Black Mountains to the east), a bleak moorland expanse dominated by the craggy ridge of Carmarthen Fan. In the south the Waterfall Country is a tremendous series of waterfalls along the gorges of the Hepste, Mellte and Nedd. Sgwd yr Eira is a magnificent waterfall where, if you are brave enough, you can squeeze your way along a ledge behind the curtain of the fall.

🖼 457 E–F17 ℹ Old Cattle Market Car Park, Brecon LD3 8ER, tel 01874 623156

CAERLEON ROMAN FORTRESS AND BATHS

www.cadw.wales.gov.uk
One of three Roman legionary bases in Britain founded in AD75, Caerleon retains a well-preserved rectangular fortress, with a 6,000-seat amphitheatre and excavated remains of the barracks. Amid the modern town and preserved under cover are the baths, which included an open-air pool, heated changing rooms and an exercise hall. Excavated items are on display at Caerleon Legionary Museum (Mon–Sat 10–5, Sun 2–5). Demonstrations of a Roman legionary's life take place in the museum's Capricorn Centre, with a reconstructed barrack room and replica armour to try on.

🖼 457 F18 ℹ High Street, Caerleon, Gwent NP6 1AE, tel 01633 423134 🕐 Apr–end Oct daily 9.30–5; rest of year Mon–Sat 9.30–5, Sun 11–4 💷 Baths: adult £2.90, child (5–16) £2.50 🏛

CAERNARFON

www.caernarfon.com
This market town is dwarfed by the magnificent harbourside Caernarfon Castle (Jun–end Sep daily 9.30–6; Apr–end May, Oct daily 9.30–5; Nov–end Mar Mon–Sat 9.30–4, Sun 11–4), built in 1283 by Edward I (1239–1307) to consolidate his conquest of Wales (▷ 31). Edward I's son, the future Edward II (1284–1327), was born here. In 1969 the castle was the setting for Prince Charles's investiture as Prince of Wales. Substantial lengths of the medieval town wall still snake through the town.

On a hill above the town lie the foundations of the Roman settlement fort of Segontium, which was founded in AD77, with a museum displaying finds from this far-flung outpost of the Roman Empire. On Caernarfon Airparc, where the RAF Mountain Rescue Service was formed in 1943, is Caernarfon Airworld Museum (daily 9–4), an indoor interactive museum with historic and modern aircraft, trial flights and pleasure flights.

🖼 460 D14 ℹ Castle Ditch, Castle Street, Caernarfon LL55 1SE, tel 01286 672232

Below *Illuminated Caernarfon Castle*

INFORMATION

www.visitcardiff.com

457 F18 The Old Library, The Hayes, Cardiff CA10 1AH, tel 0870 1211 258 Cardiff Central

CARDIFF

FROM VILLAGE TO CAPITAL

From its beginnings as the site of a Roman fort on the River Taf (Taff), Cardiff grew up as a village protected by a Norman castle and, later, a modest harbour town. By the early 20th century it was the biggest coal-exporting dock in the world. The heart of the city has handsome Victorian and Edwardian shopfronts and arcades, a 19th-century covered market and gleaming civic buildings. Redevelopment of the docks area began in the 1980s, and the docks' connection with the city was gradually re-established. Cardiff is now the home of the National Assembly for Wales and the Millennium Centre which hosts opera, ballet and musicals); both are dramatic, modern buildings.

THE CASTLE AND CIVIC CENTRE

The focus of the city is Cardiff Castle (Mar–end Oct daily 9–6, rest of year 9.30–5), a Norman fortress dating from Roman times. In the 19th century it was transformed into a flamboyant, neo-Gothic extravaganza by the third Marquess of Bute and his designer William Burges. Northeast of the castle, the white Portland-stone buildings of the Civic Centre are laid out on broad avenues. In front is the elaborate City Hall and the National Museum and Gallery (Tue–Sun 10–5), with an Evolution of Wales exhibition and the largest collection of Impressionist and post-Impressionist paintings outside France.

ON THE WATERFRONT

Cardiff's docks have become vibrant Cardiff Bay, fringed with restaurants, bars and shops. Among the attractions are Techniquest (Mon–Fri 9.30–4.30, Sat–Sun 10.30–5), a science discovery complex and planetarium; arts and crafts exhibitions in a restored warehouse; Butetown History and Arts Centre (Tue–Fri 10–5, Sat–Sun 11–4.30); and the Pierhead Building (Mon–Fri 9.30–4.30, Sat–Sun and public hols 10.30–6). The white-wood Norwegian Church is a cultural centre built for Scandinavian sailors who brought timber beams for the coal mines.

Above *Cardiff's restored Pierhead Building, which was designed by William Frame and built in 1897*

CAERPHILLY CASTLE

www.cadw.wales.gov.uk

The largest medieval fortress in Wales, and one of the largest in Britain, Caerphilly Castle has a somewhat incongruous setting beside a modern industrial town. Its design was complex, with concentric outer walls—walls within walls—further defended by a water-filled moat and artificial lakes and islands. One of the towers has been permanently leaning to one side since the 17th century, when Parliamentarians tried to blow it up during the Civil War (▷ 34). The walls stand once again at their original height following restoration in the 19th and 20th centuries. There is an exhibition of working replica siege engines, which are periodically demonstrated (call in advance to find out times).

✚ 457 F18 ✉ Castle Street, Caerphilly CF83 1JD ☎ 02920 883143 ◉ Jun–late Sep daily 9.30–6; Apr–end May, Oct daily 9.30–5; rest of year Mon–Sat 9.30–4, Sun 11–4 (closed 24 Dec–1 Jan) ✋ Adult £3.50, child (5–16) £3, family £10 ▣ Caerphilly ⌂

CALDICOT CASTLE

www.caldicotcastle.co.uk

Set in a country park, Caldicot is a restored 13th-century castle on a Norman motte, built by Humphrey de Bohun, Earl of Hereford. Its elaborate defences included portcullises, heavy gates and murder holes.

Although the castle was restored by the antiquarian J. R. Cobb from 1855, much of the original stonework is still intact. Other surviving architectural details include latrine turrets, a hooded fireplace and window-seats. Remember to take a look at the sculpted heads and ornate windows on the twin turrets of the main gatehouse.

✚ 457 F18 ✉ Church Road, Caldicot NP26 4HU ☎ 01291 420241 ◉ Mar–end Oct daily 11–5 ✋ Adult £3.75, child (5–17) £2.50, family £12; additional charges for special events/activities ▢ ⌂

CARREG CENNEN CASTLE

www.cadw.wales.gov.uk

Carreg Cennen perches on an inland cliff on the western side of the Brecon Beacons National Park (▷ 227). Built in about 1300, it was originally an Anglo-Norman stronghold, designed to repel Welsh advances. Even in its ruinous state, its massive towers are still very impressive, while on the south side a sheer 90m (295ft) drop forms a natural defence. Despite this, the Welsh rebel Owain Glyndwr (c1350–1416) took the castle in the 15th century, and the Yorkists later destroyed it during the Wars of the Roses (1455–85) to prevent its use as a Lancastrian base. Make sure you investigate the passageway cut into the cliff which leads to a natural cave beneath the fortifications.

✚ 456 E17 ✉ Trapp, near Llandeilo SA19 6UA ☎ 01558 822291 ◉ Apr–end Oct daily 9.30–6.30; rest of year daily 9.30–dusk ✋ Adult £3.50, child (5–16) £3, family £10 ▢ ⌂

CASTELL COCH

www.cadw.wales.gov.uk

On the edge of Cardiff is this unfinished Victorian Gothic fantasy, designed in 1875 by William Burges (who also designed Cardiff Castle) for John Patrick Crichton Stuart, third Marquess of Bute (1713–92), as a hunting lodge. Burges created a fairy-tale place with sharp conical roofs and outrageously lavish interiors with painted ceilings and walls, sculpted and gilded figures, and elaborate furnishings. There are some clever details in the wall decoration of the drawing room—such as painted ribbons that seem to support the family portraits, and the frog holding a bottle of cough mixture for the frog that is placed in its own throat.

✚ 457 F18 ✉ Castle Road, Tongwynlais, near Cardiff CF15 7JQ ☎ 029 2081 0101 ◉ Apr–end May, Oct daily 9.30–5; Jun–end Sep daily 9.30–5; rest of year Mon–Sat 9.30–4, Sun 11–4. Usually closed for six weeks in Jan–Feb for conservation work ✋ Adult £3.50, child (5–16) £3, family £10 ⌂

CELTICA

www.celticawales.com

Welsh and Celtic history is vividly brought to the fore in this unusual museum housed in Y Plas, a Victorian mansion set in grounds which include a Celtic maze. Headsets guide visitors through a series of themed rooms, where life-size electronic figures tell their own tales. An interpretive centre uses murals and replicas to explore history, while the Historium is devoted to temporary exhibitions.

✚ 460 E16 ✉ Y Plas, Aberystwyth Road, Machynlleth SY20 8ER ☎ 01654 702702 ◉ Daily 10–6 (last admission to main exhibition 4.20) ✋ Adult £5, child (5–16) £4, family £16 ▣ Machynlleth ? Discounted rail/admission ticket available ▢ ⌂

Left *Caerphilly Castle and moat dating from the 13th century, with large towers, walls, and wide water defences*

CENTRE FOR ALTERNATIVE TECHNOLOGY

www.cat.org.uk

Within a disused slate quarry on a remote hillside in mid-Wales, a community of half a dozen self-sufficient families has been established to showcase how 'green' energy and alternative technology can be used in various aspects of everyday life. It has been arranged foremost with visitors in mind: A water-powered cliff railway (summer only) carries you up to the site from the parking area. From there you can wander among the solar-powered buildings, pumps and turbines, and see the organic gardens and farm animals.

✚ 460 E16 ✉ Near Machynlleth SY20 9AZ ☎ 01654 705950 ⊕ Easter–end Oct daily 10–5.30; Nov–Easter daily 10–dusk; extended opening hours during school summer holidays; closed Christmas and two weeks in Jan ⊕ Easter–end Oct: adult £8.40, child (5–18) £4.20, discount if you arrive by foot, bus, bike or train ▢ ⊞

CHIRK CASTLE

www.nationaltrust.org.uk

On a rise in the hills of the northern Welsh borderlands, 14th-century Chirk Castle is one of the few erected by Edward I (1239–1307) to survive intact, with its squat towers and forbidding exterior walls. Inside, however, much has changed: The Myddelton family, resident since 1595, added state rooms with Adam-style furniture, tapestries, a 17th-century Long Gallery, and decorations in a medieval idiom by the 19th-century designer Augustus Pugin (1812–52). The grounds are also beautiful and there is a lovely circular woodland walk.

✚ 461 F15 ✉ Chirk, near Wrexham LL14 5AF ☎ 01691 777701 ⊕ Early Feb to mid-Feb Sat–Sun 11–4; mid-Feb to Easter, Oct, Wed–Sun 11–4; Easter–end Jun Wed–Sun 11–5; Jul–end Aug Tue–Sun 11–5; Sep Wed–Sun 11–5; Garden 10–6 ✋ Adult £8, child (5–16) £4.40, family £20. Garden only: adult £5.58, child £2.79, family £13.95 🚉 Chirk 🍴 ⊞

CONWY

▷ 231.

DAN-YR-OGOF NATIONAL SHOWCAVES

www.showcaves.co.uk

The focus of this complex of attractions in the Brecon Beacons National Park (▷ 227) was discovered by local farmers Jeff and Tommy Morgan in 1912. Their voices are used to guide visitors through the caves, which include the Bone Cave, where 42 Bronze Age skeletons were found, and the Dome of St. Paul's in the Cathedral Cave, where waterfalls feed into an underground lake. Elsewhere are a Dinosaur Park, Barney Owl's Adventure Playground, a replica Iron Age farm, a Shire Horse Centre and Victorian Farm. Separate charges give entrance to a dry-skiing slope and trekking facility.

✚ 457 E17 ✉ National Showcaves Centre for Wales, Dan-yr-Ogof, near Abercrave, Upper Swansea Valley SA9 1GJ ☎ 01639 730801, 01639 730284 (winter helpline) ⊕ Apr–end Oct daily from 10. First admission to caves 10.30; last admission varies (usually about 3). Also open school holidays at Christmas and Feb half-term ✋ Adult £11, child (4–16) £6.50 ▢ ⊞

DOLAUCOTHI GOLD MINES

www.nationaltrust.org.uk

Britain's only known Roman gold mine may date back as early as the Bronze Age. It was also in use from Victorian times until the 1930s.

A long guided tour (children under 5 are not admitted) leads through the most recent site and explores the Roman/Victorian caves and passages. Visitors are kitted out with helmets and lamps for the underground sections, and are encouraged to pan for gold in the mine yard. Look out for the Roman axe marks which are still visible in the rock at the entrance to the mining passage.

✚ 460 E17 ✉ Pumsaint, Llanwrda SA19 8US ☎ 01558 825146 (recording), 01558 650177 ⊕ Mar–end Oct daily 10–5 (last underground tour 4.30) ✋ Site only (includes gold-panning): adult £3.09, child (5–16) £1.54, family £8.50. Underground tour: adult £3.45, child £1.72, family £8.63 ▢ ⊞

ELAN VALLEY

www.elanvalley.org.uk

Created between 1893 and 1952 to provide water for the city of Birmingham, this Welsh version of the Lake District (▷ 312) has dams and reservoirs within the Cambrian Mountains. Initially the scheme caused controversy as it involved flooding existing communities; the lakes are now recognised as attractions in themselves.

The earlier dams are built in an elaborate Victorian style, and the area is rich in wildlife, including the rare red kite (identified by its large wingspan and forked tail). Some of the birds fly over to Gigrin Farm (not open to the public) near Rhayader.

The Elan Valley Visitor Centre has an exhibition, a café and maps with details of routes which are suitable for walkers, cyclists and those on horseback, including the easy-to-follow Elan Valley Trail. This 8-mile (13km) route is suitable for all, including pushchairs and wheelchairs. It also has information on which birds to look out for.

✚ 460 E16 ℹ Elan Valley Visitor Centre, Rhayader LD6 5HP, tel 01597 810880 (Rangers' Office), 01597 810898 (Visitor Centre) ⊕ Visitor Centre: mid-Mar to end Oct daily 10–5.30 ▢ ⊞

Below *Caban Coch Reservoir bridge*

CONWY
THE FORTIFICATIONS

The best-preserved medieval town in Wales memorably evokes the era of English rule. It makes an excellent base for exploring Snowdonia and the coast. Conwy was built by Edward I after his conquest of the area in 1283 (▷ 30). His military architect, James of St. George, created a walled and fortified town based on those in Switzerland and France. By the 18th century Conwy had settled into its role as a trading post and river-ferry port on the route to Holyhead and Ireland. The town's most striking feature is the virtually intact 1,280m (4,200ft) town wall that extends from the castle and contours above the streets. Three double-towered gateways and 21 towers punctuate the wall; a walk along it gives wonderful views over the town rooftops, the surrounding countryside and the River Conwy. Also built by Edward I, the formidable castle (Apr–end May daily 9.30–5; Jun–end Sep daily 9.30–6; Oct daily 9.30–5; Nov–end Mar Mon–Sat 9.30–4, Sun 11–4) has eight massive round towers guarding the estuary. Inside, only one stone arch remains of the eight that were constructed in the 1340s to support the roof of the great hall.

DOMESTIC ARCHITECTURE

One of Conwy's greatest treasures is Plas Mawr (Apr–end May Tue–Sun 9.30–5; Jun–end Aug 9.30–6; Sep 9.30–5; Oct 9.30–4), the Elizabethan town house completed in 1585 for Robert Wynn. Designed to spread upwards rather than outwards, the house was partly influenced by European architecture— such as the canalside houses of Bruges in Belgium. In 1993 the Welsh heritage body Cadw embarked on a meticulous restoration project that resulted in a re-creation of Wynn's great hall, kitchen, bedrooms and banqueting room.

On the corner of Castle Street, Aberconwy House (Apr–end Oct Wed–Mon 11–5), with its stone steps and overhanging upper storey, represents the sole surviving merchant's building of medieval Conwy. It contains period furniture, and a video traces its history. On the quayside is the Smallest House (Apr–end Oct daily 10–6; Aug daily 10–8), a very narrow one-up, one-down dwelling.

INFORMATION

www.conwy.gov.uk

✚ 460 E14 🛈 Conwy Castle Visitor Centre, Conwy LL32 8LD, tel 01492 592248 🚉 Conwy

Above *Conwy Castle and Telford's Suspension Bridge*

ERDDIG

www.nationaltrust.org

For 240 years this 17th-century red-brick mansion was occupied by the Yorke family, but it then fell into near dereliction and was rescued by the National Trust in the 1970s. It is chiefly of interest not for its architecture, but for the unusually close bond between its owners and their staff. You enter not through the front door but through the servants' quarters. The house is set in formal gardens overlooking a canal lined with lime trees. Make sure you see the portraits of servants, dating from the 1790s and 1830s, along with verses about them.

➕ 461 F15 ✉ Near Wrexham LL13 0YT ☎ 01978 315151 (recording), 01978 355314 🕐 House: late Mar–end Sep Sat–Wed, Good Fri 12–5, also Thu Jul–Aug; Oct Sat–Wed 12–4; last admission 1 hr before closing. Tapestry Room and small Chinese Room: Wed and Sat. Garden: late Mar–end Jun, Sep Sat–Wed, Fri 11–6; Jul–end Aug Sat–Thu 10–6; Oct Sat–Wed 11–5; Nov–end Dec Sat–Sun 11–4 💷 Adult £8.54, child (5–16) £4.27, family £21.35. Garden and outbuildings only: adult £5.45, child £2.72, family £13.63 🍴 🏧

GOWER PENINSULA

www.enjoygower.com

The Gower Peninsula is something of a scenic microcosm on the doorstep of industrial Swansea (▷ 238) and the old-fashioned seaside resort of Mumbles. Its sandy beaches attract crowds at weekends in summer, and footpaths skirt virtually the entire length of its dramatically varied coastline, along the cliff-bounded heights of the southern shores and the lower-lying marshes on the north side.

For stunning views and great walks along this beautiful coastline, head up the moorland ridge of Cefn Bryn, near the sweeping sands of Three Cliffs Bay. At the western tip of Gower, Rhossili Down provides a walk at two levels—along its crest and along the beach far below, where shipwrecks are revealed at low tide. From there you can walk past Worms Head, a long finger of rock which

is accessible via a causeway and across a natural arch (Devil's Bridge) for two hours before and after low tide. The coast turns a corner to enter Mewslade Bay with startlingly jagged cliffs. At Oxwich Bay there are nature trails through dunes and woods. On the north coast the village of Llanrhidian overlooks salt marshes and tidal sandbanks, where cockles are harvested.

Make sure you leave time to see Gower's castles. Oxwich and Pennard are eerie ruins on the south coast, while to the north Weobley Castle (Apr–end Oct daily 9.30–6; rest of year daily 9.30–5) is a more substantial survival, a fortified manor house dating mainly from the 13th and 14th centuries.

➕ 456 D18 ℹ Gower Heritage Centre, Parkmill, Gower, Swansea SA23 2EM, tel 01792 371206

GREENWOOD FOREST PARK

www.greenwoodforestpark.co.uk

Children of all ages can let off plenty of steam in this imaginative forest park in the foothills of Snowdonia (▷ 237). There are boisterous activities such as a sled run down a 70m (230ft) slide, a jungle boat ride and mini tractors. Elsewhere are longbow archery, traditional craft displays, ducks, peacocks, rabbits, an arboretum and gardens, a sculpture trail and a rainforest boardwalk.

➕ 460 E14 ✉ Greenwood Forest Park (Gelli Gyffwrdd), Y Felinheli LL56 4QN ☎ 01248 671493, 01248 670076 (infoline) 🕐 Easter , Jul–end Aug, daily 10.30–6; Mar–end Apr, May–end Jun 10–5.30; Sep–end Oct 11–5 💷 Varies according to season and number of activities. Adults £4.95–£7.50, child (under 16) £3.95–£6.50, family £15.65–£24.95 🍴 🏧

HARLECH CASTLE

www.cadw.wales.gov.uk

The walls and six drum towers of this 13th-century castle stand virtually at their original height. Built as one of Edward I's iron ring of fortresses designed to subdue the Welsh, it is defended by a massive gatehouse and commands views of the sea, the Snowdonia mountains

Above *The old slate mines of Llanberis*

and the Lleyn Peninsula. Fortified steps (open in summer only) lead to the foot of the castle.

The song *Men of Harlech* was inspired by a long siege against the castle when it was held by the Lancastrians during the 15th-century Wars of the Roses.

➕ 460 E15 ✉ Castle Square, Harlech LL46 2YH ☎ 01766 780552 🕐 Mar–end May, Oct daily 9.30–5; Jun–Sep 9.30–6; Nov–end Mar Mon–Sat 9.30–4, Sun 11–4 💷 Adult £3.50, child (5–16) £3, family £10 🚉 Harlech 🏧

LAUGHARNE

www.dylanthomasboathouse.com

Pronounced *larn*, this quiet town on the Taf Estuary grew up around 12th- to 16th-century Laugharne Castle (Apr–end Sep daily 10–5), which is now an imposing ruin.

The celebrated Welsh poet Dylan Thomas (1914–53) settled here in 1949, and his boathouse (daily 10–5.30) and writing shed, where he lived and worked in his final, tragic and alcohol-blighted years, make a poignant visit. Creating the right atmosphere is the paper-strewn desk (with discarded papers on the floor) where Thomas wrote his best-known work, *Under Milk Wood* (1954), basing the town of Llareggub on Laugharne. He and his long-suffering wife Caitlin are buried in St. Martin's churchyard.

➕ 456 D17 ℹ Visitor Centre, 113 Lammas Street, Carmarthen SA31 3QA, tel 01267 231557

LLANBERIS

www.llanberis.org

Llanberis is a busy mountain resort spread out at the foot of Snowdon, the highest mountain in Wales. From here steam trains on the rack-and-pinion Snowdon Mountain Railway (mid-Mar to end Nov daily, weather permitting) grind their way to the summit, from where you can walk back via a number of contrasting routes. At a lower level, the Llanberis Lake Railway (for timetable, www.lake-railway.co.uk) steams its way along Llyn Padarn. Electric Mountain (rest of year 10–4.30) offers a tour of one of Europe's largest pumped storage stations, hidden deep inside a mountain.

In Padarn Country Park, the National Slate Museum (Easter–end Oct daily 10–5; rest of year Sun–Fri 10–4) paints a vivid picture of the daily lives of workers in the slate quarries that functioned here from 1861 to 1969.

➕ 460 E14 ℹ Visitor Office, 41b High Street, Llanberis LL55 4EU (closed winter), tel 01286 870765

LLANDRINDOD WELLS

www.llandrindod.co.uk

Period shopfronts, frilly wrought-iron canopies, and broad avenues lined with villas and hotels assert Llandrindod as one of the best-preserved Victorian spa towns in Britain. Within Rock Park you can sample the rusty-tasting waters that gush from a fountain, or visit the restored Pump Room, while the lake is a popular strolling area. Among many period buildings is the Automobile Palace, an early motor showroom (1909) housing the National Cycle Collection (Mar–end Oct daily 10–4), a collection of some 250 historic bicycles from Victorian examples to more comfortable-looking modern racing bikes.

It's worth trying to visit in late August, when the whole town dresses in period costume during Llandrindod's Victorian Week.

➕ 460 F16 ℹ The Groe Car Park, Builth Wells LD2 3BT, tel 01982 553307 🚉 Llandrindod Wells

LLANDUDNO

www.visitconwy.org.uk

A well-preserved example of Victorian seaside architecture, Llandudno has an elegant seafront, with hotels and guesthouses overlooking a pebble beach and iron-railed pier. Venture by cable-car or steep tramway to Great Ormes Head for fine views over Conwy Bay and the Snowdonia mountains. The Great Orme Mines (Easter–early Nov daily 9.30–5) were dug for copper by Bronze Age settlers around 4,000 years ago and claim to be the oldest metal mines in the world open to the public; excavations can sometimes be seen in progress.

➕ 460 E14 ℹ Library Building, Mostyn Street, Llandudno LL30 2RP, tel 01492 876413 🚉 Llandudno

LLANGOLLEN

▷ 235.

LLEYN PENINSULA

www.gwynedd.gov.uk

This tranquil arm of land jutting out between Tremadog and Caernarfon bays forms part of an unspoiled, rugged coastline and a rural, hilly interior. At the base of the peninsula is Porthmadog, a small town linked to Snowdonia by two steam railways—the Welsh Highland Railway (timetable, www.whr.co.uk) and the Ffestiniog Railway (timetable, www.festrail.co.uk).

Two other popular places on the southern coast are Criccieth, with a castle on a headland overlooking the beach, and Pwllheli. Elsewhere, the peninsula is all about wildlife, tranquillity, and ancient and sacred sites. Tre'r Ceiri is an Iron Age settlement memorably set beside the coastal mountain of Yr Eifl; Bardsey Island, off the tip of the Lleyn Peninsula, was the site of a 5th-century Celtic monastery. Don't miss Plas yn Rhiw on the south coast (Easter–end Apr Thu–Sun 12–5; May–end Jun, Sep Thu–Mon 12–5; Jul–end Aug Wed–Mon 12–5; Oct Thu–Sun 12–4), a 16th-century manor house with ornamental gardens overlooking the bay known as Hell's Mouth.

➕ 460 D15 ℹ Min y Don, Station Square, Pwllheli LL53 5HG, tel 01758 613000 🚉 Pwllheli

MONTGOMERY

www.montgomery-powys.co.uk

While none of the border towns of mid-Wales are of great size, Montgomery is scarcely more than a village, yet with imposing Georgian buildings recalling its once greater status as a county town. The finest buildings are in Broad Street, and include the 1748 Town Hall. Overlooking the town are the sparse ruins of the 13th-century castle, well worth climbing for its views. A 16th-century former inn, The Old Bell (Easter–end Sep Wed–Fri, Sun 1.30–5, Sat 10.30–5) houses local history displays about the town and the Cambrian Railway.

➕ 461 F16 ℹ Vicarage Garden, Church Street, Welshpool SY21 7DD, tel 01938 552043

Below *The Snowdon Mountain Railway goes from Llanberis to the top of Snowdon*

NATIONAL BOTANIC GARDEN OF WALES

www.gardenofwales.org.uk

When it opened in 2000 this was Britain's first new national botanic garden in nearly 200 years. Essentially a teaching and research facility, the garden is laid out with visitors in mind, with plants along a broadwalk linking a Japanese garden, a double-walled garden and a marsh lining the lake and pond. The gardens occupy the estate of a Georgian mansion that has long since vanished, from which time Paxton's Tower, a two-storey triangular eyecatcher, survives. The Great Glasshouse is a striking glass dome designed by Norman Foster, which houses plants of Mediterranean ecosystems.

🛨 456 E17 ✉ Middleton Hall, Llanarthne SA32 8HG ☎ 01558 668768 🕙 Nov–end Mar daily 10–4.30; rest of year daily 10–6; last admission 1 hr before closing 🖐 Adult £8, child (5–15) £3, family £17 🍴 ▢ 🏛

NATIONAL WETLANDS CENTRE WALES

www.wwt.org.uk

One of nine centres in Britain to be run by the Wildfowl and Wetlands Trust (WWT), this reserve lies on the east side of Carmarthen Bay. Hundreds of ducks, geese, swans and flamingoes enjoy life here—some are tame enough to be fed by hand. The little egret is a success story here—their numbers have shot up from just two in 1995 to several hundred now. There are observatory hides for birdwatching, as well as a Millennium Discovery Centre and a play area with tunnels and a maze.

🛨 456 E18 ✉ Llwynhendy, Llanelli SA14 9SH ☎ 01554 741087 🕙 Summer daily 9.30–5 (grounds 9.30–6); winter daily 9.30–4.30 (grounds 9.30–5) 🖐 Adult £6.95, child (4–16) £3.85, family £19.45 ▢ 🏛

NATIONAL WOOL MUSEUM

www.museumwales.ac.uk

This museum doubles as a working woollen mill, producing modern goods that are offered for sale.

Right *Taking a Canoe Safari at the National Wetlands Centre*

Yarns are produced on 19th-century machinery and woven on both hand and power looms. You can also watch demonstrations of traditional hand-carding, spinning and weaving. The museum traces the history of Dre-Fach Felindre and its heyday as the 'Huddersfield of Wales' (referring to the major textile-producing town in northern England), when 40 mills were based here.

🛨 460 D17 ✉ Dre-Fach Felindre, Llandysul SA44 5UP ☎ 01559 370929 🕙 Apr–end Sep daily 10–5; rest of year Tue–Fri 10–5 🖐 Free ▢ 🏛

OAKWOOD PARK

www.oakwoodthemepark.co.uk

One of Pembrokeshire's biggest family attractions, Oakwood Park has rides such as the wooden roller-coaster Megafobia, the 46m (150ft) high skycoaster, Vertigo, and Wales's only shoot-and-drop tower, The Bounce, which shoots riders into the air at high speed—and watches them drop. Playtown is aimed at younger children, while Techniquest is an indoor science discovery centre. In August there are fireworks displays when the park opens late.

🛨 456 D17 ✉ Canaston Bridge, Narberth, Pembrokeshire SA67 8DE ☎ 08712 206211 🕙 Easter–end Jul daily 10–5; Aug 10–10; Sep 10–5 🖐 Adult £14.75, child (3–9) £13.50. After 5.30 (Aug) £10 🍴 ▢ 🏛

PEMBROKE CASTLE

Surrounded by water on three sides, this massive Norman fortress remained invincible until the 17th-century Civil War (▷ 34), when the Parliamentarians took it. During the Wars of the Roses, Lady Margaret Beaufort came here and gave birth to the future king, Henry VII (1457–1509), the first Tudor king of England. Life-size figures in the great hall of the gatehouse represent Earl William de Valence and his family at a medieval banquet. Other displays trace the story of Henry VII and describe the horrors of punishment in the castle dungeon.

🛨 456 C18 ✉ Pembroke SA71 4LA ☎ 01646 681510 🕙 Apr–end Sep daily 9.30–6; Mar, Oct 10–5; Nov–end Feb 10–4 🖐 Adult £3.50, child (over 5) £2.50, family £10 ❓ Guided tours (Jun–end Aug daily) £1 extra 🚻 Pembroke ▢ 🏛

LLANGOLLEN
LLANGOLLEN TOWN

A romantic, green vale and home of the world-famous musical Eisteddfod, The Vale of Llangollen has attracted tourists since the late 18th century. A good starting point is the market town of Llangollen, which has hosted the International Eisteddfod every July for more than 50 years. At the festival, held in the impressive Royal International Pavilion, performers from all over the world compete in dance, song and music. Indoor attractions here include the Motor Museum and Canal Exhibition (Mar–end Oct daily 11–5), with cars and cycles dating from 1912 and a display about the building of the canals, and the Llangollen Museum (daily 10–4), recording the social and industrial history of this fascinating corner of Wales.

On a hill above town is the half-timbered house, Plas Newydd (House: Easter–end Oct Sat–Wed 12–5; Gardens: Easter–end Oct Sat–Wed 11–5.30). This was the home of the Ladies of Llangollen—Lady Eleanor Butler and Miss Sarah Ponsonby—who fled their families in 18th-century Ireland in order to live together, and who welcomed a stream of celebrated visitors to their much-extended cottage between 1780 and 1829. The house is furnished as it was in their day and an exhibition in one room tells the ladies' remarkable story.

THE GREAT OUTDOORS

The canal wharf is the starting point for horse-drawn barge trips through the vale, including a dizzy stretch across Thomas Telford's monumental Pontcysyllte Aqueduct, 38m (126ft) above the River Dee, and reaching the river at the weir of Horseshoe Falls. Steam trains on the Llangollen Railway lead through 13km (8 miles) of scenery, stopping at Berwyn, above the river gorge and a 15-minute walk from Horseshoe Falls. There are great views of the vale beyond Llangollen from the ruins of Castell Dinas Brân (Crow City Castle), on a hill above town.

INFORMATION
www.llangollen.org.uk
✚ 461 F15 🛈 Town Hall, Castle Street LL20 5PD, tel 01978 860828

Above *View of Llangollen, across the River Dee*

235

PEMBROKESHIRE COAST NATIONAL PARK

www.visitpembrokeshire.com
www.pcnpa.org.uk

The Pembrokeshire Coast Path, a 186-mile (300km) National Trail, weaves around an intricate seaboard, giving excellent sea views. The scenery divides between the more rugged north and the level cliffs in the south.

Near St. David's (▷ 237), Whitesands Bay is a long beach, with St. David's Head a short walk north looking across towards Ireland. Strumble Head, at the tip of the cliffs, has some of the best views to the south from the Iron Age hillfort site of Garn Fawr. Fishguard is a harbour town with ferries over to Rosslare in Ireland. Inland, the Preseli Hills are dotted with prehistoric sites, including Bronze Age stone circles and Neolithic burial chambers; it was from here that the bluestones of Stonehenge originated (▷ 143). On the hillfort site of Castell Henllys (Apr–end Oct daily 10–5; rest of year 11–3) you'll find a reconstruction of an Iron Age village.

One of many outstanding coastal viewpoints is Wooltack Point near Marloes, which overlooks Skomer and Skokholm islands (▷ opposite). Bosherston Lily Ponds lie close to the beach of Broad Haven; the coast path going west passes the rock pillars of Elegug Stacks and the natural arch known as the Green Bridge of Wales. Many tidal creeks drain into the harbour of Milford Haven; overlooking one inlet is Carew Castle (Apr–end Oct daily 10–5; rest of year 11–3), the ruined shell of a medieval fortress-turned-Elizabethan-mansion. The ancient, primitive hermitage chapels of St. Non, St. Justinian and St. Govan (near Bosherston), are each sheltered remotely in the cliffs. 🕂 460 C17 🛈 National Park Visitor Centre, The Grove, St. David's SA62 4NW, tel 01437 720392

PENRHYN CASTLE

www.nationaltrust.org.uk

This stately mock-castle overlooking the Menai Strait and Anglesey follows the 19th-century fashion for neo-Norman architecture. Ostentatious in the extreme, it was built by Thomas Hopper between 1820 and 1840 and has more than 300 rooms.

The Pennant family flaunted their wealth here (gained from Jamaican sugar, slavery and Welsh slate) with a slate bed weighing 1 tonne, which was made for Queen Victoria, stained-glass windows in the great hall, and a grand staircase with ornate lamp-holders, carved masks and encrusted pillars.

You can tour the grounds in a staff-driven buggy (reservation necessary). Look out for a walled garden and exotic tree and shrub collection. 🕂 460 E14 ✉ Llandygai, Bangor LL57 4HN ☎ 01248 353084; 01248 371337 infoline ⏰ Mar–end Jun, Sep–end Oct Wed–Mon 12–5; Jul, Aug Wed–Mon 11–5. Garden: Mar–end Jun and Sep, Oct Wed–Sat 11–5; Jul, Aug Wed–Mon 10–5 👆 Adult £7, child (5–16) £3.50, family £17. Gardens and stable block exhibitions only: adult £5, child £2.50 🍴 🏛

PISTYLL RHAEADR

www.pistyllrhaeadr.co.uk

At the end of a long, sparsely populated valley is this dramatic waterfall (the name means 'waterfall spout'), the tallest in Wales. A narrow ribbon of water drops into a wooded rock basin from a height of 73m (240ft), broken in mid-flight by a man-made rock arch placed there to enhance the whole effect.

During a tour of Wales in the 19th century, the English writer and traveller George Henry Borrow (1803–81) recorded the fall as 'an immense skein of silk agitated and disturbed by tempestuous blasts'. Visitors can walk to the top or watch the spectacle from the picnic area at ground level. 🕂 460 F15 🛈 Vicarage Gardens, Church Street, Welshpool SY21 7DD, tel 01938 552043

PORTMEIRION

www.portmeirion-village.com

The Italian Riviera comes to the shores of Snowdonia in this surreal 20th-century creation, by architect

Above *Puffins are excellent fishers*

Sir Clough Williams-Ellis, occupying a headland overlooking the Dwyryd estuary. His aim was to show that a beautiful location could be developed without its being spoiled. The result is a storybook version of a Mediterranean village in which parts of other buildings from elsewhere in Britain have been recycled.

Portmeirion has a piazza at its heart and buildings that include a belvedere, campanile, pantheon and triumphal arch, overlooked by pastel-hued cottages decorated with carvings and paintings. A Victorian mansion, Castell Deudraeth, houses a restaurant and rooms; cottages are let as self-catering accommodation. The village shop sells distinctive Portmeirion pottery. 🕂 460 E15 🛈 Portmeirion LL48 6ET ☎ 01766 770000 ⏰ Daily 9.30–5.30 👆 Adult £7, child (over 5) £3.50, family £17 🚉 Boston Lodge 0.6 miles (1km) on Ffestiniog Railway 🍴 🏛

POWIS CASTLE

www.nationaltrust.org.uk

The border fortress with red sandstone walls conceals an elegant stately home, influenced by 600 years of architecture. The Herbert family, who acquired it in 1584, added an Elizabethan long gallery and 17th-century state bedroom. Yet the grounds steal the show: During the 18th century the architect William Winde laid out the terraced gardens, planted with huge clipped yew hedges. There are statues, an aviary and an orangery, with views across the Severn Valley. Edward Clive, son of Clive of India, was made Earl of Powis in 1804 and restored the castle. You can visit the Clive Museum.

461 F16 Welshpool SY21 8RF 01938 551944 (recording), 01938 551929 Castle: Easter–end Jun, Sep Thu–Mon 1–5; late Sep, Oct 1–4. Jul, Aug Wed–Mon 1–5. Garden: Easter–end Jun, Sep Thu–Mon 11–5.30; late Sep–Oct Thu–Mon 11–5; Jul–Aug Wed–Mon 11–5.30 Adult £9.45, child (5–16) £4.73, family £23.63. Garden only: adult £6.75, child £3.38, family £16.88 Welshpool 2 miles (3km) via footpath

RHONDDA HERITAGE PARK

www.rhonddaheritagepark.com

Based at the former Lewis Merthyr Colliery, this heritage park evokes the sounds, smells and sights of what life was like in a working coal mine (until the large-scale closures of South Wales' mines in the 1970s and 1980s).

The underground tour, led by ex-miners, vividly recreates working conditions on a shift—there is even a simulated explosion. The multimedia exhibition Black Gold uses the lives of a real miner and his predecessors to illustrate the Rhondda's coal industry from the 1850s, and there are displays about the mining valley communities. For children of all ages there is the Energy Zone play area (Easter–end Sep).

457 E18 Trehafod, Rhondda Cynon Taff CF37 2NP 01443 682036 Daily 10–6 (last tour 4); Oct–Easter Tue–Sun Adult £5.60, child (5–16) £4.30, family

£16.50. Energy Zone: adult free, child £2 Trehafod

ST. DAVID'S

www.stdavids.co.uk

Its cathedral raises St. David's to the status of a city, yet it is scarcely more than a village in character and size. Tucked away in a dip next to the substantial ruins of the Bishop's Palace (Jun–end Sep daily 9.30–5; Oct–end May 9.30–4), St. David's Cathedral dates from the 12th century but is on the site of a sixth-century monastery founded by David, the patron saint of Wales. He was thought to have been born at a point marked by Non's Well, close by on a grassy headland on the coast. The cathedral's many highlights include its beautiful 16th-century wooden ceiling in the nave and a brightly decorated tower lantern ceiling.

460 C17 Pembrokeshire Coast National Park Visitor Centre, The Grove SA62 4NW, tel 01437 720392

ST. FAGANS NATIONAL HISTORY MUSEUM

www.museumwales.ac.uk

Set in the 100 acres (40ha) of St Fagans Castle parkland just 4 miles (6km) from the centre of the Welsh capital, St Fagans is an open-air museum which recreates many lost aspects of Welsh life and culture. Here you'll find a chapel, a farm, a school and a workmen's institute as well as more than forty other buildings, which were moved from their original sites and reconstructed here as museum pieces. There are also native breeds of farm animals and a series of galleries with displays of everday items covering home life, work, festivals and music. The Welsh language is also celebrated and explained.

457 F18 Cardiff CF5 6XB 029 2037 3500 Daily 10–5 Free 32, 320 from Cardiff

SKOMER AND SKOKHOLM

www.welshwildlife.org

These two island reserves off the western tip of the Pembrokeshire

mainland are (together with more remote Grassholm Island) among Europe's foremost breeding sites for seabirds. Porpoises and dolphins are regular visitors.

Skokholm has the first bird observatory built in Britain, founded here in the 17th century. Colonies of guillemots, razorbills and storm petrels live here, along with about 160 grey seal pups, born each year around the beaches and caves of the island. Skomer is also where 160,000 pairs of Manx shearwaters live. Ferries leave from Martinshaven (Easter–end Oct). It is also possible to stay on Skokholm (call tourist office for information and contact details).

456 C18 Tourist information, 19 Old Bridge, Haverfordwest SA61 2EZ, tel 01437 763110

SNOWDONIA NATIONAL PARK

www.eryri-npa.gov.uk

Covering a large chunk of northwest Wales, Snowdonia National Park takes its name from Snowdon (1,085m/ 3,560ft), the highest mountain in Wales. This area of wild peaks and lakes draws great numbers of walkers and climbers, and Glyder Fawr, Carnedd Dafydd and Moel Siabod are among the shapely peaks. There are easier walks in the forests around Betws-y-Coed and along the Aberglaslyn Pass near the village of Beddgelert.

Built of sturdy stone around a spacious square, Dolgellau, near looming Cader Idris), is the only town situated inside the national park. Other towns lying close to the park boundary include the historic castle towns of Conwy and Caernarfon, the noteworthy Victorian seaside resort and town of Llandudno and Blaenau Ffestiniog, in its industrial setting amid mountains of slate scraps. Something not to be missed, and beloved by all is the Snowdon Mountain Railway which goes from Llanberis to the mount's summit.

460 E15 Snowdonia National Park Authority, Penrhyndeudraeth LL48 6LF, tel 01766 770274

Above *Sunrise over Swansea's working docks*

SWANSEA
www.visitswanseabay.com
This industrial city on the south coast boasts two fine museums, virtually adjacent in the regenerated dockland district. The National Waterfront Museum (daily 10–5, admission free) opened in time for the 200th anniversary of Nelson's victory at Trafalgar in 1805. The theme is mostly industrial history—Nelson's fleet was kitted out with copper hulls and cannonballs from the city's giant metal manufacturers, and a focal point among the modern interactive displays is a tin-plate rolling mill. The nearby Swansea Museum (Tue–Sun, 10–5, free) tells the city's own story, with floating exhibits as well as graphic accounts of the Blitz in World War II (▷ 41), the Mumbles lifeboat and Cape Horn coal trade.
➕ 456 E18 🚹 Plymouth Street, Swansea SA1 3QG, tel 01792 468321; 🕐 Mon–Sat 9.30–5.30 (and also Easter–Sep Sun 10–4)

TENBY
www.virtualtenby.co.uk
Sections of its 13th-century wall, notably the fine Five Arches gateway, still stand around this cheerful harbour town and resort whose beaches make it a popular choice with families. Georgian houses crowd around the harbour, where a 19th-century fort can be seen on St. Catherine's Island (which can be reached on foot at low tide). The Tudor Merchant's House (Mar–end Oct Sun–Fri 11–5) is a restored building dating from the late 15th century. The boat trip (Easter–end Oct, weather dependent) to Caldey Island is fun. Since 1929 it's been home to a Cistercian community that has restored the medieval monastery. The monks make perfumes, craft items and honey and sell them in the monastery shop.
➕ 456 D18 🚹 Upper Park Road, Tenby SA70 7LT, tel 01834 842402 🚉 Tenby

TREDEGAR HOUSE
www.newport.gov.uk
Regarded as the finest Restoration (dating from the 1660s) house in Wales, Tredegar was the seat for 500 years of the Morgan family, and they had it built in red brick around two sides of a courtyard. One wing survives from the 15th-century building, while interior highlights include the Brown Room, completely furnished in 17th-century oak, and the King's Room, furnished as it was in the 1930s and 1940s, when it was occupied by Evan Morgan, the last member of the family to live here. The unusual window sundial has two painted flies.
➕ 457 F18 ✉ Newport NP10 8YW ☎ 01633 815880 🕐 Easter–end Sep Wed–Sun 11–4 👋 Adult £6.05, child (under 15) free 🍴 🔲 🏛

TREFRIW WOOLLEN MILLS
www.t-w-m.co.uk
The busy clatter of machinery makes it clear that this is very much a working mill. It has been owned by the same family for more than 140 years and they make traditional tapestry-style, double-weave products on machinery dating from the 1950s and 1960s. You can see the weaving process and the hydroelectric turbines that replaced the waterwheels in the 1930s and 1940s. Beautiful, hard-to-resist rugs, bedspreads, cushions, scarves and skirts are all for sale in the shop.
➕ 460 E14 ✉ Trefriw LL27 0NQ ☎ 01492 640462 🕐 Mon–Sat 9.30–5.30, Sun 10–5.30. Weaving and upper floors: Mon–Fri 10–5 👋 Free 🔲 🏛

WELSH WILDLIFE CENTRE
The nature reserve here covers woods, meadows, reedbeds and marshes along the River Teifi, as well as a former slate quarry and former railway bed. The diversity of habitats gives rise to an abundance of wildlife, including otters and one of the largest British colonies of Cetti's warblers. The limestone plantlife features rare species. For birdwatching make for the treetop hide; for children there's a wildlife adventure playground.
➕ 460 D17 ✉ Cilgerran, near Cardigan SA43 2TB ☎ 01239 621600 🕐 Easter–end Sep daily 10–5. Reserve open daily, all year 10.30–5 👋 Included in car-parking charges: £3 per car 🔲 🏛

YNYSLAS
www.ccw.gov.uk
Seven species of orchid grow in the dunes on this fine section of coastline north of Aberystwyth (▷ 225). The reserve juts out into the watery expanses of the Dovey estuary, looking across to Aberdovey and the southern border of Snowdonia National Park (▷ 237).

It is fascinating to watch how the dunes are constantly changing as they shift in the wind. The visitor complex explains how the dunes are formed, gives information on the indigenous wildlife and conducts walks through the reserve.
➕ 460 E16 🚹 Ynyslas Information Centre, c/o Countryside Council for Wales, Plas Gogerddan, Aberystwyth SY23 3EE, tel 01970 871640 🕐 Apr–end Sep daily 9.30–5.30 👋 Freeconwy

WYE VALLEY
▷ 239.

WYE VALLEY

The River Wye builds up to a glorious finale as it meanders through the steep-sided wooded Wye Valley, at its best in autumn when the leaves turn russet red. The Wye Valley was once busy with charcoal burning which supplied local ironworks. During the latter years of the 18th century the valley became popular with Romantic poets in their quest for a deeper appreciation of nature.

MONMOUTH

This small market town of Georgian and older buildings stands where the Monnow flows into the River Wye. The Monnow itself is spanned by a uniquely designed 13th-century fortified bridge. The arcaded Shire Hall dominates the marketplace, Agincourt Square, while Monmouth Castle was the birthplace of Henry V (1387–1422). East of town rises The Kymin, a hill with fine views and two Georgian follies, both of which are owned by the National Trust.

William Wordsworth's poem *Composed a Few Miles above Tintern Abbey* was inspired by the majestic ruins of Tintern Abbey (Apr–end May and Oct daily 9.30–5; Jun–end Sep daily 9.30–6; Nov–end Mar Mon–Sat 9.30–4, Sun 11–4). Although turned into a roofless shell during the Dissolution of the Monasteries under Henry VIII, parts of the 12th- to 13th-century Cistercian abbey stand at their original height, notably the abbey church, where elaborate window tracery survives. The Cistercians tended to choose beautiful settings for the sites of their abbeys, and this is no exception, with lovely views along the gorge. Further south, the Wynd Cliff gives expansive views over the area.

CHEPSTOW

Guarding a vital crossing point into Wales and at the foot of the hilly town of Chepstow, the impressive fortress of Chepstow Castle (Apr–end May and Oct daily 9.30–5; Jun–end Sep daily 9.30–6; Nov–end Mar Mon–Sat 9.30–4, Sun 11–4) was built in 1067 as the Norman invaders pushed westwards. The stone keep is original, but the towers, walls and gatehouses were added later.

INFORMATION

www.monmouth.org.uk
✚ 457 G17–18 ℹ Shire Hall, Agincourt Square, Monmouth NP25 3DY, tel 01600 713899 🚂 Chepstow

TIPS

» The best of the walks through the gorge are along the waymarked Offa's Dyke Path and (lower level) Wye Valley Walk.

» There's a good viewpoint overlooking a huge loop of the river at Symonds Yat, northeast of Monmouth.

Above *Looking along the Wye Valley from Symonds Yat*

BRECON BEACONS NATIONAL PARK

From the literary town of Hay-on-Wye this upland tour takes in some magnificent scenery around the Black Mountains, one of the national park's four distinct areas.

THE DRIVE
Distance: 91 miles (147km)
Allow: 4–5 hours
Start/end: Hay-on-Wye

★ Hay-on-Wye stands high above the south bank of the River Wye. Welsh rebel leader Owain Glyndwr (c1350–1416) destroyed its castle during the 15th century, but the keep, some parts of the walls and a gateway remain. The town's cinema has become the world's biggest second-hand bookshop; in fact the whole town seems to be taken up with second-hand books. Appropriately, Hay hosts a world-famous literary festival every summer attracting thousands.

From Hay drive southwest for 8 miles (13km) along the B4350 and A438 to Bronllys.

❶ From Bronllys there are clear views of the Brecon Beacons ahead and the Black Mountains, which dominate the scenery to the left. The 12th-century church here, now rebuilt, has a distinctive detached tower. Bronllys Castle (open access) is 0.5 mile (800m) along the A479.

From Bronllys continue along the A438 and A470. Turn right on to the B4602 to Brecon.

❷ At the confluence of the rivers Usk and Honddu, Brecon is a magnet for walkers. East of town is the terminus of the Monmouth and Brecon Canal, and to the south is the Brecon Beacons National Park. The city's cathedral dates mainly from the 13th and 14th centuries. The Brecon Cathedral Heritage Centre in the converted tithe barn traces the history of the priory. Brecon Castle is now in the grounds of the Castle Hotel. The County Hall houses the Brecknock Museum of Local History and nearby the South Wales Borderers Museum has relics from the Zulu War of 1879 to World War II and later.

From Brecon continue southwards along the A470 towards Merthyr Tydfil and the heights of the Brecon Beacons. At Libanus, a right-hand dead-end turn leads up to the Brecon Beacons Mountain Centre.

❸ The Mountain Centre makes an ideal introduction to the park. There are easy walks around the common that surrounds the centre, with views of the highest parts of the park.

Before reaching Merthyr Tydfil turn on to an unclassified road north to Pontsticill.

❹ Walking and boating are major attractions in this area, as well as the Brecon Mountain Railway, which runs for 4 miles (6.5km) up the valley through unspoiled scenery.

Continue on unclassified roads past Talybont Reservoir to the village of Talybont-on-Usk.

5 Talybont-on-Usk is now a base for walkers and outdoor activities, with the Outdoor Education Centre in the old train station.

6 The 18th-century Monmouthshire and Brecon Canal, which passes through the village, was built to carry coal and iron ore. It closed in 1962, but was reopened by volunteers in 1970 for use by pleasure craft.

From Talybont-on-Usk, follow the B4558 to Llangynidr, then the B4560 and an unclassified road to Crickhowell.

7 The name Crickhowell is derived from the Iron Age fort Crug Hywel ('Hywel's cairn'). The town grew up around Alisby's Castle, which was captured and destroyed by Owain Glyndwr in 1403 and is now a ruin. The River Usk is crossed by an old bridge dating from the 17th century, which appears to have 13 arches on one side but only 12 on the other— the result of 19th-century alterations.

From Crickhowell take the A40 to Abergavenny.

8 At the edge of the Brecon Beacons National Park, Abergavenny is overlooked by the Sugar Loaf mountain, 596m (1,955ft) high, and Ysgyryd (Skirrid) Fawr (488m/1,601ft). The castle, now in ruins, was founded in 1090.

From Abergavenny take the A465 northeast towards Pontrilas. At Llanvihangel Crucorney turn left on an unclassified road to Hay-on-Wye via Llanthony.

9 This route leads up through the wild, remote scenery of the Black Mountains, past the ruins of Llanthony Priory (▷ 227), where a hotel occupies the former refectory and whose pub in the vaulted cellar is one of the most architecturally unusual in Wales. The road climbs to the top of Gospel Pass (542m/ 1,778ft) for a sweeping view into mid-Wales; you can get even higher by walking up the nearby summit of Hay Bluff (676m/2,217ft), to the right of the summit parking area.

Continue down the steep gradient back to Hay-on-Wye.

PLACES TO VISIT
ABERGAVENNY CASTLE
✉ Castle Street, Abergavenny NP7 5EE
☎ 01873 854282
🕐 Mar–end Oct daily 11–5; Nov–end Feb Mon–Sat
✋ Free

BRECKNOCK MUSEUM
✉ Captain's Walk, Brecon LD3 7DW
☎ 01874 624121
🕐 Apr–end Sep daily 10–5; rest of year Mon–Sat
✋ Adult £1, child (under 15) free

BRECON CATHEDRAL HERITAGE CENTRE
✉ Cathedral Close, Brecon LD3 9DP
☎ 01874 625222
🕐 Mon–Sat 10.30–4, Sun 12.30–4
✋ Free

BRECON MOUNTAIN RAILWAY
✉ Pant Station, Merthyr Tydfil CF48 2UP
☎ 01685 722988
🕐 Visit www.breconmountainrailway.co.uk for timetable
✋ Adult £8.50, child (3–15) £4.25

SOUTH WALES BORDERERS MUSEUM
✉ The Barracks, Brecon LD3 7EB
☎ 01874 613311
🕐 Daily 10–5, Sat–Sun 10–4
✋ Adult £3, child (under 16) free

WHERE TO EAT
Oscar's, High Town, Hay-on-Wye (tel: 01497 821193) is a bistro with salad bar and home-made cakes. Both the White Swan Inn (tel 01874 665276) and the Felin Fach Griffin are outstanding pubs in Brecon.

WHEN TO GO
The summer months offer long days and the chance of sunnier weather; perfect for active days in the National Park.

Opposite *Looking down on to the Talybont Reservoir*

LLANGORSE LAKE

The crannog (artificial island) in Llangorse Lake is thought to be the ancient seat of the kings of Brycheiniog. This walk circumnavigates the lake before a modest ascent offers striking views of the Brecon Beacons (▷ 227).

THE WALK
Distance: 8 miles (13km)
Allow: 4 hours
Start/end: Parking area beside public toilets, between caravan park and sailing club, map ref 434 F17
OS Landranger map: 160
OS Explorer map: OL13

★ Nestling beneath the Mynydd Llangorse (Llangorse mountain), and overlooked by the shapely Mynydd Troeg, is Llangorse Lake. This shallow lake is popular with watersports enthusiasts and attracts plenty of birdwatchers too.

From the parking area, aim for a concrete footbridge to the left of the caravan park on Llangorse Common. Go diagonally left.

❶ Soon you can see the crannog, the only known example in Wales, a few paces from the shore. Its access causeway has long since disappeared, and today there is (to the uninitiated) nothing to see—just a clump of reeds on a pile of stones. But it is rather more than that. The perimeter of this little island is made of pointed oak piles, hewn using a metal adze (an early chisel). The crannog is thought to have supported early medieval dwellings. In 1925 a dugout canoe, dated at around AD800, was found nearby; it's now kept in the Brecknock Museum in Brecon (▷ 240).

When the Mercians (English) invaded parts of Wales from about AD850, this site—thought to be the heart of the kingdom of Brycheiniog ('land of Brychan')—did not escape their attention. These words are anglicized to Brecknock and Brecon; the name Brecon Beacons is still commonly used, while Brecknock is an alternative name for the old county of Breconshire. According to legend, the lake conceals an ancient city; its Welsh name, Llyn Syfaddan, means 'lake of the sunken island'.

Cross more fields, skirting the lake, to reach the church of St. Gastyn at Llangasty-Talyllyn.

❷ The 'llan' prefix, meaning church, is very common in Wales. This name translates as 'the church of St. Gastyn at the end of the lake'.

Turn right. After Llan (a house) take a waymarked footpath on the left. Soon there will be a hedge to your left. Turn right and cross two fields diagonally to a sunken lane, to the left of a farm. Turn right and take the minor road.

Go left. Take the first left turn, signed Cathedine 0.5 mile (1km). Turn right beside Rectory Cottage. Take stiles through three fields; cross the fourth field diagonally to the B4560 (beware of traffic as you emerge on to this road). Turn right along it for 50m (55 yards), then take a rough track to the right of some farm buildings.

F17

❸ The village of Llangors consists of little more than a sinuous road, a church, chapel, shop and sub-post office, and a couple of pubs. At its heart is the church of St. Paulinus, on the site of a sixth-century building.

At a blind corner immediately before the churchyard, take a narrow signed footpath beside a house. Cross fields to return to the start of the walk.

WHERE TO EAT
The Red Lion Hotel at Llangorse is an old village pub serving hot meals. (tel 01874 658238).

PLACES TO VISIT
ST GASTYN CHURCH
✉ Llangasty, Brecon LD3 7PX
☎ 01874 658298
🕐 Mon–Sun 9–5

WHEN TO GO
The lake is a mini hotspot for watersports enthusiasts on summer weekends, and also attracts its fair share of birdwatchers.

Opposite *The thatched roof of a crannog on Llangorse Lake*
Below left *Sailing boats on the lake*
Below right *Golden-ringed dragonflies are a common sight in the area*

Take a less distinct track (marked by a blue arrow) before the ford, ascending along the left-hand side of a lightly wooded stream. In an eroded gully find a gate up to the left. Follow this sunken lane until it peters out.

Turn left, above a fence and broken wall, then go through an old gate (blue waymarker) to pass a farmhouse ruin. Continue on a path, now through bracken, until 50m (55 yards) before the track descends to a gate.

Turn sharp right, uphill, on a zigzagging green path. Turn left at a fence, then left again at a fence corner. Descend to a converted barn. Continue along the field's left edge. Go down to a gate among larch trees, beside an old wall.

Walk through the forest, back into bracken. About 90m (100 yards) beyond a stream crossing, descend beside a farm track, taking the line of greatest slope down the field to the riding and climbing centre below.

Turn right, then right again towards Cae-cottrel farm. Take a stile on the left. Skirt this field to the left. Pass into the next field through a gap in the hedgerow, skirting left again, to farm buildings and a track.

Turn right, following the lanes to Llangors.

PEMBROKESHIRE COAST NATIONAL PARK

The magnificent coastline of the Pembrokeshire Coast National Park can be elusive, as the roads tend to steer inland and away from the sweeping beachesalong the coast. This route glimpses some of the most scenic stretches, but the best way to explore is to walk a section of the Pembrokeshire Coast Path, which weaves along the seaboard.

THE DRIVE
Distance: 108 miles (172km)
Allow: Half a day
Start/end: Tenby,

★ On this drive you will see castles, historic towns and sense the primeval-feeling Preseli Hills.

Leave Tenby on the A4139, then turn left on to the B4585 to Manorbier.

❶ Manorbier was the birthplace of the medieval explorer and scholar Giraldus Cambrensis (c1146–1223)—locally known as Gerald of Wales—who described it as 'the pleasantest spot in Wales'.

Return to the A4139 for 5 miles (8km) to Lamphey.

❷ The romantic ruins of a 13th-century Bishop's Palace lie to the northeast of Lamphey. The palace originated as a country retreat for the bishops of St. David's (▷ 237), and has ornate parapets, fish ponds and a 16th-century chapel.

Continue along the A4139 for a further 2 miles (3km) to get to Pembroke.

❸ The ancient town of Pembroke was built around the 12th- to 13th-century Pembroke Castle, the birthplace of Henry VII (1457–1509). It still has its fine circular keep, and beneath it is a huge natural cavern known as The Wogan.

Head north towards Haverfordwest, picking up the A477 to cross the estuary.

❹ The estuary forms part of the huge natural harbour of Milford Haven, with its oil refineries. This part is the most industrialized stretch, but farther west there are some isolated headlands such as St. Ann's Head near Dale and Wooltack Point, overlooking the bird reserve of Skomer Island, west of Marloes.

On the far side of the bridge turn right on to an unclassified road, through Burton, Port Lion and Llangwm.

❺ Along these back roads you get glimpses of the wide rivers and the labyrinth of tidal creeks that drain into Milford Haven and form part of the national park. The Western and Eastern Cleddau rivers merge just above the village of Llangwm.

Carry on past Hook, along back roads, to Haverfordwest. At the roundabout on the south side of town pick up signs for St. David's, leading northwest on the A487.

6 The 12th-century castle on the hill above Haverfordwest is now a ruin. There is more history close by at Castle House, the location of the town museum.

Continue on the A487 to Solva, where the road dips into a steep-sided valley. Solva, once a busy port where steamships embarked for points as far as America, is a thriving sailing village today. Proceed along the A487 to St. David's.

7 The smallest cathedral city in Britain, St. David's was founded by an early Christian community. The cathedral stands next to the ruins of the Bishop's Palace. West of St. David's, Whitesands Bay is an excellent swimming beach, and the starting point for walks to St. David's Head, where you can sometimes see the Irish coast.

Take the A487 towards Fishguard but, before the edge of St. David's, turn left on the B4583 towards Whitesands Bay. At the first junction

stay on an unclassified road heading past Trevine, and carry on through the tiny coastal village of Abercastle.

8 Just west of Abercastle, at Longhouse Farm, Carreg Sampson is a 5,000-year-old burial chamber comprising massive stones.

At Abercastle follow the road as it turns right inland, continue through Mathry and turn left on the A487 to Fishguard.

9 Fishguard has two parts. Upper Fishguard stands back from the sea; from there the road falls steeply to Lower Fishguard, a quaint and largely unspoiled town. Ferries leave here for Rosslare in Ireland.

From Fishguard stick to the A487 and head east to Newport.

10 Just outside Newport is the Pembrokeshire Candle Centre, where you can see handmade candles being produced. The remains of Newport's 12th-century castle can still be seen behind the main street. Southeast of town, reached by back lanes, Pentre Ifan

burial chamber is one of the finest Neolithic monuments of its type in Wales.

Continue along the A487. On the left, signposted from the road, is Castell Henllys.

11 At Iron Age Castell Henllys, reconstructed thatched circular huts show the life of the original residents.

Turn right on the B4329 towards Haverfordwest. This road rises up on to the main ridge of the Preseli Hills.
　Turn left on the B4313 to Narbeth. From here head south on the A478, then turn right on the A4115 to Cross Hands and turn left on the A4075 to Carew. South of Carew turn left on the A477 and then right on the B4318 back to Tenby.

PLACES TO VISIT
BISHOP'S PALACE
✉ Cathedral Close, St. David's SA62 6PE
☎ 01437 720517
🕐 Daily 9.30–6
💷 Adult £2.50, child (under 18) £2

CASTELL HENLLYS
✉ Pany Glas, Meline, Crymych SA41 3UT
☎ 01239 891319
🕐 Apr–end Oct daily 10–5
💷 Adult £3, child £2, family £8

PEMBROKE CASTLE
✉ Main Street, Pembroke SA71 4LA
☎ 01646 681510
🕐 Daily 9.30–6
💷 Adult £3, child £2, family £8

PEMBROKESHIRE CANDLE CENTRE
✉ The Cilgwyn Candles, Trefelin, Cilgwyn, Newport SA42 0QN
☎ 01239 820470
🕐 Easter–end Oct daily 11–5; Nov–Dec 12–4
💷 Free

Opposite *Carew Castle, the ruined shell of a medieval fortress-turned-Elizabethan mansion*

STRUMBLE HEAD AND THE FRENCH INVASION

This glorious stretch of coastline is so well endowed with heady scenery and the promise of seals and dolphins that the drama of its history seems superfluous. But this is the place where Britain confronted her last invaders.

THE WALK

Length: 6 miles (10km)

Allow: 3 hours

Start/end: parking area opposite Strumble Head lighthouse, map ref 433 C17

OS Landranger map: 157

OS Explorer map: OL35

★ Each headland and inlet of the beautiful and dramatic Pembrokeshire National Path has its own story. At Strumble Head the French invaded Britain but got too drunk on contraband liquor to fight.

From the parking area at Strumble Head, turn right, away from the lighthouse, and walk with the sea on your left. When the road turns right, inland, cross a stile on the left-hand side to proceed along the signposted coast path. Descend almost to sea level at the bay of Porth Sychan.

❶ The French invasion of 1797 boasts its own tapestry, housed at Fishguard, but this is the only thing it has in common with the more successful venture at Hastings in 1066 (▷ 30). Led to believe that the Welsh peasants were ready to rise up against the English Crown, a company of 1,400 French troops landed in Pembrokeshire on 22 February 1797. They weren't crack troops, but mostly convicts under the leadership of an Irish-American colonel, and issued with four days' food and double rations of brandy.

Continue along the signposted coast path. It's important to ignore paths going inland on your right; they lead to farm tracks. Cross several footbridges, keeping the sea on your left. Climb to pass the site of St. Degan's Chapel. Ignore a signposted path going inland before crossing a footbridge at Penrhyn. Keep the sea on your left until you reach the memorial to the French invasion at Carregwastad Point.

❷ They landed at Carregwastad Point, on a calm, moonlit night, after the alarm had been raised at Fishguard, a little farther along the coast.

Bear right with the coast path and cross the first stile after the memorial. Turn right here to leave the coast path and take another signposted path, which begins with

the sea to your right, up through the gorse shrubs, then swings left inland to reach a marked post near a wall. Turn right, keeping the wall on your left in a second field. Cross a stile beside a gate to follow a lane. This bends left. Continue inland, ignoring another green lane on your right. Pass through a gate, ignoring another track signposted on your left, shortly before bearing right to Tre-Howel Farm.

❸ The invaders made their headquarters at Tre-Howel Farm and eagerly set about drinking Portuguese wine salvaged from a shipwreck the previous month. By the afternoon of 24 February most were helplessly drunk. And Lord Cawdor had already assembled 575 local men to save the kingdom. Tradition has it that it was the appearance of Jemima Nicholas and her cloaked and bonneted female companions that persuaded the French soldiers to surrender. The ladies circled the invaders from the hillsides; their red cloaks may have been mistaken for defenders' uniforms.

Take Tre-Howel's access drive through the yard and then turn left up a quiet road and turn right to enjoy sweeping views over the sea on your right.

❹ The French lost 20 soldiers in early skirmishes and drownings. The only Welsh casualty was a woman killed accidentally when a pistol was being loaded. The centenary of the invasion was marked by a monument on Carregwastad Point. Strumble Head lighthouse was built on Ynys Meicel in 1908.

Bear right at a fork to follow the road down to Strumble Head's lighthouse. Ignore a drive for Llanwnwr Farm on your left. Return to the parking area to the left.

Opposite *Strumble Head lighthouse*
Above *The memorial at Carregwastad Point marks the spot of the last hostile invasion of Britain*

WHERE TO EAT
There are several pubs, cafés and shops in Fishguard, but no places to buy food along the walk.

PLACE TO VISIT
MELIN TREGWYNT MILL
✉ Castlemorris, Haverfordwest, Pembrokeshire SA62 5UX
☎ 01348 891288 ⏰ Mon–Fri 9–4.30, Sat 10–5, Sun 11.30–4.30

WHEN TO GO
Avoid windy or wet weather that can create treacherous walking conditions and make route-finding more difficult.

TIPS
» Avoid straying inland from the path before the memorial because there is a confusing network of paths through the muddy fields between the coast and the lane.
» If you lose the path inland, retrace your steps back to the coast path rather than try navigating to Tre-Howel farm.
» Strumble Head is signposted from the steep road up from Fishguard, but don't continue to the very end of the track as turning becomes difficult. Park opposite the lighthouse; you can walk across the causeway.

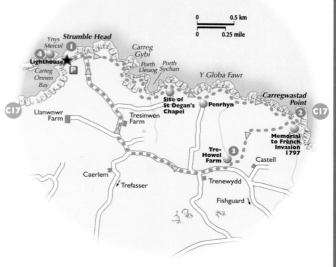

SNOWDONIA NATIONAL PARK

Although driving can be a little limited in Wales's largest and most dramatic national park (▷ 237), this tour of the principality's extensive mountainous region has plenty to offer.

THE DRIVE

Distance: 73 miles (117km)
Allow: 4 hours
Start/end: Snowdonia National Park

★ From the information office turn right on to the A5 and head north along this road through Betws-y-Coed.

❶ The route passes the entrance to Swallow Falls on the right. This waterfall has an attractive sylvan setting, making it one of the most frequented beauty spots in Snowdonia.

Continue along the A5, past the strange Tŷ Hyll (Ugly House), said to have been built overnight—traditionally a way of claiming freehold rights. Continue on the A5 past Capel Curig and Llyn (lake) Ogwen. From the parking area at the far end of Llyn Ogwen a short path leads to Llyn Idwal, beneath the vast crags of the Devil's Kitchen.

❷ Llyn Idwal, a popular haunt of rock climbers, was where Idwal, son of the 12th-century Prince of Gwynedd, was pushed to a watery end by his jealous cousin.

Still on the A5, on entering Bethesda (after about 4 miles/6.5km) turn left on to the B4409. The road passes the spoil heaps of a slate quarry and continues through the village of Tregarth. Turn left (signed Caernarfon/Llanberis) on to the B4366 and continue to a roundabout. Take the first exit for Llanberis on the B4547 and presently turn left on to the A4086, which takes you in to Llanberis itself.

❸ Llanberis (▷ 233) is the site of the Welsh Slate Museum as well as the base station of the Snowdon Mountain Railway, which carries passengers to the summit of Snowdon.

From Llanberis, carry on along the A4086 up the Llanberis Pass.

❹ As the road leaves Llanberis the grey slateworks loom up over Llyn Peris, site of the Electric Mountain, which conducts underground tours into Dinorwig Power Station, built into Elidir mountain.

❺ The route now winds through dramatic craggy scenery and over the Llanberis Pass for views of the valley below. At the top of the Llanberis Pass, the Miners' Track and Pyg Track provide exciting ascents of the mountain. To get superb close-up views of Snowdon without making an ascent, walk the first section of the Miners' Track along a well-graded path, past two lakes and as far as Glaslyn lake, then return the same way.

Not long after crossing the pass the road reaches a T-junction. Turn right on to the A498 for Beddgelert. There are more outstanding views as the road descends to pass Llyn Gwynant, a long lake at the foot of

Y Lliwedd. Continue along the road to Beddgelert, passing the Sygun Copper Mine on the left.

6 Beddgelert is a popular walkers' village crammed with hotels and eateries and always busy in high season.

From Beddgelert, turn left over the stone bridge by the Prince Llywelyn Pub and follow the road (A498) past the Royal Goat Hotel and along the Pass of Aberglaslyn, where the Afon (River) Glaslyn follows the road at the foot of Moel y Dyniewyd. Continue along the road as it twists higher above the river. Just as the landscape begins to open out take the left turning on to the B4410 (signed Llanfrothen/Garreg). Follow this road as it crosses the river and continues (with fine mountain views) to a crossroads. Turn right and then left, following signs for Tan-y-Bwlch/ Ffestiniog Railway and continuing on the B4410.

7 The road climbs through woodland with good views over Porthmadog before it reaches Rhyd.

From here the route winds over the craggy uplands, then drops through a pine forest and past Tan-y-Bwlch, a station on the Ffestiniog Railway.

At the A487 turn left (signed Dolgellau) and, after crossing the bridge, turn left again on to the A496 (signed Blaenau Ffestiniog). Fork left, staying on the A496 and following signs for Blaenau Ffestiniog. Soon Blaenau Ffestiniog comes into view and the road passes a left turn to the hydroelectric power station at Tanygrisiau. At the roundabout take the first exit (A470) for Betws-y-Coed.

8 The road leads past Llechwedd Slate Caverns and the, grey heaps of slate that dominate this area.

9 To the left of the road there is access to Dolwyddelan Castle.

The A496 continues as a scenic mountain route. At the next major junction, take the left turn on to the A470 and keep left on the A5, crossing the bridge into Betws-y-Coed to return to the starting point of the drive.

PLACES TO VISIT
DOLWYDDELAN CASTLE
✉ Betws-y-Coed
☎ 01690 750366
🕐 Apr–end Nov daily 9.30–6.30; rest of year Mon–Sat 9.30–4, Sun 11–4
💷 Adult £2, child £1.50

ELECTRIC MOUNTAIN
✉ Llanberis LL55 4RU
☎ 01286 870636
🕐 Jun–end Aug daily 9.30–5.30; Apr– end May, Sep–end Oct 10.30–4.30; Oct–end Nov, Feb–end Mar Wed–Sun 10.30–4.30
💷 Tours: adult £6.50, child £3.25, family £16

LLECHWEDD SLATE CAVERNS
✉ Blaenau Ffestiniog LL41 3NB
☎ 01766 830306
🕐 Mar–end Oct daily 10–5.15; Nov–end Mar 10–4.15
💷 Tours, adult £8.75, child £6.50

SNOWDON MOUNTAIN RAILWAY
www.snowdonrailway.co.uk
✉ Llanberis LL55 4TY
☎ 0870 4580033
🕐 Mid-Mar to end Nov daily, every 30 min
💷 Return fare, adult £20, child £14

WHERE TO EAT
Plas Derwen, Holyhead Road, Betws-y-Coed (tel 01690 710388) for snacks and meals.

WHEN TO GO
Save this lovely drive for a fine, clear day when you will be able to appreciate the awesome views from Llanberis Pass.

Opposite *The village of Beddgelert has been famous for the grave of Gelert, the brave hound supposedly killed in a rage by his master, Prince Llywelyn*

SNOWDON AND THE WATKIN PATH

Even at its lower levels, this walk encounters some of the most varied and spectacular scenery in Snowdonia (▷ 237).

THE WALK
Length: 4 miles (6.5km)
Allow: 2 hours
Start/end: Parking area at Pont Bethania, on A498 between Capel Curig and Beddgelert, map ref 433 E15
OS Explorer map: OL17

★ This glorious route follows the path named after Sir Edward Watkin—a Victorian railway magnate and Liberal politician who gave the trail to the nation after his retirement.

From the parking area cross the bridge and follow the road towards Beddgelert for 45m (50 yards), then cross it to reach a signed path. Cross the cattle grid and follow the tarmac lane away from the road, with a river on the right and woodland on the left.

❶ The ancient oak woods of Parc Hafod-y-Llan once stretched far up Cwm Llan, but were cleared for mining and sheep-rearing.

Leave the tarmac lane at the footpath sign, bearing left through a gate on a rough track, with a wall on the left. Go ahead through gates and follow the track as it climbs to reach a wooden gate above the waterfalls.

❷ After heavy rain these falls are among the most spectacular in the national park.

The wooden gate allows access to Snowdon National Nature Reserve. Within the reserve this track runs near the river. Continue past ruined copper mines and cross a bridge of massive sleepers over the river. Pass more ruins and a tall cypress tree. Ahead now is the bulky rock outcrop of Gladstone Rock.

❸ This rock was where W. E. Gladstone gave an address to the people of Snowdonia on 13 September 1892, when he was 83 and prime minister for the fourth time. The event, held to commemorate the opening of the Watkin Path, took place in pouring rain, but Gladstone asked for an encore from the choir that Sir Edward Watkin had organized.

Past Gladstone's Rock, the track continues into Cwm Llan, eventually bearing right by old slate quarry buildings. Y Lliwedd, towering ahead, and Yr Aran, to the left, form the vast walls of the valley.

❹ Above the quarry buildings the track gives superb views of Snowdon to the left and Y Lliwedd to the right, with Bwlch y Saethau and Bwlch Ciliau between them. Bwlch y Saethau (the Pass of the Arrows) is the legendary site of King Arthur's last battle against Mordred, his treacherous nephew.

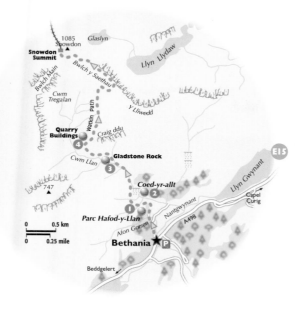

WHERE TO EAT

There are no refreshment places on this route, but there is a café at the summit of Snowdon.

PLACE TO VISIT

SNOWDON MOUNTAIN RAILWAY

✉ Llanberis LL55 4TY

☎ 0870 4580033

🕐 Mid-Mar to end Nov daily, every 30 min, www.snowdonrailway.co.uk

✋ Return fare, adult £20, child £14

WHEN TO GO

A bright, still day with good visibility. If you want to walk in peace avoid the weekends.

If you are not ascending to the summit of Snowdon, retrace your steps at this point to return to the starting point.

If you wish to walk up to the summit, the path climbs steeply up to the left, eventually reaching a saddle and continuing northwest (even more steeply) to the summit. From the top there are several ways down, and you do not need to retrace your steps (frequent buses connect various trailheads around the mountain in summer; details are available at the local tourist information offices).

The easiest (but least interesting) way down is alongside the rail track to Llanberis. More spectacular are the Pyg Track and Miners' Track that head east to Pen-y-Pass parking area on the A4086. The Snowdon Ranger Path heads west from the summit to the A4085. The notoriously vertiginous Snowdon Horseshoe takes in knife-edge ridges and the ridge of Crib Goch, and is definitely not for the faint-hearted. Alternatively, you can take the Snowdon Mountain Railway down.

SAFETY

» This is the first part of one of the routes up Snowdon. You can turn round after the quarry buildings (point 4), where the main ascent up Wales' highest mountain begins, or continue to the top.

» Although many people tackle Snowdon each weekend, it is full of dangers and you should only climb to the top if you have a good level of fitness and are wearing walking boots with good, gripping soles. Part of the path involves clambering over boulders and is very uneven, and descending from the top must be done with care (although the Snowdon Mountain Railway is an option when operating). Mobile phones may not have a signal and should not be relied upon to call for help.

» It is important to check the weather forecast before venturing out, and be aware that the summit is often shrouded in cloud, and that weather conditions can change very suddenly.

» Take OS Explorer map OL17 and a compass, allow plenty of time, and carry spare clothing, food and drink.

Opposite *View from the summit of Snowdon to Crib Goch (on the left) and Moel Siabod (in the distance)*
Below *Looking out towards the Glyderau mountain range and Y Garn*

ABERGAVENNY

SKIRRID INN
www.skirridmountaininn.co.uk
Celebrated for its food, this pub is said to be the oldest in Wales, dating back to the 12th century.
✉ Llanfihangel Crucorney, Abergavenny NP7 8DH T ☎ 01873 890258 🕐 Mon 5.30pm–11pm, Tue–Fri 11.30–3, 5.30pm–11pm; Sat 11.30–11; Sun noon–5.30

ABERYSTWYTH

SIOP Y PETHE
An established stockist of Welsh-language books, CDs and other items, including publications of prize-winning eisteddfod literature.
✉ 17 Rhodfa'r Gogledd, Aberystwyth SY23 2JH ☎ 01970 617120 🕐 Mon–Sat 9–5 (sometimes later) 🚉 Aberystwyth

ABERYSTWYTH ARTS CENTRE
www.aberystwythartscentre.co.uk
Theatre, concert hall, cinema, various galleries and shops, all located on the university campus.

✉ The University of Wales, Penglais Campus, Aberystwyth SY23 3DE ☎ 01970 623232 🕐 Box office: Mon–Sat 10–8, Sun 1.30–5.30 🖐 Various 🍴 ⬜ 🅿 🚉 Aberystwyth

BETWS-Y-COED

BRYN TYRCH HOTEL
www.bryntyrch-hotel.co.uk
Traditional pub with beamed bar. Specializes in vegetarian and wholefood meals and has some accommodation. Within sight of Snowdon, and popular with walkers.
✉ Capel Curig, Betws-y-Coed LL24 0EL ☎ 01690 720223 🕐 Daily 12–11

BRECON

MOUNTAIN AND WATER
www.mountainandwater.co.uk
The Wye Valley is an accessible and highly rated destination for paddle sports, running through 150 miles (240km) of striking scenery. Mountain and Water rents canoes and runs rafting trips.

✉ Brecon LL3 ☎ 01873 831825 🖐 Canoe taster days from £65 per day

CAPEL CURIG

PLAS Y BRENIN
www.pyb.co.uk
Rock climbing and mountaineering sessions, canoeing, dry-slope skiing. No children under 8 or unaccompanied children under 10. Same-day booking possible.
✉ Plas y Brenin National Mountain Centre, Capel Curig LL24 0ET ☎ 01690 720214 🕐 All year 🖐 Sample prices: climbing £165–£600, mountaineering/hillwalking £167–£490, kayaking and canoeing £172–£440 🍴

CARDIFF

CASTLE WELSH CRAFTS
Opposite the entrance to Cardiff Castle, this giftshop has good-quality traditional products such as carved love spoons, Celtic-design jewellery, slate carvings and lamps. There are also excellent handmade Welsh-

Left Horse-riding at Druidston, St. Bride's Bay, Pembrokeshire Coast National Park

language cards, artwork by Welsh artists and tapestries.

✉ 1–3 Castle Street, Cardiff CF10 1BS ☎ 029 2034 3038 ◷ Mon–Sat 9–5.30, Sun 10–4 🚉 Cardiff Central

CHAPTER ARTS CENTRE
www.chapter.org

Theatre, dance, film, art exhibitions and workshops, with performances in English and in Welsh.

✉ Market Road, Canton, Cardiff CF5 1QE ☎ 029 2030 4400 ◷ Box office: Mon–Fri 11–8.30, Sat 2–8.30, Sun 3–8.30. Chapter gallery and shop: Tue–Sun 11–8, during exhibitions 👆 Various ▭ 🚉 Cardiff Central

CLWB IFOR BACH
www.clwb.net

Important Welsh-language oriented club, especially keen on local Indi bands—but also catering to a wide range of clubbers' favourite musical tastes.

✉ 11 Womanby Street, Cardiff CF10 1BR ☎ 029 2023 2199 ◷ Mon–Sat 7.30pm– late 👆 Free–£11 🚉 Cardiff Central

COAL EXCHANGE
www.coalexchange.co.uk

This iconic venue at the heart of the rejuvenated Welsh capital saw the world's first recorded million pound business deal in the city's 19th-century coal trading heyday. Closed for major renovation work in 2007 and will reopen in 2009.

✉ Mount Stuart Square, Cardiff CF10 6EB ☎ 029 2049 4917 ◷ Closed until 2009 🚉 Cardiff Central

GLAMORGAN CRICKET CLUB
www.glamorgancricket.com

Welsh cricket's only first-class team hold their own with the English counties.

✉ Sophia Gardens, Cardiff CF1 9XR ☎ 0871 282 3400 ◷ Apr–end Sep 👆 £8–£15

LIQUID-LIFE
www.liquidclubs.com

This branded city-centre super-club

is all lava lamps and light shows. Music is from the dance mainstream with some R&B.

✉ St. Mary's Street, Cardiff CF10 1FA ☎ 029 2064 5464 ◷ Tue, Thu 10pm– 2.30am, Fri 10pm–3am, Sat 10pm–4am 👆 Usually free before 10, then various

MILLENNIUM STADIUM
www.millenniumstadium.com

State-of-the-art sports stadium with retractable roof, hosting major sports and music events.

✉ St. Mary's Street, Cardiff CF10 1GE ☎ 0870 013 8600; ticket hotline 0870 5582582 ◷ Tours (non-match days): Mon– Sat 10–5, Sun 10–4 👆 Tours: adult £6.50, child £4, family £21 🍴 ▭ 🚉 Cardiff Central

NEW THEATRE
www.newtheatrecardiff.co.uk

A traditional theatre—mostly touring English language productions—with gigs and dance.

✉ Park Place, Cardiff CF10 3LN ☎ 029 2087 8889 ◷ Box office: Mon–Sat 10–8 🍴 ▭ ♿ 🚉 Cardiff Queen Street

ST. DAVID'S HALL
www.stdavidshallcardiff.co.uk

Wales' national concert hall, home of the BBC National Orchestra of Wales and a venue for the biennial Cardiff Singer of the World. Pop, rock and classical music, comedy, children's shows and dance.

✉ The Hayes, Cardiff CF10 1SH ☎ 029 2087 8444 ◷ Box office: Mon–Sat 9.30–8 (or 5 if no performance) 👆 Various 🍴 ▭ ♿ 🚉 Cardiff Central

SHERMAN THEATRE
www.shermancymru.co.uk

A mixture of conventional and radical productions, including those by the Sherman Theatre Company.

✉ Senghennydd Road, Cathays, Cardiff CF24 4YE ☎ 029 2064 6900 ◷ Box office: Mon–Sat 10–8 (10–5.30 if no performance) ▭ 🚉 Cardiff Queen Street

CEREDIGION
LLWYNHELYG FARM SHOP

Farm shop with strong emphasis on Welsh produce, including 60 types of cheese.

✉ Sarnau, Llandysul, Ceredigion SA44 6QU ☎ 01239 811079 ◷ Mon–Sat 8.30–6.30, Sun 9.30–1.30

CHEPSTOW
CHEPSTOW RACECOURSE
www.chepstow-racecourse.co.uk

Jumps and flats course hosting Coral Welsh National.

✉ Chepstow NP16 6BE ☎ 01291 622260 ◷ Over 30 meetings a year—some evenings 👆 Members' enclosure £19, public enclosure £14 (under 16s free with paying adult) 🍴 ▭ 🚉 Chepstow

CORWEN
WHITE LION HOTEL (Y LLEW GWYN)

Traditional inn by a village square, with garden, real ales and home-made food; 12 rooms. Live Welsh music Friday.

✉ Cerrigydrudion, Corwen LL21 9SW ☎ 01490 420202 ◷ Mon–Thu 12–11, Fri–Sat 12–12, Sun 12–10.30

DALE
WEST WALES WINDSURF AND SAILING CENTRE
www.surfdale.co.uk

Sailing and watersports centre for all levels of experience in windsurfing, sailing, surfing and kayaking. No children under 8. Advance reservation necessary.

✉ Dale, near Haverfordwest SA62 3RB ☎ 01646 636642 ◷ All year 👆 Rental rates from £5 per hour for surfboards, dinghies and gear

DOLGELLAU
COED Y BRENIN FOREST
www.mbwales.com
www.forestry.gov.uk

One of the world's 25 best moun-tain-biking locations, Coed Y Brenin has many waymarked trails. Bicycle rental available.

✉ Coed Y Brenin, Dolgellau ☎ 01341 440728 ▭ 🅿

HARLECH
ROYAL ST. DAVID'S GOLF CLUB
www.royalstdavids.co.uk

Scenic 18-hole course by dunes between Harlech Castle and the sea. Not suitable for beginners or those with high handicaps. Players must hold current handicap certificate. There is also a dress code. Confirm starting time in advance.

✉ Harlech LL46 2UB ☎ 01766 780857; secretary 01766 780361 ◷ Daily except during events 👹 Mon–Fri from £34 per day; Sat–Sun from £38 per day depending on season 🍴 🚗 Harlech

KNIGHTON
OFFA'S DYKE PATH
www.offasdyke.demon.co.uk
A National Trail, the 177-mile (285km) Offa's Dyke Path follows the England–Wales border from Sedbury Cliffs to Prestatyn, skirting the eighth-century defence built by Mercia's King Offa (died AD796). Hay-on-Wye, Knighton and Llangollen make good bases.

✉ Offa's Dyke Centre, West Street, Knighton LD7 1EN ☎ 01547 528753 ◷ Centre: Easter–end Oct Thu–Mon 10–5, Tue–Wed 12–5; Nov–Eater Mon, Wed 9.30–12.30, Tue, Thu–Fri 2–5 🚗 🅿

LLANBERIS
V12 OUTDOOR
www.v12outdoor.com
A range of outdoor equipment and clothing for outdoor enthusiasts and walkers and climbers.

✉ High Street, Llanberis LL55 4EN ☎ 01286 871534 ◷ Sun–Fri 9–5, Sat 9–6,

LLANDUDNO
VENUE CYMRU
www.venuecymru.co.uk
A modern waterfront theatre that has the largest stage in Wales; a good venue for drama, concerts and other live shows.

✉ The Promenade, Llandudno LL30 1BB ☎ 01492 872000 ◷ Box office: Mon–Sat 9.30–8.30, Sun 12–4 or 2–8 depending on show 👹 Various 🚗 🍷 🚗 Llandudno

LLANIDLOES
THE GREAT OAK BOOKSHOP
A rambling building full of new and second-hand books, plus a good selection of greetings cards and other stationery.

✉ 35 Great Oak Street, Llanidloes, SY18 6BW ☎ 01686 412959 ◷ Mon–Fri 9.30–5.30, Sat 9.30–4.30

LLANWRTYD WELLS
LLANWRTYD WELLS
There's plenty of easy-going mountain biking around Britain's smallest town: low-level routes on minor roads, green lanes and hilly tracks. Bicycle rental available.

✉ Llanwrtyd Wells, Powy ☎ 01591 610666 (visitor information) 🚗 🅿

MOLD
CLWYD THEATR CYMRU
www.clwyd-theatr-cymru.co.uk
Home of the Theatr Clwyd Cymru company, staging modern and classical drama, plus visiting companies and artists.

✉ County Civic Centre, Mold CH7 1YA ☎ 0845 330 3565 (box office) ◷ Box office: Mon–Sat 10–8 🍴 🚗 🍷 With view of Clwyd hills

PORTMEIRION
PORTMEIRION VILLAGE AND GARADENS
www.portmeirion.com
On the coast of Snowdonia, this attractive village and gardens makes for a great family day out. There are places to eat and drink, lovely woodland walks and some interesting architecture. The first organised plantings in the gardens took place in Victorian times.

✉ Portmeirion, Gwynedd LL48 6ER ☎ 01766 770000 ◷ Daily 9.30–5.30

THE SHIP SHOP
www.portmeirion.com
Ceramics produced at Portmeirion Potteries in Stoke-on-Trent are sold in this delightful shop.

✉ Portmeirion LL48 6ET ☎ 01766 770000 ◷ Daily 9.30–5.30 🚗 Boston Lodge on Ffestiniog Railway

ST. DAVID'S
TWR-Y-FELIN CENTRE
www.tyf.com
Coasteering was invented here and involves a mix of climbing, jumping and swimming around sheltered stretches of coastline. Equipment and guides provided.

✉ 1 High Street, St. David's, Dyfed SA62 6SA ☎ 01437 721611 ◷ Courses all year 👹 Variable

SWANSEA
ESCAPE
www.escapegroup.com
Mainstream super-club with bars and music over several levels. Varied selection of dance music.

✉ Northampton Lane, Swansea SA1 4EH ☎ 08448 845279 ◷ Fri 9pm, Sat from 10pm 👹 £12 🚗 Swansea

LOVESPOON GALLERY
www.lovespoons.co.uk
Devoted to love spoons carved by Welsh craftspeople.

✉ 492 Mumbles Road, Mumbles, Swansea SA3 4BX ☎ 01792 360132 ◷ Mon–Sat 10–5.30 🚗 Swansea

SWANSEA MARKET
Wales' largest covered market. Fresh produce from the Gower peninsula includes cockles and laver bread.

✉ Oxford Street, Swansea ☎ 01792 654296 ◷ Mon–Thu 8.30–5.30, Fri 8–5.30, Sat 7.30–5.30 🚗 Swansea

SWANSEA GRAND THEATRE
www.swanseagrand.co.uk
Traditional theatre in the heart of the city with opera, dance, drama, musicals, children's shows, comedy and jazz.

✉ Singleton Street, Swansea SA1 3QJ ☎ 01792 475242; box office 01792 475715 ◷ Box office: Mon–Sat 9.30–8 🍴 🚗 Footlights café-bar 🚗 Swansea

Y FELINHELI
GREENWOOD FOREST PARK (GELLI GYFFWRDD)
www.greenwoodforestpark.co.uk
Children can let off steam in this forest park in Snowdonia. Activities include a sled run, pedal-powered quad bikes, family roller-coaster, mini tractors, a toddlers' village and boat rides. Don't miss the animals and open-air theatre in August.

✉ Greenwood Forest Park, Y Felinheli LL56 4QN ☎ 01248 671493/670076 (info line) ◷ Mid-Feb, Sep–Oct, daily 11–5; Easter–early Sep 10–5.30 👹 Adult £6.85–£9.80, child (under 17) £5.75–£8.95, family £22.50–£33.60 🚗 🍴

FESTIVALS AND EVENTS

APRIL–SEPTEMBER
HARBOUR AND BAY FESTIVAL
Celtic food and drink fair, plus musical events and maritime walkabouts.
☎ Cardiff Bay, Cardiff ☎ 029 2087 3690
🕐 Apr–end September 🚉 Cardiff Bay

MAY–JUNE
HAY FESTIVAL
www.hayfestival.co.uk
Popular internationally renowned annual literary festival, held over 10 days.
✉ Hay-on-Wye ☎ 0870 990 1299
🕐 Late May–early June

URDD NATIONAL EISTEDDFOD
www.urdd.org
The biggest youth festival in Europe, with over 460 competitions in music, the arts, literature and performance. A total of 96 local and 17 regional eisteddfods are held throughout Wales to choose 15,000 competitors for this culminating week. There are stands and exhibitions on eisteddfod field.
✉ Different venue every year ☎ 0845 2571613 🕐 Late May–early June

JUNE
CARDIFF SINGER OF THE WORLD
www.stdavidshallcardiff.co.uk
www.bbc.co.uk/wales
www.newtheatrecardiff.co.uk
Biennial international competition for singers of opera (in St. David's) and songs (New Theatre), attracting worldwide TV audiences.
✉ St. David's Hall, The Hayes, Cardiff CF10 1SH ☎ 029 2087 8444
✉ New Theatre, Park Place, Cardiff CF11 1FH ☎ 029 2087 8889 🕐 Late June, odd-numbered years (2007, 2009)

JULY
INTERNATIONAL MUSICAL EISTEDDFOD
www.international-eisteddfod.co.uk
Week-long international festival and competition of singers and dancers,
first held in 1947 as post-war bid to unite nations.
✉ Llangollen ☎ 01978 862001 🕐 Early July

CARDIFF FESTIVAL
www.cardiff-festival.com
Live outdoor music, international street entertainment, pre-Edinburgh comedy and carnival parade at various venues.
☎ Tel: 029 2087 2087 🕐 Mid-July to early August 🚉 Cardiff Central

ROYAL WELSH SHOW
www.rwas.co.uk
Major agricultural event, with livestock, machinery and equipment, stands and displays over four days.
✉ Llanelwedd, near Builth Wells
☎ 01982 553683 🕐 Late July 🚉 Builth Road

LATE JUNE/EARLY JULY
RUTHIN FESTIVAL
www.ruthinfestival.co.uk
The streets of this lovely North Wales market town are given over to pedestrians for the Top of Town finale of the week long festival of arts, music and drama.
☎ 01824 702703 🕐 First week in July

JULY
SESIWN FAWR
www.sesiwnfawr.co.uk
Now maturing as one of Europe's most important World music events, the Sesiwn Fawr (it means 'Mighty Session' in Welsh) takes over the town of Dolgellau for a weekend in July. Welsh-language pop, folk and rock are still to the fore on the festival site by the river.
☎ 8712301314

AUGUST
NATIONAL EISTEDDFOD OF WALES
www.eisteddfod.org.uk
Wales' most important cultural gathering, with competitions in
literature, art, drama and music.
✉ Different venue each year, alternating between south and north Wales ☎ 029 2076 3777 🕐 First week in August

BRECON JAZZ FESTIVAL
www.breconjazz.co.uk
Three-day international jazz festival.
✉ Brecon ☎ 01874 611622 🕐 Early August

VICTORIAN FESTIVAL
www.vicfest.co.uk
About 300 events, including street theatre, walks, talks, exhibitions, drama and music, with Victorian themes.
✉ Llandrindod Wells ☎ 01597 823441
🕐 Mid- to late August, one week
🚉 Llandrindod

OCTOBER–NOVEMBER
THE DYLAN THOMAS FESTIVAL
www.dylanthomasfestival.com
An annual literary festival is held around the dates of Dylan Thomas's birth and death, with various guest speakers, performances and films celebrating the writer's work and life.
✉ Dylan Thomas Centre, Somerset Place, Swansea SA1 1RR ☎ 01792 463980
🕐 End October to early November
🚉 Swansea

NOVEMBER
SOUNDTRACK FILM FESTIVAL
www.soundtrackfilmfestival.com
International celebration of film and music in the Welsh capital.

EATING

PRICES AND SYMBOLS

The restaurants are listed alphabetically within each town. The prices are for a two-course lunch (L) and a three-course à la carte dinner (D). Prices in pubs are for a two-course lunchtime bar meal and a two-course dinner in the restaurant, unless specified otherwise. The price for wine is for the least expensive bottle.

For a key to the symbols, ▷ 2.

ABERDYFI
PENHELIG ARMS

www.penheligarms.com

This lovely old inn overlooks the waters of the Dydi estuary, in the far south of the Snowdonia National Park. The modern British menu in the restaurant has built up a reputation for its excellent use of local fish and seafood—cod stew with king prawns, pan fried halibut with chorizo—while the panelled bar has decent real ales and wine by the glass.

✉ Aberdyfi, Gwynedd LL35 0LT ☎ 01654 7672155 ⊕ Daily 12–2.30, 6–9.30 ✋ Telephone for prices ☐ 9 miles from Machynlleth on A439

ABERGAVENNY
WALNUT TREE INN

Freshness and seasonal availability dictate the content of the menu. Seafood is a consistent theme though, and well-sourced meat such as Berkshire pork and local game.

✉ Abergavenny NP7 8AW ☎ 01873 852797 ⊕ Tue–Sat 12–2.30, 7–10 ✋ L £15, D £29, Wine £15 ☐ 3 miles (5km) northeast of Abergavenny on B4521

ABERYSTWYTH
CONRAH HOTEL

www.conrah.co.uk

You'll find the cream of Welsh produce at this country house hotel (▷ 260), where exceptional quality classical and modern, international dishes with strong Welsh influences are served in the luxurious Harry's Restaurant. Expect to find baked cod, perhaps with a pastry crust and Welsh red mustard potatoes, as well as local lamb and vegetarian options.

✉ Ffosrhydygaled, Chancery, Aberystwyth SY23 4DF ☎ 01970 617941 ⊕ Closed 22–30 Dec, D Sun in low season ✋ L £20.60, D £26, Wine £14 ☐ On A487, 3 miles (5km) south of Aberystwyth ☐ Aberystwyth

ANGLESEY
YE OLDE BULLS HEAD INN

www.bullsheadinn.co.uk

This central inn now includes a modern restaurant decorated in chic, minimalist style. It has acquired a loyal following for its equally up-to-date British cooking, underpinned by good-quality produce. A meal might include steamed fillet of bream with crab noodles and fresh oyster sauce, followed by medallions of venison and pigeon breast with Puy lentils and morel jus. No children under seven.

✉ Castle Street, Beaumaris LL58 8AP

☎ 01248 810329 ⏱ 7–9.30; closed 1 Jan and 25–26 Dec 🖐 D £37, Wine £13.50

BRECON
THE FELIN FACH GRIFFIN
www.eatdrinksleep.ltd.uk

Staff at this pub are very positive, and the food, while familiar, is consistent and carefully conceived. The kitchen garden is certified organic and the chef makes use of the seasonal produce, accompanying local lamb or beef, venison or Welsh cheeses.
✉ Felin Fach, Brecon LD3 0UB ☎ 01874 620111 ⏱ 12.30–2.30, 7–9.30; closed L Mon and two weeks late Jan–early Feb 🖐 Bar L £12, D £38, Wine £10.95 🚗 4.5 miles (7km) north of Brecon on A470

CARDIFF
LE GALLOIS-Y-CYMRO
www.legallois-ycymro.com

This stylish restaurant has a split-level dining area and a menu of innovative European cuisine. Creative combinations have included a starter of wood-pigeon, basil and Carmarthen ham with lentils and Pant-ysgawn goat's cheese and main courses such as turbot with watercress sauce, brandade, leek fondue and morel cream. Set lunch menus are excellent value.
✉ 6–10 Romilly Crescent, Canton, Cardiff CF11 9NR ☎ 029 2034 1264 ⏱ Tue–Sat noon–2.30, 6.30–9.30 (to 10pm Fri and Sat), Sun noon–3. Closed 7–10 days over Christmas and New Year 🖐 L £25, D £36, W £13.95 🚗 5 minutes' drive west of city centre via A4119 and Llandaff Road

THE ST. DAVID'S HOTEL AND SPA
www.thestdavidshotel.com

Tides Restaurant is adjacent to this hotel's (▷ 261) stylish cocktail bar. The menu features the best of Welsh ingredients, such as braised shank of lamb, and is supplemented by a daily market menu focusing on in-season produce.
✉ Havannah Street, Cardiff CF10 5SD ☎ 029 2045 4045 ⏱ 12.30–2.15, 6.30–10.30 🖐 L £18.50, D £35, Wine from £15 🚗 M4 junction 33/A4232 for 9 miles (15km) for Techniquest at top exit slip

road; first left at roundabout then first right 🚉 Cardiff Central

CREIGIAU
CAESARS ARMS
Just a short drive from Cardiff, but as you approach along narrow country lanes this popular dining pub could be a world away. Fresh seafood is a highlight—Pembroke dressed crab, sea bass baked in rock salt, but there's Welsh black beef too and venison from the Brecon Beacons to tempt meateaters.
✉ Cardiff Road, Creigiau CF15 9NN ☎ 029 2089 0486 ⏱ bar 11–11, restaurant 12–2.30, 6–10.30 (Sun 12–4) 🖐 L £12, D £22 Wine £14 🚗 1 mile from M4 Junct 34

HAY-ON-WYE
OLD BLACK LION
www.oldblacklion.co.uk

This fine old coaching inn (▷ 262) has charm and character. Service is friendly, and a wide range of competently prepared food is provided. The impressive menu utilises fresh local ingredients wherever possible, including organic meats and seasonal herbs and vegetables from the pub's own garden. No children under five.
✉ 26 Lion Street, Hay-on-Wye HR3 5AD ☎ 01497 820841 ⏱ 11–11 🖐 L £15, D £20, Wine £12.95 🚗 From tourist information office parking area turn right along Oxford Road, pass NatWest bank and take next left (Lion Street); hotel soon on right

LAUGHARNE
THE CORS RESTAURANT
www.the-cors.co.uk

Hidden from the main street, this intimate restaurant is located within a former Victorian vicarage in the village made famous by Dylan Thomas. Once simply a bog ('cors' in Welsh), the glorious garden now provides a delightful setting with ponds and modern sculptures. The unremarkable exterior doesn't prepare first-time visitors for what's inside, however. With no draught beer, no optics, no credit cards, no printed menus and walls painted with bold colours, the place exudes

an air of Bohemian splendour, with Modernist paintings placed alongside antiques to create a quirky, eclectic feel. The kitchen makes fine use of produce from the region: smoked haddock crème brûlée perhaps, accompanied by excellent home-made bread, or tournedos of organic Pembrokeshire beef fillet with a gratin of wild mushrooms and red wine jus.
✉ Newbridge Road, SA33 4SH ☎ 01994 427219 ⏱ Daily 7-9.30pm 🖐 L £15, D £30, Wine £12.50 🚗 From Carmarthen follow A40, turn left at St Clears & 4m to Laugharne

LLANBERIS
Y BISTRO
www.ybistro.co.uk

Y Bistro is a spacious, period restaurant in the heart of Llanberis, run by a husband-and-wife team. The modern Welsh menu of simple dishes (described in English and Welsh) includes unfussy main courses such as Welsh lamb with red wine and rosemary sauce on potato rosti. A good opportunity to try one of the three Welsh wines on the approachable list.
✉ Glandwr, 43–45 Stryd Fawr (High Street), Llanberis LL55 4EU ☎ 01286 871278 ⏱ 7.30pm–10pm 🖐 D £15, Wine £10.50 🚗 In village centre at foot of Mount Snowdon by Lake Padarn

LLANWRTYD WELLS
CARLTON RIVERSIDE
www.carltonrestaurant.co.uk

Picking up the award for AA Restaurant of the Year for Wales in 2007–08, this modest restaurant with rooms sits right on the bridge over the River Irfon in the centre of Llanwrtyd Wells. The menus are down to earth too, with fixed price simplicity—you might follow seared scallops, home-made egg noodles and a shellfish velouté with pan-fried fillet of local beef topped with fried onions, served with mashed potato, buttered spinach and a red wine jus.
✉ Dolycoed Road LD5 4RA ☎ 01591 610248 ⏱ D 7–8.30 🖐 D £22.50 🚗 On the A483 in the centre of town.

MONTGOMERY
DRAGON HOTEL
www.dragonhotel.com
This is a historic black-fronted coaching inn with a homely interior. The menu makes good use of Welsh ingredients, offering traditional dishes with an occasional modern twist. Close to Montgomery Castle.
✉ Market Square SY15 6PA ☎ 01686 668359 🕐 12–2, 7–9 🖐 D £16, Wine £10.50 🚌 Behind town hall

NANTGAREDIG
Y POLYN
www.ypolyn.co.uk
Located in tranquil countryside a few miles outside Carmarthen, Y Polyn is a cosy bar and restaurant with a serious approach to food, and a setting which oozes rustic, unpretentious charm. Think shabby chic, with solid farmhouse-style tables and a miscellany of comfy chairs set on quarry-tiled floors and sisal-style carpet runners, and dark terracotta-painted walls hung with paintings by local artists or menus from renowned restaurants. Service is very personable, suitably relaxed but efficient. The kitchen delivers modern, British-themed bistro-style fare using the best local produce. Dishes and flavours are clean cut and unfussy, with the main ingredient allowed to shine; think fish soup with rouille, croûtons and Gruyére cheese, followed by roast rump of salt marsh lamb with onion, garlic and thyme purée.
✉ Nantgaredig SA32 7LH ☎ 01267 290000 🕐 Tue–Sun 12–2, 7–9; closed D Sun 🖐 L £17 D£23, Wine £13.50 🚌 Follow brown tourist signs to National Botanic Gardens, Y Polyn is signed from roundabout in front of gardens

NEWPORT
THE INN AT THE ELM TREE
Fresh local produce is the key to the menu's success at this modern, stylish restaurant—Welsh lamb, Welsh Black beef, game in season from local estates, as well as lobsters and oysters from Cardigan Bay. No children under 12.
✉ St. Brides, Wentlooge, Newport NP10

8SQ ☎ 01633 680225 🕐 12–2.30, 6–9.30 🖐 L £7, D £22, Wine £11 🚌 From M4 junction 28 take A48 towards Castleton. At first roundabout turn left; continue 1.5 miles (2.4km) right on to Morgan Way. Turn right at T-junction on to B4239 for 2.5 miles (4km)

PORTMEIRION
CASTELL DEUDRAETH BAR AND GRILL
www.portmeirion-village.com
Flooded with natural light and furnished in chic brasserie style, with light wood tables and dark upholstered chairs, this restaurant has a pleasant atmosphere of simple informality. The kitchen draws on the finest fresh local ingredients to produce dishes such as braised Welsh lamb shank with sage mash and red wine sauce, roast cod with pea purée, onion gravy and crispy smoked bacon, or pork sausage with leek and Hen Sir Welsh cheese potatoes and onion gravy. Vegetarian options are always available. Lunch and dinner menus are fixed-price, with supplementary charges for some of the dishes.
✉ Portmeirion Village, Gwynedd LL48 6ER ☎ 01766 772400 🕐 Daily, lunch and dinner 🖐 L £18.50, D £30, W £13.50 🚌 Near Minffordd, off the A487 between Porthmadog and Penryndeudraeth

PWLLHELI
PLAS BODEGROES
www.bodegroes.co.uk
This Georgian manor house restaurant is contemporary, both in decor and cuisine. Local produce is used imaginatively, as in a warm salad of monkfish or the rosemary kebab of mountain lamb with minted couscous. Puddings might include barabrith and butter pudding with Welsh whisky ice cream.
✉ Nefyn Road, Pwllheli LL53 5TH ☎ 01758 612363 🕐 12–2, 7–9; closed Mon, L Tue–Sat and Dec–end Feb 🖐 L £18 D £42.50, Wine £16 🚌 On A497 1 mile (1.6km) west of Pwllheli

ST. ASAPH
THE PLOUGH INN
This 18th-century former coaching inn on the original Holyhead–London

road buzzes throughout the day and has become a notable dining venue by night.
✉ The Roe, St. Asaph LL17 0LU ☎ 01745 585080 🕐 Daily 12–11 (10.30 Sun) 🖐 L £10.95, D £20, Wine £11.95 🏪 Wine shop 🚌 Rhyl and St. Asaph turning from A55 left at roundabout; pub 180m (200yds) on left

ST DAVID'S
MORGAN'S
www.morgans-restaurant.co.uk
Tucked away in the back streets of this tiny city, Morgan's has been consistently impressing diners for several years. The menu draws on the modern British style. Look for Gressingham duck breast, roasted in sweet spices with mandarin purée and maple-roast parsnip mash, or hake fillet poached in a cider and black peppercorn sauce with caramelised apple and chive oil from the fish menu and keep an eye open for weekly changing specials. Good vegetarian selection too.
✉ 20 Nun Street, St David's SA62 6NT ☎ 01437 720508 🕐 Wed–Mon, 6.30–11.30 🖐 D £22 🚌 Just off main square, 100yds (90m) from cathedral

SKENFRITH
THE BELL AT SKENFRITH
Normally two fish courses are available in the bar and one in the restaurant, at this 17th-century coaching inn. Main courses might include pan roasted halibut or wild sea bass, tidenham chase duck or a vegetarian tagliatelle with wild mushrooms and globe artichokes. Try the real ales or the scrumpy.
✉ Skenfrith NP7 8UH ☎ 01600 750235 🕐 12–2.30, 7–9.30; closed first two weeks of Feb 🖐 L £15, D £25.75, Wine £14

SWANSEA
FAIRYHILL
www.fairyhill.net
Fairyhill (▷ 263) is a beacon for all that's good about Welsh produce and dedicated cooking. On the menu are modern twists of traditional dishes using the best local produce, such as an open lasagne of seafood, shellfish and herb sauce, all complemented

by one of Wales' most comprehensive wine lists and excellent service. No children under eight.

✉ Reynoldston, Swansea SA3 1BS
☎ 01792 390139 🕐 12–2.30, 7.30–9; closed 1–16 Jan and 26 Dec ✋ L £15.95, D £40, Wine £15 🚗 Just outside Reynoldston off A4118 from Swansea

THE RESTAURANT @ PILOT HOUSE WHARF

The seafood served here is as fresh as it comes, and there are panoramic views from the harbourside location. The chefs take a modern approach to cooking such dishes as wild sea bass with sun-dried tomato couscous and roasted Mediterranean vegetables, and though the menu specialises in fish there are good meat choices too.

✉ Pilot House Wharf, Trawler Road, Swansea Marina, Swansea SA1 1UN
☎ 01792 466200 🕐 Tue–Sat noon–2, 6.30–9.30 ✋ L £22, D £30 🚗 South of city centre off A4067 Oystermouth Road

Below *Cardiff Bay's Mermaid Quay*

TALYBONT-ON-USK
THE USK INN
www.uskinn.co.uk

This refurbished free house has long been welcoming travellers with a good range of real ales. Look for the roast monkfish or local lamb in some creative presentations. Blackboard specials supplement the excellent menu, which includes a fish menu.

✉ Talybont-On-Usk, LD3 7JE ☎ 01874 676251 🕐 12–3, 6.30–9 (dress code); closed 25–26 Dec ✋ L £10.95, D £16.65, Wine £11.95 🚗 6 miles (10km) east of Brecon, just off the A40 to Abergavenny, if coming through Talybont turn onto Station Road alongside rail bridge, pub on right

TREDUNNOCK
THE NEWBRIDGE
www.thenewbridge.co.uk

This restaurant has a faintly Tuscan look to its bar/bistro-style interior. Although the Newbridge is tucked away in rural Monmouthshire, its menu draws extensively on the Mediterranean side of modern British food, using local produce to good effect in daily changing pork and beef dishes, as well as excellent changing fish choices.

✉ Tredunnock NP15 1LY ☎ 01633 451000 🕐 Mon–Sat 11–2.30, 6.15–9.30, Sun 12–3, 6.15–8.30 ✋ L £13.25, D £24.50, Wine £13.50 🚗 South of Usk, drive through Tredunnock village and inn is by River Usk

WOLF'S CASTLE
THE WOLFE INN

This stone, oak-beamed inn consists of four distinctive rooms, which, together with a secluded patio garden, offer a relaxed atmosphere. The freshest local produce is used to create the fine cuisine in the restaurant and the simplest of dishes in the brasserie. These range from chicken piccante and salmon in cream and pernod to mussels and garlic in white wine. There's a monthly guest beer, and a selection of coffees and teas.

✉ Wolf's Castle SA62 5LS ☎ 01437 741662 🕐 Mon–Sat 12–2, 7–9 ✋ L £11.90, D £15, Wine £8.25 🚗 On A40 between Haverfordwest and Fishguard

PRICES AND SYMBOLS

Prices are the starting price for a double room for one night, unless otherwise stated. Breakfast is included unless noted otherwise. All the hotels listed accept credit cards unless otherwise stated. Note that rates vary widely throughout the year.

For a key to the symbols, ▷ 2.

ABERGAVENNY
LLANWENARTH HOTEL AND RIVERSIDE RESTAURANT

www.llanwenarthhotel.com

Dating back to the 16th century, this charming hotel is set in the magnificent surroundings of the Brecon Beacons National Park, high up on the eastern bank of the River Usk. The conservatory lounge and restaurant take full advantage of the spectacular views and many of the bedrooms have balconies overlooking the river.

✉ Brecon Road, Abergavenny, Monmouthshire NP8 1EP ☎ 01873 810550

🖐 £85–£105, including breakfast ❶ 7
🅿 On the A40 towards Brecon, 3 miles beyond the hospital

ABERYSTWYTH
CONRAH HOTEL

www.conrah.co.uk

The elegant public rooms at this country-house hotel include a choice of comfortable lounges with inviting open fires, especially in the winter months. Bedrooms are located in both the main house and a nearby wing. There is also an excellent restaurant at this charming hotel. No children under five.

✉ Ffosrhydygaled, Chancery, Aberystwyth SY23 4DF ☎ 01970 617941 🕐 Closed 22–30 Dec, Sun in low season 🖐 £125 ❶ 17 🔄 🅿 On A487, 3 miles (5km) south of Aberystwyth 🚉 Aberystwyth

BETWS-Y-COED
TAN Y FOEL COUNTRY HOUSE

www.tyfhotel.co.uk

A refreshing small hotel in many respects, this 16th-century stone-built house offers fine views along the Conwy valley from its elevated position. The lounge and breakfast room are decorated in a modern style with a slight Eastern influence, while the conservatory restaurant is more traditional and warmed by a wood-burning stove. Dinner is a highlight of any stay. Individually furnished bedrooms, including the imaginative use of an old hayloft, are designed for comfort and relaxation. No children under seven. No dogs.

✉ Capel Garmon, Betws-y-Coed LL26 0RE ☎ 01690 710507 🕐 Closed Dec–end Jan 🖐 £141 ❶ 6 🅿 Off A5 at Betws-y-Coed on to A470, travel 2 miles (3km) north, signed Capel Garmon on right; turn towards Capel Garmon for 1.5 miles (2.5km), hotel sign on left

TY GWYN

www.tygwynhotel.co.uk

Situated on the edge of the village, close to Waterloo Bridge, this historic coaching inn retains many original features, and quality furnishings and

memorabilia throughout enhance the intrinsic charm of the property.
✉ Betws-y-Coed LL24 0SG ☎ 01690 710383 ⊙ Closed Jan 🖐 £34; discount for under-16s ① 12 🚃 Junction of A5/A470 by Waterloo Bridge 🚃 Betws-y-Coed

BEAUMARIS
BISHOPSGATE HOUSE
www.bishopsgatehotel.co.uk
With fabulous views across the Menai Strait, this lovely Georgian town house is in the heart of the town not far from the castle. It is a small, personally run hotel with attractive bedrooms, two of which have four-poster beds, and a good restaurant serving meals based on fresh local produce. Throughout the hotel there are antiques and notable architectural features include a Chinese Chippendale staircase and fine wood panelling in the lounge.
✉ 54 Castle Street, Beaumaris, Anglesey LL58 8BB ☎ 01248 810302 🖐 £65–£100, ① 9 🚃 On the main street

CAERNARFON
SEIONT MANOR
www.handpicked.co.uk
Imaginatively created out of the stone farmstead of a country manor house, this luxurious hotel is set in 150 acres (60ha) of beautiful gardens and grounds within Snowdonia. The bedrooms are furnished in country-house style, with nice antiques and some interesting artefacts, and each has a balcony or terrace. The four-poster rooms and junior suites are particularly spacious. Cooking at the manor is as accomplished as it is artistic, and less formal options include the provision of picnic hampers to enjoy alfresco.
✉ Llanrug, Caernarfon, Gwynedd LL55 2AQ ☎ 0845 072 7550 ✉ 🖐 £190–£250, ① 28 ☁ Indoor 🌀 🚃 On the A4086, 2.5 miles (4km) east of Caernarfon

CARDIFF
THE BIG SLEEP HOTEL
www.thebigsleephotel.com
Part of Cardiff's skyline, this city centre bed-and-breakfast hotel opposite Cardiff International Arena offers well-equipped bedrooms

ranging from standard to penthouse, with spectacular views over the city towards the bay. Continental breakfast is served or 'breakfast to go'is an alternative for the visitor wishing to make an early start. There is a bar on the ground floor and secure parking. No dogs.
✉ Bute Terrace, Cardiff CF10 2FE ☎ 029 2063 6363 🖐 £45; discount for under-12s ① 81 🚃 Cardiff Central

MARLBOROUGH GUEST HOUSE
This family-run guest house is just a few minutes from the city centre and has a warm and friendly atmosphere. Not all the bedrooms are spacious but the bathrooms are particularly well fitted. A comfortably furnished lounge is available for residents, and hearty breakfasts are served in the pleasant breakfast room. No dogs.
✉ 98 Newport Road, Cardiff CF24 1DG ☎ 029 2049 2385 🖐 £45; discount for under-10s ① 8 🚃 Cardiff Queen Street

THE ST. DAVID'S HOTEL AND SPA
www.thestdavidshotel.com
This imposing contemporary building sits in a prime position on Cardiff Bay. A seven-storey atrium provides a dramatic first impression on entering, and leads to the practically laid-out and comfortable bedrooms. A lounge on the first floor suits guests seeking a quiet place. There is a good restaurant (▷ 257).
✉ Havannah Street, Cardiff CF10 5SD ☎ 029 2045 4045 🖐 £200 ① 132 🚗 🌀 🚃 M4 junction 33/A4232 for 9 miles (15km) for Techniquest at top exit slip road; first left at roundabout then first right 🚃 Cardiff Central

CHEPSTOW
BEAUFORT HOTEL
www.beauforthotelchepstow.com
This 16th-century coaching inn is centrally located in town. The bedrooms are brightly decorated, and the public areas include a friendly bar and a pleasant restaurant where well-prepared meals are served. A large meeting and function room is also available.

✉ Beaufort Square, Chepstow NP6 5EP ☎ 01291 622497 🖐 £59; discount for under-14s ① 22 🚃 Chepstow

CONWY
BRYN DERWEN
Sympathetically restored and retaining many of its original Victorian features, Bryn Derwen is in an elevated position near the castle with views over the town. The brightly furnished bedrooms offer modern facilities. The breakfast room overlooks the garden, and guests also have use of the period-style lounge. No dogs.
✉ Woodlands, Conwy LL32 8LT ☎ 01492 596134 🖐 £45; discount for under-15s ① 6 🚃 Llandudno

GROES INN
www.groesinn.com
With its comfortable, well-equipped bedrooms in a separate building, this 16th-century inn has managed to retain many of its traditional features. The modern additions complement it well, notably the conservatory extension to the restaurant, which opens out on to the lovely rear garden. Several of the bedrooms have private terraces or balconies.
✉ Tyn-y-Groes, LL32 8TN ☎ 01492 650545 ⊙ Closed 24, 25, 26 Dec 🖐 £95 ① 14 🚃 2 miles (3.2km) out of Conwy town on B5106 towards Trefriw

DOLGELLAU
FRONOLEU COUNTRY HOTEL
www.fronleu.co.uk
This 16th-century farmhouse, carefully extended to retain many original features, lies in the shadow of Cader Idris mountain. The bar and lounge are located in the old building where there are exposed timbers and open fires. Most of the bedrooms are in the modern extension. The restaurant attracts a large local following. Private fishing available.
✉ Tabor, Dolgellau LL40 2PS ☎ 01341 422361 🖐 £50; discount for under-16s ① 11 🚃 Junction of A487/A470 towards Tabor opposite Cross Foxes and continue for 1.25 miles (2km). From Dolgellau take road for hospital and continue another 1.25 miles (2km) up the hill 🚃 Fairbourne

EGLWYSFACH
YNYSHIR HALL
www.ynyshirhall.co.uk

Once owned by Queen Victoria, this luxurious country house is one of the finest hotels in Wales, set in beautifully landscaped grounds which are themselves surrounded by one of Britain's best RSPB nature reserves. The house is a study in understated elegance, with artistic touches such as original paintings on the walls and individually designed bedrooms. The restaurant, too, is exceptionally good, and utilises the finest local and organic produce as well as vegetables, fruit and herbs from the hotel's own kitchen garden. The sense of wellbeing gleaned from relaxing and eating well is enhanced by a range of expert beauty treatments and exercise classes, from massage and reflexology to yoga and tai chi, and there are wonderful country walks all around.

✉ Eglwysfach, Machynlleth, Powys SY20 8TA ☎ 01654 781209 ⊙ £275 ❶ 9 🚌 Off the A487, 5.5 miles (9km) south of Machynlleth

HAVERFORDWEST
LOWER HAYTHOG FARM
www.lowerhaythogfarm.co.uk

Located in an expanse of unspoiled countryside, this 14th-century farmhouse provides high standards of comfort and good facilities. Bedrooms, some of which are in former farm buildings, are filled with thoughtful extras, and an elegant oak-beamed dining room is the perfect setting for imaginative home-cooked dinners. Private fishing and pony rides available. Credit cards not accepted.

✉ Spittal, Haverfordwest SA62 5QL ☎ 01437 731279 🛏 £50; discount for under-12s ❶ 6 🚌 5 miles (8km) north of Haverfordwest off B4329, continue along this road until rail bridge; entrance on right 🚃 Haverfordwest

HAY-ON-WYE
OLD BLACK LION
www.oldblacklion.co.uk

This fine old coaching inn, with a history stretching back several centuries—it was occupied by Oliver Cromwell (1599–1658) during the siege of Hay Castle, then a loyalist stronghold—has charm and character. Privately owned and personally run, it offers comfortable and well-equipped bedrooms, some of which are in a building next door. Excellent food is available. No children under five. No dogs (except guide dogs).

✉ 26 Lion Street, Hay-on-Wye HR3 5AD ☎ 01497 820841 🛏 £80 ❶ 6 🚌 From tourist information office parking area turn right along Oxford Road, pass NatWest bank and take next left (Lion Street); hotel soon on right

LLANBERIS
QUALITY HOTEL SNOWDONIA
www.hotels-snowdonia.com

This hotel sits near the foot of Snowdon, between the Peris and Padarn lakes. Pretty gardens and grounds make an attractive backdrop for the many weddings held here. The refurbished bedrooms are well equipped, and there are spacious lounges and bars, plus a large dining room with conservatory overlooking the lakes. Activities for outdoor enthusiasts include mountaineering, cycling and walking.

✉ Llanberis LL55 4TY ☎ 01286 870253 🛏 £100; discount for under-15s ❶ 106 🚌 On A4086 Caernarfon to Llanberis road directly opposite Snowdon Mountain Railway 🚃 Bangor

LLANDRINDOD WELLS
HOTEL METROPOLE
www.metropole.co.uk

The centre of the famous spa town of Llandrindod Wells is dominated by this Victorian hotel, which has been personally run by the same family for more than 100 years. The lobby leads to a choice of bars and an elegant lounge. Bedrooms vary in style, but all are moderately spacious and well equipped. Leisure facilities include a sauna and beauty salon.

✉ Temple Street, Llandrindod Wells LD1 5DY ☎ 01597 823700 🛏 £98; discount for under-16s ❶ 120 🚌 🏊 🚃 Llandrindod Wells

LLANGOLLEN
THE WILD PHEASANT HOTEL AND RESTAURANT
www.wildpheasanthotel.co.uk

Some bedrooms at this friendly hotel have luxury four-poster beds; guests can also request rooms and rooms on the ground floor. There is a reception area (resembling an old village square) and a large function suite. The fixed-price menu in the formal restaurant changes daily.

✉ Berwyn Road, Llangollen LL20 8AD ☎ 01978 860629 🛏 £84; discount for under-15s ❶ 46 🚃 Ruabon

LLANWDDYN
LAKE VYRNWY
www.lakevyrnwy.com

With lake and mountain views, this hotel enjoys a superb location on the edge of Snowdonia amid a vast area of woodland. Nearly half of the bedrooms have balconies, and all have an individual style of decor. There's a good restaurant, a bar and a country pub, plus a spa that includes a dry sauna, spa pool and mud therapy as well as a range of treatments. Outside, there are tennis courts and facilities for clay and game shooting, sailing and canoeing.

✉ Llanwddyn, Powys SY10 0LY ☎ 01691 870692 ✉ 🛏 £105 ❶ 52 🏊 🚌 On east side of the lake on the B4393; turn sharp right 200m (220 yds) past the dam

MERTHYR TYDFIL
NANT DDU LODGE HOTEL
www.nant-ddu-lodge.co.uk

Close to the Brecon Beacons and with origins stretching back 200 years, this delightful hotel has seen many improvements in the caring hands of the present owners. Decor throughout is contemporary and the bedrooms are thoughtfully furnished.

✉ Cwm Taf, Nant Ddu, Merthyr Tydfil CF48 2HY ☎ 01685 379111 🛏 £80; discount for under-12s ❶ 28 🚌 On main A470, 6 miles (10km) north of Merthyr Tydfil and 12 miles (19km) south of Brecon 🚃 Merthyr Tydfil

Right *Boats moored in Tenby's harbour*

PORTMEIRION

THE HOTEL PORTMEIRION

www.portmeirion-village.com

Saved from dereliction in the 1920s, this elegant hotel enjoys one of the finest settings in Wales, nestling beneath the wooded slopes of the village, overlooking the sandy estuary towards Snowdonia. Many rooms have private sitting rooms and balconies with spectacular views. The mostly Welsh-speaking staff offer warm hospitality. Facilities include beauty salon and tennis courts.

✉ Portmeirion LL48 6ET ☎ 01766 770000 🖐 £175 ⓘ 51 ⛴ 🚗 2 miles (3km) west of Portmeirion village, which is south off A487

SWANSEA

FAIRYHILL

www.fairyhill.net

Not so many years ago this fine 18th-century house had foliage poking through the roof and wild ponies running amok on its untended pastures. To stay here today is a delight, deep in the heart of the Gower Peninsula. Relaxing day rooms, leading out to the front patio, are a perfect setting to picking at the mandatory deep-fried Penclawdd cockles and laver bread before dinner (▷ 258).

✉ Reynoldston, Swansea SA3 1BS ☎ 01792 390139 ⊘ Closed 1–16 Jan and 26 Dec 🖐 £140 ⓘ 8 🚗 Just outside Reynoldston off A4118 from Swansea

THE GROSVENOR HOUSE

www.grosvenor-guesthouse.co.uk

This immaculate house is in the fashionable Uplands district, convenient for touring the Gower Peninsula and the Mumbles. After a warm welcome from the hosts, guests are shown to their pleasant bedrooms. Guests also have access to secure parking, a lounge and the dining room at this bed-and-breakfast. No children under four.

✉ Mirador Crescent, Uplands, Swansea SA2 0QX ☎ 01792 461522 ⊘ Closed 18 Dec–2 Jan 🖐 £54; discount for under-16s ⓘ 7 🚗 Off A4118 in the Uplands area of town 🚉 Swansea

TALSARNAU

MAES Y NEUADD COUNTRY HOUSE

This 14th-century hotel enjoys stunning views over the Snowdonian mountains and across the bay to the Lleyn Peninsula. The team here are committed to highlighting and restoring some of the hidden features of the house. Bedrooms are individually furnished and many have fine antique pieces. Public areas display a similar welcoming character, including the restaurant which serves locally sourced and home-grown ingredients. Activities, such as clay pigeon shooting and cooking lessons, can be arranged.

✉ Talsarnau LL47 6YA ☎ 01766 780200 🖐 £141 including breakfast and dinner ⓘ 16 🚗 3 miles (5km) northeast of Harlech, signposted on an unclassified road off B4573

TENBY

ATLANTIC HOTEL

www.atlantic-hotel.uk.com

This hotel has an enviable position looking out over South Beach and Caldy Island. Inside there is a traditional feel and the bedrooms have homely touches. Guests can relax in the comfortable lounge or enjoy a drink in the cocktail bar before taking dinner in one of two restaurants. Other facilities include a heated indoor swimming pool, solarium, spa and sauna.

✉ The Esplanade, Tenby SA70 7DU ☎ 01834 842881 ⊘ Closed 19–28 Dec 🖐 £94; discount for under-16s ⓘ 42 ⛴ 🚉 Tenby

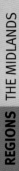

SIGHTS 266

WALKS AND DRIVES 282

WHAT TO DO 286

EATING 292

STAYING 296

THE MIDLANDS

Dominated by the valleys of the River Severn and the River Trent, the English Midlands are usually split between east and west. To the east and north, the Trent collects its water from the rising limestone hills of the Peak District. Not a place full of mountains as the name suggests but a beautiful slice of green and brown upland, wedged between the cities of central northern England, the Peak is protected by National Park status. As well as the natural treasures of caves and dramatic gorges, this is also home to Chatsworth House, one of the stateliest homes of the English aristocracy, and the mills of the Derwent Valley, so important in the history of industry that they form one of the region's two World Heritage sites. The other site, which sits in a wooded gorge on the River Severn, is perhaps one of the best-known industrial monuments in the world. The graceful Iron Bridge, spanning the river at Coalbrookdale in Shropshire, was the very first to use cast iron, and sits at the heart of a fascinating early industrial landscape, now mostly protected as a living museum.

The region's cities—Birmingham, Leicester, Stoke, Derby, Sheffield, Nottingham, Coventry—are famous for their no-nonsense industriousness, but Stratford-upon-Avon has an altogether different fame. Here England's greatest playwright, William Shakespeare, first found his muse. Now the Royal Shakespeare Company dominates the town, with several different theatres keeping the dramatic tradition alive. Close to Stratford, Warwick Castle is the most impressive of the region's many medieval fortifications.

ALTHORP

www.althorp.com

Following her death in a car crash in Paris, Diana, Princess of Wales (1961–97), was buried on a private island in a lake within the grounds of her family estate. As home of the Spencers since 1508, Althorp has become something of a shrine to her, and a six-room exhibition celebrates her life. The old Tudor mansion, modified in the 18th century in Classical style, sits among trees and pastures, and some private apartments are open to the public.

✚ 458 J16 ✉ Althorp, near Northampton NN7 4HQ ☎ 01604 770107 ◷ Ju–end Aug daily 11–5 ⛏ Adult £12.50, child (5–17) £10.50, family £29.50. Extra fee for visiting upstairs. Discounts for online or telephone reservations 🖥 🏛

ALTON TOWERS

www.altontowers.com

As theme parks go, Alton Towers rates as one of Europe's biggest, with plenty of new attractions added each year. There are knuckle-whitening roller-coaster rides such as the unmissable Nemesis, Air, Ripsaw, Submission, Rita—Queen of Speed, and features for younger children such as Cred Street and Old MacDonald's Farmyard. There are also extensive landscaped gardens. Reservations are available for major rides, and are recommended at busy times. At Halloween some of the rides take place in the dark.

✚ 461 H15 ✉ Near Alton ST10 4DB ☎ 0870 520 4060 ◷ Daily 10–5 or later according to season ⛏ Premium season: adult £34, child (4–11) £24, family £90. Special internet tariffs available 🍴 🖥 🏛

AVONCROFT MUSEUM OF HISTORIC BUILDINGS

www.avoncroft.org.uk

More than 20 historic buildings spanning 600 years of history have been rescued and reconstructed on a large open site in the Worcestershire countryside. This fascinating collection ranges from the venerable to the humble, from 15th- and 16th-century timber-framed buildings to a 1940s prefab of a kind erected hastily across Britain to house those who had lost their homes during World War II bomb raids. The National Telephone Kiosk Collection pays homage to the very British red phone box, while other exhibits include a cock-fighting pit and a working windmill.

✚ 458 G16 ✉ Stoke Heath, Bromsgrove B60 4JR ☎ 01527 831363 ◷ Easter–end Jun–end Sep, Oct Tue–Sun 10.30–5; Jul–end Aug daily 10.30–5; Nov–Easter Fri–Sun 10.30–4 ⛏ Adult £6.60, child (5–16) £3, family £16.50 🖥 🏛

BELVOIR CASTLE

www.belvoircastle.com

Pronounced beaver, the castle is a startling Regency-Gothic edifice in pinkish stone, with a jumble of towers and turrets. It has been home to the dukes of Rutland since 1508, although the present structure, the third on the site, dates from the early 19th century. It contains some opulent interiors, notably the Picture Gallery, including works by Thomas Gainsborough, Nicolas Poussin and Hans Holbein. Beneath the castle terrace are the Rose and Statue Gardens; farther away are the lush Duchess's Spring Gardens, restored to their former glory and with plants fed by natural springs close to a summer house.

✚ 462 J15 ✉ Near Grantham NG32 1PD ☎ 01476 870262 ◷ Easter–end Apr Thu–Sun 11–5, Sat 11–4; May, Jun Sun–Thu 11–5, Sat 11–4; Ju–end Aug Sat–Thu 11–5; Sep Sat–Sun 11–5, end Oct Sun–Thu ⛏ Castle and grounds: adult £12, child (5–16) £6, family £32. Gardens: adult £6, child £2 🍴 🖥 🏛

BIRMINGHAM

www.beinbirmingham.com

Britain's second city is at the heart of the industrial Midlands. While lacking the townscape of Britain's major historic cities, Birmingham does have notable pockets of interest. Since the 1980s there has been a marked improvement in the city's image, and around its remarkably intricate canal network, new walkways, shops and public areas have been created. Gas Street Basin, where narrowboats are often moored, makes a good starting point for waterside walks along the canal's towpaths.

Birmingham's obvious central point is around Victoria Square and Centenary Square, by the Grecian Town Hall. Close by is the eclectic Birmingham Museum and Art Gallery (Mon–Thu and Sat 10–5, Fri 10.30–5, Sun 12.30–5) with one of the world's largest collections of Pre-Raphaelite paintings (free). A stylish art gallery with changing exhibitions and free admission is the Ikon Gallery in Brindleyplace (Tue–Sun and public holidays 11–6).

A canalside stroll leads north from the centre to the Jewellery Quarter, which retains much Victorian character and is still the focal point for jewellery-making; there are great numbers of specialist workshops operating on a small scale. The Museum of the Jewellery Quarter in Vyse Street (Apr–end Oct Tue–Sun and public holidays 11.30–4, Nov–end Mar Tue–Sat 11.30–4) occupies the extraordinarily antiquated workshops of Smith and Pepper, in operation from 1899 to 1981 for the manufacture of bangles. In that time, virtually nothing changed, and when the factory closed down it was left untouched until it became a museum (entrance free).

Birmingham noticeably lacks green space and trees, and so the Birmingham Botanical Gardens (Apr–end Sep Mon–Sat 9–7, Sun 10–7; Oct–end Mar closes 5 or dusk if earlier) in Westbourne Road, Edgbaston, can be a welcome contrast. This is the foremost plant collection in the Midlands, with four glasshouses, themed gardens and aviaries. A visit to Cadbury World (▷ 268) is a must for chocolate lovers.

✚ 461 H16 ℹ The Rotunda, 150 New Street, Birmingham B2 4PA, tel 0844 888 3883

Opposite City Museum and Art Gallery, *Birmingham*

BLACK COUNTRY LIVING MUSEUM

www.bclm.co.uk

The industrial area of the West Midlands known as the Black Country has changed immeasurably over the past 50 years, and this brilliant evocation turns the clock back to the early years of the 20th century. All kinds of buildings from around the area have been moved here and rebuilt to create a canalside village, with shops, school, a mill, boat dock, brass foundry and back-to-back houses. You can take a canal trip into limestone caverns, watch a silent film in the 1920s Limelight Cinema, have a beer in the Bottle and Glass Inn, or have fun at the old-fashioned fairground. There's always lots happening in the way of glass-cutting, metalworking, sweet-making and other crafts. Visitors can try out a lesson in the old-fashioned school, where strict discipline is observed. The coal mine gives a glimpse of the miners' working day.

✚ 461 G16 ✉ Tipton Road, Dudley DY1 4SQ ☎ 0121 557 9643 🕐 Mar–end Oct daily 10–5; Nov–end Feb Wed–Sun 10–4; call for Christmas opening 💷 Adult £12.50, child (5–18) £6.75, family £33.50 🚻 🏧

BUXTON

www.visitbuxton.co.uk

Buxton makes an excellent base for exploring the Peak District National Park (▷ 275). This former spa town has a distinctly genteel air, with the old pump room (now an art gallery), well-manicured Pavilion Gardens, its own Opera House, the grand, domed former Devonshire Royal Hospital and the grandiose Palace Hotel. The 1854 thermal baths are now the modern Cavendish Arcade, crammed with shops, but they still feature the original plunge baths. Close to St. Ann's Well, which dispenses pure water, is the Crescent, built in the 1780s and Buxton's architectural glory. On the southern edge of town, Poole's Cavern (Mar–end Oct daily 9.30–5) is a show cave with the longest horizontal view of any cave in Britain.

✚ 461 H14 🖻 The Crescent, Buxton SK17 6BQ, tel 01298 25106

CADBURY WORLD

www.cadburyworld.co.uk

Chocoholics should beat a path to this extremely popular attraction next door to the Cadbury factory. The history section tells the story of chocolate and there are interactive exhibits, a ride through the chocolate world, free samples, and a shop from which only the most self-restrained will walk away empty-handed. You can also taste melted chocolate straight from the production line.

✚ 458 H16 ✉ Linden Road, Bournville, Birmingham B30 2LD ☎ 0845 4503599 🕐 Reservation essential, times vary. 20 Jan–end Dec usually daily (closed some days in Feb, Nov and Dec) 💷 Adult £13, child (4–15) £9.95, family £40 🚻 🚻 🏧

CALKE ABBEY

www.nationaltrust.org.uk

Despite its name, Calke Abbey is a baroque country mansion mostly built between 1701 and 1703. Little changed over the years, and, oc-cupied by the reclusive Harpur Crewe family up to 1924, it steadily decayed. The National Trust took it over and opened it to the public in 1989, deliberately leaving some of the rooms in their unrestored state. It makes a poignant visit—with the family wealth long gone, the atmo-sphere is of lost grandeur. The park, designated as a National Nature Reserve and managed for its nature conservation value, has 19th-century glasshouses, an ice house, walled flower garden and an orangery.

✚ 462 H15 ✉ Ticknall, near Derby DE73 1LE ☎ 01332 863822 🕐 House: late Mar–end Oct Sat–Wed 12.30–5.30. Garden and church: late Mar–end Oct Sat–Wed 11–5; daily Jul, Aug. Park: most days until 9 or dusk 💷 House and garden: adult £7.72, child (5–16) £3.81, family £19.54. Garden only: adult £4.81, child £2.45, family £12 🚻 🏧

Below left *View from Bandstand in the Pavilion Gardens to the domed conference centre in the old town of Buxton in the Peak District, Derbyshire*
Below *Jason, his Groom and Sir Harry Harpur by Sawrey Gilpin (1733–1807) from Calke Abbey*

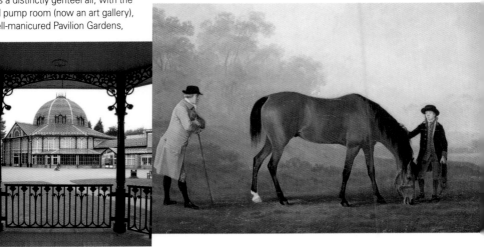

CHATSWORTH HOUSE

England's answer to the Palace of Versailles, Chatsworth is a country house on the grandest scale, with furniture and art to impress, and plenty to keep children entertained in the grounds.

THE HOUSE

This palatial home of the Duke and Duchess of Devonshire is set in the Peak District. The original house dates from 1551, but most of what you see was built between 1686 and 1707. The Painted Hall is magnificently baroque, with marble floors, a painted ceiling and a spectacular staircase. Among the 30 rooms on show are the State Bedroom, where George II (1683–1760) died. The present queen's grandparents, George V (1865–1936) and Queen Mary, slept in this room when they visited Chatsworth in 1933. Great works of art are spread throughout the house, and among the highlights are works by Antonio Canova, Rembrandt van Rijn, Paolo Veronese and Tintoretto. The library contains around 17,000 books.

THE GROUNDS AND ESTATE

The 18th-century landscaper Capability Brown laid out the park, and in the 19th century Joseph Paxton (1803–65) was head gardener before he went on to design the Crystal Palace in London for the Great Exhibition of 1851.

There is plenty to explore on the estate, including a cottage garden, a kitchen garden, an excellent farm shop, a maze, 5 miles (8km) of paths leading past rare trees and shrubs, ponds, artful fountains and outdoor sculptures. Perhaps the most memorable feature outside is the 200m (660ft) water cascade. It was designed in 1696, with every step of the stone slope built slightly differently to vary the sound that the water makes. Children are encouraged to splash and paddle in the water, which is shallow and safe. Elsewhere are a play area for younger children and a woodland adventure playground among the trees. A daily milking display takes place at 3.30pm.

INFORMATION

www.chatsworth.org
➕ 462 H14 ✉ Chatsworth, Bakewell DE45 1PP ☎ 01246 565300 ⊕ Park: all year. House, garden, farmyard and adventure playground: late Mar to mid-Dec daily. House: daily 11–5.30. Garden 11–6 (Jun–end Aug opens at 10.30). Farmyard and adventure playground: daily 10.30–5.30 ✋ Park: free. House and garden: adult £11.25, child (5–16) £6, family £28. Garden only: adult £7.50, child £4.50, family £21. Farmyard and adventure playground: adult or child (over 3) £5.25, family pass (all attractions) £46 📖 House £3.50, gardens £3.50, park £1, children's guide £1
🍴 💻 ♿

Above *Emperor Fountain, Chatsworth House, in the Peak District National Park*

CHARLECOTE PARK

www.nationaltrust.org.uk

This grand country house in the Warwickshire countryside has been the home of the Lucy family and their forbears, the Montforts, for 900 years, although the present rose-pink brick structure dates from 1551. Guests have included Elizabeth I (1533–1603), and the young William Shakespeare (1564–1616), who is alleged to have been caught poaching on the estate. Estate buildings open to visitors include the brewhouse, gatehouse, coach house and tack room. The fascinating Victorian kitchen, gives an idea of what life was like below stairs. The grounds were landscaped by Capability Brown.

✚ 458 H17 ✉ Wellesbourne CV35 9ER ☎ 01789 470277 🕐 House: Mar–end Oct Fri–Tue 12–5; mid Dec Sat–Sun 12–4. Grounds: Mar–end Oct Fri–Tue 10.30–6; Nov to mid-Dec, early Feb Sat–Sun 11–4 (also shop and restaurant) 🖐 Adult £7.45, child (5–16) £3.70, family £18.10 ▢ ▦

CHATSWORTH HOUSE

▷ 269.

Above *Houses across the River Wye, Hereford*
Opposite *Long Gallery, Hardwick Hall*

CHURCH STRETTON AND LONG MYND

www.visitsouthshropshire.co.uk

Some of the highest and least spoiled uplands in central England, Long Mynd has bracken- and bilberry-covered hillsides. The open moors are home to red grouse, with ring ouzels and wheatears favouring rocky outcrops. There are a few steep roads leading over the top, or you can walk into deep valleys such as Ashes Hollow and the Carding Mill Valley.

At the foot of the hills, Church Stretton, popular with the Victorians who came to sample its natural springs waters, makes a useful base for the area's activities, which include horseback riding, golf and gliding. East of the town, Caer Caradoc is perhaps the area's finest viewpoint, and is capped by the ramparts of an Iron Age hillfort. For more information about the area, visit the Shropshire Hills Discovery Centre (Apr–end Oct daily 10–5.30; Oct–Mar daily 10–4.30) near Craven Arms. Don't miss Stokesay Castle (Mar–end May, Sep–end Oct Thu–Mon 10–5; Jun–end Aug daily 10–6; rest of year Fri–Sun 10–4), one of England's best-preserved fortified medieval manor houses.

✚ 461 F16

CLUMBER PARK

www.nationaltrust.org.uk

One of the largest country parks in Europe, Clumber is the 1,500ha (3,700-acre) estate of a country house that was demolished in 1938. However, several features remain, including an estate village and Gothic Revival chapel. Encompassing forest, parkland, heathland and a huge serpentine lake, the park is large enough for a half day's walking, or you can follow one of several bicycle trails (bicycle rental Apr–end Oct, including tandems and child carriers).

The walled organic kitchen garden features a palm house, conservatory, vines, fig trees and herbaceous borders. There is a lively variety of special events most weekends from Easter to the end of September.

✚ 462J14 ✉ The Estate Office, Clumber Park, Worksop S80 3AZ ☎ 01909 544917 🕐 Daily dawn–dusk; Apr–end Sep only some facilities 🖐 Pedestrians, cyclists and those arriving by public transport free, cars £4.80 🍴 ▢ ▦

COVENTRY CATHEDRAL

www.coventrycathedral.org

On 14 November 1940 a bomb destroyed the medieval cathedral at Coventry. Its ruins now stand alongside the new cathedral, designed by the Scottish architect Sir Basil Spence (1907–76) and consecrated in 1962. Widely regarded as a masterpiece of modern architecture, Spence's edifice shows that contemporary style can still produce a feeling of spirituality. It has a great sense of internal space, height, peace and light, and is further distinguished by a parade of modern works of art. Most notable are the tapestry *Christ in Glory* by Graham Sutherland (1903–80), bronzes by Sir Jacob Epstein (1880–1959) and the Great Baptistry Window by John Piper (1903–92). See the West Screen before you leave, which is a wall of glass engraved with saints and angels.

✚ 458 H16 ✉ 1 Hill Top, Coventry CV1 5AB ☎ 024 7652 1200 🕐 Daily 9–5 🖐 Suggested donation £3.50 ▢ ▦

HADDON HALL

www.haddonhall.co.uk

One of the finest examples of an English medieval manor house, Haddon Hall has been in the family of the present owner, Lord Edward Manners, for over 800 years. It was modified between the 12th and 16th centuries, but has changed little since, although restoration of the house began in 2000. Intricately carved panelling adorns the Long Gallery, and the chapel has 15th-century wall paintings.

Outside, the castellations and towers are for picturesque effect rather than the defence of the estate. The garden terraces above the River Wye feature clipped yews and roses.

✚ 462 H14 ✉ Bakewell DE45 1LA ☎ 01629 812855 🕐 Apr Sat–Mon 12–5, May–end Sep daily 12–5, Oct Sat–Mon 12–5 ✋ Adult £8.50, child (5–16) £4.50, family £22 🍽 ▦

HARDWICK HALL

www.nationaltrust.org.uk

Built for the intruiging Bess of Hardwick, properly known as Elizabeth, Countess of Shrewsbury (1527–1608) in the 1590s, this late 16th-century house strongly evokes life in the Elizabethan period. Much of the original furniture and tapestries remain, and there is needlework by Mary, Queen of Scots (1542–87), who was held prisoner here for 15 years (▷ 32). The orchard and herb garden lie within the original walled courtyards, while beyond spreads a park grazed by rare breeds of cattle and sheep.

✚ 462 H14 ✉ Doe Lea, near Chesterfield S44 5QJ ☎ 01246 850430 🕐 Hall: Mar–end Oct Wed–Thu, Sat–Sun (also public holidays) 12–4.30. Garden: Apr–end Oct Wed–Sun 11–5.30. Park: daily 8–6 or dusk ✋ Adult £8.63, child (5–16) £4.31, family £21.59. Garden only: adult £4.31, child £2.09, family £10.72 🍽 ▦

HEREFORD

www.visitherefordshire.co.uk

Hereford looks its best in the area towards the River Wye, with a striking Georgian streetscape in Castle Street, and tree-shaded walks in Castle Green and along the river.

Dominating the skyline since the 12th century, Hereford Cathedral (daily 7.30–5.30) is built of golden sandstone and was modified during late medieval times. Highlights include the chained library and the Mappa Mundi, a unique world map which dates from 1290. To the north, the half-timbered Old House (Tue–Sat 10–5), built in 1621, is one of the city's finest town houses. The Hereford Cider Museum (Apr–end Oct Tue–Sat and public holidays 10–5; rest of year Tue–Sat and public holidays 11–3) in Pomona Place looks at the world of cider-making.

✚ 461 G17 ℹ 1 King Street, Hereford HR4 9BW, tel 01432 268430

INFORMATION

www.ironbridge.org.uk

✚ 461 G16 ✉ Coach Road, Coalbrookdale TF8 7DQ ☎ 01952 884391 🕐 Apr–end Oct daily 10–5, Nov–end Mar daily 10–4, smaller sites vary so check website for details. Pipeworks May–end Sep daily 1–5 🎟 Passport to all sites: adult £14.95, child (5–16) £9.95, family £48 🍴 🖥 🏛

IRONBRIDGE GORGE MUSEUMS

Several outstanding museums stand in the true birthplace of the Industrial Revolution. The Iron Bridge of 1779 did more than just span the modest River Severn: It was the first structure of its kind to be built of iron, and has come to symbolize the start of the Industrial Revolution. It was in this valley in 1709 that the ironmaster and engineer Abraham Darby I (1678–1717) pioneered the smelting of iron ore with coke rather than charcoal, making the mass-production of metal feasible.

The Gorge is dotted with nine sites that all belong to the museum. The largest is Blists Hill Victorian Town, reconstructed on the site of an 18th-century industrial estate, with working factories, shops and workers' cottages staffed by costumed actors and craftspeople. Coalport China Museum occupies what was the Coalport China Works. Close by is the entrance to the Tar Tunnel, where you go underground to see what was a natural source of bitumen when Ironbridge was functioning. Across the river stands the Jackfield Tile Museum, within a huge Victorian tile factory that is again making decorative tiles for sale.

South of Jackfield Bridge the Broseley Pipeworks, which used to manufacture clay tobacco pipes, has been left as it was when it closed in 1957 after 350 years of production. Beyond the Iron Bridge (which has an exhibition in its tollhouse) the Museum of the Gorge gives an overview of the development of the gorge as a whole, including a scale model of the area as it was in 1796. North of here the Coalbrookdale Museum of Iron contains the original blast furnace built by Abraham Darby I, while the Darby Houses were homes to the ironmasters. Enginuity, a hands-on attraction aimed at children, invites them to try such engineering tasks as stoking a furnace. The Hay Inclined Plane at Blists Hill is an astonishing engineering feat linking two canals by means of a steep tramway.

Above *Iron Bridge over the River Severn, Ironbridge*

JODRELL BANK OBSERVATORY AND ARBORETUM

www.jb.man.ac.uk

Find out about gravity, space travel, radio waves and the movement of the planets at the Observatory Visitor Centre. The main focus is the Lovell Telescope, in operation since 1957 and one of the largest fully steerable radio telescopes in the world. You can zoom in with a remote camera to see what the telescope is receiving through radio waves. Also on site is the second largest planetarium in Britain after London, and many child-friendly exhibits. Outside, the arboretum has national collections of rowan and apple tree species, and a birdwatching hide.

✚ 461 G14 ✉ Near Macclesfield SK11 9DL ☎ 01477 571339 ⏱ Easter–end Oct daily 10.30–5.30; rest of year daily 10.30–3 or 4 (check website for changes) ✋ Adult £2, child (4–16) £1. Planetarium/3D Show £1 (children under 4 free) 🅿 📷

KENILWORTH CASTLE

www.english-heritage.org.uk

No other English castle ruin even approaches 12th-century Kenilworth for sheer size. It has huge sandstone walls, a Great Hall and a mighty Norman keep. Robert Dudley (c1532–88), the Earl of Leicester, transformed it into a Tudor palace, and Elizabeth I (▷ 33), with whom he was having an affair, visited him here in 1575. Sir Walter Scott (1771–1832) stayed close by, while writing his novel Kenilworth (1821).

✚ 458 H16 ✉ Castle Mews, Kenilworth CV8 1NE ☎ 01926 852078 ⏱ Jun–end Aug daily 10–6; Mar–end May, Sep–end Oct 10–5; Nov–end Feb 10–4; closed 24–26 Dec and 1 Jan ✋ Adult £6, child (5–16) £3, family £15 🅿 Apr–end Oct 📷

LICHFIELD

www.visitlichfield.com

The glory of Lichfield is its cathedral (daily 7.40–6.15), with its trio of dark sandstone spires soaring over half-timbered houses and the former 17th-century Bishop's Palace in the cathedral close. The west front is adorned with 113 statues, including 24 English kings, while inside its many treasures include an eighth-century illuminated manuscript known as the St. Chad's Gospels, which are only on display sporadically due to restoration (tel 01543 306240). Lichfield's most famous son was the man of letters Samuel Johnson (1709–84); the house where he was born in Breadmarket Street is now The Samuel Johnson Birthplace Museum (Apr–end Sep daily 10.30–4.30; rest of year 12–4.30).

Try and time your visit to see one of the many musical events at the cathedral.

✚ 461 H16 ℹ Lichfield Garrick, Castle Dyke, Lichfield WS13 6HR, tel 01543 308209

LINCOLN

www.visitlincolnshire.com

Lincoln is visible for miles around in the low-lying landscape, with its castle and majestic twin-towered cathedral prominent on a high hill. From the modern pedestrianized shopping streets at the foot of the hill, a walk up appropriately named Steep Hill leads into Minster Yard and Lincoln Cathedral (summer Mon–Fri 7.15–8, Sat–Sun 7.15–6; winter Mon–Sat 7.15–6, Sun 7.15–5), mostly from the 13th and 14th centuries and in the top league of England's ecclesiastical architecture. Highlights include the elaborate west facade, stained-glass rose windows and 14th-century carved choir stalls. Close by are the Bishop's Palace (Apr–end Jun, Sep–end Oct daily 10–5; Jul–end Aug daily 10–6; rest of year Thu–Mon 10–4), and Lincoln Castle dating from Norman times and retaining gateways, towers and a 19th-century prisoners' chapel.

Museum attractions include the free Usher Gallery (daily 10–5) in Danes Road, with fine and decorative arts and memorabilia of the locally born poet Alfred, Lord Tennyson (1809–92), and the Museum of Lincolnshire Life (May–end Sep daily 10–5; rest of year Mon–Sat 10–5), Burton Road.

✚ 462 J14 ℹ 9 Castle Hill, Lincoln LN1 3AA, tel 01522 873213

LITTLE MORETON HALL

www.nationaltrust.org.uk

Little Moreton Hall is the perfect example of a moated timber-framed manor house. The black-and-white timbering is quite eyecatching. The Long Gallery was the final phase of building, completed 140 years after the Great Hall was begun in the 1440s. Although a visit will probably not last long, this building is a treat for those interested in English architecture. Check in advance for special Living History weekends.

✚ 461 G15 ✉ Congleton CW12 4SD ☎ 01260 272018 ⏱ Mar–end Oct Wed–Sun 11.30–5; Nov to mid-Dec Sat–Sun 11.30–4 ✋ Adult £5.25, child (5–16) £2.50, family £12.50 🍴 📷

Left *Haunting castle ruins stand proud at Kenilworth*

LUDLOW
www.ludlow.org.uk
Georgian brickwork and earlier half-timbering grace the streets of this hilltop town, with Broad Street a particularly harmonious example of townscape. Ludlow Castle (Jan Sat–Sun 10–4; Feb–end Mar, Oct–end Dec daily 10–4; Apr–end Jul, Sep daily 10–5; Aug daily 10–7), a border fortress begun in the late 11th century, was enlarged in the 14th century into a palace for the powerful Roger Mortimer. Near the ancient Butter Cross, the church of St. Laurence assumes a practically cathedral-like grandeur, and has a fine set of 15th-century carved misericords (benches in the choir). The town has emerged as a regional foodie capital, with a range of restaurants. The annual Ludlow Festival (▷ 291), has drama performances in the castle grounds.
✚ 461 G16 ⓘ Castle Street, Ludlow SY8 1AS, tel 01584 875053

LYME PARK
www.nationaltrust.org.uk
One of the finest examples of English Palladian architecture, the grey-stone Hall was begun in the 16th century and remodelled in 1725 by the Venetian architect Giacomo Leoni, giving the house Classical proportions and baroque ceilings. Some of the Elizabethan interiors survive, and contrast strongly with later rooms. In the Saloon, the great woodcarver Grinling Gibbons (1648–1721) added virtuoso carving.

The large grounds have strongly contrasting views, with urban Manchester (▷ 316) on one side and the rural Peak District (▷ opposite) on the other. There is ample scope for walks in the huge deer park, which contains woodland, ornamental gardens and an 18th-century hunting lodge known as The Cage. The scene in the 1995 BBC television adaptation of Jane Austen's *Pride and Prejudice* where the character Mr. Darcy emerges from a lake was filmed here.
✚ 461 G14 ✉ Disley, Stockport SK12 2NR ☎ 01663 766492 (recording), 01663 762023

ⓖ House: Apr–end Oct Fri–Tue 11–5. Park: Apr–end Oct daily 8am–8.30pm; rest of year daily 8–6. Garden: Apr–end Oct daily 11–5; Mar–end Nov to mid-Dec Sat–Sun 12–3 ✋ House: adult £5, child (5–16) £2.50. House and garden: adult £6.90, child £3.40, family £17.20. Park: £4.60 per car, refundable on purchase of house and garden ticket. Garden only: adult £4.30, child £2.10
🍴 ☐ ⊞

MACCLESFIELD SILK MUSEUM AND PARADISE MILL
www.silk-macclesfield.org
Three related attractions tell the story of silk production in the town of Macclesfield. The Silk Museum in Park Lane has exhibits about all aspects of the industry, including the workers' lives, the operation of looms, and manufactured silk. The Heritage Centre on Roe Street, close by, has a collection of silk costumes and displays related to the development of the silk industry in the town, housed within a former Sunday School. You can also explore a re-creation of a Victorian school room. A short walk away is Paradise Mill, a 19th-century silk-producing mill in operation until 1981. Inside, little has been changed, with handlooms that were installed in 1912 still in working order.
✚ 461 G14 ✉ Park Lane, Macclesfield SK11 6TJ ☎ Heritage Centre 01625 613210; Paradise Mill 01625 612045 ⓖ Silk Museum: Mon–Sat 11–5, public holiday Mon 12–4. Paradise Mill: guided tours Mon–Sat 11.45, 1, 2.15. Heritage Centre: Mon–Sat 11–5, Sun 12–4; closed Good Fri ✋ All three sites: adult £7.90, children free. Site Heritage Museum adult £3.90, children free 🍴 ☐ ⊞

MALVERN HILLS
www.malvernhills.gov.uk
Malvern water has been noted for its purity since the 18th century. Malvern Wells still has a spa atmosphere in its ornate Victorian buildings, although Great Malvern, to the north, is older; its magnificent priory church has some stunning 15th-century stained glass.

The long, narrow ridge of the Malvern Hills rises suddenly away from the town. From a distance they look like a jagged mountain range, but close up they appear much less daunting. Several marked walks reveal far-ranging views of the Cotswolds and along the border with Wales.
✚ 461 G17 ⓘ 21 Church Street, Malvern WR14 2AA, tel 01684 892289

MR STRAW'S HOUSE
www.nationaltrust.org.uk
From the exterior, this appears to be a perfectly ordinary Edwardian house, yet its owner, a tradesman by the name of Mr. Straw, changed virtually nothing in more than 60 years of living here from 1923. After his death it was opened to the public by the National Trust in the mid-1990s. Mr Straw's letters, photographs, clothing, furniture, wallpaper and other household items have been preserved intact, creating a fascinating time capsule. There is a lovely traditional suburban garden.
✚ 462 J14 ✉ 7 Blyth Grove, Worksop S81 0JG ☎ 01909 482380 ⓖ Late Mar–end Oct Tue–Sat 11–5 ✋ Adult £5.18, child (5–16) £2.70, family £13.50. Admission by pre-reserved timed ticket only.

NOTTINGHAM
www.visitnottingham.com
Although not the most attractive of cities, Nottingham has a real buzz, with a vibrant mix of lively bars, pubs and clubs.

The Castle Museum and Art Gallery (daily 10–5) includes the Story of Nottingham gallery and has underground tours through passages cut below the city (in which Ye Olde Trip to Jerusalem pub is built). For more underground tours, visit the City of Caves (daily 10.30–4) beneath the Broadmarsh Shopping Centre, dug out over the centuries. The Galleries of Justice (Apr–end Oct Tue–Sun and public holidays 10–4; rest of year Tue–Fri 10–3, Sat–Sun 10–4), in Shire Hall, vividly re-enact a trial in a Victorian court and the grim hardship of life in a prison cell.
✚ 462 J15 ⓘ 1–4 Smithy Row, Nottingham NG1 2BY, tel 0115 915 5330

PEAK DISTRICT NATIONAL PARK

www.peakdistrict.org

Ringed by industrial cities such as Manchester and Sheffield, the Peak District provides an exhilarating sense of freedom and space.

The Peak District is really two landscapes: The Dark Peak is an area of bleak, open gritstone moors with rocky edges, such as Stanage Edge, while the White Peak is formed of classic limestone country with stone-walled pastures cut by deep dales (valleys), such as Dovedale, Lathkill Dale and Monsal Dale.

Of the many villages worth a look in the area are Tissington, with wide grassy borders and a Jacobean hall, and Eyam, where you can follow the moving story of a village that, finding itself ravaged by plague in 1665, deliberately isolated itself from the outside world. The canalside village of Cromford had the world's first water-powered mill in 1771, now a museum.

The ruins of Peveril Castle (May–end Aug daily 10–6; Apr and Sep–end Oct daily 10–5; Nov–end Mar Wed–Sun 10–4) overlook Castleton at the heart of the Peak's cave district, with several caverns open to the public. The Blue John Cavern at Castleton (summer daily 9.30–5.30; rest of year 9.30–dusk), with its vast stalactite- and stalagmite-covered interior, also includes the Blue John Mine that extracts Blue John stone, one of the rarest and most beautiful forms of fluorspar. Also worth visiting in the Peak District are Buxton (▷ 268), Chatsworth House (▷ 269), Haddon Hall (▷ 271), and Lyme Park (▷ opposite). For a walk and tour, ▷ 282–285.

✚ 462 H14 ⓘ Old Market Hall, Bridge Street, Bakewell DE45 1DS, tel 01629 813227

QUARRY BANK MILL AND STYAL COUNTRY PARK

www.quarrybankmill.org.uk

On the wooded fringes of Manchester, the River Bollin runs through Styal Country Park, a rewarding area for walks marred only by the noise of aircraft from Manchester Airport near by.

The main focus of the park is Quarry Bank Mill, a water-powered cotton mill built in 1784, and restored by the National Trust. The looms clatter away, and exhibits evoke the working life of the mill. You can also see spinning and weaving demonstrations. The Apprentice House shows how a mill apprentice would have lived 160 years ago; reserve your ticket as soon as you arrive as places are limited.

✚ 461 G14 ✉ Quarry Bank Road, Styal SK9 4LA ☎ 01625 445896 ⓦ Estate: daily, dawn–dusk. Mill: Mar–end Oct daily 11–5; Nov–end Jan Wed–Sun 11–4. Apprentice House: Mar–end Oct daily; Nov–end Jan Wed–Sun, timed tickets necessary. Garden: Mar–end Oct daily 11–5 ♿ Mill and Apprentice House: adult £8.63, child (5–16) £4.36, family £20.63. Mill only: adult £6.09, child £3.36, family £15.45 🍴 🖥 🏛

Above *View over Ladybower Reservoir in the Peak District National Park, Derbyshire*

INFORMATION

www.shakespeare-country.co.uk
www.shakespeare.org.uk
🔁 458 H17 ℹ️ Bridgefoot, Stratford-upon-Avon CV37 6GW, tel 0870 160 7930
❓ Avon Boating runs short river cruises in Victorian and Edwardian craft from near the theatres; www.avon-boating.co.uk 🚉 Stratford-upon-Avon

Above *The timber-framed Grammar School of Stratford-upon-Avon*

INTRODUCTION

Home of Britain's greatest playwright and the Royal Shakespeare Company, Stratford has become a very popular stop on the tourist route, but is still the top destination for literary pilgrims. A wealth of Tudor architecture and plenty of other attractions await.

Before the birth of the world's greatest playwright (▷ 32, 33), to John and Mary Shakespeare, Stratford was a busy but unexceptional market town, where merchants built imposing half-timbered houses. Even without the Shakespeare connection, Stratford is a very appealing town on the River Avon, with many historical buildings. One of the most photogenic spots is Church Street. Many of the buildings have Georgian frontages, but the 15th-century almshouses are timber-framed, and the King Edward VI School is thought to be where Shakespeare was educated. The Guildhall Chapel dates from the 13th century and is still a place of worship.

WHAT TO SEE

SHAKESPEARE'S BIRTHPLACE

The site most visitors head for first is this building in the middle of town. Whether this marks the Bard's true birthplace is open to question, but it has become his shrine. Since his birth in 1564, this half-timbered Tudor house has changed, but the interior has been refurbished to give a good impression of the young Shakespeare's life.

✉️ Henley Street CV37 6QW ☎️ 01789 204016 🕐 Apr–end May, Sep–end Oct daily 10–5; Jun–end Aug daily 9–5; Nov–end Mar Mon–Sat 10–4, Sun 10.30–4

ROYAL SHAKESPEARE COMPANY

The Royal Shakespeare Company (RSC) maintains Stratford's theatrical traditions. Its principal theatre, the Royal Shakespeare, was designed in cinema-style in the 1930s. This, and its smaller sister theatre, The Swan, are now being comprehensively redesigned to bring them up to 21st-century standards. The work is due for completion in 2010. In the meantime the company is performing in different venues around Stratford-upon-Avon, as well as in the Courtyard Theatre, a temporary structure built onto the existing studio theatre (known as The Other Place). To rub shoulders with thespians, visit the 16th-century Dirty Duck, near the theatre complex, which is a favourite watering hole of RSC actors.

ANNE HATHAWAY'S COTTAGE
Shakespeare's wife lived in this pretty thatched cottage. You can walk along the country lane from Hall's Croft to avoid the traffic. The house stayed in the Hathaway family until the 19th century, and much of the family furniture remains.
✉ Cottage Lane, Shottery CV37 9HH ☎ 01789 204016 🕓 Apr–end May, Sep–end Oct Mon–Sat 9.30–5, Sun 10–5; Jun–end Aug daily 9–5; Nov–end Mar daily 10–4

MARY ARDEN'S HOUSE AND THE SHAKESPEARE COUNTRYSIDE MUSEUM
The childhood home of Shakespeare's mother is 3 miles (5km) north of town. Walk along the towpath of the Stratford-upon-Avon Canal or take the train one stop beyond Stratford. The Shakespeare Countryside Museum surrounds the cottage and has displays about life and work here, and Glebe Farm, a working blacksmith's and falconer's.
✉ Station Road, Wilmcote CV37 9UN ☎ 01789 204016 🕓 Apr–end May, Sep–end Oct daily 10–5; Jun–end Aug daily 9.30–5; Nov–end Mar daily 10–4

HOLY TRINITY CHURCH
Out of town by the river is the 13th-century church where Shakespeare was baptized in 1564 and buried in 1616, as shown by the baptismal entry and burial notice in the parish register here. His gravestone is in front of the altar.
✉ Old Town CV37 6BG ☎ 01789 415563 🕓 Apr–end Sep Mon–Sat 8.30–6, Sun 12.30–5; rest of year Mon–Sat 9–4, Sun 12.30–5

HALL'S CROFT
This half-timbered house is named after the respected physician Dr. John Hall, who married Shakespeare's daughter, Susanna, in 1607. It contains period furnishings and there is also a small display of medicine that would have been used in Shakespeare's day.
✉ Old Town CV37 6BG ☎ 01789 204016 🕓 Nov–end Mar daily 11–4; Apr–end May, Sep–end Oct daily 11–5; Jun–end Aug Mon–Sat 9.30–5, Sun 10–5

HARVARD HOUSE
Now containing the Neish Collection of Pewter, this ornate timbered house was the home of Katherine Rogers, mother of clergyman John Harvard (1607–38), who emigrated to Massachusetts shortly before his death. His generous bequests to the newly founded US college at Cambridge led to its being named after him.
✉ High Street CV37 6HP ☎ 01789 204016 🕓 End May–end Jun and mid-Sep to end Oct Fri–Sun 12–5; 4 Jul–end Aug Wed–Sun 12–5; public holidays in May and Aug 12–5

MORE TO SEE
NEW PLACE
The house where Shakespeare died in 1616 no longer exists, but its site in Chapel Street is marked by a garden next to Nash's House (daily), itself owned by the first husband of his granddaughter Elizabeth and now containing displays on the town's history.
✉ Chapel Street CV37 6EP ☎ 01789 204016 🕓 Jul–end Aug Mon–Sat 9.30–5, Sun 10–5; Apr–end May and Sep–end Oct daily 11–5; Nov–end Mar daily 11–4

TIPS
» Hop-on hop-off tours, run by City Sightseeing are a useful way to get to Anne Hathaway's Cottage and Mary Arden's House.
» Combined tickets are sold for the Shakespeare houses: New Place, Nash's House, Hall's Croft, Anne Hathaway's Cottage and Mary Arden's House.

Above *Old Market Hall, Shrewsbury*

SHREWSBURY

www.visitshrewsbury.co.uk

Black-and-white Tudor houses and Georgian red brick distinguish the old town of Shrewsbury, on a peninsula tightly enclosed by a great loop of the River Severn, guarded on its landward side by Shrewsbury Castle (Mon–Sat 10–5, Sun 10–4), which contains the Shropshire Regimental Museum. Examples of half-timbered buildings include Owen's Mansion and Ireland's Mansion, close to the arcaded Old Market Hall of 1596, while the narrow alley of the Bear Steps leads past a timber-framed hall now housing an art gallery.

About 6 miles (9.5km) southeast of Shrewsbury, Wroxeter Roman City (Apr–end Oct daily; Nov–end Mar Wed–Sun) had a population of 6,000 in Roman times, but was later abandoned. It has the remains of a second-century municipal baths and a museum.

⊕ 461 F15 ⓘ The Music Hall, The Square, Shrewsbury SY1 1LH, tel 01743 281200

SHUGBOROUGH ESTATE

www.shugborough.org.uk

The ancestral home of the earls of Lichfield is a crisply classical 17th- and 18th-century mansion. During the 1740s, rococo plasterwork was added to the sumptuous state rooms. In addition to period furniture, paintings, ceramics and silver, there are photographs by the late Patrick, Earl of Lichfield (1939–2005), a celebrated photographer. You can visit the servants' quarters, kitchen, brewhouse and coach house, plus a Victorian schoolroom and puppet shop. The park has some unusual classical monuments, as well as Park Farm, with an agricultural museum and rare farm breeds.

⊕ 4461 G15 ✉ Milford, near Stafford ST17 0XB ☎ 01889 881388 ⓒ Late Mar–end Oct daily 11–5 ♿ Whole site: adult £12, child (5–16) £7, family £30. National Trust members: house free; all sites £6 🍴 🖥 🏛

SNIBSTON DISCOVERY PARK

www.leics.gov.uk/museums

Snibston is a well-designed museum where learning and fun go hand in hand—though not to the detriment of the seriousness of subjects such as conditions down a 19th-century coal mine, where men, women and children worked in sometimes appalling situations. Using former industrial buildings and the Coalville mine buildings, the park mixes indoor and outdoor educational activities, including outdoor science and water playgrounds.

⊕ 462 H15 ✉ Ashby Road, Coalville LE67 3LN ☎ 01530 278444 ⓒ Apr–end Sep daily 10–5; Oct–end Mar Mon–Fri 10–3, Sat–Sun 10–5 ♿ Adult £6.40, child (5–15) £4.20, family £19.20 🖥 🏛

SOUTHWELL

www.southwellminster.org.uk
www.nationaltrust.org.uk

The minster (Apr–end Sep daily 8–7; rest of year daily 8–dusk) is the architectural highlight of this small Nottinghamshire town (pronounced suthall). Dating from Norman times, the chapterhouse (begun 1292) has superbly delicate carving, celebrating the foliage of Sherwood Forest in stone. In Upton Road, The Workhouse (early Mar, Oct Sat–Sun 11–4; late Mar Wed–Sun 11–4; Apr–end Sep Wed–Sun 12–5), the best-preserved building of its kind in Britain, evokes the grim life of the destitute. Opened in 1824 to shelter and feed the sick and poor, the workhouse is typical of the many that once dotted the country.

⊕ 462 J15 ⓘ The Gilstrap Centre, Castlegate, Newark NG24 1BG, tel 01636 655765

STOKE-ON-TRENT

www.visitstoke.co.uk

Potteries are known to have existed since at least 1300 in the Six Towns (Burslem, Fenton, Hanley, Longton, Stoke and Tunstall) that make up the Stoke-on-Trent conurbation. Some of the most desirable ceramics in the world have come from this region. Twelve of the potteries have factory tours, and two of these are large-scale attractions with visitor centres—Wedgwood (Mon–Fri 9–5, Sat–Sun 10–5; closed 24 Dec–2 Jan) and Spode (Mon–Sat 9–5, Sun 10–4); the Spode factory dates from the 18th century, and tours run on weekdays. These and many other potteries have factory shops with big discounts.

For an interesting overview of the history of Staffordshire pottery, visit the free Potteries Museum and Art Gallery (Mar–end Oct Mon–Sat 10–5, Sun 2–5; rest of year Mon–Sat 10–4, Sun 1–4) in Hanley. The Gladstone Pottery Museum (daily 10–5), in Longton, occupies the area's last working Victorian pottery factory.

⊕ 461 G15 ⓘ Bagnall Street, Hanley, Stoke-on-Trent ST1 3AD, tel 01782 236000

STONELEIGH ABBEY

www.stoneleighabbey.org

Stoneleigh is a country house occupying a medieval monastic site. Visitors are taken to the room where Queen Victoria (1819–1901) slept, the dining room where she and her husband, Prince Albert (1819–61) dined in 1858, and the bath that was made specially for her visit. It is also recorded that novelist Jane Austen (1775–1817) paid a visit to the house in 1806.

✚ 458 H16 ✉ Stoneleigh, near Kenilworth CV8 2LF ☎ 01926 858535 ◷ House: Good Fri–end Oct Tue–Thu, Sun and public holidays 11–4. Grounds: 10–5 ♿ Grounds only, £3 per person. Guided tours of West Wing and Stables: adult £6.50, first child (5–12) free, additional child £3 ❓ Abbey: 90-min guided tours only at 11am, 1pm and 3pm; reservations not essential, but advisable to arrive slightly early ▣ 🏛

STRATFORD-UPON-AVON

▷ 276–277.

SUDBURY HALL AND NATIONAL TRUST MUSEUM OF CHILDHOOD

www.nationaltrust.org.uk

Considered one of the finest houses of its period in England, Sudbury Hall dates from the late 17th century. Its greatest qualities are the interiors, with carving by Grinling Gibbons (1648–1721), painted ceilings and murals of mythological subjects by Louis Laguerre, and a spectacular staircase carved by Edward Pierce. The Gallery—one of the longest in England—has an opulent decorative plasterwork ceiling.

In the 19th-century service wing, the National Trust Museum of Childhood looks into the world of the child, past and present, with collections of antique toys and dolls. Younger visitors also get the opportunity to play the role of chimney-sweep and climb inside a chimney.

✚ 462 H15 ✉ Sudbury, Ashbourne DE6 5HT ☎ 01283 585305 ◷ Apr–end Oct Wed–Sun 1–5; early Dec Sat–Sun 11–4 ♿ Hall and Museum (including gardens): adult £11.25, child (5–16) £6.12, family £27.90. Hall or museum: adult £6.48, child £3.78, family £16.74 ▣ 🏛

TATTON PARK

www.tattonpark.org.uk

The Classical Georgian mansion and 405ha (1,000-acre) park at Tatton stage a lively variety of events throughout the year, including flower shows, antiques fairs, vintage car shows, drama and concerts with fireworks. The house has furniture that was specially made by furniture makers Waring and Gillow of Lancaster, and paintings by Canaletto (1697–1768). The Tudor Old Hall was its precursor.

The grounds have plenty to entice, with a Japanese garden, rose garden, fern house, maze and rare-breeds farm, as well as woodland walks and several bicycle trails.

✚ 461 G14 ✉ Near Knutsford WA16 6QN ☎ 01625 534435 (recording), 01625 534400 ◷ Park: Easter–end Sep daily 10–7; rest of year Tue–Sun 11–5. Gardens: Apr–end Sep Tue–Sun 10–6; rest of year Tue–Sun 11–4. Mansion: Apr–end Sep Tue–Sun 1–5. Farm: Apr–end Sep Tue–Sun 12–5; rest of year Sat–Sun 11–4. Old Hall: Apr–end Sep Sat–Sun guided tours only. ♿ Mansion, gardens, Tudor Old Hall and farm (per attraction): adult £4, child (4–15) £2, family £10; car entry to park £4.50 ▣ 🏛

Below *Tatton Park, Georgian mansion and gardens owned by the National Trust*

WALL ROMAN SITE (LETOCETUM)

www.english-heritage.org.uk

There is little above foundation level to be seen here, yet the museum and audiotour help to bring the place back to life.

Known to the Romans as Lectocetum, Wall was established as a military base in around AD50 at the junction of two routes—Watling Street and the Rykneld Way—and grew into a busy town, providing overnight accommodation for travelling Roman officials and imperial messengers. The bathhouse is one of the most complete Roman relics of its kind in Britain, and there are also remains of a mansion.

🕇 461 H16 ✉ Watling Street, Wall WS15 0AW ☎ 0121 625 6820 🕔 Mar–Oct daily 10–5 ✋ Free

WARWICK CASTLE

▷ 281.

WEST MIDLANDS SAFARI PARK AND LEISURE PARK

www.wmsp.co.uk

The 4-mile (6.5km) drive through this hugely popular safari park takes about an hour and gives visitors a close encounter with lions, giraffes, zebras and more, as well as with some endangered species such as white rhinoceroses and Bengal tigers. You may also get the chance to feed antelopes. Throughout the day there are live shows that might feature a reptile encounter, feeding the hippos or a sea-lion show.

The leisure park area has lots of entertaining rides, as well as the heart-stopping Venom Tower Drop, which takes you gently to the top of its 30m (98ft) tower, then plummets back to earth. Younger children will enjoy pets' corner where they can touch and feed the animals.

🕇 461 G16 ✉ Spring Grove, Bewdley DY12 1LF ☎ 01299 402114 🕔 Mid-Mar to end Oct daily from 10 (closing time varies, the earliest is 3) ✋ All visitors over 4 years old £10.50, under 3s free 🍴 🖥 🏛

WORCESTER

www.visitworcester.com

The city of Worcester is a mix of the sublime and the mundane: Amid some insensitive 20th-century development and fine streets of Georgian mansions and timber-framed buildings is the cathedral (daily 7.30–6), with a superb crypt, cloister and monuments, including that of King John (1167–1216) and the 14th-century Beauchamp tomb. The Royal Worcester Porcelain Works (visitor centre: Mon–Sat 9–5.30, Sun 11–5, closed Easter Sun; tours Mon–Fri, reservations advised) dates from 1751 and offers a factory tour and a museum, where examples of this delicate china through the ages are on display in period settings.

During the Battle of Worcester in 1651, Charles II (1630–85) made his headquarters near the cathedral at the 11th-century Commandery (Mon–Sat 10–5, Sun 1.30–5), which now houses the Civil War Visitor Centre, focusing on the trial of Charles I and Cromwell's campaign (▷ 34, 35).

Another famous person associated with this area is one of England's greatest composers, Edward Elgar (1857–1934), whose statue stands near the cathedral. He was born outside the city at Lower Broadheath, at what is now the Elgar Birthplace Museum (daily 11–5; closed 23 Dec–31 Jan).

🕇 461 G17 🛈 The Guildhall, High Street, Worcester WR1 2EY, tel 01905 726311

Below *Interior of Worcester Cathedral, Worcester*

WARWICK CASTLE

Architecturally, Warwick is one of the finest examples of a medieval castle in England, with its exteriors dating back to the 14th and 15th centuries. To appreciate this almost too perfect-looking to be real castle from the outside, walk around the walls and through the gardens, landscaped by Capability Brown in the 1750s, with the subsequent addition of a Victorian Rose Garden and Peacock Garden. The castle is owned by the Merlin Group (which also runs the London Eye and Madame Tussaud's in London, ▷ 81) and is run as a modern tourist attraction.

The interior was thoroughly upgraded between the 17th to 19th centuries, and the private apartments are furnished as they would have been in 1898. The Royal Weekend Party uses waxwork figures to replicate aristocratic life of that time, one guest being the young Winston Churchill (1874–1965). The Dream of Battle feature asks you to imagine the experiences of a 12-year-old boy on the eve of the battle of Barnet in 1461. Through a mix of live action and computer generated graphics it portrays the noise and terror of wartime in medieval England.

WARWICK

Many visitors to the castle unfortunately miss the town of Warwick itself, which was given a handsome makeover after a disastrous fire in 1694. As a result, it has some of the finest 18th-century streetscapes in England, notably in the High Street and Northgate Street. Predating the fire are two medieval gateways, the old houses in Castle Lane, the 15th-century Beauchamp tomb in the Church of St. Mary and (near the West Gate) Lord Leycester Hospital (closed Mon). The last of these is a wonderfully complete group of half-timbered buildings (mostly 16th-century). Visitors can look into the chapel, courtyard and great hall.

INFORMATION

www.warwick–castle.co.uk

✚ 458 H16 ✉ Warwick CV34 4QU
☎ 0870 442 2000 🕐 Apr–end Sep daily 10–6; rest of year daily 10–5
✋ Summer: adult £18.95, child (4–16) £11.95, family £56 ❓ Audiotour £2.50
📖 £3.95 🍴 🏬 📷 🏛 Warwick

Above *Warwick Castle stands beside the River Avon*

THE PEAK DISTRICT NATIONAL PARK

This drive explores the gentler southern White Peak, with its high, close-cropped sheep pasture, limestone dry walling and wooded valleys. It also offers a glimpse of the Dark Peak—bleaker moorland and angular outcrops of blackened millstone grit.

THE DRIVE
Distance: 57 miles (92km)
Allow: 2 hours
Start/end: Castleton

★ Perched above Castleton is Peveril Castle, built by William Peveril—the illegitimate son of William the Conqueror—and immortalized in Sir Walter Scott's 1825 novel *Peveril of the Peak*. Castleton is surrounded by show caves (▷ 284), of which Peak Cavern has the best entrance.

From Castleton go east on the A625 through Hope, then turn right on to the B6049. Soon turn left on unclassified roads to Great Hucklow, via Foolow to Eyam.

❶ In 1665, the year of the Great Plague, a chest of infected cloth was sent from London to Eyam. Soon, four out of every five villagers were dead. The villagers resolved to isolate themselves and prevent the disease from wiping out other communities nearby. The churchyard graves reflect this sad story, and every August a service is held in a nearby dell, Cucklets Church.

Leave Eyam on the B6251, then go left on to the A623. At Baslow turn right on to the A619, then left on to the B6012. After 5 miles (8km) turn left at Edensor for Chatsworth.

❷ Chatsworth (▷ 269) is one of the grandest country houses in England, and is popularly known as the 'Palace of the Peak'. Edensor is its village.

Leave Chatsworth, then turn left on to the B6012. At Rowsley turn left on to the A6 for Matlock and carry on through to Matlock Bath.

❸ Adjoining Matlock is Matlock Bath, the 19th-century spa town where tall Victorian villas scale the hillside. The spa pavilion now houses the Peak District Mining Museum, which includes access to the disused lead and fluorspar workings of Temple Mine. A cable-car takes you from the river at Matlock Bath to the 305m (1,000ft) Heights of Abraham, a park with zigzagging paths, a maze and a playground. At the top you can climb the Victoria Prospect Tower, and below ground there are two caverns to explore: Great Rutland and Great Masson.

Leave Matlock Bath on the A6 to reach Cromford.

❹ Cromford marks a significant point in the emergence of England as an industrial nation. It was here in 1771 that Sir Richard Arkwright (1732–92)—the inventor of mechanical spinning (▷ 36)—erected Cromford Mill, the world's first mechanized textile factory. Close by is the Cromford Canal, which once had a busy wharf, but now offers a tranquil towpath towards the old rail station. The defunct trackbed is now the High Peak Trail, a route for walkers and cyclists.

5 The National Tramway Museum at Crich, south of Cromford, has more than 40 trams from all over the world, built between 1873 and 1953. Volunteers keep the vehicles in pristine condition, and several trams run on any given day. The admission price allows unlimited rides along the 1-mile (1.5km) route.

From Cromford turn right on the A5012, signposted Buxton. Turn right on to the B5056, then left on the A6 to the little market town of Bakewell.

6 The fine, five-arched stone bridge, built in 1300 to span the River Wye, is the principal feature of Bakewell. The Romans came here for the warm springs and the Saxons named it Bad Quell or 'bath well'. Most of the buildings are 17th- and 18th-century, but the Old House Museum, with wattle-and-daub walls, is at least 100 years older, and contains ancient objects. The town is the headquarters of the Peak District National Park (▷ 275), and its best-known shop is the Old Original Bakewell Pudding Shop. Bakewell puddings (never called Bakewell tarts here) originated in the kitchens of the Rutland Arms Hotel (▷ 292), when the cook accidentally poured an egg mixture on to the jam instead of the pastry. Just outside town is Haddon Hall, one of England's best medieval manor houses (▷ 271).

Go north on the A6 from Bakewell. At Ashford in the Water turn right on to the B6465 and in 4 miles (6.5km) turn left on to the A623, then left into Tideswell.

7 Tideswell expanded with the medieval wool trade, but over the years it has become a sleepy backwater, and little remains to indicate the town's heyday. One glorious exception is the 14th-century church of St. John the Baptist—known as 'the Cathedral of the Peak'—with a

soaring tower. Tideswell is a venue for well-dressing, the local tradition of decorating wells and springs with pictures made from living plants and flowers, which takes place at the end of June or in early July.

From Tideswell follow the B6049 south, then the A6 to Buxton.

8 Buxton is one of the highest towns in England, at 307m (1,007ft), and has plenty of reminders of its spa days (▷ 268).

Continue north on the A6 towards Chapel-en-le-Frith. Before reaching it, turn right on the A623, then left followed by a fork to the right on unclassified roads down the Winnats Pass, and back into Castleton.

WHERE TO EAT
The French Renaissance Restaurant in Bath Street, Bakewell (tel 01629 812687), is in a converted barn with stone walls and beamed ceiling, and would make a treat for lunch, with dishes such as pork fillet stuffed with black pudding. There are plenty of pubs and eateries in Castleton.

PLACES TO VISIT
CROMFORD MILL
✉ Cromford DE24 3RQ ☎ 01629 824297 🕐 Daily 9–5 ✋ Tours: adult £2, child £1.50

NATIONAL TRAMWAY MUSEUM
✉ Matlock DE4 5DP ☎ 0870 758 7267 🕐 Mid-Mar to end Oct daily 10.30–5; rest of year 10.30–4 ✋ Adult £8.50, child £4.50

OLD HOUSE MUSEUM
✉ Heald Bank, The Yeld, Bakewell DE45 1FH ☎ 01629 813165 🕐 Apr–end Oct daily 11–4 ✋ Adult £2.50, child £1

PEAK DISTRICT MINING MUSEUM
✉ Pavilion, Matlock DE4 3NR ☎ 01629 583834 🕐 Summer daily 10–5; winter 11–4 ✋ Adult £3, child £2

PEVERIL CASTLE
✉ Castleton S33 8WQ ☎ 01433 620613 🕐 May–end Sep daily 10–6; Apr, Oct daily 10–5; rest of year Wed–Sun 10–4 ✋ Adult £3, child £1.50

WHEN TO GO
Go in June or July if you want to see the dressed wells of the Peak villages.

CAVE DALE AND THE CASTLETON CAVES

Castleton is where the shales and gritstone of the Dark Peak and the limestone plateau of the White Peak meet in the Peak District National Park (▷ 275). Here countless generations of miners have dug shafts and enlarged the natural caves that riddle the bedrock in search of ore. This route passes all the area's show caves and also takes in the hidden gorge of Cave Dale.

THE WALK

Length: 5 miles (8km)
Allow: 3 hours
Start/end: Castleton parking area, Derbyshire, map ref 435 H15
www.peakdistrict.org,
OS Landranger map: 110
OS Explorer map: OL1

★ Castleton is the last settlement before the Hope Valley narrows and squeezes into the rocky ravine of Winnats. It is a bustling tourist town with a history stretching back to Norman times, and a geology that has given rise to many of its successes.

From the parking area turn left down the main street, then right along Castle Street, passing the church and youth hostel. On reaching the marketplace, turn left to Bar Gate, where a signpost points to Cave Dale. Go through a gate, and enter the limestone gorge of Cave Dale.

❶ Cave Dale has a narrow and dramatic entrance, with the ruined keep of Peveril Castle (▷ 282) crowning the cliff to the right. Geologists once thought that Cave Dale was a collapsed cavern, but now believe that it is a valley carved by glaciers in the last ice age.

Continue along the path to pass several cave entrances. As you gain height the gorge gets shallower. Go through a gate in the dry-stone wall and then follow a well-defined track across pastureland. It then passes through a gate in another wall before merging into a path dropping from the grassy slope to the right. The track divides at a T-junction soon after: Take the left fork, leading uphill and slightly away from the wall on the right to reach the top corner of the field. Go through a gate at this point and follow a section of track between walls to reach a crossing of routes near the old Hazard Mine.

At this point turn right along a stony walled lane, which swings right to reach a minor road near Oxlow House Farm. Take the path across the road to reach a disused quarry on Windy Knoll.

❷ The path directly opposite is an optional diversion to the windswept summit of Mam Tor, known as the 'shivering mountain' because of its many landslips. This detour is well marked, as it crosses stiles, then the next road goes up a steep flight of steps on the right. The summit is capped by the ramparts of an Iron Age hillfort, and there's an exhilarating ridge walk along the 2-mile (3.5km) path to Lose Hill.

At the quarry, turn right on a footpath to a minor road. After turning left to the next road junction, take the old Mam Tor road straight ahead. The road was once the main A625, but landslides from Mam Tor

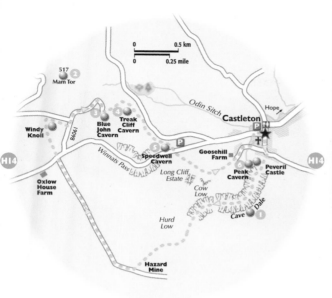

have closed this section of it and it no longer runs through to Castleton. After 370m (400 yards) turn right down the tarmac approach road to the Blue John Cavern, then turn left by the ticket office.

3 The Blue John Cavern has some fine examples of the fluorspar known as Blue John which is fashioned into ornaments and jewellery. There are no natural stalagmites or stalactites, but the cave has deep vertical views.

Go through the gate and trace the path as it crosses a series of fields. Beyond a gate the path curves right, crosses the steep-sided, grassy slope of the hill. The path passes the Treak Cliff Cavern ticket office.

4 Treak Cliff Cavern is a small cavern that has been mined for Blue John and has the bonus of some natural stalactite formations.

Go left down the concrete steps by the ticket office, then turn right on a concrete path with handrails. Half-way down, take the hillside path on the right, signposted 'Winnats Pass'. On the approach to Speedwell Cavern the path becomes indistinct, but there's an obvious stile straight ahead which will take you out on to the Winnats road.

5 A visit to Speedwell Cavern includes an underground boat trip through a level excavated by lead miners, forming a subterranean canal 500m (1,640ft) long. It took them 11 years, but low yields and high costs forced the early closure of the mine. The boat trip takes you down the canal to a landing stage just short of the 'bottomless pit', part of a natural cavern.

A path on the far side of the road takes the route through the National Trust's Longcliff Estate. This path follows roughly the line of a wall and veers left beneath the hill of Cow Low to reach Goosehill Farm. Here, follow the lane called Goosehill back into Castleton. Beyond Goosehill

Bridge, turn left down a surfaced path alongside a stream and back to the parking area.

6 You can detour to Peak Cavern on the right, just before reaching the bridge; it's well worth going to just for the huge cave entrance, Britain's largest. There is still evidence here of the ropemakers who lived and worked in the cavern, and whose speciality was hangman's nooses.

PLACE TO VISIT
PEAK CAVERN

✉ Castleton, Derbyshire S33 8WS
☎ 01433 620285 ⏰ Easter–end Oct daily 10–5; Nov–Easter Sat–Sun 10–5 💷 Adult £6, child £4

WHERE TO EAT

Castleton has cafés and several pubs, including the 17th-century Castle pub in Castle Street.

WHEN TO GO

This walk, and the caves, are perfect for a dry, dull day.

BAKEWELL

OLD ORIGINAL BAKEWELL PUDDING SHOP

One of Britain's most famous traditional pastry treats has been sold in this shop for more than 50 years. There's some controversy about whether they really have the original recipe, but they certainly taste good enough to back up the claim. Take one away or enjoy it in the shop's upstairs café.

✉ The Square, Bakewell, Derbyshire DE45 1BT ☎ 01692 812193 ⏰ Daily 9–6

PEAK DISTRICT NATIONAL PARK AUTHORITY

www.peakdistrict.org

The Peak District is the main draw for walkers in the Midlands, with more than 1,600 miles (2,575km) of public footpaths across moors and limestone gorges. National park rangers take guided walks throughout the year.

The superlative crags and caverns of the Peak District attract many climbers and cavers. Whether you're going up or down, reserve a tour with a qualified instructor from one of the area's outdoor activities operators who provide equipment. The National Park Authority can supply names of operators.

The Peak District is also popular with cyclists, who can try everything from off-road riding to the disused and flat railway route, the Tissington Trail. You can pre-reserve bicycles for rental from one of the National Park Authority's three bicycle rental shops.

✉ Aldern House, Baslow Road, Bakewell DE45 1EA ☎ 01629 816200

BIRMINGHAM

BIRMINGHAM HIPPODROME THEATRE

www.birminghamhippodrome.com

Home of the Birmingham Royal Ballet, which performs three times a year. Touring shows include the Welsh National Opera, West End shows, musicals and comedy.

✉ Hurst Street, Birmingham B5 4TB ☎ 0870 730 1234 ⓘ Box office: Mon–Sat, 10–8 ♿ £10–£46 🍴 🛒 🎭
🚉 Birmingham Moor Street

BIRMINGHAM REPERTORY THEATRE

www.birmingham-rep.co.uk

In existence since 1913, with two theatres—Main House (seating 900) and The Door Studio theatre (140).

✉ Broad Street, Centenary Square, Birmingham B1 2EP ☎ 0121 245 2000; box office 0121 236 4455 ⓘ Box office:

Mon–Sat 10–8 (6 when no performance), Sun when a performance (check times)
🍴 🛒 🎭 Birmingham New Street, Birmingham Moor Street, Birmingham Snow Hill

THE BULLRING

www.bullring.co.uk

Shoppers are spoiled for choice in Birmingham. The rebuilt Bullring shopping area joins Brindley Place and the Gas Street Basin, all retail nirvanas.

✉ Birmingham B5 4BU ☎ 0121 632 1500 ⓘ Mon–Fri 9.30–8, Sat 9–8, Sun 11–5 🍴 🛒 🎭 Birmingham New Street, Birmingham Moor Street

Q CLUB

www.queclub.co.uk

A giant among club venues, the old Methodist Central Hall re-opened its doors to the club scene in late 2007 after a five-year closure. The ground floor has seven rooms, including the vast main arena; upstairs the smaller Q2 is more intimate. Look for big name-DJs from Ministry of Sound, Cream, Sundissential and Raveology.

✉ 212 Corporation Street, Birmingham B4 6QB ☎ 0121 212 1212 ⓘ 10pm–6am; check website for details ♿ £13.50
🚉 Birmingham New Street

ST. MARTIN'S MARKET

www.ragmarket.com

Known as the 'Rag Market', this market has 350 stalls selling a very wide variety of crafts, including jewellery and pottery, plus fabrics, household items, new and designer clothes, and second-hand clothes.

✉ Edgbaston Street, Birmingham B5 4RB ☎ 0121 303 0300 🕐 Tue, Fri–Sat 9–5 🍴 ◻ 🚆 Birmingham New Street

WARWICKSHIRE COUNTY CRICKET CLUB

www.thebears.co.uk www.edgbaston.com

The second Test ground in the Midlands also boasts Edgbaston Cricket Museum, with more than 100 years of cricketing memorabilia.

✉ The County Ground, Edgbaston, Birmingham B5 7QU ☎ 08700 621902 🕐 Apr–end Sep 🖱 Varies, depending on the match. From £10 🍴 ◻ 🚆 Birmingham Five Ways

BROMSGROVE
JINNEY RING CRAFT CENTRE

www.jinneyringcraft.co.uk

Rural craft centre with artists and craftspeople in converted farm buildings. Includes pottery, jewellery, candles, art, stained glass, garden design, violins, fabrics and picture framing.

✉ Hanbury, near Bromsgrove B60 4BU ☎ 01527 821272 🕐 Mon–Sat 10–5, Sun 11–5 🖱 Free 🍴

BUXTON
BOOKSTORE BRIERLOW BAR

www.bookstore-derbyshire.co.uk

If you find yourself short of holiday reading, you'll find around 20,000 titles to choose from in one of the largest discount bookshops in the UK. A full range of subjects includes local interest, walks and maps. It also has an indoor play area for kids and a coffee shop.

✉ Ashbourne Road, near Buxton, Derbyshire SK17 9PY ☎ 01298 71017 🕐 Mon–Sat 9.30–5.30, Sun 11–5 (from 10.30am for viewing) 🚗 5km (3 miles) south of Buxton on A515 Ashbourne road

Opposite *Mountain biker beside Ladybower Reservoir, Peak District National Park*

BUXTON OPERA HOUSE

www.buxtonoperajouse.org.uk

Not just opera but rock, jazz and classical music, contemporary and classical theatre, stand-up comedy and pantomime. Home to the annual summer arts festival.

✉ Water Street, Buxton SK17 6XN ☎ 01298 72050; box office: 08451 272190 🕐 Box office: Mon–Sat 10–8 (6 when no performance), Sun from 4 on performance days 🖱 Various 🖱 🚆 Buxton

CASTLE DONINGTON
DONINGTON PARK

www.donington-park.co.uk

Home of the British Motorcycle Grand Prix and a track for cars and motorcycles. Also on site, the Donington Grand Prix Collection.

✉ Castle Donington, near Derby DE74 2RP ☎ 01332 810048; Museum: 01332 811027 🕐 Races most weekends, Mar–end Nov. Museum: daily 10–5 (later on race days) 🖱 Adult from £10, child (under 15) free. Museum: adults £7, child (6–16) £2.50, family £14 🍴 ◻

DERBY
ROYAL CROWN DERBY FACTORY SHOP

www.royalcrownderby.co.uk

Fine bone china has been made in Derby for more than 250 years, and the factory shop is the best place to buy it. Weekday factory tours.

✉ 194 Osmaston Road, Derby, Derbyshire DE23 8JZ ☎ 01332 712800 🕐 Mon–Sat 9–5, Sun 10.30–4.30; closed public holidays and Sun of Bank Holiday weekends 🖱 Factory tour £4.95 (refunded on sales of £50 or more in the shop) 🚗 South of Derby on A514

DROITWICH
DROITWICH SPA BRINE BATHS COMPLEX

www.brinebath.co.uk

The water at this natural brine spa is pumped from an underground lake 61m (200ft) below the town and used for its therapeutic proper-ties. Rehabilitation, physiotherapy, hydrotherapy, massage and beauty therapy services are available. There is also a sauna and fitness centre.

✉ St. Andrews Road, Droitwich WR9

8DN ☎ 01905 794894 🕐 Mon–Fri 11.30–9, Sat 10–5, Sun 10–4 🖱 Adult £8 (couples £14.50), child (10–16) £4.50 🍴 ◻ 🚆 Droitwich Spa

FLASH
NORTHFIELD FARM RIDING AND TREKKING CENTRE

www.northfieldfarm.co.uk

Pony-trekking in the Peak District from 40 minutes to two days. Riders of all ages and standards, and riders with disabilities, welcomed.

✉ Flash, near Buxton SK17 0SW ☎ 01298 22543 🕐 Normally starting 10.30 or 2 🖱 1 hour from £18, 2 hours from £30, 1 day from £60, short breaks available. Booking essential 🚆 Macclesfield (9 miles/14km)

GREAT MALVERN
MALVERN SPLASH LEISURE COMPLEX

www.slm-leisure.co.uk

Swimming pool with fitness suite, wave machine and flume, dance studio, sunbeds and sauna. Children's activities and soft play.

✉ Priory Road, Great Malvern WR14 3DS ☎ 01684 893423 🕐 Daily 7am–10pm 🖱 Swim: adult £2.95, child £2.25, family £8.75 ◻ 🚆 Great Malvern

HEREFORD
THE COURTYARD

www.courtyard.org.uk

Performance venue covering music, film, theatre, comedy, dance and the visual arts.

✉ Edgar Street, Hereford HR4 9JR ☎ 01432 346500; box office: 08701 122330 🕐 Box office: Mon–Sat 10–8 🖱 Free–£20 🍴 🚆 Hereford

IRONBRIDGE
JONATHAN HARRIS STUDIO GLASS

www.jhstudioglass.com

Handcarved cameo glassware, plus bowls, vases, perfume bottles and paperweights, with glassmaking demonstrations.

✉ Coalport China Museum, Coalport, Ironbridge TF1 6TH ☎ 01952 246381 🕐 Contact for details 🖱 Free ◻ 🚆 Telford (5 miles/8km), then shuttle bus (Sat–Sun and public holidays) to Ironbridge Gorge Museums

LEEK
PEAK DISTRICT HANG GLIDING CENTRE
www.peakhanggliding.co.uk
The oldest British Hang Gliding and Paragliding Association-approved school in Britain; learn to fly in four to seven days.
✉ York House, Ladderedge, Leek ST13 7AQ ☎ 07000 426445 ◷ Courses usually 4–7 days ✋ £475

LEOMINSTER
THE MOUSETRAP
www.mousetrapcheese.co.uk
Small, central shop run by cheesemakers Karen and Mark Hindle, selling farmhouse and Continental cheeses. Also biscuits, pickles, chutneys, local beers, ciders and cider brandy. Other branches in Hereford and Ludlow.
✉ 3 School Lane, Leominster HR6 8AA ☎ 01568 615512 ◷ Mon–Sat 9–5 🚆 Leominster

MATLOCK
HEIGHTS OF ABRAHAM
www.heightsofabraham.com
From the cable-car ride to the top of the cliff to the tour of the caverns beneath it, children will love this attraction. The modern cable-cars can carry pushchairs (strollers) and wheelchairs too, and there are stunning views on the way up. Atop the cliff there's a 24ha (60-acre) park with an exciting play area, and the cave tours explore old mine workings, one of which includes a fabulous light show.
✉ Derby Road, Matlock Bath, Matlock, Derbyshire DE4 3PD ☎ 01629 582365 ◷ Early Feb–early Nov, daily 10–5 (4.30 in Feb) ✋ Adult £10.50, child (5–16) £7.50, under 5s free (one per full-paying adult) family £33–£39 ☕ Coffee shop and bar ⊞ 🚆 In village of Matlock Bath, on A6 29km (18 miles) north of Derby

MELTON MOWBRAY
TWINLAKES PARK
www.twinlakespark.co.uk
Large-scale outdoor and indoor play areas for all ages set in 32ha (80 acres) of Leicestershire Wolds countryside.

✉ Melton Spinney Road, Melton Mowbray LE14 4SB ☎ 01664 567777 ◷ Daily 10–5 (varies). Closed 24–26 Dec ✋ Easter to mid-Nov adults and children over 92cm (3ft) £9.49, children under 92cm (3ft) free; mid-Nov to Easter adults £5.99, children over 92cm (3ft) but under 16 years of age £5.99, children under 92cm (3ft) free 🍴 ☕ ⊞ 🚆 Melton Mowbray

YE OLD PORK PIE SHOPPE
www.porkpie.co.uk
Dickinson and Morris have been baking pork pies since 1851 and are the last remaining producers of authentic Melton Mowbray pork pies in Melton Mowbray.
✉ Dickinson and Morris, 10 Nottingham Street, Melton Mowbray LE13 1NW ☎ 01664 482068 ◷ Mon–Sat 8.30–5 (until 4pm Jan, Feb) 🚆 Melton Mowbray

NOTTINGHAM
BROADWAY CAFÉ BAR
A movie-mad clientele congregates at the bar of this independent cinema for a good selection of beers. Mezzanine bar upstairs.
✉ Broadway Cinema, 14 Broad Street, Nottingham NG1 3AL ☎ 0115 952 1551 ◷ Mon–Fri 9am–11pm, Sat 11–11, Sun 12–10.30 🚆 Nottingham

BROADWAY CINEMA
www.broadway.org.uk
Classy cinema and the best in the East Midlands, screening main-stream titles, as well as an impressive selection of art-house films.
✉ 14–18 Broad Street, Nottingham NG1 3AL ☎ 0115 952 6600; box office: 0115 952 6611 ◷ Box office: Mon–Fri 9–8.45, Sat–Sun, one hour before the first film–8.45pm ✋ Adult £5.90, children (under 12) £2.50 ☕ See above 🚆 Nottingham

GATECRASHERLOVES NOTTINGHAM
www.gatescrasher.com/nottingham
Given the Gatecrasher brand make-over during the winter of 2007, this vast club continues to attract the big-name DJs.
✉ The Elite Building, Queen Street, Nottingham NG1 2BC ☎ 0115 910 1101 ◷ Daily 9/10pm–4am ✋ From £4 🚆 Nottingham

THE LACE CENTRE
Possibly the last shop in a city famed for lace, but undoubtedly the most unusual, in a 14th-century timbered house. Has displays of lacemaking and also the chance for visitors to try pillow lacemaking.
✉ Severns Building, Castle Road, Nottingham NG1 6AA ☎ 0115 941 3539 ◷ Apr–end Oct Mon–Sat 10–5, Sun 11–4; Nov–end Mar Mon–Sat 10–4, Sun 11–4. Lacemaking: Apr–end Oct Thu 2–4 ✋ Free 🚆 Nottingham

NATIONAL ICE CENTRE
www.national-ice-centre.com
Huge modern ice rink.
✉ Bolero Square, The Lace Market, Nottingham NG1 1LA ☎ 0115 853 3000 ◷ Mon, Wed, Fri 1.30–4, 7.30–10, Tue 10–12, Thu 10–12, 7.30–10, Sat 10–12, 2.30–5, 7.30–10.30, Sun 10–12, 2.30–5 ✋ Fri night, Sat–Sun and local school holidays £5.50; off peak £4; skate hire £2; under 5s £2.50 plus free skate hire ☕ 🍴 🚆 Nottingham

NOTTINGHAM ARENA
www.nottingham-arena.com
Large modern ice rink and 10,000-seater concert venue, used for Holiday on Ice shows as well as concerts.
✉ National Ice Centre, Bolero Square, The Lace Market, Nottingham NG1 1LA ☎ 0115 853 3000; tickets: 08701 210123 (24 hours) ◷ All year ✋ £10–£50 ☕ 🍴 🚆 Nottingham

NOTTINGHAM ROYAL CENTRE
www.royalcentre-nottingham.co.uk
Houses both the Theatre Royal, Nottingham's top venue for plays, musicals, comedy, opera and classical concerts, and the Royal Concert Hall, a venue that attracts major names of classical and pop music.
✉ Theatre Square, Nottingham NG1 5ND ☎ 0115 989 5500; box office: 0115 989 5555 ◷ Box office: Mon–Sat 8.30–8.30 ✋ Various 🍴 ☕ 🍴 🚆 Nottingham

Right Cable-cars travel up the slopes of Matlock Bath

NOTTINGHAMSHIRE COUNTY CRICKET CLUB

www.nottsccc.co.uk

One of two Test (international) cricket grounds in the Midlands.

✉ Trent Bridge, Nottingham NG2 6AG ☎ 0115 982 3000; tickets: 0870 168 8888 ◷ Apr–end Sep ✋ Adult £12–£18, child (under 16) £7–£16, family £31–£40 🚆 Nottingham

ROCK CITY

www.rock-city.co.uk

One of the biggest and best rock clubs in the country, with amps turned up to 11.

✉ 8 Talbot Street, Nottingham NG1 5GG ☎ 0871 310 0000 ◷ Tue 9.30pm–2am, Thu–Fri 9pm–2am, Sat 8.30pm–2.30am ✋ Free–£10 🚆 Nottingham

YE OLDE TRIP TO JERUSALEM

www.triptojerusalem.com

Dates back to the 12th century and claims to be the oldest inn in England, where Crusaders would meet on their way to the Holy Land.

✉ 1 Brewhouse Yard, Castle Road, Nottingham NG1 6AD ☎ 0115 947 3171 ◷ Mon–Sat 11.30–midnight, Sun 11.30–11 🚆 Nottingham

RAGDALE

RAGDALE HALL HEALTH HYDRO

www.ragdalehall.co.uk

A luxurious spa with three swimming pools, two exercise studios and 400 staff administering beauty treatments.

✉ Ragdale, near Melton Mowbray LE14 3PB ☎ 01664 434831 ◷ All year ✋ Day spa package from £69 🍴 🚆 Melton Mowbray

SHREWSBURY

THE PARADE SHOPPING CENTRE

www.paradeshops.co.uk

A concentration of 30 shops and a coffee house in central Shrewsbury, contained in a Grade II-listed (landmark) building with a grand classical entrance with columns and a pediment. Crafts and specialist shops offering picture framing, dolls'

houses, hobby horses and a variety of clocks.

✉ St. Mary's Place, Shrewsbury SY1 1DY ☎ 01743 343178 ◷ Mon–Sat 9.30–5 🚆 Shrewsbury

SILVERSTONE

SILVERSTONE CIRCUIT

www.silverstone-circuit.co.uk

The home of British motor racing, with over 40 motor racing events a year, including F1. Also tuition in driving a racing car yourself.

✉ Silverstone NN12 8TN ☎ 08704 588200; tickets: 08704 588290 ◷ All year ✋ Various 🍴 🚆

STOKE-ON-TRENT

EDWARDS' CHINA

www.edwardschina.co.uk

One of the best shops in Stoke for examples of work by all the major local china manufacturers, as well as top-quality crystal.

✉ 2–10 Market Lane, Hanley, Stoke-on-Trent ST1 1LA ☎ 01782 260345 ◷ Mon–Sat 9–5, Sat 8.30–5 🚆 Stoke-on-Trent

THE SNOWDOME
www.snowdome.co.uk
Indoor slope for skiers and snow-boarders of all abilities.
✉ Leisure Island, River Drive, Tamworth B79 7ND ☎ 0870 500 0011 🕔 Daily 8am–11pm 💷 Adult from £16 per hour, child (8–16) from £11 per hour 🖥 💷 🚉 Tamworth

TOWCESTER
CATANGAR LLAMAS
www.llamatrekking.co.uk
Llama trekking along bridleways and country lanes.
✉ 18 High Street, Weston, Towcester NN12 8PU ☎ 01295 768676 🕔 All year, reservation essential 💷 Adult from £25, child (8–12) free if sharing a llama with an adult

WORCESTER
PERDISWELL PARK GOLF CLUB
Pay and play on this 18-hole, par-68 course in parkland.
✉ Bilford Road, Worcester WR3 8DX ☎ 01905 754668 🕔 All year 💷 Mon–Fri £10.15, Sat–Sun £13.85 🍴 💷

SWAN THEATRE
www.huntingdonhall.com
Varied and eclectic mix of drama, music, comedy, pantomime and poetry.
✉ The Moors, Worcester WR1 3EF. Box office: Worcester Live, Huntingdon Hall, Crowngate, Worcester WR1 3LD ☎ 01905 611427 🕔 Box office: Mon–Sat 10–5pm 💷 Varies 💷 🚉 Worcester Foregate Street

WORCESTER RACECOURSE
www.worcester-racecourse.co.uk
Racecourse in a picturesque setting by the river. Twenty race meetings.
✉ Pitchcroft, Worcester WR1 3EJ ☎ 0870 220 2772 🕔 Apr–end Oct 💷 £7–£22 🍴 🖥 💷 🚉 Worcester Forgate (10-min walk)

STRATFORD-UPON-AVON
ROYAL SHAKESPEARE COMPANY COURTYARD THEATRE
www.rsc.org.uk
Home of the Royal Shakespeare Company (RSC), presenting Shakespeare's plays and other works. You can take a guided tour behind the scenes including an insight into the transformation of the Royal Shakespeare Theatre due for completion in 2010.
✉ Waterside, Stratford-upon-Avon CV37 6BB ☎ 01789 403404; box office: 08706 091110 🕔 All year 💷 £5–£30 🍴 💷 🚉 Stratford-upon-Avon

STRATFORD PICTUREHOUSE
www.picturehouses.co.uk
Modern two-screen cinema showing the latest blockbuster and art-house releases. Works by local artists on display in the roof-top terrace bar.
✉ Windsor Street, Stratford-upon-Avon CV37 6NL ☎ 9871 704 2067 information 🕔 All year 💷 Adults: £6–£6.75, child £5–£5.75 🖥 💷 🚉 Stratford-upon-Avon

WILDMOOR SPA
www.wildmoorspa.com
After a cultural session in Shakespeare's home town you may feel the need for a bit of pampering at this sleak, modern spa and health club, based around an old farmhouse on the edge of town. Individual treatments and day sessions are available.
✉ Alcester Road, Stratford-upon-Avon CV37 9RJ ☎ 01789 299666 🕔 Daily 💷 Taster sessions from £59 🚉 Stratford-upon-Avon

TAMWORTH
DRAYTON MANOR THEME PARK
www.draytonmanor.co.uk
More than 100 innovative rides, including Apocolypse and Shockwave, plus a zoo.
✉ Near Tamworth B78 3TW ☎ 0844 472 1950 🕔 Mid-Mar to late Oct daily 9.30–5, (closed some days in Sep and Oct) 💷 Adult £23 or over, child (4–11) £19, family tickets available 🍴 🖥

Above Stratford-Upon-Avon is the home town of William Shakespeare
Opposite Castleton Garland Ceremony

APRIL

SHAKESPEARE'S BIRTHDAY CELEBRATIONS

www.shakespeare.org.uk

Shakespeare was not born on 23 April, but that was the date of his baptism and therefore the date on which his birthday is celebrated annually with a weekend of events. ✉ Various locations, Stratford-upon-Avon ☎ 01789 204016 ⚙ Nearest weekend to 23 April, parade Saturday starts at 10.55am ✋ Free 🚉 Stratford-upon-Avon

MAY

CASTLETON ANCIENT GARLAND CEREMONY

An annual summer ceremony with a parade to the market square (see below). Participants wear garlands and stopping for refreshment at every pub on the way. ✉ Castleton, Derbyshire ☎ 01433 621192 ⚙ Last Saturday in May ✋ Free

JUNE

THE THREE COUNTIES SHOW

www.threecounties.co.uk

Find out about rural England at this agricultural show of produce and crafts from Herefordshire, Gloucestershire and Worcestershire. ✉ Malvern Showground, Malvern ☎ 01684 584900 ⚙ Friday–Sunday, mid-June ✋ Adults £15, child (5–15) £7.50, family £34 🚉 Great Malvern

LUDLOW FESTIVAL

www.ludlowfestival.co.uk

Open-air theatre in the grounds of Ludlow Castle, with music, opera, dance, comedy, street performers, culminating in a firework finale. ✉ Castle Square, Ludlow SY8 1AY ☎ 01584 872150 ⚙ Two weeks, late June–early July ✋ Various 🚉 Ludlow

JULY

BUXTON FESTIVAL

www.buxtonfestival.co.uk

An established opera and arts festival in the town's lovely Opera House and other venues. ✉ Various locations in Buxton ☎ 01298 70395 ⚙ Two weeks, mid-July ✋ Various 🚉 Buxton

LEICESTER COMEDY FESTIVAL

www.comedy-festival.co.uk

For about 15 years, this top-class festival of fun has been attracting big names such as Jack Dee, Jo Brand, Bill Bailey, Lee Mack, Jason Byrne, Alan Davies and many others. As well as the main shows there are workshops and other events. ✉ Various venues in Leicester (contact: LCB Depot, 31 Rutland Street, Leicester LE1 1RE) ☎ 0116 261 6812 ⚙ Early to mid-July

AUGUST

THREE CHOIRS FESTIVAL

www.3choirs.org

Europe's oldest choral festival, held in rotation in each of the cathedrals of Hereford, Gloucester and Worcester. Rotates around the cities with Hereford in 2009. ✉ Hereford, Gloucester, Worcester ☎ 01452 529819 ⚙ Early August ✋ Free–various 🚉 Hereford, Gloucester or Worcester

SEPTEMBER

LUDLOW MARCHES FOOD AND DRINK FESTIVAL

www.foodfestival.co.uk

Britain's premier food and drink festival featuring local produce and related events. ✉ The Buttercross, Ludlow SY8 1AW ☎ 01584 873957 ⚙ Friday–Sunday, early September ✋ Free 🚉 Ludlow

ARTSFEST

www.artsfest.org.uk

Over 300 performances throughout the city make this Britain's largest free arts festival. ✉ Various venues, Birmingham ☎ 01214 645678 ⚙ Friday–Sunday, early September ✋ Free 🚉 Birmingham New Street

EATING

Above *East Gate old gateway, Chester*

PRICES AND SYMBOLS

The restaurants are listed alphabetically within each town. The prices are for a two-course lunch (L) and a three-course à la carte dinner (D). Prices in pubs are for a two-course lunchtime bar meal and a two-course dinner in the restaurant, unless specified otherwise. The wine price given is for the least expensive bottle.

For a key to the symbols, ▷ 2.

ALDERLEY EDGE
ALDERLEY EDGE HOTEL

www.alderleyedgehotel.com
The air-conditioned, split-level conservatory restaurant at this country-house hotel (▷ 296) has a comprehensive, Modern European à la carte menu—including a mosaic of local game birds served with pickled young turnips, foie gras beignet and damson chutney—and also fixed-price meals. Home-grown herbs, fish from Fleetwood and a dizzying array of breads also feature. There is an impressive wine list.
✉ Macclesfield Road, Alderley Edge SK9 7BJ ☎ 01625 583033 🕐 12–2, 7–10; closed D 25–26 Dec, 1 Jan 🖐 L £17.95, D £29.50, Wine £11.50 🔄 🚌 Off A34 in Alderley Edge on to B5087 towards Macclesfield. Hotel 200m (220yds) on right

ASTON CANTLOW
KING'S HEAD

www.thekh.co.uk
A pub so old that Shakespeare's parents may have celebrated here, the wisteria-clad King's Head is the epitome of the English country pub. The food is a notch above the rest though—look for the creative lamb and fish dishes on the à la carte menu. Simpler bar food is also offered, alongside decent real ales, including local micro-brews.
✉ 21 Bearley Road, Aston Cantlow B95 6HY ☎ 01789 488242 🕐 11–3, 5.30–11 food 12–2.30, 6.30–9.30 (Sun 12.30–3) 🖐 L £12, D £15, Wine £12.50 🚌 Call for directions

BAKEWELL
RUTLAND ARMS HOTEL

www.bakewell.demon.co.uk
In this hotel's (▷ 296) restaurant local ingredients are to the fore and cooking is traditional but with a modern influence. A wild mushroom risotto and roast summer quail on crushed pea mash are typical of the fixed-price menu.
🕐 The Square, Bakewell DE45 1BT ☎ 01629 812812 🕐 Daily 12–2, 7–9 🖐 L £13.95, D £28.50, Wine £12.50 🚌 On A6 in centre of Bakewell, opposite war memorial 🚉 Bakewell

BAMFORD
YORKSHIRE BRIDGE INN

www.yorkshire-bridge.co.uk
Food is available in the bar or dining room of this historic inn (▷ 296). Dishes may include pork and leek sausages and prosciutto ravioli, or traditional favourites such as steak and kidney pie. Grills, baked potatoes, sandwiches and salads make filling snacks. Food can be served in the garden.

Ashopton Road, Hope Valley S33 0AZ
☎ 01433 651361 ● 11–11. Restaurant
Mon–Fri 12–2, 6–9, Sat 12–2, 6–9.30,
Sun 12–8.30 🍴 L £7.25, D £16, Wine
£10.25 🚗 A57 (Sheffield–Glossop road),
at Ladybower Reservoir take A6013 Bamford
road, inn 1 mile (1.6km) on right

BASLOW
FISCHER'S BASLOW HALL
www.fischers-baslowhall.co.uk
Baslow Hall (▷ 296) has all the
trademarks of a 17th-century
manor—built in 1907, it is in fact
a clever architectural fake. There
is however, nothing fake about
Max Fischer's cooking, a lifetime's
dedication to food means that he,
and his dedicated team, deliver
sophisticated, elegant fare that is
pricey for the area but well worth it.
No children under 12.
● Calver Road, Baslow DE45 1RR
☎ 01246 583259 ● 12–2, 7–10; closed L
Mon, D Sun (except hotel residents), 25–26
Dec 🍴 L £23, D £38, Wine £18.50 🚗 On
A623 between Baslow and Calver

BIRMINGHAM
PASCAL'S
www.pascalsrestaurant.co.uk
Pascal Cuny's stylish eatery picked
up the baton from Jessica's on the
same site in 2007. Although the
name has changed, the restaurant
has kept to the atmosphere
that made its predecessor so
successful. Menus are simple and
change seasonally. Expect good
fish and seafood creations, roast
Gressingham duck, and bold use of
roast beef.
● 1 Montague Road, Edgbaston B16 9HN
☎ 0121 455 0999 ● Tue–Fri 12–2, Tue–
Sat 7–10 🍴 L £18.50 (3 courses), D £27.95
(a la carte), Wine £15.90 🚉 Birmingham
New Street

BROADWAY
THE LYGON ARMS
www.thelygonarms.co.uk
The choice and range of menus are
the strengths of this historic hotel
(▷ 297). The Modern European
dishes produce gutsy flavours from
the simple use of quality ingredients.
Look for the panfried red mullet, beef

and lamb from the hotel's own farm,
and the daily changing vegetarian
choices.
✉ High Street, Broadway WR12 7DU
☎ 01386 852255 ● 12–2, 7–9.30; closed
L Mon–Fri 🍴 L £12.75, D £18, Wine £12.75
🚗 Turn off A44, signed Broadway, hotel on
High Street

CHACOMBE
GEORGE AND DRAGON
This is an attractive, honey-stoned,
16th-century pub tucked away in a
pretty village. Blackboards list the
interesting choice of food, from
sandwiches and out-of-the-ordinary
pasta dishes to venison kebabs.
Highchairs available.
● Silver Street, Chacombe, near
Banbury OX17 2JR ☎ 01295 711500
● 12–11. Restaurant 12–2.30, Mon–Sat
6.30–9.30 🍴 L £10, D £13.50, Wine £11.50
🚗 Banbury 3 miles (4.5km) 🚗 From
junction 11 of M40 take A361 to Daventry,
then first right to Chacombe and second left
in village

CHESTERFIELD
HARDWICK INN
www.harwickinn.co.uk
By the south gate to the
National Trust's Hardwick Hall, this
15th-century sandstone inn has a
historic feel about it. Open fires in
winter keep up the ambience, but
it's the traditional carvery that draws
diners. There's a choice of three
locally sourced meats, alongside

generous Yorkshire puddings and
fresh, seasonal vegetables. There's
also a daily changing specials board,
vegetarian options and fresh fish
from Scarborough. As well as real
ales such as Theakston's XB and Old
Peculiar in the bar, you can enjoy
lighter bar food such as sandwiches
or afternoon tea.
✉ Hardwick Park, Doe Lea, Chesterfield
S44 5QJ ☎ 01246 850245 ● 11.30–11
food 11.30–9.30 (Sun 12–9) 🍴 L £11.60
D £14.25 🚗 From M1 Junction 29 take
A6175. In 0.8km (0.5 miles) go left (signed
Stainsby/Hardwick Hall). After Stainsby
continue for 3km (2 miles) then go left at
staggered junction and follow signs.

CLIPSHAM
THE OLIVE BRANCH
www.theolivebranchpub.com
Don't be fooled by the laid-back
atmosphere at this popular
restaurant—food is taken very
seriously here, and the casual
approach is due simply to a lack
of pretension. Starters tend to be
simple combinations of high-quality
ingredients (panfried scallops, fennel
and citrus salad), while main courses
might include pot-roast partridge
from a local estate, Herdwick lamb
or farm-produced Lincolnshire
sausages.
✉ Main Street, Clipsham LE15 7SH
☎ 01780 410355 ● 12–2, 7–9.30; closed
D Sun 🍴 L £14.50, D £16.90, Wine £14
🚗 9 miles (15km) north of Stamford on A1

Left *The 18th-century church spire rises above houses in Church Lane, Ludlow*

GRINDLEFORD
MAYNARD ARMS
www.themaynard.co.uk
The modern interior of this 1898 coaching inn (▷ 297) is matched by the contemporary British menus in the Longshaw Bar and Padley Restaurant. Local produce features strongly in dishes such as roast rack of Derbyshire pork glazed with mozzarella and served with sautéed greens and charcuterie sauce. For a traditional finish, go for the original Bakewell pudding and custard.
✉ Main Road, Grindleford S32 2HE
☎ 01433 630321 🕐 Mon–Sat 11–3, 5.30–11, Sun 12–10.30. Restaurant 12–2, 6–9.30 (closed L Sat) 🖐 L £8.95, D (4 courses) £27.95, Wine £13 🚉 Grindleford 🚌 From Sheffield take A625 to Castleton. Left into Grindleford on B6521. After Fox House, hotel on left

HEREFORD
CASTLE HOUSE
www.castlehse.co.uk
The cuisine at this Victorian mansion (▷ 297) is exceptionally good. The food makes good use of the surrounding countryside with Herefordshire beef, Gloucester Old Spot pork, organic poultry and free-range eggs. Highlights might include caramelized breast of maize-fed chicken or a tian of local asparagus, crispy hereb pastry, poached egg and white wine sauce.
✉ Castle Street, Hereford HR1 2NW

☎ 01432 356321 🕐 12.30–2, 7–10 🖐 L £12, D £25, Wine £12.50 🚉 Hereford 🚌 Follow signs to City Centre East. At junction of Commercial Road and Union Street, follow Castle House hotel signs

LEDBURY
FEATHERS HOTEL
www.feathers-ledbury.co.uk
Dinner is served in this hotel's (▷ 297) sedate Quills Restaurant, or in Fuggles, the friendly bar/brasserie. The menu includes steaks alongside more complex dishes such as loin of Herefordshire venison with pear and rosemary tart tatin, curly kale, salsify and game jus.
✉ High Street, Ledbury HR8 1DS
☎ 01531 635266 🕐 12–2, 7–9.30 🖐 L £13.75, D £19.20, Wine £13 💳 🚌 Ledbury 🚌 South from Worcester on A449; east from Hereford on A438; north from Gloucester on A417

LINCOLN
WIG & MITRE
www.wigandmitre.com
This pub restaurant is justifiably popular. Among the noteworthy dishes are salt roast hake with herb mash and the slow braised blade of Derbyshire beef.
✉ 30–32 Steep Hill, Lincoln LN2 1TL
☎ 01522 535190 🕐 8am–midnight. Restaurant 8am–11pm 🖐 L £11, D £22, Wine £12.55 🚉 Lincoln 🚌 In town centre next to Lincoln Castle car park, at the top of Steep Hill

LUDLOW
LA BÉCASSE
www.labecasse.co.uk
Alan Murchison took on the premises of the former Hibiscus restaurant in 2007. The cooking has retained its predecessor's French fixation with a firm footing in locally sourced and seasonally available produce. That might mean coq au vin or crispy pork belly, Mortimer Forest venison or saddle of rabbit. Desserts make good use of plums, apples, pears and rhubarb.
✉ 17 Corve Street, Ludlow SY8 1DA
☎ 01584 872325 🕐 Wed–Sun 12–2, Tue–Sat 7–9 🖐 L £20, D £24. Wine £17 🚉 Ludlow 🚌 Town centre, bottom of hill below Feathers Hotel

MR. UNDERHILLS
www.mr-underhills.co.uk
Dinner at this smart-looking restaurant is a set six courses, consisting of skilfully prepared Modern International dishes that emphasize the freshness of the excellent produce. A typical dinner menu might include foie gras custard with sweetcorn cream and sesame glaze, roasted pavé of halibut, roasted rack and slow-cooked shoulder of local lamb with sorrel, mint and baby spinach, then dessert and cheeses. Wines come from a Euro-centric list, with a range of half bottles. Children welcome; vegetarian by request only.
✉ Dinham Weir, Ludlow SY8 1EH
☎ 01584 874431 🕐 D only, 7.30–8.30; closed Mon, Tue, one week Jan, one week Jul 🖐 D £45, Wine £17 🚌 From Castle Square, facing castle, turn left around castle; turn right before bridge, restaurant on left

NORTON
THE HUNDRED HOUSE HOTEL
www.hundredhouse.co.uk
The 'hundred herb house' might be a more fitting name for this comfort-able inn (▷ 298), given the huge variety of aromatic plants flourishing both indoors and out. Bowls of fresh herbs on the tables invite diners

to flavour their own food, while bunches of drying herbs dangle from the wooden rafters. The home-grown herbs also bring a terrific aroma to the Modern British dishes that celebrate the local produce, such as rack of Shropshire spring lamb, while desserts include apricot and almond flan.

✉ Bridgnorth Road, Norton, Shifnal TF11 9EE ☎ 01952 730353 🕐 12–2.30, 6–10 ♨ L £12, D £22, Wine £12.95 🚗 Midway between Telford and Bridgnorth on A442, in centre of village

NOTTINGHAM
HART'S HOTEL
www.hartsnottingham.co.uk
This Modern British brasserie offers creatively conceived dishes that pack in the flavours. chicken and ham hock tortellini could be followed by line-caught sea bass, with tomato and crab rissoto and a ginger foam, accompanied by a glass of wine from the reasonably priced list.

✉ Standard Hill, Park Row, Nottingham NG1 6FN ☎ 0115 988 1900 🕐 12–2, 7–10.30; closed D 25 Dec, 26 Dec, 1 Jan ♨ L £12.95, D £22.50, Wine £14.50 🚗 From junction 24 of M1, take A453 to city centre. Hotel at junction of Park Row and Rope Walk, close to city centre

ROSS-ON-WYE
THE MOODY COW
This old stone inn has been popular since the early 1990s for its good, homemade food. The extensive, imaginative menu includes pan-fried duck breast with a sweet raspberry compote, and desserts such as lavender crème brûlée. The friendly, farmhouse-style bar serves meals and real ales. Children's meals available.

✉ Upton Bishop, Ross-on-Wye HR9 7TT ☎ 01989 780470 🕐 Tue–Sat 12–3, 6.30–11, Sun 12–3, ♨ L £16, D £21, Wine £11.95 🚗 Off junction 3 of M50, then 2 miles (3km) into Upton Bishop

STAMFORD
THE GEORGE OF STAMFORD
www.georgehotelofstamford.com
A beautiful 16th-century coaching inn (▷ 299) in the heart of the stone-

built town of Stamford. The bars offer snacks such as sandwiches using locally baked bread, home-ground beefburgers or a cold buffet. More elaborate dishes are served in the candlelit restaurant, or sample a lighter menu in the garden lounge or in the ivy-clad courtyard. No children under 10.

✉ 71 St. Martins, Stamford PE9 2LB ☎ 01780 750750 🕐 Mon–Fri 11–2.30, 6–11, Sat–Sun 11–11. Restaurant 12.30-2.30, 7.30–10.30 ♨ L £17.50, D £31, Wine £15.45 🚗 Stamford 🚗 Turn off A1, 15 miles (24km) north of Peterborough on to B1081, 1 mile (1.6km) on left

STOW-ON-THE-WOLD
THE EAGLE AND CHILD
www.theroyalisthotel.co.uk
This excellent pub is a relaxing place in which to sample real ales and excellent food from the hotel kitchen, including first-class sausage and mash using local Gloucester Old Spot sausages. Reserving in advance is advisable at this ever popular place.

✉ The Royalist Hotel, Digbeth Street, Stow-on-the-Wold GL54 1BN ☎ 01451 830670 🕐 11–11 (12–11 in winter). Restaurant Tue–Sat 12–3, 7–10, Sun 12–3 ♨ L £14, D £20, Wine £13 🚗 Moreton-in-Marsh 🚗 From junction 8 of M40 follow A40 to Burford. Join A424 to Stow-on-the-Wold. Turn right on to A436 downhill and hotel is on left of green

947AD AT THE ROYALIST HOTEL
www.theroyalisthotel.co.uk
The restaurant in the ancient inn, the George of Stamford (▷ 299) offers high-quality cooking with a seasonal menu ranging from caramelized belly of pork with langoustines and a black pudding filo parcel to artichoke ravioli or poached pave of turbot in red wine. Delicious desserts might include pear tarte tatin or Baileys pannacotta. Canapés and *amuse bouche* are included in the fixed price.

✉ Digbeth Street, Stow-on-the-Wold GL54 1BN ☎ 01451 830670 🕐 Tue–Sat 7–9.30, Fri–Sun 12–2.30 ♨ L £21.95, D £350, Wine £17.15 🚗 Moreton-in-Marsh 🚗 See Eagle and Child above

STRATFORD-UPON-AVON
FOX AND GOOSE INN
www.foxandgoose.co.uk
Matching the decor and ambience of this stylish pub/restaurant is a daily-changing menu from a team of talented young chefs—a mix of traditional dishes and more à la mode offerings, such as coconut and saffron risotto with caramelized pineapple.

✉ Armscote, near Stratford-upon-Avon CV37 8DD ☎ 01608 682293 🕐 11–3, 6–11. Restaurant 12–2.30, 7–9.30; closed 25–26 Dec, 1 Jan ♨ L £16, D £16.20, Wine £11.95 🚗 Stratford-upon-Avon 🚗 From Stratford-upon-Avon take A3400 south for 7 miles (11km). After Newbold-on-Stour turn right towards Armscote (signed), then 1 mile (1.6km) to village

STRATFORD VICTORIA
www.qhotels.com
The spacious restaurant at this eye-catching, modern hotel (▷ 299) features European-themed dishes. The likes of braised duck with spiced red cabbage or lentil, chickpea and spinach crumble might be followed by a competent crème brûlée or a warm chocolate tart.

✉ Arden Street, Stratford-upon-Avon CV37 6QQ ☎ 01789 271000 🕐 12.30–2, 6–9.45 ♨ L £16, D £21.50, Wine £15.95 🚆 🚗 Stratford-upon-Avon 🚗 A439 into Stratford town, then follow A3400 (Birmingham). At traffic lights turn left into Arden Street and hotel is 150m (165 yds) on right

WORCESTER
BROWN'S RESTAURANT
This former warehouse and foundry is today a welcoming restaurant on the riverbank opposite Worcestershire County Cricket ground. A sample fixed-price dinner menu takes in roast chump of Welsh mutton, spotted dick and a good cheese selection.

✉ The Old Cornmill, South Quay, Worcester WR1 2JJ ☎ 01905 26263 🕐 12–2.30, 6.30–10; closed Mon ♨ L £19.95, D £31.95, Wine £16 🚗 Worcester 🚗 From M5 junction 7 follow signs to city centre. At traffic lights turn into Copenhagen Street parking area, next to restaurant

PRICES AND SYMBOLS

Prices are the starting price for a double room for one night, unless otherwise stated. Breakfast is included unless noted otherwise. All the hotels listed accept credit cards unless otherwise stated. Note that rates vary widely throughout the year.

For a key to the symbols, ▷ 2.

ALDERLEY EDGE
ALDERLEY EDGE HOTEL
www.alderleyedgehotel.com
This well-furnished hotel, with charming grounds, was built in 1850. The attractive bedrooms and suites offer excellent quality and comfort. The bar and adjacent lounge lead into the split-level conservatory restaurant (▷ 292).
✉ Macclesfield Road, Alderley Edge SK9 7BJ ☎ 01625 583033 🖐 £110 🛈 50
🚌 Off A34 in Alderley Edge on to B5087 towards Macclesfield. Hotel 200m (200yds) on right

Above *A view over Bakewell with the church*
Opposite *Buxton Opera House*

BAKEWELL
RUTLAND ARMS HOTEL
www.bakewell.demon.co.uk
The delightful antique furniture, comfortable chairs and welcoming open fires of the public rooms in this 19th-century hotel create a homely ambience of bygone times, while the friendly staff are attentive and welcoming. There is a good restaurant (▷ 292).
🖐 The Square, Bakewell DE45 1BT ☎ 01629 812812 🖐 £95 🛈 35
🚗 Matlock 🚌 On A6 in centre of Bakewell, opposite war memorial

BAMFORD
YORKSHIRE BRIDGE INN
www.yorkshire-bridge.co.uk
Despite the name, this 19th-century inn is in Derbyshire and surrounded by majestic Peak District scenery. Excellent food is available (▷ 292). Bedrooms are attractively furnished, comfortable and well equipped.
✉ Ashopton Road, Hope Valley S33 0AZ ☎ 01433 651361 🖐 £90 🛈 14 🚌 A57 (Sheffield–Glossop road), at Ladybower Reservoir take A6013 Bamford road, inn 1mile (1.6km) on right

BASLOW
FISCHER'S BASLOW HALL
www.fischers-baslowhall.co.uk
Located at the end of a chestnut tree-lined drive on the edge of the Chatsworth estate is this beautiful manor house. It offers sumptuous accommodation and facilities throughout. Staff provide very friendly and attentive service. The main house contains traditional and individually themed rooms, while the Garden House has spacious, more contemporary rooms with Italian marble bathrooms. The memorable cuisine in the restaurant (▷ 292) is a highlight of any stay.
✉ Calver Road, Baslow DE45 1RR ☎ 01246 583259 🕐 Closed 25–26 Dec 🖐 £140 🛈 11 🚌 On A623 between Baslow and Calver

BIRMINGHAM
WESTBOURNE LODGE
www.westbournelodge.co.uk
This bed-and-breakfast has 24 bedrooms, including family rooms on the ground floor. Facilities include a comfortable lounge, a relaxing bar with access to the patio and garden,

and a pleasant dining room.
🖐 25–31 Fountain Road, Edgbaston B17
8NJ ☎ 0121 429 1003 🕐 Closed 24
Dec–1 Jan 🖐 £69 🛈 24 🚇 Birmingham
University 🚗 50m (150ft) from A456, 1.25
miles (2km) from Five Ways

BROADWAY
BOWERS HILL FARM
www.bowershillfarm.com
Located in immaculate farmhouse
gardens, this Victorian house has
been sympathetically renovated
to provide comfortable bedrooms
and modern bathrooms. Breakfast
can be taken in the dining room or
conservatory, and a guest lounge
with open fire is also available.
✉ Bowers Hill, Willersley WR11 5HG
☎ 01386 834585 🖐 £60 🛈 3 🚗 From
A44 Broadway to Evesham, follow signs to
Willersley. At village follow signs to Badsey
industrial estate from mini roundabout, farm
2 miles (3km) on right by postbox

THE LYGON ARMS
www.barcelo.com
A hotel with a wealth of historic
charm and character in the heart of
the Cotswolds. Dating back to the
16th century, it offers comfortable
bedrooms with modern facilities and
some fine antique furniture. Public
rooms include a variety of lounge
areas and a choice of dining options.
There is a health spa that includes a
heated swimming pool, gym, sauna,
steam room and beauty treatments,
plus there are tennis facilities,
a croquet lawn, bicycle hire and
horseback riding nearby.
✉ High Street, Broadway WR12 7DU
☎ 01386 852255 🖐 £109 🛈 64 🚾 🚾
🚗 Turn off A44, signed Broadway, hotel on
High Street

BUXTON
ROSELEIGH HOTEL
www.roseleighhotel.co.uk
This impressive stone building
overlooking the Pavilion Gardens provides clean and spacious bedrooms.
The public rooms are comfortable,
while the resident owners of this
bed-and-breakfast establishment offer excellent hospitality. No dogs.
✉ 19 Broad Walk, Buxton SK17 6JR

☎ 01298 24904 🕐 Closed 16 Dec–10
Jan 🖐 £70 🛈 14 🚇 Buxton 🚗 A6 to
Morrisons roundabout, turn on to Dale Road,
right at lights. In 100m (110yds) turn left by
Swan pub downhill and right into Hartington
Road

GRINDLEFORD
MAYNARD ARMS
www.maynardarms.co.uk
In the heart of the Peak District National Park, a delightful country hotel
set in immaculately kept gardens
with views of the Derwent Valley
and beyond. Bedrooms are tastefully
furnished and decorated, some
with four-poster beds and two with
separate sitting rooms. A lounge on
the first floor overlooks the garden.
Excellent bar food and restaurant
(▷ 294).
✉ Main Road, Grindleford S32 2HE
☎ 01433 630321 🖐 £95 🛈 10
🚇 Grindleford 🚗 From Sheffield take
A625 to Castleton. Left into Grindelford on
B6521. After Fox House, hotel on left

HEREFORD
CASTLE HOUSE
www.castlehse.co.uk
This Georgian town house hotel
is just a short stroll from the
cathedral. Unashamedly plush,
it is the epitome of elegance
and sophistication. The character
bedrooms are equipped with every
luxury to ensure a memorable stay
and are complemented by the well-
proportioned and restful lounge and
bar. The experience is completed
by award-winning cuisine in the
restaurant (▷ 294).
✉ Castle Street, Hereford HR1 2NW

☎ 01432 356321 🖐 £175 🛈 15
🚇 Hereford 🚗 Follow signs to City Centre
East. At junction of Commercial Road and
Union Street, follow Castle House hotel signs

KENILWORTH
VICTORIA LODGE
www.victorialodgehotel.co.uk
Situated on the fringe of the historic
town, Victoria Lodge is a family-run
establishment. All of the highly
appointed rooms are en suite and
are thoughtfully furnished with
homely extras. There is a car park
and a Victorian walled garden for
guests' use. Victoria Lodge is within
walking distance of Kenilworth
Castle and the town's many
acclaimed restaurants.
✉ 180 Warwick Road, CV8 1HU ☎ 01926
512020 🕐 Closed 24 Dec–1 Jan 🖐 £72
🛈 10 🚗 230m (250yds) southeast of town
centre on A452, opposite St. John's Church

LEDBURY
FEATHERS HOTEL
www.feathers-ledbury.co.uk
This historic, timber-framed hotel
in the middle of Ledbury has a
king-sized helping of old-fashioned
charm. The bedrooms don't
disappoint and excellent meals can
be enjoyed in the rustic brasserie
(▷ 294), with its adjoining bar.
Facilities include a leisure centre
with solarium, Jacuzzi, steam room
and a heated indoor pool.
✉ High Street, Ledbury HR8 1DS
☎ 01531 635266 🖐 £120 🛈 19 🚾 🚾
🚇 Ledbury 🚗 South from Worcester on
A449; east from Hereford on A438; north
from Gloucester on A417. Hotel in centre of
town in High Street

LEICESTER
REGENCY HOTEL
This friendly hotel is located on the edge of town and provides smart accommodation, suitable for both business and leisure guests. Dining options include a cosy conservatory brasserie and a formal restaurant. A relaxing lounge bar is also available, along with good banqueting and conference facilities. Bedrooms come in a variety of styles and sizes and include some spacious and stylish rooms.

✉ 360 London Road, Leicester LE2 2PL ☎ 0116 270 9634 💷 £62 ① 32 🚗 On A6, 2.5km (1.5 miles) from city centre

LUDLOW
BROMLEY COURT B&B
www.ludlowhotels.com
Situated in the Georgian/early Victorian area of this historic town, this smart little bed-and-breakfast hotel is a combination of separate houses, all retaining original features and enhanced by period furnishings. A relaxed and friendly atmosphere prevails and a freshly prepared breakfast, which relies heavily on local produce, is served in the comfortable dining room.

✉ 73 Lower Broad Street, Ludlow SY8 1PH ☎ 01584 876996 💷 £110 ① 3 🚉 Ludlow 🚗 Just off B4361; over Ludford Street, forward 20m (22yds) on right

MARKET DRAYTON
TERNHILL FARM HOUSE & THE COTTAGE RESTAURANT
www.ternhillfarm.co.uk
This elegant Grade II-listed Georgian farmhouse stands in a large pleasant garden and has been carefully modernised to provide quality accommodation. There is a choice of comfortable lounges, and the Cottage Restaurant features imaginative dishes using local produce. Secure parking is an additional benefit.

✉ Ternhill TF9 3PX ☎ 01630 638984 💷 £60 ① 5 🚗 On junction of A53 and A41, archway off A53 to back of property

MARKET HARBOROUGH
BEST WESTERN THREE SWANS HOTEL
Public areas in this former coaching inn include an elegant fine-dining restaurant and cocktail bar, a smart foyer lounge and popular bar areas. Bedroom styles and sizes vary, but they are very well appointed and equipped. Those in the wing are particularly impressive, offering high quality and spacious accommodation.

✉ 21 High Street, LE16 7NJ ☎ 01858 466644 💷 £80 ① 61 🚗 M1 junction 20, take A4304 to Market Harborough. Through town centre on A6 from Leicester, hotel on right

MUCH WENLOCK
RAVEN HOTEL
www.ravenhotel.com
This town-centre hotel is made up of several historic buildings with a 17th-century coaching inn at the centre. Accommodation includes some rooms on the ground floor, and all are well furnished and equipped to a high standard. There's also a restaurant.

✉ Barrow Street, Much Wenlock TF13 6EN ☎ 01952 727251 💷 £120 ① 15 🚉 Telford Central 🚗 From M54 junction 4 or 5 take A442 south, then A4169 to Much Wenlock

NORTON
THE HUNDRED HOUSE HOTEL
www.hundredhouse.co.uk
Primarily Georgian, but with some parts of the hotel dating back to the 14th century, this one-time coaching inn and courthouse is now a friendly, family-owned hotel. It offers individually styled, well-equipped bedrooms which have period furniture and attractive soft furnishings. Public areas include intimate bars and dining areas (▷ 294).

✉ Bridgnorth Road, Norton, Shifnal TF11 9EE ☎ 01952 730353 🕐 Closed 25 Dec night and 26 Dec night 💷 £99 ① 10 🚗 Midway between Telford and Bridgnorth on A442, in centre of village

Above *A birds-eye view from the tower of Worcester Cathedral*
Below left *A narrow boat passes Worcester Cathedral on the River Severn*

NOTTINGHAM
LACE MARKET HOTEL
www.lacemarkethotel.co.uk
This smart building—a conversion of two Georgian town houses opposite the Galleries of Justice—is located in the trendy Lace Market area of the city, once famous for Nottingham's prime industry. The stylish, contemporary bedrooms include a selection of spacious superior rooms and split-level suites. Equipment includes CD players and mini bars. Public areas include the popular Merchants Restaurant and Saints Bar. There's also complimentary use of the nearby health club.
✉ 29–31 High Pavement, Nottingham NG1 1HE ☎ 0115 852 3232 🖐 £109 ⓘ 42
🅿 Nottingham 🚌 Follow tourist signs for Galleries of Justice which are opposite hotel

STAMFORD
THE GEORGE OF STAMFORD
www.georgehotelofstamford.com
Steeped in hundreds of years of history, this delightful coaching inn provides spacious public areas including a choice of dining options (▷ 295), comfortable lounges, a business centre and a range of quality shops. Bedrooms are stylishly appointed, ranging from traditional to contemporary in design. A highlight is afternoon tea, taken in the brightly planted courtyard, weather permitting.
✉ 71 St. Martins, Stamford PE9 2LB ☎ 01780 750750 🖐 £105 ⓘ 47
🅿 Stamford 🚌 Turn off A1, 15 miles (24km) north of Peterborough on to B1081, 1 mile (1.6km) on left

STOW-ON-THE-WOLD
THE ROYALIST HOTEL
www.theroyalisthotel.co.uk
Dating from AD947 and certified as the oldest inn in England, this superb hotel has a wealth of history and character. The public areas and bedrooms (some with Jacuzzi) are pleasant. The 947AD restaurant (▷ 295) is excellent.
✉ Digbeth Street, Stow-on-the-Wold GL54 1BN ☎ 01451 830670 🖐 £100
ⓘ 14 🅿 Moreton-in-Marsh 🚌 From junction 8 of M40 follow A40 to Burford. Join A424 to Stow-on-the-Wold. Turn right on to A436 downhill and hotel is on left of green

STRATFORD-UPON-AVON
AMBLESIDE
www.amblesideguesthouse.com
A welcoming B&B close to the centre of town, the Ambleside is attractive and always immaculately clean. Rooms are individually decorated and well-equipped. Breakfasts are taken in the bright and spacious dining room, which looks out on to a pleasing front garden area. There is free parking for guests at the rear of the property.
✉ 41 Grove Road, Stratford-upon-Avon CV37 6PB ☎ 01789 297 239 🖐 £50 ⓘ 7
🚌 On A4390, opposite Fir Park

STRATFORD VICTORIA
This eye-catching modern hotel, with its red-brick facade, is within walking distance of the town centre. The open-plan public areas include a lounge, a small bar and a larger restaurant (▷ 295) with exposed beams and ornately carved furniture. As well as a mini-gym, there is access to leisure facilities at the nearby Stratford Manor.

✉ Arden Street, Stratford-upon-Avon CV37 6QQ ☎ 01789 271000 🖐 £74
ⓘ 102 🍴 🅿 Stratford-upon-Avon
🚌 A439 into Stratford town then follow A3400 (Birmingham). At traffic lights turn left into Arden Street and hotel is 150m (165yds) on right

TAMWORTH
GLOBE INN
www.theglobetamworth.com
Situated in the centre of Tamworth, this popular inn provides well-equipped and pleasantly decorated accommodation. The refurbished public areas include a spacious lounge bar and a relaxed dining area where a varied selection of dishes is available. There is also a function room and adjacent parking.
✉ Lower Gungate, Tamworth B79 7AW ☎ 01827 60455 🕐 25 Dec 🖐 £50
ⓘ 18

WORCESTER
BURGAGE HOUSE
www.burgagehouse.co.uk
Ideally located adjacent to the cathedral and many historic attractions, this impressive Georgian house retains many original features. Bedrooms, one of which is located on the ground floor, are large and homely and the elegant dining room is the setting for a full English breakfast. No dogs.
✉ 4 College Precincts, Worcester WR1 2LG ☎ 01905 25396 🕐 Closed 23–30 Dec 🖐 £65 ⓘ 4 🚌 From M5 junction 7 head for city centre, at seventh traffic lights turn left into Edgar Street, College Precinct is pedestrian-only street on right

WORKSOP
BEST WESTERN LION HOTEL
This former coaching inn lies on the edge of the main shopping precinct, with a car park to the rear. It has been extended to offer modern accommodation that includes excellent executive rooms. A wide range of interesting dishes is offered in both the restaurant and bar.
✉ 112 Bridge Street S80 1HT ☎ 01909 477925 🖐 £75 ⓘ 46 🚌 A57 to town centre, turn at Walkers Garage on right, follow to Norfolk Arms, turn left

SIGHTS 302
WALKS AND DRIVES 326
WHAT TO DO 342
EATING 348
STAYING 354

THE NORTH

Northern England tumbles down either side of the Pennine Hills, which run the length of its spine. These rough moorland tracts, seldom rising above 600m (2,000ft), serve to both divide the region east and west, and also to define much of its character. It was from these uplands that the Brontës fashioned their evocative prose and that the water flowed which powered the textile mills and factories which clothed the industrial revolution in the 19th century. Wool, cotton, mining and shipbuilding created new towns and cities in Lancashire, West Yorkshire and the northeast, around the rivers Tyne, Wear and Tees. Today, the cities of Manchester, Liverpool, Leeds and Newcastle are vibrant, modern, exciting places, but their industrial past is never far away. The past is the key to some of the North's other great attractions. In Durham and York, the colossal medieval cathedrals tower over ancient streets. In Northumberland it is the castles that capture the eye, dominating towns and villages such as Alnwick and Bamburgh. Defence may have been the inspiration for another of the North's most important features. Hadrian's Wall marked the very northern limits of the vast Roman Empire. Now you can trace its well-preserved remains as it snakes across the northern borderlands from Wallsend, on the Tyne to Bowness on the Solway Firth. But this isn't just a region of towns and cities. There are four National Parks too, protecting some of the most exquisite and distinctive countryside in Europe. The Lake District needs little introduction and the Yorkshire Dales are famous throughout the world, but the connoisseur will also find delight in the solitude of Northumberland and in the airy, heathered space of the North York Moors.

Opposite *The impressive restored fortress of Bamburgh Castle is perched on a basalt outcrop on the edge of the North Sea*
Below right *Beamish Open Air Museum*

ALNWICK CASTLE
www.alnwickcastle.com
Alnwick Castle is the quintessential medieval English fortress, with towers and battlements set in parkland by the River Aln. The Harry Potter movies were filmed here. The castle was founded in 1095, and by 1147 it had the appearance that it essentially has today. The Percy family, later the dukes of Northumberland, have owned it since 1309. The interiors are a surprise, remodelled in the 19th century in sumptuous neo-Renaissance style, with much gilding and carving.

The Alnwick Garden (from 10am, check website: www.alnwickgarden. com) was created by the Duchess of Northumberland on a 42-acre (17ha) site next to the castle and opened its first phase in 2002. The Poison Garden, pavilion and visitor centre followed, making this one of Britain's most popular gardens.
✚ 465 H9 ✉ Alnwick NE66 1NQ
☎ 01665 510777 ◉ Castle: Easter–end Oct daily 11–5 (last admission 4.30). Grounds: daily 10–6 ♿ Castle and grounds: adult £10.50, child (5–15) £4.50, family £27.50 ▣ ⊞

BAMBURGH CASTLE
www.bamburghcastle.com
Sitting on an outcrop of rock overlooking the North Sea, Bamburgh has huge walls and turrets, and a massive square keep. Despite its apparent strength, it was the first castle ever to be taken by artillery—by King Edward IV's army in 1464. Its shattered remains were restored in the 18th and 19th centuries. The interiors were remodelled in the 19th century, but are still impressive—especially the King's Hall—while the armoury and dungeon are exciting for children.
✚ 465 H9 ✉ Bamburgh NE69 7DF
☎ 01668 214515 ◉ Mar–end Oct daily 10–5 ♿ Adult £7, child (5–15) £3 ▣ ⊞

BEAMISH, THE NORTH OF ENGLAND OPEN AIR MUSEUM
www.beamish.org.uk
A reconstruction of a northern town from a bygone era, full of buildings transported from other places, Beamish is filled with details of past times. It tells the story of the people of northeast England between 1825 and 1913. Costumed staff welcome visitors to shops stocked with period goods, and to the pub and newspaper office. You can take part in a lesson in the village school, ride on an electric tram, visit the dentist's surgery, catch a replica 1825 steam train and visit a factory. The schoolroom teaches how hard schooldays were, and the chapel shows how religion dominated many lives.
✚ 465 H11 ✉ Beamish DH9 0RG
☎ 0191 370 4000 ◉ Easter–end Oct daily 10–5. Town and tramway: Nov–end Mar Tue–Thu, Sat–Sun 10–4 ♿ Apr–end Oct: adult £16, child (5–16) £10; rest of year: £6 for all ⊟ Bus 28 or 28a from Newcastle ⊠ Newcastle (12 miles/19km) ▣ ⊞

BEMPTON CLIFFS
www.rspb.org.uk
One of the major bird sites on the east coast, these sheer 120m (400ft) chalk cliffs are home to more than 200,000 breeding seabirds. There are five safe viewing points (two accessible to wheelchairs) and a visitor office, run by the Royal Society for the Protection of Birds (RSPB). Bird species (depending on the season) include puffins, guillemots, razorbills, kittiwakes, fulmars and migrating birds. It is one of the country's most important breeding sites for Britain's largest seabird, the gannet, with several thousand nests.

Also look out for seals and porpoises. A footpath follows the coast to the east around the spectacularly indented cliffs of Flamborough Head.
✚ 463 K12 ✉ Bempton Cliffs Nature Reserve, 11 Cliff Lane, Bempton, Bridlington YO15 1JD ☎ 01262 851179 ◉ Visitor office: Mar–end Nov daily 10–5; Feb and Dec Sat–Sun 9.30–4 ⊠ Bempton, 1 mile (1.5km) ♿ £3.50 per car ▣ ⊞

BERWICK-UPON-TWEED
www.exploreberwick.co.uk
Positioned near the Scottish border, Berwick was long under threat of invasion and is guarded by Britain's only complete set of 16th-century ramparts, which you can walk around in their entirety. Here, three great bridges span the River Tweed—the Royal Border Railway Bridge, the Royal Tweed Bridge and the Berwick Bridge.

Berwick itself reveals its quirky side within the walls, a place full of unexpected levels and grey stone houses. Prominent in the town, Berwick Guildhall (guided tours Easter–end Sep Mon–Fri 10.30am and 2pm) houses the Cell Block Museum in the Town Gaol. Berwick Barracks (Wed–Sun), the earliest surviving in Britain, date from the early 18th century and contain The King's Own Scottish Borderers Regimental Museum as well as the Berwick Museum and Art Gallery, including Chinese ceramics, medieval carvings and Impressionist paintings.

The Breakyneck Steps, beside the White Wall of the castle, plunge from the heights to the riverbank.
✚ 467 G9 ▌ 106 Marygate TD15 1BN, tel 01289 330733 ⊠ Berwick-upon-Tweed

BEVERLEY

www.eastriding.gov.uk

Beverley is one of the best-looking old market towns in the north of England. The main attraction is its architecture. It has streets lined with mostly 18th- and 19th-century houses, two marketplaces and the North Bar of 1409, a rare early brick gateway. Beverley Minster dates mostly from the 13th century. It is a large, long building with twin towers and an interior full of light and elaborate carving. The Percy Tomb in Beverley Minster is a masterpiece of the mid-14th-century Decorated style, with a very elaborate stone canopy, carved with fruit, flowers, figures and angels.

Though smaller, St. Mary's Church, at the other end of the town, is equally impressive. It was mostly rebuilt in the 15th century, and its painted roof, dating from around 1445, depicts 40 English kings. The carving of a rabbit in St. Michael's Chapel is reputedly the inspiration for the White Rabbit in Lewis Carroll's *Alice's Adventures in Wonderland* (1865). Also take a look at the Minstrels in St. Mary's Church, carvings of five players at the top of a nave pillar.

✚ 462 K13 🛈 34 Butcher Row HU17 0AB, tel 01482 391672 🚌 Beverley

BLACKPOOL

www.visitblackpool.com

What Blackpool does, it does extremely well: donkey rides, amusement arcades and big rides. During the 19th century, local factory workers traditionally came here for their annual week's holiday to enjoy the promenade, the sandy beach and the theatres. Blackpool Tower (daily; closed Mon–Fri in winter, except Feb half-term), a scale copy of Paris's Eiffel Tower, dates from this time and you can still visit the Grand Theatre. Blackpool Pleasure Beach (Apr–end Oct, Dec daily; Nov, Mar Sat–Sun) is the main draw. The original Big Dipper was opened here in 1923 and is still going strong, rivalled today by one of Europe's biggest roller-coasters, The Big One.

The best time to visit is in the autumn, when you can see the famous Blackpool Illuminations, huge moving tableaux of fairytales and brilliantly lit trams.

✚ 464 F13 🛈 1 Clifton Street FY1 1LY, tel 01253 478222 🚌 Blackpool

BLACKWELL, THE ARTS AND CRAFTS HOUSE

www.blackwell.org.uk

One of the most important examples of an Arts and Crafts houses in Britain, Blackwell was designed by the English architect Mackay Hugh Baillie Scott (1865–1945), and completed in 1900 for Edward Holt. After a restoration project costing £3.25 million, the Lakeland house was opened to the public in 2001. Baillie Scott was influenced by William Morris (1834–96) and author John Ruskin (1819–1900), and the Arts and Crafts' rural motifs are evident everywhere: stained-glass windows, and tiles and friezes of wild flowers, berries and animals. Overall, however, the interior is strikingly modern, even minimalist. The house hosts art exhibitions throughout the year.

✚ 464 F12 ✉ Bowness-on-Windermere LA23 3JR ☎ 015394 46139 🕓 Apr–end Oct daily 10.30–5; rest of year daily 10–4 🎟 Adult £6, child (under 16) £3.50, family £16 🖵 🎫

BRADFORD

www.visitbradford.com

Bradford played a major role in the wool trade during the Industrial Revolution. European merchant settlers brought wealth and prestige and with it the city became the wool capital of the world. Legacies of this past include fine, gritstone buildings and early Victorian architecture. The City Hall, with its Italianate clock tower, and the neo-Gothic Wool Exchange are two fine examples.

The main attraction is the National Media Museum (Tue–Sun and public holidays), housed in a curved, glass-walled building. Inside are five floors of interactive displays on all forms of visual media, including an IMAX cinema. There's something here

for all the family—exhibits on the earliest days of television, methods of advertising and news gathering, and plenty of buttons to press and games to play.

Learn more about the city's past in the Bradford Industrial Museum (Tue–Sat, Sun pm and public holidays), housed in the former Moorside Mills northeast of the city itself. There are working textile machines, workers' cottages and shire horses like those that once pulled the city's trams and buses.

Now a World Heritage Site, Saltaire, 4 miles (7km) north of central Bradford, is a remarkable Victorian factory village. It was built in the 1850s by the philanthropic wool baron Sir Titus Salt to house his workers in decent conditions around his colossal Italianate woollen mill. A school, hospital, two churches, Sunday school, washhouse and shops were all part of Salt's design. Today, Salt's Mill has shops, businesses and the 1853 Gallery (Mon–Fri 10–5.30, Sat–Sun 10–6, free), the world's largest permanent collection of paintings by the local artist David Hockney (born 1937). Walk along the back streets of Saltaire to see how the 19th-century mill workers lived.

✚ 462 H13 🛈 City Hall, Centenary Square BD1 1HY, tel 01274 433678 🚌 Bradford Interchange, Saltaire

BRIMHAM ROCKS

www.brimhamrocks.co.uk

Aspiring rock climbers beat a path to this vast series of strange rock formations scattered across nearly 400ha (1,000 acres) of elevated moorland on the edge of the Yorkshire Dales (▷ 338–339). The varied and strange sculptural effects of wind, ice and rain have produced a series of grit-stone towers and pinnacles, some seemingly on the flimsiest of foundations. Look for the Dancing Bear, David's Writing Desk and the Idol.

✚ 465 H12 ✉ Brimham Rocks, Summerbridge, Harrogate HG3 4DW ☎ 01423 780688 🕓 Daily 8–dusk 🎟 Free 🚌 Bus 24 Harrogate/Pateley Bridge with a 2-mile (3km) walk from Summerbridge 🖵 🎫

DURHAM

The heart of the university city of Durham, a World Heritage Site, is compact, historic and largely traffic-free. High on the cliff above the River Wear is the mighty three-towered cathedral (Mon–Sat 9.30–6, Sun 12.30–5.30; until 8pm late Jul, Aug). It was built mostly over 40 years from 1093 and both rounded Norman and pointed Gothic arches can be seen. Huge cylindrical pillars are carved with geometric designs, while at the east end lies the body of St. Cuthbert, one of the region's major saints. The Bishop's throne is the most elevated in Britain—fittingly, for the prince-bishops of Durham were a law unto themselves, and even the king needed permission to enter their lands. The cloisters and precincts represent the most complete survival of a medieval monastery in England; off the cloister, the Treasury (Mon–Sat 10–4.30, Sun 2–4.30) has relics of St. Cuthbert. The Galilee Chapel, at the cathedral's west end, is decorated with carved zigzags, giving a jazzy setting for the tomb of the Venerable Bede (c673–735), Britain's first historian.

On the opposite end of the hilltop is the Norman castle (Jul–end Sep daily; rest of year Mon, Wed, Sat, Sun afternoons), whose great circular keep contains the Gallery and Chapel, and the medieval Great Hall. There is also a series of 18th-century state rooms. Since 1832 it has been part of Durham University. In an attractive cobbled street, the Durham Heritage Centre (Jun–end Sep daily 11–4.30; Apr–end May, Oct Sat–Sun 2–4.30) in St. Mary le Bow Church in North Bailey tells the city's story.

Other attractions in the city include the Oriental Museum (daily), with art and antiquities from the Middle East, India, China, Korea and Japan, the Durham Miners Heritage Centre (Tue–Thu and Sat) and the lovely Houghall Gardens (daily), on Stockton Road. The 25-acre (10ha) gardens include an arboretum with the National Collection of Whitebeams, water, heather and woodland gardens. In summer, official 'Blue Badge' guides lead walks, and river cruises are available from Elvet Bridge. When it's time to hit the shops, head for Fowlers Yard, where 'creative workspaces' are occupied by artists and craftspeople—and a microbrewery.

INFORMATION

www.visitdurham.com
465 H11 ℹ Millennium Place DH1 1WA, tel 0191 384 3720 🚃 Durham

Above Durham's 14th-century castle

CAMELOT THEME PARK

www.camelotthemepark.co.uk

Camelot is a medieval fantasy theme park featuring roller-coasters, a go-karting circuit, a farm and gardens.

🚻 461 G13 ✉ Charnock Richard, Chorley PR7 5LP ☎ 08702 204820 🕐 Easter, May–end Aug daily 10–5; Apr, May, Sep, Oct Sat–Sun ✋ Adult £19, child £19, child under 1m (3ft) free, family £64 🍴 🖥 🏛

CASTLE HOWARD

www.castlehoward.co.uk

A ruler-straight road leads through the estate of this palatial baroque house, the first building to be designed by the playwright and architect Sir John Vanbrugh (1664–1726), in 1699, with the assistance of the vastly more experienced Nicholas Hawksmoor (1661–1736).

The domed hall and wide facades are familiar to millions of Britons through the fondly remembered 1981 television adaptation of Evelyn Waugh's *Brideshead Revisited,* and for many people Castle Howard has come to epitomize a nostalgia for England before World War II. It is still the home of the Howard family.

The dome and many rooms were destroyed in a fire in 1940, but the damage was repaired and the house's restoration continues. You can take a tour through rooms deco-rated with Howard family heirlooms, and paintings by Peter Paul Rubens, Canaletto and Hans Holbein. There are exhibitions dedicated to the filming of *Brideshead Revisited,* the building of the house, and the role of women at the house.

The gardens feature the formal Italianate Temple of the Four Winds, the great Pyramid and the huge Mausoleum. There is also an adven-ture playground, farm shop, plant nursery and holiday park.

🚻 465 J12 ✉ Castle Howard, near Malton YO60 7DA ☎ 01653 648333 🕐 House: Mar–end Nov daily 11–4. Garden: daily 10–6.30 or dusk all year ✋ House and garden: adult £10.50, child (4–16) £6.50, family £27.50. Garden: adult £8, child £5, family £21 🚌 Bus 840 from York train station mid-Apr to end Sep 🍴 🖥 🏛

CATALYST MUSEUM

www.catalyst.org.uk

The chemical industry is the focus of this family-oriented attraction in a former soap factory. It makes an unusual day out, with plenty of hands-on exhibits, including puzzles, touch-screen computers and a giant bubble machine. Archive footage and lifelike reconstructions delve into the chemical industry through the ages, from the production of medicines and soaps to toys, photography and clothing. An all-glass lift whisks you to the Observatory Gallery for views of the River Mersey.

🚻 461 G14 ✉ Mersey Road, Widnes WA8 0DF ☎ 0151 420 1121 🕐 Tue–Fri, public holidays 10–5; Sat–Sun 11–5. Also most Mon 10–5 during school holidays ✋ Adult £4.95, child (5–16) £3.95, family £15.95 🚉 Runcorn (far side of Runcorn–Widnes Bridge) 🖥 🏛

CHESTER

www.visitchester.com

A Roman city called Deva, then a medieval port and cathedral city, and, after the River Dee silted up, a place where prosperous Georgian merchants settled. Chester has the most complete medieval city walls in Britain. You can walk along or beside them to get an overview of the city. One of the original city gate-ways is Eastgate, surmounted by a highly ornate clock dating from 1897; just to the south, the wall passes the partly excavated site of the largest Roman amphitheatre in the country, and close by the Roman Garden has re-erected Roman columns.

The best Roman remains are in the Grosvenor Museum (Mon–Sat 10.30–5, Sun 1–4), with tombstones and displays on the city's history. The Dewa Roman Experience (Mon–Sat 9–5, Sun 10–5), on the site of the original Roman fort, evokes Roman Chester with a re-created street.

Central Chester has the striking black-and-white buildings of The Cross. These are 19th-century Tudor replications, but Chester has many original examples of half-timbered architecture. To the north is Chester Cathedral (Mon–Sat 9–5, Sun 12.30–4), which forms part of the most complete medieval monastic complex in Britain.

You can see Europe's largest bat enclosure, called the Twilight Zone, at Chester Zoo (daily from 10; for times call 01244 380280).

🚻 461 F14 ℹ Town Hall, Northgate Street CH1 2HJ, tel 01244 402111

CRAGSIDE

www.nationaltrust.org.uk

This spectacular 19th-century house was built for the industrialist and inventor William Armstrong (1810–1900) and was the first house in the world to be lit entirely by electric light, powered by a hydroelectric plant that he installed. The house has Arts and Crafts furniture and interiors, and conveys the lifestyle of a rich 19th-century businessman. The grounds include a deep wooded valley and one of Europe's largest rock gardens. There is also a devious maze, and the grounds are one of the red squirrel's last strongholds. Displays recall Armstrong and his inventions, which include the breech-loading gun.

🚻 465 H10 ✉ Cragside, Rothbury, Morpeth NE65 7PX ☎ 01669 620150 🕐 House: mid-Mar to end Sep Tue–Sun 1–5.30. Estate and garden: mid-Mar to end Oct Tue–Sun 10.30–5.30; Nov–end Dec 11–4 ✋ House, gardens and estate: adult £11, child £5.50, family £26.50. Gardens and estate: adult £7 (£3.50 in winter), child £3 (£1.60 in winter), family £17 (£8 in winter) 🍴 🏛

DUNSTANBURGH CASTLE

www.english-heritage.org.uk

The castle ruin stands on an outcrop of rock, 1 mile (1.6km) from the road. The site was fortified during the Iron Age and the present structure was begun in 1314 by Thomas, Earl of Lancaster.

🚻 465 H9 ✉ Near Alnwick NE66 2RD ☎ 01665 576231 🕐 Apr–end Sep daily 10–6; Oct 10–4; Nov–end Mar Thu–Mon 10–4 ✋ Adult £3.50, child (under 16) £1.80 🚌 Craster (via Alnwick) from Newcastle upon Tyne

DURHAM

▷ 305.

FOUNTAINS ABBEY AND STUDLEY ROYAL WATER GARDEN

Heart-stopping vistas greet visitors to Britain's most complete monastic ruins, with a medieval deer park and elegant 18th-century water gardens.

Fountains Abbey was established in 1132 by 13 monks looking for a simple life, and this damp, rocky, desolate ravine fitted the bill perfectly, with a supply of stone and timber for building, shelter from the rough northern weather and an abundance of spring water. The abbey became extremely wealthy, but Henry VIII closed it down during his dissolution of the country's monasteries in 1539 (▷ 32). Yet it has survived as Britain's largest abbey ruin and you can still see the church tower, dating from around 1500, soaring above the Norman nave. Wander too among the remains of the monastic quarters and into the vaulted interior of the cellarium (storehouse).

The later owners beautified the estate and it was sold to Sir Stephen Proctor, who commissioned the building of Fountains Hall (1598–1604), partly from stone taken from the abbey.

In the 18th century the neighbouring estate of Studley Royal fell into the hands of local MP John Aislabie, who began to landscape the grounds, a project begun in 1720 and completed after his death in 1746 by his son, William. The result is a remarkable creation, a water garden of geometric pools, follies and a landscape of rocky outcrops. In 1768 William acquired Fountains Abbey and Fountains Hall. He extended the gardens to include the sweeping lawn as an approach to the abbey and added Anne Boleyn's Seat, a viewpoint above the valley with a framed view of the ruins.

Close by are the Banqueting House, the Temple of Piety, the Temple of Fame, the Gothic Tower and the fishing lodges that overlook the lake at the garden's eastern end.

To see more, take the path that rises steeply from the Water Gardens via the Serpentine Tunnel to Anne Boleyn's Seat; the Seven Bridges Walk goes through re-created wilderness.

INFORMATION

www.fountainsabbey.org.uk
✚ 465 H12 ✉ Ripon HG4 3DY
☎ 01765 608888 ◉ Abbey, Hall and Water Garden: Mar–end Oct daily 10–5; Nov–end Feb 10–4. Deer Park: daily dawn–dusk 🖐 Adults £7.15, child (5–16) £3.80, family £19 🚆 Harrogate 🍴 🏛

Above *The arched frame of the beautiful 12th-century Cistercian Fountains Abbey*

INFORMATION

www.hadrianswallcountry.org
🗺 465 G10 ℹ Wentworth Car Park, Hexham NE46 1QE, tel 01434 652220
🖐 Vindolanda Fort: adult £5.20, child (5–18) £3. Birdoswald Fort: adult £4.10, child £2.10 🚌 Stagecoach AD122 service: Apr–end Oct (limited service rest of year), linking Carlisle, Hexham, Haltwhistle, Brampton and main Roman sites along the wall; call 01434 322002
📖 £12.99

TIP

» Use the AD122 bus to return to your starting point if you want an extended walk along the wall.

HADRIAN'S WALL

Northumberland preserves the best remains of this once 76-mile (122km) monument, built between AD122 and 128 on the orders of the Roman emperor Hadrian (AD76–138). He had it built to control trade over the border rather than to keep out the barbarians to the north. The B6318 road, which runs parallel to it for part of the way, follows the line of the Roman military way that served the regular forts and observation turrets along the wall. A deep defensive rampart—the vallum—was dug later on the south side of the wall.

HIGHLIGHTS

In many places the wall has long since disappeared, but there are well-preserved sections between Chollerford in the east and Haltwhistle in the west. At Housesteads Roman Fort (Apr–end Sep daily 10–6; Oct–end Mar daily 10–4) the latrines have seating for 12 soldiers and a water channel for sponges (used in place of toilet paper). Close to here is Vindolanda Fort (Apr–end Sep daily 10–6; Feb–end Mar, Oct–end Nov 10–5; Dec–end Jan 10–4), with reconstructions of part of the wall and buildings, and a museum displaying local excavations.

Chesters Roman Fort (Apr–end Sep daily 10–6; rest of year daily 10–4) was a cavalry fort with the remains of the bathhouse (look for the niches where clothes were placed), headquarters and barracks. Corbridge Roman Site (Apr–end Sep daily 10–5.30; Oct 10–4; Nov–end Mar Sat–Sun 10–4) is a former Roman garrison town and was the supply base for the Roman invasion of Scotland in AD80, with some well-preserved granaries.

For an idea of Roman-style bathing, visit the reconstructed bathhouse at Hadrian's outpost, Segedunum Roman Fort (Apr–end Oct daily 10–5; Nov–end Mar daily 10–3) at Wallsend. A 35m (115ft) tower gives a superb view of the remains of the fort itself. At South Shields, Arbeia Roman Fort (Apr–end Oct Mon–Sat 10–5.30; rest of year Mon–Sat 10–3.30) has a reconstructed gatehouse and re-created scenes of camp life. At the west end of the wall, the finest monument is Birdoswald Fort (Apr–end Sep daily 10–5.30, Oct daily 10–4).

The Mithraic Temple at Carrawburgh has the remains of a place of worship for the soldiers, dedicated to the god Mithras.

Above *Roman Hadrian's Wall winding away from Cuddy's Crag, Northumberland National Park*

HAWORTH

When Haworth was home to the Brontë family in the 19th century, it was still a textile-manufacturing village. The steep, cobbled streets are surrounded by wild moorland, and the look of the village has changed little since the Brontës lived here, despite the gift shops and tea rooms.

THE PARSONAGE

Haworth became home to the Brontës in 1820 when Patrick Brontë (1777–1861) was appointed its rector. It was while living at the Parsonage here that the three sisters—Charlotte (1816–55), Emily (1818–48) and Anne (1820–49)—wrote their most famous novels, respectively *Jane Eyre* (1847), *Wuthering Heights* (1847) and *The Tenant of Wildfell Hall* (1848). You can follow well-trodden paths past the Brontë Falls to the ruins of Top Withins farmhouse, reputedly the model for nature-loving Emily's *Wuthering Heights*. There's a tiny statue of Charlotte in the cabinet to your left as you enter her room, together with the description of her by her biographer, friend and fellow novelist Mrs Elizabeth Gaskell (1810–65).

The Parsonage sits at the top of Main Street, overlooking the church. Built in 1778, it has been restored to how it would have looked in the Brontës' day. Mementoes include the children's handwritten miniature books, the sofa on which Emily died and Charlotte's wedding bonnet.

The great tragedy of the family is that they all died at a young age. The girls' brother, Branwell, an alcohol and opium addict, died of tuberculosis in 1848 at the age of 31. Emily also succumbed to the disease and died three months later, at the age of 30. Anne faded away, dying in Scarborough in 1849, having journeyed there to see if the sea air would cure her. Charlotte died on 31 March 1855 at the age of 39 in the early stages of pregnancy. Two other sisters, Maria and Elizabeth, died in childhood.

OTHER SIGHTS

Inside the Parish Church of St. Michael and All Angels, where Patrick Brontë was vicar for 41 years, are memorials to the family. Visit the Brontë Weaving Shed (Mon–Sat 10–5.30, Sun 11–5), on North Street, where you can see traditional 19th-century commemorative Brontë Tweed being made.

INFORMATION
www.visithaworth.com
✚ 465 H13 ﹟ 2–4 West Lane, Haworth BD22 8EF, tel 01535 642329
🚂 Keighley and Worth Valley Railway (01535 645214), connecting with mainline services at Keighley 📅

TIP
»» Steam trains from Keighley run by the Keighley and Worth Valley Railway are a good way to get to the village.

Above *Haworth seen on a wintery day from Penistone Hill, West Yorkshire*

Above *A row of puffins on a rock in the Farne Islands*

FARNE ISLANDS

www.nationaltrust.org.uk

The National Trust specifically advise wearing a hat when visiting this archipelago of 28 islands during the breeding season, to protect visitors from dive-bombing terns. The Farne Islands are one of Britain's foremost seabird breeding grounds. On the boat trip from Seahouses harbour you may spot seals bobbing in the water before you land on Inner Farne and Staple Island, which support populations of puffins, razorbills, eiders, kittiwakes, cormorants and oystercatchers. Other islands can be viewed from the boat.

🔵 465 H9 ✉ c/o The Sheiling, 8 St. Aidan's, Seahouses NE68 7SR ☎ 01665 721099/720651 🌐 Landing permitted on Inner Farne and Staple Island: Apr, Aug–end Sep daily 10.30–6. May–end Jul (breeding season) Staple Island 10.30–1.30, Inner Farne 1.30–5 ✋ (Excluding boat): May–end Jul: adult £5.60, child (5–16) £2.80. Apr, Aug–end Sep: adult £4.60, child (5–16) £2.30 🚢 From Seahouses harbour (2.5 hr) ❓ Wheelchairs have access to Inner Farne only, preferably at high tide

FOUNTAINS ABBEY AND STUDLEY ROYAL WATER GARDEN

▷ 307.

HADRIAN'S WALL

▷ 308.

HALIFAX

www.calderdale.gov.uk

In the heart of the Pennine Hills, Halifax became a powerhouse of the textile industry during the Industrial Revolution. The focus of its pre-industrial heritage is Piece Hall, built as a woollen market in 1779, with 350 small rooms set on a series of colonnaded tiers around a vast open space. Today, the hall has small gift shops, cafés, a market and open-air concerts. The main tourist attraction is Eureka! The Museum for Children (daily), aimed at 3- to12-year-olds, where children can learn about themselves and the world.

🔵 461 H13 ℹ️ Piece Hall, Halifax HX1 1RE, tel 01422 368725 🚇 Halifax

HAREWOOD HOUSE AND BIRD GARDEN

www.harewood.org

This showpiece country house was designed for the Lascelles family (the earls of Harewood) by John Carr in 1759. Much of the furniture is by Thomas Chippendale (1718–79) from nearby Otley. There's plenty to enjoy outside, with an adventure playground, a rose garden, lakeside walks, a Spiral Meadow in the kitchen garden and a Bird Garden with over 100 species of bird.

🔵 462 H13 ✉ Harewood, near Leeds LS17 9LQ ☎ 0113 218 1010 🌐 Grounds and Bird Garden: daily 10–4.30 (last admission 4.30). House: daily 11–4.30. Terrace Gallery: daily 11–4.30. Old Kitchen: daily 12–4.30 ✋ Late Jun–early Sep: adult £12, child £7.70, family £42; rest of season: adult £10, child £6.20, family £36. Half-price tickets available to visitors who arrive by bicycle or bus 🚌 Bus 36 from Harrogate or Leeds 🍴 🛒 🏛

HARROGATE

www.harrogate.gov.uk

Its spa days may have declined, but Harrogate still exudes style, with Victorian buildings and hotels ranged around the expansive 80ha (200-acre) green known as The Stray. Why not sample the waters from Europe's strongest sulphur well at the Royal Pump Room Museum (Apr–end Oct Mon–Sat 10–5, Sun 2–5; rest of year Mon–Sat 10–4) in Crown Place, or look into the former Promenade Room that now houses the Mercer Art Gallery (Tue–Sun and public holidays)? The 1897 Royal Baths in Crescent Road still have the original Turkish baths, decorated appropriately in Moorish style with plush tiles, in addition to saunas and solariums.

Harrogate is a leading events venue and the annual Antiques Fair attracts dealers from around the world. The Royal Horticultural Society's Harlow Carr Botanical Garden (Mar–end Oct daily 9.30–6; Nov–end Feb 9.30–4) is one of the show gardens of the north.

Having afternoon tea at Betty's Tearoom on Parliament Street is a Harrogate institution.

🔵 462 H13 ℹ️ Royal Baths Assembly Rooms, Crescent Road HG1 2RR, tel 01423 537300 🚇 Harrogate

HAWKSHEAD

www.hawksheadtouristinfo.org.uk

With its whitewashed houses, narrow streets and cobbled alleyways, Hawkshead has hardly changed since the days when William Wordsworth (1770–1850) attended school here. The traffic-free central area has allowed it to keep its dignity. For centuries Hawkshead was a thriving market town at the heart of the local woollen industry, but it dwindled into insignificance in the 19th century. Wordsworth carved his name on his desk at Hawkshead Grammar School, now a museum (Easter–end Sep Mon–Sat 10–1, 2–5, Sun 1–3.30; Oct Mon–Sat 10–1, 2–3.30, Sun 1–3.30), and as a boy attended Hawkshead church. The Beatrix Potter Gallery (Easter–end Oct Sat–Thu 10.30–4.30) has

illustrations by the famous children's author Beatrix Potter (1866–1943), who lived at Near Sawrey.
✠ 464 F12 ℹ Main Street, Hawkshead LA22 0NS, tel 01539 436946

HAWORTH
▷ 309.

HEBDEN BRIDGE
www.calderdale.gov.uk
This spectacular little Pennine town is set in the steep-sided valley of Calderdale, with double-decker houses—one house at the top entered from one street, another underneath entered from a street below—clinging tenaciously to the hillsides. Heptonstall, above Hebden Bridge, became the local focus for hand-weaving in the pre-Industrial age, but was overtaken by the large mills in Hebden Bridge during the 19th century.

If you have time, take the walk from Hebden Bridge to Heptonstall via the packhorse bridge and the steep cobbled lane known as The Buttress.
✠ 461 G13 ℹ Hebden Bridge Visitor and Canal Centre, New Road, Hebden Bridge HX7 8AF, tel 01422 843831 🚉 Hebden Bridge

HEXHAM
www.hadrianswallcountry.org
Hexham, a market town on the River Tyne, is dominated by its abbey church. Begun by St. Wilfrid in about AD675, it contains the crypt built by the saint, but otherwise dates mostly from 1180 to 1250. Look for the Roman standard-bearer's tombstone, the ancient crypt and the Frith Stool (a Saxon seat in the chancel). Moot Hall, near the marketplace, is a miniature castle pierced by a gateway, erected in the late 14th century as the entrance to barracks for the local garrison; it now houses an art gallery and library. Hexham makes a good base for exploring the most impressive parts of Hadrian's Wall (▷ 168).
✠ 465 G10 ℹ Wentworth Car Park, Hexham NE46 1QE, tel 01434 652220 🚉 Hexham

HOLKER HALL
www.holker-hall.co.uk
The hall itself dates from the 17th century, but much of what you see today is from the 1870s, when architects Paley and Austin added a new wing, a cantilevered staircase and well-disguised modern comforts such as fake books to hide the light switches. The grounds overlook Morecambe Bay, and have woodland trails as well as formal gardens. The Lakeland Motor Museum has more than 100 vehicles on display, including the Campbell Bluebird exhibition dedicated to the father-and-son team of Sir Malcolm (1885–1949) and Donald Campbell (1921–67), who between them set a series of water-speed records on nearby Coniston Water from the 1930s to the 1960s.
✠ 464 F12 ✉ Cark-in-Cartmel, near Grange-over-Sands LA11 7PL ☎ 015395 58328 🕐 Apr–end Oct Sun–Fri 11–4. Lakeland Motor Museum: Apr–end Oct Sun–Fri 10.30–4.45. Gardens: Apr–end Oct Sun–Fri 10–5.30 👆 All sights: adult £11.50, child (6–15) £6.50, family £32 🍽 💻 🎁

HULL
www.hullcc.gov.uk/visithull
The large port of Kingston upon Hull is only patchily inviting at first look. World War II bombing devastated large areas of the city. However, much investment has gone into rejuvenating the waterfront and the old town. The best areas are the narrow cobbled High Street, with old warehouses, Victorian shopping arcades, a lively covered market and the streets around the vast Holy Trinity Church.

There is also still considerable activity along the quaysides as trawlers land their catches.

The Deep (daily 10–6, last entry 5) is billed as 'the world's only submarium'. It puts the marine world into chronological context, from the Big Bang onwards, and has all kinds of marine life and push-button gadgets. Hull's other museums (Mon–Sat 10–5, Sun 1.30–4.30) are all free and include the lively trio of Wilberforce House, the home of slavery abolitionist William Wilberforce

(1759–1833); Streetlife, a transport museum popular with children; and the more sober Hull and East Riding Museum, with recreations of an Iron Age village and a well-displayed Roman section. The charmingly old-fashioned Hull Maritime Museum (Mon–Sat 10–5, Sun 1.30–4.30), in Queen Victoria Square, has details on the city's history of whaling, fishing and shipping, and nearby is the equally absorbing Ferens Art Gallery (Mon–Sat 10–5, Sun 1.30–4.30).

Two impressive modern structures are the Tidal Surge Barrier (1980), at the entrance to the River Hull from the Humber, and the mighty Humber Bridge (1981).
✠ 462 K13 ℹ 1 Paragon Street, HU1 3NA, tel 01482 223559 🚉 Hull

ISLE OF MAN
www.visitisleofman.com
Best known perhaps for the annual motorcycle races—the Isle of Man Tourist Trophy (TT), held on various courses for almost a century—the Isle of Man is a curious fragment of the British Isles. Measuring 33 miles by 13 miles (53km by 21km) and in the Irish Sea off the northwest of England, the island is a Crown dependency, not part of the UK, and has lenient taxation and the world's oldest continuous parliament (the Tynwald). But the landscape has much more to interest the visitor: sandy beaches, dramatic moors and mountains, and a generous smattering of Celtic crosses, standing stones and ancient burial grounds.

The capital, Douglas, has a Victorian waterfront, horse-drawn trams and the Manx Museum (Mon–Sat 10–5), but Peel makes a characterful base. Train enthusiasts should take a trip on the island's narrow-gauge railway.

Peel Castle and Castle Rushen in Castletown are both impressive places to visit.
✠ 464 D12 ℹ Isle of Man Welcome Centre, Sea Terminal Buildings, Douglas IM1 2RG, tel 01624 686766 🚢 Isle of Man Steam Packet Company ☎ 01624 661661, www.steam-packet.com (Heysham, Liverpool–Douglas)

KENDAL

www.golakes.co.uk

For 600 years up to the 19th century, this town of grey stone on the eastern threshold of the Lake District (▷ 172) also flourished as a milling town. Today, although the manufacturing industries have dwindled, Kendal still has many former weavers' yards as well as numerous ginnels (alleyways), most just off Highgate and Stricklandgate.

The town's best-known former residents are Henry VIII's sixth wife Catherine Parr (1512–48), born in the now-ruined hilltop castle, and portraitist George Romney (1734–1802). Some of Romney's works are displayed in Abbot Hall Gallery (Mon–Sat), with paintings by J. M. W. Turner and John Constable.

The Museum of Lakeland Life (Mon–Sat) recalls local life from the 17th to 19th centuries.

🚩 465 G12 🚹 Town Hall, Highgate LA9 4QL, tel 1539 725758 🚆 Kendal

KESWICK

www.keswick.org

Keswick's position on Derwentwater is the key to its appeal as the major centre in the northern Lake District. Walkers venture from here all year round to the summit of Skiddaw, into the crag-lined valley of Borrowdale or along the gentle paths by the lake. The Keswick Launch (Easter–end Nov daily from 10am; rest of year Sat, Sun and public holidays) connects points around the lake.

Neolithic Castlerigg Stone Circle, to the east, comprises 38 chunks of volcanic stone (▷ 329).

🚩 464 F11 🚹 Moot Hall, Market Place CA12 5JE, tel 017687 72645

LAKE DISTRICT NATIONAL PARK

www.lake-district.gov.uk

This is an extraordinarily diverse area of mountains and lakes tucked into England's northwest corner. There's a wide choice of walking routes, from the high summits of Scafell Pike and Helvellyn to strolls through tranquil valleys and along lake shores. Or you can see it on a cruise: Options include the Victorian steam yacht

Gondola for a trip on Coniston Water, or a lake steamer on Ullswater.

There's also a range of indoor attractions, including visits to the houses of the area's most famous residents. Among them are Hill Top (Mar–end Oct Sat–thu 10.30–4.30), home of Beatrix Potter (1866–1943), and Rydal Mount (Mar–end Oct daily 9.30–5; rest of year 10–4, closed Tue), home of William Wordsworth (1770– 1850). It was Ullswater daffodils that inspired his famous poem. He and his sister Dorothy lived at Dove Cottage in Grasmere (daily 9.30–5.30).

🚩 464 F12 🚹 National Park Authority, Murley Moss, Oxenholme Road, Kendal LA9 7RL, tel 01539 724555

LEEDS

▷ 313.

LINDISFARNE (HOLY ISLAND)

www.lindisfarne.org.uk

Joined at low tide by a causeway to the mainland, Holy Island (known as Lindisfarne before 1082) retains the sense of isolation that drew monks and hermits here from early medieval times onwards. You need to take note of the signs for safe crossing times. The most famous monk was St. Cuthbert (died AD687), bishop of the monastery. The museum beside the ruins of 12th-century Lindisfarne Priory (Apr–end Sep daily 9.30–5; Oct daily 9.30–4; Nov–end Jan 10–2; Feb–end Mar 10–4) recounts the life of the early monks. Lindisfarne Castle (Apr–end Oct Tue–Sun 12–4.30 or 10.30–3 depending on tides, but check tides) was built in the 1540s and restored in 1903 by the architect Sir Edwin Lutyens; its interior is a combination of the 16th century, comfortable Edwardian furnishings and Lutyens' quirks.

While you are here, try the delicious Lindisfarne mead, an alcoholic honey drink made at St. Aidan's Winery. And take a look at the copy of the Lindisfarne Gospels (an illuminated seventh-century manuscript now kept in the British Library) in St. Mary's Church.

🚩 465 H9 ✉ Holy Island, Northumberland TD15 2SH ☎ 01289 389244

LIVERPOOL

▷ 314.

MANCHESTER

▷ 315.

MARTIN MERE

www.wwt.org.uk

Martin Mere is a wetland habitat for birds from every corner of the world. Winter is a particularly good time to visit, when thousands of pink-footed geese, and whooper and Bewick's swans can be seen under floodlight in the evening.

An exciting new development is the reintroduction of beavers, a species absent for some 500 years. Two breeding pairs were released here in 2007, in a spacious enclosure.

🚩 461 F13 ✉ The Wildfowl and Wetlands Trust, Burscough L40 0TA ☎ 01704 895181 🕓 Mar–end Oct daily 9.30–5.30; rest of year daily 9.30–5 💷 Adult £8.25, child (4–16) £4.10, family £22.50 🖱 🏛

NEWBY HALL AND GARDENS

www.newbyhall.com

A treasure house of art and furniture, this 17th-century building has sculptures and tapestries brought back from the Grand Tour of Europe in the 1760s by William Weddell, the owner. He commissioned the architect Robert Adam to extend the house, adding a sculpture gallery. Much of the furniture was designed by Adam and made by Thomas Chippendale. The gardens, developed in the 20th century, have superb borders. There is an adventure playground, miniature railway and sculpture exhibition.

🚩 465 H12 ✉ Newby Hall, Ripon HG4 5AE ☎ 01423 322583 🕓 Easter–end Sep Tue–Sun (Tue–Mon Jul, Aug). Garden: 11–5.30 (last entry 5). House: 12–5 (last entry 4) 💷 House and garden: adult £10.20, child (4–16) £7.80. Garden: adult £7, child £5.80. Miniature railway: all £1.50 🍴 🖱 🏛

NEWCASTLE UPON TYNE

▷ 316.

LEEDS

One of the fastest-growing cities in England, Leeds displays true northern grit alongside a cultural renaissance. Industry and commerce are synonymous with this city, whose architecture tells of great expansion in the 19th century. The classical Town Hall is one of Britain's grandest, and the Victorian glass-roofed arcades and elliptical Corn Exchange are period gems as well as bustling shopping venues. Nightlife, music and theatre are other major draws.

In central Leeds, the City Art Gallery (Mon–Tue 10–8, Wed 12–8, Thu–Sat 10–5, Sun 1–5), on the Headrow, has an impressive range of 19th- and 20th-century paintings and sculptures. Next door is the Henry Moore Institute (Thu–Tue 10–5.30, Wed 10–9) with major exhibits from 1850 to the present by Henry Moore, Barbara Hepworth, Andy Goldsworthy and others. Telling the story of medical treatment through the ages, the Thackray Medical Museum (daily 10–5), on Beckett Street, is of mainstream appeal, with interactive displays exploring Victorian slum life.

After many years of ignoring the River Aire and the Leeds–Liverpool Canal planners have developed along the banks of both, with a dynamic waterfront culture of pavement cafés and specialist shops. Here, the Royal Armouries Museum (daily 10–5) houses the national collection of arms and armour. Look for the elephant armour and Henry VIII's tournament armour.

Outstanding among the more outlying attractions is Leeds Industrial Museum (Tue–Sat 10–5, Sun 1–5), within Armley Mills, once the largest woollen mill in the world. The museum now tells the story of the growth of Leeds as one of the world's great industrial cities. Temple Newsam (Apr–end Oct Tue–Sun 10.30–5; Nov–end Mar Tue–Sun 10.30–4), east of the city, is a large 16th-century house with rich collections of fine art, as well as Europe's largest working rare breeds farm.

INFORMATION

www.leeds.gov.uk

✚ 462 H13 🛈 Gateway Yorkshire, The Arcade City Station LS1 1PL, tel 0113 242 5242 🚆 Leeds City ✈ Leeds/Bradford Airport

Above *Shops, cafés and a bar are in the Leeds Corn Exchange*

INFORMATION

✚ 461 F14 🛈 Atlantic Pavilion, Albert Dock L3 4EA, tel 051 237 3925
❓ Magical Mystery Tour bus from Gower street, Albert Dock, daily 2.10pm (also 11.40 in summer), tel 0151 236 1965
🚉 Liverpool Lime Street

TIPS

» Save on what could be a very expensive day out by visiting these free attractions: Walker Art Gallery, Merseyside Maritime Museum, HM Customs and Excise National Museum, Museum of Liverpool Life and Tate Liverpool.
» Ride the ferry across the Mersey (Pier Head) for the best introduction to the city.

LIVERPOOL

Its days as one of the great ports of the British Empire have long gone, but the grandeur of its architecture echoes the boom years—Liverpool has more landmark buildings than any English city outside London and was the European Capital of Culture 2008.

ARCHITECTURAL HIGHLIGHTS

Walk from Lime Street Station, past neoclassical St. George's Hall (1854), along Dale Street and Water Street to the waterfront. Here is the Royal Liver Building (1911 by W. Aubrey Thomas), a main landmark, with the famous sculptural Liver Birds perched high on the 10-storey tower.

Red-brick Albert Dock (1846) was imaginatively restored in 1988 into gift shops, cafés and major museums. Fans can visit the Beatles Story (daily 10–6), dedicated to the world-famous group. There's a mock-up of The Cavern club, the white piano on which John Lennon (1940–80) composed Imagine (1971), and other memorabilia.

At either end of Hope Street are the two cathedrals. The vast, sandstone Anglican Liverpool Cathedral was started in 1904 but inaugurated in 1978, to Giles Gilbert Scott's design; its tower can be seen from north Wales. The concrete Metropolitan Cathedral (Roman Catholic) was built in 1967 and is sometimes affectionately known as the Mersey Funnel. It was designed by Frederick Gibberd, and is brilliantly lit by blue stained-glass windows.

MUSEUMS AND GALLERIES

The Walker Art Gallery (daily 10–5), on William Brown Street, houses one of the UK's best provincial art collections, including works by local artist George Stubbs (1724–1806), noted for his paintings of horses. The impressive Maritime Museum (daily 10–5), in Albert Dock, gives an insight into the city's maritime past. Next door, Tate Liverpool (Tue–Sun 10–5.50; daily Jun–end Aug) houses an excellent collection of modern art. Just beyond Albert Dock, the old Manchester Dock is being transformed into a new Museum of Liverpool, due to open in 2010.

THE BEATLES CONNECTION

From Albert Dock, the Magical Mystery Tourbus goes to Strawberry Fields, Penny Lane and The Cavern, locations closely associated with the Beatles. Other tours take in the childhood homes of John Lennon and Sir Paul McCartney where the group often rehearsed.

Below *Liverpool's stately buildings line the docks on the River Mersey*

MANCHESTER

Manchester grew from a small town in the late 18th century to become one of the most important cities of the Industrial Revolution. It made its money from cotton, earning it the nickname Cottonopolis. Waves of decline and rebuilding followed, a highlight being Manchester's successful hosting of the 2002 Commonwealth Games, which has created entire new areas.

THE HIGHLIGHTS

Great buildings, such as the neo-Gothic Town Hall (tours Sat and Wed 2pm; book through tourist information), and the Royal Exchange (the former Cotton Exchange), speak of the wealth of the late 18th century, and you are free to wander around these buildings. The top attraction is Urbis (daily 10–6), housed in a shimmering glass building near the cathedral. Inside, state-of-the-art interactive displays and exhibits lead you through a journey exploring life in different cities of the world.

Carefully restored and given a striking new stone and glass extension to the original, stone-built, porticoed Victorian building, the Manchester Art Gallery (Tue–Sun 10–5) can show off its artistic wealth, which includes a great collection of modern pieces as well as its noted Pre-Raphaelite paintings. The ground floor is home to the Manchester Gallery, with works by L. S. Lowry (1887–1976) and others. In the Castlefield district, the Museum of Science and Industry in Manchester (daily 10–5) is an excellent free visit, with Robert Stephenson's 1830 locomotive *Planet*.

SALFORD QUAYS

Salford Quays houses two major free tourist attractions. Within a gleaming steel-built structure, The Lowry (galleries: Sun–Fri 11–5, Sat 10–5) encompasses theatres and galleries, including an exhibition of Lowry paintings, with some of his earlier, iconic images of matchstick men in the streets of industrial Manchester. Across a footbridge is the Imperial War Museum North (Mar–end Oct daily 10–6; Nov–end Feb 10–5), an ingenious building made of three shards of fractured steel to represent the world's conflicts on land, sea and air.

INFORMATION

www.manchester.gov.uk

✚ 461 G14 ℹ️ Town Hall Extension, Lloyd Street M60 2LA, tel 0871 222 8223

🚉 Manchester Piccadilly

Below *City Lowry Centre, Salford Quays, Manchester*

NEWCASTLE UPON TYNE

The locals of this resurgent city compensate for the biting North Sea winds with a natural warmth and exuberance.

AROUND THE TYNE

The River Tyne provides some of Newcastle's key landmarks. The semicircular Tyne Bridge has as its companions the High Level Bridge (1849), with two decks (the upper for trains and the lower for motorized traffic), the hydraulically operated Swing Bridge (1876) and the innovative Gateshead Millennium Bridge (2000), with its unique blinking-eye mechanism that makes it pivot to allow ships to pass. The bridges join Newcastle to Gateshead, where a major attraction is the huge Baltic Centre for Contemporary Art (gallery: Wed–Mon 10–6, Tue 10.30–6). Occupying a former flour mill, this lively arts quarter includes The Sage, an ultra-modern theatre and arts venue, and has a rooftop restaurant.

Newcastle dates back to Roman times, and the 'new castle'—of which the impressive keep and chapel survive—was begun in 1080. On the riverfront is 16th-century Bessie Surtees' House (Mon–Fri 10–4), built of timber and originally home to rich merchants. Early legacies of the boom years as a coal port include elegant Victorian architecture by John Dobson in Grey Street; climb the 164 steps of Grey's Monument for an overview. Around here is the main shopping area, with the indoor Grainger Market (Mon, Wed 9–5, Thu–Sat 9–5.30) offering all kinds of goods.

MUSEUMS AND GALLERIES

The city is known for its lively nightlife, but has enough cultural highlights (many free) to justify a visit. The Laing Art Gallery (Mon–Sat 10–5, Sun 2–5) focuses on 19th-century art. The Great North Museum (due to open 2009) pulls together the collections of several leading museums in the region. Two of Newcastle's liveliest attractions are the Centre for Life (Mon–Sat 10–6, Sun 11–6), delving into evolution, the workings of the brain and emotions, and the Discovery Museum (Mon–Sat 10–5, Sun 2–5), with interactive science, featuring shipbuilding, mirrors, magnets and a Science Maze.

Above *The Millennium Bridge illuminated at night, Newcastle upon Tyne*

NORTH YORK MOORS NATIONAL PARK

www.northyorkmoors-npa.gov.uk
www.visitnorthyorkshiremoors.co.uk
Though not the highest nor the most dramatically rugged of Britain's national parks, this is a highly distinctive corner of England. Medieval stone crosses, placed as waymarkers, punctuate the bare waste of the moors, which feature the country's largest continuous tract of heather—a really spectacular purple carpet in late summer. There's an exhilarating sense of solitude up here among the skylarks and grouse.

Below are a series of lush, green dales (valleys) such as Esk Dale and Rosedale, each with trademark attractive villages such as Hutton-le-Hole and Coxwold that sport red-tiled roofs, yellowstone walls and spacious village greens (come out of season if you want to avoid the crowds). Make a visit to Ryedale Folk Museum in Hutton-le-Hole to see reconstructed local buildings. The quiet market town of Helmsley, on the park's southern edge, makes a useful base for exploring the area, and has the jagged ruins of a 13th-century castle (Apr–end Sep daily 10–6; Mar, Oct daily 10–5; rest of year Thu–Mon 10–4) to explore.

Coastal attractions include the formidable sandstone cliffs and impossibly squashed-together fishing villages such as Robin Hood's Bay, with a famously steep main street and a smuggling history to rival any other, and Staithes, which has maintained quite a few of its traditional qualities.

You can get a good idea of the landscape by driving or cycling along the many quiet roads, or from the steam and diesel trains on the North Yorkshire Moors Railway (▷ 333). But the best views of all are from the long-distance footpath, the Cleveland Way, as it snakes along the escarpments, taking in the huge inland cliff of Sutton Bank, the mini-summit of Roseberry Topping and the entire coastal stretch from Saltburn-by-the-Sea to Filey.

Early Christians left some impressive monuments, including the monastic remains of 14th-century Mount Grace Priory (Apr–end Oct daily 10–6; rest of year Thu–Mon 10–4), 11 miles (18km) north of Thirsk, where a silent order of monks once lived, 12th-century Byland Abbey (Apr–end Oct Thu–Mon 11–6; open Wed in Aug) near Coxwold, and Rievaulx Abbey (▷ 318).

Take a trip on the North Yorkshire Moors Railway, which runs from Pickering to Grosmont through the heart of the moors.

✚ 465 J12 ℹ️ North York Moors National Park, The Old Vicarage, Bondgate, Helmsley, York YO62 5BP, tel 01439 770657

NORTHUMBERLAND NATIONAL PARK

www.northumberlandnationalpark.org.uk
This quietest and least-frequented of Britain's national parks covers an area known as the Cheviot Hills—uplands spanning the Scottish border, grazed by hardy sheep—as well as Hadrian's Wall farther south (▷ 308). Roads into the Cheviots tend to be dead ends, but the drive into Coquet Dale via Alwinton gives a good idea of the sheer emptiness of the landscape. If you want to explore further, Windy Gyle is an excellent walkers' summit, with expansive views into Scotland. West of the park boundary lie the huge plantations of Kielder Forest; this man-made landscape is not to everyone's taste, but offers forest walks, rowing boats on the reservoir of Kielder Water and outstanding cycling.

North of Redesdale, much of the land is used for military training, and parts are closed to the public, while others are accessible only on designated footpaths when the warning flags are not flying. Details are available from tourist information offices.

✚ 465 G10 ℹ️ Eastburn, South Park, Hexham NE46 1BS, tel 01434 605555

NOSTELL PRIORY

www.nationaltrust.org.uk
This mansion takes its name from the priory dedicated to St. Oswald, which was founded on the site in the 12th century. The interior is the main draw, with detailed plasterwork by Robert Adam (1728–92) and James Paine (1717–89) and furniture by Thomas Chippendale (1718–79). There are paintings by Flemish artist Pieter Brueghel the Younger (c1564–1638) and an 18th-century dolls' house, complete with original fittings and scaled-down Chippendale furniture. There are plans to restore the surviving 18th-century garden features. Enjoy the scented rose garden and the lakeside walk to the Menagerie Garden.

✚ 462 H13 ✉️ Doncaster Road, Nostell, near Wakefield WF4 1QE ☎ 01924 863892 🕐 House: Apr–end Oct Wed–Sun 1–5. Grounds: Mar–end Oct Wed–Sun 11–5.30; Nov Sat, Sun 11–4.30; mid-Dec Wed–Sun 11–4.30 👜 House and grounds: adult £7, child (5–16) £3.50, family £16.80. Grounds only: adult £3.50, child £1.50 🚌 Arriva 485, 496, B-Line 244/5 🚉 Fitzwilliam 1.5 miles (2km) 🍴 🎁

PORT SUNLIGHT

www.portsunlightvillage.com
In the industrial Wirral peninsula is this visionary garden village utopia, built in 1888 by the enlightened Sunlight Soap magnate William Hesketh Lever to house his factory workers—and now an extremely desirable place to live. No two groups of cottages are quite the same, although black-and-white Tudor and bricky Queen Anne and Elizabethan styles predominate. The Village Trail is a self-guiding walking tour available from the Sunlight Vision Museum (daily 10–4.30).

At its heart is the Lady Lever Art Gallery (Mon–Sat 10–5, Sun 1–5), built for the education of the workers, which has paintings by Edward Burne-Jones, Dante Gabriel Rossetti, J. M. W. Turner, John Constable and Joshua Reynolds, as well as Wedgwood ceramics.

✚ 461 F14 ℹ️ Sunlight Vision Museum, 23 King George's Drive, Port Sunlight, Wirral CH62 5DX, tel 0151 644 6466 🚉 Port Sunlight

QUEEN STREET MILL

www.lancashire.gov.uk/education/
museums/queen/

The last of the great steam-powered
Lancashire cotton mills, Queen
Street Mill came quite late to
the industry. Built for a workers'
cooperative betwen 1894 and 1895,
in its heyday it ran 1,138 looms
from its massive steam engine
(named 'Peace' after World War I).
Raw cotton came here the USA,
was woven into plain cloth, then
exported to India, China and South
America, as well as supplying
more local markets. It finally closed
in 1982 and was preserved as a
museum to the industry. It's also
popular with filmmakers as an
authentic set. Demonstrations of
the steam engine and looms run
12.45–1.30, 2.15–3, 3.45–4.30.
465 G13 ✉ Harle Syke, Burnley BB10
2HX ☎ 01282 412555 ⏲ May–end Sep
Tue–Sat, Apr Tue–Fri 12–5; Mar, Oct, Nov
Tue–Thu 12–4; public holiday weekends
12–3 ✋ Adult £3, accompanied child under
16 free 🚉 Burnley 🍴 🏛

RHEGED

www.rheged.com

Rheged was the name of an ancient
Celtic kingdom that dominated northwest England and southern Scotland
in the sixth century AD. Today it is
Cumbria's largest visitor complex,
and Europe's largest grass-covered
building. The central attraction is
Rheged—the Movie (daily, various
times), a film that plays on a giant
screen and charts 2,000 years of the
area's history.

As well as the theatre, cafés,
specialist food shops and shops
selling outdoor gear, books and toys,
there is a large exhibition space,
which hosts touring exhibitions from
time to time and the innovative
Discovering Cumbria feature, which
combines a scale model of the
mountainous peninsula and tells
its tale through an audio-visual
commentary. Outside, Turrets and
Tunnels is a fantastic play facility
(Mar–end Oct 11–4) for children.
464 F11 ✉ Redhills, Penrith CA11
0DQ ☎ 01768 868000 ⏲ Daily 9–5.30

✋ Discovering Cumbria: free. Giant
cinema: adult £4.95 (extra film £3), child
(5–14) £3 (extra film £2), family £14 (extra
film £8.50) 🚉 Penrith station, then bus X4
or X5 🍴 🖥 🏛

RICHMOND

www.richmond.org

Richmond is one of the most
tempting historical towns in the
Yorkshire Dales. Off cobbled Trinity
Church Square, a large marketplace,
is a steep knot of unspoiled streets
such as Frenchgate and Newbiggin
Broad, mainly with refined Georgian
buildings, and two surviving
medieval gateways.

Perched on a precipitous bank
above the fast-flowing River Swale,
Richmond Castle (Apr–end Sep daily
10–6; Oct–end Mar Thu–Mon 10–4)
dates from 1071; within it, Scollard's
Hall (1080) may be Britain's earliest
surviving domestic building. Still
very much in use, the Georgian
Theatre Royal (Mon–Sat 10–4) has
the oldest unaltered interior (1788)
in Britain. The museum displays
original playbills and painted scenery
made in 1836.
465 H12 🛈 Friary Gardens, Victoria
Road, Richmond DL10 4AJ, tel 01748 850252

RIEVAULX ABBEY

www.english-heritage.org.uk

Rievaulx (pronounced reevo) was
the first Cistercian monastery to
be founded in England, in 1132,
and by 1200 there were more than
140 monks and 500 lay brothers
leading an austere life of prayer,
fasting and work in this remote
corner of Rye Dale. Much of what
you see today dates from the 13th
century, supremely graceful in spite
of the damage following Henry VIII's
dissolution of the monasteries in
1539 (▷ 32). Particularly majestic
are the soaring arches of the now
roofless monastic church. Rievaulx
Terrace and Temples (Mar–end
Sep daily 11–6; Oct 11–5) are an
18th-century landscape feature
overlooking the abbey ruins.
465 J12 ✉ Rievaulx Abbey, Rievaulx
YO62 5LB ☎ 01439 798228 ⏲ Apr–end
Sep daily 10–6; Oct Thu–Mon 10–5; rest of

Above *12th-century Rievaulx Abbey*

year Thu–Mon 10–4 ✋ Adult £4.50, child
(under 16) £2.30. Audiotour free 🖥 🏛

RIPON

www.ripon.org

One of England's smallest cities,
with a population of around 15,000,
Ripon is known as the Cathedral
City of the Dales. Overlooking the
spacious marketplace and the knot of
narrow streets is the cathedral (daily
8–6.15). Its chief glories include the
choir stalls, with late 15th-century
carved misericords, and the Saxon
crypt—a remnant of the seventh-
century monastery.

Ripon's museums pursue the
law-and-order theme, for Ripon was
once within the jurisdiction of the
archbishops of York, who maintained
their own law. The Police and Prison
Museum (Apr–end Oct daily 1–4,
11–4 during school holidays) in St.
Marygate has a cranking machine,
turned by prisoners simply to give
them something to do, while the
Workhouse Museum (Apr–end
Oct daily 1–4, 11–4 during school
holidays), in the former workhouse
in Allhallowgate, illustrates how the
old and poor were treated during the
19th century.

The Hornblower blows the large
horn by the obelisk in Market Square
at 9pm every evening, to tell the
citizens that the watch has been set.

465 H12 🔼 Minster Road, Ripon HG4
1QT, tel 0845 389 0178 (Apr–end Oct daily;
rest of year Thu and Sat only)

SCARBOROUGH

www.scarborough.gov.uk
www.discoveryorkshirecoast.com
A headland occupied by the ruins
of 12th-century Scarborough Castle
(Apr–end Sep daily 10–6; Oct Thu–
Mon 10–5; rest of year Thu–Mon
10–4) divides the two curving sandy
bays of Scarborough, just outside
the southeast corner of the North
York Moors National Park (▷ 317).
The town became a spa in the 17th
century and has a valid claim as
Britain's first seaside resort. The
oldest part of town huddles beside
the fishing harbour in South Bay.
Most of Scarborough developed
after the railway arrived in 1845. One
of the great symbols of Scarborough
is the Grand Hotel of 1863, once
one of the largest in the world, with
its bulbous domes and elaborate
balconies.

William Smith (1769–1839),
one of the founders of modern
geology, suggested the design
for the Rotunda on Vernon Road.
It was built in 1828 and opened
amid great civic pageant, to show
a collection of fossils in their order
of strata—a revolutionary concept
at that time. The museum has been
lovingly restored and re-opened as a
museum of geology in 2008 (daily),
with Smith's personal collection
alongside the Scarborough collection
of fossils taking up the first floor
displays. Other floors bring modern
technology into action to describe
the future of geological research and
the part it plays in everyday life.

Across the Valley Gardens, the
Scarborough Art Gallery (Tue–Sun
10–5) is housed in an Italianate villa.
Alongside the municipal art collection, it keeps a running programme
of contemporary exhibitions, often
from bigger, state collections.

The Sea Life Centre and Marine
Sanctuary (Nov–end Feb daily 10–4;
Mar–end Apr 10–5; May–end Oct
10–6) in North Bay is one of the
town's main family attractions, with

rockpool habitats and a variety of
marine life.

Enjoy a concert by the Spa
Orchestra, either in the Spa Grand
Hall or outdoors in the special
band area; alternatively there are
re-enacted sea battles using model
ships on the lake in Peasholm Park
during summer. The grave of author
Anne Brontë (1820–49) is in the
churchyard near the parish church.
462 K12 🔼 Unit 15a Brunswick
Sopping Centre, Westborough, Scarborough
YO11 1UE, tel 01723 373333

SIZERGH CASTLE

www.nationaltrust.org.uk
The home of the Strickland family
for over 760 years, this ivy-clad
medieval castle/manor house has
been much extended. At its core is
a 14th-century pele (small, square,
defensive) tower; the rest is mostly
Elizabethan. Inside, there is an
exceptional series of oak-panelled
rooms set off by intricately carved
mantelpieces and early oak furniture.
Each room is hung with portraits of
the family and of royalty with whom
they have had some connection.

The grounds feature two lakes, a
rock garden and a wild garden.
464 F12 ✉ Sizergh, near Kendal LA8
8AE ☎ 015395 60951 🔵 Mar–end Oct
Sun–Thu 1–5 (garden 11–5) 🖐 Adult £6.40,
child (5–16) £3.20, family £16 🔲 🔢

SKIPTON

www.skiptononline.co.uk
The Gateway to the Dales is at its
liveliest on market days—Monday,
Wednesday, Friday and especially
Saturday. The broad, tree-lined main
street is full of shops and old pubs,
with ginnels (cobbled alleys) running
off on either side. Retaining turrets
and battlements, Skipton Castle
(Mar–end Sep Mon–Sat 10–6, Sun
12–6; rest of year Mon–Sat 10–4,
Sun 12–4) dates from Norman
times. It played a significant role in
the Wars of the Roses (1455–85) and
endured a three-year Parliamentarian
siege during the Civil War (▷ 34),
after which it had to be partly rebuilt.
465 G13 🔼 35 Coach Street BD23 1LQ,
tel 01756 792809 🔼 Skipton

TOWNEND

www.nationaltrust.org.uk
Come here to see how Lakeland
farmhouses used to look. Townend
has no electricity, and epitomizes
the remoteness of the Lake District
in centuries past. It remained the
property of the farming Browne
family for over 300 years until it was
taken over by the National Trust in
1943, though you can still meet the
current Mr Browne at the house
(most Thursdays). The mainly 17th-
century house has the Browne's
handcarved furniture and domestic
implements, and has a downhouse
for washing, cooking, pickling and
brewing, and a firehouse with living
quarters.
464 F12 ✉ Troutbeck, Windermere
LA23 1LB ☎ 015394 32628 🔵 Apr–late
Oct Wed–Sun 1–5; late Mar, late Oct 1–4
🖐 Adult £3.80, child (5–16) £1.90, family
£9.50 🔟 🔲 🔢

UPPER TEESDALE

www.northpennines.org.uk
Spring gentians and orchids are
among the rare post-Ice Age
vegetation in this tundra-like part
of the northern Pennine Hills. The
main settlement is Barnard Castle,
named after the substantial ruins
of its 11th-century castle (Apr–end
Sep daily 10–6; Oct daily 10–4; rest
of year Thu–Mon 10–4), used as
a stronghold of the Balliol family.
On the edge of town, the Bowes
Museum (Mar–end Oct daily 10–5;
Nov–end Feb daily 10–4) of fine arts
occupies an unexpectedly grand
building, built in 1869 in the style of
a French château. However, the real
drama of the valley lies to the west.
High Force, a spectacular 21m (70ft)
waterfall, is part of the Raby Castle
estate and is at its most raging after
a heavy rainfall. Take the 10-minute
walk down through woodland from
the B6277.

Cauldron Snout waterfall, near
the vast reservoir of Cow Green,
is spectacular as it tumbles down
the hillside.
465 G11 🔼 Woodleigh, Flatts Road,
Barnard Castle DL12 8AA, tel 01833 690909
🖐 High Force: adult £1, child £0.50

INFORMATION
www.discoveryorkshirecoast.com
✚ 465 J11 ℹ Langbourne Road YO21
1YN, tel 01947 602674 🚉 Whitby

WHITBY AND THE NORTH YORK MOORS COAST

Whitby is a blend of fishing port and Victorian seaside resort, set along the slopes of the deep valley of the River Esk. Prominent among the boats that pack the harbour are the traditional flat-bottomed fishing cobles. The 13th-century ruins of Whitby Abbey (Apr–end Sep daily 10–6; Oct daily 10–5; Thu–Mon 10–4 rest of year) are reached by 199 steps. The visitor complex gives a vivid audio-visual guide from the days of the abbey's seventh-century founder, St. Hilda, to its shelling by German warships in World War I. The abbey, steps and graveyard of St. Mary's Church feature in Irish writer Bram Stoker's classic novel *Dracula* (1897).

A statue of the great explorer Captain James Cook (1728–79) looks over the town from the West Cliff. He was born close by in Marton and his ships were built at Whitby; the house where he lodged in Grape Lane while an apprentice is now the Captain Cook Memorial Museum (Mar daily 11–3; Apr–end Oct daily 9.45–5), telling the story of his life and voyages of discovery.

Whitby's other strength is as a base for visiting the North York Moors and coast (▷ 317, 330–331). Three extraordinary fishing villages are located near the town. Staithes has escaped prettification and is set along a narrow, steep-sided creek, often bearing the brunt of storms and floods. A 20-minute clifftop walk leads to the village from Runswick Bay, smaller and neater, tightly packed beneath the cliff. Farther south, Robin Hood's Bay was rife with smuggling in the 18th century. It hugs a steep slope, and is densely packed with red pantiled roofs, tiny alleys and crooked lanes. From here there are breezy walks south along the highest cliffs on England's east coast.

Whitby Museum (Tue–Sun 9.30–4.30, some Mon in school holidays) is in Pannett Park and has an idiosyncratic collection of fossils, natural history, Whitby jet and seafaring memorabilia. The Dracula Experience (Apr–end Oct daily 10–5; rest of year Sat–Sun 10.30–4, later in summer) provides a blood-curdling encounter with Whitby's fictional past.

Above *The haunting ruins of St. Hilda's Abbey, Whitby*
Right *Lake Windermere, Lake District National Park*

WINDERMERE

www.golakes.co.uk

Windermere town and Bowness merge together on the east shore of Windermere, England's longest lake (10.5 miles.17km).

For most visitors, the lake, whose wooded shores are dotted with houses, is the major attraction: Steamers ply its length from near Ambleside at the north end to Lakeside at the southern extremity. A vehicle ferry connects the Bowness shore with Claife, where the National Trust manages a lovely stretch of wooded shoreline which was popular with 19th-century tourists. To the north on the A591, the Brockhole Visitor Centre (Easter–end Oct daily 10–5) supplies information on the area, plus guided walks and some children's activities.

✚ 464 F12 ❗ Victoria Street, Windermere LA23 1AD, tel 015394 46499 🚉 Windermere

YORKSHIRE DALES NATIONAL PARK

www.yorkshiredales.org.uk

The Yorkshire Dales comprise some of the most enticing terrain of the Pennine Hills, the backbone of northern England. Below the bleak gritstone moors run a series of limestone valleys (dales), each with its own subtle character. The villages, built of stone and often ranged around greens, are very

much part of the landscape, and many grew up around the now-vanished lead mining industry in the 18th and 19th centuries.

✚ 456 G12–H12 ❗ Yorkshire Dales National Park Authority, Colvend, Hebden Road, Grassington BD23 5LB, tel 01756 752748

WHARFEDALE, SWALEDALE AND WENSLEYDALE

Corridor-like Wharfedale begins at Bolton Abbey, with its ruined 12th-century priory beside the still-functioning priory church, then continues past the mini-gorge of The Strid and the village of Grassington and the overhang of Kilnsey Crag. Farther north, the scenery is more mellow and expansive in Wensleydale, a valley renowned for waterfalls, Wensleydale cheese and the forbidding castle ruins of Middleham and Bolton Castle.

Swaledale is a remote place studded with stone barns and relics of lead-mining, and with the fast-flowing River Swale linking Reeth and the market town of Richmond (▷ 318).

✚ 465 G12–H12

THE WESTERN DALES

To the west are the Yorkshire Dales' most spectacular limestone landscapes, including the Three Peaks (the three highest hills—Whernside, Ingleborough and Pen-y-Ghent).

North of Malham is Malham Cove, a limestone cliff beneath a deep-fissured limestone pavement. Over to the east, Gordale Scar was formed by glacial meltwaters, leaving a gorge shadowed by huge, formidable crags.

At the northwestern extremity of the park, the Howgill Fells are a great contrast, formed by high, rounded hills of slate. There are stern, hikes over them, but the walk up the summit of Winder from the town of Sedbergh provides a good taster.

✚ 465 G12

YORKSHIRE SCULPTURE PARK

www.ysp.co.uk

The sculpture park was set up in 1977 and was a pioneer in placing sculpture outdoors. A trail takes you on a tour of the highlights, and there are plenty of places for picnicking.

There are permanent and changing exhibits in this expansive parkland, with works by some of the leading figures of the last 100 years, including Dame Barbara Hepworth (1903–75), Dame Elisabeth Frink (1930–93) and Sir Anthony Caro (born 1924), plus gallery space for smaller exhibits.

✚ 432 H13 ✉ West Bretton, Wakefield WF4 4LG ☎ 01924 832631 🕓 Mar–end Oct daily 10–6; Nov–end Feb daily 10–5 ✋ Free ▯ ▦

YORK

▷ 322–325.

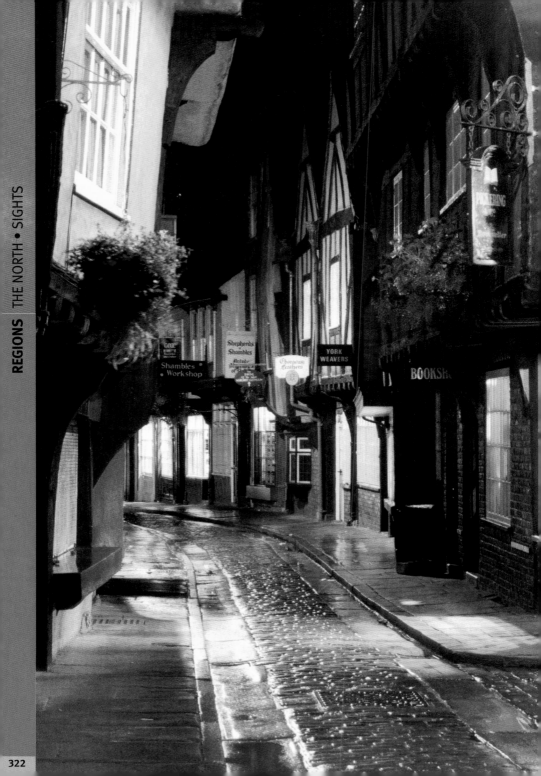

INTRODUCTION

This strikingly beautiful city straddling the River Ouse is one of Britain's premier sights and has a multitude of museums and buildings spanning a range of historic periods. Much of the city's compact heart is pedestrianized, so it's a great place to explore on foot, taking in its wealth of shops and vibrant street performers. Among the most evocative streets are The Shambles, originally a street of butchers' shops and retaining overhanging, jettied, timber-framed buildings, and Stonegate, where shop signs and frontages span several centuries. Also look for York's distinguished clutch of medieval churches (some no longer used for services). Arguably the finest is Holy Trinity (Goodramgate) with its inward-facing box pews and late 15th-century stained glass.

York was founded by the Roman army in AD71 as the town of Eboracum. The Roman fortress and the roads that led to it form the basis of the city's outline today, and a few remains are visible above ground, such as the walls of the fortress in the foundations of York Minster. After the Romans left, Viking settlers took over, and the town became Jorvik. They established the city's gateways and named the streets, many of them on the Roman lines. In the Middle Ages, York flourished as a trading city, and the walls begun in Roman times were rebuilt.

WHAT TO SEE

YORK MINSTER

www.yorkminster.org

Dating from 1220–1472, this is Europe's largest Gothic cathedral north of the Alps, with two towers, richly traceried windows and a massive west front. Its medieval stained glass represents a quarter of all the stained glass of the period in England. Look particularly for the *Five Sisters* within a quintet of lancet windows, and for the depictions of Genesis and Revelation in the superb east window of *c*1250—the world's largest area of medieval stained glass within a single window. The stone choir screen is carved with images of English monarchs from William I (1028–87) to Henry VI (1421–71), while around the nave and choir are painted stone shields dating from the time when Edward II (1284–1327) held a parliament in York.

There are separate admission charges for certain other parts of the Minster— the treasury, featuring the 11th-century Horn of Ulf, and the crypt, containing part of the 11th-century church that preceded the Minster. Also below ground level, the foundations (or undercroft) reveal an absorbing cross-section of history, from the remains of a Roman fort to the drastic building works carried out in the 1960s to support the collapsing central tower (whose foundations turned out to be completely inadequate). The octagonal Chapter House has lively carvings of flowers and fruits and is unusual in that it lacks a central structural pillar. The long climb up the central tower is rewarded by a panoramic view over the city (extra admission charge).

✚ 325 B1 ✉ Deangate YO1 7HH ☎ 01904 557216 🕐 Easter–end Oct Mon–Sat 9–5, Sun 12–3.45; Nov–end Mar Mon–Sat 9.30–5, Sun 12–3.45; no sightseeing Good Fri, Easter Sun 💷 Adult £5.50, child (under 16) free. Combined ticket (includes undercroft, treasury and crypt): adult £9.50, child free. Tower: adult £4, child £2

CITY WALL

You get an immense sense of historic continuity in York, which is enclosed by its virtually complete wall, pierced by bars (gateways). The section between Bootham Bar (on the site of the Roman gateway) and Monk Bar gives some of the choicest views of the old city. Monk Bar, the best-preserved gateway, houses the Richard III Museum (Mar–end Oct daily 9–5; rest of year daily

INFORMATION

www.visityork.org

✚ 462 J13 🛈 20 George Hudson Street YO1 6WR, tel 01904 554455 🚉 York

Opposite *York's medieval streets are more commonly known as The Shambles*

TIPS

» The York Pass (www.yorkpass.com) gives free entry to more than 30 attractions in and around the city, plus numerous special offers for shopping and dining (adult: one day £21, two days £27, three days £34).

» The city wall (3 miles/5km) is worth walking, but you may prefer to skip the southern part, which looks over relatively modern suburbs.

» A boat trip on the River Ouse is a great alternative way of seeing York and its surroundings, and also offers a glimpse of the Archbishop of York's palace at Bishopthorpe.

Above *Medieval York Minster is adorned with gargoyles*
Below *A red-coated town crier in York*

9.30–4), presenting the story of the monarch (1452–85) portrayed (possibly unfairly) as a murderer by Shakespeare and others, and giving you a chance to reach your own verdict. The heads of criminals and enemies were placed on spikes on Micklegate Bar during the Wars of the Roses (1455–85), and there's a small social history display inside (Feb–end Oct daily 9–5; rest of year Sat–Sun 9–dusk).

THE SHAMBLES
A short walk south from York Minster leads through some of the city's most memorable streets, where jettied half-timbered buildings overhang the narrow thoroughfare. This was originally a row of butchers' stalls (hence the hooks and rails, from which the meat was hung, still visible above some windows). It has since been smartened up into one of the city's most famous sights and costumed characters such as town criers (below) entertain sightseers. Stonegate has an array of old shopfronts and has such curios as a red devil figurine above a former printer's shop. Farther east, near Aldwark, is the half-timbered Merchant Taylors' Hall (tel 01904 624889 to arange a visit), with a 14th-century roof beyond a 17th- and 18th-century facade.
✚ 325 C2

YORK CASTLE MUSEUM
Housed in the former Debtors' Prison of 1705 and Female Prison of 1780, this museum alone justifies a visit to York. Displays include full-size reconstructions of Victorian and Edwardian shopping streets, collections of costumes and uniforms, and the very cell in which notorious highwayman Dick Turpin (1706–39) spent his last days before facing death on the gallows.
✚ 325 C3 ✉ The Eye of York YO1 1RY 🕐 Daily 9.30–5

JORVIK VIKING CENTRE
Another of York's must-see sights is the fruition of an excavation that uncovered the Viking settlement of Jorvik. The centre presents a unique journey back to 10th-century York, with sights, sounds and smells of life based on archaeological evidence. It ends with a display of finds from the site and a hologram of the Viking helmet found here—the original is in the Yorkshire Museum in Museum Gardens.
✚ 325 B2 ✉ Coppergate YO1 9WT ☎ 01904 543400 🕐 Apr–Oct daily 10–5; rest of year daily 10–4

NATIONAL RAILWAY MUSEUM
In the west of the city, the National Railway Museum is the definitive national collection of railwayana, and it's free. Over 100 restored locomotives are on display here, including the record-breaking steam locomotive *Mallard*, which reached a heady 126mph (202kph) and is the world's fastest steam engine, a full-size working replica of the *Rocket*, originally built by railway pioneer George Stephenson (1781–1848), the sumptuous royal saloon carriage (car) built for Queen Victoria (1819–1901), and a modern Japanese bullet train. Other displays include railway posters, paintings and photographs. Rail buffs may also like to visit York Model Railway (Mon–Sat 9–6, Sun 10–5), in York Station.
✚ 325 A2 ✉ Leeman Road YO26 4XJ ☎ 0844 815 3139 🕐 Daily 10–6

MUSEUM GARDENS
This is a pearl of a picnic place, where you can spread out on the lawn and survey the scene. There are ruins of 13th-century St. Mary's Abbey, the 13th-century remains of St. Leonard's Hospital (including a chapel and vaulted undercroft), a Roman tower known as the Multangular Tower and a large chunk of Roman wall standing at its original height. Also in the gardens is the Yorkshire Museum (daily 10–5), whose exhibits include Roman sculptures and

mosaics, Anglo-Saxon finds such as the Ormside Bowl and much-embellished Gilling Sword, Viking weaponry and medieval treasures.

✚ 325 B2

MORE TO SEE

TREASURER'S HOUSE

This house beside the Minster was mostly rebuilt in the 17th century—long after the post of Treasurer to the Minster was abolished (in 1547)—after which it passed into private hands. It is now owned by the National Trust.

✚ 325 B1 ✉ Minster Yard YO1 7JL ☎ 01904 624247 🕓 Apr–end Oct Sat–Thu 11–4.30; Nov Sat–Thu 11–3

THE MERCHANT ADVENTURERS' HALL

York's largest (27m by 12m/ 89ft by 40ft) and most impressive medieval half-timbered building is still in use. It has a complex roof with vast crossbeams.

✚ 325 C2 ✉ Fossgate YO1 9XD ☎ 01904 654818 🕓 Easter–end Sep Mon–Thu 9–5, Fri–Sat 9–3.30, Sun 12–4; rest of year Mon–Sat 9–3.30

CLIFFORD'S TOWER

The four-lobed stone keep of the castle dates from 1245, and replaced a wooden tower built by William I in 1068.

✚ 325 B3 ✉ Tower Street YO1 1SA ☎ 01904 646940 🕓 Easter–end Sep daily 10–6; Oct 10–5; Nov–Easter 10–4

FAIRFAX HOUSE

Witness wealthy living during the 18th century at this Georgian town house, which was saved from collapse in 1984. It contains select items from centuries past, notably a collection of 17th- and 18th-century English clocks.

✚ 325 B2 ✉ Castlegate YO1 9RN ☎ 01904 655543 🕓 Mon–Thu and Sat 11–4.30, Sun 1.30–4.30, Fri guided tours, 11 and 2

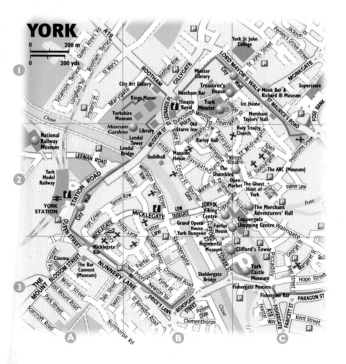

THE LAKE DISTRICT NATIONAL PARK

This circuit takes in the best of the Lake District, from Wordsworth's Grasmere and the beautiful Langdale valley, to the spectacular high passes of Wrynose and Hardknott and the less-visited western areas of the national park (▷ 312).

THE DRIVE

Distance: 80 miles (129km)
Allow: One day
Start/end: Keswick

★ The road passes Thirlmere, originally two small lakes, but both now dammed to form one large reservoir supplying Manchester with its water; you can take the unclassified road along the western shore (with paths along part of it). To the east, Helvellyn rises steeply.

Head south out of Keswick on the A591 (signposted Ambleside). Follow the A591 as far as Grasmere.

❶ At the edge of the village is Dove Cottage, the home of William Wordsworth (▷ 312).

Just beyond Dove Cottage the road twists and follows the lake of Grasmere before joining the banks of Rydal Water just before entering Rydal village. At St. Mary's Church in Rydal turn left and head up the steep hill to a parking area for Rydal Mount.

❷ Rydal Mount was the last of Wordsworth's homes in the Lakes (▷ 312).

After a visit to Rydal Mount, return to the A591 and continue south into Ambleside.

❸ Ambleside is a popular spot, and busy at most times of the year. There are plenty of tea rooms and cafés here to make this a good lunchtime stop. Its most celebrated landmark is Bridge House, a tiny house over babbling Stock Ghyll, the trickle of a river that runs parallel to the main street. Legend has it that it was built like this so that the owner could avoid paying land taxes.

From Ambleside bear right at the mini roundabout (traffic circle) along the A591. South of Ambleside turn right, following signs for the A593 to Coniston, and continue to Skelwith Bridge. Just before Skelwith Bridge, turn right on the B5343 to the valley of Langdale.

❹ Langdale is dominated by the formidably craggy bulks of the Langdale Pikes, with the more distant summit of Bow Fell beyond.

At the end of the valley the road turns sharply left and passes a lone house before climbing steeply out of the valley over a cattle grid. At a T-junction turn right, following signs for the Wrynose and Hardknott passes.

At the top of the climb, the road drops steeply to Wrynose Bottom before crossing the River Duddon and climbing steeply again over Hardknott Pass.

5 The lonely ruins of Hardknott Roman Fort appear on the right as you drop down.

Carry on down into Eskdale, a gentle ride due west along narrow country lanes. The road passes Dalegarth Station, terminus for the miniature Ravenglass and Eskdale Railway (steam and diesel services). At the T-junction bear right, following signs for Ravenglass and heading straight through Eskdale Green and up to Santon Bridge. At Santon Bridge, you can make a 4-mile (6.5km) detour along a right-hand turn following signs for Wasdale Head and Wast Water.

6 Here, England's highest mountain, Scafell Pike (978m/ 3,210ft), rises above its deepest lake.

From Santon Bridge, continue north, following signs to Gosforth.

7 At Gosforth, outside St. Mary's Church, at the eastern end of the village, is a remarkable 10th-century wheel-head cross (signposted as the Viking Cross), richly carved with a fusion of pagan and Christian symbolism.

Continue through Gosforth, and follow signs for the A595 to Whitehaven. Turn left at the first T-junction, right at the mini roundabout and right again on to the A595.

8 You can detour (left) from here to the Sellafield Visitor Centre, which has plenty of interactive exhibits explaining the workings of the Sellafield nuclear reprocessing plant, which you can tour.

Follow the A595 through New Mill to Calder Bridge, then turn right on a minor road signposted Ennerdale. This road rises gently to gain views along the coast, where the surreal massiveness of Sellafield looms large. At the T-junction turn right to head

into Ennerdale Bridge and straight on through the next village, Kirkland, to reach the A5086. Turn right on to this main road and into Lamplugh. In Lamplugh, take the first turning right, and follow signs to Loweswater.

Soon after Loweswater village, keep forward at a crossroads, then right at a T-junction with the B5289 (signposted Buttermere, but the sign may be obscured in the hedgerow on the left).

9 The B5289 drops down to follow the left bank of Crummock Water, then goes through Buttermere village and on past the banks of its lake before climbing up through Honister Pass, at the top of which is the working Honister Slate Mine.

The road then drops from the top of the Honister Pass into rolling Borrowdale, via Rosthwaite and Grange, before following the bank of Derwent Water (pic opposite). The road leads back into Keswick. Bear left at the first roundabout and right at the second into the town.

PLACE TO VISIT
SELLAFIELD VISITOR CENTRE
✉ Seascale CA20 1PG
☎ 019467 27027
🕐 Apr–end Nov daily 10–5; rest of year 10–4
🖐 Free

WHERE TO EAT
The Old Dungeon Ghyll Hotel (tel 015394 37272) on the road into Great Langdale serves bar meals (12–2).

WHEN TO GO
Choose a dry, clear day because the twisting turns of Hardknott Pass can make for strenuous driving, even in the best road conditions.

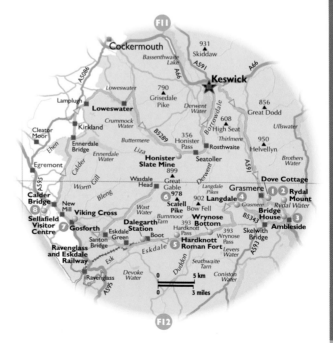

FRIAR'S CRAG AND CASTLERIGG STONE CIRCLE

The northeast shores of Derwent Water provide a magnificently varied walk, taking in some of the choicest views of this lake and the surrounding peaks. The later stages include the best-known prehistoric stone circle in the Lake District (▷ 312).

THE WALK

Length: 7 miles (11km)
Allow: 3–4 hours
Start/end: Parking area at Derwentwater, just south of Keswick and signposted off the B5289, map ref 439 F11
OS Landranger map: 89, 90
OS Explorer map: OL4

Take the lakeside road beside the Derwentwater landing stages and go along the tree-lined track to the end of Friar's Crag for a lake view.

❶ Derwentwater is ringed by mountain peaks and dotted with mysterious little tree-clad islands. The writer John Ruskin (1819–1900) described this outlook from Friar's Crag as one of Europe's finest scenic viewpoints.

Retrace your steps to follow the path that swings right to a gate and proceed along the lake shore. Cross two footbridges, then go through a gate into a wood. Continue along the woodland fringe and across a footbridge, then bear right to go through a gate. Turn left along a metalled road. Shortly before reaching the B5289, turn right on a path through the trees.

Continue for about 350m (380 yards) parallel to the road, and at the end of the fence, bear right into the wood. Go over the first of the two wooden bridges and turn left up to the road. Cross into Great Wood parking area. Take the path from its right-hand corner and climb gently for about 270m (295 yds) to a track that comes down on your left. Turn up this and continue for 0.5 miles (800m) uphill through woodland. The path begins to level out: soon bear right to a T-junction, signposted Rakefoot and Walla Crag. Shortly the path ascends to a stile. Go over the stile, leave the woodland and go forward between a wall and a fence. At a T-junction turn right through a gate signed Castle Rigg, Walla Crag.

Continue along the edge of the ravine and through another gate. After 90m (100 yds), cross a footbridge on the left and go up the steps, through the gate and turn left on to a metalled track. After 18m (20 yds) turn right through a gate signposted Castlerigg Stone Circle.

Continue on the left-hand edge of the field between a wall and a fence. Cross two stiles; turn left at the second stile following the sign for the stone circle. Follow the left-hand edge of the field, crossing further stiles to reach a gate in the A591 Keswick to Windermere road. Turn

Left *Catbells and Friar's Crag reflecting in Derwent Water*

right, then take the first left on to a track passing houses (High Nest). Continue through a field gate, then across stiles and fields to a lane next to a wood. Turn left on to a road.

② Castlerigg Stone Circle is in a field on your left. Dating from late Neolithic times to the early Bronze Age (*c*2500–2000BC), this is one of the most imposing prehistoric monuments in northern England. Its purpose remains a mystery, but it seems likely that its builders particularly valued the site's great view of Derwent Water.

After viewing the stone circle, keep your back to the entrance gate and cross the fields to the right by a stile (by a wall and fence junction) on to a lane. Turn left and continue for 0.5 mile (800m) back to the A591. Turn right along the footpath beside this often busy road.

After 0.5 mile (800m), take a minor road left, signposted to Rakefoot. Beyond a house on the right, turn

right through a gate by a fingerpost, and follow a path that goes under a footbridge heading downhill through woodland to a stream.

Cross a footbridge over the stream, turn right and follow the stream downhill to a gate. Continue past Springs Farm, and cross a bridge on a surfaced lane leading into Springs Road. After 0.5 miles (800m), passing houses on the way, bear left down a narrow path to a gate. Ascend some steps and continue uphill, bearing right through dense woodland. Towards the top, climb steeply left to the viewpoint of Castle Head.

③ This low wooded hillock gives a surprisingly extensive view of Derwentwater, with the jagged outlines of Cat Bells and Causey Pike rising above the opposite shore. The largest of the lake's islands is St. Herbert's Island, named after its inhabitant from AD685. Lord's Island once had a house on it belonging to the Earl of Derwentwater, while Derwent Isle was home in the 16th century to a colony of German miners who came here to work in

the nearby Goldscope Mine. Return through the trees, bearing left to the lower slopes of the hill, to join up with a path that descends to the left to steps at a gap in the wall and the B5289. Cross over the road and bear left to steps and a ramp on the right. Descend the steps, then keep to the path ahead to reach a wood. Turn right to return to the parking area.

PLACE TO VISIT
THE CUMBERLAND PENCIL MUSEUM
✉ Southey Works, Keswick, CA12 5NG
☎ 017687 73626
🕐 Daily 9.30–5
✋ Adult £3, Child £1.50, Family £7.50

WHERE TO EAT
Rembrandts in Station Road, Keswick (tel: 017687 72008) is a traditional, family-friendly English eating house, with panelled divisions between tables. It offers full English breakfast, soup-and-sandwich deals, and casseroles and fish suppers.

WHEN TO GO
Castlerigg is magical at any time of year, but is best appreciated on a cold, clear winter's day when a light frost makes the stones sparkle.

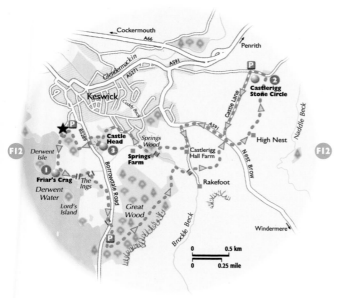

NORTH YORK MOORS NATIONAL PARK

Exhilarating high moorland with superb views contrasts with fertile, green dales and stone-built villages in this tour of the North York Moors (▷ 317).

THE DRIVE

Distance: 55 miles (89km)
Allow: 3–4 hours
Start/end: Pickering

★ Pickering, the southern terminus of the North Yorkshire Moors Railway, is a market town on the northern edge of the vale. Of interest are the Beck Isle Museum of Rural Life and the 15th-century wall paintings in the Church of St. Peter and St. Paul.

From Pickering follow the A169 Whitby road, gradually climbing towards the moors. After 5 miles (8km) pass a turning on the left to Lockton.

❶ You can detour can be made to the attractive hilltop villages of Lockton and Levisham, on the edge of the Tabular Hills, before descending to the steep valley of Newton Dale.

Continue the main tour, climbing to 280m (920ft) on Lockton Low Moor.

❷ The road passes the Hole of Horcum (pictured above), a spectacular natural hollow popular with hang-gliders. The road then drops. After 3 miles (5km), beyond the Saltersgate Inn, turn left on to an unclassified road marked Goathland.

❸ To the right of the main road before the turning is the truncated triangular pyramid that houses the Fylingdales Ballistic Missile Early Warning Radar Station.

Cross Goathland Moor before descending to Goathland. Go right at the T-junction and pass the Mallyan Hotel to enter the village, which is close to Mallyan Spout waterfall (▷ 332).

Follow signs for Whitby and cross the railway. Climb on to the moors and after 2 miles (3km) turn left on to the A169. In another 0.5 miles (800m) turn left on to an unclassified road, signposted Grosmont and

Egton. The road crosses Sleights Moor. As you descend there are fine views along Esk Dale. The road drops steeply into Grosmont.

❹ Grosmont village developed in the 19th century to house miners for the local iron industry. The northern terminus of the North Yorkshire Moors Railway is here, running steam and diesel trains to Pickering.

Go over the level (train) crossing and River Esk, then ascend steeply to Egton. In the village bear right (signed Whitby) and opposite the Wheatsheaf Inn turn left, signed Glaisdale. Follow the road that descends steeply into Glaisdale. From the higher part of Glaisdale follow the signs to Castleton, and after 1 mile (1.6km) bear right. In another 0.75 mile (1km), at the T-junction, turn right for Lealholm. Recross the River Esk then turn left, signed Danby. Continue through Esk Dale.

❺ After 3.5 miles (5.5km) you reach the Moors Centre (Mar– end Dec daily; Jan–end Feb weekends only), which has local information and walks signposted from the grounds.

Keep left to Danby village.

❻ Here are remains of 14th-century Danby Castle, and the high-arched Duck Bridge over the River Esk, built in 1386.

Go over the staggered crossroads and continue to Castleton. Just beyond the village, bear left (signed Rosedale) to climb along the 348m (1,140ft) Castleton Rigg. After 4 miles (6.5km) turn left to Rosedale Abbey.

Just before you turn, note Ralph Cross, the symbol of the national park, on your right. After the turn, another small medieval white cross, known as Fat Betty (the shaft of which has disappeared), is to the left. From Ralph Cross go across the plateau of Rosedale Moor for 4 miles (6.5km) and then descend into Rosedale, before bearing left for Rosedale Abbey.

❼ This quiet village became a busy mining centre after the discovery of ironstone in 1856. Next to the church are the remains of the 12th-century Cistercian nunnery after which the village was named.

At the end of the village turn right and ascend the very steep Rosedale Chimney Bank. To avoid this, continue straight ahead in Rosedale Abbey, turning right after 4.5 miles/7km, signed Lastingham; then follow the road though Lastingham and into Hutton-le-Hole.

❽ Rosedale Chimney Bank gets its name from a previous landmark, a 30m (100ft) high chimney. This remnant of the iron industry was demolished in 1972 for safety reasons, but the arches of iron kilns can be seen on the right. The summit of Rosedale Chimney Bank has far-ranging views. Lastingham church

is worth a detour for its remarkably intact Norman crypt.
Cross Spaunton Moor. After 3 miles (5km), at the T-junction, turn right for Hutton-le-Hole.

❾ This streamside village has a large, hummocky central green and contains the Ryedale Folk Museum, with a variety of buildings of different ages erected from all over the area.

Turn left on to the Kirkbymoorside road. In 3 miles (5km), at a T-junction, turn left on to the A170, signed Scarborough. Return through the agricultural countryside of the Vale of Pickering, passing beside the village of Wrelton and through Aislaby and Middleton to return to Pickering.

PLACES TO VISIT
BECK ISLE MUSEUM OF RURAL LIFE
✉ Pickering YO18 8DU
☎ 01751 473653
🕐 Apr–end Oct daily 10–5
✋ Adult £3, child £1.50, family £7.50

PICKERING CASTLE
✉ Pickering YO18
☎ 01751 474989
🕐 Apr–end Sep daily 10–6; Oct 10–4
✋ Adult £2.50, child £1.30

RYEDALE FOLK MUSEUM
✉ Hutton-le-Hole YO62 6UA
☎ 01751 417367
🕐 Apr–end Oct daily 10–5; Nov–end Mar 10–dusk, closed 21 Dec–21 Jan
✋ Adult £4.50, child £3, family £12

WHERE TO EAT
There are plenty of tea shops in Pickering and Helmsley. For meals, the Star Inn (tel 01439 770397) in Harome, near Helmsley, serves excellent food and local ales. It has three bedrooms.

WHEN TO GO
Take this drive in early spring and enjoy the lush greeness of the Moors.

MALLYAN SPOUT AND WADE'S CAUSEWAY

Starting at a village set around a large open common, this walk takes in some of the most stunning scenery in the North York Moors (▷ 317). A lush wooded ravine provides a view of Mallyan Spout waterfall, before you cross peaceful farmland.

THE WALK

Length: 4.5 miles (7km); extension to Wade's Causeway adds 1.5 miles (2.4km)
Allow: 2 hours (plus 30 min to Wade's Causeway)
Start/end: Goathland church, at west end of village, map ref 440 J12
OS Landranger map: 94
OS Explorer map: OL27

★ Opposite the church go through a kissing gate beside the Mallyan Spout Hotel, signposted Mallyan Spout. A lush wooded ravine provides a view of Mallyan Spout waterfall, before you cross peaceful farmland.

❶ Goathland is a stop on the North Yorkshire Moors Railway, and the station is in the valley below the village. Running from Pickering to Grosmont, the line was laid out by rail pioneer George Stephenson (1781–1848) in 1836 for horse-drawn trains. It operated until 1957 and was reopened by enthusiasts in 1973. Most of its trains are steam-hauled. Part of the original route went up an incline between Goathland and Grosmont, but this proved too steep for horses or steam traction, and in 1865 a 'deviation line' was built by blasting away sections of bedrock. The original route is still open as a footpath, and passes a terrace of railway cottages at Esk Valley between the two villages.

Follow the path to a streamside signpost and turn left. Continue past the waterfall, which tumbles down from a tributary stream to the left; take care here, as the rocks can be slippery.

❷ In the valley of the West Beck, and especially near the waterfall of Mallyan Spout (21m/70ft), ferns grow prolifically. You may spot the male fern, with its pale green stems, the buckler fern, which has scales with a dark central stripe and pale edges, and the hartstongue fern with its distinctive strap-like fronds.

Follow the footpath signs over two footbridges, across a stile and up a flight of steps, to ascend a stile on to a road beside a bridge. Turn left along the road and climb

To continue the main walk, just after crossing the ford go straight ahead along the track (but if you have come from the Roman road, do not recross the ford but turn right), eventually to reach a road by farm buildings. Turn right up to this road and, just before a wooden garage, turn left on a green track up the hillside.

Go ahead at a crossing track, passing a small cairn (stone mound) and bending left along the ridge. The obvious path is marked by a series of little cairns, eventually taking a left fork where the path divides, to go down a small stream and join a clear track. Goathland church soon comes into sight. Pass the bridleway sign and descend the road near the church to return to the start.

TIP

>> An optional extension takes in Wade's Causeway (also known as Wheeldale Roman Road), an exceptionally well-preserved stretch of ancient trackway crossing the moor.

PLACE TO VISIT
NORTH YORKSHIRE MOORS RAILWAY

www.northyorkshiremoorsrailway.com

✉ Pickering YO18 7AJ

☎ 01751 472508

🕐 Easter–end Oct daily; Nov–Feb some weekends and school holidays.

WHERE TO EAT

Goathland Hotel (tel 01947 896203) and Mallyan Spout Hotel (tel 01947 896486).

WHEN TO GO

Visit the falls after a few days of rain to enjoy them in full spate.

the hill. Where the road bends left, go right along a bridleway through a gate. Turn left down a path to go over a bridge, then ahead between the buildings, through a gate and across the field.

Part of the way across the field, go through a gate to the right into woodland. Ascend a stony track; go through a gate to reach a facing gate as you leave the wood. Do not go through this gate, but turn right up the field, going left at the top through a gateway. Continue with a wall on your right and go through a marked gateway in the wall and up the field, to emerge on to a metalled (paved) lane.

Turn left along the lane, go through a gate and follow the sign for the Roman road. Go through another gate, still following the public bridleway signs as you join a track. Continue through a small gate to descend to another gate, and then carry on until you cross the ford. A highly recommended detour

at this point is to turn right immediately over a footbridge, signposted 'Roman road'. Go right at the end of the bridge and follow the path. Cross a stile and continue to the left, again signposted to the Roman road. Ascend to a wooden stile in the corner of the field and continue along the field edge with a wall on your left. Go through a gate to reach a sign giving details of the Roman road. From there, retrace your steps to return to the ford.

❸ At the ancient stony track, known as Wade's Causeway (pictured opposite) or Wheeldale Roman Road, you'll learn the legend of giant Wade who was said to have built the road to take his cattle to market. You can still make out the ditches at each side of the road and the culverts (tunnels) still covered by stone capping in places. The road certainly took legionnaires from Malton to the signal station near Whitby, but its complete route has not been fully authenticated.

REGIONS • THE NORTH • DRIVE

NORTHUMBERLAND NATIONAL PARK AND THE BORDER FOREST PARK

Hadrian's Wall—part of a World heritage Site that spans the northern frontier of the Roman Empire—also lines one side of the vast Border Forest Park, stretching beyond the Scottish border.

THE DRIVE

Length: 140 miles (225km)
Time: 4–5 hours
Start/end: Bellingham

★ In the small market town of Bellingham, the church of St. Cuthbert has a unique barrel-vaulted roof with six-sided stone ribs to give added protection from fire. In the churchyard is a well whose waters are traditionally believed to have healing powers.

Leave Bellingham on the B6320, signposted Hexham and, after 0.5 miles (800m), bear left and over a river. Take the next right turn, an unclassified road through North Tynedale. Continue for 4 miles (6.5km), cross a river bridge and turn right. At a T-junction turn left and continue past Stannersburn. After a while enter Kielder Forest and drive to Kielder Water.

❶ Kielder Forest is a vast plantation of larch, spruce, Scots pine and lodgepole pine blanketing the Cheviot Hills. It forms part of the Border Forest Park, spanning the border into Scotland and creating the largest expanse of planted forestry in Britain. To the east its landscapes merge with the open moorland horizons of Northumberland National Park. Kielder Water, the largest reservoir in western Europe, offers a variety of activities.

❷ Continue to Kielder village. This village developed with the area's forestry industry. Kielder Castle is an 18th-century shooting lodge that now serves as the Border Forest Park information office and a Forest Museum.

Continue for 3 miles (5km) and cross the Scottish border, then turn left on to the B6357, signposted

Newcastleton. At a junction with the B6399 you can make a detour from the main route to Hermitage Castle by turning right for 4 miles (6.5km), then turning left on to an unclassi-fied road.

❸ Romantically associated with Mary, Queen of Scots (1542–87), brooding Hermitage Castle punctuates the desolate landscape. Its mighty towers and grim walls entirely suit their windswept situation. It was a stronghold of the Douglas family of Scottish nobles in the 14th century, and much later became the property of Mary's lover (and subsequently husband) James Bothwell (c1535–78).

On the main route, bear left on the B6357 to Newcastleton.

❹ The village of Newcastleton was planned in the 18th century and was a flourishing weaving centre before forestry became important to local life in 1921.

Drive to the far end of the village and turn left on an unclassified road, signposted Roadhead. Cross a river bridge and turn right following signs for Roadhead. After 3 miles (4.8km) cross Kershope Burn to enter the English county of Cumbria. Ascend a winding road through Kershope Forest and continue to reach a white house. Turn left here, signposted Carlisle. After 4 miles (6.5km) bend right then left around another white house. Follow the road for 1.5 miles (2.5km) to reach the B6318. Turn left, and immediately left again on to an unclassified road and drive to Bewcastle.

⑤ Several ancient remains can be seen in the bleak open moorland that surrounds Bewcastle. Materials from a Roman fort that was once an outpost of Hadrian's Wall were used to build a castle here, but it has succumbed to the ravages of time. In the village churchyard is the remarkable seventh-century AD Bewcastle Cross, intricately carved with runic inscriptions and patterns.

The road bears right to bypass the middle of Bewcastle and crosses a river bridge. After 5 miles (8km) cross the B6318, and after another 2.5 miles (4km) meet a T-junction. Turn left, signposted Birdoswald, and follow the line of Hadrian's Wall for 0.5 miles (800m) to Banks.

⑥ One mile (1.6 km) southwest of Hadrian's Wall lies the Augustinian Lanercost Priory (founded 1166). Its nave is still in use.

Continue from Banks to Birdoswald.

⑦ At Birdoswald you can see the large and impressive outer defences of a Roman fort known as Camboglanna, and well-preserved sections of Hadrian's Wall extend east and west. Close by are the substantial remains of Harrow's Scar Milecastle.

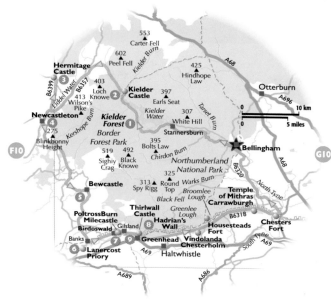

Turn right on to the B6318, signposted Gilsland, and after 1 mile (1.6km) turn right to Gilsland.

⑧ Hadrian's Wall runs south of this former spa and includes Poltross Burn Milecastle. Close to the village is an attractive waterfall. For details of Hadrian's Wall, ▷ 308. At Banks, a turret on the Roman wall was once manned by troops garrisoned at the nearest milecastle. A footpath leads east to the Pike Hill signal tower, part of a beacon system by which a warning of attack could be sent the length of the wall with surprising speed.

From Gilsland turn left along the B6318, signposted Greenhead, and meet a junction; turn left to enter Greenhead.

⑨ Close to Greenhead is a dramatic series of ravines known as the Nine Nicks of Thirlwall. Nearby are the ruins of 14th-century Thirlwall Castle.

From Greenhead, continue east on the B6318 to Chesters Fort, near which turn left on the B6320 to Bellingham. You pass the most famous features of Hadrian's

Wall along this stretch, including Vindolanda, Housesteads Fort, the Temple of Mithras at Carrowburgh and Chesters Fort (▷ 308).

PLACES TO VISIT
BIRDOSWALD ROMAN FORT
✉ Gilsland CA8 7DD
☎ 01697 747602
🕐 Mar–end Nov daily 10–5.30
✋ Adult £3.60, child £1.80, family £9

FOREST MUSEUM
✉ Kielder Castle NE48 1ER
☎ 01434 250209
🕐 Late Mar–end Oct, Dec daily 10–5; Nov weekends only

HERMITAGE CASTLE
✉ Newcastleton SY7 8AX
☎ 01387 376222
🕐 Apr–end Oct daily 9.30–6.30
✋ Adult £2.50, child £1

LANERCOST PRIORY
✉ Lanercost CA8 2HQ
☎ 01697 73030
🕐 Apr–end Sep daily 10–6; Oct Thu–Mon 10–4
✋ Adult £2.60, child £1.30

Opposite *Hadrian's Wall, Northumberland National Park*

HADRIAN'S WALL AND THIRLWALL CASTLE

A stretch of the Roman wall and a medieval castle are highlights of this varied walk.

THE WALK

Length: 4 miles (6.5km)
Allow: 2.5 hours
Start/end: Parking area at Walltown, northwest of Haltwhistle, map ref 439 G10
OS Landranger map: 86
OS Explorer map: OL43

★ From the car park, follow the Pennine Way eastwards alongside the road for 0.5 mileS (800m), and over a cattle grid. At a footpath sign for Walltown Crags turn left towards Hadrian's Wall.

Started by Emperor Hadrian in around AD122, the 76-mile (122km) barrier ran from the River Tyne to the Solway Firth, across the neck of northern England. One of the best surviving monuments of the Roman world, it separated Roman civilization from the 'barbarians' to the north. For much of its length it follows the Great Whin Sill, a natural barrier.

On reaching Hadrian's Wall the route goes right, but a short diversion to the left gives good views towards the Cumbrian hills. Returning to the wall, follow it along the top of Walltown Crags, past Turret 45a.

❶ There were originally nine gaps—the Nine Nicks of Thirlwall—along this stretch of the Great Whin Sill, but only five remain because of quarrying. Turret 45a was built before the rest of the wall and may have been a signal post used while the wall was being constructed.

From Turret 45a the route leaves the course of Hadrian's Wall after descending into the valley north of Walltown Farm and turning left along a track.

❷ Walltown was once a village but is now no more than a farm. Close by was the site of a fortified tower once inhabited by John Ridley, whose brother Nicholas was a Protestant martyr burned at the stake in 1555.

Following the track as it bends left and then right, go through a gateway and diagonally left past a waymark sign towards the roofs of High Old Shield. Go over a ladder stile in the wall, walk downhill across a footbridge and turn left on the metalled track.

Turn right up the entrance to High Old Shield, signposted Cairny Croft. Where the track bends left, go over two stiles and follow the waymarked route behind the farm to go over another stile.

Follow the stone wall and then descend to a stile. Cross another field, go over a stile in a stone wall and turn left. Follow a track to a further stile, and walk left of a wooden hut to a footpath sign.

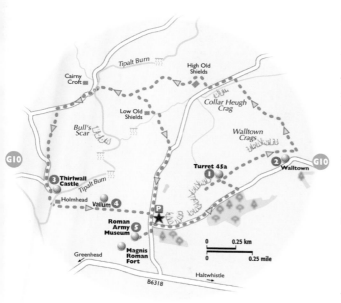

and nearby Vindolanda as they were in Roman times.
From the museum carry on back to the parking area.

TIPS

» Waterproof footwear is needed at all times; crossing the Tipalt Burn on stepping stones needs care and should not be attempted after heavy rain (a walking stick may help).

» A shorter, alternative route goes through Low Old Shield, missing out the stepping stones, Thirlwall Castle and the vallum.

PLACES TO VISIT
ROMAN ARMY MUSEUM

✉ Carrovan, Greenhead CA6 7SB
☎ 01697 747485
🕐 Mid–Feb to mid–Nov daily
✋ Adult £4.20, child (5–18) £2.50

THIRLWALL CASTLE

✉ Greenhead
☎ 01434 344430 (Ranger Service)
🕐 Daily
✋ Free

WHERE TO EAT

The Milecastle Inn (tel 01434 321372) in Haltwhistle serves food daily, with sandwiches and home-made pies available at lunchtime.

To avoid the stepping stones across a stream, Tipalt Burn, turn left towards Low Old Shield to join the metalled track in 0.5 mile (800m), turning right to Walltown parking area.

For the full route, continue straight ahead, then make towards the white cottage in the valley. Descend to cross a stile beside the stream, turn left and carefully go over the stepping stones.

Follow the road uphill for 400m (440 yards) to a footpath sign in the fence on the left. Go over the stile, cross a field to another stile and walk diagonally to a gate in the corner of the next field. On the road turn left to descend to Thirlwall Castle.

❸ Built in the 14th century to defend a gap in the wall against the Scots, Thirlwall Castle is a grim tower built of stones taken from Hadrian's Wall itself. Edward I (1239–1307) is said to have stayed here on his way to fight the Scots in 1306. Legend says a dwarf guards a solid gold table somewhere in the castle.

Take the farm track to the right of the castle, go over a footbridge and along the track by the buildings. After a right-hand bend, turn left up a track beyond a single stone gatepost. Where the track hairpins left, go straight ahead through a gate and uphill to the vallum.

❹ The earth rampart known as the vallum, 3m (10ft) wide at the bottom and 6m (20ft) wide at the top, was constructed parallel to the wall, at a distance of between 55m and 90m (180ft and 300ft). Crossed only at the forts, it was the result of new military ideas that came in around AD124.

Follow the vallum over two stiles and turn right on the metalled (paved) track to visit the Roman Army Museum.

❺ Next to the fort of Magnis, the Roman Army Museum contains Roman excavation finds, life-size displays of army equipment and models, films evoking the harsh life of the Roman soldier, and a video showing representations of the wall

Opposite *Hadrian's Wall seen from Walltown, Northumberland National Park*

YORKSHIRE DALES NATIONAL PARK

This tour takes in some of the subtle variety of the Yorkshire Dales (▷ 321), from remote Nidderdale to Richmond—one of the best-preserved market towns in northern England—to Swaledale, Wensleydale and the tranquil beauty of Wharfedale.

THE DRIVE
Length: 75 miles (120km)
Time: 3 hours
Start/end: Pateley Bridge

★ The Yorkshire Dales are a series of beautiful valleys spreading out from the high Pennine watershed to the north of the industrial heartlands of West Yorkshire. Starting from the heart of Pateley Bridge take a minor road from near the bridge itself that leads north into Nidderdale towards Ramsgill and Lofthouse. Pass Gouthwaite Reservoir on your right.

❶ Just west of Lofthouse is How Stean Gorge, a dramatic ravine edged by small cliffs and honeycombed with pot-holes, and with a footpath on its edge giving views along the gorge.

In Lofthouse turn right to take the steep road out of the village, over the moors towards Masham.

Continue for about 6 miles (10km), passing two more reservoirs on the right. Take the third left turn, as you approach Healey, towards Ellingstring, turning left to the junction with the A6108, which you follow through Middleham to Leyburn.

❷ On the way to Leyburn you pass the remains of Jervaulx Abbey on the right, near the village of Middleham (▷ 340–341). Leyburn is a busy Wensleydale town with many tea shops and a market on Friday. Tennants in Harmby Road is the largest antiques and house clearance auction room in Europe.

In Leyburn turn left then right, following the A6108 to the edge of Richmond. The route turns left just before the town centre. After passing a right turn to Catterick, turn immediately left up Hurgill Road, past a parking area on the left.

❸ You can take a detour and continue into Richmond, with its formidable castle towering high over the river and, beyond the huge market place, the remarkable Georgian Theatre Royal (▷ 318).

Hurgill Road takes you back along the River Swale, but climbs high above the river before dropping steeply down to Marske. Cross the bridge and turn right towards Reeth, then turn left on the B6270 to Grinton.

❹ Up to the 16th century the church at Grinton was the only one in Swaledale, and coffins had to be carried great distances over rough tracks on a route that became known as the Corpse Way. The church is called 'the Cathedral of the Dales', and was substantially rebuilt in the 15th century.

In Grinton turn right on to a minor road and take the right fork,

Left *How Stean Gorge in Nidderdale, Yorkshire Dales*

following signs for Redmire along a high moorland road passing disused lead mines. When the road finally descends, take the first turning on the right for Castle Bolton.

❺ Castle Bolton is the estate village for the towering bulk of Bolton Castle, completed in 1399 and the former stronghold of the Scrope family. Mary, Queen of Scots (1542–87) was imprisoned here for six months. The castle was besieged and captured by Parliamentarian forces in 1645.

Turn right for Carperby. Turn left to the Aysgarth Falls.

❻ This is a very popular scenic spot. Although the falls consist of three different sections, only the Upper Falls are visible from the road. Nearby is a watermill, gift shop and tea room.

Beyond Aysgarth Falls turn left on to the A684, signposted Leyburn, then take the second turning on the right on to the B6160, following the signs into West Burton.

❼ West Burton is a picture-book village and has the largest village green in the Dales, with space for horses to graze. In the centre there is a pub and a pottery workshop, but no church or market. At the north end of the village is a small waterfall.

Rejoin the B6160, which now takes you along the lesser-known Bishopdale and down through Wharfedale.

❽ Buckden is a starting point for walks around northern Wharfedale. To walk the Dales Way follow the river northwest and join a lane past Hubberholme, a remote little hamlet where the church has a rood loft (forward choir loft) of 1558—a rare survival of a decree by Elizabeth I that such adornments should be removed from churches.

The drive then passes Kettlewell, once a hub of the lead-mining industry. Farther down Wharfedale look out for Kilnsey Crag on your right, easily identified as it juts out dramatically towards the main road. This is a popular target of climbers and is a haunt of peregrine falcons.

Carry on to Grassington.

❾ This is a large village with narrow cobbled streets, 18th-century houses, pubs, the Yorkshire Dales National Park office and the Upper Wharfedale Folk Museum.

Go into Grassington and leave on the B6265 to return to Nidderdale and Pateley Bridge.

❿ Along this road you'll see a a sign for the Stump Cross Caverns, lit show caves that you can walk around without a guide. Wolverine Cave has particularly fine stalactites and stalagmites.

PLACES TO VISIT
BOLTON CASTLE
✉ Leyburn DL8 4ET
☎ 01969 623981
🕐 Apr–end Sep daily 10–5; Oct–end Mar 10–4
🎫 Adult £5, child £3.50, family £12

UPPER WHARFEDALE FOLK MUSEUM
✉ The Square, Grassington
🕐 Apr–end Sep daily 11–1, 2–4.30; Sep–end Oct 2–4.30
🎫 Adult 75p, child 50p, family £2

WHERE TO EAT
Drinks and snacks are available at Yore Mill Visitor Centre (tel 01969 663399) near the Aysgarth Falls.

WHEN TO GO
Visit in the height of summer and enjoy the fertile scenery of the Dales.

MIDDLEHAM AND JERVAULX ABBEY

This is an easy walk by the riverside and through woodland, mostly on marked tracks, with the added historical interest of Middleham Castle and the substantial ruins of Jervaulx Abbey.

THE WALK

Length: 7.5 miles (12km)
Allow: 3 hours
Start/end: Middleham marketplace map ref 439 H12
OS Landranger map: 99
OS Explorer maps: OL30, 302

★ From the royally connected Middleham Castle and back via the gallops for today's throughbreds.

Starting at the marketplace walk to the side of Middleham Castle and go left into the cobbled alley by the Castle Keep Tea Rooms in Canaan Lane.

❶ Middleham is a famous racehorse-training centre, sometimes called 'the Lambourn of the North'. Middleham Castle was a favourite place of Richard III (1452-85). Edward IV (1442–83) and Henry VI (1421–71) were both

imprisoned in the castle during the Wars of the Roses in the 15th century. The central keep, one of the largest in England, dates back to the 12th century.

The Middleham Jewel, a magnificent gold and sapphire pendant of the late 15th century, was unearthed close to Middleham Castle in 1985. It fetched £2.5 million at auction, when funds were raised to keep it in Britain. The original is now in the Yorkshire Museum in York (▷ 324), and there is a replica at Middleham Castle.

Walk ahead, with Middleham Castle on your left. Continue through the gate and field. At the end of the field, go through the gate and continue in the same direction, but with the wall now on your left. Walk down to the River Cover. Turn left over a stile in the fence and walk along the river. This woodland path is easy to

follow. Continue along the riverbank. Go through the gate into a field and head to the right of the gate at the far side. Stay by the river to reach some stepping stones.

❷ The track from Middleham to Jervaulx dates back to the 11th century, and these are believed to be the original stepping stones. They were thought to be lost until a few years ago when plans were made to reinstate the ancient path using concrete slabs, but workmen found these stones buried in the riverbed and replaced them.

Cross the river here, continue up the path, through the gate and turn left along the embankment. The path is clear, with occasional stiles and signposts leading to Cover Bridge.

Cross the road and pass through a gate marked 'public footpath,

private fishing', and follow the wide embankment. Go through a gate and, after 0.5 mile (800m), go through another. The path continues for another 0.5 mile (800m) until you leave it through another gate, turning right along a track that leads to a road. Turn left on to the road and continue until you reach Jervaulx Abbey on your left.

❸ Founded in 1156 by Savigny monks who later became Cistercians, Jervaulx is known as the original home of Wensleydale cheese, and for the breeding of racehorses, the latter continued today in Middleham.

After visiting the abbey, retrace your steps to Cover Bridge and the Cover Bridge Inn.

❹ Without this ancient, beamed inn there might be no Wensleydale cheese. Created at Jervaulx Abbey, the recipe for the cheese was passed to the landlord after the dissolution of Jervaulx in 1536. He sold the cheese for 40 years as Coverham cheese,

before passing on the recipe—which then reverted to the famous name of Wensleydale.

Cross the bridge and turn left past the pub at the bungalow. Here a narrow gap in the wall leads you back to the River Cover, where you turn right to skirt the pasture. Go through a gate and follow the path along the riverbank. The path is well defined and after a few minutes' walking look for a stile in the wall on your right, which leads to another wall with a stile and two yellow arrows above it (beyond this wall are the

stepping stones you crossed earlier). Do not cross this stile but turn right up the field, and go out through a gate. This leads into Straight Lane, a path that becomes a wider track. Some way beyond a house on your right, turn left through a tiny gap in the wall. Go up the field, turning left when you reach the wall at the far end and skirt around to a small stile to your right. Climb this and cross the field to another stile that takes you down a high-hedged path to rejoin Canaan Lane.

PLACES TO VISIT

JERVAULX ABBEY
✉ Jervaulx HG4 4PH
☎ 01677 460391
🕐 Dawn to dusk
✋ Adult £2, child £1.50

MIDDLEHAM CASTLE
✉ Middleham DL8 4RJ
☎ 01969 623899
🕐 Mar–end Sep daily 10–6; Oct–end Mar Mon, Thu–Sun 10–4
✋ Adult £3.30, child £1.70

WHERE TO EAT

There are pubs and cafés in Middleham and the Cover Bridge Inn. Tea room at Jervaulx Abbey (mid-Mar to end Oct).

WHEN TO GO

Avoid coming at weekends when Jervaulx Abbey can be very busy with visitors.

Opposite *The Norman Middleham Castle*
Above *Jervaulx Abbey ruins*

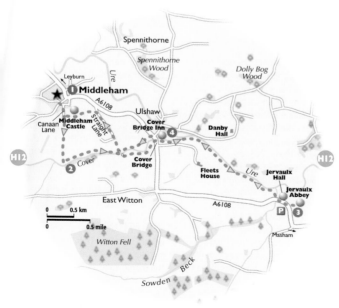

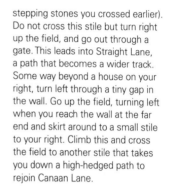

ALNWICK
BARTER BOOKS
www.barterbooks.co.uk
Huge, eccentric second-hand
bookshop in grandiose former train
station. Books are displayed in the
former waiting rooms and platform
area, and a model railway runs along
shelves. Substantial local interest
section, plus rare books.
✉ Alnwick Station, Alnwick NE66 2NP
☎ 01665 604888 🕒 Apr–end Sep daily
9–7; rest of year Fri–Wed 9–5, Thu 9–7 💻

BEVERLEY
THE WHITE HORSE
Traditional 16th-century pub also
known as Nellie's.
✉ 22 Hengate, Beverley HU17 8BL
☎ 01482 861973 🕒 Mon–Sat 11–11,
Sun 12–10.30pm 🚍 Beverley

BRADFORD
ALHAMBRA THEATRE
www.bradford-theatres.co.uk
This traditional theatre hosts visiting
ballet, opera, classical and modern
drama companies.

✉ Morley Street, Bradford BD7 1AJ
☎ 01274 432000 🕒 Box office: Mon–Sat,
10–8 🖐 From £16 🚻 🚍 Bradford
Interchange

CHESTER
CHESHIRE WORKSHOPS
Large, modern collection of
buildings in a rural setting outside
Chester where you can see candles
being made and a candle-dipping
Ferris wheel. Also glassmaking
demonstrations and workshops
for children.
✉ Burwardsley, near Chester CH3 9PF
☎ 01829 770401 🕒 Daily 10–5
🖐 Free 🚻

CHESTER MARKET
www.visitchester.com
This interesting covered market in
a modern building in the heart of
Chester has been in existence on
this site from the 14th century.
✉ Princess Street, Chester ☎ 01244
402340 🕒 Mon–Sat 8–5 💻
🚍 Chester

Above Cycling at Wastwater, Lake District

CHESTER RACES
www.chester-races.co.uk
Small racecourse, known as the
RodeeThe country's oldest, dating
from the 16th century.
✉ The Racecourse, Chester CH1 2LY
☎ 01244 304600 🕒 14 flat-racing fixtures,
May–end Sep 🖐 £7–£40, reserve festival
days in advance 🍴 💻 🚻 🚍 Chester

OLD HARKERS ARMS
This lively pub is in a converted
Victorian canalside warehouse.
✉ 1 Russell Street, Chester CH3 5AL
☎ 01244 344525 🕒 Mon–Sat 11.30–11,
Sun 12–10.30 🚍 Chester

CONISTON
CONISTON BOATING CENTRE
For boating enthusiasts, here you
can hire a range of dinghies, motor
boats and canoes.
✉ Lake Road, Coniston ☎ 015394 41366
🕒 Daily 10–4.30 🖐 From £9 per hour
rowing boat, £18 per 2 hours canoe

GATESHEAD
THE SAGE
www.thesagegateshead.org
One of the foundation pillars of the revitalised Newcastle/Gateshead waterfront, the Sage is a distinctive venue, with a range of performance and exhibition spaces. The eclectic programme ranges from pop legends to experimental orchestras , with home gigs by the Northern Sinfonia and the Folkworks traditional music organisation.

✉ St Mary's Square, Gateshead Quays, Gateshead, NE8 2JR ☎ 0191 443 4661 ◔ Box office: 9am–9pm
💻 🔊 🍴 🚆 Newcastle Central Tube: Gateshead Interchange 🚌 Q1

GRIZEDALE
GO APE
www.goape.co.uk
A section of Grizedale Forest has been transformed into a fun adventure course, where, after a bit of instruction (and being fitted with a climbing harness to attach to the safety system), you can clamber and swing through the trees to your heart's content using the rope ladders, rope bridges, rope swings and zip slides that have been fixed up in the tree tops. Minimum age is 10 (but no unaccompanied children under 18), so this is a great family outing. Allow about 3 hours, more to walk the forest trails or rent a mountain bike and cycle along them.

✉ Grizedale Forest Visitor Centre, Grizedale, Hawkshead, Ambleside, Cumbria LA22 ☎ Tel 0845 643 9215 ◔ Mid-Mar to end Oct, daily 9–5 (may vary depending on season); weekends Nov and Feb 🖐 Adult £25, child (10–17) £20 💻

HARROGATE
BETTY'S CAFÉ AND TEA ROOMS
www.bettys.co.uk
High-class baker's and patisserie (opened 1919), that has a quintessentially English tea room attached. Specialities include Yorkshire curd tarts and Fat Rascals. Shops in Ilkley, Northallerton and York too.

✉ 1 Parliament Street, Harrogate HG1 2QU ☎ 01423 502746 ◔ Daily 9–9, closed 1 Jan and 25–26 Dec 💻 🚆 Harrogate

THE HYDRO
www.harrogate.gov.uk
The Hydro is a modern swimming pool and fitness complex, offering beauty therapies, massage and crèche.

✉ Jennyfield Drive, Harrogate HG1 2RP ☎ 01423 556767 ◔ Daily 7.30am–9.30pm
🖐 Swimming: adult £3.65, child (3–18) £1.80, under 4 free; creche available (3–5) 💻 🚆 Harrogate

MONTEY'S
www.monteys.co.uk
Friendly café and bar serving food. Live music most evenings.

✉ 3 Corn Exchange Buildings, The Ginnel, Harrogate HG1 2RB ☎ 01423 526652 ◔ Daily 5pm–midnight 🚆 Harrogate

THE TURKISH BATHS AND HEALTH SPA
www.harrogate.gov.uk/turkishbaths
The baths first opened in 1897 and have since been stylishly renovated. The Moorish interiors are reason enough to visit, but keenly priced spa treatments are tempting. Admission includes use of the steam room, plunge pool and frigidarium (relaxation room).

✉ Royal Baths, Parliament Street, Harrogate HG1 2WH ☎ 01423 556746 ◔ Sun–Fri 9.30–7.30, Sat 9.30–4.30
🖐 Admission £10.50; massage: from £18; reflexology: from £27 🚆 Harrogate

HAWES
WENSLEYDALE CREAMERY
www.wensleydale.co.uk
Where better to buy delicious Wensleydale cheese than from the maker. If you visit on a cheese-making day, you can watch the process from a viewing gallery. Any day you can taste it in the restaurant or with a sample in the shop, which has an incredible range of cheeses. There's also a museum.

✉ Gayle Lane, Hawes, North Yorkshire DL8 3RN ☎ 01969 667664 ◔ Mon–Sat 9.30–5, Sun 10–4.30

HULL
HULL TRUCK THEATRE
www.hulltruck.co.uk
Even in a new home in the city's St. Stephen's development, this remains a small theatre, which punches way above its weight thanks to its outstanding company and some inspired directors.

✉ St. Stephens, Hull ☎ 01482 323638 ◔ Box office: Mon–Fri, 11–8 (performance days), 11–5 (non-performance days), Sat 1–8 (performance days only), Sun 5.30–7.30pm (performance days only) 🚆 Hull Paragon

KENDAL
LAKE DISTRICT NATIONAL PARK AUTHORITY
www.lake-district.gov.uk
A magnet for lovers of the outdoors, 'the Lakes' have attracted poets, artists and writers as well as countless hikers and day trippers. A network of narrow valleys (dales) radiates out from a central core of mountains including England's highest, Scafell Pike 978m (3210ft). Well-maintained paths give a fantastic range of walks from easy strolls to challenging long-distance hikes.

✉ Murley Moss, Oxenholme Road, Kendal LA9 7RL ☎ 01539 724555

KESWICK
THEATRE BY THE LAKE
www.theatrebythelake.com
From its origins in the back of a trailer, parked in a car park, Keswick's theatre has grown to become one of the most respected regional theatres in the north, with a main auditorium and a studio for smaller productions.

✉ Lake Road, Keswick CA12 5DJ ☎ 017687 74411 ◔ Box office: 9.30–8
💻 🔊

KIELDER WATER
LEAPLISH WATERSIDE PARK
www.nwl.co.uk
Europe's largest man-made lake offers a wide range of water-based pursuits, from canoeing and sailing to fishing and pleasure cruises on the ferry *Osprey*. The waterside park also has an innovative children's play garden.

✉ Kielder NE48 1AX ☎ 01434 250312 ◔ All year 🖐 Ferry around lake: adult £6, child £3.75

KIRBY MISPERTON

FLAMINGOLAND THEME PARK AND ZOO

www.flamingoland.co.uk

White-knuckle experiences, rides for small children and a zoo with over 1,000 animals.

✉ Kirby Misperton, near Malton YO17 6UX ☎ 0871 911 8000 ⏰ Mar–end Oct Mon–Fri 10–5, Sat–Sun 10–6 (times vary later in year according to daylight) 🖑 Adult £22 (including child over 4), under 4 free, family £82 🍴 ⊟ 🏛 🚌 Malton 5 miles (8km)

KNARESBOROUGH

BLUE SKY BALLOONS

www.blueskyballoons.co.uk

Hot-air balloon rides over the Yorkshire countryside.

✉ Moor Lane, Arkendale, Knaresborough HG5 0RQ ☎ 01423 340140 ⏰ Apr–end Sep daily evenings, 🖑 Balloon ride: £185 per person 🚌 Knaresborough

LEEDS

CITY VARIETIES

www.cityvarieties.co.uk

Typical 19th-century music hall. Actors Lillie Langtry (1853–1929) and Charlie Chaplin (1889–1977) appeared here.

✉ Swan Street, Leeds LS1 6LW ☎ 0845 644 1881 ⏰ Box office: Mon–Sat 10 to curtain up 🖑 Various ⊟ 🚆 🚌 Leeds

GRAND THEATRE AND OPERA HOUSE

www.leedsgrandtheatre.com

Grand Victorian theatre—base of Opera North—staging opera, ballet, classical and modern drama, musicals, shows and gigs.

✉ 46 New Briggate, Leeds LS1 6NZ ☎ 0870 121 4901 ⏰ Box office: Mon–Sat 10–8, Sun only if show 🖑 Varies ⊟ 🚆 🚌 Leeds

HARVEY NICHOLS

www.harveynichols.co.uk

The Leeds' branch of the London department store is just as chic as the original. Expensive designer clothes are a speciality, and the beauty salon and fourth-floor restaurant are extremely popular.

✉ 107–111 Briggate, Leeds LS1 6AZ

☎ 0113 2048888 ⏰ Mon–Wed 10–6, Thu 10–8, Fri, Sat 10–7, Sun 11–5 ⊟ 🚌 Leeds

MOJO

Intimate, modern bar in central Leeds, serving superb cocktails to rock and indie music.

✉ 18 Merrion Street, Leeds LS1 6PQ ☎ 0113 2446387 ⏰ Sun–Thu 5pm–2am; Fri–Sat 5pm–3am 🚌 Leeds

VICTORIA QUARTER

Classy, covered shopping area built in 1898, with a stained-glass roof. A wide range of top-quality stores, from Paul Smith to Louis Vuitton, as well as Harvey Nick's.

✉ Briggate, Leeds LS1 6AZ ☎ 0113 2455333 ⏰ Mon–Sat 10–5, Sun 11–5. Times vary; some shops closed Sun ⊟ 🚌 Leeds

WEST YORKSHIRE PLAYHOUSE

www.wyplayhouse.com

Modern theatre hosting a regular season of classical and modern plays.

✉ Playhouse Square, Leeds LS2 7UP ☎ 0113 213 7700 ⏰ Box office: Mon–Sat 9–8 🖑 From £5 🍴 ⊟ 🚆 🚌 Leeds

YORKSHIRE CRICKET CLUB

www.yorkshireccc.com

International ground with fine facilities for spectators.

✉ Headingly Cricket Ground, St. Michael's Lane, Leeds LS6 3BU ☎ 0870 429 6774 ⏰ Reservations: Mon–Fri 9–5 🖑 County match (3–4 days): adult £15, child £10. One-day match: adult £15, child £10 ⊟ 🚌 Headingley, Burley Park or Leeds City

LIVERPOOL

AINTREE RACECOURSE

www.aintree.co.uk

Home to the Grand National, the world's most famous steeplechase (▷ 347 Festivals and Events).

⏰ Ormskirk Road, Aintree, Liverpool L9 5AS ☎ 0151 5232600

ALBERT DOCK

www.albertdock.com

Touristy, with some quirky gift and homeware stalls, but visit for souvenirs, the Tate Liverpool or the Beatles Story.

✉ Albert Dock, Liverpool L3 4AF

⏰ Generally Mon–Sat 9–6, Sun 11–5 🍴 ⊟ 🚌 Liverpool Lime Street

LE BATEAU

This alternative music nightspot has two floors full of indie, punk, nu-wave and '60s rock, depending on what night it is. Friday's Indiecation is seriously eclectic and will even drag in a bit of disco in a genre-hopping dancefest for the MySpace generation.

✉ 62 Duke Street, Liverpool L1 5AA ☎ 0151 709 6508 ⏰ From 10.30pm 🖑 From £2 🚌 Liverpool Central

CAVERN WALKS

wwww.cavern-walks.co.uk

Named for the famous club where the 1960s group The Beatles made their name, offers designer fashion, jewellery and gift shops on two floors. Cricket has chic, stylish, quality fashions.

✉ Matthew Street, Liverpool L2 6RE ☎ 0151 2369082 ⏰ Mon–Sat 9–6 🍴 ⊟ 🚌 Liverpool Lime Street

EVERYMAN THEATRE

A wide range of productions—from Shakespeare to modern playwrights—as well as concerts, exhibitions and dance.

✉ 5–9 Hope Street, Liverpool L1 9EL ☎ 0151 7094776 ⏰ Box office: Mon–Sat 10–7 🖑 Various 🍴 🚆 🚌 Liverpool Lime Street

JEFFS

Affectionately known as the 'Harrods of Liverpool', this place specializes in women's wear, fashions and accessories. Take a break in the Victorian tea room.

✉ 80 Bold Street, Liverpool L1 4HR ☎ 0151 7070880 ⏰ Mon–Sat 9.30–5.30 ⊟ 🚌 Liverpool Central

PHILHARMONIC HALL

www.liverpoolphil.com

Art deco building, home to the Royal Liverpool Philharmonic; also hosts jazz, pop and world music.

✉ Hope Street, Liverpool L19 BP ☎ 0151 7093789 ⏰ Daily; box office: Mon–Sat 10–5.30, Sun 12–5 🍴 Varies 🍴 🚆 🚌 Liverpool Central

PROBE RECORDS
www.probe-records.com
Legendary record shop and part of Liverpool's music scene for decades, selling vinyl and CDs covering rock, indie, electronic and more.
✉ 9 Slater Street, Liverpool L1 4BW
☎ 0151 7088815 ⏰ Mon–Sat 10–6
🚇 Liverpool Central

RAWHIDE COMEDY CLUB
www.royalcourtliverpool.co.uk/rawhide
Liverpool's favourite comedy club is enjoying its second sojourn in this historic bar and restaurant. Thursday nights see local wannabes standing up to national talent.
✉ Prohibition Bar & Grill, Lyceum Building, 1A Bold Street, Liverpool L1 4DJ ☎ 0870 787 1866 ⏰ Wed–Sat from 6pm 💷 Wed £3, Thu £7, Fri £12, Sat £15. Over 18s only
🍴 🚇 Liverpool Lime Street

MANCHESTER
BRIDGEWATER HALL
www.bridgewater-hall.co.uk
Home of the Hallé and BBC Philharmonic orchestras, this is one of Europe's finest venues for classical music.
✉ Lower Mosley Street, Manchester M2 3WS ☎ 0161 9079000 ⏰ Box office: Mon–Sat 10–8, Sun 12–6 (8 on concert nights) 💷 Various 🚇 Manchester Piccadilly

THE COMEDY STORE
www.thecomedystore.co.uk
Live stand-up performances at the only Comedy Store outside London.
✉ Deansgate Locks, Whitworth Street, Manchester ☎ 0870 593 2932 ⏰ Performances Wed–Sun 💷 £5–£18
🍴 🚇 Manchester Deansgate

CRAFT AND DESIGN CENTRE
wwww.craftanddesign.com
Buy funky jewellery, candles, furniture and the like from the artists' workshops here.
✉ 17 Oak Street, Manchester M4 5JD
☎ 0161 8324274 ⏰ Mon–Sat 10–5.30, Sun in Dec 🚇 Manchester Piccadilly

CRUZ 101
www.cruz101.com
A popular Gay Village destination,

Cruz 101 is one of Manchester's best gay clubs, with a range of entertainment from club nights to live acts.
✉ 101 Princess Street, Manchester M1 6DD ☎ 0161 9500101 ⏰ Wed–Mon 11pm–3.30/5/6am 🚇 Manchester Piccadilly

THE LOWRY
www.thelowry.com
Two theatres in an iconic modern building offering a range of music, opera, comedy and drama.
✉ Salford Quays, Salford, Manchester M50 3AZ ☎ 0870 787 5780 ⏰ Daily 💷 From £10 🍴 🚇 Salford Central

MANCHESTER ROADHOUSE
www.theroadhouselive.co.uk
Excellent venue to catch young Mancunian bands searching for fame. Also hosts club nights.
✉ 8–10 Newton Street, Manchester M1 2AN ☎ 0161 2379789 ⏰ Mon–Thu 7pm–2am, Fri–Sun 9pm–3am 💷 Free–£8
🚇 Manchester Piccadilly

MANCHESTER UNITED FOOTBALL CLUB
www.manutd.co.uk
Match tickets may be virtually impossible to obtain, but a visit to Old Trafford's Theatre of Dreams museum—covering the history of the club from 1878 to the present day—is the next best thing.
✉ Sir Matt Busby Way, Old Trafford, Manchester M16 0RA ☎ 0161 868 8000; 0870 442 1994 ⏰ Daily 9.30–5
💷 Stadium tour and museum: adult £10, child £7, family £30; museum only: adult £6.50, child £4.75, family £20

ROYAL EXCHANGE THEATRE
www.royalexchange.co.uk
The city's best-known theatre with a superb setting in the Royal Exchange and 'in-the-round' aspect.
✉ St. Ann's Square, Manchester M2 7DH
☎ 0161 8339833 ⏰ Box office: 9.30–6 (7.30 in person) 💷 Various 🍴 💷
🚇 Manchester Piccadilly

SELFRIDGES
www.selfridges.com
This branch of the fabulous London store aims to be funkier and focused on fashion.

✉ Exchange Square, Manchester M3 1BD
☎ 0800 123 400 ⏰ Mon–Fri 10–8, Sat 9–8, Sun 11–5 🍴 💷 🚇 Manchester Piccadilly

THE TRIANGLE
www.trianglemanchester.co.uk
The former Corn Exchange has been redeveloped into a complex housing mainstream chains and independent shops.
✉ Exchange Square, Manchester M4 3TR ☎ 0161 8348961 ⏰ Mon–Wed 10–6, Thu–Sat 10–7, Sun 11–5
🍴 💷 🚇 Manchester Victoria

TRIBAL SESSIONS AND REDLIGHT AT SANKEYS SOAP
One of Manchester's trendy and popular club nights.
✉ Jersey Street, Manchester M4 6JG
☎ 0161 6619668 ⏰ Fri 10pm–3am, Sat 10.30pm–4am 💷 Fri £8–£12, Sat £10–£12. Programme may differ during student vacations 🚇 Manchester Piccadilly

NEWCASTLE UPON TYNE
GRAINGER MARKET
www.newcastle.gov.uk
This traditional, early 19th-century indoor market contains the oldest surviving branch of Marks & Spencer, opened in 1895. The market consists of the Grainger Arcade and the impressive vegetable market, with its curved glass roof. There are over 100 stores.
✉ Grainger Street, Newcastle upon Tyne NE1 5QN ☎ 0191 2115540 ⏰ Mon and Wed 9–5, Tue, Thu–Sat 9–5.30
🍴 🚇 Newcastle

THEATRE ROYAL
www.theatreroyal.co.uk
The northeast England venue of choice for the Royal Shakespeare Company, the National Theatre and Opera North, the Theatre Royal dates from 1837 and also hosts shows and musicals from London's West End. Dance and comedy fill out the impressive listings.
✉ 100 Grey Street, Newcastle upon Tyne NE1 6BR ☎ 0844 811 2121 ⏰ Box office: Mon–Sat 9–8 (Wed 10–8, Sun from 2 hours before performance) 🍴 💷 🚇 Newcastle Central 🚇 Monument

TYNESIDE CINEMA

www.tynecine.org

Art-house and foreign-language films.

✉ 10 Pilgrim Street, Newcastle upon Tyne NE1 6QG ☎ 0191 2328289 ⏰ Box office: Mon–Sat 10–8.30, Sun from 15 min before first lunchtime screening ♿ From £5 🖪 🖫 🚇 Newcastle

OSWALDTWISTLE
OSWALDTWISTLE MILLS

www.o-mills.co.uk

One of Lancashire's legendary old cotton mills has been imaginatively converted to house around 80 retail outlets and other attractions, such as a working sweet factory (with viewing gallery), garden centre, events area, indoor and outdoor play areas, and donkey rides in summer. Development includes the huge gourmet food area. Much of the character of the old buildings have been retained, and it's a great place for a shopping outing.

✉ Moscow Mill, Colliers Street, Oswaldtwistle, Lancashire BB5 3DE ☎ 01254 871025 ⏰ Mon–Sat 9.30–5.30 (till 8 Thu), Sun 11–5 🍴 🚌 Off the B6231, just south of Church & Oswaldtwistle railway station

PENRITH
RHEGED CENTRE

www.rheged.com

This award-winning centre is Europe's largest grass-covered building, its rough stone walls cleverly concealing a dozen craft shops, a giant cinema screen showing nine specially-made films, two exhibition halls and various children's activities, plus special events. People come here just to see the building, which has an admirable sustainability ethic.

✉ Redhills, Penrith, Cumbria CA11 0DQ ☎ 01768 868000 ⏰ Daily 9.30–5. Closed 25–26 Dec ♿ Free; separate charges for films and children's activities 🚌 Off the M6 at Junction 40

RICHMOND
THE GEORGIAN THEATRE ROYAL

www.georgiantheatreroyal.co.uk

The only functioning 18th-century theatre surviving in Britain stages various productions.

✉ Victoria Road, Richmond DL10 4DW ☎ 01748 825252 ⏰ Box office: Mon–Sat 10–5, 7pm on performance days ♿ From £5 🍴 🖫

RIPON
DAVILLS OF RIPON

Make a bee-line for this tiny shop near Market Square, for excellent bread, cakes and even more superb handmade chocolates.

✉ 24 Westgate, Ripon HG4 2BQ ☎ 01765 603544 ⏰ Mon–Tue, Thu–Sat 8.30–4, Wed 10–1

ROTHERHAM
MAGNA SCIENCE ADVENTURE CENTRE

www.visitmagna.co.uk

Discover science at this awesome, disused steelworks which has been turned into an educational adventure centre. Its four pavilions—Earth, Air, Fire and Water—are aimed at children, with plenty of hands-on activities.

✉ Sheffield Road, Templeborough, Rotherham S60 1DX ☎ 01709 720002 ⏰ Daily 10–5 ♿ Adult £9.95, child (5–15) £7.95, family £32.95 🍴 🖪 🏛 🚇 Meadowhall

SCARBOROUGH
STEPHEN JOSEPH THEATRE

www.sjt.uk.com

Theatre hosting both repertory and touring productions plus premières of dramas by playwright and director Sir Alan Ayckbourn.

✉ Westborough, Scarborough YO11 1JW ☎ 01723 370541 ⏰ Box office: Mon–Sat 10–6 (8 when performances are running) ♿ From £11 🖪 🖫 🚇 Scarborough

SHEFFIELD
THE LEADMILL

www.leadmill.co.uk

A Sheffield institution, the Leadmill continues to thrive with a mixture of club nights and live gigs by up-and-coming bands and more established ones looking for an intimate venue.

✉ 6 Leadmill Road, Sheffield S1 4SE ☎ 0114 221 2828 ⏰ Club nights from 10pm, gigs from 7pm ♿ Varies 🖪 🖫

🚇 Station: Sheffield, Tram: Sheffield Station/Sheffield Hallam University

MEADOWHALL

www.meadowhall.co.uk

This is a mega-mall including all the main chain stores and a massive range of shops, plus several restaurants, cafés and an 11-screen cinema.

✉ Meadownhall Centre, Sheffield S9 1EP ☎ 0114 256 8800 ⏰ Mon–Fri 10–9, Sat 9–7, Sun 11–5 (some shop hours may vary) 🚌 Northwest of city, just off M1 at junction 34

STOCKTON-ON-TEES
TEES WHITE WATER CENTRE

www.4seasons.co.uk

Purpose-built whitewater canoe course beside the River Tees, with rapids and slalom course—perfect for adrenaline junkies.

✉ Tees Barrage, Stockton-on-Tees TS18 2QW ☎ 01642 678000 ⏰ Daily 8–8, in summer; 8–6, in winter ♿ Whitewater rafting: £99–£200 group of 6. Day ticket £8.50 🖪 🚇 Thornaby

YORK
BARBARA CATTLE

www.hl-brown.co.uk

A treasure house in York's historic centre, with fine silver and jewellery, especially 18th- and 19th-century English silverware and York silver. A must for collectors.

⏰ 45 Stonegate, York YO1 8AW ☎ 01904 623862 ⏰ Mon–Sat 9–5.30 🚇 York

ROBERT THOMPSON'S CRAFTSMEN LTD

www.robertthompsons.co.uk

Run by the grandsons of founder Robert Thompson (1876–1955), the woodcarver whose work is seen in many of Yorkshire's churches and great houses. Items are finished with Thompson's celebrated trademark mouse.

⏰ Mouseman Visitor Centre, Kilburn, York YO61 4AH ☎ 01347 869100 ⏰ Mon–Thu 9–5, Fri 9–3.45, Sat 10–12; closed Christmas and New Year. Visitor Centre: Easter–end Sep daily 10–5; Oct Tue–Sun 10–5; Nov, Dec Wed–Sun 11–4 🍴 🚇 Thirsk (7 miles/11km)

FEBRUARY

VIKING FESTIVAL
www.yorkfestivals.com
Longship races and battle re-enactments draw around 10,000 people to York for this jovial salute to its 200-year Viking occupation.
✉ York, various locations ☎ 01904 615505

MARCH

WORDS BY THE WATER
www.wayswithwords.co.uk
Based in the Theatre by the Lake, this literature festival brings many big names from the media, politics and the arts to the Cumbrian town.
✉ Keswick ☎ 017687 74411 ⊕ First two weeks in March

APRIL

GRAND NATIONAL
www.aintree.co.uk
This famous horse race is broadcast live and has many a betting novice laying a wager.
⊕ Ormskirk Road, Aintree, Liverpool ☎ 0151 5232600 ⊕ First Saturday in April ✋ From £10

MAY–JUNE

ISLE OF MAN TT RACES
www.iomtt.com
Perhaps the most famous (and notorious) motorcycle races in the world take place over two weeks on this mountainous island.
⊕ Douglas, Isle of Man ☎ 01624 644644 ⊕ May to June

JUNE

MERSEY RIVER FESTIVAL
www.visitliverpool.com
Europe's biggest free maritime gala, held annually.
⊕ Albert Dock, Liverpool ☎ 0151 233 2008 (tourist office)

JULY

YORK EARLY MUSIC FESTIVAL
www.yorkfestivals.com
Held over two weeks, this is Britain's leading early music festival.
✉ York, various locations ☎ 01904 632220

GREAT YORKSHIRE SHOW
www. greatyorkshireshow.com
The largest of northern England's agricultural and country shows.
✉ Great Yorkshire Showground, Harrogate ☎ 01423 541000 ⊕ From 2nd Tuesday in July for 3 days

AUGUST

INTERNATIONAL BEATLE WEEK
www.visitliverpool.com
The biggest annual celebration of The Beatles' music in the world takes place over five days lin Liverpool.
✉ Atlantic Pavilion, Albert Dock, Liverpool ☎ 0151 239 9091 ⊕ Late August

MANCHESTER PRIDE
www.manchesterpride.com
One of the largest Gay Pride events in Europe.
✉ Manchester, various locations ☎ 0161 236 7474

SEPTEMBER

GREAT NORTH RUN
www.greatrun.org
A half-marathon on the streets of Newcastle and Gateshead.
✉ Newcastle, Gateshead

OCTOBER

CHESTER LITERATURE FESTIVAL
www.chester-literature-festival.org.uk
Literary events around Chester.
✉ Festival Office, Viscount House, River Lane, Saltney CH4 8RH ☎ 01244 409113 ⊕ October ✋ Various ⊞ Chester

PRICES AND SYMBOLS

The restaurants are listed alphabetically within each town. The prices are for a two-course lunch (L) and a three-course à la carte dinner (D). Prices in pubs are for a two-course lunchtime bar meal and a two-course dinner in the restaurant, unless specified otherwise. The price for wine is for the least expensive bottle.

For a key to the symbols, ▷ 2.

ALTRINCHAM
JUNIPER

This is one of the North's best restaurants, lurking behind a suburban facade south of Manchester. There are also exciting changes to the Modern French food, with creative, idiosyncratic combinations of superbly sourced ingredients. Service is slick, and the wine list is good.

✉ 21 The Downs, Altrincham WA14 2QD ☎ 0161 9294008 🕐 Fri–Sat 12–2, 7–9.30, ,Tue–Thu 7–9.30. Closed 1 week in Feb, 2 weeks in summer 🍴 L £20, D £40, Wine £20 🚗 A556 Chester to Manchester road

APPLEBY-IN-WESTMORLAND
THE ROYAL OAK INN

The interior of this historic pub consists of a classic tap room with blackened beams, oak panelling and open fire, a comfortable lounge and two dining rooms. Ingredients are sourced locally wherever possible and menus change regularly. Options include home-made soups, Sunday lunches and vegetarian meals.

✉ Bongate CA16 6UN ☎ 017683 51463 🕐 Mon–Sat 11–11 (10.30 Sun) 🍴 L £15, D £20, Wine £10 🚗 Take A66 east from M6 junction 38, village on B6542 to right

BAMBURGH
VICTORIA HOTEL

www.victoriahotel.net

A Victorian hotel with a modern brasserie and indoor children's play area, beneath the shadow of Bamburgh's great castle. Good use is made of local fish, from the Seahouses smoked haddock fishcakes to the pan-fried sea bream, whilst elsewhere you can expect modern British brasserie standards such as pheasant stuffed with haggis or duck breast on sweet and sour red cabbage.

✉ Front Street, Bamburgh NE69 7BP ☎ 01668 214431 🕐 11–11, food 12–9 🍴 L £12.70, D £17.20 🚗 In centre of village

BEAMISH
BEAMISH PARK HOTEL

www.beamish-park-hotel.co.uk

The Conservatory Bistro, reached through the welcoming lounge of this stylish hotel, is effortlessly relaxed. Modern and chic, with a contemporary colour scheme, artistic lighting and distinctive fabrics, it boasts a host of individual design features. Like the ambience, the restaurant's regularly-changing menu is modern in style and includes a selection of British dishes with a smattering of international influences - all making good use of local, seasonal produce. Try the pressed ham hock terrine with home-made pease pudding to start, followed by a main course of slow-cooked organic beef blade with two celeries and rich gravy, making room for a delicious dessert of warm lemon polenta cake, lime syrup and mascarpone.

✉ Beamish Burn Road, NE16 5EG ☎ 01207 230666 🕐 Daily 12–2.30, 7–10.30 🍴 L £12.50, D £25 🚗 A1(M) turn off onto A692, continue for 2m (3km) into Sunniside. At traffic lights take A6076 signposted Beamish Museum & Tanfield Railway. Hotel is situated behind Causey Arch Inn

BEVERLEY
THE PIPE AND GLASS
www.pipeandglass.co.uk
Blending the contemporary with the traditional, this pantiled inn is both rustic and modern. The food follows the same theme, with good value hearty dishes featuring local produce such as roast Gloucester Old Spot pork, black pudding forcemeat, sage and scrumpy gravy or Burdass lamb and kidney casserole with rosemary dumpling and Tibthorpe honey carrots. Puddings make good use too of local fruit such as rhubarb or plum.

✉ West End, South Dalton HU17 7PN ☎ 01430 810246 🕐 12–2, 6.30–9.30 Closed Mon, D Sun, 25 Dec, 2 weeks Jan 🍴 L £10.50, D £15.75, Wine £XXXX 🚗 Leave Beverley N on A164, at Molescroft roundabout take the 2nd exit on B1248 for 4 miles (6km), turn left on Mere Lane, then right on Main Street and left at West End

BLACKBURN
MILLSTONE AT MELLOR
www.shireinns.co.uk
This old coaching inn in the beautiful Ribble Valley retains a feel of period authenticity while conjuring up surprisingly sophisticated Modern British food. There is a healthy nod to local traditions and local produce still features in dishes like chicken and black pudding terrine, or braised Pendle lamb shank in a port wine jus.

✉ Church Lane, Mellor BB2 7JR ☎ 01254 813333 🕐 12–2.15, 6.30–9.15 🍴 L £16.95, D £25.95, Wine £13.95 🚗 Call for directions

BOLTON ABBEY
DEVONSHIRE ARMS COUNTRY HOUSE HOTEL
There is nothing starchy about the elegant Burlington Restaurant at this beautiful hotel (▷ 354), nor indeed its modern Anglo-French cuisine. You can glide effortlessly from pan-seared langoustine with artichoke pannacotta and a shellfish dressing, to pumpkin and truffle risotto, before lingering over a tantalizing dessert menu.

✉ Bolton Abbey BD23 6AJ ☎ 01756 710441 🕐 12–2.30, 7–10; closed L Mon–Sat 🍴 L £15, D £25, Wine £11.95 (in Brasserie). D £58 in restaurant 🚗 On B6160 to Bolton Abbey 230m (250 yards) north of junction with A59 roundabout junction 🚗 Ilkley 4.5 miles (7km)

BOROUGHBRIDGE
THE DINING ROOM RESTAURANT
www.thediningroomonline.co.uk
Behind the restaurant's shop-style, bow-fronted exterior lies a traditional lounge-style bar, perfect for pre- and post-dinner drinks. In contrast, the dining room is a more light, spacious and contemporary affair, decked out with wooden beams, high-backed chairs, crisp linens and good quality crockery and silverware. In fine weather the new terrace is perfect for relaxed alfresco dining.

✉ 20 St James Square, YO51 9AR ☎ 01423 326426 🕐 12–2, 7–9.30, closed Mon, L Tue–Sat, D Sun; 26–28 Dec, 1 Jan, public holidays 🍴 L £20, D £27 🚗 A1(M), Boroughbridge junct, sign to town. Opposite fountain in the town square

CHESTER
OLD HARKERS ARMS
www.harkersarms-chester.co.uk
There's a good selection of sandwiches and paninis in the restaurant at lunchtime at this canalside pub, and an interesting range of dishes that might include Moroccan lamb with couscous, baked salmon or spicy meatballs. Local ice cream and cheeses add a bit of sustainable credibility to the desserts. Children not allowed.

✉ 1 Russell Street, Chester CH1 5AL ☎ 01244 344525 🕐 11.30–11. Restaurant 12–9.30 🍴 L £10, D £17.20, Wine £12 🚗 Chester 🚗 Down the steps off City Road on the banks of the canal

CRATHORNE
CRATHORNE HALL HOTEL
www.handpicked.co.uk
Savour the stunning period elegance of Crathorne Hall, a magnificent Edwardian property set in 15 acres (6ha) of landscaped grounds. Wood panelling, an impressive carved stone fireplace, ornate ceilings and imposing oil paintings are just some of the original features in the formal Leven Restaurant, forming the period backdrop for white-linen dressed tables, darkwood leather chairs and stunning views. The formal service is appropriately skilled and professional but friendly. Impressive British cooking—underpinned by classical roots—is characterised by interesting combinations with the emphasis on local and seasonal ingredients and accomplished simplicity. Grand reserve blade of beef served with roasted foie gras and pumpkin mash, and Yorkshire curd tart accompanied by elderflower ice cream and sloe gin jelly show the style.

✉ TS15 0AR ☎ 01642 700398 🕐 Daily 12.30–2.30, 7–9.30 🍴 L £30, D £40 🚗 Off A19, 2m E of Yarm. Access to A19 via A66 or A1, Thirsk

DURHAM
BISTRO 21
Bistro 21 is an intimate, laidback dining experience in a restored farmhouse with a loyal, local following. The list of daily specials is announced on a blackboard. A modern take on traditional English cooking, using simple combinations of fresh flavours. Children are welcome.

✉ Aykley Heads House, Aykley Heads DH1 5TS ☎ 0191 3844354 🕐 12–2, 7–10.25; closed Sun, 25 Dec 🍴 L £14, D £16.50, Wine £13 🚗 Off B6532 from Durham centre; pass County Hall on right, turn right at double roundabout into Aykley Heads 🚗 Durham

Opposite *The Millennium and Tyne Bridges in Newcastle upon Tyne*

EAST WITTON

THE BLUE LION

www.thebluelion.co.uk

There is excellent food available in the bar of this traditional pub, but serious diners reserve ahead for the dining room, where dishes might include chargrilled beef with a shiraz sauce, shallots, lardons and mushrooms.

✉ East Witton, near Leyburn DL8 4SN ☎ 01969 624273 ⏰ Mon–Sat 11–11, Sun 12–10.30. L served 12–2.15, D served 7–9.30 ♿ L £16, D £25, Wine £12.95 🚌 Telephone for directions

HALIFAX

SHIBDEN MILL INN

www.shibdenmill.com

This 17th-century inn retains much charm and character. A cosy bar and candlelit restaurant attract plenty of drinkers and diners and the chef offers a wide selection of dishes. Interesting starters may be followed by seared sea bass in an asparagus and hollandaise sauce, confit of duck leg with puy lentils and a carrot and coriander jus—or you could look for something simpler from the bar menu. Food can be served outside in the garden.

✉ Shibden Mill Fold HX3 7UL ☎ 01422 365840 ⏰ 12–2, 6–9.30 ♿ L £8.95, D £24, Wine £12.95 🚉 Halifax

HARROGATE

THE BOAR'S HEAD HOTEL

www.boarsheadripley.co.uk

This converted coaching inn is part of the Ripley Castle estate, owned by the Ingilby family for over 27 generations. By all accounts Lady Ingilby is a rigorous taskmaster and taster, taking a personal interest in the inventive, reliable Modern British menu, while her husband, Sir Thomas, shows the same interest in assembling the 200-bin wine list. Main courses encompass grilled fillet steak and a selection of veg-etarian alternatives, while desserts include lemon and lime soufflé.

✉ Ripley Castle Estate HG3 3AY ☎ 01423 771888 ⏰ 12–2, 7–9.30 ♿ L £15, D £30, Wine £12.95 🚗 On A61 Harrogate–Ripley road, in village centre

HOTEL DU VIN & BISTRO

www.hotelduvin.com

The hotel was created from a row of eight Georgian town houses overlooking the 200-acre (80ha) common, The Stray. It has operated as a hotel since the 1930s and Hotel du Vin Harrogate offers a luxurious experience. Both food and wine are very important here, and the bistro menu changes daily. Classic dishes are featured, supporting the HdV philosophy of quality food cooked simply, using the freshest of local ingredients. Kick off with seared scallops with celeriac purée, Cox's apple and parsnip crisps, followed by a main course of roast rabbit loin with tagliatelle, broad beans, girolle mushrooms and Pommery mustard and tarragon velouté. In summer you can dine outside in the courtyard.

✉ Prospect Place, HG1 1LB ☎ 01423 856800 ⏰ 12–2, 6.30–10 ♿ L £15.50, D £35 🚗 From A1 follow signs for Harrogate & town centre. Take 3rd exit on Prince of Wales rdbt (marked town centre). Hotel is 400yds (365m) on right

HAWORTH

WEAVERS RESTAURANT

www.weaversmallhotel.co.uk

Occupying three village cottages is this restaurant serving traditional but Modern British food in this famous literary town (▷ 309). The à la carte and blackboard menus typically might include lamb shank, poached chicken breast or griddled fillets of Dales-bred beef. Vegetarian options are available, and alongside the desserts is an excellent cheese selection.

✉ 15 West Lane BD22 8DU ☎ 01535 643822 ⏰ 11.30–2.30, 6.30–9.30; closed L Tue and Sat, D Sun, Mon ♿ L £13.50, D £16.50, Wine £13.50 🚗 From A629 take B6142 to Haworth centre by Brontë Museum parking area

HELMSLEY
STAR INN
www.thestararharome.co.uk
Unpretentious, hearty British food cooked with great skill from fine fresh ingredients (much of it home-grown or produced locally to order) is the winning formula here. The thatched 14th-century restaurant/pub off the tourist track serves the same food in a small bar and cosy dining room, each with open fires. A refreshing degree of simplicity is evident in the North Sea fish pie or the pan-roast lamb.
✉ Harome, Helmsley YO6 5JE ☎ 01439 770397 ◷ 11.30–3, 6.30–11, D Tue–Sun; closed two weeks Jan ✋ L £25, D £35, Wine £13 ⬛ From Helmsley take A170 towards Kirkbymoorside. After 1.5 miles (2.5km) turn right towards Harome. After another 1.5 miles (2.5km) Star Inn is first building on right

ILKLEY
BOX TREE RESTAURANT
www.theboxtree.co.uk
The old stone farmhouse has for 300 years stood in this part of Yorkshire, first making its mark as a serious restaurant in 1962. The current incumbents, Simon and Rena Gueller, are clearly respectful of the past while taking the restaurant forward. Service is highly professional and, while a touch old school, the atmosphere is friendly and unstuffy. The wine list has something for everyone and the sommelier is on hand if needed.
✉ 35–37 Church Street, LS29 9DR ☎ 01943 608484 ◷ Tue–Sun 12–2, 7–9.30; closed Mon, L Tue–Thu, D Sun, 27–31 Dec, 1–5 Jan ✋ L £20, D £50, Wine £22 ⬛ On A65 from Leeds through Ilkley, main lights approx. 200 yds (180m) on left

KESWICK
THE HORSE AND FARRIER INN
Popular with fell walkers, this 300-year-old stone inn has traditional bars and dining room. Imaginative dinners include chicken breast with mushroom, bacon and sherry cream sauce on herb risotto. Food is also served on the patio.
✉ Threlkeld Village CA12 4SQ ☎ 01768 779688 ◷ Mon–Sat 11–11, Sun 12–10.30 ✋ L £13, D £20, Wine £9.95 ⬛ Telephone for directions

LANGHO
NORTHCOTE MANOR
www.northcotemanor.com
Built in the 1870s for a wealthy Victorian textile mill owner, today Northcote Manor is a gastronomic haven that continues to go from strength to strength, its famous kitchen twice producing the Young Chef of the Year. Contemporary in style with a modern minimalist feel, high quality lighting and eye-catching local modern art, the restaurant is a light-and-airy, spacious affair with a conservatory front that enjoys excellent views of chef-patron Nigel Haworth's organic garden and the distant hills of the Ribble Valley through its bay windows. Crisp white linen, a wine list of some 450 bins and service with a formal air of professionalism all play their part at this foodie destination. Nigel creates an enticing repertoire which has its roots firmly in Lancashire, making the most of the North West's abundant local larder to create dishes of true terroir. The cooking is intelligently simple and exudes high technique. Roast halibut with Shorrocks cheese fondue, tempura cauliflower and bacon makes a fine starter, followed by a superb main course of breast of corn-fed Gossnargh chicken with Périgord truffles, Jerusalem artichoke, puréed spinach and white leek fritter.
✉ Northcote Road BB6 8BE ☎ 01254 240555 ◷ Daily 12–2, 7–9.30, closed 25 Dec, 1 Jan ✋ L £17.50, D £40 ⬛ Directions M6 junction 31 take A59, follow signs for Clitheroe. Left at 1st traffic light, on to Skipton/Clitheroe Road for 9m (14km). Left into Northcote Road, hotel on right

LEEDS
BRASSERIE FORTY 4
This riverside restaurant in a converted grain store attracts interest in its slick, contemporary Mediterranean menus. Busy and buzzy Forty 4 attracts loyal legions of foodies, but the lunchtime menu also provides a budget option for shoppers. There's a growing global influence on the food as spicy chicken in a mango salsa vie with fillet of Yorkshire beef. Early-bird menus offer very good value.
✉ 44 The Calls LS2 7EW ☎ 0113 2343232 ◷ 12–2, 6–10; closed Sun ✋ L £13.50, D £19.95, Wine £12.25 ⬛ From Crown Point Bridge turn left past church and left into High Court Road; on river ⬛ Leeds

LIVERPOOL
SIMPLY HEATHCOTES
www.heathcotes.co.uk
Opposite Liverpool's pier head is this stylish and sophisticated, minimalist designer eaterie serving Modern British cuisine with plenty of twists and specialities from the north of England. Typical dishes might include a starter of potted Morecambe Bay shrimps with chilli and mace followed by a main course of slow-cooked pork belly with freshwater crayfish, pea purée and red-wine vinegar. Vegetarian options are available.
✉ Beetham Plaza, 25 The Strand L2 0XL ☎ 0151 2363536 ◷ 12–2.30, 7–10; closed 25–26 Dec, 1–2 Jan ✋ L £15.50, D £18, Wine £14.95 ⬛ Opposite pier head

MANCHESTER
GRADO
www.heathcotes.co.uk
This Spanish-style eatery in the heart of Manchester is owned by the Heathcotes restaurant group, which also owns Simply Heathcotes (above). The menus are pleasingly authentic: Duck with figs and honey roast chicory and aged Jerez vinegar, braised rabbit with rioja prunes, sage, pine nuts and bomba rice, spatchcock chicken, roasted over charcoal. There's a daily roast and unlike actual Spain, you'll find a vegetarian option.
New York Street, Piccadilly, Manchester M1 4BD ☎ 0161 238 9790 ◷ 11.30–2, 5–11 (Tapas bar 11–11) ✋ L £16.50, D £22, Wine £13.95 ⬛ Manchester Piccadilly

MASHAM
VENNELL'S

www.vennellsrestaurant.co.uk
The decor in this Grade II, listed, shop front-style restaurant, which overlooks the main street through the village, is traditional and comes in muted shades of beige, while plenty of artwork adorns the walls. There's a snug-style lounge downstairs to peruse the sensibly concise, appealing, classically-inspired menus and, while wife Laura runs front of house with relaxed informality, chef-patron Jon (who worked for many years at Haley's Hotel in Leeds) is at the stove. Quality local ingredients and assured skill are evident throughout the menu; think home-smoked salmon, followed by hare saddle and ravioli with beetroot purée and wild mushrooms. Finish with a trio of passionfruit desserts: a soufflé, sorbet and posset.
✉ 7 Silver Street, HG4 4DX ☎ 01765 689000 ◷ 12–2, 7.15–9.15, closed Mon, L Tue–Thu, D Sun; 26–29 Dec, 1–14 Jan, 1 week Sep, public holidays 🍴 L £16.95, Telephone for prices 🚗 Telephone for directions

NEWCASTLE UPON TYNE
CAFÉ 21

This stylish eatery with French café service is located underneath the Tyne Bridge. Blackboards list the day's menu of French bistro food with healthy British and Asian over-tones. It is busy day and night offering fishcakes with buttered spinach, parsley cream and chips, or baked fillet of pork with sage and onion mousse and black pudding fritters.
✉ Queen Street, Newcastle Quayside NE1 3UG ☎ 0191 2220755 ◷ 12–2.30, 6–10.30; closed Christmas 🍴 L £14, D £16.50, Wine £13 🚗 Telephone for directions

PICKERING
FOX AND HOUNDS COUNTRY INN

www.thefoxandhoundsinn.co.uk
It always inspires confidence to see a restaurant that is used by local people for both eating and

drinking. The welcoming atmosphere of the bar extends into the more formal dining area, where you can experience not just good, hearty cooking (including vegetarian options), but also some delicate intricacies of flavours and styles. Modern and traditional British dishes are side by side on this menu.
✉ Main Street, Sinnington, York YO62 6SQ ☎ 01751 431577 ◷ 12–2, 6.30–9; closed 25–26 Dec 🍴 L £15, D £20, £11.75 🚗 In centre of Sinnington, 274m (900ft) off A170 between Pickering and Helmsley

ROCHDALE
NUTTERS

www.nuttersrestaurant.com
Housed in a 19th-century manor in over six acres (2.5ha) of groomed parkland, this high-ceilinged restaurant has superb Gothic arches that add a sense of theatre to the overall dining experience. Overlooking Ashworth Moor, the restaurant offers formal dining but with a relaxed feel. Impressive, top-notch Modern British cuisine is served, conjured from the finest local and regional produce. Ham hock and foie gras roulade is served with brioche crisps to start, while mains range from caramelised Goosnargh duck breast with ginger and garlic roasted sweet potato with pak choi, to seared sea bass with a basil and flat leaf mousse with potato splinters and lemon and tomato butter. Gourmet menu and afternoon teas also available.
✉ Edenfield Road, Norden, OL12 7TT ☎ 01706 650167 ◷ 12–2, 6.30–9.30; closed Mon, 1–2 days after Christmas and New Year 🍴 L £12.95, D £30 🚗 From Rochdale take A680 signed Blackburn. Nutters is on Edenfield Road.

ROMALDKIRK
ROSE AND CROWN

www.rose-and-crown.co.uk
On the village green, overlooking the old stocks and water pump, this ivy-clad pub is relaxed but hides a surprising degree of sophistication inside. You can eat informally in the brasserie and bar or head for starched-linen elegance in the restaurant. Whichever you choose,

you can expect award-winning food from menus that might include pan-fried local game, roasted Teesdale lamb or fish, well-kept ale and a good selection of wines. There are also 12 en-suite rooms to tempt you to stay the night.
✉ Romaldkirk, Barnard Castle DL12 9EB ☎ 01833 650213 ◷ 11.30–3, 5.30–11, food served 12–1.30, 6.30–9.30 🍴 L £10, D £18.75 🚗 6 miles (10km) north west of Barnard Castle on B6277

SHEFFIELD
THE FAT CAT

This consistently top-rated pub is a place of quiet relaxation free from music and slot machines, with good home-cooked food and fine beers. The food always includes a variety of vegetarian and gluten-free fare as well as daily specials. Typical dishes include tikka mushrooms with rice and nutty parsnip pie, followed by jam roly-poly.
✉ 23 Alma Street S3 8SA ☎ 0114 2494801 ◷ Mon–Sat 12–3, 5.30–11, Sun 12–3, 7–10.30; closed 25–26 Dec 🍴 L £3.50, D £3.50, Wine £8.20 🚗 Sheffield

WEST WITTON
WENSLEYDALE HEIFER

www.wensleydaleheifer.co.uk
You might not expect to find a great seafood restaurant in the Yorkshire Dales, but this unassuming country pub is just that. There's an informal fish bar with seagrass flooring, wooden tables and rattan chairs, and a contemporary-styled restaurant—all chocolate and linen. favourites from the a la carte might include thick roast Whitby cod, goat's cheese, Parma ham, tomato fondue, basil pesto and spring onion mash or Atlantic halibut, salmon and tiger prawn curry, roast aubergine and French beans, coconut cream, cardamom rice and cucumber salad, but they also do fish and chips and meat dishes.
✉ West Witton, Leyburn DL8 4LS ☎ 01969 622322 ◷ 12–2.30, 6–9.30 🍴 L £14, D £16.50, Wine £13.50 🚗 On A684, 3 miles (5km) west of Leyburn

Right *The Abbey steps, Whitby*

WHITBY

ESTBEK HOUSE

www.estbekhouse.co.uk

In a hamlet just a mile or so up the coast from Whitby, Estbek House is a restaurant with rooms. In summer you can sit outside in the cobbled courtyard, or upstairs in the rather chic dining room. Expect a lot of local fish on the menu, but it's not the only thing they do well here—the fillet steak and mushroom basket is popular, and the pinenut and wild mushroom ravioli should console vegetarians. For dessert look for the stem ginger trifle with homegrown rhubarb.

✉ East Row, Sandsend YO21 3SU
☎ 01947 893424 🕐 6–9 🖐 D £25.85, Wine £16.50 🚗 From Whitby follow A174 towards Sandsend; Estbek is just before bridge.

WINDERMERE

HOLBECK GHYLL

www.holbeckghyll.com

Dining is an integral part of the experience at this hotel overlooking Windermere and the Langdale Fells. Both the formal and traditional restaurant and the more contemporary terrace provide diners with stunning views. The latter has French doors which open out on to a heated patio. Food is a mixture of classic French and English cooked with skill and precision to create fresh, unfussy dishes with an intense clarity of flavours. Start with roast quail with creamed baby leeks and black pudding tortellini, followed by roasted brill with apple, potato, celery and sider foam. Meals are served in a professional manner but without stuffiness. An extensive wine list includes some serious French and Italian heavyweights. A jacket and tie is preferred in the restaurant. No children under eight.

✉ Holbeck Lane LA23 1LU ☎ 01539 432375 🕐 12.30–2, 7–9.30; closed 5–25 Jan 🖐 L £22.50, D £49, Wine £19.50
🚗 3 miles (5km) north of Windermere on A591, turn right into Holbeck Lane

THE SAMLING

www.thesamling.com

Tucked away in a 27ha (67-acre) estate of woodland, meadow and landscaped garden, the Samling is a chic oasis of contemporary cuisine above one of England's loveliest lakes. The ambitious menus ooze creativity with the occasional slice of traditional French cooking. The three-course fixed-price menu is a good place to start, but aspiring gourmets will enjoy the eight-course extravaganza.

✉ Ambleside Road, LA23 1LR ☎ 015394 31922 🕐 12.30–2, 7–10 🖐 L £55, D £55, Wine £30 🚗 On A591 towards Ambleside, first right after Low Wood Hotel, 2 miles (3.2km) from Windermere town.

YORK

BLUE BICYCLE

www.thebluebicycle.com

A popular city-centre bistro, the Blue Bicycle caters for locals and tourist alike. They come for the Modern European menu, which features local fish and game in season as well as tasty vegetarian choices such as borlotti bean and leek pie with goat's cheese mash and a vegetarian gravy. There's tasteful accommodation available, too, if you fancy making a night of it.

✉ 34 Fossgate, York YO1 9TA ☎ 01904 673990 🕐 12–2.30, 6–9.30 (Sun 9) 🖐 L £13.50, D £30, Wine £12.50 🚗 Just off Parliament Street 🅿 York

MELTON'S RESTAURANT

www.meltonsrestaurant.co.uk

The Modern British cooking at this inviting shopfronted restaurant has influences from Europe, Asia and North America—smoked haddock with sorrel pesto, corn-fed chicken breast with saffron risotto—from the à la carte or set-price lunch/early evening menu. It is a family-run establishment (rather than part of an impersonal chain). Details are impressive, from the varied canapés to the home-made cheese biscuits, and the warm service shows pride in the food.

✉ 7 Scarcroft Road YO23 1ND ☎ 01904 634341 🕐 12–2, 5.30–10; closed L Mon, Sun, 3 weeks at Christmas, 1 week in Aug 🖐 L £17.50, D £24.50, Wine £15 🚗 South from city centre across Skeldergate Bridge, opposite Bishopthorpe Road parking area

STAYING

Above *Lake District National Park*

PRICES AND SYMBOLS

Prices are the starting price for a double room for one night, unless otherwise stated. Breakfast is included unless noted otherwise. All the hotels listed accept credit cards unless otherwise stated. Note that rates vary widely throughout the year.

For a key to the symbols, ▷ 2.

ALTRINCHAM

ASH FARM COUNTRY HOUSE

www.ashfarm.co.uk

This 18th-century farmhouse bed-and-breakfast is peacefully located on a country lane. The bedrooms boast handmade furniture. The many personal touches include homemade biscuits, fresh fruit, bathrobes and hot-water bottles for cooler nights. There is a large lounge and separate breakfast area with beautiful views over the Cheshire countryside. No children under 12 or dogs.

🕙 Park Lane, Little Bollington WA14 4TJ 🕾 0161 9299290 🕙 Closed 5 Jan–15 Jan 🛏 £78 🛈 3 🚗 Turn off A56 beside Stamford Arms

BAMBURGH

VICTORIA HOTEL

www.victoriahotel.net

In the centre of town overlooking the village green, this hotel has been sympathetically upgraded and offers an interesting blend of tradition and modernity. The bedrooms, some with views to Bamburgh Castle and Holy Island, are elegantly furnished. The bar is popular with locals. There's also a restaurant.

🕙 Front Street NE69 7BP 🕾 01668 214431 🛏 £90 🛈 29 🚗 Off A1 north of Alnwick turn on to B1342 near Belford and then follow signs to Bamburgh 🚉 Chathill

BOLTON ABBEY

DEVONSHIRE ARMS COUNTRY HOUSE HOTEL

This beautiful hotel dates back to the 17th century and has the feel of a country house. There are log fires in the sitting rooms and the rooms in the older part of the house have four-poster beds. There is an excellent restaurant (▷ 349).

🕙 Bolton Abbey BD23 6AJ 🕾 01756 710441 🛏 £235 🛈 40 🚗 On B6160 to Bolton Abbey 230m (250 yards) north of junction with A59 roundabout junction 🚉 Ilkley 5 miles (7km)

CATLOWDY

BESSIESTOWN FARM

www.bessiestown.co.uk

This delightful farmhouse is a useful place to break a journey to or from Scotland. Bedrooms are stylish and

include family rooms and a luxury suite with spa bath. There's also an indoor swimming pool. Freshly prepared dinners and hearty breakfasts with home-made bread set travellers up for the day. No dogs.
🌐 Catlowdy CA6 5QP ☎ 01228 577219 🛏 £78 🛈 5 🚗 From Bush Hotel in Longtown, 6.5 miles (10km) to Bridge Inn, turn right onto B6318, 1.5 miles (2km) to Catlowdy, farm first left

CHESTER
MACDONALD NEW BLOSSOMS
www.macdonald-hotels.co.uk
Right in the heart of this historic city, just a few paces from the pedestrianised centre, New Blossoms has a venerable history and has retained some of its Victorian-era features in the public rooms. Bedrooms are well appointed with internet access and flat-screen TVs, and many have evocative views across the city's rooftops. The Snooty Fox restaurant is open all day, and there is also a bar menu for less formal eating.
✉ St. John Street, Chester CH1 1HL ☎ 01244 323186 🛏 £90 🛈 67 🚗 M53 Junction 12 follow city centre signs for Eastgate, continue through pedestrianised zone, hotel on left

CONISTON
CONISTON LODGE
www.coniston-lodge.com
Coniston Lodge bed-and-breakfast is ideally situated for exploring the Lake District. All bedrooms are attractively decorated. Cooking may include homemade pâté, local game and fish, can be sampled in the dining room. No dogs.
🌐 Station Road LA21 8HH ☎ 01539 441201 🛏 £107 🛈 6 🚗 At crossroads on A593 close to filling station; turn uphill at crossroads into Station Road 🚉 Windermere

DURHAM
KINGSLODGE HOTEL AND RESTAURANT
www.kingslodge.info.co.uk
With the illusion of a secluded setting, this stylish modern hotel is popular with both business and leisure guests. Accommodation is

provided in compact but well-designed rooms. For meals, Knights is a contemporary restaurant and champagne bar, and there is also a less formal bar and beer terrace, and a bright and comfortable lounge.
🌐 Flass Vale DH1 4BG ☎ 0191 3709977 🛏 £110 🛈 21 🚗 A1 junction 62 over first three roundabouts, then right at fourth. Take first left then first right; hotel is at end of road 🚉 Durham

GRASSINGTON
ASHFIELD HOUSE HOTEL
www.ashfieldhouse.co.uk
Guests are greeted like old friends at this beautifully maintained 17th-century house, peacefully tucked away a few paces from the village square. The bedrooms of this luxury bed-and-breakfast are attractively decorated. The smart lounges offer a high level of comfort where guests can relax or enjoy pre-dinner drinks from an honesty bar. A freshly prepared four-course dinner is available by arrangement (except Saturday). No children under 12. No dogs.
🌐 Summers Fold, Grassington, Skipton BD23 5AE ☎ 01756 752584 🛏 £90 🛈 8 🚗 Take B6265 to village centre then turn left off Main Street into Summers Fold 🚉 Skipton

HARROGATE
ALEXA HOUSE & STABLES COTTAGES
www.alexa-house.co.uk
With rooms divided between the main house and the former stables, this is a popular guest house on the edge of the town. The proprietors are attentive and the facilities reach high standards, so there is a loyal clientele. Public rooms make good use of natural light, giving them a bright and spacious feel.
🌐 26 Ripon Road, Harrogate HG1 2JJ ☎ 01423 501988 🛏 £85 🛈 13 🚗 On A61 0.25 miles (0.4km) from junction with A59

HAWKSHEAD
QUEEN'S HEAD HOTEL
In this prettiest of Lakeland villages, the Queen's Head pub doesn't spoil the show. The 16th-century building

stands in Hawkshead's traffic-free centre, festooned with hanging baskets and window boxes. The interior has bare beams, a real fire and plenty of curios. Bedrooms are decorated in a country style.
🌐 Main Street LA22 0NS ☎ 01539 436271 🛏 £75 🛈 14 🚗 A590 to Newby Bridge, take first right to Hawkshead

HAWORTH
OLD WHITE LION HOTEL
www.oldwhitelionhotel.com
Over 300 years old and steeped in history, this delightful hotel is at the top of an old cobbled street, just 0.5 miles (800m) from Haworth station on the Worth Valley railway. There is an oak-panelled lounge and a choice of homey bars serving a range of meals. Formal dining is available in the popular restaurant. The comfortably furnished bedrooms are well equipped and vary in size and style.
🌐 Main Street, Haworth, Keighley BD22 8DU ☎ 01535 642313 🛏 £79.50 🛈 15 🚗 Turn off A629 on to B6142 into Haworth 🚉 Haworth, Keighley

HELMSLEY
FEVERSHAM ARMS HOTEL
www.fevershamarmshotel.com
The bedrooms in this comfortable hotel are furnished to a high standard and there is a comprehensively equipped leisure centre with a gym. Tennis courts and a heated swimming pool can be found in the pleasant grounds. Diners have a choice of formal or informal styles of eating, and menus offer a wide choice.
🌐 1 High Street YO62 5AG ☎ 01439 770766 🛏 £135 🛈 24 🛉 🚗 From junction 49 of A1 take A168 to Thirsk then A170 to Helmsley. From York take B1363 north, turn left on to B1257 and then A170. Hotel is 125m (140 yds) from Market Place 🚉 Malton

ISLE OF MAN
DREEM ARD
This quiet B&B to the north of Douglas was joint winner of Visit Britain's Best Small Hotel on the Isle of Man in 2007. The spacious rooms are well equipped and the hosts are genuinely hospitable. Convivial and

informal meals are served around a big table and there are fine views across the surrounding countryside.

🅖 Ballanard Road, Douglas IM2 5PR ☎ 01624 621491 💷 £59 🛈 3 🅿 From St. Ninian's Church, along Ballanard Road for 1 mile (1.6km), over Johnny Wattersons Lane crossroads, past farm on left Dreem Ard on left.

KESWICK
DERWENTWATER HOTEL
www.derwentwater-hotel.co.uk
This is a popular and friendly holiday hotel with gardens that stretch down to the shores of Derwentwater. Some of the bedrooms have good views of the lake. Inviting public areas include a conservatory, lounge and shop, and a restaurant. Outdoor facilities include a croquet lawn and putting green, private fishing, and access to local leisure facilities, including free use of a nearby health spa.

✉ Portinscale CA12 5RE ☎ 01768 772538 💷 £160 🛈 46 🅿 Off A66 turn into Portinscale and through village then when road turns right take left turn as signposted 🅿 Penrith

LEEDS
MALMAISON HOTEL
www.malmaison.com
Close to the waterfront, this stylish property offers striking air-conditioned bedrooms. The bar leads into a brasserie, where guests can choose between a full three-course meal or a substantial snack. Service is both enthusiastic and friendly. A small fitness centre and impressive meeting rooms complete the package.

✉ Sovereign Quay LS1 1DQ ☎ 0113 3981000 💷 £99 🛈 100 🅿 From M621/M1 junction 3 follow signs to Leeds city centre. At KPMG building turn right into Sovereign Street; Malmaison is at end of street on right 🅿 Leeds City

LIVERPOOL
LIVERPOOL MARRIOTT HOTEL CITY CENTRE
www.marriott.co.uk
The Marriott is a large, impressive modern hotel located in the heart of

the city. The elegant public rooms include a café bar, cocktail bar and Oliver's Restaurant, for dining in stylish surroundings. The bedrooms benefit from many facilities. The hotel also has a well-equipped health club with heated indoor pool, plus sauna, solarium and Jacuzzi.

✉ 1 Queen Square L1 1RH ☎ 0151 476 8000 💷 £99 🛈 146 🅿 From city centre follow signs for Queen Square parking, hotel is adjacent 🅿 Liverpool Lime Street

MANCHESTER
THE LOWRY HOTEL
www.thelowryhotel.com
This superbly located hotel is part of the Chapel Wharf development on the banks of the River Irwell, and this forms the backdrop for the hotel. The decorative style throughout is contemporary, with good use made of light and space to create an environment that is modern yet welcoming. The River Room restaurant is justly renowned. Facilities include a sauna and gym, with spa and swimming pool available offsite.

✉ 50 Dearmans Place, Chapel Wharf, Salford M3 5LH ☎ 0161 827 4000 💷 £125 🛈 165 🅿 Manchester Piccadilly or Victoria

MALMAISON
www.malmaison.com
Even more chic and stylish following substantial building work, the well-presented Malmaison now offers extra comfort, including some additional air-conditioned bedrooms. Good meals are served in the busy brasserie, and other facilities include a small but exclusive spa, plus sauna, solarium, Jacuzzi and gym.

✉ Piccadilly M1 3AQ ☎ 0161 2781000 💷 £99 🛈 167 🅿 Follow city centre signs then signs to Piccadilly station to find hotel opposite at bottom of station approach 🅿 Manchester Piccadilly

MASHAM
SWINTON PARK
www.swintonpark.com
The original part of this imposing castle dates from the 17th century,

and it was extended during the Victorian and Edwardian eras. The bedrooms are tastefully furnished and come with features such as CD players, and there is also a gym and Jacuzzi. Samuel's restaurant uses local produce, much of it from the Swinton estate. A superb range of activities and outdoor facilities includes private fishing, croquet, putting, shooting, falconry and horseback riding. There's also a golf course nearby.

✉ Masham, Ripon HG4 4JH ☎ 01765 680900 💷 £160; discount for under-12s 🛈 30 🅿 Turn off A1 left (west) on to B6267 to Masham. Follow signs through Masham town centre and turn right on to Swinton Terrace. Follow road 1 mile (1.6km) over bridge and up hill. Swinton Park is on right 🅿 Northallerton

MORECAMBE
CLARENDON HOTEL
www.mitchellshotels.co.uk
This well-maintained seafront hotel has been completely refurbished to offer bright, cheerful public areas and smartly appointed bedrooms, all with fully tiled bathrooms. Its position offers fine views over Morecambe Bay and the mountains of the Lake District beyond. There is a restaurant, and afternoon teas and bar meals are also available. The popular Davy Jones Locker bar is in the cellar.

✉ 76 Marine Road West, West End Promenade LA4 4EP ☎ 01524 410180 💷 £90 🛈 29 🅿 From M6 junction 34 follow Morecambe signs. At roundabout with The Shrimp on corner take first exit to Westgate and follow to waterfront. Turn right at traffic lights and hotel is third block along Central Promenade 🅿 Morecambe

NEWCASTLE UPON TYNE
MALMAISON QUAYSIDE
www.malmaison.com
Overlooking the river and the new Millennium Bridge, this hotel has a prime position in the new up-and-coming redeveloped quayside district. Bedrooms are spacious and contemporary in style, offering large beds, music and communications systems as standard. Public areas

include spa, sauna, solarium and gym facilities, some meeting rooms and the popular riverside brasserie. ✉ Newcastle upon Tyne NE1 3DX ☎ 0191 245 5000 🍴 £99 🛏 120 ▽ 🚇 Follow signs for Newcastle city centre and take road for Quayside/Law Courts. Hotel is 100m (110yds) past Law Courts 🚉 Newcastle Central

ROSEDALE ABBEY
THE MILBURN ARMS HOTEL
www.milburnarms.co.uk
Hidden deep in the folds of the North York Moors National Park, this charming country-house hotel acts as a perfect retreat from the modern world. Dating back to 1776, the family-run hotel offers 13 beautifully furnished bedrooms with a welcoming bar and log fires in the public rooms. The hotel's Priory restaurant is well regarded. ✉ Rosedale Abbey, Pickering YO18 8RA ☎ 01751 417312 ⊘ Closed 25 Dec 🍴 £90 🛏 13 🚇 A170 west from Pickering, right at Rosedale sign then 7 miles (11km) north

SCARBOROUGH
OX PASTURE HALL COUNTRY HOTEL
www.bw-oxpasturehall.co.uk
This delightful country hotel is a lovely conversion of a farmhouse, set in the North Riding Forest Park. Six of the bedrooms are in the main house and the others around an attractive garden courtyard. Public areas include a split-level bar, a quiet lounge and attractive restaurant offering à la carte and fixed-price menus. Outside is a croquet lawn and putting green. Fishing available. ✉ Lady Ediths Drive, Raincliffe Woods YO12 5TD ☎ 01723 365295 🍴 £112; discount for under-12s 🛏 24 🚇 Take A171 out of Scarborough. After passing hospital follow tourist sign for Forge Valley and Raincliffe Woods. Turn left and hotel is 1.5 miles (2.5km) on right 🚉 Scarborough

WHITBY
ESTBEK HOUSE
www.estbekhouse.co.uk
In a tiny fishing village north of Whitby, this lovely restaurant with

rooms, has four individually styled bedrooms for you to retire to after dinner. Each room has a different character, and on the second floor the exposed former ship's timbers of the roof are exposed. ✉ East Row, Sandsend YO21 3SU ☎ 01947 893424 🍴 £90 🛏 4 🚇 On Cleveland Way, next to East Beck

WINDERMERE
CEDAR MANOR COUNTRY LODGE
This neat hotel is set in large gardens on the edge of town. Some of the bedrooms are in a former coach house, all are smartly presented and have private bathrooms. Public areas include a lounge and split-level breakfast room. ✉ Ambleside Road LA23 1AX ☎ 015394 43192 🍴 £92 🛏 9 🚇 From M6 junction 36 stay on A591 beyond Windermere turning, hotel is on left past St. Mary's Church

YORK
ALEXANDER HOUSE
www.alexanderhouseyork.co.uk
Guests are made to feel very much at home at this Victorian terraced house, just a short walk from the city centre. The owners of this stylish bed-and-breakfast delight in sharing their home with guests, and have created four superbly equipped rooms. Delicious breakfasts featuring quality local produce are served in the well-appointed dining room. No children under 12. ✉ 94 Bishopthorpe Road YO23 1JS ☎ 01904 625016 ⊘ Closed 25 Dec–1 Jan 🍴 £65 🛏 4 🚇 From A64 take A1036 York road west into city centre. Turn right at Scarcroft Road, at the end turn right and Alexander House is 100m (110yds) on left 🚉 York

THE GRANGE HOTEL
www.grangehotel.co.uk
This bustling Regency town house is conveniently placed. The bedrooms have been thoughtfully equipped, and the public rooms are comfortable and stylish. There are three dining options—a seafood bar,

The Brasserie in the cellar, which has an informal atmosphere, and The Ivy, which is lavishly decorated and offers a fine dining menu. ✉ 1 Clifton, York YO30 6AA ☎ 01904 644744 🍴 £139 🛏 30 🚇 On A19 York–Thirsk road about 500m (550 yds) from city centre 🚉 York

HAZELWOOD
www.thehazelwoodyork.com
The Hazelwood bed-and-breakfast is an elegant Victorian town house quietly situated in the heart of the ancient city, only 350m (400 yards) from York Minster. The bedrooms are individually styled and tastefully fitted to very high standards using designer fabrics. There's a wide choice of breakfasts. No children under eight. No dogs. ✉ 24–25 Portland Street, Gillygate YO31 7EH ☎ Tel: 01904 626548 🍴 £75 🛏 14 🚇 Approaching York from north on A19 turn left before City Gate and take first turning left 🚉 York

YORK
LINTHWAITE HOUSE HOTEL AND RESTAURANT
www.inthwaite.com
Linthwaite House is set in 6ha (14 acres) of hilltop grounds that include its own fishing tarn, and enjoys stunning views of Windermere lake—particularly from its bright, attractive conservatory. Other public rooms include a comfortable lounge, a smokers' bar and a restaurant serving carefully prepared meals. The bedrooms, which are individually decorated in both contemporary and traditional styles, are thoughtfully equipped. Service and hospitality are real strengths at this hotel. There's also a croquet lawn, putting green, private fishing and free use of the nearby leisure spa. ✉ Crook Road, Windermere LA23 3JA ☎ 01539 488600 🍴 £99; discount for under-12s 🛏 26 🚇 Take A591 towards the lakes for 8 miles (13km) to large roundabout. Take first exit (B5284) and continue for 6 miles (10km). Hotel is on left, 1 mile (1.6km) past Windermere golf club 🚉 Windermere

SIGHTS 360
WALKS AND DRIVES 386
WHAT TO DO 394
EATING 400
STAYING 406

SCOTLAND

A nation in its own right, Scotland has successfully redefined itself since devolution restored its parliament in 1999. It's hard not to see it as a country of two cities. In the east, the capital Edinburgh has the graceful curves of its Georgian New Town and the intriguing streets surrounding its celebrated Royal Mile, leading up to the Royal Palace and parliament building at Holyrood. In the west, Glasgow's image is far more gritty based on its heritage as the industrial powerhouse of the British Empire. Even the city's architects went their own way, producing the distinctive styles of Alexander 'Greek' Thomson and Charles Rennie Mackintosh. Both cities boast nationally important museums and galleries and a thriving nightlife. The capital also holds the great Edinburgh Festival, one of the largest arts festivals in the world.

But for many, Scotland is not about cities, it's about stunning scenery. The Highlands rise from banks of the Clyde on the very edge of Glasgow, their glens and mountains stretching far to the north. From their western seaboard, the Inner and Outer Hebrides spill, a complex pattern of islands and peninsulas as beautiful and wild as any in Europe. The Gaelic culture of this remote region spread its fame far across the world, but there is something very special about seeing the strongholds of the original MacDonalds, as well as the many other clan names that once made the Highlands a place to be feared and subjugated. To the far north, beyond John O'Groats, the Orkney and Shetland islands have a different cultural heritage again. Amid place names more Norse than Gaelic you'll find remains of the earliest northern European cultures, their stone monuments predating even those of the Celts.

ABBOTSFORD

www.scottsabbotsford.co.uk

This delightful, overblown, turreted grey mansion is a must for an insight into the eclectic mind of the writer Sir Walter Scott (1771–1832), best known for epic romantic poems such as *The Lady of the Lake* (1810) and novels including *Ivanhoe* (1819).

He built Abbotsford in 1812 on the banks of the River Tweed, 3km (2 miles) west of Melrose, and it is filled with historical curiosities, some of which are built into the fabric of the house. Take a look at the great man's library, the gracious dining room, whose windows look down to the river, and the bristling armoury, its walls covered with guns, knives and other weapons. The overall effect is one of mock, almost theatrical, antiquity—a distillation of the ambience of his novels.

✚ 467 G9 ✉ Melrose TD6 9BQ ☎ 01896 752043 🕐 Easter–end May, Oct Mon–Sat 9.30–5, Sun 2–5; Jun–end Sep daily 9.30–5 💷 Adult £6.20, child £3.10, under 8s free 🅿 🏛

ABERDEEN

www.agtb.org

Scotland's third city was once its biggest seaside resort, thanks to the miles of golden sands which stretch north from the mouth of the River Don. Today Aberdeen has a businesslike air and is better known as the oil capital of Europe. Its foundations as a royal burgh date back to the early 12th century, and it grew into a major port for access to the Continent, trading in wool, fish and scholars from its two universities. In fact, the harbour is still the heart of the city. In the late 18th century, the town expanded, and many of Aberdeen's finest granite buildings in the New Town date from the 19th century. Architect Archibald Simpson (1790–1847) is associated with many, including the Union Buildings and Assembly Rooms Music Hall on Union Street.

Opposite *Aberdeen is often referred to as the 'Granite City'*

Provost Ross's House (1593) houses the lively Aberdeen Maritime Museum (Mon–Sat 10–5, Sun 12–3), with an 8.5m (28ft) scale model of an oil rig. The Aberdeen Art Gallery on Schoolhill has an outstanding collection of 18th- to 20th-century paintings (Mon–Sat 10–5, Sun 2–5).

✚ 470 G6 🛈 23 Union Street AB11 5BP, tel 01224 288828 🚉 Aberdeen

ARRAN, ISLE OF

This scenic island between the Ayrshire coast and the Kintyre Peninsula has been a popular holiday resort for generations of Clydesiders. The mountain of Goat Fell (874m/2,867ft) dominates the skyline to the north, and there is plenty of opportunity for outdoor activities, including walking, golf and pony-trekking around the island. The red sandstone Brodick Castle (Castle: Apr–end Oct daily 11–4.30. Country park: all year daily 9.30–dusk) is the single biggest attraction.

✚ 466 C9 🛈 The Pier, Brodick KA27 8AU, tel 01770 302140 ⛴ Ferry from Ardrossan to Brodick or Kintyre to Lochranza (summer)

BLAIR CASTLE

www.blair-castle.co.uk

This white-turreted mansion north of Pitlochry seems the archetypal Scottish castle. It's been the ancestral home of the Murrays and Stewarts, dukes and earls of Atholl, for more than 700 years, and has its own private army, the Atholl Highlanders, thanks to a favour granted in 1845 by Queen Victoria. The Highlanders are the only remaining private army in Europe—visitors in May can see them parade under inspection of the Duke of Atholl.

The medieval castle occupied a strategic position on the main route to Inverness and was seized by Cromwell's army in 1652 (▷ 34). In more peaceful times, it was recast as a Georgian mansion by the second duke, and with the advent of the railway in 1863, a Victorian-style remodelling took place, leaving the pretty building you see today. There's lots to see inside, including

an original copy of the National Covenant and the small tartan-clad room where Bonnie Prince Charlie slept in 1745.

✚ 467 E6 ✉ Blair Atholl, Pitlochry PH18 5TL ☎ 01796 481207 🕐 Mar–end Oct daily 9.30–4.30; Nov–end Mar Tue, Sat 9.30–12.30 💷 House and grounds: adult £7.90, child £4.90 (5–16), family £20.50. Grounds only: adult £2.70, child £1.40, family £6 🚉 Blair Atholl Village 🅿 🏛

BRAEMAR AND DEESIDE

www.aberdeen-grampian.com

In 1852, when Queen Victoria and Prince Albert picked an estate between Ballater and Braemar on which to build their holiday home, the Dee Valley acquired a cachet which it has never quite lost. Members of the royal family still spend their summers at Balmoral Castle (exhibition Apr–end Jul daily 10–5).

To the east of the Cairngorms, the Dee valley offers good walking country. West of the small town of Braemar, a narrow road leads upstream to the Linn of Dee, where the river plunges down between polished rocks into foaming pools. This is part of the 29,340ha (72,500-acre) Mar Lodge Estate, managed by the National Trust for Scotland (NTS), with signposted walks. The road ends near the Earl of Mar's Punchbowl, another beauty spot, where, it is said, the earl brewed punch in a natural bowl in the rocks before the Jacobite uprising of 1715.

From Braemar, the A93 follows the course of the river as it flows east for 60 miles (96km) to the coast at Aberdeen. Ballater is a pleasing little granite-built town, once the terminus of a railway branch line. This is celebrated at the Old Royal Station, now an information centre and tea room (Jul–end Sep daily 9–6; Oct–end May 10–5) which recalls the days when famous guests would alight here on their way to Balmoral.

East lies Glen Tanar, with birch woods at the Muir of Dinnet, and good walking over the Grampian Hills to the Glens of Angus.

✚ 469–470 F6 🛈 The Mews, Mar Road, Braemar AB35 5YL, tel 01339 741600

INFORMATION

✚ 469 F6 ℹ Cairngorms National park
Authority ✉ 14 The Square, Grantown-
on-Spey PH26 3HG, tel 01479 873535

Aviemore

✚ 469 E5 ℹ Grampian Road, PH22
1RH, tel 0845 2255121 🚆 Aviemore

THE CAIRNGORMS

The highest massif in Britain, with alpine plants and rare wildlife, is a winter
playground for climbers and skiers.

The Cairngorm Mountains lie between Speyside (▷ 382) and Braemar
(▷ 361), dominated by the four peaks of Ben Macdhui (1,309m/4,295ft),
Braeriach (1,295m/4,249ft), Cairn Toul (1,293m/4,242ft) and Cairn Gorm
(1,245m/4,085ft). Between them runs the ancient north–south pass of Lairig
Ghru, and around the northwest edge are the settlements of Speyside and the
skiing resort of Aviemore. The remoteness of the Cairngorms has left them
the haunt of golden eagles, ptarmigan, capercaillie and other species that thrive
in the deserted corries amid unusual alpine plants. The area was designated
Scotland's second national park in 2003.

The once-sleepy station of Aviemore was developed in the 1960s as a ski
centre, and while some of the most brutal specimens of architecture from this
period have been demolished, it has little to recommend it unless you are part
of the ski scene. The Rothiemurchus Estate, 1.5 miles (2.5km) to the south
(daily 9–5.30), offers a variety of outdoor pursuits in a beautiful setting of mountains, lochs and Caledonian pine forest. This is the remains of the Old Wood of
Caledon that once covered much of the country, harbouring wolves and bears.

Aviemore is linked by the Strathspey Steam Railway (tel 01479 810725) to Boat
of Garten. The Royal Society for the Protection of Birds (RSPB) has a visitor complex here—a camera watches the ospreys nesting on nearby Loch Garten with
a fabulous backdrop of the ancient landscapes of Rothiemurchus. A funicular
railway in the Cairngorm ski area east of Aviemore takes visitors up Cairn Gorm
to the highest shop and restaurant in Britain (May to mid-Jun, Sep–end Nov daily
10–4; sunset dining Jun–end Aug Fri–Sat).

Above *Ben Macdui seen from Glen Lui
near Braemar, Cairngorms National Park*

CAERLAVEROCK CASTLE
www.historic-scotland.gov.uk
The remains of three huge round towers mark out the corners of this ruined, triangular castle, once the home of the Maxwell family. It is set close to the Solway shore, about 8 miles (13km) southeast of Dumfries. Two sides were protected by an arm of the sea, while the third had a moat, earthworks and a mighty gatehouse. The castle saw lots of action before extensive rebuilding during the 15th century. In the 1630s it was remodelled for more comfortable living.

✚ 464 F10 ✉ Glencaple, Dumfries DG1 4HD ☎ 01387 770244 ◉ Apr–end Sep daily 9.30–5.30; Oct–end Mar daily 9.30–4.30 ✋ Adult £5, child (5–15) £2.50 🖵 🏛

CALLANDER
www.lochlomond-trossachs.org
Callander is a bustling little town, the eastern gateway to the Trossachs (▷ 379). The architecture of its long main street reflects the town's hey-day in the late 19th century as a spa, and today it is lined with interesting shops. The surrounding area is best known as Rob Roy Country. Rob Roy Macgregor (1671–1734) was a local outlaw, whose life was celebrated and fictionalized, first by Daniel Defoe then by Sir Walter Scott. Liam Neeson played the role in the 1995 film version. Rob Roy was born at Glen Gyle and you can see his grave at nearby Balquhidder. The 79-mile (127km) Rob Roy Way is a walking trail which passes through Callandar on its way from Drymen to Pitlochry.

✚ 467 E8 ℹ Ancaster Square FK17 8ED, tel 08452 255121

CAWDOR CASTLE
www.cawdorcastle.com
The name of Cawdor has echoes of Shakespeare's *Macbeth*, and this marvellous castle does not disappoint. It stands inland, between Inverness (▷ 376) and Nairn, with a central tower dating from 1454, a drawbridge and proud turrets. It is the home of Angelika, Dowager Countess of Cawdor, and the

presentation of family portraits and treasures is refreshingly light-hearted. The influence of the owner and her late husband is most clearly seen in the gardens, which are symbolically themed. They include a holly maze surrounded by a tunnel of golden laburnum, and the mysterious Paradise Garden with a seven-pointed star at its core.

✚ 469 E5 ✉ Nairn IV12 5RD ☎ 01667 404401 ◉ Daily 10–5.30, May to mid-Oct ✋ Adult £7.90, child (5–15) £4.90, family £24. Gardens only £3.50 🍴 🏛

CRARAE GARDEN
www.nts.org.uk
This hillside garden lies on the shores of Loch Fyne, between Inveraray and Lochgilphead. It was the creation of Lady Grace Campbell and continued by her son, Sir George Campbell, who began the transformation of a narrow Highland glen into a Himalayan gorge in 1925. One of its highlights is the the Neolithic chambered cairn (c2500BC). Today the garden is cared for by the National Trust for Scotland (NTS), and has more than 400 species of rhododendron and azalea. This is primarily a woodland garden, with paths winding through eucalyptus and other trees.

✚ 466 C8 ✉ Inveraray PA32 8YA ☎ 01546 886614 ◉ Daily 9.30–dusk. Visitor centre: Apr–end Sep daily 10–5 ✋ Adult £5, child £4, family £14 🖵 🏛

CRATHES CASTLE
www.nts.org.uk
In 1323, Robert the Bruce gave a parcel of land east of Banchory to Alexander Burnard (Burnett) of Leys. In 1553 a castle was begun on the site and it is now a great example of a baronial-style tower house, famous for its Jacobean ceilings, boldly painted with figures, designs and mottoes.

While the interior of the castle presents the comfortable setting of mellow furnishings, oak-carved panels and family portraits you might expect, it is the 1.5ha (3.75-acre) walled garden glimpsed from the windows that steals the show.

Massive hedges of Irish yew topiary dominate the upper garden, and the deep herbaceous borders of the lower garden are breathtaking.

✚ 470 G6 ✉ Banchory AB31 5QJ ☎ 01330 844525 ◉ Gardens: all year daily 9–dusk. Castle and visitor centre: Apr–end Sep daily 10.30–5.30; Oct daily 10.30–4.30 ✋ Castle or gardens: adult £10, child (5–16) £7, family £25 🖵 £3.50 🍴 🏛

CULLODEN
www.nts.org.uk
The Jacobite defeat at the Battle of Culloden, fought on 16 April 1746, was the dismal outcome of a civil war that had split families and hastened the end of the clan system in Scotland.

Prince Charles Edward Stuart (1720–88), nicknamed Bonnie Prince Charlie, was brought up in European exile, the heir to the throne of Scotland, which the Catholic Stuarts still claimed through James, the Old Pretender.

Encouraged by the French, Charles landed at Glenfinnan (▷ 371) in 1745 and raised a mixed bag of Highland fighters. Initially the Prince's army was successful, and reached Derby in central England before running out of steam. The Highlanders then retreated north, but by the spring of 1746 the Hanoverian forces were closing in.

When the two armies met at Culloden, a tactical blunder placed the Prince's Highlanders within range of the government artillery, and the Jacobites were blown away in under an hour. Today memorial stones and flags show where indi-vidual clans fell on the battlefield.

The admission price includes a guide to the battlefield, but it's a good idea to watch the audio-visual exhibition in the visitor complex before exploring the battlefield.

✚ 469 E5 ✉ Culloden Moor, Inverness IV2 5EU ☎ 0844 4932159 ◉ Site: daily, all year. Visitor centre: Apr–end Oct 9–6, Nov–end Mar 10–4 ✋ Adult £10, child (5–18) £7.50, under 5 free, family £24 🖵 🍴 🏛 ❓ Audio-visual tour in French, Gaelic, German, Italian and Japanese

Left *The Town House at Culross. The ground floor was once used as a prison*
Above *The ruins of Doune Castle, Stirling*

CULROSS

Your first impression of this little town may be one of familiarity: Culross (pronounced *cure-oss*) looks like the paintings of very old Scottish burghs, with its winding, cobbled streets and crow-stepped gables. It had an early involvement in coal-mining and salt-panning, mostly through George Bruce, the town's 16th-century entrepreneur. As the local coal ran out, the emphasis on industrial activity swung to other parts of the Forth Valley and Culross became a backwater. Many of the 17th- and 18th-century houses were never replaced, so it was Culross's poverty that created the picturesque groupings admired today.

In the 1930s the National Trust for Scotland started buying up properties approaching dereliction. Decades later, many of the houses are fully restored and inhabited. Exceptional buildings, such as the ochre Culross Palace (Bruce's mansion of 1597) and the Town House (1626, where suspected witches were locked in the attic), are open to the public (Easter–end May Thu–Mon 12–5, Jun–end Sep daily 12–5). Other buildings in the town are closed.

✚ 672 E8 ℹ 1 High Street, Dunfermline KY12 7DL, tel 01383 720999

CULZEAN CASTLE AND COUNTRY PARK

www.nts.org.uk
Culzean (pronounced *cullane*) is the National Trust for Scotland's most popular property, thanks in part to the surrounding country park—228 lush green hectares (563 acres) of wild gardens and leafy woodland filled with trails.

The golden stone castle, set right at the edge of the cliffs, is handsome rather than beautiful, with its baronial towers and castellated roofline. It is reached via a bridge, and rises high above the terraced garden. Inside, it is like an 18th-century show home, the masterpiece of Scottish architect Robert Adam (1728–92), who worked on it from 1777 to 1792. Highlights include the graceful oval staircase and the Circular Saloon. The top floor was granted to US General Eisenhower in 1945, for his lifetime, as thanks from the people of Scotland for American help during World War II. You can stay in the Eisenhower apartment.

✚ 466 D9 ✉ Maybole KA19 8LE ☎ 0844 4932149 ⏰ Castle: Easter–end Oct daily 10.30–5. Country park: daily 9.30–dusk, all year 🖐 Castle and country park: adult £12, child (5–16) £8, family £30. Park only: adult £8, child £5, family £20 🍴 ▢ 🏛

DEEP SEA WORLD

www.deepseaworld.com
This mega-aquarium lies just off the north side of the Forth road bridge, and is an underwater wonderworld. The complex has one of the world's longest underwater walkways (110m/360ft), where a perspex tunnel allows visitors to share the sharks' domain without getting wet. Beware—it's quite easy to lose excited small children on the conveyor belt.

Explore the tanks full of piranhas, sharks, stingrays and deadly poisonous frogs, and get your hands wet in the rock pool area with safer creatures such as starfish. There is also a seal sanctuary. If you're over 16, and a certified diver, don't miss the chance to join a shark dive—reservation is essential.

✚ 467 F8 ✉ Battery Park, North Queensferry KY11 1JR ☎ 01383 411880 ⏰ Mon–Fri 10–5, Sat–Sun 10–6 🖐 Adult £11, child (3–15) £7.50, family £36 🚉 North Queensferry ▢ 🏛

DOUNE CASTLE

www.historic-scotland.gov.uk
The village of Doune lies 8 miles (13km) northwest of Stirling, and it would be easy to pass through and miss the castle completely. Look for the signs, however, that lead you down a narrow road to this substantial grey ruin, hidden in the trees on a curve of the River Teith.

Built by the powerful Regent of Scotland, Robert Stewart, Duke of Albany, in the late 14th century, the castle is comparatively simple in construction, with a main block of buildings set around a courtyard, and contained by a great curtain wall.

It is an admirable example of medieval concerns for security, with gates to secure the courtyard, further gates to defend the buildings should the courtyard be taken in battle, and separate stairs to the lord's hall and the retainers' hall to ensure that each could be defended in its own right. Even the Duke's bedroom has its own emergency exit.

✚ 467 E8 ✉ Castle Road, Doune FK16 6EA ☎ 01786 841742 ⏰ Apr–end Sep daily 9.30–5.30; rest of year Sat–Wed 9.30–4.30 🖐 Adult £4, child (5–15) £2 🏛

DUNDEE

www.angusanddundee.co.uk

Dundee sprawls along the northern shore of the Firth of Tay, but speed past inland on the ring road and you'll miss a treat, for Dundee's waterfront has undergone a transformation.

The focus is Discovery Point and a famous heroine of polar exploration, the three-masted Royal Research Ship *Discovery*, which was built here in 1901. The story of her planning and construction is told in the museum alongside (Easter–end Oct Mon–Sat 10–6, Sun 11–6; rest of year Mon–Sat 10–5, Sun 11–5), with models and sailors' belongings that bring the city's shipbuilding history to life. Be sure to see the poky corner on board *Discovery* where the ship's doctor Edward Wilson (1872–1912) painted watercolours of the trip. *Discovery*'s maiden voyage, under the command of a young Robert Falcon Scott (1868–1912), was to Antarctica, where in 1902 she became frozen in the pack ice. She was to remain there for two long winters, while scientific research was undertaken and Scott made an unsuccessful attempt to reach the South Pole. It's a fascinating story, making the tour of the ship's cramped quarters even more interesting.

On the other side of the rail station, Sensation Dundee is a tribute to modern research (daily 10–5). It's a lively hands-on science centre dedicated to the five senses.

Dundee's second major attraction is an excellent industrial museum in the middle of the city, called the Verdant Works (Easter–end Oct Mon–Sat 10–6, Sun 11–6; rest of year Wed–Sat 10.30–4.30, Sun 11–4.30). It's a good idea to watch the short film first. Save money by buying a joint entrance ticket for Verdant Works and *Discovery*.

🚻 443 F7 🛈 21 Castle Street DD1 3AA, tel 01382 527527

DUNKELD AND HERMITAGE

With the exception of the diminutive 13th-century cathedral, the original settlement of Dunkeld was destroyed by the Jacobites after their victory at Killiecrankie in 1689. It was rebuilt, with terraced houses packed tightly into just two main streets, Cathedral Street and High Street, with a tidy little square, the Cross. Many of the houses are whitewashed, and its pleasing uniformity owes much to restoration by the National Trust for Scotland. By the partly restored cathedral stands the Parent Larch, a tree imported from Austria in 1738 and the parent of many of the trees in the nearby forests, planted between 1738 and 1830 by the dukes of Atholl.

A pleasant walk beside the River Braan leads past the tallest Douglas fir in Britain (64.3m/ 211ft) to the Hermitage, an 18th-century folly. To the east, the Loch of the Lowes is in the care of the Scottish Wildlife Trust and is famous for breeding ospreys (Apr–end Sep daily).

🚻 442 F7 🛈 The Cross, Dunkeld PH8 0AN, tel 01350 727688 🚌 Dunkeld and Birnam

EAST NEUK

Neuk is the Scottish word for a corner, and East Neuk is the name given to eastern Fife, where old fishing villages face south to Edinburgh and the Lothians. These old towns have narrow streets that quickly get congested in summer, so be prepared to explore on foot.

Crail is the farthest east of the string, with a charter dating to 1178 and a photogenic 16th-century harbour. Former trading links with the Netherlands show up in the architecture, characterized by pantile roofs and high, stepped gables. The square-towered tolbooth even has a Dutch bell, cast in 1520.

Next in line to the west is Anstruther, a larger resort town and former herring port. The Scottish Fisheries Museum (Apr–end Sep Mon–Sat 10–5.30, Sun 11–5; rest of year Mon–Sat 10.30–4.30, Sun 12–4.30) is in historic waterfront buildings around a courtyard, and illustrates the past and present life of Scottish fishermen and their families. The town also has a history of smuggling, which took place mainly on the Dreel stream and the 16th-century Smuggler's Inn.

Continue west to Pittenweem, the main fisheries port for the East Neuk. The town began in the seventh century when St. Fillan based himself in a cave here (in Cove Wynd) while converting the local Picts to Christianity. Artists seem to be attracted to the town and there are several small art galleries to explore.

The tiny houses of the next village, St. Monans, crowd around its harbour, where shipbuilding as well as fishing brought prosperity in the 19th century. The splendid, squat Auld Kirk (old church), standing alone at the western end, was built in 1362.

Elie is the farthest west of the East Neuk villages, and its golden sands made it a popular holiday resort during the late 19th century. A causeway leads to a rocky islet with views out to sea and a busy watersports complex. The stone windmill on the coast between Pittenweem and St. Monans, once used to evaporate seawater for the valuable salt industry.

🚻 443 G8 🛈 Museum and Heritage Centre, 62–64 Marketgate, Crail KY10 3TL, tel 01333 450869 (seasonal) 🛈 Tourist Information Office, Harbourhead, Anstruther KY10 3AB, tel 01333 311073 (seasonal) ❓ Fife Coastal Path links the villages

Below *The remains of the Cathedral in Dunkeld*

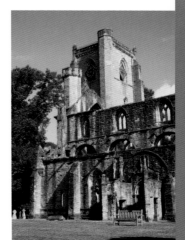

is not used.

EDINBURGH

INFORMATION

www.edinburgh.org

🔖 467 F8 ℹ️ 3 Princes Street (above Mall) EH2 2QP, tel 0131 473 3800; Apr, Oct Mon–Sat 9–6, Sun 10–6; May–end Jun, Sep Mon–Sat 9–7, Sun 10–7; Jul–end Aug Mon–Sat 9–8, Sun 10–8; Nov–end Mar Mon–Sat 9–5, Sun 10–5

🚆 Edinburgh Waverley

INTRODUCTION

The Scottish capital is divided into two distinct halves by the the Water of Leith. The Old Town to the south has historic routes such as Grassmarket and Canongate and a medieval network of alleys. More breathing space can be found in the striking Georgian streets of the New Town to the north.

The name Edinburgh derives from the city's original name, Dunedin, and the 12th-century term burgh, denoting a town with certain rights, such as trading or taxation. Edinburgh was a royal burgh, and by the time Robert the Bruce (▷ 30) granted a new charter to the city in 1329, it was on the road to becoming the capital of Scotland. The 16th and 17th centuries saw religious and political turmoil, but the city survived. Unlike Glasgow (▷ 372–375), Edinburgh's people didn't get their hands dirty during the Industrial Revolution, preferring to develop services such as banking. In the 1990s, political power was devolved from London to the Scottish capital.

WHAT TO SEE

EDINBURGH CASTLE

www.edinburghcastle.gov.uk

Edinburgh Castle towers over the city from its volcanic rock. Bronze Age people settled on the top around 850BC, and by the Middle Ages it was a fortified site and royal residence. The views from the ramp at the entrance are great. The Half Moon Battery is the defensive wall and walkway on the east side, built after the Lang (long) Siege of 1567–73. Since 1861 a field gun has boomed out here Monday to Saturday at precisely 1pm to enable mariners to fix the time accurately. The Crown Room displays the ancient regalia of Scotland—crown, sceptre and sword—locked away after the parliamentary union with England in 1707 (▷ 35) and unearthed by Sir Walter Scott in 1818. The Stone of Destiny is also here, on which Scottish kings were crowned. Originally at Scone Palace, it was stolen by Edward I and remained

Above *Fireworks explode over the city of Edinburgh, illuminating the night sky to celebrate the Edinburgh Festival*

in London until recovered from Westminster Abbey in 1996. The Scotch Whisky Heritage Centre (Sep–end Apr daily 10–6; rest of year daily 9.30–6.30) is below the castle.

➕ 368 B2 ✉ Castle Hill EH1 2NG ☎ 0131 225 9846 ⏰ Apr–end Sep daily 9.30–6; rest of year daily 9.30–5 🖐 Adult £11, child (under 16) £5.50 🎧 Guided tours 📷

PALACE OF HOLYROODHOUSE

www.royal.gov.uk

Filled with works of art from the Royal Collection, this towered palace sits at the foot of the Royal Mile and is the Queen's official residence in Scotland, which means it may be closed at short notice. The palace started in the 15th century as a guest house for Holyrood Abbey, and its name is said to come from the Holy Rood, a fragment of Christ's cross belonging to David I (c1080–1153). Bonnie Prince Charlie (1720–88) held court here in 1745, followed by George IV on his triumphant visit to the city in 1822. The state rooms, designed for Charles II and hung with Brussels tapestries, are particularly good.

➕ 369 E1 ✉ EH8 8DX ☎ 0131 556 5100 ⏰ Easter–end Oct daily 9.30–6; rest of year daily 9.30–4.30 🖐 Adult £9.80, child (under 17) £7.50, under 5 free, family £33.50 🎧 Guided tours only Nov–end Mar 📷

NATIONAL GALLERY OF SCOTLAND

www.nationalgalleries.org

Designed by New Town architect William Playfair (1789–1857), the National Gallery of Scotland has a collection of 20,000 paintings, sculptures and drawings. The main focus are paintings by Europe's great masters but Scottish artists are displayed in their own section downstairs. Favourites include Sir Henry Raeburn's tartan-clad chieftan, *Colonel Alastair Mcdonnell of Glengarry* (1812), and the land- and seascapes of William McTaggart (1835–1910).

➕ 369 C2 ✉ The Mound EH2 2EL ☎ 0131 624 6200 ⏰ Fri–Wed 10–5, Thu 10–7 🖐 Free 🚌 Free bus runs between all four national galleries 📷

NATIONAL MUSEUM OF SCOTLAND

www.nms.ac.uk

This entertaining museum showcases the Scottish collections from the Royal Museum next door. It is a superb, well-explained collection that covers the shaping of Scotland through geology and glaciation, what is known of the lives of the earliest settlers in Scotland and the founding of Scottish identity.

➕ 368 C3 ✉ Chambers Street EH1 1JF ☎ 0131 225 7534 ⏰ Tue 10–8, Mon, Wed–Sat 10–5, Sun 12–5 🖐 Free 🎧 Free tours daily 🍴 📷

NEW TOWN

The New Town covers 2.5sq km (1sq mile) to the north of Princes Street, and is characterized by broad streets of grand, terraced houses with large windows and ornamental door arches. The Georgian House (Mar daily 11–4; Easter–end Jun, Sep–end Oct daily 10–5; Jul–end Aug daily 10–6; Nov daily 10–3), on Charlotte Square's north side, is a meticulous recreation of an 18th-century home, down to the Wedgwood dinner service on the dining table.

➕ 368 B1

ROYAL MILE

The Royal Mile is the name of the long street that links Holyrood Palace with Edinburgh Castle. About 60 narrow closes lead off on either side. Lady Stair's Close, near St. Giles' Cathedral, is the best known and leads through to the Writers' Museum (Mon–Sat 10–5, Sun 2–5 during Edinburgh Festival). Drop into the Museum of Edinburgh (Sep–end Jul Mon–Sat 10–5; Aug Mon–Sat 10–5, Sun 1–5) to get a feeling of the interiors of these old houses. The 1490 John Knox House (Jul Mon–Sat 10–5, Sun 12–4; Aug Mon–Sat 10–7, Sun 12–4;

TIPS

»A free bus service links the four national galleries.

» The exact fare is required for Lothian Buses and First Edinburgh, but journeys shouldn't cost much more than £1 (£2 on night buses).

Below *John Knox House on the Royal Mile*

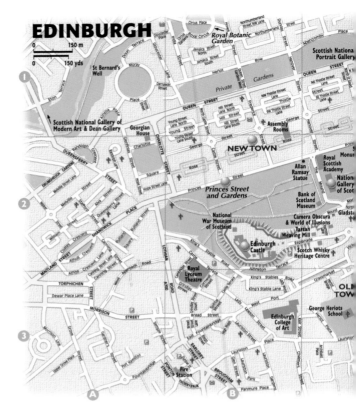

EDINBURGH

Sep–end Jun Mon–Sat 10–5), on the corner of Royal Mile, is where John Knox (c1505–72), the founder of the Church of Scotland, preached.
✛ 369 C2

NATIONAL GALLERY OF MODERN ART AND DEAN GALLERY

A sweeping, living sculpture of grassy terraces and ponds is the first thing you see as you arrive here. Among the works in the permanent collection are those by Pablo Picasso, Georges Braque, Henri Matisse and Barbara Hepworth. The work of the early 20th-century group of painters known as the Scottish Colourists is striking. Across the road is the Dean Gallery. This collection majors on Dada and the Surrealists, and Scottish sculptor Eduardo Paolozzi (1924–2005).
✛ 368 off A1 ✉ 75 Belford Road EH4 3DR ☎ 0131 624 6200 ⏰ Daily 10–5 ✋ Free, may be a charge for temporary exhibitions 💻

MORE TO SEE

ARTHUR'S SEAT

Arthur's Seat is the 251m (823ft) high remains of a 325-million-year-old volcano. There is access to Holyrood's hills and lochs.
✛ 369 off E2

ROYAL BOTANIC GARDEN

The garden has 15,500 species in 28ha (70 acres) of landscaped grounds and 10 greenhouses.
✛ 368 off B1 ✉ 20A Inverlieth Row EH3 5LR ☎ 0131 552 7171 ⏰ Mar, Oct daily 10–6; Apr–end Sep daily 10–7; Nov–end Feb daily 10–4 ✋ Free

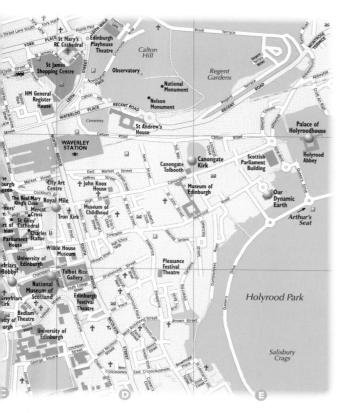

CANONGATE KIRK

Canongate Kirk was built in 1688 after James VI of Scotland converted the abbey church at Holyrood to a chapel. Some of Edinburgh's finest are buried in the graveyard.

🔢 369 E2 ✉ Canongate EH8 8BR ☎ 0131 556 3515 🕐 Jun–end Oct Mon–Sat 10.30–4, Sun 10–12.30 ✋ Free 💻

OUR DYNAMIC EARTH

This science park tells the story of the Earth in slick, easy chunks of virtual-reality science. The planet is explored inside out through 11 galleries, from the effect of erupting volcanoes to the icy chill of the polar regions.

🔢 369 E2 ✉ Holyrood Road EH8 8AS ☎ 0131 550 7800 🕐 Jul–end Aug daily 10–6; Nov–end Mar Wed–Sun 10–5 ✋ Adult £9.50, child £5.95

GREYFRIARS BOBBY

This bronze statue is of a Skye terrier, Bobby, the devoted companion of a farmer who regularly dined in Greyfriars Place.

🔢 369 C2 ✉ George IV Bridge

SCOTTISH NATIONAL PORTRAIT GALLERY

Scottish worthies—including the great and the good, the vain and the bad, the beautiful and the long-forgotten—and the national photography collection are represented in this gallery.

🔢 368 C1 ✉ 1 Queen Street EH2 1JD ☎ 0131 624 6200 🕐 Fri–Wed 10–5, Thu 10–7 ✋ Free 💻

Opposite *Princes Street is Edinburgh's main artery*
Below *Greyfriars Bobby*

Above *Rebuilt in 1912 but dating back to 1220, Eilean Donan Castle on Loch Duich*

EILEAN DONAN CASTLE

www.eileandonancastle.com

Probably the most photographed castle in Scotland, Eilean Donan is perched on a rock near the northern shore of Loch Duich, joined to the mainland by a bridge. There has been a fortification on the site since the 13th century, and a MacRae stronghold was destroyed here by government troops in 1719. The Eilean Donan you see today, complete with stone walls up to 4.3m (14ft) thick, is the result of rebuilding between 1912 and 1932. It is said that its creator, Lieutenant Colonel John MacRae-Gilstrap, saw an image of how it might look in a dream. It has starred in films such as *The World Is Not Enough*.

✚ 468 C5 ✉ Dornie, by Kyle of Lochalsh IV40 8DX ☎ 01599 555202 ⏱ Mid-Mar to mid-Nov daily 10–6 (last admission 5pm) ✋ Adult £4.95, child £3.95, family £10.50 ▢ ♿

FALKIRK WHEEL

www.thefalkirkwheel.co.uk

Is it engineering or art? That's one of the questions that comes up at first sight of this unique 35m (115ft) structure. It opened in 2002 to link the canals that run across the middle of Scotland, replacing 11 locks, which had been dismantled in 1933. The wheel is a cross between a lock and a lift, a state-of-the-art method of raising and lowering boats between two different levels of the Forth and Clyde Ship Canal and the Union Canal. Watch from the glass-sided visitor centre as the great structure rotates, and take a 40-minute boat ride up on to the higher canal, through a tunnel, and back down on the wheel.

✚ 467 E8 ✉ Lime Road, Tamfourhill, Falkirk FK1 4RS ☎ 0870 050 0208 ⏱ Feb–Easter, Nov–end Dec Mon–Fri 10–4.30, Sat–Sun 10–6; Sep–end Oct, Easter–end Jul daily 9.30–6; Aug Mon–Fri 9.30–6, Sat–Sun 9.30–7 ✋ Free. Boat ride: adult £8, child (5–16) £4.25, under 5s free, family £21.50 🚆 Falkirk Grahamston ▢ ♿ ❓ Advance reservation essential for boat trips

FALKLAND PALACE

www.nts.org.uk

Stuart monarchs used this handsome Renaissance-fronted fortress in the heart of Fife as a hunting lodge and retreat. The twin towers of the palace gatehouse dominate the little town of Falkland, with its clusters of 17th-century red-roofed houses. The palace itself dates to the 15th century. Mary, Queen of Scots (1542–87) spent part of her childhood here, but when the future Charles II (1630–85) fled to exile in 1651, it fell into ruin. In 1887 its fortunes changed when John Patrick Crichton Stuart, third Marquess of Bute, started rebuilding and restoring it. A series of rooms reflect the different periods of occupation, including the Chapel Royal and the King's Room.

✚ 467 F8 ✉ Falkland, Cupar KY15 7BU ☎ 0844 493 2186 ⏱ Mar–end Oct Mon–Sat 10–5, Sun 1–5 ✋ Adult £10, child £7, family £25 ♿

FORT WILLIAM

Fort William's location on a road and rail junction at the head of Loch Linnhe and the foot of the Great Glen makes it a convenient touring base for the northwest of Scotland. The town's heyday as a military outpost is long gone—the fort, which withstood Jacobite attacks in 1715 and 1745, was demolished in 1864 for a rail station. The town grew after this period, and is unappealing in itself, but its position makes it popular with walkers and climbers.

Fort William's biggest attraction lies to the east: the rounded bulk of Ben Nevis (1,343m/4,406ft), Britain's highest mountain. Conditions at the top can be extremely cold even on warmer days below, and visitors should take all necessary precautions before attempting to climb it. On the first Saturday in September you may be overtaken by runners—entrants in the annual Ben Nevis Race, established in 1937. The record currently stands at 1 hour 25 minutes.

✚ 466 D6 ℹ Cameron Square PH33 6AJ, tel 08452 255121 🚆 Fort William

FYVIE CASTLE

www.nts.org.uk

Magnificent Fyvie Castle, set in a landscaped park in the valley of the River Ythan, has a 46m (150ft) frontage, dominated by a large gatehouse. It is said that five of Scotland's great families—the Prestons, Meldrums, Setons, Gordons and Leiths—each built a tower as they owned the castle in turn. The oldest part dates from the 13th century and incorporates the architectural highlight: a spiral staircase of broad stone steps known as a wheelstair, a 17th-century addition by Alexander Seton. Opulent interiors were created in the early 20th century, making a rich backdrop to the weapons collections and portraits.

✚ 470 G5 ✉ Near Turriff AB53 8JS ☎ 0844 493 2182 ⏱ Jul–end Aug daily 11–5; Apr–end Jun, Sep–end Oct Sat–Wed 12–5. Grounds: all year daily 9.30–dusk ✋ Adult £8, child (5–16) £5, under 5s free, family £20 ▢ ♿

GLAMIS CASTLE

www.glamis-castle.co.uk

A grand, turreted building 5 miles (8km) west of Forfar, Glamis (pronounced *glahms*) Castle has been the seat of the earls of Strathmore and Kinghorne since 1372. It's essentially a medieval tower house that was extended and remodelled to palace proportions. Explore the castle on a guided tour and then roam the stunning park.

Glamis was the childhood home of Queen Elizabeth, the Queen Mother (1900–2002), and there is a special exhibition on her life in the Old Coach House. In the village of Glamis, the Angus Folk Museum (Easter–end Jun, Sep–end Oct Sat–Sun 12–5; Jul–end Aug Mon–Sat 11–5, Sun 1–5) gives an idea of life at the other end of the social scale.

✚ 467 F7 ✉ By Forfar DD8 1RJ ☎ 01307 840393 ◉ Mar–end Oct daily 10–6; Nov–end Dec 11–5 💷 Adult £8, child (5–16) £5, under 5s free, family £22.50 🍴 🎦

GLASGOW

▷ 372–375.

GLEN AFFRIC

This peaceful valley, 48km (30 miles) southwest of Inverness and running parallel with the Great Glen, is one of the best-loved beauty spots in the Highlands. Its scenery combines forest and moorland, river and loch with mighty mountains such as Carn Eighe (1,182m/3,878ft). A narrow road leads up from Cannich to where you can park at the River Affric, passing the Dog Falls and a picnic area at Loch Beinn a Mheadhoin on the way up. Crested tits and crossbills may be seen all year in the woods, while golden eagles and capercaillie are rarer sightings.

✚ 469 D5 🛈 Castle Wynd, Inverness IV2 3BJ, tel 0845 225 5121

GLEN COE

Whether your first approach to Glen Coe is from the wide, watery wasteland of Rannoch Moor, or up from Loch Leven, you cannot fail to be impressed by the majesty of this long, steep-sided valley. On a clear day you can see the tops of the Aonach Eagach ridge to the north (966m/3,169ft) and the peaks of the Three Sisters to the south, leading down from Bidean nam Bian (1,148m/3,766ft). At the top, eastern end, the glen is guarded by Buachaille Etive Mor, the Great Shepherd of Etive (1,019m/3,343ft).

This is prime mountaineering country, and not for the unfit or unwary. In winter it offers an extra challenge to climbers. There is a ski station with a chairlift at the eastern end, on the flanks of Meall a'Bhùiridh (1,108m/3,635ft). Learn more about the glen's remarkable geology at the Inverrigan Visitor Centre (Mar–Easter daily 10–4; Easter–end Aug daily 9.30–5.30; Sep–end Oct daily 10–5; Nov–end Feb Thu–Sun 10–4).

Memories last long in the Highlands, and there is still a frisson between the Macdonalds and Campbells that dates back to a February night in 1692. At a time when clan leaders were required to swear allegiance to the monarchs, William and Mary, Alastair Macdonald of Glencoe postponed the task. When he missed the deadline, Campbell of Glenlyon was sent to make an example of him. Campbell's men were billeted here for two weeks before turning on their hosts in an act of cold-blooded slaughter that left 38 dead. The betrayal has never been forgotten.

✚ 66 D7 🛈 Ballachulish PA39 4JR, tel 01855 811296 (seasonal)

GLENFINNAN

On 19 August 1745, Prince Charles Edward Stuart (Bonnie Prince Charlie) raised his standard here at the top of Loch Shiel, a rallying cry to supporters of his father's claim to the throne of Scotland. It was the start of the Stuarts' final campaign, which would end in disaster at Culloden (▷ 363). The occasion is recalled by a pillar monument topped by the statue of a kilted soldier, built here in 1815, which provides a focus for the magnificent view down the loch. The National Trust for Scotland has an informative visitor office near by (Apr–end Jun, Sep–end Oct daily 10–5; Jul–end Aug daily 9.30–5.30).

✚ 468 C6 🛈 Cameron Square, Fort William PH33 6AJ, tel 0845 225 5121 🚉 Glenfinnan

HADDINGTON

This handsome market town is set in prime agricultural country on the River Tyne, 18 miles (29km) east of Edinburgh. It was granted the status of a royal burgh in the 12th century, and later became the county town for East Lothian. Protestant reformer John Knox was born here around 1513. The original medieval town was laid out to a triangular streetplan that can still be traced along High Street, Market Street and Hardgate. The painted 18th-century Georgian buildings of the High Street make an attractive facade.

✚ 467 G8 🛈 Quality Street, North Berwick EH39 4HJ, tel 01620 892197

Below *A view down Glen Coe from the pass, with the Three Sisters on the left*

INFORMATION

www.seeglasgow.com

467 E8 Greater Glasgow and Clyde Valley Tourist Board, 11 George Square, Glasgow G2 1DY, tel 0141 204 4400; Easter–end Sep Mon–Sat 9–8, Sun 10–6; rest of year Mon–Sat 9–6

Glasgow Central and Queen Street

Glasgow Underground (or Clockwork Orange) links different parts of the city, tel 0141 333 3708

INTRODUCTION

Once Scotland's industrial powerhouse, Glasgow has rediscovered its artistic side in recent years. It was European City of Culture in 1990, then City of Architecture and Design in 1999—a long way from its roots in ironworks and shipbuilding. The industrial decline of the 1960s and 1970s caused big problems but, in typical style, the city picked itself up and is now, arguably, a more exciting place than its east coast rival, Edinburgh (▷ 366–369).

Trade and religion have shaped Glasgow. St. Kentigern (518–603) is said to have built Glasgow's first church, where the cathedral now stands. The settlement became a royal burgh in 1611 and the Protestant Revolution later that century allowed commerce to flourish. As a port on the west coast, Glasgow was perfectly located for trade with the English colonies in America, importing tobacco, cotton and rum. The Industrial Revolution helped Glasgow become the workshop of the Western world. Money flowed in as ships built on the Clyde flowed out; the opulent City Chambers (Mon–Fri 9–5) on George Square suggest how wealthy the city was. The city is now adapting to post-industrial life, with an emphasis today on culture and entertainment.

WHAT TO SEE

BURRELL COLLECTION

This priceless collection of 9,000 pieces of art from around the world was given to Glasgow in 1944 by Sir William Burrell (1861–1958). You'll find August Rodin's *The Thinker* in the Courtyard. Intriguing old stone doorways lead into different parts of the museum. In the Ancient Greece and Rome section, look for fragments of delicate Roman mosaics. Don't overlook the Islamic Art section at the farthest end of the museum, dripping with Oriental carpets. The corridor between the café and the entrance is aglow with medieval glass, suspended along the windows that form the outer skin of the building.

374 A3 Pollok Country Park, 2060 Pollokshaws Road G43 1AT 0141 287 2550 Mon–Thu, Sat 10–5, Fri, Sun 11–5 Free; charge for some special exhibitions Pollokshaws West Free guided tours

Above *Looking across George Square to the City Chambers*

GALLERY OF MODERN ART (GoMA)

GoMA, in a former tobacco baron's mansion, is set on four floors linked by a glass lift. Among the ever-changing displays, look for Peter Howson's painting *Patriots* (1991), with three loutish men and their snarling bulldogs, as well as huge striped canvases by pop artist Bridget Riley (born 1931) and works by Andy Warhol (1927–87) and David Hockney (born 1937).

➕ 374 C2 ✉ Royal Exchange Square, Queen Street G1 3AZ ☎ 0141 229 1996 🕐 Mon–Wed, Sat 10–5, Thu 10–8, Fri, Sun 11–5 ✋ Free 🚇 Queen Street, Glasgow Central 🚌 Tours most weekends 📷 🏛

GLASGOW SCIENCE CENTRE

The main attraction at the Science Centre is the Science Mall, with four floors of 500 interactive exhibits. Highlights include distorting mirrors, seeing how an artificial arm picks up signals from your body, and a walk-on piano for those under seven. The other main elements on the site are the 24m (80ft) screen in the IMAX theatre, and the dizzying 122m (400ft) viewing tower designed to turn 360 degrees in the wind.

➕ 374 A2 ✉ 50 Pacific Quay G51 1EA ☎ 0871 540 1000 🕐 Easter–end Oct daily 10–5, Nov–end Mar Tue–Sun 10–5 ✋ Science Centre: adult £7.95, child (3–16) £5.95; combination tickets available 🚇 Cessnock 🚇 Exhibition Centre 🍴 🏛

GLASGOW NECROPOLIS

This is Glasgow's 'city of the dead', stuffed with ostentatious monuments to the wealthy 19th-century industrialists who developed the city. Their competitive spirit showed even after death, with extraordinary monuments commissioned from the finest architects of the day. There's a great view of the crowded Necropolis skyline from the third floor of St. Mungo Museum (▷ 375).

➕ 374 C2 ✉ Castle Street ℹ 11 George Square G2 1DY, tel 0141 204 4400 🕐 Daily 7am–dusk ✋ Free

HUNTERIAN MUSEUM AND ART GALLERY

www.hunterian.gla.ac.uk

William Hunter (1718–83) was a Glasgow-trained physician who left his scientific collections—including anatomical specimens used in teaching—to his old university. The collection was opened for show in 1807, making this the oldest public museum in Scotland. The magnificent art collection, in a separate building on campus, originates from Hunter's own purchases of 17th-century Flemish, Dutch and Italian masters. There's also a coin collection and displays of geology and archaeology, including Roman finds from Scotland.

➕ 374 A1 ✉ University of Glasgow, 82 Hillhead Street G1 8QQ ☎ 0141 330 5431/4221 🕐 Mon–Sat 9.30–5 ✋ Free 🚇 Hillhead 🚇 Glasgow Queen Street 📷 🏛

THE MACKINTOSH TRAIL

Charles Rennie Mackintosh (1868–1928) was born in Glasgow, and at the age of 16 was apprenticed to a firm of architects. He was an outstanding student, praised for the originality of his architecture, a distinctive fusion of the flowing lines of art nouveau with the simplicity of the Arts and Crafts Movement. He left his mark on Glasgow, with principal points of interest forming the Rennie Mackintosh Trail.

The Glasgow School of Art (tours Apr–end Sep daily 10.30, 11, 11.30, 1.30, 2, 2.30; Oct–end Mar Mon–Sat 11, 2) was founded in 1845. Mackintosh won the competition to design the new building at 167 Renfrew Street in 1896. It is known as his masterpiece and still looks fresh and modern over 100 years later.

The Willow Tearooms, opened in 1903, are a short walk away above a jewellery shop at 217 Sauchiehall Street and offer a restored Mackintosh interior upstairs in the Salon de Luxe.

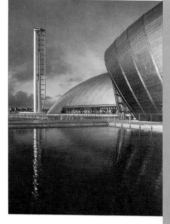

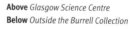

Above *Glasgow Science Centre*
Below *Outside the Burrell Collection*

GLASGOW

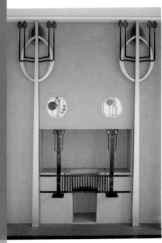

The House for an Art Lover (Apr–end Sep Mon–Wed 10–4, Thu–Sun 10–1; Oct–end Mar Sat–Sun 10–1) is a fantasy, designed in 1901 without the imposed limitations of budget or client, by Mackintosh and his wife, Margaret MacDonald (1864–1933). In 1996 artists and craftspeople made the dream a reality at 10 Dumbreck Road in leafy Bellahouston Park.

At the university's Hunterian Gallery, Mackintosh House is the exquisite recreation of the interior of the home which the Mackintoshs made together, with original furniture, as it appeared in 1906. You can clearly see the influence of Japanese style.

At Queen's Cross, 870 Garscube Road, northwest of the city, St. Matthew's Free Church is Mackintosh's only complete church, designed in 1897. It follows a simple Gothic Revival style, the attention to detail extending to the carvings of birds and foliage on the oak pulpit. The church was restored and is home to the Charles Rennie Mackintosh Society (Mar–end Oct Mon–Fri 10–5, Sun 2–5).

Hidden down Mitchell Lane, between Buchanan and Union streets, the Lighthouse is Glasgow's museum of architecture and design. Completed in 1985, the building was the first public commission by Mackintosh. It later became the

headquarters of the *Glasgow Herald* newspaper. As well as a permanent Mackintosh display, there are extensive temporary exhibitions. There's a breathtaking view from the top of the Lighthouse (Mon, Wed–Sat 10–5, Tue 11–5, Sun 12–5).
🛈 11 George Square G2 1DY, tel 0141 204 4400

MORE TO SEE

ST. MUNGO MUSEUM OF RELIGIOUS LIFE AND ART
www.glasgowmuseums.com
Enter this modern museum near the medieval cathedral through a Zen gravel garden. It is set out over three floors, with an art collection, religious items and a section about religion in Glasgow.
➕ 374 C2 ✉ 2 Castle Street G4 0RH ☎ 0141 553 2557 🕒 Mon–Thu, Sat 10–5, Fri, Sun 11–5 👆 Free 🚇 High Street 🍴 🏛

THE TENEMENT HOUSE
www.nts.org.uk
In the 19th and early 20th centuries, most Glaswegians lived in tenement houses, sharing communal facilities. They could be overcrowded, with families sharing one room. This example was the home of Agnes Toward from 1911. Agnes never threw anything away and when she died in 1975, her house became a unique time capsule of social history.
➕ 374 B1 ✉ 145 Buccleuch Street, Garnethill G3 6QN ☎ 0141 333 0183 🕒 Mar–end Oct daily 1–5 👆 Adult £5, child (5–16) £4, family £14 🚇 Cowcaddens 🚉 Charing Cross

TALL SHIP AT GLASGOW HARBOUR
www.thetallship.com
The best view of this fine steel-hulled sailing ship is from the windows of the Science Centre opposite. The SV *Glenlee*, built on the Clyde in 1896, is one of five Clyde-built ships left afloat.
➕ 374 A2 ✉ 100 Stobcross Road G3 8QQ ☎ 0141 222 2513 🕒 Mar–end Oct daily 10–5; rest of year daily 10–4 👆 Adult £4.95, child (5–16) one child free with every adult, additional child £2.50 🚇 Partick 🚉 Finnieston/Exhibition Centre 🅿 🏛

PEOPLE'S PALACE
www.glasgowmuseums.com
Set on Glasgow Green, this museum captures the character of the city.
➕ 374 C2 ✉ Glasgow Green G40 1AT ☎ 0141 271 2951 🕒 Mon–Thu, Sat 10–5, Fri, Sun 11–5 👆 Free 🚇 High Street, Argyle Street, Bellgrove 🅿 🏛

CLYDEBUILT
www.scottishmaritimemuseum.org
Runs through Clydeside's golden age of shipbuilding in the 19th and 20th centuries.
➕ 374 off A2 ✉ Braehead Shopping Centre, Kings Inch Road G51 4BN ☎ 0141 886 1013 🕒 Mon–Sat 10–5.30, Sun 11–5.30 👆 Adult £4.25, child (5–16) £2.50, family £10 🚉 Gilmour Street 🚤 Waterbus

SCOTTISH FOOTBALL MUSEUM
www.scottishfootballmuseum.org.uk
Hampden Park is Scotland's national football stadium.
➕ 374 C3 ✉ Hampden Park G42 9BA ☎ 0141 616 6139 🕒 Mon–Sat 10–5, Sun 11–5 👆 Adult £8, child (5–16) £4, family £20 🚇 Bridge Street 🅿 🏛

BOTANIC GARDENS
The highlight is the Kibble Palace, a huge domed glasshouse.
➕ 374 A1 ✉ 730 Great Western Road G12 0UE ☎ 0141 334 2422 🕒 Daily 7–dusk; glasshouses: Apr–end Oct daily 10–4.45; rest of year daily 10–4.15 👆 Free 🚇 Partick

Above *The SV* Glenlee *at rest*
Below *Inside the Kibble Palace, part of the Botanic Gardens*
Opposite *Example of Mackintosh's work at the House for an Art Lover*

HIGHLAND FOLK MUSEUM

www.highlandfolk.museum

Two sites in Kingussie and Newtonmore, 2.5 miles (4km) apart and signposted from the A9, make up the Highland Folk Museum. Together they offer an unsanitized picture of rural life in the Highlands over the centuries, through reconstructed buildings, a working croft and collections of everyday objects. Kingussie has a large collection of farming implements and machinery, and a reconstructed blackhouse, a traditional stone cottage, from Lewis (▷ 380). Newtonmore has a reconstructed 18th-century village, including a tailor's workshop, a church and a school. Staff in traditional costume demonstrate farming skills and crafts. The Kingussie site is only open to pre-booked groups.

469 E6 Duke Street, Kingussie PH21 1JG 01540 661307 Easter–end Aug daily 10.30–5.30; Sep–end Oct 11–4.30 Kingussie: adult £2.50, child (5–16) £1.50. Newtonmore: adult £5, child £3. Kingussie Newtonmore

INNER HEBRIDES

▷ 378.

INVERARAY

Spread out along a bay near the head of Loch Fyne, Inveraray was for centuries the capital of Argyll. The ruling family, the Campbell dukes of Argyll, had a castle near by, and when the untidy village threatened the view, the third duke moved the lot to its present purpose-built site. This creates a harmony in the buildings. They include the parish church, which causes the main street to flow around it. The tall brown-stone tower belongs to All Saints' Episcopalian Church, famous for its peal of 10 bells and with panoramic views from the top (mid-May to end Sep daily 10–1, 2–5).

The town's courthouse and jail of 1820 now house an entertaining exhibition about prison life (Apr–end Oct daily 9.30–6; rest of year daily 10–5).

To the north, Inveraray Castle is an 18th-century mansion (Apr–end Oct Mon–Sat 10–5.45, Sun 12–5.45; last admission 5pm).

If you have time, visit the original Loch Fyne Oyster Bar for fresh and smoked seafood, at the head of Loch Fyne.

466 D8 Front Street PA32 8UY, tel 0845 225 5121

Above *View of Inveraray over Loch Fyne*

INVEREWE GARDENS

www.nts.org.uk

In 1862 Osgood Mackenzie (1842–1922) inherited the Inverewe estate from the Laird of Gairloch, his stepfather, and on this barren, wind-blown promontory started to plant sheltering belts of trees. Inverewe benefits from the warmth of the Gulf Stream, and although the garden is on a latitude more northerly than Moscow, it rarely suffers from extreme frosts. Masses of soil and fertilizing seaweed had to be imported, and this seemed to be an unpromising start to what has become Scotland's best-known woodland garden. In fact, Mackenzie had to wait 20 years before the trees were sufficiently established for him to begin serious planting. The planting is varied and exotic, with something flowering at most times of the year.

Inverewe is surrounded by some of the most beautiful scenery in the Highlands; make the most of a visit to this remote spot and explore the area.

468 C4 Poolewe, Achnasheen IV22 2LG 0844 493 2225 Garden: Apr–end Oct daily 9.30–8; rest of year 10–3. Visitor centre: Easter/Apr, Sep daily 9.30–5; May–end Aug daily 9.30–6; Oct daily 10–4 Adult £8, child (5–16) £5.25, family £20 Private jetty in the garden allows access by private or cruise boat. Free guided tours Apr–end Sep Mon–Fri 1.30pm

INVERNESS

The administrative capital of the Highland region, Inverness is a service town for the surrounding area, filled in summer with visitors planning Highland expeditions.

Inverness's lack of antiquities is due, the locals will tell you, to the Highlanders' habit of burning the town down at regular intervals after Oliver Cromwell (1599–1658) built a fort here in 1652. The architecture is mostly 19th century, including the red sandstone castle with its monument to Flora MacDonald, who helped Bonnie Prince Charlie to escape in 1746 after his defeat at nearby Culloden Moor (▷ 363).

A 60-mile (100km) slash across the country from Inverness to Fort William, the Great Glen follows a geological fault. It is lined with roads and a series of lochs, of which the longest and best known is Loch Ness. Narrow and up to 230m (750ft) deep in places, some believe Loch Ness harbours a monster (known as Nessie). The first recorded sighting was in the seventh century, and you can find out about more recent searches in Drumnadrochit where two exhibition centres vie for your custom: the Lochness Exhibition Centre and the Original Loch Ness Monster Visitor Centre (both open daily).

469 E5 Castle Wynd IV2 3BJ, tel 08452 255121 Inverness Inverness

JEDBURGH

www.visitscottishborders.com

Jedburgh lies on the old main road into Scotland, and has witnessed many conflicts—in fact, so frequently was the town's castle attacked, rebuilt and attacked again that it was finally demolished in 1409. In its place is the former county jail, now Jedburgh Castle Jail and Museum (Easter–end Oct Mon–Sat 10–4.30, Sun 1–4). The broken tower and red sandstone walls of the ruined abbey (Apr–end Sep daily 9.30–5.30; rest of year 9.30–4.30) still dominate the town.

This was one of the great medieval Border abbeys (along with Kelso, ▷ right, Dryburgh, and Melrose, ▷ 380), and the shepherding skills of the monks were the basis on which the town's weaving industry and wealth grew. Mary, Queen of Scots reputedly stayed in a house in the town in 1566, leaving it briefly to visit her wounded lover, the Earl of Bothwell (c1535–78). Her death mask, at Mary, Queen of Scots' House (Mar–end Nov Mon–Sat 10–4, Sun 11–4.30), was taken from her severed head.

➕ 467 G9 ℹ️ Murray's Green TD8 6BE, tel 0870 608 0404 (seasonal)

JOHN O'GROATS

www.visitjohnogroats.com

In popular imagination, John o'Groats is the most northerly settlement on the British mainland, 873 miles (1,405km) from Land's

End in Cornwall (▷ 134), although the inhabitants of tiny Scarfskerry, a few miles to the northwest, have been known to take exception to the claim. It is named after a Dutchman, Jan de Groot, who lived here in 1509, and his octagonal house overlooks the wild waters of the Pentland Firth; today there are souvenir shops and cafés.

In 1952, Queen Elizabeth the Queen Mother (1900–2002) acquired and restored the nearby Castle of Mey as a holiday home (May–end Jul, mid-Aug to end Sep Sat–Thu 10.30–4). It contains an appealing blend of kitsch, comfort and grandeur.

The true most northerly point in Britain is the exposed headland of Dunnet Head, between John o'Groats and Thurso.

➕ 470 F2 ℹ️ County Road, John o'Groats KW1 4YR, tel 0845 225 5121 (seasonal)

KELSO

www.visitscottishborders.com

Kelso is one of the most elegant of the Border towns, with a wide cobbled square at its heart. A poignant fragment is all that remains of Kelso Abbey, once the largest of the Border abbeys, destroyed by the English in 1545. Nearby is the handsome five-arched bridge over the River Tweed built by John Rennie in 1803. From the parapet there is a fine view across to Floors Castle (Easter, May–end Oct daily 10–5), the largest inhabited house in Scotland, a monument to the wealth and privilege of the dukes of Roxburghe. Fine art, tapestries and French furniture are all on view.

An 18th-century mansion northwest of Kelso, Mellerstain House (Easter, May–end Jun, Sep, Sun, Wed 12.30–5; Jul–end Aug Sun–Mon, Wed–Thu 12.30–5; Oct Sun 12.30–5) is famous for its architecture and elegant interiors, and is still the family home of the Earl of Haddington. The delicate plasterwork is reminiscent of the decoration of Wedgwood pottery.

Left *The Falls of Dochart at Killin*

➕ 467 G9 ℹ️ Town House, The Square TD5 7HF, tel 0870 608 0404

KILLIN

www.killin.info

The flower-filled village of Killin lies at the western end of Loch Tay, in the ancient district of Breadalbane, and is a popular touring, walking and fishing area. It has its own attractions, notably the Falls of Dochart, which run through the middle. The hills are full of colourful legends, brought to life at the Breadalbane Folklore Centre in St. Fillan's Mill (Apr–end Jun, Sep–end Oct daily 10–5; Jul–end Aug daily 10–5.30). If you can't tell your fairies from your kelpies, this is the place to get educated.

➕ 467 E7 ℹ️ Breadalbane Folklore Centre, Falls of Dochart, Main Street FK21 8XE, tel 01567 820254

KINTYRE

www.kintyre.org

In 1098, Norse king Magnus Barelegs hauled his ship over the narrow neck of land at Tarbert to claim the beautiful Kintyre peninsula. Despite swift, modern access it still has the feeling of a world apart. The eastern road, via the holiday village of Carradale, is slower, allowing time to enjoy the views to Arran (▷ 361).

The Mull of Kintyre was made famous by Sir Paul McCartney in his hugely successful song (the former Beatle owns a home and a recording studio in the area). It is the southernmost tip of this peninsula, looking across to Northern Ireland, only 12 miles (20km) away. Tarbert, at the top, is an appealing little port, while Campbeltown, at the southern end, remains an important focus for the local farming community, and the home of the Springbank distillery. Try to visit the golden sands in Machrihanish Bay—they are often deserted.

➕ 466 C9 ℹ️ Harbour Street, Tarbert PA29 6UD, tel 08452 255121 ℹ️ Mackinnon House, The Pier, Campbeltown PA28 6EF, tel 08452 255121 ❎ Campbeltown 🚢 Ferry: Lochranza on Arran to Claonaig (summer) and Tarbert (winter)

INFORMATION

466 and 468. The main islands are identified by a red dot

The Pier, Craignure, Isle of Mull PA65 6AY, tel 01680 812377

Bowmore, Islay PA43 7JP, tel 01496 810254

Harbour Street, Tarbert PA29 6UD, tel 01880 820429 Mull: ferry from Oban, Kilchoan and Lochaline. Coll, Tiree, Colonsay: ferry from Oban. Islay and Jura: ferry from Tarbert. Gigha: ferry from Tayinloan on the Kintyre peninsula. All Caledonian MacBrayne, tel 01475 650100 (recording), 0870 565 0000 (reservations); www.calmac.co.uk

Islay has a whisky trail leaflet, detailing the opening times for the Laphroaig, Lagavulin and Bowmore distilleries

TIPS

» Ferry services to the islands are infrequent and may change according to weather conditions; plan your visit carefully.

» Reserve ahead; accommodation on the smaller islands is limited.

Above *The pretty harbour and town of Tobermory, Isle of Mull*

INNER HEBRIDES

The islands of the Inner Hebrides hug the western shores of Scotland and include Mull, Iona, Coll, Tiree, Colonsay, Islay, Jura and Gigha.

MULL

Mull, the largest island, covers 900sq km (350sq miles), with high mountains in the south and the rugged inlets of Loch Scridain and Loch na Keal in the west. The main settlement is Tobermory. The remoteness of the western coast, its sculpted appearance created by lava flow 50 million years ago, makes it an ideal habitat for golden eagles, buzzards and peregrines. To see birds of prey up close, visit Wings Over Mull, a conservation complex at Craignure (Apr–end Oct daily 10.30–5.30). A short ride away on a narrow-gauge railway (Apr–end Oct daily 10–4.30), Torosay Castle is a stately home built in 1858 (house: Apr–end Oct daily 10.30–5; gardens: summer daily 9–7).

IONA AND STAFFA

Fionnphort on Mull is the main access point for Iona, a magical island and the cradle of Christianity in Scotland since the sixth century. Make straight for the abbey (Apr–end Sep daily 9.30–5; Oct–end Mar daily 9.30–4.30), but spare time for the remains of the 13th-century priory. Excursions take in the island of Staffa, with its hexagonal basalt columns and Fingal's Cave.

THE OTHERS

To the west of Mull, the low-lying islands of Coll, Tiree, Colonsay and Oronsay are known for sandy beaches and rare birds. By comparison, Islay is positively cosmopolitan, a working island with seven distilleries, the Museum of Islay Life at Port Charlotte (Apr–end Oct Mon–Sat 10–5, Sun 2–5), and an annual festival of music and whisky, the Feis Ile (late May/early Jun). With its three high conical mountains, Jura is easily recognized. Standing stones and cairns date habitation here back to 7000BC. Gigha is famous for the gardens of Achamore House (daily, all year). Canna, Rum, Eigg and Muck make up the Small Isles south of Skye and are reached from Mallaig. Each has its own identity, but they share a reputation for unusual birdlife. Rum is the biggest, with the mountains of Askival (812m/2,664ft) and Sgùrr nan Gillean (764m/2,506ft), and Muck is the smallest, occupied by just one farm.

LOCH LOMOND AND THE TROSSACHS NATIONAL PARK

The romantic beauty of the Highland landscape, epitomized by this accessible and scenic area, was first 'discovered' in the late 18th century. It was novelist and poet Sir Walter Scott who did much to bring it to the popular eye, with his poem *The Lady of the Lake* (1810), set in identifiable locations across the Trossachs, ending at Loch Katrine. Today, Scotland's first designated national park (in 2002) stretches from the western shores of Loch Long across to Callander (▷ 363), and from Killin (▷ 377) in the north to Balloch in the south.

This is great hiking country, with waymarked trails and an attractive stretch of the West Highland Way long-distance footpath running along the eastern shore of Loch Lomond. Stretching for 38.6km (24 miles), the loch is a watersports' playground, with 38 pretty islands scattered throughout. Ben Lomond, on the eastern shore, is a popular Munro hill climb (974m/3,195ft). Luss, off the A82, is the best village to explore. The Loch Lomond Shores Visitor Centre explains the geology and history of the region (Easter–end Jun daily 9.30–6; Jul–end Aug 9.30–6.30; rest of year 10–5).

The Trossachs is the area to the east of Loch Lomond, including the wooded hills of the Queen Elizabeth Forest Park, and the peaks of Ben Venue (729m/2,391ft) and Ben Ledi (879m/2,883ft). Some of the best scenery is between Aberfoyle and Loch Katrine, with easy walking and a steamboat ride among the islands.

If you have time, visit the dramatic pass to the high point of Rest and Be Thankful, on the A83 west of Arrochar.

INFORMATION

www.lochlomond-trossachs.org

✚ 466 D7/8 ℹ National Park Gateway Centre, Loch Lomond Shores, Ben Lomond Way, Balloch G83 3QL, tel 0845 345 4978

🚆 Balloch, Tarbet and Ardlui on west side of Loch Lomond

Below *The sun sets behind the hills of Luss on Loch Lomond*

REGIONS SCOTLAND • SIGHTS

Above *The ruins of Maclellan Castle in Kirkcudbright*

Left *The Spinning Mill's new buildings by the banks of the River Clyde in New Lanark.*

KIRKCUDBRIGHT

This pretty harbour town lies southwest of Castle Douglas and has retained much character. The street plan is medieval, the castle ruin 16th-century, and its popularity with painters dates from 1901, when artist E. A. Hornel (1864–1933) settled here. Broughton House, where he lived and worked, is now a gallery and museum. It is said that local residents approached Hornel and his friends for their advice on colour schemes whenever their house fronts needed repainting—hence the harmonious shades seen in the High Street.

More paintings by Kirkcudbright artists can be seen in the Tolbooth Art Centre (Nov–end Apr Mon–Sat 10–4; May–end Jun, Sep Mon–Sat 11–5, Sun 2–5; Jul–end Aug Mon–Sat 10–5, Sun 2–5; Oct Mon–Sat 11–4, Sun 2–5).

✚ 464 E11 ℹ️ Harbour Square DG6 4HY, tel 01557 330494

LEWIS AND HARRIS

Lewis and Harris are joined by a narrow neck of land, but retain strong individual identities. They share a strong Gaelic culture and a traditional observance of the Sabbath—so plan ahead if you're here on a Sunday.

Lewis has large undulating peat moors scattered with lochs. Steornabhagh (Stornoway) is the administrative focus and a busy fishing port. Good roads lead through the crofting communities that hug the shore and to the mountainous southwest corner, where the white sands of Uig and Reef compete with green islands to steal the view.

Harris is the most beautiful of the Outer Hebrides, with high mountains and deep-cut bays. The browns, greens and greys of the landscape are reflected in its most famous export, Harris tweed, a high-quality, hand-woven cloth.

The island has many prehistoric monuments and monoliths, including the remarkable avenue and circle of 13 stones at Calanais (Callanish), dating to around 3000BC (Visitor Centre: Apr–end Sep Mon–Sat 10–6; rest of year Wed–Sat 10–4). Just up the coast, Dun Carloway Broch is an excellent example of a circular Iron Age dwelling. Set back from the beach at Bosta is a reconstructed Iron Age house that can be compared to the evocative 19th-century Black House at Arnol (Apr–end Sep Mon–Sat 9.30–6.30; Oct–end Mar 9.30–4.30).

✚ 468 B3/4 ℹ️ 26 Cromwell Street, Stornoway, Isle of Lewis H51 2DD, tel 01851 703088 ℹ️ Pier Road, Tarbert, Isle of Harris HS3 3DJ, tel 01859 502011 🚢 Ferry from Uig on Skye to Tarbert, from Otternish on North Uist to An T-ob (Leverburgh) and from Ullapool to Stornoway ✈️ Flights from Glasgow and Edinburgh to Stornoway ❓ No public transport on Sundays

MELROSE

www.visitscottishborders.com

The Romans built a massive fort here, by a bridge over the River Tweed, and called it Trimontium after the three peaks of the Eildon Hills. There's little left to see now, but the Three Hills Roman Heritage Centre in this compact Borders town sets it all in context (Mar–end Oct daily 11.30–4.30).

The more visible history of Melrose dates from 1136, when David I (c1085–1153) founded the pink sandstone abbey (Apr–end Sep daily 9.30–5.30; rest of year daily 9.30–4.30). Repairs in the 19th century were at the instigation of novelist Sir Walter Scott; the ruins are majestic, and the stone carving outstanding—look up to see saints, dragons, flowers and a pig playing the bagpipes. The burial place of Robert the Bruce's heart in the abbey is marked by an engraved inscription.

✚ 467 G9 ℹ️ Abbey House TD6 9LG, tel 0870 608 0404

NEW LANARK WORLD HERITAGE SITE

www.newlanark.org

Robert Owen (1771–1858) bought the cotton mills here in 1799 and established a utopian society—a model community with improved conditions for the workers and their families. There was a school, day nursery, institute for adult education and village store run by a cooperative. The site declined, but in 1973 the New Lanark Conservation Trust started to restore it, with the results seen today.

✚ 467 E9 ✉️ New Lanark Mills, Lanark ML11 9DB ☎️ 01555 661345 🕐 Visitor Centre: Jun–end Aug daily 10.30–5, rest of year 11–5 🎫 Adult £5.95, child (5–16) £4.95, family £17.95 🛒 🎁

ORKNEY ISLANDS

This low-lying group of more than 90 islands and skerries lies 20 miles (32km) off the northern coast of Scotland. Orkney joined Scotland in the 13th century as part of a dowry when Margaret of Denmark married the Scottish king James III (1452–88). Today these islands ring with Norse-sounding place names, although Picts and Celts pre-dated the Vikings by at least 4,000 years, leaving extraordinary signs of their presence at Maes Howe and Skara Brae.

Hoy is the second-largest of the Orkney islands. Its best-known feature is the columnar stack of red sandstone, known as the Old Man of Hoy. Standing at 137m (450ft), it's a challenge for climbers.

The heather-covered hills of Cuilags and Ward Hill offer excellent walking country, with views over Scapa Flow. This sheltered natural harbour was home to the Royal Navy during both world wars, and was the site of the scuttling of the German fleet after the end of World War I. Learn more at the fascinating Scapa Flow Visitor Centre and Museum at Lyness (May–end Sep Mon–Sat 9–4.30, Sun times depend on ferry timetable; rest of year Mon–Fri 9–4.30). A group of Italian prisoners of war confined on the islands during World War II created the Italian Chapel (daily, dawn–dusk) in two Nissen huts.

The buildings of Kirkwall's narrow streets date from the 16th to the 18th centuries. Dominating everything is St. Magnus Cathedral on Broad Street (Apr–end Sep Mon–Sat 9–6, Sun 1–6; rest of year Mon–Sat 9–1, 2–5).

A 7m (23ft) grassy mound in a field to the south of Loch of Harray, on the road from Stromness to Finstown, Maes Howe (Apr–end Sep daily 9.30–5; Oct–end Mar 9.30–4) looks unpromising at first sight. Under the turf, however, lies a chambered grave dating from around 2800BC that is a treasure of World Heritage status. While the contents are long gone, the structure itself has survived undamaged, barring some runic graffiti left by passing Vikings. Don't miss the nearby Ring of Brodgar, a magnificent stone circle.

A visit to Skara Brae (Apr–end Sep daily 9.30–5.30; rest of year daily 9.30–4.30) is essential. Northwest of Kirkwall, it is the site of a village inhabited between 3100 and 2500BC. The sands subsequently encroached and covered the houses, which lay undiscovered until a storm in 1850 revealed stone structures. Excavations showed six similar houses linked by passageways. As you walk around the site, you look down into the houses from above, through what would have been roofs of skin and turf. Slabs of stone created hearths, cupboards in the walls, bed surrounds, clay-lined troughs in the floor, and even a dresser, suggesting a delightfully unexpected degree of sophistication.

Orkney's second town, Stromness, boomed in the early 19th century. The winding main street is paved and cobbled; follow it all the way to its southern end, to the maritime displays in the Stromness Museum on Alfred Street (Apr–end Sep daily 10–5; Oct to mid-Feb, mid-Mar to end Apr Mon–Sat 11–3.30).

INFORMATION
www.visitorkney.com
➕ 471 F2 ℹ️ 6 Broad Street, Kirkwall KW15 1NX, tel 01856 872856 🚢 Ferry: from Aberdeen (6 hr) or Scrabster, by Thurso (90 min) ✈️ Kirkwall

REGIONS SCOTLAND • SIGHTS

Above *Abandoned and overgrown croft buildings, Rackwick, Hoy*

Above *Rosslyn Chapel, one of the finest examples of medieval stone carving in Britain*

PERTH

The Roman settlement of Perth was founded in the first century AD. Today it is a lively city, with great shops and cafés. The Perth Mart, in the old cattle market, is the venue for the pedigree bull sales, held in October and February.

Open-top bus tours depart from the rail station to Scone Palace (Apr–end Oct daily 9.30–5.30). In the grounds of this stately home is Moot Hall, the earliest crowning place of Scottish kings and first home of the Stone of Destiny (▷ 366).
✚ 467 F7 ℹ️ Lower City Mills, West Mill Street PH1 5QP, tel 01738 450600 (seasonal) 🚆 Perth

PITLOCHRY

Pitlochry has one long main street. It's been a popular holiday resort since the 19th century, and has two distilleries: Bell's Blair Atholl (Easter–end Apr Mon–Sat 9.30–5; Jun–end Oct Mon–Sat 9.30–5, Sun 2–5; Nov–Easter tours only at 11am, 1pm, 3pm) and Edradour (Mar–end Oct Mon–Sat 9.30–6, Sun 11.30–5; Nov–end Dec Mon–Sat 9.30–4, Sun 11.30–4; Jan–end Feb Mon–Sat 10–4, Sun 12–4). A footbridge leads to the Festival Theatre and Plant Collectors Garden (Easter–end Oct daily 10–5).
✚ 467 E7 ℹ️ 22 Atholl Road PH16 5DB, tel 01796 472215 🚆 Pitlochry

ROSSLYN CHAPEL

www.rosslynchapel.org.uk
This is the most mysterious building in Scotland: It was made famous by Dan Brown's *The Da Vinci Code*. A church was founded here in 1446. It was to be a large cruciform structure, but only the choir was ever built, along with parts of the east transept walls. It is linked with the Knights Templar and believed by some to be the hiding place of the Holy Grail.
✚ 467 F8 ✉️ Roslin EH25 9PU ☎️ 0131 440 2159 🕐 Mon–Sat 9.30–6, Sun 12–4.45 ✋ Adult £7, under 16s free ♿

ST. ANDREWS

St. Andrews has a sandy bay and a narrow harbour, and Scotland's oldest university, founded in 1413. It is also the home of the Royal and Ancient Golf Club, founded in 1754 and still the ruling authority on the game. Check out its history at the British Golf Museum on Bruce Embankment (mid-Mar to end Oct Mon–Sat 9.30–5.30, Sun 10–5; Nov to mid-Mar daily 10–4).

Near the ruins of the cathedral stand the remains of the 12th-century St. Rule's Tower. Climb the spiral stairs of the 33m (108ft) tower for views that reveal the medieval grid of the city streets.

North along the shore lie the spectacular ruins of the castle, rebuilt in 1390, where a battle and siege took place in 1546 (Apr–end Sep daily 9.30–5.30; rest of year daily 9.30–4.30).
✚ 467 G7 ℹ️ 70 Market Street KY16 9NU, tel 01334 472021

SCOTTISH CRANNOG CENTRE

www.crannog.co.uk
Crannogs were circular, communal dwellings built on stilts above the surface of a loch, and 2,000 years ago central Scotland was apparently littered with them. One has been reconstructed near Kenmore at the eastern end of Loch Tay. Informative tours show some of the remarkable discoveries from the site, and take you across the uneven pier into the hut itself, where you can learn how archaeologists have gleaned clues to the way of life of the original crannog dwellers. Back on land, there are demonstrations of ancient skills such as fire-making. Reserving ahead is essential in mid-summer.
✚ 467 E7 ✉️ Kenmore, South Loch Tay, near Aberfeldy PH15 2HY ☎️ 01887 830583 🕐 Mid-Mar to end Oct daily 10–5.30; Nov Sat–Sun 10–4 ✋ Adult £5.75, child (5–16) £4, family £14 ♿

SPEYSIDE

www.maltwhiskytrail.com
The River Spey flows from the Cairngorms (▷ 362) near Aviemore and winds northeast through gentle hills and woodland to pour into the sea between Lossiemouth and Buckie. On the way, it flows under a magnificent iron bridge at Craigellachie designed by engineer Thomas Telford (1757–1834). It lends its name to the historic Strathspey Railway and the town of Grantown-on-Spey, and picks up a long-distance trail, the Speyside Way. Speyside is a name associated with the area between Elgin, Grantown and Keith, and more particularly with the production of some of Scotland's famous single malt whiskies. Eight distilleries are linked by the signposted Malt Whisky Trail: Glen Grant, Glen Moray, Cardhu, Strathisla, Glenlivet, Benromach, Dallas Dhu and Glenfiddich. Each offers tours and whisky tastings, but opening times and admissions vary so check ahead (the tourist office has a leaflet with all the information).
✚ 469 F5 ℹ️ 17 High Street, Elgin IV30 1EG, tel 01343 542666 ℹ️ High Street, Grantown-on-Spey PH26 3EH, tel 01479 872773 (seasonal)

SHETLAND ISLANDS

Shetland has an unusually cosmopolitan air, thanks to its northern trade routes, and a culture that is more Viking than Scottish.

Shetland, a grouping of more than 100 islands, is the most northerly part of Britain, lying as close to Bergen in Norway as to Aberdeen.

The capital is the harbour town of Lerwick. Dutch herring fishermen used its sheltered harbour in the 17th century. In the shops, traditional knitwear is the thing to buy; if you can't see what you want, dextrous workers will make you a bespoke garment. The Shetland Museum in a splendid new building on Hays Dock is a terrific introduction to the islands (Mon–Wed, Fri–Sat 10–5, Thu 10–7, Sun 12–4).

Complex layers of history were uncovered at Jarlshof Prehistoric and Norse Settlement (Apr–end Sep daily 9.30–5.30), near Sumburgh, when a storm dislodged the covering turf. The obvious survivor is the shell of the 17th-century Laird's House, which overlies a broch (a prehistoric circular stone tower). Around it are the remains of a Viking farm with a communal longhouse. Further layers have revealed a settlement from the second century BC, and a 14th-century medieval farm, creating an intriguing record of life here.

The double-skinned circular tower of Mousa Broch dates from 100BC to AD300, and is the best-preserved example of its kind in Scotland. Access in summer is via a small passenger boat from Leebitton, in Sandwick (boat trips on *Solan N* mid-Apr to mid-Sep weather permitting. Reservations essential, tel: 01950 431367 or 07901 872339).

A tiny grass-covered island off the southwest coast, St. Ninian's Isle is a green jewel. It is joined to the land by a curved tombolo of silvery shell sand, which permits access except during the highest tides of the year, and is a lovely area for walks. St. Ninian was the first Christian missionary to reach Shetland, and the ruins of a 12th-century church still stand. In 1958 a hoard of intricately worked Pictish silver was discovered, buried under the nave. The treasure is now in the National Museum of Scotland in Edinburgh (▷ 367), but replicas can be seen in the Shetland Museum in Lerwick.

Much of Unst's fame rests on its status as the most northerly of the Shetland isles. The nature reserve at Hermaness is home in summer to 100,000 screaming seabirds who nest on and around the cliffs. There's a regular ferry service from Yell to Unst.

INFORMATION

www.visitshetland.com

⊞ 471 G3 🚶 Market Cross, Lerwick ZE1 0LU, tel 01595 693434 🚢 Ferry to Lerwick from Kirkwall (8 hr) or Aberdeen (14 hr) ✈ Sumburgh

Above *St. Magnus Bay, Mainland*

INFORMATION

➕ 468 B5 ℹ️ Bayfield House, Bayfield Road, Portree IV51 9EL, tel 01478 612137
🛳️ Ferry: Mallaig to Armadale (40 min, summer), Glenelg to Kylerhea (15 min, summer), Skye Bridge at Kyle of Lochalsh

Above *The Cuillin Hills looking across Loch Scavaig from Elgol*
Below *Dunvegan Castle, seen from across the bay*

SKYE

Skye is the largest and best known of the Inner Hebrides, its name woven into the story of Bonnie Prince Charlie's flight after the Battle of Culloden (▷ 363) in the 18th century, and the loss of a way of island life and emigration to the New World in the 19th century. Every view of the island is dominated by the Cuillin (pronounced *coolin*), jagged mountains that reach their highest peak in the south with Sgurr Alasdair (1,009m/3,310ft). These are the Black Cuillin, distinct from the scree-covered granite of the lower Red Cuillin, but all are challenges for climbers. In the north of the island, ancient lava flows have produced sheer cliffs, with crags and pinnacles such as the Old Man of Storr, created where softer rocks buckled under the weight of the lava. The unusual formations of the Quiraing on the Trotternish peninsula can be examined more closely if you walk with care.

The harbour town of Portree is the focus of island life, and its Aros Experience offers the best introduction to Skye's natural history (daily 9–5.30).

The Skye bridge sets one massive concrete foot firmly on the little 2.4ha (6-acre) island of Eilean Ban, a nature reserve run by a charitable trust for the local community. Access is via the Bright Water Visitor Centre on the pier at Kyleakin (times vary, tel 01599 530040), which has information on local wildlife and history.

The western side of Skye is wilder, with the long fingers of Waternish and Duinish stretching to the Outer Hebrides. Dunvegan is the family seat of the MacLeods, and claims to be Scotland's oldest inhabited castle, occupied since the 13th century (mid-Mar to end Oct daily 10–5.30; rest of year daily 11–4, last entry 30 min before closing). Among its treasures is the Fairy Flag, a now tattered scrap of cloth, with apparently potent powers to rescue the clan at times of peril.

Broadford is the main place in the south, with access to the magnificently scenic road to Elgol. If you haven't already seen otters in the coastal waters, take a look at them at the Kylerhea Otter Haven (daily dawn–dusk).

Skye offers some excellent dining (▷ 405). At Carbost, the Talisker Distillery produces a fragrant, peaty single malt whisky (Easter–end Jun, Sep–end Oct Mon–Sat 9.30–5; Jul–end Aug Mon–Sat 9.30–5, Sun 12.30–5; Jan–Easter tours 1.30pm, 3.30pm; Nov–end Dec tours by appointment only).

STIRLING

www.stirling.co.uk

Stirling Castle's strategic position high on a rocky outcrop, commanding the narrow waist of land between the Forth estuary and the marshlands of the west (now drained), has given it a prominent role in Scottish history. The castle, where Mary, Queen of Scots spent her childhood, served as a royal palace and was remodelled many times (Apr–end Sep daily 9.30–6; rest of year daily 9.30–5). Mary was crowned in the Chapel Royal in 1543. The town behind and below the castle has other interesting buildings and was of particular importance in the Wars of Independence fought against England in the 13th and 14th centuries. Notable Scottish victories include Stirling Bridge (1297), fought at the Old Bridge, when William Wallace (c1270–1305) cleverly split the opposing army, and Bannockburn (1314), when Robert the Bruce (1274–1329) took charge. Both men are commemorated as local heroes: Wallace with the National Wallace Monument on the hill of Abbey Craig (Nov–end Feb daily 10.30–4; Mar–end May, Oct daily 10–5; Jun daily 10–6; Jul–end Aug daily 9–6; Sep daily 9.30–5.30), and Bruce with a heritage centre on the field of Bannockburn, below the castle (Apr–end Oct daily 10–5.30).

🞤 467 E8 ℹ 41 Dumbarton Road, Stirling, FK8 2QQ, tel 08452 255121 🚆 Stirling

THREAVE GARDEN AND ESTATE

www.nts.org.uk

Threave is an investment in the future. The National Trust for Scotland has created a teaching garden, where horticulturalists come to learn and try out new ideas. It offers a mixture of established splendours such as a vast walled garden alongside less formal, more experimental areas. The garden was created during the Victorian era and Threave House dates from 1872.

🞤 464 E10 ✉ Castle Douglas DG7 1RX ☎ 0844 493 2245 🕓 Garden and estate: daily, all year. Visitor centre and countryside centre: Mar–end Oct daily 9.30–5.30; Feb,

Nov–end Dec daily 10–4. House: Mar–end Oct Wed–Fri, Sun, 11–3.30 (guided tours only, admission by timed ticket) 🖐 Garden: adult £10, child (5–16) £7, family £25 🍴 🏛

TORRIDON

A spectacular wilderness of massive, bare mountains, Torridon, Scotland's first national nature reserve, lies on the northwest coast. The 1,000m (3,282ft) bulk of Beinn Eighe looms above the lonely pass between Shieldaig and Kinlochewe, shedding white quarzite scree like snow. To the west, Liathach (1,055m/3,460ft) is the tallest peak in the range, closely followed by Beinn Alligin (985m/ 3,232ft). The mountains are for serious walkers only, but there's a more accessible path along the north shore of Loch Torridon to Red Point. The National Trust for Scotland has a visitor centre by Torridon village (Easter–end Sep daily 10–5).

🞤 468 C5 ℹ Auchtercairn, Gairloch IV21 2DN, tel 01455 712071 (seasonal)

TRAQUAIR

www.traquair.co.uk

An air of romance and secrecy surrounds Traquair, a beautiful old castle buried in the trees about 6 miles (10km) southeast of Peebles. It started out as a royal hunting lodge for King James III (1452–88), and at one point the River Tweed ran so close that he could fish from his windows. In the 17th century, however, the river was re-routed by Sir William Stuart. The castle has been in the continuous ownership of the Maxwell Stuarts since 1491.

Traquair's sense of mystery comes from its connections with the doomed Stuart cause to take over the Scottish throne. Mary, Queen of Scots called by here in 1566, and the famous Bear Gates have not been opened since 1745, when Bonnie Prince Charlie last rode through. The fifth earl of the Maxwell Stuarts was incarcerated for helping him and promised that the gates would not be opened until a Stuart was on the throne.

Above *Shellfish baskets on the quayside at Ullapool*

The Traquair Brewery was successfully revived in 1965. Taste the results in the shop.

🞤 467 F9 ✉ Innerleithen EH44 6PW ☎ 01896 830323 🕓 May–end Sep daily 12–5; Jun–end Aug daily 10.30–5; Oct daily 11–3; Mar–end Apr Sat–Sun 12–5; Nov Sat–Sun 11–3 🖐 House and grounds: adult £6.50 child (5–14) £3.50, family £18 🍴 🏛

ULLAPOOL

www.ullapool.com

This small town stretches along a spit of land on the shore of Loch Broom. An 18th-century planned town, Ullapool may no longer be the hub of the North Atlantic fishing industry, but it is a good touring base. The road north leads into a sparsely populated country of peatbog and loch, heather moorland and bare, rocky mountains. This is the 11,000ha (27,180-acre) national nature reserve of Inverpolly, and the prominent lumps of rock are mountains of weathered, red Torridonian sandstone, of which the most accessible is Stac Pollaidh (612m/2,008ft). The area is rich in wildlife and there are sandy beaches at Achnahaird, Garvie, Reiff and Badentarbat.

Remote Achiltibuie, north of Ullapool and reached via a winding, single-track road, has views to the Summer Isles.

🞤 469 D4 ℹ Argyle Street, Ullapool IV26 2UR, tel 08452 255121 🚢 Badentarbat to Summer Isles cruises, summer; ferry to Lewis

DRIVE

SCOTTISH BORDERS

This circular drive from Moffat takes in some of the loveliest landscapes of the Scottish Borders, chasing literary connections with novelists John Buchan (1875–1940) and Sir Walter Scott (1771–1832), and poets William Wordsworth (1770–1850) and James Hogg (1770–1835).

THE DRIVE

Distance: 120 miles (193km)
Allow: 1–2 days
Start/end: Moffat

★ Leave the attractive 17th-century spa village of Moffat by the A701, which follows the Tweed valley. Turn right at the B712 to Dawyck Botanic Garden.

❶ This is an outpost of the Royal Botanic Garden, Edinburgh. Established over 300 years ago, it is noted for its trees, with magnificent autumnal displays from beeches and maples.

Return along the B712, turn right at the A701, and follow this to Broughton.

❷ In a converted church in Broughton, the John Buchan Centre details the history of the master storyteller whose best-known novel is *The*

Thirty-nine Steps. Buchan was also a historian, and wrote biographies of Sir Walter Scott and the 17th-century Scottish general James Montrose. Don't miss Broughton Gallery, set in a fairy-tale castle up the hill.

Continue on the A701 and turn right at the A72. Turn left at the A721 and right at the A702. Follow this into the narrow streets of West Linton.

❸ In the 17th century West Linton became famous for its stonemasons, who were the chief gravestone carvers in the area. Gifford's Stone, a well-worn bas relief on a wall in the main street, is by James Gifford. Opposite it is another of his works, the Lady Gifford Well, which he carved in 1666. The Cauld Stane Slap, an ancient road across the Pentland Hills, passes nearby.

Leave the village by the B7059. Turn right at the A701 and left at

the B7059. Turn left at the A72 for Peebles. Pass the tower of Neidpath Castle on the right, above the River Tweed, as you enter the town of Peebles. Leave the town on the A72, passing the Kailzie Gardens. After 6 miles (9.6km) reach Innerleithen.

❹ Innerleithen is Scotland's oldest spa. It boomed in the 19th century after Sir Walter Scott named one of his novels *St. Ronan's Well* (1823), after the town's mineral wells. In the High Street, Robert Smail's Printing Works is a tiny print shop started in 1840, when the press was powered by water. Historic Traquair House lies just over 1 mile (1.6km) to the south.

Stay on the A72 for 12 miles (19km) to reach the busy textile town of Galashiels.

❺ Galashiels is famous for its weaving. The story of the mills is told in the Lochcarron Cashmere

Above *Grey Mare's Tail waterfalls*
Opposite *Dawyck Botanical Gardens*

Wool of Scotland Visitor Centre; entertaining factory tours show the entire process of tartan manufacture. Look for Old Gala House, founded around 1583. The nearby mercat (market) cross, which marks the centre of the old town, dates from 1695. It features in the Braw Lads Gathering, an annual festival dating from 1599, during which the boundaries of the town are confirmed by being ridden on horseback.

Leave by the A7, signposted to Selkirk. Turn right at the B7060, then left at the A707 at Yair Bridge. Continue on this road, which becomes the A708 near Selkirk. Follow Ettrick Water and then Yarrow Water on the A708 to Yarrowford, a distance of 13 miles (21km).

❻ This scattered village lies on Yarrow Water, the river that inspired William Wordsworth to compose three poems in its praise. The former royal hunting lodge of Newark Tower lies downstream and dates from 1423. Hunting took place in the hills of Ettrick Forest until the 16th

century, when sheep farming was introduced.

❼ The ruins of Foulshiels House also lie this way. It was the birthplace of explorer Mungo Park (1771–1806), who died in his search for the source of the Niger (▷ 388). Bowhill House, a 19th-century mansion, is surrounded by a country park.

Continue on the A708, passing along the northwestern shore of St. Marys Loch.

❽ At 3 miles (4.8km) long, St Marys Loch is one of the best places in southern Scotland for watersports. At the southern end of the loch, on a spit of land which separates it from the smaller Loch of the Lowes, a red sandstone monument recalls local poet James Hogg, known as the Ettrick Shepherd. Hogg spent many an evening in the nearby Tibbie Shiels Inn with his friend Sir Walter Scott.

Continue on the A708 for 9 miles (14.5km) and follow signs to the

parking area at the Grey Mare's Tail waterfall. Stay on the A708 for 10 miles (16km) to reach Moffat.

PLACES TO VISIT
BOWHILL HOUSE
✉ Selkirk TD7 5ET
☎ 01750 22204
🕐 Jul daily 1–4.30; park only: mid-Apr to end Aug Sat–Thu 11–5
✋ House £6, park £2

DAWYCK BOTANIC GARDEN
✉ STOBO EH45 9JU
☎ 01721 760254
🕐 Apr–end Sep daily 10–6; Mar, Oct 10–5; rest of year 10–4
✋ Adult £3.30, child £1, family £8

ROBERT SMAIL'S PRINTING WORKS
✉ 7–9 High Street, Innerleithen EH44
☎ 01896 830206
🕐 Easter, Jun–end Sep Thu–Mon 12–5, Sun 1–5
✋ Adult £5, child £4, family £14

WHEN TO GO
Visit in the autumn and enjoy the blaze of colour at the Royal Botanic Garden.

FROM SELKIRK TO THE WILDS OF AFRICA

A gentle walk by Ettrick Water, laced with memories of the great explorer Mungo Park (1771–1806).

THE WALK

Length: 3 miles (4.8km)
Allow: 1 hour 40 min
Start/end: West Port Car Park, Selkirk, map ref 467 F9
OS Explorer map: 338

★ It is hard to imagine that the sleepy town of Selkirk has any connection with the wilds of Africa. But look carefully at the statue in the High Street and you'll see that it commemorates Mungo Park, a local, the noted surgeon and explorer, who was born near by at Foulshiels.

From Park's statue in the High Street walk to the Market Place, go right down Ettrick Terrace, left at the church, then sharp right down Forest Road. Follow this downhill, cutting off the corners using the steps, after No. 109, to Mill Street. Go right, then left on to Buccleuch Road. Turn right following the signs for the riverside walk and go across Victoria Park to join a tarmac track.

❶ Park was educated at Selkirk Grammar School, trained as a doctor and took a post as surgeon's mate on a ship bound for the East Indies. He returned from the voyage and promptly set off again, this time heading for Africa to map the River Niger. Park's journey lasted more than 2.5 years.

When Park returned to Scotland he published an account of his explorations, *Travels in the Interior Districts of Africa* (1799), which became a bestseller. He disappeared during a second expedition in 1806. Tragedy struck again when his son followed in his footsteps some 20 years later, and disappeared without a trace.

Turn left, walk by the river, then join the road and turn right to cross the bridge. Turn left along Ettrickhaugh Road, passing a row of cottages on your left. Just past them turn left, cross a tiny footbridge, then turn left down some steps, follow the path to the riverbank and turn right.

Follow the path along the river margin; it's eroded in places so watch your feet. Eventually join a wider track and bear left. Follow this to reach a weir (small dam) and a salmon ladder. Turn right to cross the tiny bridge.

Immediately after this go left and continue walking alongside the river until you reach a point at which Yarrow Water joins the Ettrick Water. Retrace your steps for about 91m (100yds), then turn left at a crossing of tracks.

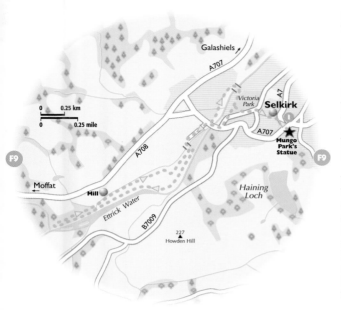

Galashiels

A707

Victoria Park

Selkirk

A7

A707

Mungo Park's Statue ★

Moffat ←

Mill

A708

Ettrick Water

B7009

Haining Loch

227 ▲ Howden Hill

F9

0   0.25 km
0   0.25 mile

don't cross the bridge but join the footpath on the left.

Follow this footpath as it goes past a sports ground, then skirts a housing estate. Continue walking until you reach the pedestrian footbridge on your right-hand side, where you cross over the river, bear right, then retrace your footsteps back over Victoria Park and uphill to the Market Place at the start of the walk.

WHERE TO EAT
There are several places to try in the centre of Selkirk. Among the hotels offering bar meals is the Cross Keys by the Market Place, which serves toasted sandwiches and light snacks. There's also a small tea room. Look for the famous Selkirk bannock, a small fruitcake, on sale in the town bakeries.

PLACE TO VISIT
SIR WALTER SCOTT'S COURTROOM
✉ Market Place, Selkirk TD7 4BT
☎ 01750 20761
🕐 Easter–end Sep Mon–Sat 10–4;
Jun–end Aug Sun 10–2; Oct Mon–Sat 1–4
✋ Free

WHEN TO VISIT
In spring and summer the waterside route is sprinkled with wild flowers.

Your route now takes you through the woods, until you cross over the little bridge by the weir again. Take the footpath to the left and follow the cinder/gravel track around the meadow until you come to the mill buildings.

Bear right (but don't cross the bridge) and continue, walking with the mill lade (small canal) on your

left. Where the path splits, take the track on the left to follow a straight, concrete path beside the water to reach an abandoned fish farm.

Walk around the buildings, then bear left to continue following the mill lade. Go left over the footbridge, then right, passing the cottages again. At the main road go right to reach the bridge. At this point

Opposite Market Place, Selkirk
Left Selkirk in the Tweed Valley
Below Statue of explorer Mungo Park in Selkirk

WESTERN HIGHLANDS

'The Road to the Isles', an old cattle drovers' road, leads into the western Highlands at the start of one of the most scenic routes in Scotland.

THE DRIVE

Distance: 205 miles (330km)
Allow: 2–3 days
Start/end: Fort William

★ Leave Fort William on the A82 towards Inverness, then turn left at the A830, signposted Mallaig. Turn right at the B8004 toward Banavie to admire Neptune's Staircase, the flight of locks on the Caledonian Canal (▷ 392–393). Return to the A830, then turn right and follow the road along Loch Eil to Glenfinnan.

❶ Glenfinnan, at the head of Loch Shiel, is famous for its links with the ill-fated Jacobite rebellion of 1745. Take the short path behind the National Trust for Scotland's visitor office to view the 21-arch Glenfinnan viaduct, by Sir Robert 'Concrete Bob' MacAlpine (1847–1934), which carries the scenic West Highland Railway to Mallaig. The railway runs parallel with the road for much of the way—look for steam locomotives running in summer.

Follow the A830, passing the shores of Loch nan Uamh.

❷ A cairn marks the spot where, after defeat at Culloden in 1746 and months in hiding in the Western Isles, Bonnie Prince Charlie finally fled to exile in France. He was helped during this time by many ordinary people, and despite a well-publicized reward of £30,000, nobody betrayed him.

Continue on the A830, passing through woodland of beech, oak and birch to the village of Arisaig.

❸ During World War II, agents of the Special Operation Executive (SOE) trained in the area around Arisaig, honing their fieldcraft skills before being dropped behind enemy lines in Europe. Their base was nearby Arisaig House, a private manor house in a magnificent setting (private).

Continue on the A830 up the coast to Morar, with views out to the islands of Eigg and Skye.

❹ Morar is famous for its silvery silica sands, and for its very own monster, Morag, who is believed to live in the murky depths of Loch Morar, 310m (1,020ft) down.

Continue on the A830 to Mallaig.

❺ Mallaig's busy fishing harbour, facing the island of Skye across the Sound of Sleat, is the mainland terminal for ferries to the Inner Hebrides, including the group of Rum, Eigg, Muck and Canna, known as the Small Isles. Mallaig rose to prominence after the arrival of the railway in 1901. That was during the herring boom—now prawns are a mainstay. See them in Marine World, an aquarium on the harbour front. At the road's end, Mallaigvaig looks across to the hills of Knoydart, one of the remotest areas of Scotland.

Return along the A830 to Lochailort. Turn right at the A861 and follow it to Kinlochmoidart and Acharacle.

6 Acharacle lies at the southwest tip of Loch Shiel. A detour on to the B8044 leads to the dramatic ruin of Castle Tioram, on Loch Moidart (free access). It lies on a rocky islet at the end of a sandy spit, and dates from the early 13th century, although the central keep is newer. It was the seat of the Macdonalds of Clanranald, and was deliberately burned down when Allan, the 14th chief, set off in 1715 to join the Jacobite uprising, to prevent its use by Campbell enemies.

Continue on the A861 to Salen, then turn right at the B8007, to explore the Ardnamurchan peninsula. Continue on the B8007, passing through the scattered community of Kilchoan, to Ardnamurchan Point.

7 The most westerly point on the British mainland, Ardnamurchan is marked with a lighthouse, and has superb views to the islands of the Inner Hebrides, Barra and South Uist.

Return to Salen along the B8007, then turn right at the A861 to the Highland village of Strontian.

8 Strontian gives its name to the element strontium, extracted from the mineral strontianite, discovered here in 1764. Strontium has a deep crimson flame when burned, and is used in fireworks. The area was extensively mined between 1722 and 1904 for lead, zinc and silver; it now supplies minerals for the lubrication of oil rigs. There are walks through the nearby Ariundel woods.

Continue on the A861, then turn right on to the A884. Follow this to Lochaline.

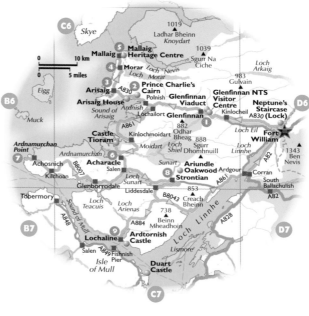

9 Lochaline stands on the Sound of Mull, with a ferry service to Fishnish, and views to the ruins of Ardtornish Castle, and Duart Castle on Mull.

Return on the A884 to the junction (right) with the B8043. Follow this road to meet the A861. Turn right and follow this up Loch Linnhe to Ardgour. Take the Corran ferry across the loch at the Corran Narrows. At the other side turn left on to the A82 and return to Fort William.

PLACE TO VISIT
MALLAIG MARINE WORLD

✉ Mallaig Harbour PH41 4XP

☎ 01687 462292

🕐 Jun–end Aug Mon–Sat 9–6, Sun 11–6; Apr–end May, Sep–end Oct Mon–Sat 9–5, Sun 11–5; Nov–end Mar Mon–Sat 9–5

✋ Adult £2.75, child £1.50

WHEN TO GO

Choose a fine day for the drive to enjoy the superb views at Ardnamurchan Point.

Opposite *A steam train in Glenfinnan Valley*
Below *On the banks of Loch Linnhe*

THE CALEDONIAN CANAL

A walk alongside—and underneath—Thomas Telford's masterpiece of civil engineering.

THE WALK
Length: 4.5 miles (7.2km)
Allow: 1 hour 45 min
Start/end: Kilmallie Hall, Corpach
OS Explorer map: 392

★ The first survey for a coast-to-coast canal across Scotland, linking the lochs of the Great Glen, was made by James Watt, inventor of the steam engine, in 1767. For this great enterprise, only one name was seriously considered: Thomas Telford (1757–1834).

From Kilmallie Hall, go down past Corpach Station to the canal and cross the sea lock that separates salt water from fresh water.

❶ Each of the 29 locks on the Caledonian Canal was designed to accommodate the width and length of a 40-gun frigate of Lord Nelson's navy fleet.

Follow the canal (on your left) up past another lock, where a path on the right has a Great Glen Way marker. It passes under tall sycamores to the shore. Follow the shoreline path past a soccer pitch and then turn left, across grass to the end of a back street. A path ahead leads up a wooded bank to the towpath.

Just before the bridge, turn right at signs for the Great Glen Way and the Great Glen Cycle Route.

❷ The Great Glen Way is a spectacular 75-mile (120km) coast-to-coast walking route between Fort

William and Inverness on low-level woodland tracks and the towpath which runs alongside the Caledonian Canal. Cyclists can use the Great Glen Cycle Route which follows a similar route, sharing some of the trail.

❸ The Caledonian Canal was a tremendous feat of civil engineering. Some 200 million wheelbarrow-loads of earth were shifted over the next 19 years. Four aqueducts let streams and rivers pass below the waterway, and there was a dam on Loch Lochy and diversion of the rivers Oich and Lochy. Loch Oich needed to be deepened, and for this task a steam dredger had not only to be built, but invented and designed too. After falling into a state of neglect in the 20th century, the canal

Opposite *The lochs at Corpach Basin on the Caledonian Canal, Highlands*
Right *Ben Nevis rises up in the background behind Loch Linnhe*

was on the verge of closure when, in 1996, the government promised £20 million for a complete refurbishment.

Continue along the towpath to Neptune's Staircase.

❹ This fanciful name was given to the group of eight locks by Thomas Telford himself. It takes about 90 minutes for boats to work through the system. As each lock fills, slow roiling currents come up from underneath, and as each empties, water forced under pressure into the banks emerges from the masonry in little fountains. The 18m (60ft) of ascent alongside the locks is the serious uphill part of this walk.

A gate marks the top of the locks. About 183m (200yds) later, a grey gate on the right leads to a dump for dead cars; ignore this one. Over the next 90m (100yds) the canal crosses

a little wooded valley, with a black fence on the right. Now comes a second grey gate. Go through, to a track turning back sharp right and descending to ford a small stream.

On the right, the stream passes right under the canal in an arched tunnel, and alongside is a second tunnel which provides a walkers'

way to the other side. Water from the canal drips into the tunnel, which has a fairly spooky atmosphere. At the tunnel's end, a track runs up to join the canal's northern towpath. Turn right, back down the towpath. After passing Neptune's Staircase, cross the A830 to a level crossing without warning lights. Continue along the right-hand towpath. After a mile (1.6km) the towpath track leads back to the Corpach double lock.

WHERE TO EAT
The Moorings Inn at Banavie offers restaurant and bar meals. On the other side of both the A830 and canal, the unassuming Lochy family pub has picnic tables and promises 'massive portions'. At the walk start, a Spar shop sells hot pies, and Kilmallie Hall has a community garden with picnic tables to eat them at.

PLACE TO VISIT
INVERLOCHY CASTLE
✉ Fort William, Invernesshire
✋ Free

WHEN TO VISIT
This is an enjoyable, easy walk at any time of the year.

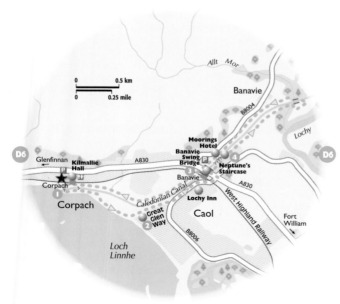

ABERDEEN

THE BELMONT

www.picturehouses.co.uk

This popular art-house cinema also screens classic films and holds French and Italian film festivals.

✉ 49 Belmont Street, Aberdeen AB10 1JS ☎ 01224 343536 🕐 Daily ✋ From £3.70 🖥 🚇 Aberdeen

ESSLEMONT & MACINTOSH

This large independent department store has been a fixture of Aberdeen's 'Granite Mile' since 1873. On a site split between two buildings, discover emporia of clothes, cosmetics, perfume, china, gifts and things for the home.

✉ 26–38 Union Street, Aberdeen AB10 1GD ☎ 01224 647331 🕐 Mon, Wed, Fri–Sat 9–5.30, Tue 9.30–5.30, Thu 9–7.30, Sun 12–4 🖥 🚇 Aberdeen

LEMON TREE

www.lemontree.org

The best music venue in Aberdeen, with classical, traditional Irish, funk, blues and rock concerts. Also hosts theatre, dance and comedy. Close to the top of Union Street.

✉ 5 West North Street, Aberdeen AB24 5AT ☎ 01224 642230 🕐 All year 🖥 Food Thu–Sun 12–3; live jazz Fri and Sun 🚇 Aberdeen

MUSIC HALL

www.musichallaberdeen.com

Big classical concerts are held here, including performances by the Royal Scottish National Orchestra. Also jazz concerts.

✉ Union Street, Aberdeen AB10 1QS ☎ 01224 641122 (box office) 🕐 All year 🛒 🚇 Aberdeen

OLD BLACKFRIAR'S

Cosy pub dating back to the time of Mary, Queen of Scots.

✉ 52 Castle Street, Aberdeen AB11 5BB ☎ 01224 581922 🕐 Mon–Sat 11am– midnight, Sun 12.30–11.30 🚇 Aberdeen

ABERFELDY

HIGHLAND ADVENTURE SAFARIS

www.highlandadventuresafaris.co.uk

Explore the Highlands on a Land Rover tour. Local wildlife includes grouse, deer and golden eagles.

✉ The Highland Safari Lodge, Dull, Aberfeldy PH15 2JQ ☎ 01887 820071

🕐 All year ✋ 2 hour 30 min tour: adult £32.50, child (under 12) £12.50, (13–18) £17.50 🖥 🚇

ARRAN (ISLE OF)

ARRAN AROMATICS

www.arranaromatics.com

Natural bath and beauty products are handmade on the farm, signposted from Brodick Pier. As well as the Arran Aromatics shop, there is a gift shop on site.

✉ The Home Farm, Brodick KA27 8DD ☎ 01770 302595 🕐 Mon–Sat 9–5.30

ISLE OF ARRAN DISTILLERS

www.arranwhisky.com

The distillery in the north of the island produces Arran's own single malt whisky. Take the guided tour, enjoy the exhibition and buy a gift or bottle of Arran whisky in the shop. Tours include a taste of the whisky.

✉ Distillery and Visitor Centre, Lochranza KA27 8HJ ☎ 01770 830264 🕐 Mid-Mar to end Oct daily 10–6; Nov to mid-Mar check ahead ✋ Adult £4, child £2.50, under 12 free 🍴 Restaurant serves good local food, Italian coffee and home baking 🚇

AVIEMORE

ROTHIEMURCHUS ESTATE
www.rothiemurchus.net
The Rothiemurchus Estate south of Aviemore has forests, rivers, lochs and mountains to explore and is home to rare species such as the capercaillie. The activity centre offers guided walks, fishing, shooting and off-road driving.
✉ Near Aviemore PH22 1QH ☎ 01479 812345 ◷ Daily 9–5.30 ⛛ Variable 🚌 🚉 Aviemore

DUMFRIES

THE GLOBE INN
This 400-year-old pub was Robert Burns's local. You'll find it down an alley near the foot of the High Street.
✉ 56 High Street, Dumfries DG1 2JA ☎ 01387 252335 ◷ Mon–Wed 10am–11pm, Thu–Sun 10am–midnight 🚉 Dumfries

THEATRE ROYAL
www.theatreroyaldumfries.co.uk
The Theatre Royal is Scotland's oldest working theatre, offering plays and pantomimes performed by the resident amateur Guild of Players and touring productions of music and drama.
✉ Shakespeare Street, Dumfries DG1 2JH ☎ 01387 254209 ◷ All year ⛛ From £6 🚌 🚉 Dumfries

DUNDEE

CAMPERDOWN WILDLIFE CENTRE
www.dundeecity.gov.uk/camperdown
This wildlife park just outside the city has 85 species of native Scottish and other European wildlife including lynx, bears, wolves, bats, Arctic foxes and pine martens. In the summer you can see the animals being fed. Special events year-round include popular animal handling and feeding days.
✉ Camperdown Country Park, Coupar Angus Road DD2 4TF ☎ 01382 432661 ◷ Mar–end Sep daily 10–4.30; rest of year daily 10–3.30 ⛛ Adult £3.30, child (3–15) £2.75, family £9.25

Opposite *Jenners store, Edinburgh*

DUNDEE REP
www.dundeerep.co.uk
Scotland's leading repertory theatre is in Dundee's West End, the up-and-coming cultural quarter. Also hosts touring productions and shows by the contemporary Scottish Dance Theatre.
✉ Tay Square, Dundee DD1 1PB ☎ 01382 223530 ◷ All year. Box office: 10am–8pm 🚌 🚉 Dundee

SOCIAL
The glass-walled side of this trendy bar overlooks Tay Square. Cool, contemporary decoration inside, with different events each night, including live music from R&B to reggae.
✉ 10 South Tay Street, Dundee DD1 1PA ☎ 01382 202070 ◷ Mon–Sat 11am–midnight, Sun 12–12 🚉 Dundee

DUNKELD

BROUGHTON-STUART JEWELLERY LTD
www.broughton-stuartjewellery.co.uk
Craig Stuart uses an ancient technique called Mokume Gane to achieve a delicate wood-grain effect on his jewellery, combining gold, platinum and diamonds into unique miniature works of art.
✉ 25 Atholl Street, Dunkeld PH8 0AR ☎ 01350 727888 ◷ Mon–Wed, Fri–Sat 10–4

EASDALE

SEA.FARI
www.seafari.co.uk
Enjoy an exhilarating trip on a rigid inflatable boat to see wildlife such as seals, seabirds, dolphins and the occasional minke whale.
✉ Easdale Harbour, Seil Island, near Oban ☎ 01852 300003 ◷ Trips run all year, weather permitting, but mainly Easter–end Oct ⛛ 2 hours: adult £26, child £19.50, family £82.50

EDINBURGH

BELUGA
The Beluga bar-nightclub is the place to see and be seen: a laid-back venue to lunch in by day, and home of the beautiful people by night. A huge waterfall dominates the opulent interior.

✉ 30a Chambers Street, Edinburgh EH1 ☎ 0131 624 4546 ◷ Daily 11am–1am ⛛ Free entry 🚉 Edinburgh Waverley

BLUE MOON
Everybody is welcome at this gay bar, noted for serving the best food in the area all day. The staff are very knowledgeable on the best club nights (both gay and straight).
✉ 1 Barony Street, New Town, Edinburgh EH1 ☎ 0131 556 2788 ◷ Mon–Fri 11–11, Sat–Sun 10am–11.30pm 🚉 Edinburgh Waverley

DOMINION
www.dominioncinema.com
This cinema screens independent and mainstream movies, and has traditional leather Pullman seats. Bag a sofa and free wine or beer with the Gold Class service.
✉ 18 Newbattle Terrace, Morningside, Edinburgh EH10 4RT ☎ 0131 447 4771 (box office) ◷ Daily 🚉 Edinburgh Haymarket

EDINBURGH FESTIVAL THEATRE
www.eft.co.uk
Prestigious concert venue hosts touring productions of theatre, dance, musicals, comedy, ballet and Scottish Opera productions.
✉ 13–29 Nicolson Street, Edinburgh EH8 9FT ☎ 0131 529 6000 ◷ All year. Box office: Mon–Sat 11–8, Sun 11–4 ⛛ From £8 🚌 🚉 Edinburgh Waverley

EDINBURGH FLOATARIUM
Enjoy floating in a float tank, reflexology, massages and facials. The aromatherapy massage is particularly recommended.
✉ 29 North West Circus Place, Edinburgh EH3 6TP ☎ 0131 225 3350 ◷ Mon–Fri 9–8, Sat 9–6, Sun 9.30–4 ⛛ 1-hour float £25; 1-hour aromatherapy massage £32 🚉 Edinburgh Waverley

EDINBURGH PLAYHOUSE
www.getlive.co.uk
The best venue for touring productions of big-budget musicals and dance. A five-minute walk from the east end of Princes Street.
✉ 18–22 Greenside Place, Edinburgh EH1 3AA ☎ 0870 606 3424 ◷ All year ⛛ From £12 🚌 🚉 Edinburgh Waverley

JENNERS

www.jenners.com

Jenners is an Edinburgh institution, founded in 1838. It sells everything from high-quality clothes and shoes to toys, glassware, groceries and perfume. Slightly more expensive than Princes Street's other department stores.

✉ 48 Princes Street, Edinburgh EH2 2YJ ☎ 0131 225 2442 🕐 Mon, Wed, Fri–Sat 9–6, Tue 9.30–6, Thu 9–8, Sun 11–5 🚇 Edinburgh Waverley

JOLLY JUDGE

Seek out this 17th-century pub for its malt whiskies. At the top of the Royal Mile go down East Entry into James Court.

✉ 7a James Court, Old Town, Edinburgh EH1 2PB ☎ 0131 225 2669 🕐 Mon, Thu–Sat 12–12, Tue–Wed 12–11, Sun 12.30–11

MURRAYFIELD STADIUM

www.sru.org.uk

Rugby is Edinburgh's most popular sport, so reserving in advance for matches is essential. Behind-the-scenes tours are also available.

✉ Off Roseburn Terrace, Murrayfield, Edinburgh EH12 5PJ ☎ 0131 346 5000 🕐 Call for match information. Stadium tours Mon–Fri 11 and 2.30 🖐 Varies. Tour: adult £5, child (5–18) £3, family £12 🛒 🚇 Edinburgh Haymarket

OCEAN TERMINAL CENTRE

www.oceanterminal.com

Designed by Jasper Conran and opened in 2001, Ocean Terminal is a vast shopping and cinema complex overlooking the Firth of Forth and the Royal Yacht *Britannia*.

✉ Ocean Drive, Leith, Edinburgh EH6 6JJ ☎ 0131 555 8888 🕐 Mon–Fri 10–8, Sat 10–7, Sun 11–6 🛒 🍽 Zinc Bar & Grill (tel 0131 553 8070)

QUEEN'S HALL

www.queenshalledinburgh.co.uk

A more intimate venue than the Usher Hall, this is a real hot spot for jazz, blues and soul, as well as classical music and comedy, attracting names such as Courtney Pine and Ruby Turner.

✉ Clerk Street, Edinburgh EH8 9JG ☎ 0131 668 2019 🕐 All year 🖐 From £10 🛒 🚇 Edinburgh Waverley

ROYAL MILE WHISKIES

www.royalmilewhiskies.com

This specialist whisky shop opposite St. Giles' Cathedral stocks a vast range of malt whiskies, some of which are 100 years old. It's the best place to buy rare whiskies if you want them shipped home.

✉ 379 High Street, Royal Mile, Edinburgh EH1 1PW ☎ 0131 225 3383 🕐 Mon–Sat 10–6, Sun 12.30–6 🚇 Edinburgh Waverley

STAND COMEDY CLUB

www.thestand.co.uk

Enjoy live comedy from new and well-known comedians at this dark and intimate basement bar. Weekend shows often sell out, so reserving in advance is recommended.

✉ 5 York Place, Edinburgh EH1 3EB ☎ 0131 558 7272 🕐 Mon–Sat 7.30pm–1am, Sun 12.30–midnight 🖐 Free–£9 🚇 Edinburgh Waverley

TARTAN WEAVING MILL AND EXHIBITION

www.tartanweavingmill.co.uk

You can hear the weaving looms in the basement everywhere in this massive tartan shop at the top of the Royal Mile. On the way down you can have your photo taken in full Highland rig, consult the 'Clans and Tartans Bureau' for information about your own clan history, then have a go at weaving yourself.

✉ 555 Castle Hill, The Royal Mile, Edinburgh EH1 2ND ☎ 0131 226 4162 🕐 Daily 9–5.30 🖐 Free 🛒 🚇 Edinburgh Waverley

USHER HALL

www.usherhall.co.uk

Edinburgh's most prestigious concert hall attracts excellent orchestras. A distinctive circular building towards the West End, its high dome can be seen from many parts of the city.

✉ Lothian Road, Edinburgh EH1 2EA ☎ 0131 228 1155 🕐 All year 🖐 From £10 🛒 🚇 Edinburgh Haymarket

Above *Sign for Edinburgh's Jolly Judge pub*

ELGIN

JOHNSTON'S OF ELGIN CASHMERE VISITOR CENTRE

www.johnstonscashmere.com

Take a tour of the only Scottish mill still to turn beautiful cashmere into clothes: it has been spun, dyed and woven here for over 200 years. The shop sells high-quality cashmere clothes in glorious shades.

Tax-free shopping for visitors from outside the EU. Signposted from central Elgin.

✉ Newmill, Elgin IV30 4AF ☎ 01343 554099 🕐 Mon–Sat 9–5.30; also Jun–end Oct Sun 11–4.30 🛒 🚇 Elgin

FORT WILLIAM

JACOBITE STEAM TRAIN

www.steamtrain.info

The steam train that had a cameo role as the Hogwarts Express in the Harry Potter films follows the scenic Road to the Isles via Glenfinnan (where scenes were shot at the great viaduct).

✉ Fort William Railway Station, Fort William ☎ 01463 239026 🕐 Mid-Jun to early Oct Mon–Fri 10.20am 🖐 Day return: adult £26, child £15 🛒 📅

NEVIS RANGE

www.nevisrange.co.uk

Ski and snowboarding resort north of Fort William, with the highest altitude skiing in Scotland, from easy to difficult.

✉ Torlundy, Fort William PH33 6SW ✉ 01397 705855 🕐 Daily; closed early Dec 🖐 Gondola: adult £8, child £4.90; ski rental: £15.50 daily; snowboard rental £17.50 daily 🍽 🛒

GLASGOW

ARCHES
www.thearches.co.uk
The nightclub in the Arches complex, with its industrial-style interior, is Glasgow's biggest. The music varies and can include hip-hop, house, soul or big name DJs.

✉ 253 Argyle Street, Glasgow G2 8DL ☎ 0870 240 7528 ◉ Club nights Fri–Sun, until late ♨ From £5 🚇 St. Enoch 🚆 Glasgow Central

BARROWLANDS
www.glasgow-barrowland.com
Big-name pop and rock acts play at this engaging venue. Tickets from Ticket Scotland (tel 0141 204 5151).

✉ 244 Gallowgate, Glasgow G4 0TS ☎ 0141 552 4601; 0870 903 3444 ◉ All year ♨ From £9 🚇 🚆 St. Enoch 🚆 Glasgow Central, Queen Street

CENTRE FOR CONTEMPORARY ARTS (CCA)
www.cca-glasgow.com
Various contemporary art forms, including music, visual art and alternative cinema are catered for at this cutting-edge venue. Films include classics, foreign films and work by leading directors.

✉ 350 Sauchiehall Street, Glasgow G2 3JD ☎ 0141 352 4900 (cinema tickets) ◉ Daily 🍴 🚇 🚆 Cowcaddens

GEOFFREY (TAILOR) KILTMAKERS & WEAVERS
www.geoffreykilts.co.uk
One of Scotland's top kiltmakers and Highland dress specialists, brimming with every kind of kilt, tartan and accessory. Made-to-measure outfits can be sent to you abroad.

✉ 309 Sauchiehall Street, Glasgow G2 3HW ☎ 0141 331 2388 ◉ Mon–Wed, Fri–Sat 9–5.30, Thu 9–7, Sun 11–5 🚆 Glasgow Charing Cross

GLASGOW ROYAL CONCERT HALL
www.grch.com
Glasgow's most prestigious venue and home of the Royal Scottish National Orchestra, this concert hall has a varied schedule of classical, pop and rock music and holds the

Celtic Connections winter festival of concerts and ceilidhs.

✉ 2 Sauchiehall Street, Glasgow G2 3NY ☎ 0141 353 8000 ◉ All year ♨ £5–£30 🚇 Buchanan Street 🍴 🚇 🎫 🚆 Glasgow Queen Street

KING TUT'S WAH WAH HUT
www.kingtuts.co.uk
The heart of the Glasgow music scene. It's an unpretentious, relaxed venue playing cutting-edge indie, pop and rock. Tickets from Ticketmaster.

✉ 272a St. Vincent Street, Glasgow G2 5RL ☎ 0141 221 5279/0870 169 0100 (Ticketmaster) ◉ All year ♨ From £4.50 🚇 🚆 Glasgow Central, Queen Street

PRINCES SQUARE
www.princessquare.co.uk
An art deco-style doorway on Buchanan Street announces this smart indoor shopping complex. Good shops sell clothes, shoes and gifts, including Jo Malone perfumes.

✉ 48 Buchanan Street, Glasgow G1 3JX ☎ 0141 204 1685 ◉ Mon–Wed, Fri 9.30–6, Thu 9.30–8, Sat 9–6, Sun 12–5 🚇 🚆 🍴 🚆 Glasgow Argyle Street

SCOTIA BAR
This traditional pub is Glasgow's oldest, established in 1792. Live folk music on most evenings and poetry readings on Sundays.

✉ 112–114 Stockwell Street, Glasgow G1 4LW ☎ 0141 552 8681 ◉ Mon–Sat 11am–midnight, Sun 12–12 🚇 St. Enoch 🚆 Glasgow Central

THEATRE ROYAL
www.theatreroyalglasgow.com
The best in opera, ballet, dance and theatre at the home of Scottish Opera and Scottish Ballet.

✉ 282 Hope Street, Glasgow G2 3QA ☎ 0141 240 1133 ◉ All year ♨ From £4 🍴 🚇 🚆 Cowcaddens, Buchanan Street 🚆 Queen Street

TISO GLASGOW OUTDOOR EXPERIENCE
www.tiso.com
This place has a great selection of outdoor equipment, clothing and books. The interactive features—a 15m (50ft) rock pinnacle, waterfall

and 7m (23ft) ice wall—enable you to try out the gear.

✉ Couper Street, off Kyle Street, Glasgow G4 0DL ☎ 0141 550 5450 ◉ Mon–Tue, Fri–Sat 9–6, Wed 9.30–6, Thu 9–7, Sun 11–5 🚆 Glasgow Queen Street

JEDBURGH

CHRISTOPHER RAINBOW
Bicycles can be rented here, or delivered. Ideal for the peaceful Four Abbeys Cycleway through Melrose, Dryburgh and Kelso along the Tweed and Teviot rivers.

✉ 8 Timpendean Cottages, Jedburgh TD8 6SS ☎ 01835 830326 ◉ All year ♨ Bicycle rental from £18 a day

KINGUSSIE

HIGHLAND WILDLIFE PARK
www.highlandwildlifepark.org
This interesting reserve, which has a children's trail, activities and play area, also has a viewpoint from where you can watch red deer, Highland cattle and bison. A raised walkway takes you over the wolf enclosure.

✉ Kincraig, Kingussie PH21 1NL ☎ 01540 651270 ◉ Apr–end May, Sep–end Oct daily 10–6; Jun–end Aug 10–7; rest of year 10–4 ♨ Adult £8.50, child £6.50 🚇 🚆 Kingussie 4 miles (6.5km)

KIRKCUDBRIGHT

JO GALLANT
www.jogallant.co.uk
Sumptuous textiles are displayed in this stone-fronted building near the Tolbooth Art Centre. The price of the embroidered wall-hangings, cushions and scarves may be high, but so is the quality.

✉ Ironstones, 70 High Street, Kirkcudbright DG6 ☎ 01557 331130 ◉ Mon–Sat 10–5 (call first if travelling specially)

LEWIS

OISEVAL GALLERY
www.oiseval.co.uk
Enjoy beautiful photographs of Hebridean landscapes by James Smith, displayed in a small gallery in the photographer's house. Mail-order service available.

✉ Brue, Isle of Lewis HS2 0QW ☎ 01851 840240 ◉ Mon–Sat 10.30–5.30

LOCH KEN
GALLOWAY SAILING CENTRE
www.lochken.co.uk
Activities on Loch Ken include sailing, windsurfing, kayaking, canoeing, quad biking and gorge scrambling.
✉ Castle Douglas, Loch Ken Marina DG7 3NQ ☎ 01644 420626 ◷ Apr–end Oct ✋ Lessons from £20. Call for rental rates ▢

MELROSE
ABBEY MILL
This large store selling knitwear, clothes, toys and Scottish food occupies a corn mill, which dates back to the Middle Ages, just outside town, beyond Melrose Abbey.
✉ Annay Road, Melrose TD6 9LG ☎ 01896 822138 ◷ Daily 9–5.30, may vary in winter ▢

PENICUIK
EDINBURGH CRYSTAL VISITOR CENTRE
www.edinburgh-crystal.com
See the famous Edinburgh crystal being made in the factory and choose from beautiful decanters, vases and whisky glasses in the shop. You can talk with the master craftspeople as they work, and see how glass has been made through the ages.
✉ Eastfield, Penicuik EH26 8HB ☎ 01968 675128 ◷ Mon–Sat 10–5, Sun 11–5 ▢

PENTLAND HILLS ICELANDICS
www.phicelandics.co.uk
Enjoy short rides or all-day treks in the Pentland Hills on Icelandic ponies from a Trekking and Riding Society of Scotland-approved centre. Tough shoes and warm clothing essential. Minimum age 8 years.
✉ Windy Gowl Farm, Carlops, Penicuik EH26 ☎ 01968 661095 ◷ Fri–Wed, all year, rides at 10 and 2.30 ✋ £30 for two hours

PERTH
CAITHNESS GLASS VISITOR CENTRE
www.caithnessglass.co.uk
Vases, whisky tumblers, decanters and paperweights are sold at discount prices in the factory shop. Glassmaking can be watched on weekdays year-round and weekends in July and August. The shop offers overseas posting.
✉ Inveralmond, Perth PH1 3TZ ☎ 01738 637373 ◷ Mid-Jun to early Sep Mon–Sat 9–6; Oct–end May Mon–Sat 9–5, also Sun 10–5, Mar–end Nov, and 12–5 Dec–end Feb ✋ Free ❙❙ ⊞ ▢ Perth 2.5 miles (4km)

FAMOUS BEIN INN
www.beininn.com
The Bein Inn, 5 miles (8km) south of Perth, was built as a resting place for travellers on the route from Edinburgh to the Highlands. It is famous for its small stage, attracting folk, country and rock musicians. There are 10 gigs monthly.
✉ Glenfarg, Perth PH2 9PY ☎ 01577 830216 ◷ Daily to 11.30pm

PITLOCHRY
FREESPIRITS
www.freespirits-online.co.uk
This outdoor activities company majors in adrenalin sports around the River Tay, River Tummel and Perthshire. Activities are suitable for age 8 and over.
✉ Riverside Inn, Grandtully, Pitlochry PH9 0PL ☎ 0845 644 4755 ◷ All year ✋ Rafting from £30; canyoning £30 ▢ ▢ Pitlochry

HERITAGE JEWELLERS
www.heritage-jewellers.co.uk
This small, exclusive shop sells gold and silver jewellery, cultured pearls, Celtic jewellery made in Orkney and Scottish gold.
✉ 104 Atholl Road, Pitlochry PH16 5BL ☎ 01796 474333 ◷ Mon–Sat 10–5, Sun 12–4 ▢ Pitlochry

ST. ANDREWS
CENTRAL BAR
A St. Andrews institution in the heart of the town, popular with students and locals. Food served until 9pm. On the corner of College Street and Market Street.
✉ 79 Market Street, St. Andrews KY16 9NU ☎ 01334 478296 ◷ Mon–Thu noon–midnight, Fri–Sat noon–1am ▢ Leuchars

DAVID BROWN GALLERY
The gallery is worth a visit if you love antiques and golf. Unassuming on the outside, but an Aladdin's cave within, crammed full of silverware, prints and vintage golfing books.
✉ 9 Albany Place, St. Andrews KY16 9HH ☎ 01334 477840 ◷ Mon–Sat 9–5.30

ST. ANDREWS LINKS
www.standrews.org.uk
The largest golf complex in Europe consists of six public golf courses, including the Old Course, the New Course and the Jubilee Course. Advance reservation essential—the waiting list is anything from weeks to years. Check the website for the complex rules and requirements.
✉ Pilmour House, St. Andrews KY16 9SF ☎ 01334 466666 ◷ All year ✋ Strathtyrum Course £22; Old Course £115 ▢ ▢ Leuchars

STOBO
STOBO SPA
www.stobocastle.co.uk
Treat yourself at this luxurious spa south of Edinburgh. Lunch and dinner are included. Reserve in advance. Not suitable for children.
✉ Stobo Castle, Stobo EH45 8NY ☎ 01721 725300 ◷ All year ✋ Day visit from £160 ❙❙

TAIN
GLENMORANGIE DISTILLERY
www.glenmorangie.com
Take a tour of the 'Glen of Tranquillity' distillery and see how this famous whisky is made before tasting the real thing. Advance reservation recommended.
✉ Tain IV19 1PZ ☎ 01862 892477 ◷ Mon–Fri 9–5; also Jun–end Aug Sat 10–4, Sun 12–4 ✋ Adult £2.50 ⊞

ULLAPOOL
HIGHLAND STONEWARE
www.highlandstoneware.com
See this distinctive pottery being made and hand-painted by crafts-people at the Ullapool factory. You can commission your own designs.
✉ Mill Street, Ullapool IV26 2UN ☎ 01854 612980 ◷ Easter–end Oct Mon–Fri 9–6, Sat 9–5

JANUARY

CELTIC CONNECTIONS
www.celticconnections.com
Scotland's biggest folk festival attracts musicians from all over the world for concerts and ceilidhs for two weeks across the city.
✉ Glasgow ☎ 0141 287 5511
🕐 Mid-January

UP HELLY AA
www.shetlandtourism.com
Viking celebrations in Lerwick, with torchlight processions, a ceremonial ship burning and partying. Local Up Helly Aa festivals are held around the islands during February and March.
✉ Lerwick, Shetland ☎ 01595 693434
🕐 Last Tuesday in January

APRIL

SPIRIT OF SPEYSIDE WHISKY FESTIVAL
www.spiritofspeyside.com
Four days of whisky-flavoured fun all over Speyside, from vintage tastings on trains to tours of unusual distilleries. Book ahead.
✉ Speyside ☎ 01343 542666
🕐 Late April–early May

JUNE

ROYAL HIGHLAND SHOW
www.royalhighlandshow.org
Scotland's biggest agricultural show: top livestock judging, show jumping, heavy horses, crafts, trade stands and other country activities.
✉ Ingliston, near Edinburgh ☎ 0131 335 6200
🕐 Late June

JULY

GLASGOW JAZZ FESTIVAL
www.jazzfest.co.uk
Five days of the best in international jazz. Sample the Fringe, too.
✉ Glasgow, various venues ☎ 0141 552 3552
🕐 Early July

AUGUST

INTERNATIONAL ARTS FESTIVAL
www.eif.co.uk
The three-week event is the world's largest arts festival, offering opera, dance, music and theatre.
✉ Edinburgh, various venues ☎ 0131 473 2099

EDINBURGH FRINGE FESTIVAL
www.edfringe.com
The ever-expanding Fringe hosts hundreds of productions of varying quality in any venues with available space.
✉ Edinburgh, various venues ☎ 0131 226 5257 🕐 Mid- to end August

COWAL HIGHLAND GATHERING
www.cowalgathering.com
The biggest Highland games in Scotland fields 3,500 competitors from as far afield as Canada and New Zealand. Highland dancing, piping and athletics events over three days.
✉ Dunoon ☎ 01369 703206
🕐 Late August

SEPTEMBER

BRAEMAR GATHERING
www.braemargathering.org
Gatherings of competitive pipers, dancers and athletes have occurred here for around 900 years, and the Queen is a regular visitor.
✉ Braemar ☎ 01339 755377
🕐 Early September

DECEMBER

HOGMANAY
www.edinburghshogmanay.org
Celebrate the New Year with live music and fireworks at Scotland's biggest annual party. Entry is free but you need to obtain a pass in advance–see website.
✉ Princes Street, Edinburgh ☎ 0131 473 3800
🕐 31 December

Below *Dancing features at many festivals and games especially in the Highlands*

PRICES AND SYMBOLS

The restaurants are listed alphabetically within each town. The prices are for a two-course lunch (L) and a three-course à la carte dinner (D). Prices in pubs are for a two-course lunchtime bar meal and a two-course dinner in the restaurant, unless specified otherwise. The wine price is for the least expensive bottle.

For a key to the symbols, ▷ 2.

ABERDEEN
MARYCULTER HOUSE

www.maryculterhotel.com
Enjoy a candle-lit dinner with fillet of Aberdeen Angus with potato and celeriac purée, rack of lamb on fried potatoes with wild mushroom ragout, and venison with pommes dauphinoise, red cabbage and Madeira jus. No children under 4.
✉ South Deeside Road, Maryculter AB12 5GB 01224 732124 ⏱ D only, 7.15–9.30 ✋ D £27, Wine £16.95 🚌 From Aberdeen take B9077 (South Deeside Road) for 8 miles (13km)

NORWOOD HALL

www.norwood-hall.co.uk
Dishes are classic with the odd Scottish twist: Breast of pheasant is stuffed with haggis, while Grampian chicken is accompanied by black pudding mousse and a whisky sauce.
✉ Garthdee Road, Cults AB15 9FX
☎ 01224 868951 ⏱ 12–2, 7–9.30
✋ L £23, D £29, Wine £18.50 🚌 From the south, leave the A90 at 1st roundabout, cross bridge and turn left at roundabout into Garthdee Road; continue for 1.5 miles (2.4km)

ACHILTIBUIE
THE SUMMER ISLES HOTEL

www.summerisleshotel.co.uk
In summer, long daylight hours afford excellent views of the islands late into the evening from this spectacularly located hotel. The style is broadly modern British, so a meal from the daily changing five-course menu could include filo parcel of monkfish tails with a tamarind sauce followed by Summer Isles langoustine and spiny lobsters with hollandaise sauce. After this, roast rib of Aberdeen Angus beef with mushrooms, red onion and red wine sauce then a selection from the sweet trolley. No children under six.
✉ Ullapool IV26 2YG ☎ 01854 622282
⏱ 12.30–2, D at 8; closed mid-Oct to Easter
✋ L £26, D £47, Wine £15 🚌 10 miles (16km) north of Ullapool. Turn left off A835

on to single-track road. 15 miles (24km) to Achiltibuie. Hotel 90m (100yds) after post office on left

APPLECROSS
APPLECROSS INN
A traditional white-painted inn on the shore of Applecross Bay. The lively kitchen staff have the pick of the rich local produce to create some stunning dishes, including seafood, Aberdeen Angus steaks and game. Favourites include king scallops in garlic butter with crispy bacon on rice, and fresh monkfish and squat lobster in a rich prawn sauce on home-made tagliatelle. Meat-eaters will relish the Applecross venison casserole with braised red cabbage on apple and wholegrain mustard mash, and to finish try raspberry cranachan or cardamom pannacotta. ✉ Shore Street IV54 8LR ☎ 01520 744262 ◉ Mon–Sat 11–11, Sun 2.30–11 (12.30–7, Sun, Dec–end Jan) 🍴 L £12, D £18, Wine £10 🚗 From Lochcarron to Kishorn, then left on to unclassifed road to Applecross over 'Bealach Na Ba'

ARRAN, ISLE OF
EIGHTEEN 69 AT AUCHRANNIE COUNTRY HOUSE
www.auchrannie.co.uk
Superior local ingredients star on the short dinner menu. Try freshly caught langoustines served in a butter and coriander (cilantro) sauce or fillet of Angus beef with potatoes. Hearty desserts are popular, and the wine list is good. ✉ Brodick, KA27 8BJ ☎ 01770 302234 ◉ D 6.30–9.30 🍴 D £32, Wine £13 🚗 From ferry terminal turn right and follow coast road through Brodick, then take 2nd left past golf club

AUCHTERARDER
ANDREW FAIRLIE AT GLENEAGLES
www.gleneagles.com
Applaud Andrew Fairlie's bold move in taking his talents to such a revered institution as Gleneagles. He created a totally new restaurant in an area of the hotel previously used as a champagne bar. This is an evenings-only venue with pitch-black walls punctuated by paintings and dramatic lighting. There is an element of theatre at work with an earthy dish of pan-fried langoustines and shellfish cappuccino having the cloche removed at the table to reveal a rich, aromatic foam. Staff are young, knowledgeable and quick to enthuse about the cooking, which is neat, unpretentious and often inspired. ✉ Gleneagles PH3 1NF ☎ 01764 694267 ◉ 7–10 D only; closed Sun, Jan 🍴 D £60, Wine £25 🚗 Signposted from A9 🚆 Gleneagles

BANCHORY
BANCHORY LODGE HOTEL
Cooking is traditional and sound at this 16th-century coaching inn (▷ 406), relying on quality ingredients, such as Aberdeen Angus beef, with complementary saucing and garnishing. ✉ AB31 5HS ☎ 01330 822625 ◉ 12–2, 6–9 🍴 Bar L £6, D £50, Wine £12.50 🚗 Off A93 18 miles (29km) west of Aberdeen

CALLANDER
ROMAN CAMP COUNTRY HOUSE
www.roman-camp-hotel.co.uk
Highly accomplished cooking draws on excellent Scottish produce. The four-course dinner menu changes daily; the shorter lunch menu offers good value. ✉ FK17 8BG ☎ 01877 330003 ◉ 12.30–2, 7–8.30 🍴 L £25, D £44, Wine £18 🚗 Turn left at east end of Callander High Street, go down a 274m (300yds) driveway into the hotel grounds

CAWDOR
CAWDOR TAVERN
Arbroath smokie and citrus mousse to start, then the traditional haggis, neeps and tatties. A daily specials menu might focus on confit of pheasant leg on a bed of clapshot, collops of Scottish beef fillet. ✉ The Lane IV12 5XP ☎ 01667 404777 ◉ May–end Oct daily 11–11; rest of year daily 11–3, 5–11; closed 25 Dec, 1 Jan. Bar meals: Mon–Sat 12–2, 5.30–9, Sun 12.30–3, 5.30–9. Restaurant: Mon–Sat 12–2, 6.30–9, Sun 12.30–3, 5.30–9 🍴 L £12, D £25, Wine £12.95 🚗 From A96, Inverness–Aberdeen road, take B9006 and follow signs for Cawdor Castle. Pub is in village centre

EDINBURGH
BLUE BAR CAFÉ
This modern brasserie goes from strength to strength with a menu that is flexible, good value and imaginative. Lunch could be as simple as a crayfish sandwich or a bowl of white bean and chorizo soup. A more substantial meal would be carpaccio of beef with Parmesan followed by corn-fed chicken with aromatic leek risotto and bacon dressing. Deftly prepared desserts such as chocolate tart with caramelized oranges also feature. ✉ 10 Cambridge Street EH1 2ED ☎ 0131 2211222 ◉ 12–3, 6–11; closed Sun, 25–26 Dec 🍴 L £9.95, D £18, Wine £12.95 🚗 From Princes Street turn into Lothian Road second left, first right, above the Traverse Theatre

THE BRIDGE INN
www.bridgeinn.com
Dating back to around 1750 the Bridge Inn is famous for its fleet of restaurant boats and sightseeing launches. Local produce is freshly prepared and served, and top-quality Scottish meat has been a speciality for over 30 years. Typical dishes include shank of Lothian lamb, roast Barbary duck breast, Thai green curry, and salmon and asparagus pie. Principal beers on offer include Bellhaven 80/-. ✉ 27 Baird Road, Ratho EH28 8RA ☎ 0131 333 1320 ◉ Mon–Fri 12–11, Sat 11am–12am, Sun 12.30–11pm; closed 26 Dec, 1–2 Jan. Bar meals: daily 12–9. Restaurant: daily 12–2.30, 6.30–9.30 🍴 L £10, D £22, Wine £11.25 🚗 From Newbridge B7030 junction (intersection) follow signs for Ratho

OFF THE WALL RESTAURANT
This Royal Mile restaurant has an uncomplicated approach to cuisine: no fussiness or unnecessary flourishes, just perfectly prepared food that speaks for itself. The decor's based on the same mantra of simplicity. Expect modern cooking made from the finest Scottish ingredients: beef fillet, perhaps, with red cabbage, port sauce and

buttery truffle mash; or venison with celeriac and a chocolate sauce. And as befits its name, Off the Wall delivers a few unexpected combinations—squab pigeon with black pudding and orange sauce, for instance. Vegetarian options available on request.

✉ 105 High Street, Royal Mile EH1 1SG ☎ 0131 558 1497 🕐 12–2, 6–10; closed Sun, 25–26 Dec, 1–2 Jan 🍴 L £16.50, D £38, Wine £13.95 🚉 On Royal Mile near John Knox House. Entrance via stairway next to Baillie Fyfes (first floor)

RESTAURANT MARTIN WISHART

Serious French staff are intent on communicating their passion for food and wine. This is sophisticated territory. There's a juggernaut of a carte with enough eye-catching flair, luxury and creativity to compete with any national restaurant. Terrine of confit duck, foie gras with sweet and sour pear, duck bonbon and walnut toast is a flawlessly executed dish, while fillet of Buccleuch beef, confit of bone marrow, celeriac purée, beignets of salsify and marchand de vin sauce is similarly precise. Smart dress is preferred.

✉ 54 The Shore, Leith EH6 6RA ☎ 0131 553 3557 🕐 12–2, 7–10; closed L Sat, Sun–Mon, 25 Dec 🍴 L £20.50, D £45, Wine £19.50 🚉 Telephone for directions

STAC POLLY

Two low-ceilinged rooms make for an intimate atmosphere in this charming restaurant in the heart of the city, with its cream parchment walls, red carpet and tartan-covered chairs. Modern Scottish cuisine dominates the menu, for example baked supreme of Scottish salmon served with braised leeks, bacon dumplings and a lemon butter sauce. Desserts, and the wine list, are appealing.

✉ 8–10 Grindlay Street EH3 9AS ☎ 0131 229 5405 🕐 12–2, 6–11; closed L Sat and Sun 🍴 L £14.95, D £30, Wine £14.95 🚉 In town centre, beneath Castle, near Lyceum

Right View over the water to the pretty little harbour town of Kirkcudbright (pronounced Kirkoobree)

THE WITCHERY BY THE CASTLE

www.thewitchery.com

Heavy with theatrical, Gothic charm, the entire restaurant is candlelit and is the place to come for a special night out. The menu provides a contemporary spin on modern classics—typically, game, fish and shellfish feature highly in dishes such as jambonette of Borders guinea fowl served with a blanquette of baby vegetables, caramelized apples and smoked garlic. There's an extensive global wine list.

✉ Castlehill, Royal Mile EH1 2NF ☎ 0131 225 5613 🕐 12–4, 5.30–11.30; closed 25–26 Dec 🍴 L £12.95, D £43, Wine £15.95 🚉 At the gates of Edinburgh Castle, at the top of the Royal Mile

FORT WILLIAM

INVERLOCHY CASTLE

www.inverlochycastlehotel.com

Creative, seasonal Scottish food such as roast loin of roe deer with a fig crust, and baked rice pudding with spiced pineapple. Dinner is a four-course set menu.

✉ Torlundy PH33 6SN ☎ 01397 702177 🕐 12.30–1.30, 6 for 6.30 or 9 for 9.30 for non-residents 🍴 L £28, D £65, Wine £75 🚉 Hotel is 3 miles (4.8km) north of Fort William on A82

MOORINGS

www.moorings-fortwilliam.co.uk

The menu is modern, and West Coast seafood and Highland game are regular features. Classics such as bangers and mash, or fisherman's creel pie are typical. There are several vegetarian choices.

✉ Banavie PH33 7LY ☎ 01397 772797 🕐 D only, 7–9.30 🍴 D £19, Wine £13.95 🚉 3 miles (4.8km) north, off A830. Take A830 for 1 mile (1.6km), cross the Caledonian Canal, then take 1st right

GLAMIS

CASTLETON HOUSE

www.castletonglamis.co.uk

The menu draws on influences from all over the world—try fillet of Tamworth pig with black pudding and perhaps the Cointreau crème caramel with cardamom ice cream.

✉ Castleton of Eassie DD8 1SJ ☎ 01307 840340 🕐 12–2, 7–9 🍴 L £15.95, D £35, Wine £14 🚉 On A94 midway between Forfar and Cupar Angus, 3 miles (4.8km) west of Glamis

GLASGOW

THE BUTTERY

The Buttery is something of a hidden gem. The menu features wild boar with creamed, apple-scented

barley, iced fudge and marshmallow parfait. Check directions before you set off.
✉ 652 Argyle Street G3 8UF ☎ 0141 221 8188 🕐 12–2, 7–10 🍴 L £16, D £38, Wine £16 🚇 From roundabout at end of Elderslie Street, take left. 600m (620yds) on left down Argyle Street.

SHISH MAHAL
Fast and friendly restaurant cooking meals in the classic Pakistani tradition. Black-clad waiters serve a selection of lamb favourites like kashmiri, rogan josh and bhoona, along with baltis in cast-iron bowls, a wonderful pakora medley featuring fish, chicken and vegetable, a delicious tarka daal, and freshly baked naan bread. Reservation essential.
✉ 60–68 Park Road G4 9JF ☎ 0141 339 8256 🕐 12–2, 5–11; closed L Sun 🍴 L £5.50, D £12.95, Wine £9.95 🚇 Glasgow Charing Cross

UBIQUITOUS CHIP
No trip to Glasgow would be complete without a visit to this city institution to sample some fine, Modern Scottish cuisine, which applies a modern slant to original and traditional recipes. Just stepping inside the glass-roofed, green leafy courtyard provides a special experience after the busy streets of Glasgow. Diners can choose from several menu options, all of which successfully pay homage to Scotland's fine fresh produce and national specialities. So expect to find such things as free-range Perthshire pork, braised for 36 hours with truffle oil and served with leeks and basil mashed potatoes.
✉ 12 Ashton Lane G12 8SJ ☎ 0141 334 5007 🕐 12–2.30, 6.30–11; closed 25 Dec, 1 Jan 🍴 L £22, D £39, Wine £14.95 🚇 In the West End of Glasgow off Byres Road. Beside Hillhead underground station

HARRIS, ISLE OF
SCARISTA HOUSE
www.scaristahouse.com
The set menu might feature a rich and intense langoustine bisque, followed by navarin of Harris lamb with dauphinoise potatoes. Pudding

might feature brown bread ice cream with glazed fresh figs and port syrup. No children under 7.
✉ Scarista HS3 3HX ☎ 01859 550238 🕐 L 12–3, D daily at 8; closed 25 Dec 🍴 L £15, D £34.50, Wine £13.50 🚇 On A859 15 miles (24km) south of Tarbert

INNERLEITHEN
TRAQUAIR ARMS HOTEL
The food at this traditional inn (▷ 408) has a distinctive Scottish flavour with dishes of Finnan savoury, salmon with ginger and coriander (cilantro), and fillet of beef Traquair. A selection of omelettes, salads and baked potatoes is also available.
✉ Traquair Road EH44 6PD ☎ 01896 830229 🕐 Daily 11am–midnight; closed 25–26 Dec, 1 Jan. Restaurant: daily 12–9 🍴 L £12, D £20, Wine £11 🚇 9.5km (6 miles) east of Peebles on A72. Hotel 90m (100yds) from junction with B709

INVERNESS
BUNCHREW HOUSE HOTEL
This hotel's (▷ 408) well-proportioned Classical dining room looks out across the Beauly Firth. Despite the romantic location, there is nothing whimsical about the food or the dedication to combining quality produce with sound cooking practices. Expect West Coast crab cake with braised scallops, roast loin of west Highland lamb, and caramelized lemon tart with an Armagnac sauce.
✉ Bunchrew IV3 8TA ☎ 01463 234917 🕐 12.30–1.45, 7–8.45; closed 24–26 Dec 🍴 L £20, D £35.50, Wine £13.50 🚇 2.5 miles (4.5km) from Inverness on A862 towards Beauly

RIVERHOUSE
Start with fresh oysters served with lemon, red wine and shallot dressing. Mains range from Dover sole and pan-seared scallops to Aberdeen Angus fillet steak. No children under 8.
✉ 1 Greig Street IV3 5PT ☎ 01463 222033 🕐 12–2.15, 5.30–10; closed Mon and Sun Sep–end Apr 🍴 L £11.50, D £28.95, Wine £18.50 🚇 On the corner of Huntly Street and Greig Street

ISLAY, ISLE OF
THE HARBOUR INN
This lovely old hotel (▷ 409) overlooks Loch Indall and houses an elegant restaurant specializing in 'Tastes of Islay'. These might include pheasant, partridge and woodcock in various guises along with the finest local fish—Loch Gruinart oysters, perhaps, or a special recipe fish chowder. Many dishes are paired with whiskies from the distilleries on the island.
✉ The Square, Bowmore PA43 7JR ☎ 01496 810330 🕐 12–2.30, 6–9; closed L Sun, 25 Dec, 1 Jan 🍴 L £12.50, D £25, Wine £11.65 🚇 Bowmore is situated 8 miles (13km) from the ports of Port Ellen and Port Askaig

KILCHRENAN
ARDANAISEIG HOTEL
www.ardanaiseig.com
This old country house hotel (▷ 409) has its own herb garden, helping to enhance the predominantly Scottish-led ingredients and flavours, particularly seafood, in the restaurant. A set menu might feature Inverawe smoked trout with potato salad, trout caviar and herb oil, to be followed by mains such as herb crusted saddle of lamb with Provençale vegetables and tomato and cumin sauce. The wine list is impressive. No children under seven.
✉ PA35 1HE ☎ 01866 833333 🕐 12.30–2, 7–9; closed 2 Jan–10 Feb 🍴 L £12, D (6 courses) £42, Wine £18 🚇 Take A85 to Oban. At Taynuilt turn left on to B845 towards Kilchrenan. In Kilchrenan turn left by pub. Hotel in 3 miles (5km)

KIRKCUDBRIGHT
SELKIRK ARMS HOTEL
www.selkirkarmshotel.co.uk
The restaurant in this comfortable hotel (▷ 409) conjures up some innovative, Modern British cooking with creative flavour combinations such as gateaux of prawns and cream cheese on a pear salad with a red pepper sauce and saddle of venison on a confit of vegetables served with a juniper reduction to follow. Local produce,

particularly seafood, puts in a regular appearance on the menu, and there's a good-value selection of wines as well as an extensive range of malt whiskies to sample.
✉ Old High Street DG6 4JG ☎ 01557 330402 ◷ 7–9.30 🍴 L £12, D £25, Wine £12.50 🚗 5 miles (8km) south of A75 junction with A711

MELROSE
BURT'S
www.burtshotel.co.uk
The bar is popular for informal lunches and suppers. In the restaurant try avocado cheesecake to begin, while typical mains range from sea bream, venison and chicken through lamb chops and steaks to a vegetarian platter. Selkirk Bannock Pudding is served with shortbread ice cream. No children under 10.
✉ Market Square TD6 9PL ☎ 01896 822285 ◷ 12–2, 7–9 🍴 L £15.50, D £31.50, Wine £13.25

ORKNEY ISLANDS
CREEL RESTAURANT
There's a warm welcome at this waterfront restaurant. Simple use of fresh local produce, particularly fish and seafood, ensures honest, flavoursome fare. Begin with velvet crab bisque or perhaps steamed lemon sole. Sea scallops and roasted monkfish tails served with leeks, fresh ginger and beans or grilled chicken fillet with roasted red pepper marmalade could follow. Strawberry shortcake, pannacotta or possibly chocolate mascarpone torte will leave you happily satisfied with just enough room for coffee with handmade chocolates and fudge.
✉ Front Road, St. Margaret's Hope KW17 2SL ☎ 01856 831311 ◷ D only; closed Jan–end Mar, Nov 🍴 D £30, Wine £11 🚗 13 miles (20km) south of Kirkwall. On A961 on waterfront in village

PEAT INN
THE PEAT INN
www.thepeatinn.co.uk
Using the very best Scottish produce, this country inn serves up the highest-quality French-infused cuisine. There's a great tasting menu

and the à la carte is of a manageable size to try cassoulet of lamb, pork and duck, or fillet of halibut on a lobster risotto. The fixed-price lunch is very good value and the wine list is like a taster's guide to French wine.
✉ Peat Inn KY15 5LH ☎ 01334 840206 ◷ 12.30–2, 7–10; closed Sun–Mon, 25 Dec, 1 Jan 🍴 L (3 courses fixed price) £22, D fixed price £32, Wine £18 🚗 At junction of B940/B941, 6 miles (9.2km) southwest of St. Andrews.

PERTH
HUNTINGTOWER HOTEL
www.huntingtowerhotel.co.uk
The restaurant of this stately hotel is a great place for formal dining. Two menus provide choice and value, with simpler specials and a more hearty contemporary menu including Scottish seafood and game. Breast of duck with plum tarte tatin, and roast loin of venison with dauphinoise potato and red cabbage are just two selections.
✉ Crieff Road PH1 3JT ☎ 01738 583771 ◷ L 12–2.30, D 6–9.30 🍴 L £12.95, D £33, Wine £12.95 🚭 🚗 10 minutes from Perth on A85, towards Crieff

LET'S EAT
Close to the River Tay in the centre of town, this comfortable establishment appeals to a wide audience and has built up a good reputation for its light, modern bistro food. A team of competent staff provide polite, understated service of dishes such as a simply prepared and well-balanced fillet of halibut with Skye langoustines, Glamis sea kale, asparagus and a prawn essence, and a divine dessert of Valrhona chocolate tart with a white chocolate sorbet. The wine list offers plenty of choice from new and old world regions, as well as good-value house wines.
✉ 77–79 Kinnoull Street PH1 5EZ ☎ 01738 643377 ◷ 12–2, 6.30–9.45; closed Sun, Mon; two weeks Jan, two weeks Jul 🍴 L £13.95, D £22.50, Wine £12.50 🚗 On corner of Kinnoull Street and Atholl Street, close to North Inch

PITLOCHRY
MOULIN HOTEL
www.moulinhotel.co.uk
This hotel produces its own Braveheart beer, which appears on the food menu too, giving local

venison dishes that extra flavour.
✉ 11–13 Kirkmichael Road, Moulin PH16
5EW ☎ 01796 472196 ◐ Sun–Thu 12–11,
Fri–Sat 12–11.45. Bar meals: 12–9.30.
Restaurant: D only, 6–9 ♨ L £10, D £23.50,
Wine £11.95 🚗 From A924 at Pitlochry
take A923

ST. ANDREWS
THE INN AT LATHONES
Full of character and individuality,
this lovely country inn has a
colourful, cosy restaurant. Select
from one of three menus—including
a seven-course delicacy option—all
offering Modern Scottish and
European cuisine. Good-quality
raw ingredients tell in the tartare of
salmon starter and again in the rib-
eye of mature Glenfarg Angus beef
with a Lagavulin, smoked bacon and
wild mushroom sauce. Thick chips
cooked in beef dripping deserve
a mention too. Balance your
cholesterol intake with a simple red
berry soup to finish.
✉ Largoward KY9 1JE ☎ 01334 840494
◐ 12–2.30, 6–9.30; closed Christmas,
two weeks Jan ♨ L £14.50, D £27.50,
Wine £12.50 🚗 5 miles (8km) south of St.
Andrews on A915. In 0.5 miles (800m) before
Largoward on left just after hidden dip

ROAD HOLE GRILL
www.oldcoursehotel.kohler.com
Enjoy classic fine dining in
sumptuous surroundings. The menu
is marked out by clear flavours
and quality Scottish produce, such
as Highland venison with wild
mushroom fricasée, and the wine
list has 235 choices. There's a smart
dress code.
✉ Old Course Hotel KY16 9SP ☎ 01334
474371 ◐ Dinner only, 7–10; closed 24–28
Dec ♨ D £40, Wine £33

ST. MONANS
THE SEAFOOD RESTAURANT
www.theseafoodrestaurant.com
So modest is the entrance to this
restaurant that you could easily
miss it, but let the sea wall be your
guide and you won't go wrong. The
cooking style is fashionably modern,
and a penchant for contrasting
flavours and textures results in some

dazzling collaborations: A starter
salad of lobster, langoustine and
mango with radish shoots, mizuna,
basil purée and gazpacho avoids
going an ingredient too far, as does
baked fillet of halibut with shiitake
mushrooms, asparagus, crushed
potatoes and a garlic and herb
butter. Adding immeasurably to the
dining experience are the great sea
views from this simple yet elegant
restaurant. There are no vegetarian
dishes available.
✉ 16 West End KY10 2BX ☎ 01333 730327
◐ 12–2.30, 6–9.30; closed Mon, D Sun,
25–26 Dec, 1–2 Jan ♨ L £16, D £30, Wine
£18 🚗 Take A959 from St. Andrews to
Anstruther then head west on A917 through
Pittenweem. In St. Monans go to harbour,
then turn right

SKYE, ISLE OF
CUILLIN HILLS HOTEL
www.cuillinhills-hotel-skye.co.uk
Local meat, fish and game feature
largely: steamed Loch Eilort mussels might be followed by braised
saddle of venison and pigeon with
red wine, topped off with a dark
chocolate terrine.
✉ Portree IV51 9QU ☎ 01478 612003
◐ 12–2, 6.30–9; closed L Mon–Sat
♨ L £13, D £32.50, Wine £15 🚗 0.25
miles (0.5km) north of Portree on A855

ROSEDALE
www.rosedalehotelskye.co.uk
Emphasis is on fresh, local and
organic produce in the imaginative
set-price menu.
✉ Beaumont Crescent, Portree IV51 9DB
☎ 01478 613131 ◐ D only, 6.30–8.30;
closed Nov–end Mar ♨ D £28, Wine
£14.95 🚗 On harbour front

THE THREE CHIMNEYS
Situated at the end of the island,
overlooking Loch Dunvegan. Fish
and shellfish naturally feature heavily
but they don't dominate a menu
that is defined by the use of quality
produce. Starters include Loch Dunvegan langoustines with salad leaves
and herbs from Glendale and pan-
fried pigeon breast on pearl barley
risotto. Lobster bisque could serve as
the definitive version of the dish with

fathom-deep flavours and satisfying
chunks of lobster meat. Much praise
is also due for west coast halibut,
startlingly white with an accompanying lobster ravioli and basil butter
sauce. Desserts hold their own with
accomplished efforts such as brioche
bread-and-butter pudding with Seville
orange anglaise. A very special place.
✉ Colbost IV55 8ZT ☎ 01470 511258
◐ 12.30–2, 6.30–9.30; closed L Sun; three
weeks Jan ♨ L £18.50, D £45, Wine £18
🚗 From Dunvegan take B884 to Glendale

STIRLING
STIRLING HIGHLAND
www.paramount-hotels.co.uk
At the Scholars Restaurant and
adjoining Headmaster's Study
Bar dishes include roasted spring
chicken supreme with baby pak choi
in a sweet and sour sauce, penne
pasta with pesto, or salmon fillet on
lemon risotto.
✉ Spittal Street FK8 1DU ☎ 01786 272727
◐ 6.30–9.30; L bar only daily 10–10 ♨ L
£15 (bar only), D £24.50, Wine £16 🚗 On
road to Stirling Castle, follow Castle signs

SWINTON
WHEATSHEAF
www.wheatsheaf-swinton.co.uk
Overlooking the village green, this
country inn serves above-average
food. There are two dining areas—
the original dining room and a pine
sun lounge. Service is relaxed, but
efficient and Modern British cuisine
uses fresh local produce cooked to
order. The lunch menu changes daily
and offers very good choice and
value. The dinner menu is equally
appealing, with breast of wild wood
pigeon on a medallion of Scotch
beef fillet with black pudding in
madeira sauce, for instance, or fillet
of salmon on a crayfish, tomato and
coriander (cilantro) sauce.
✉ Main Street TD11 3JJ ☎ 01890 860257
◐ 12–2.15, 6–9; closed Mon (except
residents), D Sun ♨ L £10, D £20, Wine
£11.95 🚗 On A6112, halfway between Duns
and Coldstream

PRICES AND SYMBOLS

Prices are the starting price for a double room for one night, unless otherwise stated. Breakfast is included unless noted otherwise. All the hotels listed accept credit cards unless otherwise stated. Note that rates vary widely throughout the year.

For a key to the symbols, ▷ 2.

ABERDEEN
ARDOE HOUSE

www.macdonald-hotels.co.uk

This Scots baronial-style mansion stands in an elevated position above the beautiful countryside of the Dee Valley. In the main house the rooms are tastefully furnished to retain the ambience of a country house hotel, with a more modern feel to those in the extension. There is a leisure club with sauna, gym, supervised pool and solarium, and an impressive cocktail lounge serving over 180 different malt whiskies.

✉ South Deeside Road, Blairs AB12 5YP
☎ 01224 860600 ⦿ £105 ⓘ 117 ⊠
🚗 5km (3 miles) west of city off B9077

ARDUAINE
LOCH MELFORT

www.lochmelfort.co.uk

Enjoying one of the finest locations on the west coast, this popular, family-run hotel has outstanding views across Asknish Bay towards the islands of Jura, Scarba and Shuna.

✉ PA34 4XG ☎ 01852 200233 ✋ £78; discount for under-14s ⓘ 27 🚗 On the A816, midway between Oban and Lochgilphead 🚗 Oban

AVIEMORE
THE OLD MINISTER'S HOUSE

www.theoldministershouse.co.uk

The Old Minister's House is beautifully furnished and immaculately maintained while the bedrooms are spacious and equipped to a high standard. There is a lounge and a dining room where hearty breakfasts are served. No children under four.

✉ Rothiemurchus PH22 1QH ☎ 01479 812181 ✋ £60 ⓘ 4 🚗 From Aviemore take B970, signed Glenmore and Coylumbridge. Establishment is 0.75 miles (1km) from Aviemore at Inverdruie 🚗 Aviemore

BALLATER
BALGONIE COUNTRY HOUSE

www.royaldeesidehotels.com

This Edwardian house is set in neatly tended gardens. There is a homey bar and lounge, and carefully prepared meals are served in the dining room. Bedrooms and public areas offer good levels of comfort. The proprietors ensure a friendly welcome.

✉ Braemar Place AB3 5NQ ☎ 013397 55482 ⦿ Closed 6 Jan–end Feb ✋ £100; discount for under-14s ⓘ 9 🚗 Off A93 Aberdeen–Perth road, on the western outskirts of village of Ballater. Hotel is signed 🚗 Aberdeen

BANCHORY
BANCHORY LODGE HOTEL

This tranquil hotel offers the added attraction of the River Dee, famed for its salmon, running through its grounds. Victorian furnishings accentuate the sense of comfort, and traditional dining is on offer (▷ 401).

Fishing is possible from March to the end of September.

✉ AB31 5HS ☎ 01330 822625 ✋ £130
ⓘ 22 ⊘ In dining room 🚗 Off A93 18 miles (29km) west of Aberdeen

CALLANDER
ARDEN HOUSE
www.ardenhouse.org.uk
This large Victorian villa lies in mature gardens in a quiet area of the town. It starred in the 1960s TV series *Dr. Finlay's Casebook* and is a friendly, welcoming house. The bedrooms are thoughtfully furnished and equipped with little extra touches. There is a stylish lounge in addition to the breakfast room. No children under 14. Two nights minimum in high season.

✉ Bracklinn Road FK17 8EQ ☎ 01877 330235 ✋ £70 ⓘ 6 ⊗ Closed Nov–end Mar 🚗 From A84 into Callander from Stirling, turn right into Bracklinn Road signed to golf course and Bracklinn Falls. House 183m (200yds) on left

DALBEATTIE
AUCHENSKEOCH LODGE
www.auchenskeoch.co.uk
A former Victorian shooting lodge set in 8ha (20 acres) of stunning grounds with woodland and a small loch. The house is full of charm, and traditional furnishings, log fires and artwork help preserve the original character of the house. A set four-course dinner is served in the stylish dining room. No children under 12. Private fishing is available.

✉ Southwick, Dalbeattie DG5 4PG ☎ 01387 780277 ⊗ Closed Nov–Easter ✋ £60 ⓘ 3 🚗 5 miles (8km) southeast of Dalbeattie, off B793 🚉 Dumfries

DUNDEE
SANDFORD COUNTRY HOUSE HOTEL
www.sandfordhotelfife.com
The Sandford offers glorious views of the Fife countryside, log fires, local antiques and a kitchen that produces the best of the region's cuisine. A variety of bedroom sizes are available, all tastefully modern and well equipped.

✉ Newton Hill, Wormit DD6 8RG
☎ 01382 541802 ✋ £70 ⓘ 16 🚗 4 miles (6.5km) south of Tay Bridge near junction of A92 and B946

DUNKELD
KINNAIRD
www.kinnairdestate.com
This striking Edwardian mansion stands in a majestic countryside estate. Public rooms are furnished with antiques and beautiful paintings. Sitting rooms are warm and inviting with deep-cushioned sofas and open fires. Bedrooms are furnished with luxurious fabrics. Cooking is creative. No children under 12. Tennis courts, private fishing and shooting are available.

✉ Kinnaird Estate PH8 0LB ☎ 01796 482440 ✋ £275, including breakfast and dinner ⓘ 9 🚗 From Perth, take A9 north. Keep on A9 past Dunkeld and continue for 2 miles (3km), then take B898 on the left 🚉 Dunkeld or Birnam

EDINBURGH
BONNINGTON GUEST HOUSE
This Georgian house offers individually furnished bedrooms that retain many of the property's original features. The homely lounge is complemented by an attractive dining room, where a fine Scottish breakfast is served. There is a particularly warm welcome here.

✉ 202 Ferry Road EH6 4NW ☎ 0131 554 7610 ✋ £50; discount for under-11s ⓘ 6 🚗 On A902 🚉 Edinburgh Waverley

MALMAISON
www.malmaison.com
The stylish Malmaison overlooks the port of Leith. Bedrooms have striking decor, CD players, mini bars and a number of individual touches. Food and drink are equally important here, with brasserie-style dining and a café-bar.

✉ One Tower Place EH6 7DB ☎ 0131 468 5000 ✋ £99 ⓘ 101 🚗 A900 from city centre towards Leith. At end of Leith Walk continue over lights, through two more sets of lights, then left into Tower Street; hotel on right

THE SCOTSMAN
www.thescotsmanhotel.co.uk
The former head office of *The Scotsman* newspaper has been transformed into this state-of-the-art boutique hotel, where traditional elegance blends seamlessly with cutting-edge technology and friendly, attentive service. Bedrooms are all smartly furnished and very well equipped. The galleried Brasserie restaurant offers an informal dining option.

✉ 20 North Bridge EH1 1YT ☎ 0131 556 5565 ✋ £250 ⓘ 68 🚗 A8 to city centre, left on to Charlotte Street. Right into Queen Street, right at roundabout on to Leith Street. Keep straight on, left on to North Bridge, hotel on right 🚉 Edinburgh Waverley

Below *The Malmaison, Edinburgh*

FORT WILLIAM
ASHBURN HOUSE
www.highland5star.co.uk
This elegant Victorian villa, which enjoys wonderful views overlooking Loch Linnhe and the Ardgour Hills, is just five minutes from the town centre. The bedrooms are spacious, with an extensive range of amenities. No dogs.
✉ 8 Achintore Road PH33 6RQ ☎ 01397 706000 🕐 Closed Dec–end Jan ✋ £70, discount for under-14s ⓘ 7 🚗 At the junction of A82 and Ashburn Lane, 500m (550yds) from the large roundabout at the southern end of the High Street; or 400m (440yds) on the right after entering 30mph zone from the south 🚉 Fort William

LIME TREE
www.limetreefortwilliam.co.uk
The Lime Tree is a charming and contemporary small hotel, with its own art gallery. The hotel has comfortable lounges with real fires, and a restaurant serving excellent local produce. The rooms are individually designed and spacious.
✉ Achintore Road PH33 6RQ ☎ 01397 701806 ✋ £80 ⓘ 9

GAIRLOCH
THE OLD INN
The oldest hotel in Gairloch, dating from around 1792, with views across Gairloch harbour. The Inn has been sympathetically restored. There is an excellent range of real ales and plenty of accommodation.
✉ Gairloch IV21 2BD ☎ 01445 712006 ✋ £45 ⓘ 14 🚗 Just off main A832, near harbour at southern end of village

GLAMIS
CASTLETON HOUSE
www.castletonglamis.co.uk
Exemplary levels of guest care by enthusiastic owners and their young team are features of this Victorian house set in its own grounds. Bedrooms are noted for their comfortable beds. Lunches are also served here, but it is dinner that will provide a particularly memorable experience.
✉ Castleton of Eassie DD8 1SJ ☎ 01307 840340 ✋ £140, discount for under-14s

ⓘ 6 🚗 On A94 midway between Forfar and Cupar Angus, 3 miles (5km) west of Glamis 🚉 Dundee

GLASGOW
KELVINGROVE HOTEL
www.kelvingrove-hotel.co.uk
This well-maintained, friendly hotel lies just west of the city centre. Bedrooms, including several rooms suitable for families, are particularly well equipped and have fully tiled private bathrooms. There is a bright breakfast room and a reception lounge that is manned 24 hours.
✉ 944 Sauchiehall Street G3 7TH ☎ 0141 339 5011 ✋ £50 ⓘ 22 🚗 0.25 miles (400m) west of Charing Cross. From M8 junction 18 follow signs for Kelvingrove 🚉 Kelvinhall or Glasgow Central

ONE DEVONSHIRE GARDENS
www.onedevonshiregardens.com
One Devonshire Gardens is one of Glasgow's most stylish hotels. The sumptuously furnished drawing room is the focal point of the attractive day rooms, with all the elegance and comfort expected in such a grand house. An imaginatively prepared Scottish menu is served in the small dining room and there is 24-hour room service.
✉ 5 Devonshire Gardens G12 0UX ☎ 0141 339 2001 ✋ £145; discount for under-14s ⓘ 14 🚗 From M8 junction 17 turn right at slip road lights (A82). Continue 1.5 miles (2.5km). Go over first traffic lights, left at second. Take 1st right at mini roundabout. Hotel is at end of road 🚉 Glasgow Central

GLENELG
GLENELG INN
This characterful old village inn commands stunning views across the Glenelg Bay. From here the little summer-only ferry chugs across the Sound of Sleat to the Isle of Skye. As well as a bar where fiddlers often play and an excellent dining room noted for local cuisine, there are comfortable bedrooms with magnificent views.
✉ IV40 8JR ☎ 01599 522273 ✋ £100 including dinner ⓘ 7 🚗 From Shiel Bridge (A87) take unclassified road to Glenelg

GRANTOWN-ON-SPEY
THE PINES
www.thepinesgrantown.co.uk
This impressive Victorian house is set in well-tended gardens, a short walk from the heart of town. Bedrooms are generally spacious and many have views of the beautiful Speyside scenery. No children under 12.
✉ Woodside Avenue PH26 3JR ☎ 01479 872092 🕐 Closed Nov–end Feb ✋ £100 ⓘ 8 🚗 Aviemore

HARRIS, ISLE OF
SCARISTA HOUSE
www.scaristahouse.com
Food lovers will know of this restaurant with rooms. The house is run in a relaxed country house manner, so expect wellies (rubber boots) in the hall and books and CDs in one of the two lounges.
✉ Scarista HS3 3HX ☎ 01859 550238 ✋ £175 ⓘ 5 🕐 Closed Christmas 🚗 On A859, 15 miles (24km) south of Tarbert

INNERLEITHEN
TRAQUAIR ARMS HOTEL
This traditional inn is in a village setting close to the River Tweed, surrounded by lovely countryside and with a dining room (▷ 403) and homey bar.
✉ Traquair Road EH44 6PD ☎ 01896 830229 🕐 Closed Dec 25, 26, 1–3 Jan ✋ £58 ⓘ 15 🚗 9.5km (6 miles) east of Peebles on A72. Hotel 90m (100yds) from junction with B709

INVERNESS
BUNCHREW HOUSE HOTEL
www.bunchrew-inverness.co.uk
This beautifully located 17th-century mansion retains much of its original character. The dining room (▷ 403) has marvellous views.
✉ Bunchrew IV3 8TA ☎ 01463 234917 🕐 Closed 24–27 Dec ✋ £130 ⓘ 14 🚗 2.5 miles (4.5km) from Inverness on A862 towards Beauly

MOYNESS HOUSE
www.moyness.co.uk
This elegant villa offers beautifully decorated bedrooms and well-fitted bathrooms. There is a sitting room, a dining room where traditional

Scottish breakfasts are served, and a garden.

✉ 6 Bruce Gardens IV3 5EN ☎ 01463 233836 🖐 £72 ⓘ 6 🚗 Off A82 Fort William road, almost opposite Highland Regional Council headquarters

ISLAY, ISLE OF
THE HARBOUR INN

The bedrooms in this charming old hotel are stylishly furnished and the public rooms have wonderful views of the surrounding bay. There is a fine restaurant (▷ 403) which offers a menu featuring the 'Tastes of Islay'.

✉ The Square, Bowmore PA43 7JR ☎ 01496 810330 🗓 Closed 25 Dec, 1 Jan 🖐 £90 ⓘ 7 🚗 Bowmore is situated 13km (8 miles) from the ports of Port Ellen and Port Askaig

JEDBURGH
JEDFOREST HOTEL

www.jedforesthotel.com
This country house hotel is set in 14ha (35 acres) of woodland and pasture. Jedforest provides a stylish haven. Immaculately presented throughout, it offers an attractive dining room, a brasserie and a lounge. The bedrooms are very smart, with the larger ones being particularly impressive.

✉ Camptown TD8 6PJ ☎ 01835 840222 🖐 £140 including dinner; discount for under-13s ⓘ 12 🚗 3 miles (5km) south of Jedburgh, off A68

KELSO
THE ROXBURGHE HOTEL AND GOLF COURSE

www.roxburghe.net
This impressive Jacobean mansion is set in 200ha (495 acres) of mature wood and parkland. Sporting pursuits are popular, with many guests enjoying shooting, fishing and golf. Bedrooms are individually designed and a number have real fires. Comfortably furnished lounges are a perfect setting for lavish afternoon teas.

✉ Heiton TD5 8JZ ☎ 01573 450331 🖐 £140; discount for under-12s ⓘ 22 🚗 3 miles (5km) south of Kelso off A698 🚆 Berwick-upon-Tweed

KILCHRENAN
THE ARDANAISEIG HOTEL

Idyllic and tranquil, this old country house hotel sits in a striking location on the shores of Loch Awe. Grand in every sense with a good restaurant (▷ 403). No children under seven.

✉ By Loch Awe PA35 1HE ☎ 01866 833333 🗓 Closed 2 Jan–10 Feb 🖐 £103 ⓘ 16 🚗 Take A85 to Oban. At Taynuilt turn left on to B845 towards Kilchrenan. In Kilchrenan turn left by pub. Hotel in 5km (3 miles)

KIRKCUDBRIGHT
SELKIRK ARMS HOTEL

www.selkirkarmshotel.co.uk
This Best Western hotel gets its name from an historical association: it was here that Robert Burns wrote the *Selkirk Grace*. Set in secluded gardens, it is a stylish hotel just outside the city centre. Rooms are furnished in an uncluttered, contemporary style.

✉ Old High Street DG6 4JG ☎ 01557 330402 🖐 £52 ⓘ 17 🚗 On A71, 5 miles (8km) south of A75

MELROSE
BURT'S HOTEL

www.burtshotel.co.uk
Family-owned hotel in a small market town, offering an hospitable welcome. As well as comfortable rooms, the hotel also has a formal restaurant with daily changing menus, and a relaxed bistro bar.

✉ Market Square TD6 9PN ☎ 01896 822285 🖐 £58 ⓘ 20 🚗 A6091, 2 miles (3km) from A68 south of Earlston

FAUHOPE HOUSE

Here you'll find first-class hospitality and excellent breakfasts, plus a chance to savour the splendid interior of a delightful country house. Public areas are elegantly furnished; the dining room is particularly stunning. Bedrooms are a haven of luxury, all individual in style and superbly equipped. No dogs.

✉ Gattonside TD6 9LU ☎ 01896 823184 🖐 £70 ⓘ 5 🚗 Turn right off A68 on to B6360 to Gattonside. At the 30mph sign turn right, then right again and go up a long drive leading to Fauhope

MOFFAT
WELL VIEW

www.wellview.co.uk
Well View still retains many original Victorian features. The individually furnished bedrooms are comfortable and thoughtfully equipped. Dinner is the highlight of a stay; the six-course tasting menu focuses on fine, fresh ingredients, which are locally sourced where possible. The bar meals are excellent value.

✉ Ballplay Road DG10 9JU ☎ 01683 220184 🗓 Closed two weeks Feb, two weeks Oct 🖐 £110; discount for under-11s ⓘ 6 🚗 On A708 from Moffat, pass fire station and take first left

MULL, ISLE OF
HIGHLAND COTTAGE

www.highlandcottage.co.uk
Visitors are assured of a personal welcome at this charming cottage-style hotel. Bedrooms are appointed to a high standard and feature antique beds and a range of thoughtful extras. Public areas include a relaxing lounge, an honesty bar as well as an elegant dining room.

✉ Breadalbane Street, Tobermory PA75 6PD ☎ 01688 302030 🗓 Closed four weeks mid-Oct to mid-Nov 🖐 £120 ⓘ 6 🚗 A848 Craignure/Fishnish ferry terminal, pass Tobermory signs, go ahead at mini roundabout across narrow bridge, turn right. Hotel on the right opposite the fire station 🚆 Oban

PERTH
HUNTINGTOWER

www.huntingtowerhotel.co.uk
An Edwardian-era house in a delightful country setting has been refurbished to provide excellent accommodation. Lunches are served in a pleasant conservatory while more formal dining is available in the Oak Room. The spacious bedrooms have a full complement of modern facilities.

✉ Crieff Road, PH1 3JT ☎ 01738 583771 🖐 £100 ⓘ 34 🚗 3 miles (5km) west of Perth off A85

Abpve West Sands, St. Andrews' largest and best-known beach

PARKLANDS HOTEL
www.theparklandshotel.com
There are great views from this hotel over the city centre park known as the South Inch. the bedrooms are smart and furnished in contemporary style. There's a choice of restaurants at the Parklands, with fine dining offered in Acanthus.
✉ 2 St Leonards Bank PH2 8EB ☎ 01738 622451 ✋ £100 ⓘ 14 🚍 From M90 exit 10, after 1 mile (1.5km) turn left at end of park area at traffic lights, hotel is on the left

PITLOCHRY
GREEN PARK
www.thegreenpark.co.uk
This hotel is stunningly set in beautiful landscaped gardens on the shore of Loch Faskally, within strolling distance of the town centre. Many of the bright, spacious bedrooms share expansive views, and the restaurant menu includes produce from the hotel's own kitchen garden.
✉ Clunie Bridge Road PH16 5JY ☎ 01796 473248 ✋ £152; including dinner ⓘ 51 🚍 Turn off A9 at Pitlochry, follow signs 0.25 miles (0.5km) through the town, hotel on banks of Loch Faskally

PINE TREES
www.pinetreeshotel.co.uk
In extensive tree-studded grounds high above the town, this Victorian mansion has many original features, including wood panelling, ornate ceilings and a marble staircase. Public rooms overlook the lawns,

and the mood is refined and relaxing.
✉ Strathview Terrace PH16 5QR ☎ 01796 472121 ✋ £120, including dinner ⓘ 20 🚍 From the high street turn into Larchwood Road and follow hotel signs

ST. ANDREWS
EDENSIDE HOUSE
www.edenside-house.co.uk
This modernized 18th-century house is family run and offers a home from home, overlooking the Eden estuary and nature reserve. Bedrooms are bright and cheerful, and are for the most part accessed externally. There is a homey lounge, and hearty breakfasts are served.
✉ Edenside KY16 9SQ ☎ 01334 838108 ✋ £56 ⓘ 8 🚍 Clearly visible from A91, 2 miles (3km) west of St. Andrews, directly on estuary shore

ST. ANDREWS GOLF HOTEL
www.standrews-golf.co.uk
Friendly attentive service is a particular feature of this hotel, which overlooks the lovely bay and so enjoys fine views of the coastline and links. The bedrooms have a crisp, clean, contemporary design. There is a choice of bars and a wood-panelled restaurant. Lunch is very good value and the wine list has global appeal.
✉ 40 The Scores KY16 9AS ☎ 01334 472611 ✋ £170; discount for under-12s ⓘ 22 🚍 Follow signs 'Golf Course' into Golf Place and in 180m (200yds) turn right into The Scores 🚉 Leuchars

SHETLAND ISLANDS
GLEN ORCHY HOUSE
www.guesthouselerwick.com
This welcoming and well-presented hotel is within easy walking distance of the town centre. Bedrooms are modern in design. Breakfasts, as substantial as dinner, are chosen from the daily-changing menu.
✉ 20 Knab Road, Lerwick ZE1 0AX ☎ 01595 692031 ✋ £69; discount for under-12s ⓘ 22 🚍 Next to the coastguard station

SKYE, ISLE OF
HOTEL EILEAN IARMAIN
www.eilean-iarmain.co.uk
This 19th-century hotel overlooking Isle Ornsay harbour enjoys spectacular sea views. Rooms are on the simple side (not all have TVs), but the cuisine is breathtaking.
✉ Isle Ornsay, Sleat IV43 8QR ☎ 01471 833332 ✋ £80 ⓘ 12 🚍 Take A851 to Isle Ornsay harbourfront

STIRLING
STIRLING HIGHLAND
Set high above the town the hotel occupies what was once the old high-school building. The Scholars Restaurant and adjoining Headmaster's Study Bar (▷ 405) are housed in original classrooms. Bedrooms are modern and well-equipped.
✉ Spittal Street FK8 1DU ☎ 01786 272727 ✋ £115 ⓘ 96 🚍 On road leading to Stirling Castle; follow Castle signs

TORRIDON
LOCH TORRIDON COUNTRY HOUSE HOTEL
www.lochtorridonhotel.com
Most bedrooms enjoy Highland views, the day rooms are comfortable, and the whisky bar stocks over 300 malts. Wide range of outdoor activities include shooting, bicycling, horseback riding and walking.
✉ By Achnasheen IV22 2EY ☎ 01445 791242 ✋ £225, incuding dinner ⓘ 19 ⊙ Closed 3–27 Jan 🚍 From A832 at Kinlochewe, take A896 towards Torridon; do not turn into village, instead carry on for 1 mile (1.6km). Hotel on right

PRACTICALITIES

Planning gives you all the important practical information you will need during your visit from money matters to emergency phone numbers.

Essential Information	**412**
Weather	412
Documents and Customs	414
Money	415
Health	417
Basics	419
Communication	420
Tourist Information	422
Useful Websites	423
Finding Help	424
Opening Times and Entrance Fees	425
Media	426
Books, Films and Maps	427
What to Do	**428**
Entertainment and nightlife	430
Sports and Activities	431
Film and Music	434
Festivals and Events	436
Eating	**438**
Afternoon Tea	442
Whisky	443
Staying	**444**
A Brief Guide to Architectural Periods	**447**
Kings and Queens of England	**450**
Glossary for US Visitors	**452**

WEATHER

CLIMATE

Being an island, Britain's climate is naturally determined by its surrounding seas. Weather fronts move in from the west across the Atlantic—low pressure brings wind, rain and changeable conditions, and high pressure brings more settled weather. Most weather fronts that affect Britain intersect with the Atlantic's warm Gulf Stream, explaining why Britain's climate is milder than other countries on the same latitude. When this water-laden sea air meets land, rain falls. As a result the wettest areas of Britain are in the west: Cornwall and Wales. These cloudy depressions are punctuated by anti-cyclones that bring fine weather. Prevailing winds are from the southwest, but cold winds from the northeast (Scandinavia) and warm winds from the southeast (Africa) sometimes affect the country.

Winter (December to late February) is chilly, but snow is rare in southern Britain. However, it is more widespread in the hills of northern England, Wales and Scotland; Scotland's Highlands have skiable snow most winters.

WEATHER REPORTS

The Meteorological (Met) Office, founded in 1854, is the government agency responsible for weather forecasting and supplying information to broadcasters such as the BBC. It is a global service and its website is an excellent place to start with any weather-related query. Daily forecasts are given at the end of television and radio news programmes, and are also available by phone, fax, text messaging or on the Internet. The Met Office also provides detailed vital shipping and other marine forecasts.

REGIONAL FORECASTS

For regional forecasts from the Met Office for the next hour, day, five or ten days, by telephone or fax, see their website: www.metoffice.gov.uk for a full list of numbers to dial.

REGIONAL VARIATIONS

Despite the small size of the United Kingdom, there are considerable regional variations in its weather. The moderating influence of the sea affects the coastal climate for up 20 miles (32km) inland. In winter the coast is often warmer than inland

LONDON
TEMPERATURE

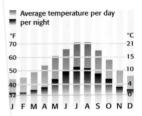

RAINFALL

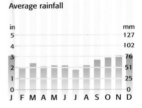

EDINBURGH
TEMPERATURE

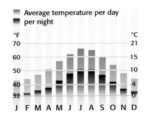

RAINFALL

BATH
TEMPERATURE

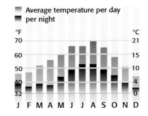

RAINFALL

YORK
TEMPERATURE

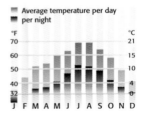

RAINFALL

areas and in summer it is often cooler. Mountainous areas (see below) are notoriously unpredictable and the weather is often harsh. The coldest areas of the country in winter are the Grampian and Tayside regions of Scotland, with average daily temperatures in January as low as -5°C (23°F). The sunniest parts tend to be flat areas near the coast, such as the Isle of Wight with up to 1,800 hours of sunshine out of 4,000 daylight hours annually. South-facing slopes receive more sunshine than north-facing slopes. The wettest areas are in the south and west of the country, while much of the east, including Cambridgeshire and East Anglia, is in a rain shadow. Cities will also have their own micro-climates and are often drier and warmer than surrounding land.

MOUNTAINOUS AREAS
The weather in Britain's mountain regions (parts of Scotland, Wales and the Lake District) can often be more changeable and dramatic than in low-lying areas, regardless of season. British mountains may not be high but in winter they can be dangerous for the unprepared. Expect temperatures to drop by about two degrees per 300m (985ft) of ascent and wind speeds to double with every 900m (about 3,000ft) of altitude. The Met Office provides twice-daily forecasts for those going into the mountains.

FLOOD-PRONE AREAS
Several areas of Britain can be susceptible to flooding, usually in flat flood basins, such as the Vale of York, close to rivers. Flooding is more of a risk to property than life, and should not be more than a very infrequent inconvenience to visitors. Warnings are issued on television and radio, or you can call the national Floodline (tel 0845 988 1188) or log on to the Environment Agency's website (www.environment-agency.gov.uk) for the latest news.

WHEN TO GO
May and June have the bonus of long daylight hours, when it stays light until well after 9pm—and after 11pm in northern Scotland.

June to the end of August is the warmest and busiest period, especially during school holidays (late July to end of August). Rural and coastal areas—such as the West Country, the national parks and the Scottish Highlands—as well as major tourist cities are very busy at Easter and in July and August. Spring and September are appreciably quieter, although the weather is less reliable.

Autumn and early spring often have the windiest conditions of the year. Global warming appears to have made winter start later and end earlier, with frosty conditions often not arriving until November.

On average January is the coldest month. The winter months can be a good time for visiting cities. Accommodation is often less expensive and sights are less crowded. However, some attractions close in winter (November to Easter), including most National Trust properties. Major city museums stay open year round.

TIME ZONES
Britain is on Greenwich Mean Time (GMT)—also known as Universal Time (UTC)—during winter. In summer (late March to late October) clocks go forward one hour to British Summer Time (BST). The chart below shows time differences from GMT in principal cities around the world.

City	Time	Time at difference
	12 noon	GMT
Amsterdam	+1	1pm
Auckland	+10	10pm
Berlin	+1	1pm
Brussels	+1	1pm
Chicago	-6	6am
Dublin	0	12pm
Johannesburg	+2	2pm
Madrid	+1	1pm
Montréal	-6	6am
New York	-5	7am
Paris	+1	1pm
Perth, Australia	+8	8pm
Rome	+1	1pm
San Francisco	-8	4am
Sydney	+10	10pm
Tokyo	+9	9pm

WEATHER SITES

ORGANIZATION	NOTES	TELEPHONE/FAX	WEBSITE
The Met Office (UK)	Highly informative site, with inshore marine forecasts and specialist forecasts for leisure activities, including images from webcams at several locations for mountain pursuits.	Tel: 0870 900 0100 Fax: 0870 900 5050	www.metoffice.gov.uk enquiries@metoffice.gov.uk
BBC	Comprehensive online information, UK and world weather reports, plus many related topics. Includes satellite imagery and five-day and regional forecasts.		www.bbc.co.uk/weather
Countryfile	Television show on Sunday morning on BBC1, also gives a five-day forecast		www.bbc.co.uk/sn/tvradio/[rogrammes /countryfile

DOCUMENTS

PASSPORTS

Foreign visitors must have a passport valid for at least six months when entering the UK.

The United Kingdom (England, Wales, Scotland and Northern Ireland), the Channel Islands, the Isle of Man and the Republic of Ireland form a common travel area. Once you have entered this area, passing through immigration control at any point of entry, you are free to travel within it. However, to take an internal flight, you should carry a passport as identification.

LOSS OF PASSPORT

If you lose your passport, contact your embassy in the UK. It helps if you have details of your passport number; either carry a photocopy of the relevant pages of your passport, or scan them and email them to yourself at an account that you can access anywhere in case of emergency (such as www.hotmail.com).

VISAS

Citizens of any one of the European Economic Area (EEA) countries—the EU, plus Switzerland, Norway and Iceland—can enter the UK on leisure or business for any length of stay without a visa. Visitors from the US, Australia, Canada or New Zealand do not require a visa for stays of up to six months. But, you must have enough money to support yourself without working or receiving money from public funds.

Those wishing to stay longer than six months, and nationals of certain other countries, require a visa.

You are usually allowed to enter and leave the UK as many times as you like during the validity of your visa. On arrival you must be able to produce documentation establishing your identity and nationality. For details see www.ukvisas.gov.uk. Visa regulations can change at short notice, so check before you travel.

CUSTOMS

Entrants to the UK will have to pass through Customs. Arrivals with 'nothing to declare' should pass through the green channel; those with 'goods to declare' should go to the red channel and arrivals from other EU countries with nothing to declare should pass through the blue channel.

VAT REFUNDS
▷ 416.

WORK PERMITS

These permits enable employers based in the UK to employ people who are not nationals of EEA countries and who are not entitled to work. Applications are made by the employer. Citizens of the Commonwealth, British Dependent Territories or British Overseas citizens between 17 and 27 can work part-time or casually for up to two years, as long as work is not the main reason for the visit.

TRAVEL INSURANCE

Insurance is recommended for personal possessions, legal liability and medical costs. See Health (▷ 417) for information on what the NHS provides. An annual policy may well be the best value for frequent overseas travellers.

CUSTOMS

Goods you buy in the EU

If you bring in large quantities of alcohol or tobacco, a Customs Officer is likely to ask about the purposes for which you hold the goods. This particularly applies if you have with you more than the following amounts:

» 3,200 cigarettes	» 110 litres of beer
» 400 cigarillos	» 10 litres of spirits
» 200 cigars	» 20 litres of fortified wine (such as port or sherry)
» 3kg (7lb) of smoking tobacco	» 90 litres of wine (of which only 60 litres can be sparkling wine)

There are limits on the amount of tobacco products you can bring into the UK from some EU countries. From Estonia: 200 cigarettes or 250g (9oz) of smoking tobacco (no limit on other tobacco products). From Hungary, Latvia, Lithuania, Poland, or Slovakia: 200 cigarettes (no limit on other tobacco products).

The EU countries are: Austria, Belgium, Cyprus*, Czech Republic, Denmark, Estonia, Finland, France, Germany, Greece, Hungary, Italy, Latvia, Lithuania, Luxembourg, Malta, Netherlands, Poland, Portugal, Republic of Ireland, Slovakia, Slovenia, Spain (but not the Canary Islands), Sweden, the UK (but not the Channel Islands).

*Though Cyprus is part of the EU, goods from any area of Cyprus not under control of the Government of the Republic of Cyprus are treated as non-EU imports.

Travelling to the UK from outside the EU

You are entitled to the allowances shown below only if you travel with the goods and do not plan to sell them.

» 200 cigarettes; or	» 100 cigarillos; or
» 50 cigars; or	» 250g (9oz) of tobacco
» 60cc/ml of perfume	» 250cc/ml of toilet water
» 1 litre of spirits or strong liqueurs over 22 per cent volume; or	
» 2 litres of fortified wine, sparkling wine or other liqueurs	
» 2 litres of still table wine	
» £145 worth of all other goods including gifts and souvenirs.	

For further information see HM Revenue and Customs website: www.hmrc.gov.uk and click on Travel Information.

MONEY

Britain can be an expensive country for visitors, so it's a good idea to explore your options for carrying and changing money.

» Expect to spend a minimum of about £40 per day, if you're travelling independently. It's not hard to spend more than £100 in a day.

» The best idea is to carry money in a range of forms—cash, at least one credit card, bank card/charge/ Maestro card and traveller's cheques. The last of these are the safest, as you will be refunded in the event of loss (keep the counterfoil separate from the cheques themselves), usually within 24 hours.

CREDIT CARDS

Credit cards are widely accepted; Visa and MasterCard are the most popular. These can also be used for withdrawing currency at cashpoinst (ATMs), where you pay a fixed withdrawal fee, making it more economical the larger the amount you withdraw, and avoiding the commission charged for changing foreign banknotes and cashing traveller's cheques. If your credit cards or traveller's cheques are stolen call the issuer immediately, then report the loss to the police; you'll need a reference number for insurance purposes.

AUTOMATIC TELLER MACHINES (ATMS)

These are widely available across the country and accept most credit and debit cards. Remember that your credit card issuer may charge you a fee for a cash advance by credit card. You will need a four-digit PIN (comprising four numbers, not letters) from your bank to use an ATM.

10 EVERYDAY ITEMS AND HOW MUCH THEY COST

Takeaway sandwich	£2.50
Bottle of water	£1.00
Cup of tea or coffee	90p–£1.75
Pint of beer	£2.20
Glass of house wine	£2.50
British national daily newspaper (Mon–Fri), more at weekends (Sun, up to £1.50)	30p–65p
Roll of camera film	£5
20 cigarettes	£5
Ice cream	£1
Litre of petrol	92p–95p

BANKS AND POST OFFICES

» Most banks open Mon–Fri, 9.30–4.30pm, some also open on Sat morning and a few on Sun morning.

» It pays to shop around for the best exchange and commission rates on currency. You do not pay commission on sterling traveller's cheques if you cash them at a bank affiliated with the issuing bank.

» You need to present ID (usually passport) when cashing traveller's cheques.

» About 1,400 post offices offer commission-free bureau de change services (tel: 08458 500900), with an online ordering service available through www.postoffice.co.uk. Payment is in cash, or by cheque, banker's draft, Visa, MasterCard,

EXCHANGE RATES AT TIME OF PUBLICATION

£1=		unit value in £ sterling
US $	$1	£0.57
Canadian $	$1	£0.50
Australian $	$1	£0.42
New Zealand $	$1	£0.37
Euro €	€1	£0.69

For up-to-date exchange rates use an online currency converter such as www.xe.com/ucc/

Maestro, Delta, Solo or Electron.

» Most main post offices are open Mon–Fri 9–5.30, Sat 9–12.30.

BUREAUX DE CHANGE

» These operate in most major streets in towns and cities in Britain, as well as at airports, rail stations and Underground stations in central London. They are mostly open 8am–10pm. Rates may be higher than at banks; it pays to shop around—Commission rates for currency and traveller's cheques should be clearly displayed.

» 'Commission free' bureaux often offer very poor rates, and should be used only for small amounts.

CONCESSIONS

Reduced fares on buses, trains and Underground services are available for the under-16s. Over- 60s can purchase a Senior Railcard for £20, giving a one-third reduction on off-peak rail services. For concessions on public transport, ▷ 53.
For discount passes, ▷ 53.

LOST/STOLEN CREDIT CARDS

American Express
01273 696933

Diners Club
01252 513500/0800 460 800

MasterCard/Eurocard
0800 964767

Maestro
0113 277 8899

Visa/Connect
0800 895082

MAJOR BANKS

There are four main clearing banks in the UK and they each have hundreds of branches. All have foreign exchange facilities.

Name	Head Office Address	Telephone
Barclays	54 Lombard Street EC3P 3AH	020 7699 5000
LloydsTSB	25 Gresham Street EC2V 7HN	020 7626 1500
NatWest	135 Bishopsgate EC2M 3UR	0800 505050
HSBC	8 Canada Square E14 5HQ	020 7991 8888

THE EURO (€)

Britain has not adopted the Euro as a currency, and it is not legal tender here. That said there are many places, particularly around the capital and some of the main entry ports that are willing to accept euros as payment. You may even see some prices expressed in euros. However you may find that the exchange rate they are offering isn't favourable and you certainly can't rely on being able to use euros instead of pounds sterling.
» Outside London, generally, the bigger the city, the more places will accept euros. Some of the chain stores that accept euros will display a sticker to advertise the fact, otherwise the best advice is to ask before you shop.

WIRING MONEY

In an emergency money can be wired to visitors from their home countries, but this can be expensive and time-consuming. Money can be wired from bank to bank, which takes up to two working days, or to agents such as Travelex (tel 01733 318922, www.travelex.co.uk) or

Western Union (tel 0800 833 833, www.westernunion.com).

VAT REFUNDS

» Value Added Tax (VAT) of 17.5 per cent is added to most purchases, including consumer durables and antiques.
» If you are a visitor from a non-EU country you can claim VAT back for large purchases from shops that operate the Global Refund scheme. When you make your purchase you can request a tax refund form, which you present to the customs officer on leaving the UK. Alternatively you can post the form back to the shop when you have returned home or collect an immediate cash

refund at 339 Oxford Street, London W1 (tel: 020 8222 0101; www.globalrefund.com).
» Refunds can be made up to three months after purchase.

Below Camping at Wast Water, Lake District

TIPPING	
Restaurants	10%
(where service is not included)	
Tour guides	£1–£2
Hairdressers	10%
Taxis	10%
Chambermaids	50p–£1 per day
Porters	50p–£1 per bag

24-HOUR EXCHANGE SERVICES IN LONDON

CHEQUEP●INT
CHANGECAMBIO

Chequepoint

550 Oxford Street W1C 1LU Tel: 0207 724 6127
Marble Arch Underground

71 Gloucester Road SW7 4SS
Tel: 020 7373 9682
Gloucester Road Underground

2 Queensway (first floor) W2 3RX
Tel: 020 7229 0093
Website: www.chequepoint.comBayswater or
Queensway Underground

HEALTH

Britain's National Health Service (the NHS) was set up in 1948 to provide healthcare for the nation's citizens based on need not the ability to pay. It is funded by taxpayers—to the tune of £104 billion per year in England alone—and managed by a government department. While NHS care for British citizens is free, private healthcare can also be bought from organizations such as BUPA. Visitors from the European Union (EU) are entitled to free NHS treatment (see below), but people of many other nationalities will have to pay for medical treatment.

BEFORE YOU DEPART

Consult your doctor at least 6–8 weeks before leaving. Free medical treatment is available for visitors from elsewhere in the European Economic Area (EEA) and Switzerland: Pick up a form from your local post office to apply for a free European Health Insurance Card (EHIC). Several countries have reciprocal healthcare agreements with the UK. In most cases a passport is sufficient identification for hospital treatment. But most countries, including the US and Canada, do not have agreements with Britain, so an insurance policy is advisable.

» No inoculations are required to enter Britain. However, it is advisable to have a tetanus booster before departure. And check with your doctor whether you need immunization or health advice for: meningococcal meningitis; hepatitis B; diphtheria; and measles/MMR (measles, mumps, rubella).

WHAT TO BRING

Visitors from Switzerland the EEA should bring their European Health Insurance Card (EHIC, see left). Those from outside the EEA should bring their travel insurance policy and a photocopy. Travel insurance is recommended. While emergency medical care is provided free of charge at Accident and Emergency departments of NHS hospitals, the cost of further medical treatment and repatriation is usually covered by a travel insurance policy.

» Visitors with existing medical conditions and allergies, for example to commonly used drugs, should wear a warning bracelet or tag. Take a first-aid kit with you. This should include: assorted adhesive plasters (Band Aids); sterile dressings; a bandage with safety pins; cotton wool (cotton balls); insect repellent; antiseptic cream; painkillers; remedies for constipation and for diarrhoea; antihistamine tablets; sunscreen; personal medicines.

STAYING HEALTHY

Tap water is safe to drink if it comes from the mains. Drinking water that comes from a tank, for example in a train toilet or in the upstairs rooms of a house, will be less fresh.

Between May and September the sun can be strong and a high-factor sunscreen (factor 15 or above) is recommended. Apply it every couple of hours, and more often if you are swimming. Remember that it is also possible to burn on a cloudy day.

» There are no malaria-carrying mosquitoes in Britain, but in the warmer months biting insects can be an annoyance, especially near water, so insect repellent is advisable. In Scotland tiny biting insects known as midges are a particular problem by the lochs and sea during May to late September.

» Major chemists (pharmacies) and larger supermarkets have a wide range of medicines that you can buy over the counter, although items such as antibiotics require a prescription from a doctor.

» Chemists rotate their opening hours, with hours of the duty chemist displayed in pharmacy windows and in local newspapers.

HEALTHY FLYING

» Visitors to Britain from as far as the US, Australia or New Zealand may be concerned about the effect of long-haul flights on their health. The most widely publicized concern is deep vein thrombosis (DVT). Misleadingly labelled 'economy-class syndrome' DVT is the formation of a blood clot in the body's deep veins, particularly in the legs. The clot can be deadly as it moves around the bloodstream.

» People most at risk include the elderly, smokers, the overweight, pregnant women and those using the contraceptive pill. If you are at increased risk of DVT see your doctor before departing. Flying increases the likelihood of DVT because passengers are often seated in a cramped position for long periods of time and may become dehydrated.

TO MINIMIZE RISK:

drink water (not alcohol)
don't stay immobile for hours at a time
stretch and exercise your legs periodically
do wear elastic flight socks, which support veins and reduce the chances of a clot forming

Other health hazards for flyers are airborne diseases and bugs spread by the plane's air-conditioning system. These are largely unavoidable but if you have a serious medical condition seek advice from a doctor before flying.

HOSPITAL EMERGENCY DEPARTMENTS IN KEY CITIES

NAME	ADDRESS	TELEPHONE
Charing Cross Hospital	Fulham Palace Road, London W6 8RF	020 8846 1234
Royal United Hospital	Coombe Park, Bath BA1 3NG	01225 428331
Royal Infirmary of Edinburgh	51 Little France Crescent EH16 4SU	0131 536 1000
John Radcliffe Hospital	Headley Way, Oxford OX3 9DU	01865 741166
York Hospital	Wiggington Road, York YO31 8HE	01904 631313
Call 999 or 112 for an ambulance		

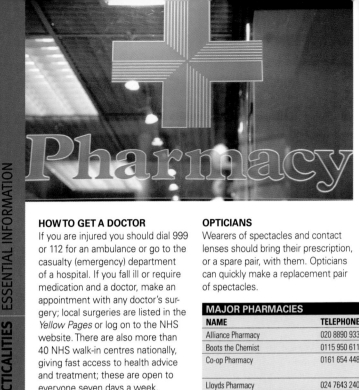

SMOKING

Passive smoking (inhaling others' cigarette smoke) has become a major issue in Britain and after many years of furious debate there is now legislation pertaining to smoking in public areas throughout the country.

» Smoking is banned in pubs, clubs, restaurants, cinemas, offices, all forms of public transport and all other enclosed public spaces in England.

» The website of Action on Smoking and Health (ASH; www.ash.org) is a useful resource.

HOW TO GET A DOCTOR

If you are injured you should dial 999 or 112 for an ambulance or go to the casualty (emergency) department of a hospital. If you fall ill or require medication and a doctor, make an appointment with any doctor's surgery; local surgeries are listed in the *Yellow Pages* or log on to the NHS website. There are also more than 40 NHS walk-in centres nationally, giving fast access to health advice and treatment; these are open to everyone seven days a week.

» Free 24-hour medical advice from a qualified nurse is available through the government service NHS Direct (tel: 0845 4647; www.nhsdirect.nhs.uk).

» If you are staying at a hotel or bed-and-breakfast the staff should be able to help you contact a doctor urgently. In many cases emergency telephone numbers will be displayed in a central area or in your room. You can also log on to www.nhs.uk and click on 'Find a local NHS services' for details about the nearest doctor, dentist, optician or pharmacy.

DENTAL TREATMENT

Patients over 16 have to pay for dental treatment, either through private practices or (slightly cheaper) through the NHS. It is sensible to go for a dental check-up before you leave home. Dentists are listed in telephone directories or you can use the British Dental Association's online service at www.bda-find-adentist.org.uk.

OPTICIANS

Wearers of spectacles and contact lenses should bring their prescription, or a spare pair, with them. Opticians can quickly make a replacement pair of spectacles.

MAJOR PHARMACIES

NAME	TELEPHONE	WEBSITE
Alliance Pharmacy	020 8890 9333	www.alliancepharmacy.co.uk
Boots the Chemist	0115 950 6111	www.boots.com
Co-op Pharmacy	0161 654 4488	www.co-operative.co.uk/en/pharmacy
Lloyds Pharmacy	024 7643 2400	www.lloydspharmacy.co.uk
Superdrug	020 8684 7000	www.superdrug.com
Sainsbury Pharmacy	020 7695 6000	www.sainsburys.co.uk
Tesco Pharmacy	0800 50555	www.tesco.com

OPTICIANS

NAME	TELEPHONE	WEBSITE
Boots Opticians	0845 1204343	www.bootsopticians.co.uk
David Clulow (London)	020 8515 6700	www.davidclulow.com
Dollond & Aitchison	0121 706 6133	www.danda.co.uk
Specsavers	01481 236000	www.specsavers.co.uk
Vision Express	0115 986 5225	www.visionexpress.com

ALTERNATIVE MEDICAL TREATMENTS

A wide range of alternative treatments is available in the UK. These treatments are not free for visitors. The listings below are a starting point; local telephone directories will have more details.

NAME	TELEPHONE	WEBSITE
British Osteopathic Association	01582 488455	www.osteopathy.org enquiries@osteopathy.org
British Chiropractic Association	0118 950 5950	www.chiropractic-uk.co.uk enquiries@chiropractic-uk.co.uk
The Society of Homeopaths	0845 450 6611	www.homeopathy-soh.org info@homeopathy-soh.org

Physiotherapists: Use a telephone directory and choose a chartered therapist

BASICS

There is very little that cannot be acquired in Britain if you have forgotten anything or need to replace something.

CLOTHES AND LUGGAGE

Bring a selection of clothing for a wide range of weather conditions. Rainwear is essential, and also recommended are a lightweight waterproof jacket for summer and a small shoulder bag or rucksack for daily use when sightseeing and walking around town. Avoid expensive-looking, cumbersome luggage if you plan to move around the country a lot.

ADAPTORS

Britain uses 240 volts AC and three-pin plugs, so you'll need an electrical adaptor or converter. Small appliances such as razors and laptops can run on a 50-watt converter, while irons and hairdryers require a 1,600-watt converter. Combination converters cover both types. An adaptor is also required for telephone sockets if you need to acces the internet.

OTHER ITEMS TO PACK

» Details of emergency contacts and friends.
» Your driving licence or permit. An International Driving Permit may be useful if your licence is not in English.
» First-aid kit with sticking plasters (adhesive tape), antiseptic cream, cream for insect stings, diarrhoea medicine, laxatives, painkillers, plus any personal medication.
» Glasses or contact lenses and solution, and prescription details.
» Photocopies of passport and travel insurance (or send scanned versions to a secure email account that you can access while you are away).
» Traveller's cheques and/or credit cards (preferably more than one card), and a small amount of cash in sterling (£).
» Numbers of credit/debit cards, registration numbers of mobile phones and cameras in case of loss.

» Compass (for finding your way in unfamiliar cities).

MEASUREMENTS

Britain officially uses the metric system, with fuel sold in litres, and food in grams and kilograms. However, imperial measurements are still used widely. Beer in pubs is still sold in pints (just over 0.5 litres), and road distances and speed limits are given in miles and miles per hour (mph) respectively. The British gallon (4.546 litres) is larger than the US gallon (3.7854 litres).

PUBLIC TOILETS

Although some unpleasant facilities survive, most public toilets are modern and well maintained. They are generally plentiful and free in built-up areas. In some city locations self-cleaning, stainless-steel cubicles (superloos) have been installed, and these normally cost 30p to use; there is a similar charge to use toilets at certain large rail stations. Major department stores, large supermarkets and all motorway service stations and filling stations have free toilets. In rural areas toilets can sometimes be found at some roadside lay-bys (rest stops)and in parking areas. It is frowned upon for non-customers to use the toilets in pubs, cafés and restaurants.
» Some public toilets for visitors with wheelchairs (for example at train stations) are opened with a special 'RADAR key' available to those with registered disabilities. If you do not have a key, ask the station staff for help.

» Toilets for people with disabilities are unisex, and often also contain baby-changing facilities.

LAUNDRY

When you book accommodation you may want to check whether there are laundry facilities. Telephone directories list launderettes and dry-cleaners. Some launderettes offer 'service washes', where the washing and drying are done for you (the typical cost is £5–£6 for a small bag), either on the same day or within 24–48 hours. Dry-cleaning is expensive (around £7 per jacket or skirt), but widely available: Some dry-cleaners also offer clothing repairs such as zip replacements.

CONVERSION CHART		
From	**To**	**Multiply by**
Inches	Centimetres	2.54
Centimetres	Inches	0.3937
Feet	Metres	0.3048
Metres	Feet	3.2810
Yards	Metres	0.9144
Metres	Yards	1.0940
Miles	Kilometres	1.6090
Kilometres	Miles	0.6214
Acres	Hectares	0.4047
Hectares	Acres	2.4710
Gallons	Litres	4.5460
Litres	Gallons	0.2200
Ounces	Grams	28.35
Grams	Ounces	0.0353
Pounds	Grams	453.6
Grams	Pounds	0.0022
Pounds	Kilograms	0.4536
Kilograms	Pounds	2.205
Tons	Tonnes	1.0160
Tonnes	Tons	0.9842

COMMUNICATION

With technology rapidly changing the way we communicate, the humble postcard is in danger of looking old-fashioned. But however you want to keep in touch with friends and family, there is a multitude of generally swift, convenient and reliable options in Britain.

TELEPHONES

The public telephone company is British Telecom (BT), which operates 63,000 payphones in the UK.

AREA CODES, COUNTRY CODES AND TELEPHONE DIRECTORIES

» When making a local call omit the initial area code.

» When making an international call dial the international code, the country code, followed by the telephone number minus the initial 0.

» Most area codes are four- or five-digit numbers beginning with 01.

» For London the code is 020. Telephone directories (phone books) and Yellow Pages show the code in brackets for each telephone number.

» There is a full list of area codes and country codes in every phone book.

PUBLIC PHONEBOXES

» Boxes are generally silver or red and are found at all main-line stations, Underground stations and on the streets in towns and cities throughout the country.

» You can use credit and debit cards to make calls from BT payphones (£1 setup charge, other calls for instance to mobiles £1; then 20p per minute all times).

» Payphones accept 10p, 20p, 50p and £1 coins; some also accept £2 coins. Only unused coins are returned, so try to avoid using high denomination coins for short calls.

» Some establishments, such as hotels and pubs, have their own payphones, for which they set their own profit margin. These can be exorbitant, and are recommended only in an emergency. Similarly, phone calls made from hotel rooms often incur high charges.

USING A MOBILE PHONE

Britain has embraced mobile phone technology, although mobiles are sometimes discouraged in pubs and elsewhere, and some train carriages (cars) have dedicated 'quiet areas'. There's a proliferation of mobile phone shops in almost every town.

» If you're visiting from overseas and have a mobile phone on the GSM system, you can purchase a SIM card for between £10 and £20 which gives you access to one of the main networks such as O2, Orange or Vodafone. Check before you leave.

» A 'pay as you go' option allows you to top up your account at supermarkets, shops and some other phone outlets. You are usually given a choice of accounts, depending on how much and when you are likely to make calls. A subscription-type account is useful if you are staying in the country for any substantial period of time.

» It is also possible to use your own phone and SIM card, depending on what sort of phone you have. You need to know if your phone operates on a GSM (Global System for Mobile Communications) frequency. Single band GSM phones, which work on 900MHz freqency, can be used in more than 100 countries, but not in the US or Canada. Most phones sold in the US work on 1900MHz and require a new SIM card for use in Britain. Dual (900 and 1900MHz) as well as tri band phones can be used in most countries around the world without any alteration.

» Note that there are still 'black

CALL CHARGES	
Minimum charge	40p
All UK calls to numbers beginning 01 and 02	40p for up to 20 minutes (10p for every 10 minutes thereafter)
Calls to mobile phones	63p per minute Mon–Fri 6am–6pm; 37.5p per minute Mon–Fri 6pm–6am and weekends
Belgium, Denmark France, Germany, Greece, Italy, Luxembourg, Netherlands, Portugal, Spain, Sweden, Switzerland	£1 per minute at all times
Australia, Canada New Zealand, United States	£2 per minute
Call Charges	Local calls and long-distance calls within Britain are the same price irrespective of time of day. Calls to mobile phones are generally more expensive than other calls

COUNTRY CODES FROM UK	
Australia	00 61
Belgium	00 32
Canada	00 1
France	00 33
Germany	00 49
Ireland	00 353
Italy	00 39
Netherlands	00 31
New Zealand	00 64
Spain	00 34
Sweden	00 46
US	00 1

holes' where you cannot get a mobile phone signal, and that these vary for each network.

» Pack an adaptor for the charger.

USING THE INTERNET

» A major network of multimedia Web phones is being installed by BT on main streets, stations, airports and motorway service stations across the country. These enable users to surf the internet and send emails and text messages. Internet access costs £1 for 15 minutes, and 10p for each 90 seconds thereafter. The cost of sending an instant email is 20p. Text messages cost 10p a message. Some payphones allow you to send texts and emails.

» Some public libraries have free Internet access; for details see www.peoplesnetwork.gov.uk. They may trival some Internet cafés (charges typically £1–£2 per hour), in major cities and towns.

WIRELESS BRITAIN

In addition to Internet cafés and web phones, BT and others have introduced more than 2,000 wireless 'hotspots' in airports, hotels, cafés and service stations across the country (to find the location of your nearest wireless hotspot in the UK go to www.wifinder.com). Wireless (WiFi) hot spots allow you to access the internet from any wireless device, such as a PC or PDA. They usually charge you by the minute or you can buy access in blocks of time over a certain period. Your wireless device should be able to detect a signal and the service's charging arrangements will appear in your browser.

USING A LAPTOP

If you intend to use your own laptop in the UK you will need to bring a power converter to recharge it and a plug socket adaptor. A surge protector is also a good idea. To connect to the internet you need an adaptor for the phone socket, available (in the UK) from companies such as Tele-adapt (www.teleadapt. com). If you use an international Internet service provider, such as Compuserve or AOL, it's cheaper to dial up a local node rather than the number in your home country. Wireless technology, such as Bluetooth, allows you to connect to the internet using a mobile phone; check beforehand what the charges will be. Dial tone frequencies vary from country to country so set your modem to ignore dial tones.

POST (MAIL)

» For all post office information, phone the customer helpline, tel 0845 722 3344.

» Post boxes are painted bright red (except some in post offices) and are either set into walls or are freestanding circular pillar boxes. Collection times are shown on each post box.

» Stamps are available from news-stands and supermarkets in addition to post offices.

» Generally airmail is preferable for mail sent outside Europe; for bulky items surface mail is substantially cheaper but typically takes around eight weeks. Airmail to North America takes about four days, to Europe around three days and to Australasia about five days.

» Large post offices have poste restante services, where items may be collected.

» To send items inland for next-day delivery, use Special Delivery. Through this service you can insure the items for various amounts, and also insure in case of loss.

VIDEOS AND DVDS

Videos, DVDs and console games purchased in Britain will be formatted to the PAL standard prevalent in Europe and Asia. They will not work in Canada or the US, where TV and video equipment is formatted to the NTSC standard.

DIALLING CODE PREFIXES	
00	international codes
01	area codes
02	area codes
07	calls charged at mobile rates
080	free calls
084	calls charged at local rates
087	calls charged at national rates
09	calls charged at premium rates

For details of charges, call the operator on 100. When dialling Britain from abroad, dial 0044 and omit the first 0 of the area code.

USEFUL TELEPHONE NUMBERS
Directory enquiries: competing services from several companies: try **118500** (BT) or **118118**
International directory enquiries: competing services from several companies: try **118505** (BT) or **118661**
International operator: 155
Operator: 100
Time: 123

POSTAGE RATES		
First class within UK	Up to 100g (3.5oz) letter	36p
	(usually arrives next day, but not guaranteed)	
Second class within UK	Up to 100g (3.5oz) letter	27p
	(usually two to three days)	
Recorded post (proof of posting)	signature on delivery	From 72p

AIRMAIL RATES		
Outside Europe	Letter (100g/3.5oz)	£2.52
	Postcard	56p
Europe	Letter (100g/3.5oz)	£1.36
	Postcard	50p

TOURIST INFORMATION

There are 800 Tourist Information Centres (TICs) across Britain, with national and regional tourist boards for England, Wales and Scotland. TICs are a useful source of maps, brochures and information on places to stay, where to eat and local events. Many supply free local area street maps.

Many TICs have accommodation services, and most will also book rooms in the local area free of charge. For bookings outside the area, you may be charged a small fee (in the region of £2.50).

VisitBritain are responsible for promoting British tourism. Its website, www.visitbritain.com is very useful, especially for details when planning your trip and for booking accommodations or researching festivals and events taking place throughout the year.

NATIONAL TOURIST BOARDS

VisitBritain:
Britain and London Visitor Centre, 1 Lower Regent Street, London SW1Y 4XT. Personal callers only: Mon 9.30–6.30, Tue–Fri 9–6.30, Sat–Sun 10–4 (Sat 9–5, Jun–end Oct); www.visitbritain.com

Visit Scotland:
Visit Scotland Centre, PO BOX 705, Edinburgh EH4 3EU, tel 0845 2255 121, fax: 01506 832121, www.visitscotland.com

Visit Wales:
VisitWales Centre, Brunel House, 2 Fitzalan Road, Cardiff CF24 0UY, tel 08701 211251, fax: 08701 211259, www.visitwales.com

REGIONAL TOURIST BOARDS

Cheshire & Warrington Tourism Board:
Grosvenor Park Lodge, Grosvenor Park Road, Chester, Cheshire CH1 1QQ, tel 01244 346543, fax 01244 343127; www.visit-cheshire.com

Cumbria Tourist Board:
Ashleigh, Holly Road, Windermere LA23 2AQ, tel 01539 444444, fax 01539 444041; www.golakes.co.uk

East of England Tourist Board:
Topplesfield Hall, Market Place, Hadleigh, Ipswich IP7 5DN, tel 08702 254800, fax 08702 254890; www.visiteastofengland.com

East Midlands Tourism:
Apex Court, City Link, Nottingham NG2 4LA, tel 0115 988 8546, fax 0115 853 3666; www.eastmidlands.com

Heart of England Tourism:
Woodside, Larkhill Road, Worcester WR5 2EZ, tel 01905 761100, fax 01905 763450; www.visitheartofengland.com

Lancashire & Blackpool Tourist Board:
St. George's House, St. George's Street, Chorley, Lancashire PR7 2AA, tel 01257 226600, fax 01257 469016; www.lancashiretourism.com

Marketing Manchester:
Churchgate House, 56 Oxford Street, Manchester M1 6EU, tel 0161 237 1010, fax 0161 228 2960; www.destinationmanchester.com

The Mersey Partnership:
12 Princes Dock, Princes Parade, Liverpool, Merseyside L3 1BG, tel 0151 227 2727, fax 0151 227 2325; www.visitliverpool.com

One North East Tourism
Stella House, Newburn Riverside, Newcastle upon Tyne NE15 8NY,tel 0191 229 6200, fax 0191 229 6201 www.visitnorthumbria.com

South West Tourism:
Tourism House, Pynes Hill, Exeter EX2 5WT, tel 08704 420880, fax 08704 420881; www.visitsouthwest.co.uk

Tourism South East:
40 Chamberlayne Road, Eastleigh, Hampshire SO50 5JH,tel 023 8062 5400, fax 01892 511008; www.southeastengland.uk.com

Visit London:
See Britain and London Visitor Centre (above), tel 08701 566366; www.visitlondon.com

Yorkshire Tourist Board:
312 Tadcaster Road, York YO24 1GS, tel 01904 707961, fax 01904 701414; www.yorkshirevisitor.com

VISITBRITAIN OFFICES OVERSEAS

Australia:
Level 2, 15 Blue Street, North Sydney NSW 2060, tel 02 9021 4400, fax 02 9021 4499; www.visitbritain.com/au

Canada:
5915 Airport Road, Suite 120, Mississauga, Ontario L4V 1T1, tel 905 405 1840/1 888 VISIT UK, fax 905 405 1835; www.visitbritain.com/ca

Ireland:
18/19 College Green, Dublin 2, tel 01 670 8000, fax 01 670 8244; www.visitbritain.com/ie

New Zealand:
Level 17, IAG House, 151 Queen Street, PO Box 105-652, Auckland 1, tel 09 309 1899/0800 700 741, fax 09 377 6965; www.visitbritain.com/nz

South Africa:
Lancaster Gate, Hyde Park Lane, Hyde Lane, Hyde Park, Sandton 2196 (visitors); PO Box 41896, Craighall 2024 (mail), tel 011 325 0342/3, fax 011 325 0344; www.visitbritain.com/za

USA:
551 Fifth Avenue, Suite 701, New York NY 10176-0799, tel 212 986 2266/1 800 462 2748, fax 212 986 1188; www.visitbritain.com/usa

USEFUL WEBSITES

A vast amount of information can be found on the Internet, with thousands of websites originating in Britain. Those listed below are good places to start.

GENERAL INFORMATION

www.metoffice.gov.uk
Met Office, the official weather service with detailed forecasts.
www.fco.gov.uk
Foreign and Commonwealth Office advice.
www.visitbritain.com
VisitBritain
www.ordnancesurvey.co.uk
Ordnance Survey, the government mapping agency.
www.multimap.co.uk
UK street maps at a range of scales by postcode or location (which you can print off for free).
www.yell.com
Yellow Pages telephone directory.
www.bt.com/directory-enquiries
Directory Enquiries for free.

NEWS AND SPORT

www.bbc.co.uk
News as it happens from the BBC, plus weather, sport, TV.

RAIL TRAVEL

www.thetrainline.com
Reserve tickets and find out fares and journey times.
www.nationalrail.co.uk
General information on rail travel and train times.

TRANSPORT TIMETABLES

www.pti.org.uk
National and local transport timetables, including bus, coach, rail, air and ferry services.

ROAD TRAVEL

www.highways.gov.uk
The offical website of the government's Highways Agency, providing real-time traffic news and information about roadworks and local conditions on roads.
www.theaa.com
Use the Automobile Association's website to plan your route.

AIRPORTS

www.a2bairports.com
Information on airports in the UK and Republic of Ireland.
www.baa.co.uk
British Airports Authority.

THE GOVERNMENT AND THE MONARCHY

www.direct.gov.uk
Links to government departments and services.
www.pm.gov.uk
Find out about Number 10 Downing Street, the home of the Prime Minister.
www.parliament.uk
This site explains how Britain is governed from the House of Commons.
www.scottish.parliament.uk
www.wales.gov.uk
www.ni-assembly.gov.uk
Information on the regional parliaments and assemblies in Scotland, Wales and Northern Ireland.
www.royal.gov.uk
The official website of the British monarchy is informative and interesting.

HERITAGE

www.english-heritage.org.uk
English Heritage.
www.cadw.wales.gov.uk
CADW (Welsh Historic Monuments).
www.historic-scotland.gov.uk
Historic Scotland.
www.thenationaltrust.org.uk
The National Trust.
www.nts.org.uk
National Trust for Scotland.
www.bbc.co.uk/history
Coverage of historical documentaries on the BBC.
www.sealedknot.org
A battle re-enactment society.

COUNTRYSIDE

www.forestry.gov.uk
The Forestry Commission manages forests, including some recreation facilities.
www.defence-estates.mod.uk
The Defence Estates manages Ministry of Defence (MoD) land and gives information on access.

NATIONAL CONSERVATION

www.english-nature.org.uk
English Nature, responsible for 200 national nature reserves.
www.snh.org.uk
Scottish Natural Heritage.
www.countrysideaccess.co.uk
Countryside Agency.
www.landmarktrust.org.uk
Landmark Trust, restores architecturally interesting buildings and lets them for holidays.
www.woodland-trust.org.uk
Woodland Trust, woodland conservation charity offering free access to 1,100 sites.

NATIONAL PARKS

www.breconbeacons.org
Brecon Beacons National Park.
www.broads-authority.gov.uk
Norfolk and Suffolk Broads.
www.cairngorms.co.uk
Cairngorms National Park.
www.dartmoor-npa.gov.uk
Dartmoor National Park.
www.exmoor-nationalpark.gov.uk
Exmoor National Park.
www.lake-district.gov.uk
Lake District National Park.
www.lochlomond-trossachs.org
Loch Lomond and the Trossachs National Park.
www.newforestnpa.gov.uk
New Forest National Park.
www.northyorkmoors-npa.gov.uk
North York Moors National Park.
www.nnpa.org.uk
Northumberland National Park.
www.peakdistrict.org
Peak District National Park.
www.pembrokeshirecoast.org.uk
Pembrokeshire Coast National Park.
www.cyri-npa.co.uk
Snowdonia National Park.
www.yorkshiredales.org.uk
Yorkshire Dales National Park.

WALKING

www.ramblers.org.uk
The Ramblers' Association, with extensive coverage of walking in Britain.
www.nationaltrail.co.uk
The official site for Britain's long-distance footpaths.

FINDING HELP

PERSONAL SECURITY

Levels of violent crime remain relatively low in Britain, but there are crime hotspots to avoid in certain larger cities. In most tourist areas the main danger is petty theft.
Be particularly wary of thieves on the London Underground, and in crowded places such as airports and main train stations. Avoid unlit urban areas at night, and carry bags close to you. If someone tries to grab your bag never fight—let go at once.

If you are going out late, arrange a ride home or a taxi. Use only reputable and licensed minicab firms or black cabs, and make sure that you get out of the car in a well-lit area. If you are driving alone take a mobile phone with you so that you can stay in your car in case of breakdown. Lock the doors, particularly at night, and don't pick uphitchhikers.

Solo women should not have problems, but should exercise caution, particularly at night. Never hitch, and use your common sense on public transport: Sit near the driver or conductor on buses and avoid empty carriages (cars) on trains and on the Underground.

LOST PROPERTY

If you lose something contact the nearest police station and complete a lost-property form. Airports have dedicated lost-property offices, but contact individual airlines if you lose belongings on board the aircraft.

Within London, items found on buses, Underground trains and in taxis are usually handed into a local police station and logged. They are then forwarded to the Transport for London Lost Property Office at 200 Baker Street, London NW1 5RT (tel 0845 330 9882); open Mon–Fri 8.30–4). You are advised to provide a stamped addressed envelope, and a finder's fee based on the value of the property is payable.

EMERGENCY PHONE NUMBERS

Telephone 999 or 112 for the police, ambulance, fire service, coastguard and mountain rescue. Tell the operator which service you require, where you are, the number of the phone you are using, what the problem is and where it has happened.

For non-emergency police matters contact the nearest police station—the phone book has details, or call directory enquiries. Similarly if you have non-urgent health concerns contact NHS Direct (tel 0845 4647), whose trained medical staff can advise you or direct you to the nearest doctor ($\triangleright$ 418).

POLICE

Britain's 166,000-plus policemen are approachable and, if asked, give information and directions. The British Transport Police work on the railways and the Tube. Call 0800 405040 to report non-emergency crimes on these services. If you are the victim of a crime you can call

Victim Support (tel 0845 3030 900) for support and legal advice.

Traffic wardens issue parking tickets and deal with traffic issues but have limited powers. Security guards are not endorsed by or part of the police force, and have no more powers of arrest than a normal member of the public.

WHAT TO DO IF YOU ARE ARRESTED

Try to remain calm and polite. In motoring incidents you are obliged to give your name and address.

On-the-spot fines (starting at about £40) can be issued for offences such as being drunk and/or disorderly. Fixed penalties are also given out for motoring offences.

EMERGENCY NUMBERS

Police, ambulance, fire services, coastguard, mountain rescue or cave rescue
999 or 112

REGIONAL POLICE TELEPHONE

Bath	0845 4567000
Birmingham	0845 1135000
Bristol	0845 4567000
Edinburgh	0131 3113131
Glasgow	0141 5323000
Leeds	0845 6060606
Liverpool	0151 7096010
London	020 7230 1212
Manchester	0161 8725050
Newcastle	01661 872555
Oxford	0845 8505505
York	0845 6060247

EMBASSIES IN LONDON

Contacting your embassy

If you lose your passport or are arrested, you should contact your embassy or high commission in London.

Country	Address	Website
Australian High Commission	Australia House, Strand WC2B 4LA, tel: 020 7379 4334	www.australia.org.uk
Canadian High Commission	Macdonald House, 1 Grosvenor Square W1K 4AB united_kingdom/	www.canada.org
New Zealand High Commission	New Zealand House, 80 The Haymarket SW1Y 4TQ tel: 020 7930 8422	www.nzembassy.com
South African High Commission	South Africa House, Trafalgar Square WC2N 5DP tel: 020 7451 7299	www.southafricahouse.com
American Embassy	24 Grosvenor Square W1A 1AE tel: 020 7499 9000	www.usembassy.org.uk

OPENING TIMES AND ENTRANCE FEES

Most businesses open Monday to Friday, and some open on Saturday. Sunday is distinctly quieter, as shops can open for only six hours. Some smaller shops, particularly in smaller towns, may close early one day in midweek (often Wednesday).

The following is a rough guide to opening times, although there are many variations.

PUBLIC HOLIDAYS

Known as **bank holidays** in the UK, as these are periods when banks and many shops close. Many tourist sites now stay open (and some open specifically on these days), but virtually everything (including public transport) shuts down on 25–26 Dec. Summer bank holidays can cause major traffic delays, especially on roads to popular areas such as Cornwall and the Lake District; accommodation over holiday weekends is often fully booked in advance.

ENTRANCE FEES

Most museums, houses, galleries, gardens, cinemas, theatres and other attractions have reduced entrance fees for under-16s, holders of student cards, the unemployed and those aged 60 and over. Season tickets are often available and can be good value.

Membership of the **National Trust** (NT, tel 0870 458 4000) gives free admission to all NT and National Trust for Scotland (NTS, tel 0131 243 9300) properties and gardens. You can join at any NT property.

English Heritage (EH, tel 0870 333 1181), its Welsh counterpart **Cadw** (tel 029 2050 0200) and its Scottish counterpart **Historic Scotland** (HS, tel 0131 668 8999) manage hundreds of historic properties in Britain. Most of them are castles, archaeological sites and ruined monasteries, plus a few stately homes and industrial monuments.

» English Heritage members get free admission to EH properties, and half-price admission to Cadw and HS properties (free after first year of membership). You can join at any EH, Cadw or HS property.

DISCOUNT PASSES

Serious sightseers can save money with a choice of discount cards available from the Britain and London Visitor Centre in Lower Regent Street, London, major tourist offices and most airports. For travel concessions ▷ 53.

London Pass

(www.londonpass.com): Gives admission to over 60 attractions in and around London (with an option of free travel on public transport) and a pocket guide. Valid for one, two, three or six days, and costs from £27.

York Pass (www.yorkpass.com): Gives admission to over 30 attractions in the city for one, two or three days, and costs from £19.

Bath Pass (www.bathpass.com): Costing from £19, passes for one, two, three or seven days give admission to over 30 attractions.

Great British Heritage Pass

(www.gbheritagepass.com): Allows free entry to 600 historic properties and gardens, including those not run by English Heritage or the National Trust (▷ this page). Passes (available only to non-UK residents) are for four, seven or 15 days or one month, with prices from £28. Contact VisitBritain (▷ 422) in your home country for details on where you can purchase this pass.

NATIONAL HOLIDAYS

Although banks and businesses close on public (bank) holidays, most tourist attractions and shops remain open, except on 25 and 26 Dec and 1 Jan. If any of these days falls on a Saturday or Sunday, the next weekday is a holiday.

New Year's Day (1 January)
Good Friday
Easter Monday
First Monday in May
Last Monday in May
Last Monday in August
Christmas Day (25 December)
Boxing Day (26 December)

OPENING TIMES	
Opening hours can vary considerably.	
Banks	Mon–Fri 9.30–4.30
	Some large brancheas also open Sat morning and a few on Sun morning.
Pharmacies	Most pharmacies open Mon–Sat 9–5 or 5.30
	Notices in the window and in local newspapers indicate extended-hour rosters of local pharmacies. You should always be able to find at least one that is open.
Galleries, Houses and Museums	These vary widely. Many open Mon–Sat 10–5, Sun 12–5
	Some do not admit visitors who arrive fewer than 30 min before closing time.
Post Offices	Mon–Fri 9–5.30, Sat 9–12.30
Pubs	Changes in licensing laws mean that now negotiate their own individual opening hours. However, most maintain the traditional hours, which for pubs are 11–11. Some close around 3–6pm. In England and Wales pubs open Sun 12–10.30pm.
Restaurants	No hard and fast rule. Typically around 12–2.30pm and 6–9pm or 6–11pm. Take-aways may stay open later than 11pm.
Shops	Smaller shops Mon–Sat 9–5 or 5.30. Department stores are open until 6pm, and on Wed or Thu until 7 or 8pm. Larger shops in cities and major towns open Sun 10am to 4pm or 11am to 5pm. Some convenience stores open longer hours—8am–10pm or 11pm, seven days a week.
Supermarkets	8am–9pm or later Mon–Sat and for six hours (such as 10–4) on Sun. Some are open 24 hours.

MEDIA

Britain has some of the world's oldest newspapers and the global presence of the BBC's (British Broadcasting Corporation) radio and TV productions.

TELEVISION

British television is undergoing a digital revolution, with the gradual replacement of analogue terrestrial channels by digital versions. The process will be completed by 2012. One effect has been the success of Freeview, a free to air digital terrestrial platform, which now covers most homes in the UK. The signal comes from the existing transmitter network and is received through a domestic aerial to a 'digibox' or internally on more recent TVs. Freeview is a bit like a cable or satellite system, but has a much more limited range of channels. These include the BBC's 1, 2 ,3 and 4 its children's channels – CBeebies and CBBC, its news and Parliament channel (similar to C-Span in the US). The major commercial provider is ITV (1, 2, 3 and 4) and other channels from the old analogue system – Five and Channel 4 (S4C in Wales). Satellite giant Sky has a small presence on Freeview (SkyNew, Sky Sports News, Sky 3) and there are several music, shopping and specialist channels, broadcasting at niche times. Both the BBC and ITV break up their main channels (BBC1, BBC2, ITV1) into nations and regions. It's here you will find locally produced news, weather, sport and current affairs.

RADIO

The viewers' television licence funds BBC radio. There are also several in-dependent and commercial stations nationwide. Analogue FM and AM stations are also available digitally; more information can be found at www.digitalradionow.com.

Radio 1: 97.6–99.8FM

Broadcasts the latest pop and rock with brief news bulletins.
www.bbc.co.uk/radio1

Radio 2: 88–90.2FM

Features classic rock, pop, country, folk, reggae and soul hits interspersed with chat, news bulletins and music documentaries.
www.bbc.co.uk/radio2

Radio 3: 90.2–92.4FM

Broadcasts music from classical and jazz to world music with cultural and drama programmes.
www.bbc.co.uk/radio3

Radio 4: 92.4–94.6FM or 198LW

Broadcasts news, comedy, art, drama and quiz shows, with radio plays and documentaries.
www.bbc.co.uk/radio4

Radio 5 Live: 909/693AM

A news and sports station with chat and current affairs debates between callers and guests.
www.bbc.co.uk/fivelive

Classic FM: 100–102FM

An advertising-funded station broadcasting classical music.
www.classicfm.co.uk

Virgin Radio: 105.8FM in London, 1215AM elsewhere

A national commercial radio station transmitting rock and new music, along with sports and music news.
www.virginradio.co.uk

NEWSPAPERS AND MAGAZINES

National newspapers in Britain have traditionally been divided into quality papers in a broadsheet format and smaller tabloids. Confusingly, most 'broadsheets' have now switched to a tabloid format. Broadsheets (costing from 65p) focus on seri-ous news reporting while tabloids (costing from 35p) cover celebrity gossip and human-interest stories. Bulky weekend newspapers are more expensive, with sections on travel, finance, sport and the arts. International and foreign-language newspapers are available.

NATIONAL NEWSPAPERS	
'Broadsheets'	
The Daily Telegraph (1855) and The Sunday Telegraph (1961)	Britain's most popular daily broadsheet with a right-of-centre political point of view www.telegraph.co.uk
The Times (1785) and The Sunday Times (1822)	In-depth national and international news, politics, arts, finance. Sunday edition is huge www.thetimesonline.co.uk
Financial Times (1888)	Predominantly financial news, with sober analysis of international news. Good Saturday edition www.ft.com
The Guardian (1821) and The Observer (1791)	Left-of-centre daily and Britain's oldest Sunday paper, The Observer. Excellent website www.guardian.co.uk
The Independent (1986) and The Independent on Sunday (1990)	Relatively young papers with a mainly urban readership, and left-of-centre agenda. Good arts and sport coverage www.independent.co.uk
'Tabloids'	
The Daily Mail (1896) and The Mail on Sunday (1982)	Strident tabloids selling more than two million copies with mix of news and gossip www.dailymail.co.uk
Daily Express (1900) and Sunday Express	National news, entertainment, gossip, sport www.express.co.uk
The Sun (1969) and The News of the World (1843)	With 3.5 million readers, Britain's most popular paper. thrives on sensationalism www.thesun.co.uk
The Daily Mirror (1903) and The Sunday Mirror (1963)	Left-wing rival to The Sun with fewer titillating stories and lower sales www.mirror.co.uk
The Daily Star (1978) and The Daily Star Sunday (2002)	Sensationalism and gossip in low-budget tabloid www.dailystar.co.uk
The People (1881)	Sunday-only newspaper which thrives on sensationalism www.people.co.uk
Sunday Sport (2002)	A Sunday-only niche paper aimed at 'lads' with a frivolous sex- and sports-based approach. www.sundaysport.com

BOOKS, FILMS AND MAPS

Britain's long-established love affair with the arts has produced some of the best-known authors and film-makers in the world and a reputation as a leading light in the arts world.

BOOKS

For a general overview of the country, look no further than Simon Schama's three-volume *A History of Britain* (2001), covering events from 3000BC to AD2001. Other areas of Britain's rich history are explored in Will Hutton's *The State We're In* (2003), and *The World We're In* (1996), an economic and political survey of modern-day Britain; *The Queen's Story* (2003) by Marcus Kiggell, following Elizabeth II's 50 years on the throne; Jeremy Paxman's *The English: a Portrait of a People* (1999), the psyche of a nation through the eyes of one of Britain's most vociferous broadcasters; and *The Buildings of England* (1951–74), a series by Nikolaus Pevsner.

Fiction writers have been no less prolific, with some of the most famous names in literature writing about and based in Britain. Eighteenth-century fiction includes *Sense and Sensibility* (1811), *Pride and Prejudice* (1813) and *Persuasion* (1815) by Jane Austen, some of the seminal works on society of the time; the Brontë sisters' *Jane Eyre* (1847, by Charlotte) and *Wuthering Heights* (1847, by Emily), capturing the angst of romance and obsession in Victorian Britain; several classics by Charles Dickens, including *Bleak House* (1853), *David Copperfield* (1850) and *Oliver Twist* (1837), all set in different parts of the country; and *Middlemarch* (1872), by George Eliot (pseudonym of Mary Ann Evans), in which the characters try to overcome the dogma of the past and embrace a burgeoning new society.

Twentieth century fiction includes *England, England* (1999) by Julian Barnes, a sharp-edged satire on Englishness, *Jamaica Inn* (1936) by Daphne du Maurier, a dramatic romance set in the author's beloved Cornwall, and E. M. Forster's *Howard's End* (1910), a study of society angst in Hertfordshire and Shropshire. *Brighton Rock* (1938), by Graham Greene, is a dark depiction of a man taken over by greed, guilt and Brighton's criminal underworld, while D. H. Lawrence's *Sons and Lovers* (1913) is about a mother's obsessive love for her sons. Virginia Woolf's *Mrs Dalloway* (1925) is set in a single day in 1923 and tells the story of society hostess Clarissa Dalloway; Laurie Lee's *Cider with Rosie* (1959) is a rural romp through the Cotswolds during the 1920s.

FILMS

From a successful and well-regarded state in the 1930s, the British film industry went into a decline for several decades. In recent years it has strived to return to its former health, supplying independent productions that can hold their own against the Hollywood studios, with global successes such as the James Bond movies, *Bridget Jones's diary* (2001) and *Love Actually* (2003).

Classic movies from the British school encompass *Brief Encounter* (1945), with Trevor Howard and Celia Johnson resisting temptation in a British railway station, *Kind Hearts and Coronets* (1949), a savage comedy on Britain's class system, with Sir Alec Guinness playing several characters in the same family, and Alfred Hitchcock's *The Thirty-Nine Steps* (1935), in which Richard Hannay gets caught up in a spy ring and ends up fleeing across the Scottish countryside.

The 1960s brought a rash of movies exploring the British class system, either through comedy or tragedy, including *If* (1968), a study of the restricted world of the English public school, the highly praised *Kes* (1969), the story of a lonely Yorkshire schoolboy who finds happiness with his kestrel, and *This Sporting Life* (1963), where the late Richard Harris acts out the frustrations of a star rugby player through violence.

Several smaller-budget British films did not make the international stage but are nonetheless memorable. *Local Hero* (1983) tells the story of a Texan oil baron who wants to buy up a remote Scottish village, until the villagers win him over. *Withnail and I* (1986) depicts the lives of two out-of-work actors in the sixties and has a cult following.

With the influx of independent production companies in the 1980s and 1990s, some famous titles have been produced in recent years, including Robert Altman's *Gosford Park* (2001), yet another study of the British class system, with an all-star cast showing the British country house in all its glory, *Billy Elliot* (2000), in which the hero, a young boy played by Oscar-winner Jamie Bell, battles his northern mining background and the desire to become a ballet dancer, *The Full Monty* (1997), with its scenes of Robert Carlyle and his cohorts practising the striptease, and *Notting Hill* (1999), written by Richard Curtis, who brought the world *Four Weddings and a Funeral*, where the west London enclave is the background of the romance between bumbling bookshop owner Hugh Grant and movie star Julia Roberts.

GUIDEBOOKS

AA City Pack London
Pocket book and map in transparent wallet. £6.99
London: A City Revealed
A visual tribute to London, with over 350 large colour photographs. £30
The AA Days Out Guide
Over 2,000 places to visit, with opening times and prices. £11.99
The AA Hotel Guide £16.99
The AA Restaurant Guide Reviews of more than 1,800 restaurants in Britain. £16.99

MAPS

AA Street by Street London
17 maps and atlases in a variety of sizes and scales. £3.99 to £30
Street by Street Z-Maps £1.50
Stanfords at 12–14 Long Acre, London (tel 020 7836 1321; www.stanfords.co.uk) is a specialist map shop with maps for all regions of the British Isles.

SHOPPING

By a considerable margin Britain has the largest amount of retail space of any European country and a population of dedicated shoppers. Beyond the cheap and cheerful mementoes—models of London buses, Union Jack T-shirts and the like—souvenir-hunting is a rewarding experience, with many distinctively British products on offer.

BRITISH SPECIALITIES

Tweed and tartan, both woven woollen cloths, are two famously Scottish textiles. Both have made a comeback on catwalks in recent years and are excellent purchases. The most highly regarded tweed is Harris tweed, which is handwoven by islanders on the Outer Hebrides. The Harris Tweed Authority (tel 01851 702269; www.harristweed. com) preserves its authenticity. Tartan, or plaid, is a relatively recent invention, having first appeared at the start of the 18th century. By the end of the 18th century tartan became established as a means of identifying Scotland's clans and districts. There are many tartan patterns today; some are authentic, others are modern designs.

Clothes are a good purchase, if expensive. Men's tailors line Savile Row in London, where Prince Charles goes to have his suits made.

Home-grown women's fashion designers range from stalwarts Jasper Conran and Katharine Hamnett to new labels such as Clements Ribeiro, and Antoni and Alison. Less dressy clothing from Britain includes hardwearing Fair Isle woollen sweaters from the Shetland Islands, Barbour and Burberry jackets, and even Wellington boots from Hunter. Although functional rather than fashionable, prices can be high for these items; a Barbour jacket costs well over £100.

Since the late 18th century the potteries of Stoke-on-Trent have produced some of Britain's finest bone chinaware. Names at the heart of the industry include Wedgwood, founded by Josiah Wedgwood (1730–95), Josiah Spode (who founded the Spode factory in 1776) and Royal Doulton, which earned a royal warrant in 1901. Details of all the factory shops, which offer keen prices, and the visitor attraction Ceramica are available from Stoke-on-Trent's Tourist Information Centre; tel 01782 236000; www.visitstoke.co.uk.

Also in the Midlands, Nottingham is renowned for lace, and the highlight of the city is the central Lace Market.

Britain is a great destination for book-lovers. Second-hand shops are found in most towns, but Hay-on-Wye has the highest concentration. The large chains—Waterstones, Borders and Ottakars, and the more academic Blackwell's—carry enormous ranges and can usually order titles within days.

Music (particularly CDs) is less of a bargain, with prices comparing unfavourably to those in North America. However, again, it's hard to fault the sheer choice on offer. The big chains cover every genre and also sell videos, DVDs and books. Specialist shops, such as the record shops of Manchester's Northern Quarter, provide vinyl records to DJs and keen collectors, who also congregrate at record fairs. Bootleg recordings, such as those sometimes sold at Camden Market, London, may disappoint.

DEPARTMENT STORES

Clothes, perfumes, jewellery, home furnishings and electrical goods are all typically found in department stores. And Britain has some of the best in the world. London boasts the greatest number, among them Harrods and Harvey Nichols in Knightsbridge, Selfridges and Liberty in the West End, and several branches of John Lewis. But most cities will have at least one good department store—look out for branches of the John Lewis Partnership and House of Fraser—and shoppers no longer have to schlep to London to shop at the most fashionable. Harvey Nichols has opened shops in Leeds, Birmingham, Manchester and Edinburgh, while Selfridges now has branches in Birmingham and Manchester.

MARKETS

Market squares were often the focal point of towns, and many towns still have a market once or twice a week. Expect to find fruit and vegetables, butcher's and fishmonger's stalls and household items. Prices are often lower than in shops. Haggling is not customary.

SHOPPING MALLS AND FACTORY OUTLETS

Britain has not escaped the shopping mall. These tend to have little to offer the visitor other than the convenience of finding the usual main street shops and brands under one roof, and lots of parking spaces. But factory outlets such as McArthurGlen and Bicester Village, which sell designer clothing at discounted prices, do attract bargain-hunters, including shoppers from other countries.

TAX-FREE SHOPPING

If the goods you buy are going to be exported to a non-EU country, you are exempt from Value Added Tax (VAT; currently 17.5 per cent), where it is applied. This can be a considerable saving (but you have to spend a minimum amount, which varies from shop to shop) and it is usually reclaimed at the airport on departure rather than deducted in the shop. Most major department stores participate and will have details of their tax-free shopping policies and help with your claim. For more information: tel 020 8222 0101; www.globalrefund.com.

SALES

Twice a year, shops slash their prices in order to sell the previous season's remaining stock. The January sales see the best bargains, starting immediately after Christmas and continuing into February. Determined bargain-hunters camp out overnight in the streets in order to be first in line when the sales open at Harrods (▷ 100) or Selfridges (▷ 101). Summer sales begin in June or July and last until the end of August.

HOURS

Core opening hours are from 9am to 5pm (with no break for lunch). In towns and cities, however, most shops stay open to at least 5.30pm or 6pm, and late opening, until 8pm, 9pm or 10pm, is common in busy areas and cities, while supermarkets are likely to remain open into the night. Many shops will open for at least a few hours on Sundays.

SHOPPERS' RIGHTS

In Britain the Office of Fair Trading (www.oft.gov.uk) safeguards the rights of shoppers and encourages a fair and competitive market. Your statutory rights ensure that the goods you purchase are of 'satisfactory quality', 'fit for their purpose' and described accurately. You may be entitled to a refund if the goods don't meet these criteria; you must keep the receipt as proof of purchase.

THE LISTINGS

In our listings prices are subject to change. We have given the closest train station, if it is within 4 miles (6km) of the site.

ENTERTAINMENT & NIGHTLIFE

Britain has relaxed its licensing laws to reduce the eleventh-hour downing of drinks and embraces European-style nightlife. In the past pubs were obliged to stop serving at 11pm—a time when citizens on the Continent would be getting ready for a night on the town—and bars and clubs had trouble securing licences to serve drinks after 2am. But today pubs can stay open all day and night (local council permitting). Despite this, many still keep to traditional hours, and may close between the lunchtime and evening sessions.

Britain's biggest cities, especially London, offer thrilling nightlife that compares with anything in New York or Sydney. Whether it's cutting-edge dance clubs or bar-clubs for a slightly older crowd, it's not difficult to find somewhere to party in London, Brighton, Bristol, Birmingham, Cardiff, Leeds, Nottingham, Manchester, Glasgow or Edinburgh.

PUBS AND BARS
The relaxation of its licensing laws is reflected in Britain's changing drinking habits. In some areas bars are taking over from pubs and nightclubs as the focal points for socializing.

Pubs today differ from their predecessors in several respects. Unlike the male-dominated bastions of the past, most now encourage female customers and families.

Most pubs serve (sometimes very good) food plus coffee and tea. Free houses (independent pubs) offer the most interesting experience: As they are not tied to a large brewing group, they can stock local beers from small, specialist brewers. In the countryside, pubs are usually the only option for a night out.

BARS
During the day they resemble cafés, serving food and coffee, while at night they often become small nightclubs, complete with DJ and dance floor. Outdoor, European-style drinking is more widespread.

CLUBS
Most towns and cities will have at least one nightclub, but choose carefully. The options might be bewildering in some cities but small towns may have just one venue, playing uninspiring chart music. Britain's cosmopolitan communities ensure that most musical preferences are represented: jazz, funk, soul, dub, rock, world, and country and western.

But dance music's many strands dominate the club scene, and regions develop their own sounds: garage in London; techno in Birmingham; drum and bass in Bristol; big beat in Brighton; and house music in Liverpool and Manchester. A few superclubs survive, such as Fabric and the Ministry of Sound in London, but smaller, intimate clubs cultivate a more loyal clientele. Dress codes vary, so check before you set out. Most places accept 'smart-casual': no T-shirts, jeans or trainers (sneakers).

LISTINGS
Local listings magazines such as London's *Time Out* (www.timeout.com) are available from newsstands and tourist information offices. You'll also find listings in the local press and on websites such as www.visitlondon.com. On Saturday *The Guardian* newspaper includes *The Guide*, a great pocket-size weekly listing of arts, entertainment and nightlife.

GAY AND LESBIAN SCENE
British society seems to have finally put its hang-ups about homosexuality behind it. A gay and lesbian scene that has existed discreetly for hundreds of years has never been so visible a today, with pubs, bars and clubs for every taste and a calendar of summer festivals and events.

SPORTS AND ACTIVITIES

It doesn't take long to realize that the British are mad about sport. After all, they invented and refined many of the world's main sports, including football (soccer), rugby, cricket, golf and boxing. The sports pages of national newspapers (particularly on the weekend), carry results of the major matches and preview forthcoming fixtures (schedules) The sport section of the BBC's website (www.bbc.co.uk) also has details of fixtures. Even small towns and villages will compete in local cricket and football leagues at weekends.

Whether it's on foot, on horseback, by bicycle or in a kayak, glider, balloon or boat, there is no better way of seeing the country than getting out in the fresh air; and Britons follow a huge range of organized pursuits.

ANGLING
Coarse and fly-fishing require a licence, which you can buy at post offices. Local tackle shops are good sources of information and equipment. Fly-fishing can be more expensive but tuition is readily organized. Fishing boats from ports may also offer trips to visitors.

BALLOONING
Hot-air ballooning is a popular way of viewing the countryside. There are many operators in England, especially in rural areas and close to Bristol, where a major balloon festival is held in August. Tourist information centres list operators.

BEACHES
Britain is not short of coastline and has some spectacular beaches—if you know where to look.

Europe's Blue Flag organization (www.blueflag.org) awards flags to beaches that meet its strict standards of safety and cleanliness. There were 114 Blue Flag beaches in the UK in 2008, with high concentrations in Wales (such as St. David's) and in Devon (such as Woolacombe). But many fine beaches don't make the grade; the Marine Conservation Society's free *Good Beach Guide* (www.goodbeachguide.co.uk) recommends good beaches.

CLIMBING
The British Mountaineering Council (BMC) represents climbers, hillwalkers and mountaineers. It provides weather reports and has databases of clubs and locations.
» BMC—tel 0161 445 6111; www.mcofs.org.uk

CRICKET
The Marylebone Cricket Club (MCC), based at London's Lord's cricket ground (www.lords.org), administers the 42 Laws of cricket.

Domestic fixtures are played between the 18 top English and Welsh county sides, over three or four days, while international Test cricket is a series of five-day matches between national teams. Test matches can sell out quickly, especially for fixtures against Australia. County games, although less passionate, are more accessible. The England and Wales Cricket Board (www.ecb.co.uk) lists fixtures and details for county clubs.

CYCLING
Most towns have cycle shops and rental facilities. Cities vary in cycle-friendliness: York has an exemplary

www.svr.co.uk); North Yorkshire Moors Railway (tel 01751 472508; www.nymr.com); and Talyllyn Railway in North Wales (tel 01654 710472; www.talyllyn.co.uk).

HORSE RACING

The British love a flutter (a small wager), and the country's bookies (betting shops) do good business on major races such as the Aintree Grand National. The flat-racing season runs from late March to early November, and National Hunt (over jumps) between August and late June. There are numerous racecourses around the country but reserve in advance for major meetings.

HORSEBACK RIDING

Britain has an extensive choice of riding centres and some beautiful locations. In England and Wales riders share bridleways and rights of ways with mountain bikers. The British Horse Society (www.bhs.org.uk) has a directory of riding holiday firms.

MOTOR RACING

Britain has a long history of motor racing, and is home to several Formula One teams, such as Williams and McLaren. The British Grand Prix takes place at Silverstone in Northamptonshire (tel 08704 588290; www. silverstone-circuit.co.uk).

MOUNTAIN BIKING

Mountain biking is well established in Britain, and a series of purpose-built trails has been developed. Those in Wales managed by Mountain Biking Wales (www.mbwales.com) offer some of the best cycling in the world. Outside these hubs mountain bikers are permitted on bridleways (including long-distance paths), rights of way, but not footpaths.

RIVER SPORTS

Kayaks and canoes can be rented along several rivers and at lakes in Britain: Rivers in Wales and the Lake District are particularly good spots. Expect sedate conditions.

network of cycle paths; cycling in London can be frightening. Cyclists are not allowed on main 'A' roads and motorways (designated 'M'), and some of the smaller 'B' roads may have fast traffic, but country lanes are safe and scenic. Sustrans publishes *Cycling in the UK* (£14.99) and detailed maps. For details about travelling with a bicycle, ▷ 59.

FOOTBALL (SOCCER)

Football tops the table as the most popular spectator sport in England and Scotland, with most towns and cities fielding a team. England's Premier League of 20 teams—including Manchester United, Liverpool, Arsenal and Chelsea—has a worldwide audience and avoids the financial problems afflicting some of Europe's other leagues.

The national season runs from August to the end of May, culminating in the FA Cup Final. Domestic leagues are governed by the Football Association (www. thefa.com) or the Scottish Football Association (www.scottishfa. co.uk). The FA lists fixtures, as do newspapers. Most matches take place on Saturday, but there are also Sunday and midweek games.

GOLF

The town of St. Andrews in Scotland is famous for being the 'home of golf'. Golf was first played on the Old Course in around 1400, and the sport remains accessible and inexpensive in Scotland. Visitor regulations at England's private clubs tend to be more complex; some require a letter of introduction or handicap certificate. Public courses are open to anyone.
»The Golfclub Great Britain—tel 020 8390 3113; www.golfclubgb.co.uk

HERITAGE RAILWAYS

Steam engines run on some 100 restored, privately operated rail lines, and make an enjoyable, nostalgic experience. Information on heritage steam railways in the UK and Ireland—details of trains, operating days and events—is available from the Heritage Railway Association (www.heritagerailways.com). Five of the best steam train trips are: The Watercress Line in Hampshire (tel 01962 733810; www.watercressline. co.uk); Keighley and Worth Valley Railway in Yorkshire's Brontë Country (tel: 01535 645214; www.kwvr. co.uk); Severn Valley Railway in the West Midlands (tel 01299 403816;

Most rivers are privately owned and may be closed at certain times of the year.

» Punting—where the punter uses a long pole to propel a flat-bottomed boat—is a speciality of Oxford and Cambridge.

» British Canoe Union—tel 0845 370 9500; www.bcu.org.uk

RUGBY

Britain's second winter sport is played between September and the end of May. In Wales rugby union—with 15 players per side—is the national sport, while the north of England is the base for rugby league, the 13-a-side variant.

Ticket and fixture information:

» Rugby Football Union, Twickenham, London: www.rfu.com

» Scottish Rugby Union, Murrayfield, Edinburgh: www.scottishrugby.org.uk

» Welsh Rugby Union, Millennium Stadium, Cardiff: www.wru.co.uk

SAILING

Many people sail yachts and dinghies on weekends. Local sailing clubs, marinas and specialist agencies offer yacht charter (with or without a skipper) and dinghy rental.

» Royal Yacht Association—tel 0845 345 0400; www.rya.org.uk

SCUBA DIVING

The British Sub-Aqua Club (BSAC) has more than 1,600 branches nationwide. Since visibility and currents change during the year local advice is essential. Dives on the coast's plentiful wrecks should be attempted only with guidance.

» BSAC–tel: 0151 350 6200; www.bsac.com

SNOWSPORTS

Each winter, snowfall in the Cairngorms draws some skiers to Aviemore in Scotland, the country's most developed ski resort.

SURFING AND WINDSURFING

The Pembrokeshire coast and the beaches of Cornwall, Devon and Dorset are some of the best surf spots in Britain. Wetsuits are essential, but all equipment can be rented from surfing bases. Windsurfers have more choice, with excellent coastal stretches and inland reservoirs. Contact the British Surfing Association (BSA) for information and weather reports. The Royal Yachting Association (see Sailing) represents windsurfers.

» BSA—tel 01637 876474; www.britsurf.co.uk

TENNIS

The annual Grand Slam tennis tournament at Wimbledon causes queues along the streets of the London suburb. Most tickets are sold in advance; a few are reserved for sale on the day, but you must turn up very early. Many players warm up for Wimbledon at the Stella Artois tournament at Queen's Club in West Kensington, London.

» Lawn Tennis Association: www.lta.org.uk

WALKING

Britain's web of footpaths is rigorously maintained. Upland areas rarely top 900m (3,000ft), but weather conditions can deteriorate rapidly. Take a compass, some food and water and a waterproof jacket; and tell someone where you are going.

» Ramblers' Association—tel 020 7339 8500; www.ramblers.org.uk

FOR CHILDREN

The premier theme parks include large, very popular places such as Alton Towers (▷ 267) and Legoland Windsor (▷ 210). Family tickets are always available, but costs can accumulate. The old dictum that 'children should be seen and not heard' no longer applies and most attractions offer reduced-price tickets, children's menus and other facilities. Look out for special offers (such as two-for-one tickets) during school holidays that may be advertised in newspapers or tourist offices.

FILM AND MUSIC

As cinema has grown in popularity, intimate, bijou venues have made way for huge but somewhat soulless multiplexes showing the latest blockbusters. So-called 'high-brow' culture—theatre, opera, ballet—is steadily becoming less élitist and more affordable. However, good seats are not cheap and popular performances are booked up quickly. Mid-week performances are often good value.

Smoking is banned in venues such as cinemas and theatres (except in designated areas), but alcohol is sometimes served in independent cinemas, and theatres have bars and cafés or restaurants. At the theatre order your interval (intermission) drinks in advance and avoid the mad scramble for the bars.

CINEMA

Every year the British film industry produces a minor hit or two and grabs a couple of sought-after Oscars, but never really challenges the likes of Hollywood. British cinemas are much the same: dominated by multiplexes but interspersed with interesting, independent picture houses such as the Cornerhouse in Manchester, the Watershed in Bristol and the Phoenix Picture House in Oxford. Usually tickets can be reserved in advance and collected at the door (a good idea with popular films), or you can just turn up and pay, but be prepared to wait.

CLASSICAL MUSIC, OPERA AND DANCE

Larger venues across London that can cater for the scale of classical music and dance performances—Barbican Hall, the South Bank Centre and the Royal Opera House—are also home to national companies. Birmingham and Bournemouth also have excellent orchestras. Both the BBC National Orchestra of Wales (tel 0800 052 1812; www.bbc.co.uk/wales/now) and Welsh National Opera (tel 029 2063 5000; www.wno.org.uk) are based in Cardiff, while Glasgow is home to Scottish Opera (tel 0141 248 4567; www.scottishopera.org.uk)

and Scottish Ballet (tel 0141 331 2931; www.scottishballet.co.uk). Multipurpose spaces, such as the Lowry in Manchester, host a range of performances. Tickets for venues around the country are available from:

» Bournemouth Symphony Orchestra—tel 01202 670611; www.bsolive.com
» City of Birmingham Symphony Orchestra—www.cbso.co.uk
» English National Ballet—www.ballet.org.uk
» English National Opera—www.eno.org
» London Symphony Orchestra—tel 020 7638 8891; www.lso.co.uk

CONTEMPORARY LIVE MUSIC AND COMEDY

Britain's rock and pop heritage has bequeathed a number of historic venues. Regardless, it's still easy to find a band raising the roof somewhere on a Saturday night. Larger venues, from Carling Academy Brixton in London to Glasgow's Barrowlands, host big-name bands, while smaller venues (including the back rooms of pubs) book up-and-coming acts. Large stadiums such as Wembley Arena are the preserve of household names and pop acts. Harder to find are jazz, blues and world music clubs—Ronnie Scott's in London is probably the best-known venue.

Comedy clubs have become increasingly evident in cities.

THEATRE

Britons are very keen theatre-goers, and theatres have an unparalleled supply of British drama to draw on—from William Shakespeare to adopted Irishman Oscar Wilde (1854–1900), and contemporary playwrights such as Harold Pinter (born 1930). Theatre-going is not the formal occasion it once was, but most of the audience make an effort to look smart.

Unsurprisingly, London has the greatest range of venues, with contemporary productions at the Donmar Warehouse, musicals in the West End and authentically staged Shakespearean plays at Shakespeare's Globe. Regional hotspots include the West Yorkshire Playhouse in Leeds, the Theatre Royal in Plymouth and Manchester's Royal Exchange. Bristol's Old Vic repertory group is highly rated, while the cliff-top Minack Theatre in Cornwall is a stunning venue.

The epicentre of Shakespearean drama is Stratford-upon-Avon, but an outdoor performance of *A Midsummer Night's Dream* by a local group on a summer evening somewhere is just as enjoyable.

One traditional festive genre is pantomime. A bawdy blend of fairytales, topicality, cross-dressing and audience participation, it's an acquired taste, but popular with families at Christmas.

TICKETS

The easiest ways to buy tickets are from the venue's box office, direct from the performance company or through a ticket agency for larger events—a debit or credit card is useful, but an extra charge may be added. Agencies accredited by the Society of Ticket Agents and Retailers ensure that booking fees and terms and conditions are clearly identified. Major agencies include:

» First Call—tel 0870 840 1111; www.firstcalltickets.com
» Keith Prowse—tel 0870 842 2248; www.keithprowse.com/uk
» Ticketmaster—tel 0870 150 0541; www.ticketmaster.co.uk

Note that the cheaper the ticket, the poorer your view will be.

Below *King's Theatre, Glasgow*

FESTIVALS AND EVENTS

If you want to catch a special event in Britain, be it major spectacle or a minor villge fête, you'll be spoiled for choice. Sporting, cultural, religious or traditional, every month is packed with dates for the diary. A select number of them form 'The Season'—an eclectic variety of fashionable occasions that are notable social gatherings rather than just events. These include the opera festivals held at Glyndebourne and Garsington, and the Royal Academy Summer Exhibition. As the socialite's handbook *Debrett's* notes, knowing what to wear and where to sit is as much of a minefield as acquiring the right tickets. In the past The Season was an opportunity for the upper classes and upwardly mobile to meet, quaff champagne and catch up on the progress of old school chums. Increasingly today it is an excuse for the business classes to meet, quaff champagne and catch up on the progress of old clients.

ARTS AND CULTURE

There are more than 100 major arts and cultural festivals taking place in Britain each year, all listed by the British Arts Festivals Association. In Wales the most important annual festival is the Royal National Eisteddfod, a celebration of Welsh song, theatre and language in August. In the same month Scotland's showpiece, the Edinburgh Festival, takes place. Perhaps the best, and certainly the largest, example of British multiculturalism is the Notting Hill Carnival in London around the public holiday at the end of August. There are music festivals for every taste, from the rock and alternative vibes of Glastonbury (June) to the rarefied opera festivals of Glyndebourne and Garsington, for which tickets are almost impossible to acquire. Other 'Season' arts events are more accessible: the Royal Academy's Summer Exhibition and the Last Night of the Proms at the Royal Albert Hall (both in London) for lovers of pomp and ceremony, and the Hay-on-Wye Literary Festival.

» British Arts Festivals Association—tel 020 7247 4667; www.artsfestivals.co.uk

SPORT

April is a busy month for sporting occasions. The Flora London Marathon—probably the biggest mass-participation sports event in the country with almost 50,000 runners—is preceded by the world's top steeplechase, the Grand National at Aintree. The annual Varsity Boat Race—a 150-year-old race between coxed rowing eights from the universities of Oxford and Cambridge—is curiously compelling, and thousands of spectators crowd the banks of the Thames between Putney Bridge and Mortlake for this free event. The 149th race in 2003 saw Oxford win by the closest ever margin: just 30.5cm (12in).

There's less stuffiness at the FA Cup Final that marks the end of the English and Welsh domestic footballing season in May, but just as much flag-waving as at the Proms. Tickets, however, are practically impossible to get. For a grandstand view and little of the hassle, reserve your place in front of a large-screen TV at any number of pubs and bars, but choose your venue carefully, as some are extremely partisan while others may be more 'neutral'. North of the border the Scottish equivalent is equally anticipated.

The end of the football season heralds the start of the 'summer' cricket matches. However, with the first games in mid-April, the weather is usually still decidedly chilly, so it's a good idea to wrap up warm and bring an umbrella. Sporting events of The Season include the two-week Wimbledon Tennis Championship, with ample television coverage; Cowes Week, a yachting jamboree on the Isle of Wight; and Glorious Goodwood, a very popular race meeting at Britain's most scenic racecourse, in West Sussex.

TRADITIONAL EVENTS

Summer brings village fetes and agricultural shows to rural areas, while in London the Queen's birthday is celebrated with the Trooping the Colour pageant in June. But the most uniquely British event takes place in the autumn: Guy Fawkes (or Bonfire) Night. Having failed to blow up the Houses of Parliament in the Gunpowder Plot of 1605, Guy Fawkes was hung, drawn and quartered. Effigies of Guy Fawkes are often burned on bonfires across England on 5 November (or the weekend nearest that day) and fireworks mark the event.

In the depths of the cold winter (25 January) the Scots celebrate their national poet Robert Burns (1759–96), while in Wales the main festival is St. David's Day, on 1 March.

» Local tourist offices have detailed events calendars or check in advance at www.visitbritain.com

» www.whatsonwhen.com allows you to search for events by category.

Right *Tradtional Punch and Judy shows still take place on some beaches in summer*

A number of clues betray Britain's improved attitude to food. Several TV chefs have become celebrities, for example, and supermarket aisles now have more fresh ingredients and fewer freezer cabinets. As a result, British palates are becoming more adventurous. Even small towns have a wide choice of cuisines. Continental café culture has infiltrated Britain and many pubs have finally picked up on the public's appetite for better food.

Is it goodbye overcooked meat and stodgy desserts? Not quite; you may still find places resistant to progress, but more mediocre restaurants are being shown the door.

One result of this new enthusiasm is a style of restaurant cooking known as 'Modern British'. Modern British menus freely mix traditional and international flavours, ingredients and techniques. Traditional Scottish menus may include Aberdeen Angus beef, salmon and game such as venison; Traditional Welsh might use cockles, lamb or leeks.

Britain's colonial past has long spiced up the culinary scene. Indian curries are a particular favourite. But their popularity is challenged by Thai and Chinese cuisine. Larger towns and cities may have Turkish,

Indonesian, Caribbean, Vietnamese, Hungarian, Russian, Mongolian or Mexican restaurants. Middle Eastern and North African restaurants are particularly strong in London. Some ethnic restaurants are entering epicurean territory with slick styling and fusion menus. Others depart from the familiar to offer authentic dishes from the sub-continent. The best destinations for ethnic cuisine are Bradford, Manchester's Curry Mile, Brick Lane in London, Bristol's East Side and Birmingham's Balti Triangleand Chinatown.

Another British favourite is Italian food. Many Italians emigrated here in the 20th century, and Italian ice cream makers soon became local institutions; Italian-run cafés and restaurants are a sound choice if you want a good cup of coffee.

RESERVATIONS

In some restaurants it is possible to walk in off the street and get a table, but if you want to dine in a particular place, it's always advisable to reserve a table in advance. Less formal establishments may not take reservations, while top restaurants are reserved for weeks in advance. It's fairly common for a table reservation to last only a couple of hours; guests will then be expected to make way for the next sitting. Many restaurants stop serving surprisingly early, so don't turn up at 10.30pm and expect a seat without checking in advance.

DRESS CODE

Restaurant etiquette is more relaxed these days but it's unwise to turn up at a chic restaurant wearing jeans and a T-shirt. Our guide indicates which establishments prefer jacket and tie, but if in doubt simply telephone and ask.

SMOKING
A strict law prohibiting smoking in the workplace has been introduced throughout Ireland. This includes all bars and restaurants, though outdoor areas may be set aside for smokers.

LICENSING LAWS
Britain's licensing laws have historically been restrictive compared to the rest of Europe. The majority of pubs still close at 11pm, although many have taken advantage of recent changes in the law and now close an hour or two later. Children aged 16–18 can drink alcohol with a meal. Restaurants with a 'bring your own' policy may charge a corkage fee.

VEGETARIAN
Most menus include some meat-free options, but these choices are often limited, so it's advisable to check in advance what's available. Some restaurants do not include vegetarian options on the menu but will prepare one if requested.

A GUIDE TO BRITISH FOOD
BREAKFAST
The traditional English breakfast is filling, fatty and enormously comforting. A typical 'fry up' is based around fried egg and bacon, but common accompaniments include sausages, mushrooms, toast, fried bread, grilled tomatoes, baked beans and black pudding (made from barley, oats and pigs' blood). In Wales it is traditional to include cockles and laverbread (a type of seaweed) in a breakfast fry up, while Scotland favours kippers (smoked herring).

MEAT
The roast is the cornerstone of British cuisine. Done well (but not over done) it's a satisfying and social meal. The meat at the heart of the meal is usually a whole bird (chicken is the most common, and

turkeys and geese are traditional at Christmas) or a leg, joint or other cut of lamb, beef or pork. This is accompanied by roast potatoes, vegetables and gravy made from the roasting juices.

Pigs have been part of the British diet for thousands of years and are the source of black pudding, bacon and sausages (bangers). Britain has plenty of game, though this varies with the country's geography: Grouse are shot in the uplands, pheasants in the wooded valleys and rabbits in the fields. In Scotland, venison is a favourite.

SANDWICHES AND PICNICS
Probably the most typically English sandwich is the dainty cucumber variety that sometimes forms part of afternoon tea, but these are generally confined to upscale hotels, and countrywide, you're more likely to encounter hearty baguettes or rustic slices of bread with a filling of cheese, meat or salad.

The British have a romantic view of picnics. These days a picnic lunch can mean anything from a packet of sandwiches eaten in the park to an elaborate exercise with wicker

hampers, tablecloths, snacks and portable crockery.

FISH
Britain's fishermen provide fish for the whole country, but for the freshest seafood head for the coast. Cornwall has an excellent reputation and Scotland is another area of excellence—look out for Loch Fyne oysters, Arbroath smokies, lobster and salmon. Other seafood hotspots include East Anglia (for oysters and Cromer crab), Northumbria for Craster kippers, South Wales for cockles and Morecambe Bay for potted shrimps. London is historically linked with whitebait and jellied eels, and the latter are still widely available in the East End.

One of Britain's favourite dishes is fish and chips (French fries): white fish is coated in batter then deep fried and served with chips. Fish and chip shops can be found throughout the country but these, too, are at their best near the coast.

ALCOHOLIC DRINKS
A little-known fact about Britain is that it has numerous wine producers. The most traditional of

these make fruit wines such as elderflower but there are also some flourishing vineyards, especially in the south of the country.

Cider remains a popular English drink, as it has been for thousands of years. Most pubs will sell clear, commercial varieties but you can track down stronger ciders made by independent producers in counties such as Somerset and Herefordshire. Cider produced in small quantities on farms is often called scrumpy.

Traditional British ale has a stronger taste and is less fizzy than lagers and European beers. There are hundreds of independent brewers in Britain, each one producing a distinctive style of ale. Well-established brewers include Shepherd Neame in Kent (the country's oldest brewery), which produces a hoppy, tawny-coloured bitter, and Marston's Pedigree, which comes from the famous brewing town of Burton-on-Trent.

WHERE TO EAT
PUB
Is it a pub? Is it a restaurant? The new breed of 'gastro pub' is both. The trend started in London several years ago and can be summed up as restaurant-quality food served in a pub environment. The gastro pub menu is more adventurous than typical pub food, frequently influenced by Mediterranean countries and Asian flavours. The pub part of the equation means that you can expect an interesting selection of beers, as well as a fully-fledged wine list. Gastro pubs are found all over the country—the stripped pine interiors and the prices (up to £16 for a main dish) are the giveaways.

The quintessential country pub has bare stone walls, open fires and low beams. The features are sometimes copied by the mock 'olde worlde' chain pubs. Some pubs in cities survive from the Victorian period; look for enamelled tiles and lots of glass and mirrors. Other traditional customs, such as a ban on children in the bar area and restricted opening hours, are gradually being left behind. These days, most (but not all) pubs welcome families and many stay open throughout the day, though food is often only available from 12 to 2 and from 6 until 9.

Pub menus feature lighter, cheaper meals including sandwiches and filled baked potatoes–but these days most will also serve substantial dishes such as steak-and-ale pie or bangers and mash.

CAFÉS, BRASSERIES AND BISTROS
Nowadays, the word café refers to the Continental-style establishments increasingly found in small towns as well as the cities, bridging the gap between pubs, restaurants and coffee bars. Workmen's cafés–affectionately called 'greasy spoons'–sell teas, snacks and meals, usually of the fried variety. Bistros and brasseries often stay open all day. The emphasis is on a simpler style of cooking.

FAST FOOD
Fast food often means take-away food, and in many cases it's possible to buy a meal for under £4.50. American fast food chains now grace many corners of Britain. Other fast food outlets include sandwich bars, fish and chip shops and a wide variety of take-aways offering food from international cuisine, particularly in the larger cities where the kebab shop might stand a few doors down from African, Chinese or Indian establishments.

MENU READER

SAVOURY DISHES

ARBROATH SMOKIES
Small hot-smoked haddock, with a more delicate flavour than kippers.

BANGERS AND MASH
Fried sausages and mashed potato.

BLACK PUDDING
Blood sausage made from pig's blood, suet and oatmeal.

COTTAGE PIE
Minced beef and vegetables topped with mashed potato.

CLOOTIE DUMPLING
Steamed sweet and spicy pudding, traditionally cooked in a cloth ('cloot').

FISH AND CHIPS
Fish, typically cod or haddock, deep fried in batter, served with chips.

HOT TODDY
Warming drink made with boiling water, a little sugar and whisky, lemon, nutmeg and cinammon.

LANCASHIRE HOTPOT
Casserole of lamb and onions topped with sliced potato.

OATCAKE
Thin, crumbly savoury biscuit made of oatmeal.

SCOTCH EGG
Hard-boiled egg covered with sausage meat; eaten cold.

SHEPHERD'S PIE
Minced lamb and vegetables topped with mashed potato.

TOAD IN THE HOLE
Sausages baked in batter.

WELSH RAREBIT
Thick cheese sauce spread on toast and grilled.

PUDDINGS

BAKEWELL PUDDING
An almond-flavoured flan, with jam, on a pastry base.

BREAD AND BUTTER PUDDING
Slices of buttered bread baked with dried fruit, milk and eggs.

DUNDEE CAKE.
Rich fruit cake, traditionally decorated with almonds on the top.

ETON MESS
Summer fruits such as strawberries or raspberries with crushed meringues and cream.

FRUIT CRUMBLE
Stewed fruit, such as apple or rhubarb, with a topping of flour and butter.

QUEEN OF PUDDINGS
A pudding of milk, sugar and eggs, topped with jam and meringue.

SCOTCH PANCAKE
Small, thick pancake, eaten hot or cold with butter and syrup.

SPOTTED DICK
A once-famous pudding made with suet pastry and currants.

AFTERNOON TEA

AFTERNOON TEA

A great British institution, afternoon tea remains hugely popular and is available in tea rooms across the country from 2 or 3pm onwards. There are numerous regional variations, but the most widely known is probably the 'cream tea' (scones served with jam and clotted cream) traditionally associated with the West Country. Tea is thought to have arrived in Britain in the 17th century with Catherine of Braganza, the Portuguese wife of Charles II. By the 19th century, it was a fashionable drink and many merchants blended teas according to the recipes of customers, such as Earl Grey, whose bergamot-scented blend is sold in most tea shops.

TEA SHOP

A delightfully English tradition, tea shops usually open from mid-morning until 4 or 5pm. They specialize in teas, cakes and light meals and are particularly common in areas popular with tourists, such as the West Country and rural Yorkshire. They are a splendid place to relax after a day's sightseeing.

Many of the tea shops retain the decor of an earlier age and are in authentic historic buildings, with beams and antiques, lace tablecloths and pretty china.

HOTEL TEAS

One of the finest afternoon tea experiences of all is to enjoy it in one of Britain's grand hotels. Here, rather than sitting at a table as you would in a tea shop, you will be seated in an elegant lounge on comfortable sofas and chairs, with your treats laid out on a coffee table. London's top hotels are particularly famous for this, and country house hotels are similarly desirable. They serve dainty sandwiches and exquisite cakes and pastries on the finest bone china in an atmosphere of utter privilege and indulgence. For the best known places you need to make a reservation quite a long way in advance and should expect the experience to come with a hefty price tag.

The first clear written record of the production of whisky in Scotland was in 1494 during the reign of James IV, when the exchequer roll granted 'to friar John Cor, by order of the King, to make aqua vitae, eight bolls of malt.' Aqua vitae was the original term for spirits (alcoholic liquor made by distillation) and translates into Gaelic as *uisce beatha*, from which we get 'whisky'.

By the 16th century whisky was being produced by everyone in Scotland from landowners to crofters. The key ingredients were close at hand: barley (which grows well in the northern climate), pure water and peat. And the tax paid on wine from continental Europe was high, making whisky an affordable alternative for ordinary people.

After the Battle of Culloden in 1746 the fortunes of Highland whisky changed dramatically. Legislation was introduced that made small-scale whisky production illegal. In 1774 it was legalized again, but its export beyond the Highlands was forbidden. Smuggling became rife, but by the time the final restrictions on Highland distilling were lifted in 1816, malt whisky production had been all but destroyed as a cottage industry.

In 1827 the invention of the continuous still heralded a major upturn in business. In the Lowlands large-scale whisky production had continued to flourish, although the quality of the drink, distilled from wheat, corn or unmalted barley, was considered inferior. It was now possible for the Lowland distillers to produce a better quality—and quantity—of grain whisky. When this was blended with the flavoursome Highland malts, an easy-drinking Scotch was created that would sell well both in Scotland and abroad.

The master blenders who emerged at the forefront of the new industry were men whose names

are still known today, including William Teacher, Johnnie Walker and Arthur Bell.

In the later 20th century whisky's popularity took a downturn, as it went out of fashion. Then, in 1971, William Grant & Sons decided to market its single malt, Glenfiddich. A huge success, it heralded the beginning of a resurgence of interest in the single malts that had been blotted out by blends over a century earlier.

Today single malts tend to be favoured by connoisseurs. No two malt whiskies are the same—it can seem that each bottle contains the distilled essence of the place in which it was created.

WHAT'S IN A MALT?

In order to malt barley, the grain is soaked until it starts to germinate, releasing starches. It is then heated and dried out to stop germination, traditionally by burning peat, whose smoke imparts a distinctive flavour into the malt. Hot water is added to the grain and the resulting wort (into which the barley's sugars have dissolved) is drained off, cooled and pumped into fermenting vessels. Yeast is added to the wort and a bubbly fermentation begins.

Around two days later, the resulting low strength liquor is distilled in large, copper pot stills. It is distilled for a second time and 'the cut' is made to separate the 'heart' of the spirit from the volatile 'heads' (the first alcohol that condenses) and 'tails' (the heavier alcoholic compounds). The heart is transferred to a vat where it is mixed with water before being sealed into oak casks and left to mature for three years or longer.

Every detail of the manufacture affects the taste of the finished whisky, including the amount of peat used in the malting, the composition of the local water, the design of the still, the length of maturation and the type of cask in which this takes place. The better-known brands are a good starting point but investigate further and you'll quickly discover different ages and distillations carry their own mystique.

If you've ever wanted to stay in a castle, a beachside cottage or on a working farm, then Britain is the place to do it. The variety is staggering, with something for every budget. We've selected some of the country's best hotels, inns and bed-and-breakfast guesthouses, and listed further options below. Most local Tourist Information Centres will have a bed- booking service—useful for last-minute hunts for rooms. The VisitBritain organization makes lists of accommodation widely available.

BED-AND-BREAKFAST

Bed-and-breakfast seems to be a particularly British arrangement: you stay overnight in somebody's house in your own room, with breakfast included in the price. There are thousands of bed-and-breakfasts across the country. Small guest houses may have just one room for guests, others up to six or seven rooms. Prices compare favourably with hotels, but the real advantage of bed-and-breakfast is that guests enjoy an intimate hospitality that hotels cannot match. They are a good way of getting inside knowledge on a place and are especially useful in more remote areas. Hosts will usually expect you to be out of the house for most of the day.

Prices range from £30 per night to more than £100. We've selected some of the best bed-and-breakfasts in all price brackets, but a local Tourist Information Centre will have a complete list. You will need to reserve in advance during peak periods and local events. Look out for quirky properties such as Lavenham Priory; chapels, windmills, barns and listed (landmark) buildings have all been converted to bed-and-breakfast properties.

BOTHIES

In the hills of Scotland, northern England and Wales, there is a network of small buildings (about 100)—called bothies—available to hillwalkers. Few are mapped or signposted and they are maintained by volunteers from the Mountain Bothies Association (www.mount-ainbothies.org.uk) so some may be on the verge of collapse while others may have beds and a fireplace. Walkers can stay the night for free, although a donation is appreciated. If you're planning to do any walking in Scotland, northern England or Wales, it is a good idea to ask about bothies close to your route in a local Tourist Information Centre.

CAMPING

Since most land is privately owned in Britain, you cannot pitch a tent just anywhere. And it is illegal to camp in national parks and nature reserves. Instead, there are designated campsites, most with facilities such as running water, some with shops and laundries. These are often signposted from roads. Expect to spend between £2 and £10 per night. Investing in a camping stove (available from outdoor activity shops) is a good idea since open fires are not permitted. You may have to share the site with caravans (trailers). The Camping and Caravanning Club (tel: 024 7669 4995; www.campingandcaravanningclub.co.uk) recommends camp (and caravan) sites and gives advice on camping (and caravanning).

CARAVANNING

Caravans and camper vans (RVs) remain a widespread feature of

Britain's roads in summer. There are numerous caravan parks, often close to seaside resorts. The Caravan Club (tel 0800 521161; www.caravanclub.co.uk) recommends certain caravan sites and offers advice on travelling in Britain with a caravan.

FARM STAYS

Staying on a farm is an increasingly popular form of accommodation with several advantages. Food is often fresh, filling and wholesome, the rural location gives an insight into life in Britain's countryside and children often find farms more interesting than hotels. Many farms have diversified and also offer activities to guests. Accommodation may be either on a bed-and-breakfast basis, or self-catering. Farms accredited by VisitBritain are found at Farm Stay UK (tel 01271 336141; www.farmstayuk.co.uk).

HOME EXCHANGE AGENCIES

Homeowners in Britain interested in swapping houses with families abroad for holidays register with home exchange agencies. They are predominantly internet-based and the leading agencies include: www.gti-home-exchange.com, www.homelink.org.uk and www.homebase-hols.com. It may be a cost-effective system, but it requires careful research.

HOSTELLING

There are more than 300 youth hostels in Britain. Those that are members of the Youth Hostels Association (YHA; tel: 0870 770 8868, www.yha.org.uk) and the Scottish Youth Hostels Association (SYHA; tel: 01786 891400, www.syha.org.uk) will be affiliated to Hostelling International (HI), but there are also independent hostels. For people living in Britain annual membership of the YHA is £15.50 (under 26s £10); for the SYHA £6 (under 18s £2.50). For all ages for those from outside Britain annual membership of Hostelling International is £10. You don't have to be a member of the YHA or SYHA to stay at their hostels—for £3 extra per night you can stay at a YHA hostel and for £1 extra you can stay at a SYHA hostel, or you can become a member at the hostel. Prices are usually lower than £20 per night and standards are generally good but hostels remain the domain of the budget traveller.

HOTELS

Britain has an enormous choice of hotels: stylish town houses, grand country houses, old coaching inns, modern conversions, roadside lodges, five-star international hotel chains and more. It's a competitive business so look out for late deals on accommodation. Some hotels, especially the big chains in cities, rely on business guests during the week and may offer discounted rooms at the weekend to fill the establishment.

Hoteliers are also well informed on ways of parting guests from their money. It is common for hotels to charge extra for items from the mini-bar; prices are often significantly higher than they might be from the bar downstairs. Similarly, if you use the phone line in your room, for calls or internet access, expect to pay higher charges. Check in advance what the rates are, rather than have an expensive surprise when you check out. Food ordered by room service also attracts a supplement. Porters and chambermaids in hotels should be tipped about £1. We have indicated where hotels have extra facilities or activities available, such as a spa, gym or swimming pool.

Most hotels will serve meals throughout the day. In fact, some hotels are better known as restaurants rather than hotels. There are also 'restaurants with rooms.' As the name suggests, these are restaurants which also have a handful of rooms available for guests. They are usually found outside cities, and mean that diners don't have to drive home after their meals. A good example is Raymond Blanc's Le Manoir Aux Quat'

Saisons. If you are doing a lot of travel by car, you are likely to use the chain hotels beside roads and in motorway service areas. They may be bland, but are usually clean, convenient and quite economical.

PUBS

If you can tolerate the possibility of a little noise, pubs can be a convenient source of accommodation. Many of the pubs in our listings will have one or more bedrooms available to travellers. Rates are generally reasonable, typically £30 per night, and accommodation is often, but not always, on a bed-and-breakfast basis.

SELF-CATERING

Many British holidaymakers prefer staying in a cottage, house or apartment and catering for themselves. It is often less expensive than staying at a hotel.

There are thousands of properties available, but the best of those in holiday hotspots, such as Cornwall and the Lake District, are often reserved very far ahead. Reservations are usually taken by the week, although in the low season shorter stays may be possible. VisitBritain approves many properties and local Tourist Information Centres will have lists of available places. Several specialist agencies manage self-catering properties. A travel agent will have brochures for reliable companies, such as Rural Retreats (tel 01386 701177; www.ruralretreats.co.uk), managing self-catering properties in Britain.

Both The National Trust (tel 0870 458 4422; www.nationaltrustcottages.co.uk) and The Landmark Trust (tel 01628 825928; www.landmarktrust.co.uk) offer interesting properties for let. The Landmark Trust specializes in conversions of historic buildings such as forts. The National Trust has holiday cottages at many of its sites, as well as less expensive properties elsewhere.

ROMAN

The Romans invaded Britain in AD43 and by AD57 they controlled most of the country. Their legacy can be seen in London (▷ 64–117), Bath (▷ 122–125), Chester (▷ 306), Cirencester (▷ 129), York (▷ 322–325) and the grand Roman villas at Fishbourne (▷ 181), Lullingstone (▷ 187) and Bignor (▷ 174). Britain's most striking Roman structure is Hadrian's Wall in the north of England (▷ 336–337).

ANGLO-SAXON

During the Anglo-Saxon period (886–1066) churches were built of stone and characterized by their simple arched windows with thick central supports. The first St. Paul's Cathedral (▷ 86) was founded in AD604 and Edward the Confessor had Westminster Abbey (▷ 94) finished in 1066.

NORMAN

In the late 11th and 12th centuries the Norman conquerors brought new styles and craftsmen from Normandy. Massive fortified buildings and churches were thrown up in the wake of the Norman invasion, recognizable by their rounded arches, heavy masonry and decorated walls and doorways.

Examples include: Westminster Hall (▷ 84), the oldest remaining part of the medieval Palace of Westminster, erected in 1097 (but renovated in the 14th century); The White Tower, at the heart of the Tower of London (▷ 90); the keep at Dover Castle (▷ 181); Restormel Castle (▷ 139).

EARLY ENGLISH AND DECORATED

Architecture of the late 12th and 13th centuries became lighter, using pointed rather than rounded arches, especially in lancet windows This period marked the move towards the long, vertical lines of the Gothic style and an increasing focus on window space. As windows became bigger, buttresses were added to transfer the outward thrust of the roof to the ground. Increasingly elaborate tracery and decoration were employed on arches, doorways and especially windows in buildings of the later 13th and 14th centuries.

Examples: Westminster Abbey, rebuilt 1245 (▷ 94); York Minster (▷ 323); the magnificent ruins of Rievaulx Abbey ▷ 318).

PERPENDICULAR GOTHIC

Evolving from the Decorated style, simpler lines and more uniform tracery on windows and walls emerged during the late 14th and 15th centuries, with much use of fan-vaulting and four-centred arches. Designs became lighter, using greater areas of glass.

Example: Henry VII Chapel, Westminster Abbey (▷ 94).

TUDOR AND EARLY STUART

Named after the royal families, these architectural styles from the late 15th and 16th centuries marked a shift from the Gothic to the Renaissance styles, with the emphasis on domestic architecture for the expanding aristocracy and gentry. Brick and wood-panelling became popular.

Examples: Hampton Court Palace (▷ 183); Shakespeare's Globe Theatre (▷ 87), a modern reconstruction of the 16th-century original; Blenheim Palace (▷ 177); Cotehele House (▷ 129).

Opposite *Hadrian's Wall at Cuddy's Crag*
Above *Hampton Court*

LATE STUART

The Palladian style, recalling the work of 16th-century Italian architect Andrea Palladio, reflected Roman influences in porticoes and symmetrical facades. Classical styles merged in the 18th century with baroque ornamentation and detail.

Major Architects: **Inigo Jones** (1573–1652): designed the Queen's House, Greenwich and London's Banqueting Hall.

Sir Christopher Wren (1632–1723): designed St. Paul's Cathedral (▷ 86), Greenwich Hospital and many of London's City churches following the Great Fire of 1666.

Nicholas Hawksmoor (1661–1736): Wren's assistant, who preferred monumental classicism. Designed many of London's churches, including St. George's Bloomsbury and Christchurch, Spitalfields.

Sir John Vanbrugh (1664–1726): designed Castle Howard (▷ 306) and Blenheim Palace (▷ 177).

GEORGIAN AND REGENCY

During the Georgian period (1714–1830) architects turned back to the Palladian style, and in the late 18th and early 19th centuries Greek Classical influences came to the fore, prompting an emphasis on simplicity and symmetry, especially in the new terraced town houses. The Regency period (named after the Prince Regent) saw the advent of floor-to-roof bow windows and ironwork in staircases and balconies.

Major Architects: **Robert Adam** (1728–92): designed London's Osterley House and Syon House, Culzean Castle (▷ 364) and Edinburgh's Charlotte Square.

William Kent (1675–1748): advocated the return to Palladianism. Designed Chiswick House and Kensington Palace (▷ 79).

John Nash (1752–1835): known for Regency houses and responsible for London's Regent's Park terraces and Brighton's Royal Pavilion (▷ 175).

Sir John Soane (1753–1837): liked austere Classical designs. Responsible for London's Bank of England and Dulwich Art Gallery.

Decimus Burton (1800–81): a leader in the Regency style, who worked with Nash on the Regent's Park terraces and designed London's Athenaeum Club.

John Wood the Elder (1704–54): designed Queen Square and The Circus in Bath (▷ 122).

John Wood the Younger (1728–81): designed the Royal Crescent and the Assembly Rooms in Bath (▷ 122).

Isambard Kingdom Brunel (1806–59): was responsible for the Clifton Suspension Bridge (▷ 127).

Lancelot 'Capability' Brown 1716–83: English landscape gardener who designed the gardens at Blenheim Palace (▷ 177), Kew Gardens (▷ 81) and Stowe in Buckinghamshire.

VICTORIAN

Architecture of the period from 1837 to 1901 called on a mish-mash of influences as new public buildings such as train stations and municipal offices sprang up. These were notable for their neo-Gothic designs, romanticized medieval motifs, rich details and extensive use of steel, iron and glass. In contrast, mass housing was built for industrial workers.

Examples: London's Houses of Parliament (▷ 84), Natural History Museum (▷ 82–83), Albert Memorial (▷ 79), St Pancras station, Tower Bridge (▷ 88); Glasgow City Chambers; National Gallery of Scotland, Edinburgh (▷ 367); Truro Cathedral.

Major Architects: **Sir Charles Barry** (1795–1860): designed the Houses of Parliament (▷ 84) after their destruction by fire in 1834, and Manchester Athenaeum.

Sir George Gilbert Scott (1811–78): designed London's St. Pancras station and the Foreign Office; Glasgow University.

Augustus Welby Northmore Pugin (1812–52): led the neo-Gothic movement, working on the Houses of Parliament.

Alfred Waterhouse (1830–1905): designed the Natural History Museum (▷ 82–83); Manchester Town Hall.

Sir Aston Webb (1849–1930): a president of the Royal Academy, who designed London's Admiralty Arch, Buckingham Palace's east facade (▷ 76), and the Victoria & Albert Museum (▷ 91).

Alexander 'Greek' Thompson (1817–75): designed churches, warehouses and tenements in Glasgow (▷ 198–200).

LATE VICTORIAN AND EDWARDIAN

In the late 19th century the Arts and Crafts Movement was promoted by William Morris as a reaction against mass production, with the aim of making hand-made objects and fine art a part of daily life. Its influence extended to architecture as suburban brick houses, with terracotta panelling, balconies and large gardens. The organic motifs of art nouveau were popular until about 1914.
Examples: Red House, Bexley Heath; Holy Trinity Church, Chelsea.
Major Architects: **Philip Webb** (1831–1915): an exponent of a simple, domestic style, designing furniture and metalwork with Morris, as well as the Red House.

Sir Edwin Lutyens (1869–1944): designed the Cenotaph in Whitehall (▷ 91) and many country houses outside London.

Sir Herbert Baker (1862–1946): worked with Lutyens. Best known for his controversial reconstruction of the Bank of England.

Charles Rennie Mackintosh (1868–1928): designed the Glasgow School of Art and other buildings mainly in Glasgow.

INTER-WAR

Public and domestic buildings made use of art deco's geometric lines, bold colours and exotic motifs, often using Egyptian themes, marking the huge public interest in archaeologist Howard Carter's discovery of the tomb of Tutankhamun. Traditional materials such as tiles and stained glass were paired with modern chromium plating.
Examples: Metropolitan Catholic Cathedral of Christ the King, Liverpool (▷ 314); BBC Broadcasting House.
Major Architects: **Berthold Lubetkin** (1901–90): prolific Russian architect who designed the Penguin Pool in ZSL London Zoo (▷ 98–99).

Sir Giles Gilbert Scott (1880–1960): grandson of Sir George Gilbert Scott, designed the Bodleian Library, Oxford (▷ 190).

POST WORLD WAR II

After 1945 designs became increasingly stark and massive, using materials such as concrete, especially in the high-rises of the 1960s. The high-tech style of the 1970s and 1980s exposed the inner workings of buildings. Stainless steel and glass were popular materials. An emphasis on lightness combined with elegant, unconventional lines is seen in Britain's newest structures.
Examples: London's South Bank Centre; Millennium Bridge.
Major Architects: **Sir Richard Rodgers** (1933–): designed the Lloyds Building, with its 'inside-out' display of pipes and lifts.

Sir Norman Foster (1935–): responsible for London's Millennium Bridge.

Opposite *Royal Crescent, Bath*
Below left *Natural History Museum, London*
Below *Lloyd's of London building, London*

ANGLO-SAXONS
Early Saxon kings 886–1042
Edward the Confessor 1042–66
Harold II 1066

NORMANS
William I 1066–87
William II 1087–1100
Henry I 1100–35
Stephen 1135–54

ANGEVINS
Henry II 1154–89
Richard I 1189–99
John 1199–1216

PLANTAGENETS
Henry III 1216–72
Edward I 1272–1307
Edward II 1307–27
Edward III 1327–77
Richard II 1377–99

LANCASTER
Henry IV 1399–1413
Henry V 1413–22
Henry VI 1422–61 and 1470–71

YORK
Edward IV 1461–1470 and 1471–83
Richard III 1483–85

TUDOR
Henry VII 1485–1509
Henry VIII 1509–47
Edward VI 1547–53
Mary I 1553–58
Elizabeth I 1558–1603

STUART
James I (James VI of Scotland)
1603–25
Charles I 1625–49

INTERREGNUM
Commonwealth 1649–53
Protectorate 1653–59

STUART
Charles II 1660–85
James II 1685–88
William III (of Orange) 1688–1702
and Mary II 1688–94
Anne 1702–14

HANOVER
George I 1714–27
George II 1727–60
George III 1760–1820
George IV 1820–30
William IV 1830–37
Victoria 1837–1901

SAXE-COBURG GOTHA
Edward VII 1901–10

WINDSOR
George V 1910–36
Edward VIII 1936
George VI 1936–1952
Elizabeth II 1952–

Above *Princess Elizabeth, Queen Elizabeth,*
King George VI, Princess Margaret
Opposite top left *King Henry VI*
Opposite top right *George I*
Opposite bottom left *George II*
Opposite bottom right *HRH Prince Albert,*
Prince of Wales

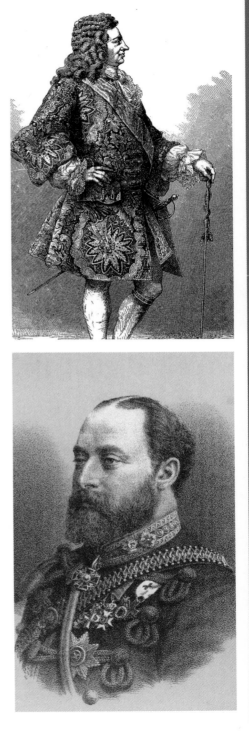

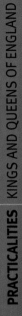

anticlockwise ....counterclockwise
aubergine ....eggplant
bank holiday ......a public holiday that falls on a Monday; there are two in May and one in August
banknote ....bill (paper money)
bill........................check (at restaurant)
biscuit....................................... cookie
bonnet...............................hood (car)
boot..trunk (car)
busker.........................street musician
caravan........................... trailer or RV
car park ....parking lot
carriage .... car (on a train)
casualty ....emergency room (hospital)
chemist.............................. pharmacy
chips ....French fries
coach .... long-distance bus
coaching inn .....pubs or hotels dating from 17th–19th centuries, located on main travel routes
concessions ....reduced fees for tickets, often available to students, children and elderly people
courgette ....zucchini
crèche.................................. day care
crisps ....potato chips
directory enquiries..............directory assistance
dual carriageway ..two-lane highway
en suite .... a bedroom with its own private bathroom; may also just refer to the bathroom
football .... soccer
full board ....a hotel tariff that includes all meals
garage...............................gas station
garden......................yard (residential)
GP..doctor
half board ....hotel tariff that includes breakfast and either lunch or dinner
high street........................ main street
hire .... rent
inland ....within the UK
jelly..Jello™
jumper, jersey.........................sweater

junction ....intersection
layby ....rest stop, pull-off
level crossing.............. grade crossing
lorry...truck
licensed...............a café or restaurant that has a licence to serve alcohol (beer and wine only unless it's 'fully' licensed)
lift...elevator
main line station ..... a train station as opposed to an underground or subway station (although it may be served by the underground/subway)
nappy ....diaper
off-licence .... liquor store
pants...................... underpants (men's)
pavement............................... sidewalk
petrol...gas
plaster ....Band-Aid or bandage
post..mail
public school............... private school
pudding.....................................dessert
purse .... change purse
pushchair .... stroller
return ticket............... roundtrip ticket
rocket..arugula
roundabout.........traffic circle or rotary
self-catering............. accommodation including a kitchen
single ticket................one-way ticket
stalls.......... orchestra seats (in theatre)
underpass .... subway
doctor's office.........................surgery
traffic jam...............................tailback
takeaway ....takeout
taxi rank ....taxi stand
ten-pin bowling ....bowling
tights ....panty-hose
T-junction .... an intersection where one road meets another at right angles (making a T shape)
toilets....................................restrooms
torch ....flashlight
trolley...cart
trousers ....pants
way out...exit

BRITISH FLOOR NUMBERING

In Britain the first floor of a building is called the ground floor, and the floor above it is the first floor. So a British second floor is a US third floor, and so on. This is something to watch for in museums and galleries in particular.

BRITISH LISTED BUILDINGS

'Listed' buildings in Britain are those that merit protection as part of the nation's architectural heritage. The list of protected buildings is compiled by the Department of Culture, Media and Sport and buildings have to meet certain criteria to be listed. Generally, they have to be architecturally or historically interesting, or have a close historical association with important events or have value as part of a group of buildings. There are three grades of listing (Grade I, Grade II* and Grade II) and buildings are graded according to their importance to the nation. All surviving buildings constructed before 1700, for example, are listed. Those in the highest grades, Grade I and II*, are eligible for grants. There are about 370,000 listed buildings.

SPEAKING SCOTTISH

Standard English is the official language of Scotland, and spoken everywhere. However, like other corners of Britain, the Scottish people have their own variations of English and the way it is spoken, and dialects of their own. In Aberdeen it is known as Doric, in the Lowlands it is Lallans, Glasgow has a patter all of its own, and in Orkney and Shetland, the local dialect has Scandinavian roots.

SCOTS

The Scots language, which stems from an older form of Lowland Scots, varies as you travel across the country from a barely detectable accent on certain words and phrases, to the broad (and very individual) patois of inner-urban Glasgow and northeast Aberdeenshire.

The Scots language has its own traditions of literature, poetry (including Robert Burns) and songs (including the Border ballads), and Aberdeen University Press publishes Scots dictionaries that celebrate the richness of the language. But it was only in 1983 that the first complete translation of the New Testament into Scots was published, the work of scholar William Laughton Lorimer (1885–1967).

NORN

In Orkney and Shetland, you'll hear a completely different accent with long 'a's and many unusual words, influenced by the Nordic languages. At its thickest, among the local people, it can sound more akin to Danish than English.

GAELIC

In the Western Isles you'll hear another accent, sometimes described as soft and lilting, which is a legacy of an entirely separate language—Gaelic (pronounced Gaallic in Scotland), still spoken by around 65,000 people.

Visitors without prior knowledge of Gaelic are most likely to see it first in place names on the map—especially of mountains—and on bilingual road signs in the west. You may hear it spoken naturally as a first language between local people in the Western Isles, see a Gaelic church service advertised, or hear it sung. And if you see 'ceud mile failte', you might recognize a warm welcome.

Gaelic language and culture arrived here with the Irish around the fifth century. It was the main tongue of northern and western Scotland until the dramatic changes of the 18th century brought about by the opening up of the Highlands after the Jacobite Rebellions, and the later land clearances which uprooted whole communities.

In the 20th century, while Gaelic might be the language spoken at home, English was the imposed language of education in schools and colleges. The whole culture might have died out, but a revival of interest in the early 1970s (spurred on by the example of a more militant Welsh language revival) helped to sustain it.

With the more recent development of interest in a separate Scottish identity, led by the emergence of the Scottish parliament in the 1990s, Gaelic is firmly back in vogue. While native speakers are steadily declining in numbers, understanding is increasing as the language is taught in schools and universities, the culture celebrated in an annual festival. Gaelic books and newspapers are published, and Gaelic speakers get their own air-time on radio and television. And as part of the wider interest in Celtic roots, Gaelic is also learned and passionately celebrated worldwide.

For more information about learning Gaelic, contact the Gaelic college Sabhal Mór Ostaig (Sleat, Isle of Skye IV44 8RQ, tel 01471 888000; www.smo.uhi.ac.uk). Comunn na Gàighlig is a government-sponsored development agency, with useful links and information (5 Mitchell's Lane, Inverness IV2 3HQ; tel 01463 234138; www.cnag.org.uk).

The Am Baile (Gaelic Village) project is a developing website sponsored by the Highland Council offering a wide variety of resources relating to Gaelic language and culture (www.ambaile.org.uk).

SCOTTISH WORDS IN COMMON USAGE

Auld Reekie	nickname for Edinburgh
aye	always/yes
bairn	baby, child
bannock	biscuit or scone
ben	hill, mountain
birle	spin, turn
bonny	pretty
brae	hill
braw	fine, beautiful
burn	stream, creek
cairn	stones forming a landmark
canny	cunning, clever
ceilidh	gathering, party, dance
coo	cow
croft	smallholding, small farm
doocote	dovecot
dour	sullen
dram	measure of whisky
een	eyes
factor	estate or farm manager
fash	bother
gae	go
gillie	hunting guide
glaur	mud
glen	valley
gloaming	evening
greet	weep
haver	to talk nonsense
heavy	dark beer
heid	head
ken	to know
kirk	church
laird	land owner
loch	lake
machair	coastal grassland
manse	minister's house
messages	shopping
nicht	night
och	oh
partan	crab
piece	sandwich
pinkie	little finger
pirrie/peerie/peedy	small
puffer	antique steamboat
Sassenach	English-speaker
sleekit	sly
stay	live
tattie	potato
tattie-bogle	scarecrow
wee	small

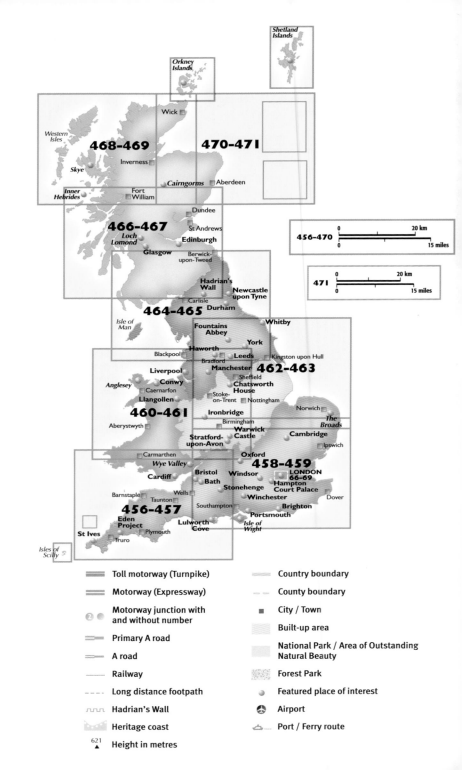

Shetland
Islands

Orkney
Islands

Wick

468-469

470-471

Western
Isles

Inverness

Skye

Cairngorms   Aberdeen

Inner
Hebrides

Fort
William

| 456-470 | 0 | | 20 km |
| | 0 | | 15 miles |

Dundee

466-467
Loch
Lomond

St Andrews

Edinburgh

Glasgow

Berwick-
upon-Tweed

| 471 | 0 | | 20 km |
| | 0 | | 15 miles |

Hadrian's
Wall

Newcastle
upon Tyne

Carlisle

464-465 Durham

Isle of
Man

Fountains
Abbey

Whitby

York

Haworth

Blackpool

Leeds

Kingston upon Hull

Bradford

Manchester 462-463

Liverpool

Sheffield

Conwy

Chatsworth
House

Anglesey

Caernarfon

Llangollen

Stoke-
on-Trent

Nottingham

460-461

Ironbridge

Norwich

The
Broads

Aberystwyth

Birmingham

Warwick
Castle

Cambridge

Stratford-
upon-Avon

Ipswich

Carmarthen

Oxford

458-459

Wye Valley

Cardiff

Bristol

Windsor

LONDON
66-69

Bath

Stonehenge

Hampton
Court Palace

Barnstaple

Wells

Winchester

Dover

Taunton

456-457

Southampton

Brighton

Eden
Project

Lulworth
Cove

Portsmouth

St Ives

Isle of
Wight

Plymouth

Truro

Isles of
Scilly

	Toll motorway (Turnpike)			Country boundary
	Motorway (Expressway)			County boundary
	Motorway junction with and without number		■	City / Town
	Primary A road			Built-up area
	A road			National Park / Area of Outstanding Natural Beauty
	Railway			Forest Park
	Long distance footpath			Featured place of interest
	Hadrian's Wall			Airport
	Heritage coast			Port / Ferry route
621 ▲	Height in metres			

MAPS

Map references for the sights refer to the atlas pages within this section or to the individual town plans within the regions. For example, Manchester has the reference ✚ 461 G14, indicating the page on which the map is found (461) and the grid square in which Manchester sits (G14).

Maps   456

Atlas index   472

13

14

DUBLIN
DUN LAOGHAIRE

Amlwch

ISLE OF ANGLESEY

Anglesey

Holyhead   Benllech

Holy Island   Llangefni   Beaumaris

Rhosneigr   Menai   Bangor
Bridge

Greenwood
Forest Park

Penrhyn
Castle

Bethesda

Caernarfon   Llanberis   1062
Carnedd
Llewelyn

Caernarfon
Bay

Snowdonia
National   Glyder Fawr
Park   1085
Snowdon

Great
Ormes
Head

Llandudno

Colwyn   Rhyl
Bay

Conwy   Abergele   A547

Bodnant
Garden   **Bodelwyddan**
Castle

Trefriw   Denbigh
Woollen
Mills

Llanrwst

CONWY   **DENB**

999   Betws-
y-coed

Capel
Curig

A498   Blaenau
Ffestiniog   *Gwydyr Forest Park*

15

Nefyn

Lleyn   *Peninsula*

Criccieth   Porthmadog

Pwllheli   **Portmeirion**

Abersoch   **Harlech**
Castle

Bardsey Island

Ffestiniog

GWYNEDD

Snowdonia

Coed-y-Brenin
Forest Park

Bala

Pistyll
Rhaeadr

Corwe

Dee

Dolgellau

Barmouth   892
Cader
Idris

Centre of
Alternative
Technology

Dyfi   A458

Glyndwr's
Way

16

Cardigan Bay

Ynyslas

Aberystwyth

Tywyn   Machynlleth

Celtica

752
Plynlimon

Llanidloes

New

POWYS

Llangurig   A470

A4120

CEREDIGION

Aberaeron

Tregaron

Elan
Valley

Llandrindod
Wells

Rhayader

Cambrian   *Mountains*

17

ROSSLARE
HARBOUR

Strumble
Head

Cardigan

Newport   Castell
Henllys

Fishguard   **Welsh**
Wildlife
Centre

St David's
Head

St David's   **Pembrokeshire Coast**
National Park

PEMBROKESHIRE

Pembrokeshire
Coast Path

St Brides Bay   Haverfordwest

Newcastle
Emlyn

Llandysul

National Wool
Museum

Lampeter

Llanwrtyd Wells

Builth
Wells

Dolaucothi
Gold Mines

Llandovery

CARMARTHENSHIRE

Llandeilo

Towy
National
Botanic Garden

Carreg
Cennen

886
Pen-y-fan

Brecon Beacons
National Park

Brecon

Dan-Yr-Ogof

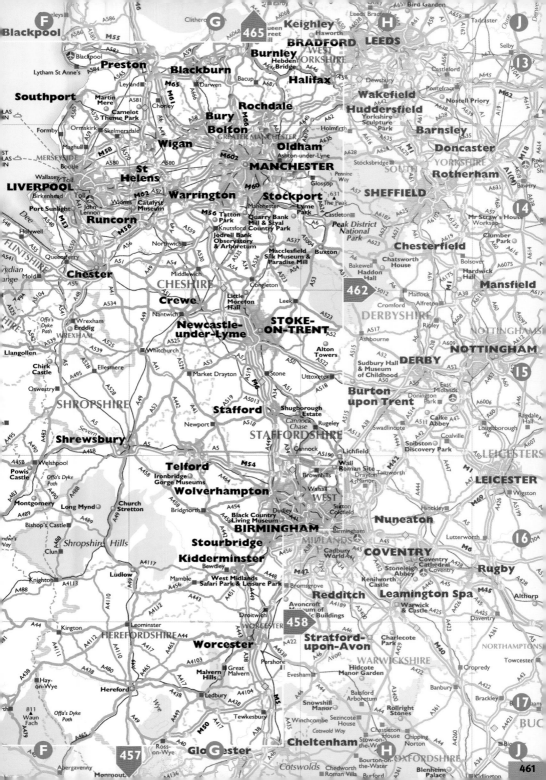

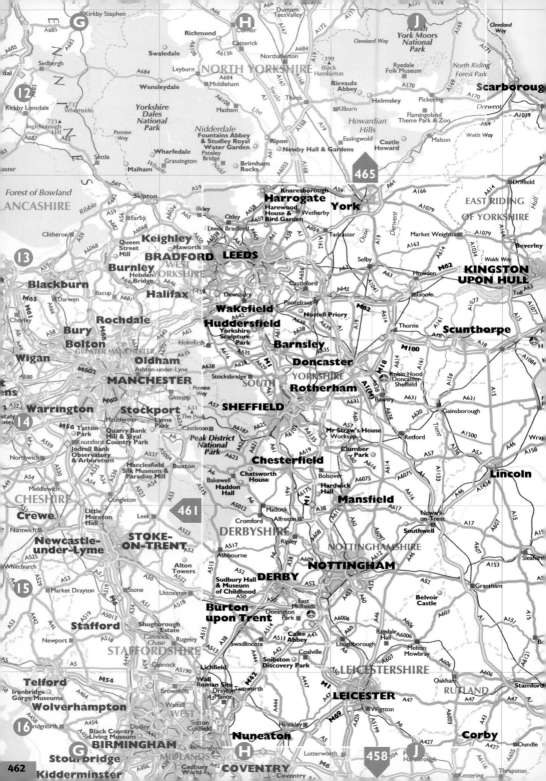

Bempton Cliffs
Flamborough Head
Bridlington

nsea

Withernsea
A1033

Humber
Immingham
Grimsby
Spurn Head
side
Cleethorpes
A46

ROTTERDAM (EUROPOORT) ZEEBRUGGE

The Wolds
A18
A16
A1031
631
Louth
A157
Mablethorpe
incolnshire Wolds
A16
Alford
A1111
A52
A153
Horncastle
A158
LINCOLNSHIRE
A158
A155
Skegness
A16
Coningsby
Tattershall Castle
A52
A17
A16
Boston
The Wash

A152
Holbeach
The Burnhams
Wells-next-the-Sea
Peddars Way & Norfolk Coast Path
Sheringham
A149
Hunstanton
Norfolk Coast
Holkham Hall
Holt
Felbrigg Hall
Cromer
Houghton Hall
A148
North Walsham
Sandringham
Castle Rising
A149
A148
A1065
Fakenham
Aylsham
A140
A151
Spalding
A17
King's Lynn
Peddars Way & Norfolk Coast Path
A47
A10
Dereham
A47
Norwich
A151
A149
The Fens
A1101
A17
Wisbech
A47
A47
Caister-on-Sea
A47
Ace
A1122
Swaffham
NORFOLK
Norwich
The Broads
Great Yarmouth
Downham Market
A1122
A134
Watton
A1075
Wymondham
A11
A146
Lowestoft
Peterborough
A605
A10
A143
A12
March
A141
A134
Thetford Forest Park
Attleborough
A140
Bungay
A145
A146
Beccles
Chatteris
A142
Littleport
A10
A11
Harles
A143
A144
CAMBRIDGESHIRE
Ely
Thetford
Diss

459

North Arran

Sound of Bute

NORTH AYRSHIRE

EAST RENFREWSHIRE

Hamilton

North Arran 874 Goat Fell dick

Dalbirnie Beith Stewarton

East Kilbride

Kilwinning

Strathaven

9 Isle of Arran

Lamlash

Ardrossan

Kilmarnock

Irvine

A71

Lanark

Firth of Clyde

Holy Island

Troon

Prestwick

Prestwick Ayr

A759

A77

A71

Galston

SOUTH LANARKSHIRE

New Lanark World Heritage Site

Stobo Castle

Peebles

Innerleithen

Galashi

Biggar

Upper Tweeddale

Traquair

Abbotsfo

LARNE

Ayr

A26

A70

Cumnock

EAST AYRSHIRE

A76

A70

Sanquhar

840 Broad Law

U p l a n d s

SCOTTISH BOR

Selkirk

A7

Hawi

466

Culzean Castle & Country Park

Maybole

Doon

Nith

Southern Upland Way

A74(M)

Moffat

A701

A708

Tweed

Ailsa Craig

Girvan

SOUTH AYRSHIRE

A77

A714

842 Merrick

Southern Upland Way

A713

Galloway Forest Park

New Galloway

A712

A702

Thornhill

A701

A709

Lochmaben

Lockerbie

DUMFRIES & GALLOWAY

Esk

Bentpath

Langholm

10 LARNE (SUMMER ONLY)

Ballantrae

BELFAST

Loch Ryan

A718

A77

Stranraer

A716

Newton Stewart

A714

710 Cairnsmore of Fleet

A762

A713

Loch Ken

Castle Douglas

A75

A711

Dumfries

Nith Estuary

A75

Annan

Longtown

A7

A607

A689

11 Portpatrick

A77

Wigtown

A75

Fleet Valley

Gatehouse of Fleet

A755

East Stewartry Coast

Caerlaverock Castle

Annan

Gretna

Solway Coast

Carlisle

M6

A747

A746

Wigtown Bay

Kirkcudbright

A711

Solway Firth

Wigton

A596

A595

Luce Bay

Whithorn

Drummore

Burrow Head

Maryport

Cockermouth

A594

A591

931 Skiddaw

A66

Rheged

A592

Mull of Galloway

Workington

A597

A595

A5086

A66

Keswick

950 Helvellyn

Ullswat

CUMBRIA

Whitehaven

899 Great Gable

964 Scafell Pike

Grasmere

902 Bow Fell

Ambleside

Rydal Mount

A592

Towne

Egremont

12 Point of Ayre

A10

Sellafield Visitor Centre

A595

Lake District National Park

Ravenglass

Windermere

Hawkshead

Blackw House

Grizedale Forest Park

A593

A592

A590

Sizergh Castle

A3 A18

Ramsey

A14

620 Snaefell

Isle of Man

Broughton-in-Furness

Ulverston

A595

Peel

Millennium Way

A18

A1

Millom

A595

Holker Hall

Arnside Silverda

A5

A3

A5

Douglas

BELFAST

Barrow-in-Furness

Carnforth

Port Erin

A5

Isle of Man (Ronaldsway)

Castletown

Isle of Walney

Morecambe

Heysham

13 Calf of Man

DUBLIN

BIRKENHEAD LIVERPOOL

LARNE

Fleetwood

Cleveleys

A586

A585

Blackpool

M55

Blackpool

Pres

Lytham St Anne's

A584

The Small Isles

Inner Hebrides

Eigg

Muck

Coll

Arinagour

Tiree
Scarinish
Tiree

Loch Morar

Sound of Arisaig

468

Morar, Moidart & Ardnamurchan

Acharacle

Tobermory

Lochaline

Loch na Keal, Isle of Mull

Ulva

Mull

966
Ben More

Iona

Fionnphort

Loch Arkaig

Great Glen Way

Glenfinnan

Loch Shiel

A830

Loch Linnhe

Spean Bridge

Nevis Range

Port William

1343
Ben
Nevis

Kinlochleven

Ballachulish

Glen Coe

1148
Bidean
Nam Bian

Ben Nevis & Glen Coe

1079
Ben
Starav

Sound of Mull

Lynn of Lorne

1074
Ben
Dorain

Tyndrum

1124
Ben
Cruachan

Dalmally

A85

Ben
Lui

Crianlarich

1171
Ben
More

Oban

Firth of Lorne

Seil

Luing

Scarba, Lunga & The Garvellachs

Scarba

Colonsay

Scalasaig

Oronsay

Jura

784
Beinn
An Oir

Port Askaig

Islay

Portnahaven

Islay

Port Ellen

Mull of Oa

Gigha

Loch Awe

ARGYLL & BUTE

Inveraray

Argyll Forest Park

973
Ben
Lomond

Queen
Fore

Crarae Garden

Loch
Katrine
Loch Lom
& The Tross
National F

West High
Wa

Loch
Lomond

Lochgilphead

Knapdale

Helensburgh

WEST
DUNBARTONSH

Kyles of
Bute

Dunoon

Colintraive

Greenock

INVERCLYDE

Dumbar

Tarbert

Rothesay

Bute

Kennacraig

Glasgow

Paisley

RENFREWSHIR

Largs

Kilbirnie

Beith

Stewarton

EAST R

Claonaig

Sound
of Bute

North
Arran

874
Goat
Fell

Kilwinning

Kilmarnock

Kintyre

Kilbrannan Sound

Brodick

NORTH
AYRSHIRE

Ardrossan

Irvine

Lamlash

Holy
Island

Firth of
Clyde

Troon

Prestwick
Ayr

Isle of
Arran

Prestwick

Ayr

Campbeltown

Campbeltown

LARNE

Culzean Castle
& Country Park

Maybole

Mull of
Kintyre

Ailsa
Craig

Girvan

SOUTH
AYRSHIRE

North Channel

Merrick

Gallow
Forest P

LARNE
(SUMMER ONLY)

Ballantrae

BELFAST

Loch Ryan

Southern Upland Way

Stranraer

Newton Stewart

Butt of Lewis

Port of Ness
(Port Nis)

A857

Oiseval
Gallery

A858

Carloway (Carlabhagh)

A857

Broad Bay

Stornoway
(Steornabhagh)

A858

A859

Stornoway

A866

The Minch

Lewis (Leodhais)

WESTERN ISLES

Outer   Hebrides

Scarp

South Lewis,
Harris &
North Uist

A859

Taransay

Tarbert
(Tairbeart)

Shiant
Islands

Pabbay

Harris
(Hearadh)

Inverewe
Gardens

A832

Berneray

Sound of Harris

Gairloch

The Little Minch

North Uist
(Uibhist a Tuath)

Lochmaddy
(Loch nam Madadh)

Trotternish

Uig

A87

A855

Sound of Raasay

Wester R

Torridon

A865

A867

Rona

Inner Sound

Benbecula

A850

A896

Benbecula
(Beinn Na Faoghla)

Dunvegan

A863

Skye

Portree

Raasay

A865

Scalpay

A890

South Uist
(Uibhist a Deas)

A863

Kyle of Lochalsh

Drynoch

Ellean Donan
Castle

South Uist
Machair

The Cuillin Hills

A87

1009
Sgurr
Alasdair

Lochboisdale
(Loch Baghasdail)

Soay

A851

Sound of Sleat

1019
Ladhar
Bheinn

Eriskay
(Eiriosgaigh)

Canna

Cuillin

Ardvasar

Knoydart

Sound of Barra

Barra

Mallaig

Loch   Morar

Barra
(Barraigh)

Rum

Castlebay
(Bagh a Chaisteil)

The Small Isles

Sound

A830

Sandray

Eigg

Glenfinnan

Mingulay

Inner   Hebrides

Muck

Sound of Arisaig

A86

Morar, Moidart &
Ardnamurchan

Loch Shiel

466

Acharacle

A861

Coll

iii

ii

i

I

2

Haroldswick

Unst

A968

Baltasound

Fetlar

Yell Sound

Yell

Shetland (North)

St Magnus Bay

A970

Scatsta

A968

Whalsay

Papa Stour

Sandness

Mainland

Shetland Islands

A971

Tingwall

A970

Lerwick

Scalloway

Bressay

Shetland (South)

A970

SHETLAND ISLANDS

Foula

Sumburgh

Sumburgh Head

ABERDEEN

Fair Isle

Papa Westray

North Ronaldsay

The North Sound

Westray

Sanday

Westray Firth

Rousay

Eday

Sanday Sound

A966

Stronsay

A967

Mainland

Shapinsay Firth

Stronsay Firth

ORKNEY ISLANDS

Hoy & West Mainland

A965

A965

A960

Kirkwall

Kirkwall

Stromness

A961

Hoy

Orkney Islands

Burray

St Margaret's Hope

South Ronaldsay

TÓRSHAVN

Pentland Firth

Island of Stroma

Gills

Scrabster

A836

John o'Groats

Thurso

A9

A99

F

ABERDEEN

G

H

J

Wick

Aberaeron	460	D16	Bedlington	465	H10	Camborne	456	C21	Cumnock	467	E9

Aberaeron	460	D16
Aberchirder	470	G5
Aberdare	457	F18
Aberdeen	470	G6
Aberfeldy	467	E7
Abergavenny	457	F17
Abergele	460	E14
Aberlour	470	F5
Abersoch	460	D15
Aberystwyth	460	E16
Abingdon	458	H18
Aboyne	470	G6
Acharacle	466	C6
Achnasheen	469	D5
Acle	463	M15
Aldeburgh	459	M17
Aldershot	458	J19
Alford	470	G5
Alford	463	K14
Alfreton	462	H15
Alloa	467	E8
Alness	469	E4
Alnwick	465	H9
Alston	465	G11
Altnaharra	469	E3
Alton	458	J19
Amble	465	H10
Ambleside	464	F12
Amersham	458	J18
Amesbury	458	H19
Amlwch	460	D14
Ammanford	456	E17
Andover	458	H19
Annan	464	F10
Appleby-in-Westmorland	465	G11
Arbroath	467	G7
Ardrossan	466	D9
Ardvasar	468	C6
Arinagour	466	B7
Arundel	458	K20
Ashbourne	462	H15
Ashford	459	M19
Ashington	465	H10
Ashton-under-Lyne	461	G14
Attleborough	463	M16
Auchterarder	467	E7
Auchtermuchty	467	F7
Aviemore	469	E5
Avonmouth	457	G18
Axminster	457	F20
Aylesbury	458	J17
Aylsham	463	M15
Ayr	466	D9
Bacup	461	G13
Bagh a Chaisteil	468	A6
Bakewell	462	H14
Bala	460	E15
Baldock	459	K17
Ballantrae	464	D10
Ballater	470	F6
Banbury	458	H17
Banchory	470	G6
Banff	470	G4
Bangor	460	E14
Barmouth	460	E15
Barnard Castle	465	H11
Barnsley	462	H14
Barnstaple	456	E19
Barrow-in-Furness	461	F12
Barry	457	F18
Basildon	459	L18
Basingstoke	458	J19
Bath	457	G18
Battle	459	L19
Bawtry	462	J14
Beaconsfield	458	J18
Beaumaris	460	E14
Beccles	463	M16
Bedford	458	K17

Bedlington	465	H10
Beith	466	D9
Benllech	460	E14
Berwick-upon-Tweed	467	G9
Bethesda	460	E14
Bettyhill	469	E2
Betws-y-Coed	460	E15
Beverley	462	K13
Bewdley	461	G16
Bexhill	459	L20
Bicester	458	J17
Bideford	456	D19
Biggar	467	F9
Billericay	459	L18
Billingshurst	458	K19
Birkenhead	461	F14
Birmingham	458	H16
Bishop Auckland	465	H11
Bishop's Castle	461	F16
Bishop's Stortford	459	K17
Blackburn	461	G13
Blackpool	461	F13
Blaenau Ffestiniog	460	E15
Blair Atholl	467	E6
Blairgowrie	467	F7
Blandford Forum	457	G20
Blyth	465	H10
Bodmin	456	D20
Bognor Regis	458	J20
Bolsover	462	H14
Bolton	461	G14
Bonar Bridge	469	E4
Bootle	461	F14
Boston	463	K15
Bourne	462	K15
Bournemouth	458	H20
Brackley	458	J17
Bradford	462	H13
Braemar	469	F6
Braintree	459	L17
Brampton	465	G10
Brechin	467	G6
Brecon	460	F17
Brentwood	459	L18
Bridgend	457	E18
Bridgnorth	461	G16
Bridgwater	457	F19
Bridlington	463	K12
Bridport	457	F20
Brigg	462	J14
Brighton	459	K20
Bristol	457	G18
Brixham	457	E21
Broadstairs	459	M18
Brodick	466	D9
Bromsgrove	458	G16
Brora	469	E4
Brough	465	G11
Broughton-in-Furness	464	F12
Brownhills	461	H16
Buckfastleigh	456	E20
Buckie	470	F4
Buckingham	458	J17
Bude	456	D20
Builth Wells	460	F17
Bungay	463	M16
Burford	458	H17
Burnham-on-Crouch	459	L18
Burnham-on-Sea	457	F19
Burton upon Trent	462	H15
Bury	461	G13
Bury St Edmunds	459	L16
Buxton	461	H14
Caernarfon	460	D14
Caerphilly	457	F18
Caister-on-Sea	463	N15
Callander	467	E8
Calne	458	G18

Camborne	456	C21
Cambridge	459	K17
Camelford	456	D20
Campbeltown	466	C9
Cannich	469	D5
Cannock	461	G15
Canterbury	459	M19
Canvey Island	459	L18
Cardiff	457	F18
Cardigan	460	D17
Carlabhagh	468	B3
Carlisle	464	F11
Carloway	468	B3
Carmarthen	456	D17
Carnforth	461	F12
Carnoustie	467	G7
Carrbridge	469	E5
Castlebay	468	A6
Castle Douglas	464	E10
Castleford	462	H13
Castletown	460	D12
Catterick	465	H12
Chard	457	F20
Chatham	459	L18
Chatteris	459	K16
Cheddar	457	F19
Chelmsford	459	L18
Cheltenham	461	G17
Chepstow	457	G18
Chester	461	F14
Chesterfield	462	H14
Chester-le-Street	465	H11
Chichester	458	J20
Chippenham	457	G18
Chipping Norton	458	H17
Chipping Ongar	459	L18
Chorley	461	G13
Christchurch	458	H20
Church Stretton	461	F16
Cirencester	458	H18
Clacton-on-Sea	459	M17
Claonaig	466	C9
Cleethorpes	463	K14
Clevedon	457	F18
Cleveleys	461	F13
Clitheroe	461	G13
Clun	461	F16
Coalville	462	H15
Cockermouth	464	F11
Colchester	459	L17
Coldstream	467	G9
Colintraive	466	D8
Colwyn Bay	460	E14
Congleton	461	G14
Coningsby	463	K15
Consett	465	H11
Conwy	460	E14
Corbridge	465	G10
Corby	462	J16
Corwen	460	F15
Coupar Angus	467	F7
Coventry	458	H16
Cowes	458	H20
Crail	467	G8
Crawley	459	K19
Crediton	457	E20
Crewe	461	G15
Crewkerne	457	F20
Crianlarich	466	D7
Criccieth	460	D15
Cricklade	458	H18
Crieff	467	E7
Cromarty	469	E4
Cromer	463	M15
Crook	465	H11
Crowborough	459	L19
Croydon	459	K18
Cullen	470	G4
Cullompton	457	F20
Cumbernauld	467	E8

Cumnock	467	E9
Cupar	467	F7
Cwmbran	457	F18
Dalbeattie	464	E10
Dalkeith	467	F8
Dalmally	466	D7
Darlington	465	H11
Dartford	459	L18
Dartmouth	457	E21
Darwen	461	G13
Daventry	458	J16
Dawlish	457	E20
Deal	459	M19
Denbigh	460	F14
Derby	462	H15
Dereham	463	L15
Devizes	458	H18
Dewsbury	462	H13
Didcot	458	J18
Dingwall	469	E5
Diss	459	M16
Dolgellau	460	E15
Doncaster	462	J14
Dorchester	457	G20
Dorking	459	K19
Dornoch	469	E4
Douglas	460	D12
Dover	459	M19
Downham Market	463	L16
Driffield	462	K13
Droitwich	461	G16
Drummore	464	D11
Drumnadrochit	469	E5
Drynoch	468	B5
Dudley	461	G16
Dufftown	470	F5
Dumbarton	466	D8
Dumfries	464	E10
Dunbar	467	G8
Dunbeath	469	F3
Dunblane	467	E8
Dundee	467	F7
Dunfermline	467	F8
Dunoon	466	D8
Duns	467	G9
Dunstable	458	K17
Dunvegan	468	B5
Durham	465	H11
Durness	469	D2
Dyce	470	G5
Earby	461	G13
Easingwold	465	J12
Eastbourne	459	L20
East Grinstead	459	K19
East Kilbride	467	E9
Eastleigh	458	H19
East Linton	467	G8
Ebbw Vale	457	F18
Edinburgh	467	F8
Egremont	464	F11
Elgin	470	F4
Ellesmere	461	F15
Ellon	470	G5
Ely	459	L16
Epping	459	K18
Esher	458	K18
Esher	458	K18
Evesham	458	H17
Exeter	457	E20
Exmouth	457	F20
Eye	459	M16
Eyemouth	467	G8
Fakenham	463	L15
Falkirk	467	E8
Falkland	467	F8
Falmouth	456	C21
Fareham	458	J20

Place	Page	Grid	Place	Page	Grid	Place	Page	Grid	Place	Page	Grid
Faringdon	458	H18	Helensburgh	466	D8	Kirkby Stephen	465	G12	Lymington	458	H20
Farnborough	458	J19	Helmsdale	469	F3	Kirkcaldy	467	F8	Lynton	456	E19
Farnham	458	J19	Helmsley	465	J12	Kirkcudbright	464	E11	Lytham St Anne's	461	F13
Felixstowe	459	M17	Helston	456	C21	Kirkwall	471	F1			
Ffestiniog	460	E15	Henley-on-Thames	458	J18	Kirriemuir	467	F7	Mablethorpe	463	L14
Filey	462	K12	Hereford	461	G17	Knaresborough	462	H13	Macclesfield	461	G14
Fionnphort	466	B7	Herne Bay	459	M18	Knighton	461	F16	Machynlleth	460	E16
Fishguard	460	C17	Hertford	459	K17	Knutsford	461	G14	Maesteg	457	E18
Fleetwood	461	F13	Hertford	459	K17	Kyle of Lochalsh	468	C5	Maghull	461	F14
Folkestone	459	M19	Hexham	465	G10				Maidenhead	458	J18
Fordingbridge	458	H19	Heysham	461	F12	Lairg	469	E4	Maidstone	459	L19
Forfar	467	F7	High Wycombe	458	J18	Lamlash	466	D9	Maldon	459	L18
Formby	461	F14	Hinckley	462	H16	Lampeter	460	E17	Mallaig	468	C6
Forres	469	F5	Holbeach	463	K15	Lanark	467	E9	Malmesbury	457	G18
Fort Augustus	469	D6	Holmfirth	462	H14	Lancaster	461	F12	Malton	465	J12
Fortrose	469	E5	Holsworthy	456	D20	Langholm	464	F10	Manchester	461	G14
Fortuneswell	457	G20	Holt	463	M15	Langport	457	F19	Mansfield	462	J14
Fort William	466	D6	Holyhead	460	D14	Largs	466	D9	March	463	K16
Fowey	456	D21	Holywell	461	F14	Lauder	467	G9	Margate	459	M18
Framlingham	459	M16	Honiton	457	F20	Launceston	456	D20	Market Deeping	462	K15
Fraserburgh	470	G4	Horncastle	463	K14	Laurencekirk	467	G6	Market Drayton	461	G15
Frinton-on-Sea	459	M17	Hornsea	463	K13	Leamington Spa	458	H16	Market Harborough	458	J16
Frome	457	G19	Horsham	459	K19	Leatherhead	459	K19	Market Rasen	462	K14
			Howden	462	J13	Lechlade on Thames	458	H18	Market Weighton	462	J13
Gainsborough	462	J14	Huddersfield	462	H13	Ledbury	461	G17	Marlborough	458	H18
Gairloch	468	C4	Hugh Town	456	C19	Leeds	462	H13	Maryport	464	F11
Galashiels	467	F9	Hungerford	458	H18	Leek	461	G15	Masham	465	H12
Galston	466	D9	Hunstanton	463	L15	Leicester	462	J16	Matlock	462	H15
Gatehouse of Fleet	464	E11	Huntingdon	459	K16	Leighton Buzzard	458	J17	Maybole	466	D9
Gateshead	465	H10	Huntly	470	G5	Leominster	461	F17	Melksham	457	G18
Gills	470	F2	Hythe	458	H20	Lerwick	471	Hii	Melrose	467	G9
Girvan	464	D10	Hythe	459	M19	Letchworth	459	K17	Melton Mowbray	462	J15
Glasgow	467	E8				Leven	467	F8	Melvich	469	E2
Glastonbury	457	F19	Ilchester	457	G19	Lewes	459	K19	Menai Bridge	460	E14
Glenrothes	467	F8	Ilfracombe	456	E19	Leyburn	465	H12	Mere	457	G19
Glossop	461	H14	Ilkley	461	H13	Leyland	461	G13	Merthyr Tydfil	457	F18
Gloucester	457	G17	Ilminster	457	F19	Lichfield	461	H16	Middlesbrough	465	H11
Godalming	458	J19	Immingham	463	K13	Lincoln	462	J14	Middlewich	461	G14
Golspie	469	E4	Inchnadamph	469	D3	Liskeard	456	D20	Midhurst	458	J19
Goole	462	J13	Innerleithen	467	F9	Littlehampton	458	K20	Mildenhall	459	L16
Grain	459	L18	Inveraray	466	D8	Littleport	459	L16	Milford Haven	456	C18
Grantham	462	J15	Inverbervie	467	G6	Liverpool	461	F14	Millom	464	F12
Grantown-on-Spey	469	F5	Invergarry	469	D6	Livingston	467	F8	Milton Keynes	458	J17
Gravesend	459	L18	Invergordon	469	E4	Lizard	456	C21	Minehead	457	E19
Great Dunmow	459	L17	Invermoriston	469	D5	Llandeilo	456	E17	Moffat	464	F10
Great Malvern	461	G17	Inverness	469	E5	Llandovery	460	E17	Mold	461	F14
Great Torrington	456	D19	Inverurie	470	G5	Llandrindod Wells	460	F16	Monmouth	457	G17
Great Yarmouth	463	N16	Ipswich	459	M17	Llandudno	460	E14	Montrose	467	G7
Greenlaw	467	G9	Irvine	466	D9	Llanelli	456	E18	Morecambe	461	F12
Greenock	466	D8	Ivybridge	456	E21	Llanfyllin	461	F15	Morpeth	465	H10
Gretna	464	F10				Llangefni	460	D14	Motherwell	467	E9
Grimsby	463	K13	Jedburgh	467	G9	Llangollen	461	F15	Muir of Ord	469	E5
Guildford	458	J19	John o' Groats	470	F2	Llangurig	460	E16			
Guisborough	465	J11				Llanidloes	460	E16	Nailsworth	457	G18
			Keighley	461	H13	Llanrwst	460	E14	Nairn	469	E5
Haddington	467	G8	Keith	470	F5	Llanwrtyd Wells	460	E17	Nantwich	461	G15
Hadleigh	459	M17	Kelso	467	G9	Lochaline	466	C7	Narberth	456	D17
Hailsham	459	L20	Kendal	465	G12	Loch Baghasdail	468	A5	Neath	457	E18
Halesworth	459	M16	Kennacraig	466	C8	Lochboisdale	468	A5	Nefyn	460	D15
Halifax	461	H13	Keswick	464	F11	Lochearnhead	467	E7	Newark-on-Trent	462	J15
Halstead	459	L17	Kettering	458	J16	Lochgilphead	466	C8	Newburgh	467	F7
Hamilton	467	E9	Kidderminster	461	G16	Lochinver	469	D3	Newbury	458	H18
Hanley	461	G15	Kidlington	458	H17	Lochmaben	464	F10	Newcastle Emlyn	460	D17
Harlech	460	E15	Kidwelly	456	D18	Lochmaddy	468	A4	Newcastle-under-Lyme	461	G15
Harleston	459	M16	Kilbirnie	466	D9	Loch nam Madadh	468	A4	Newcastle upon Tyne	465	H10
Harlow	459	K17	Killin	467	E7	Lockerbie	464	F10	New Galloway	464	E10
Haroldswick	471	Jiv	Kilmarnock	466	D9	London	459	K18	Newhaven	459	K20
Harrogate	462	H13	Kilsyth	467	E8	Longtown	464	F10	Newmarket	459	L16
Hartlepool	465	J11	Kilwinning	466	D9	Looe	456	D21	Newport	458	H20
Harwich	459	M17	Kincardine	467	E8	Lossiemouth	470	F4	Newport	457	F18
Haslemere	458	J19	Kingsbridge	456	E21	Lostwithiel	456	D20	Newport	461	G15
Hastings	459	L20	King's Lynn	463	L15	Loughborough	462	J15	Newport-on-Tay	467	F7
Hatfield	459	K18	Kingston upon Hull	462	K13	Louth	463	K14	Newquay	456	C20
Haverfordwest	456	C17	Kington	461	F17	Lowestoft	463	N16	New Romney	459	M19
Haverhill	459	L17	Kingussie	469	E6	Ludlow	461	G16	Newton Abbot	457	E20
Hawick	467	G9	Kinlochewe	469	D4	Luton	458	K17	Newton Aycliffe	465	H11
Hayle	456	C21	Kinlochleven	466	D6	Lutterworth	458	J16	Newtonmore	469	E6
Hay-on-Wye	461	F17	Kinross	467	F8	Lybster	470	F3	Newton Stewart	464	D10
Haywards Heath	459	K19	Kintore	470	G5	Lydd	459	M19	Newtown	461	F16
Heathfield	459	L19	Kirkby Lonsdale	465	G12	Lyme Regis	457	F20	Northallerton	465	H12

Northam	456	D19
Northampton	458	J16
North Berwick	467	G8
North Walsham	463	M15
Northwich	461	G14
Norwich	463	M16
Nottingham	462	J15
Nuneaton	462	H16
Oakham	462	J16
Oban	466	C7
Okehampton	456	E20
Oldham	461	G14
Oldmeldrum	470	G5
Ormskirk	461	F14
Orpington	459	K18
Oswestry	461	F15
Otley	462	H13
Oundle	462	K16
Oxford	458	J18
Padstow	456	C20
Paignton	457	E20
Paisley	466	D8
Peebles	467	F9
Peel	464	D12
Pembroke	456	C18
Pembroke Dock	456	C18
Penarth	457	F18
Pendine	456	D18
Penicuik	467	F8
Penrith	465	G11
Penryn	456	C21
Penzance	456	B21
Pershore	461	G17
Perth	467	F7
Peterborough	463	K16
Peterculter	470	G6
Peterhead	470	H5
Peterlee	465	H11
Petersfield	458	J19
Pickering	465	J12
Pitlochry	467	E7
Pittenweem	467	G8
Plymouth	456	D21
Pontefract	462	H13
Pontypool	457	F18
Pontypridd	457	F18
Poole	458	H20
Port Askaig	466	B8
Port Einon	456	D18
Port Ellen	466	B9
Port Erin	460	D12
Porthcawl	457	E18
Porthmadog	460	E15
Portnahaven	466	B9
Port Nis	468	C2
Port of Ness	468	C2
Portpatrick	464	C11
Portree	468	B5
Portsmouth	458	J20
Portsoy	470	G4
Port Talbot	457	E18
Preston	461	G13
Prestwick	466	D9
Pulborough	458	K19
Pwllheli	460	D15
Queensferry	461	F14
Radstock	457	G19
Ramsey	464	D12
Ramsgate	459	M18
Ravenglass	464	F12
Rayleigh	459	L18
Reading	458	J18
Redcar	465	J11
Redditch	458	H16
Redhill	459	K19
Redruth	456	C21
Reigate	459	K19
Retford	462	J14
Rhayader	460	E16
Rhosneigr	460	D14
Rhyl	460	F14
Richmond	459	K18
Richmond	465	H12
Ringwood	458	H20
Ripley	462	H15
Ripon	465	H12
Rochdale	461	G13
Rochester	459	L18
Romsey	458	H19
Ross-on-Wye	461	G17
Rotherham	462	H14
Rothes	470	F5
Rothesay	466	D8
Royston	459	K17
Rugby	458	J16
Rugeley	461	H15
Runcorn	461	G14
Rushden	458	J16
Ruthin	461	F15
Ryde	458	J20
Rye	459	L19
Saffron Walden	459	L17
St Albans	458	K18
St Andrews	467	G7
St Austell	456	D21
St Clears	456	D17
St David's	460	C17
St Helens	461	G14
St Ives	456	C21
St Just	456	B21
St Margaret's Hope	471	F2
St Mawes	456	C21
St Neots	459	K16
Salcombe	456	E21
Salisbury	458	H19
Saltash	456	D21
Sandness	471	Hii
Sandown	458	J20
Sandwich	459	M19
Sandy	459	K17
Sanquhar	467	E9
Saxmundham	459	M16
Scalasaig	466	B8
Scalloway	471	Hii
Scarborough	462	K12
Scarinish	466	B7
Scotch Corner	465	H12
Scourie	469	D3
Scrabster	469	F2
Scunthorpe	462	J13
Seaham	465	H11
Seaton	457	F20
Sedbergh	465	G12
Selby	462	J13
Selkirk	467	F9
Settle	461	G12
Sevenoaks	459	L19
Shaftesbury	457	G19
Shanklin	458	J20
Sheerness	459	L18
Sheffield	462	H14
Shepton Mallet	457	G19
Sherborne	457	G19
Sheringham	463	M15
Shrewsbury	461	F15
Sidmouth	457	F20
Sittingbourne	459	L18
Skegness	463	L14
Skelmersdale	461	F14
Skipton	461	G13
Sleaford	462	K15
Slough	458	J18
Southampton	458	H19
South Ballachulish	466	D7
Southend-on-Sea	459	L18
South Molton	456	E19
Southport	461	F13
South Shields	465	H10
Southwold	459	N16
Spalding	463	K15
Spean Bridge	469	D6
Stafford	461	G15
Staines	458	K18
Stamford	462	K16
Steornabhagh	468	B3
Stevenage	459	K17
Stewarton	466	D9
Stirling	467	E8
Stockbridge	458	H19
Stockport	461	G14
Stocksbridge	462	H14
Stockton-on-Tees	465	H11
Stoke-on-Trent (Hanley)	461	G15
Stone	461	G15
Stonehaven	470	G6
Stornoway	468	B3
Stourbridge	461	G16
Stowmarket	459	M17
Stow-on-the-Wold	458	H17
Stranraer	464	D10
Stratford-upon-Avon	458	H17
Strathaven	467	E9
Street	457	F19
Stromness	471	F2
Stroud	457	G18
Sudbury	459	L17
Sunderland	465	H11
Sutton	459	K18
Sutton Coldfield	461	H16
Swadlincote	462	H15
Swaffham	463	L16
Swanage	458	H20
Swansea	456	E18
Swindon	458	H18
Tadcaster	462	H13
Tain	469	E4
Tairbeart	468	B4
Talgarth	461	F17
Tamworth	462	H16
Tarbert	466	C8
Tarbert	468	B4
Taunton	457	F19
Tavistock	456	D20
Teignmouth	457	E20
Telford	461	G16
Tenterden	459	L19
Tetbury	457	G18
Tewkesbury	461	G17
Thame	458	J18
Thatcham	458	J18
Thetford	459	L16
Thirsk	465	H12
Thorne	462	J13
Thornhill	464	E10
Thrapston	458	J16
Thurso	469	F2
Tilbury	459	L18
Tiverton	457	E19
Tobermory	466	C7
Tomintoul	469	F5
Tonbridge	459	L19
Tongue	469	E3
Torpoint	456	D21
Torquay	457	E20
Totnes	457	E20
Towcester	458	J17
Tregaron	460	E16
Troon	466	D9
Trowbridge	457	G19
Truro	456	C21
Tunbridge Wells	459	L19
Turriff	470	G5
Tyndrum	466	D7
Tynemouth	465	H10
Tywyn	460	E16
Uckfield	459	K19
Uig	468	B4
Ullapool	469	D4
Ulverston	464	F12
Usk	457	F18
Uttoxeter	461	H15
Ventnor	458	J20
Wadebridge	456	C20
Wakefield	462	H13
Wallasey	461	F14
Wallingford	458	J18
Walsall	461	H16
Wantage	458	H18
Wareham	457	G20
Warminster	457	G19
Warrington	461	G14
Warwick	458	H16
Washington	465	H11
Watford	458	K18
Watton	463	L16
Wellingborough	458	J16
Wellington	457	F19
Wells	457	G19
Wells-next-the-sea	463	L15
Welshpool	461	F16
Westbury	457	G19
Weston-Super-Mare	457	F18
Wetherby	462	H13
Weymouth	457	G20
Whitby	465	J11
Whitchurch	461	G15
Whitehaven	464	E11
Whitehill and Bordon	458	J19
Whithorn	464	D11
Whitstable	459	M18
Wick	470	F3
Wickham Market	459	M17
Widnes	461	G14
Wigan	461	G14
Wigston	462	J16
Wigton	464	F11
Wigtown	464	D11
Wilton	458	H19
Wimborne Minster	458	H20
Wincanton	457	G19
Winchester	458	H19
Windermere	464	F12
Wisbech	463	K16
Witham	459	L17
Withernsea	463	K13
Witney	458	H17
Wolverhampton	461	G16
Woodbridge	459	M17
Wooler	467	G9
Worcester	461	G17
Workington	464	F11
Worksop	462	J14
Worthing	458	K20
Wragby	462	K14
Wrexham	461	F15
Wymondham	463	M16
Yarmouth	458	H20
Yeovil	457	G19
York	462	J13

A

Abbotsbury 121
Abbotsbury Swannery 121
Abbotsford 361
Aberdeen 361, 394, 400, 406
Aberdulais Falls 225
Abergavenny 241, 252, 256, 260
Aberystwyth 225, 252, 256, 260
accommodation 444–445
    bed-and-breakfast 444
    bothies 444
    camping 444
    caravanning 444–445
    farm stays 445
    home exchange agencies 445
    hostels 445
    hotels 445
    pubs 445
    self-catering 445
    (see also individual regions)
Acharacle 391
Achiltibuie 385, 400–401
adaptors 419
air travel 44–45
    airport buses 55
    airports 44
    child passengers 61
    disabilities, visitors with 62
    domestic 57–58
    health hazards for flyers 417
Aldeburgh 173, 206, 211
Alfriston 173
Allum Green 205
Alnwick Castle 303
alternative medical treatments 418
Althorp 267
Alton Towers 267
Amberley Working Museum 173
Ambleside 326
Anglesey 226, 256
Anstruther 365
Antony House 121
Arbeia Roman Fort 308
architectural periods 446–449
Ardnamurchan Point 391
Arisaig 390
Arlington Court 150–151
Arran, Isle of 361, 394, 401
Arthurian legend 133, 142, 198
arts, media and culture 24–5
Arundel 173, 211, 212, 218
Ashdown Forest 173

ATMs (cashpoints) 415
Audley End House and Gardens 174
Augustine, St. 29, 177
Austen, Jane 125, 137, 185, 279
Avebury 10, 121
Aviemore 362, 395, 406
Avoncroft Museum of Historic Buildings 267
Aysgarth Falls 339

B

Bakewell 283, 286, 292, 296
Ballater 361, 406
Balmoral Castle 361
Bamburgh Castle 303
banks 415, 425
Bannockburn 385
Bardsey Island 233
Barnard Castle 319
Barton Farm Country Park 126
Bateman's 174
Bath 10, 12, 122–125, 154–155, 159
    accommodation 166
    American Museum in Britain 125
    Assembly Rooms 124
    Bath Abbey 123–124
    Building of Bath Museum 125
    Fashion Museum and Jane Austen Centre 125
    No. 1 Royal Crescent 124–125
    Pump Room 123
    restaurants 160
    Roman Baths 123
Bath, Marquess of 18
Battle Abbey 184
beaches 431
Beachy Head 174
Beamish, the North of England Open Air Museum 303
Beatles 314, 347
Beaulieu 174
Beaumaris 226, 261
Beck Isle Museum of Rural Life 330, 331
Becket, St. Thomas 31, 177
Becky Falls 130
bed-and-breakfast 444
Beddgelert 249
Bedruthan Steps 121
Behn, Aphra 35

Bellingham 334
Belvoir Castle 267
Bempton Cliffs 303
Ben Nevis 370
Berkeley Castle 121
Berwick-upon-Tweed 303
Beverley 304, 342, 349
Bewcastle 335
Big Pit National Mining Museum 225
Bignor Roman Villa 10, 174
Birdoswald Fort 308, 335
Birmingham 47, 267 286–287, 291, 293, 296–297
    Birmingham Botanical Gardens 267
    Birmingham Museum and Art Gallery 267
    Cadbury World 267, 268
    Jewellery Quarter 267
Black Country Living Museum 268
Black House at Arnol 380
Black Mountains 227, 240, 241
Blackgang Chine 210
Blackpool 304
Blackwell, the Arts and Crafts House 304
Blaenau Ffestiniog 237, 249
Blaenavon World Heritage Site 225
Blair Castle 361
Blenheim Palalce 177
Blue John Cavern 275, 285
blue plaques 21
Boat of Garten 362
Bodelwyddan Castle 225
Bodiam Castle 177
Bodmin Moor 126
Bodnant Garden 10, 227
Bolderwood 192, 202
Bolton Abbey 321, 349, 354
Bolton Castle 321
Border Forest Park 334
Bosherton Lily Ponds 236
bothies 444
Bournemouth 126, 155, 161, 166
Bowes Museum 319
Bowhill House 387
Bowood House and Gardens 126
Bradford 304, 342
Bradford-on-Avon 126, 161, 167
Braemar 361, 399
Bratton Castle 145

Brecon 227, 240, 252, 255, 256
Brecon Beacons Mountain Centre 240
Brecon Beacons National Park 227, 240–241
Brecon Mountain Railway 240
Brighton 175, 206–7, 211, 218–19
    Brighton Museum and Art Gallery 175
    Brighton Pier 175
    Brighton Sea Life Centre 175
    Royal Pavilion 175
    restaurants 212–13
Brimham Rocks 304
Bristol 127, 155–156, 159, 161, 167
    British Empire and Commonwealth Museum 19, 127
    Clifton Suspension Bridge 38, 127
    SS *Great Britain* 127
Britain: concept of 6
British Museum 10, 74–75
Britten, Benjamin 173
Brixham 126
The Broads 176
Broadstairs 177, 211
Brockenhurst 203, 213
Brodick Castle 361
Bronllys Castle 240
Brontë sisters 309, 319
Broughton 386
Brown, Gordon 7, 16
Brownsea Island 126
Brunel, Isambard Kingdom 38, 127, 448
Bryncelli Ddu 226
Buchan, John 386
Buckden 339
Buckfast Abbey 128
Buckfast Butterfly Farm 128
Buckfastleigh 128
Buckingham Palace 76
Buckland Abbey 128
bureaux de change 415
Burghley House 196
Burnham Market 177
Burnham Overy Staithe 177
Burnham Thorpe 177
buses 12, 46, 54–55, 62
Buxton 268, 283, 287, 291, 297
Byland Abbey 317

C

Cadbury World 267, 268
Cadgwith 135
Caer Caradoc 270
Caerlaverock Castle 363
Caerleon Roman Fortress
   and Baths 227
Caernarfon 227, 237, 261
Caernarfon Castle 10, 31
Caerphilly Castle 229
Cairngorms 362
Calanais Standing Stones
   11, 380
Caldey Island 238
Caldicot Castle 229
Caledonian Canal 392–393
Calke Abbey 268
Callander 363, 401, 407
Cambridge 178–9, 207
   accommodation 219
   colleges 178–9
   Fitzwilliam Museum 179
   Kettle's Yard 179
   King's College Chapel
      178–179, 211
   restaurants 213
   University Botanic Garden
      179
Camelot Theme Park 306
Campbell, Donald 311
Campbell, Sir Malcolm 311
Campbeltown 377
Camperdown Wildlife Centre
   395
camping 444
Canterbury 177, 213, 219
car industry 17
car rental 48, 49
caravanning 444–445
Cardiff 228, 252–3, 255
   accommodation 261
   Butetown History and
      Arts Centre 228
   Cardiff Castle 228
   Norwegian Church 228
   restaurants 257
   Techniquest 228
Cardigan Bay 225
Carew Castle 236
Carisbrooke Castle 186
Carreg Cennen Castle
   229
Carreg Sampson 245
Castell Coch 229
Castell Dinas Bran 235
Castell Henllys 236, 245
Castle Bolton 339
Castle Drogo 130, 146,
   147
Castle Howard 11, 306

Castle of Mey 377
Castle Rising 180
Castle Rushen 311
Castle Tioram 391
Castlerigg Stone Circle 11,
   312, 329
Castleton 275, 282, 284–5,
   291
Catalyst Museum 306
Cauldron Snout 319
Cave Dale 284
Cawdor Castle 363
Caxton, William 33
Cefn Bryn 232
Celtica 229
Centre for Alternative
   Technology 230
Cerne Abbas 128
Charlecote Park 270
Charles, Prince of Wales 15,
   20, 42, 227
Charles Edward Stuart,
   Prince (Bonnie Prince
   Charlie) 361, 363, 371,
   384, 385, 390
Chartwell 180
Chatham Historic Dockyard
   180
Chatsworth House 11, 269,
   282
Chawton 185
Cheddar Gorge 128, 156
Cheesewring 126
Cheltenham 128–129, 156,
   159, 161, 167
Chepstow 239, 253, 261
Chesil Beach 129
Chester 306, 342, 347, 349,
   355
Chesters Roman Fort 308
Cheviot Hills 317
Chichester 180–181, 207,
   211
children 61, 433
Chiltern Open Air Museum
   181
Chirk Castle 230
Church Stretton 270
Churchill, Sir Winston 41,
   91, 177, 180, 181
Chysauster Ancient Village
   140
cinema 427, 434
Cinque Ports 195
Cirencester 129, 156
Cleveland Way 317
climate and seasons
   412–413
Clive of India 237
clothing 419

Clovelly 129, 167
clubs 430
Clumber Park 270
coaches 54, 62
Coleridge, Samuel Taylor
   137, 150
concessions 415, 425
Coniston Water 311, 312,
   342
conversion chart 419
Conwy 231, 237, 261
   Conwy Castle 231
   Plas Mawr 231
   Smallest House 231
Cook, Captain James 320
Corbridge Roman Site 308
Corfe Castle 129
Corsham Court 129
Cotehele 129
Cotswold Water Park 156
Coventry Cathedral 270
Cowes 186, 211
Coxwold 317
Cragside 306
Crail 365
Crarae Garden 363
Crathes Castle 363
credit cards 415
Criccieth 233
Crickhowell 241
crime 424
Cromford 275, 282–283
Cromwell, Oliver 34, 35, 181
Crown Jewels 90
Cuckmere Haven 174
Culloden 363
Culross 364
Culzean Castle and Country
   Park 364
Cumberland Pencil Museum
   329
customs regulations 414
cycling 59, 431–432

D

Dan-yr-Ogof National Show
   caves 230
Danby 331
Dartington Crystal 157
Dartmeet 147
Dartmoor National Park 130,
   146–149
Dartmoor Otter Sanctuary
   128
Dartmouth 130, 161–162
Darwin, Charles 181
Dawyck Botanic Garden
   386, 387
Deep Sea World 364
Deeside 361

dental treatment 418
Derwentwater 328, 329
Desert Island Discs 41
Diana, Princess of Wales 42,
   79, 267
Dickens, Charles 39, 73,
   177, 211
Dinorwig Power Station 248
disabilities, visitors with
   62, 419
distilleries 382, 384, 394,
   398
doctors 418
Dog Collar Museum 187
Dolaucothi Gold Mines 230
Dolgellau 237, 253, 261
Dolly the Sheep 26
Dolwyddelan Castle 249
Dorchester 130, 162, 167
Douglas 311
Doune Castle 364
Dove Cottage 312, 326
Dover Castle 10, 181
Down House 181
Doyle, Arthur Conan 39
Drake, Sir Francis 128, 138
Drayton Manor Theme Park
   290
dress code 438–439
drinking water 417
drives
   Brecon Beacons National
      Park 240–241
   Exmoor National Park
      150–151
   Lake District National
      Park 326–327
   New Forest 202–203
   North York Moors
      National Park 330–331
   Northumberland National
      Park and the Border
      Forest Park 334–335
   Peak District National
      Park 282–3
   Pembrokeshire Coast
      National Park 244–5
   Scottish Borders 386–387
   Snowdonia National Park
      248–249
   western Highlands
      390–391
   Yorkshire Dales National
      Park 338–339
driving 48–51
   accidents and
      breakdowns 50, 51
   car rental 48, 49
   distances and journey
      times 51

fuel 48
motorways 50
parking 49, 50
road signs 49
Druids 28
Du Maurier, Daphne 157
Dun Carloway Broch 380
Dundee 365, 395, 407
Discovery 365
Sensation Dundee 365
Verdant Works 365
Dunkeld 365, 395, 407
Dunkery Beacon 132, 151
Dunnet Head 377
Dunstanburgh Castle 306
Dunster 130
Dunvegan Castle 384
Durham 305, 349, 355
Durham Castle 305
Durham Cathedral 305
Durham Miners Heritage
Centre 305
Houghall Gardens 305
Oriental Museum 305

E
East Neuk 365
eating out 438–443
afternoon tea 442
alcohol 439–440
breakfasts 439
cafés, brasseries and
bistros 440
fast food 440
meat and fish 439
menu reader 441
pub food 440
sandwiches and picnics
15, 439
vegetarian food 439
see also restaurants
economy 6, 17, 26
Eden Project 131
Edgbaston Cricket Museum
287
Edinburgh 37, 366–9, 395–6,
399
accommodation 407
Arthur's Seat 368
Canongate Kirk 369
Edinburgh Castle
366–367
Georgian House 367
Greyfriars Bobby 369
John Knox House 367–368
Museum of Edinburgh
367
National Gallery of
Modern Art and Dean
Gallery 368

National Gallery of
Scotland 367
National Museum of
Scotland 367
New Town 37, 367
Our Dynamic Earth 369
Palace of Holyroodhouse
367
restaurants 401–402
Royal Botanic Garden
368
Royal Mile 367–368
Scotch Whisky Heritage
Centre 367
Scottish National Portrait
Gallery 369
Writers' Museum 367
Edinburgh Fringe Festival
19, 399
Eilean Ban 384
Eilean Donan Castle 11,
370
Eisteddfod 235, 255, 436
Elan Valley 230
Electric Mountain 233, 248,
249
electricity 419
Elegug Stacks 236
Elgar Birthplace Museum
280
Elie 365
Elizabeth I 33, 34, 91, 184,
273
Elizabeth II 14, 195
Elizabeth, the Queen Mother
42, 371, 377
Ely 181, 213, 219
embassies 424
emergencies 424
emergency telephone
numbers 424
entertainment and nightlife
430
listings 430
entrance fees 425
Erddig 232
Eton College 200, 201
Ettrick Water 388–389
Eureka! The Museum for
Children 310
euro 415–416
European Union 7, 42
Eurotunnel 41
Exbury Gardens and Steam
Railway 182, 203
Exeter 132, 156, 162, 167
Exford 151
Exmoor National Park 132,
150–153
Eyam 282

F
Fairhaven Woodland and
Water Garden 176
Falkirk Wheel 370
Falkland Palace 370
Falmouth 132, 156–157,
162–163, 167–168
farm stays 445
Farne Islands 310
fashion 25
Felbrigg Hall 182
ferries 56, 61, 62
festivals and events 436
London 107
Midlands 291
the North 347
Scotland 399
South East and East
Anglia 211
Wales 255
West Country 159
Ffestiniog Railway 233, 249
first-aid kit 417, 419
Fishbourne Roman Palace
181
Fishguard 236, 245
flag flying 19
Flambards Experience 157
Flamingoland Theme Park
and Zoo 344
Fleet Air Arm Museum 132
flooding 413
Floors Castle 377
Fordingbridge 202
Fort William 370, 390, 396,
402, 408
Foster, Norman 24, 192,
234, 449
Fountains Abbey 307
Fowey 132–133, 163, 168
fox hunting 21
Fox Talbot Museum 134
Freud, Sigmund 78
Friar's Crag 328
Fyfield Down 121
Fylingdales Ballistic Missile
Early Warning Radar
Station 330
Fyvie Castle 370

G
Galashiels 386–7
Garn Fawr 236
gay and lesbian scene430
George III 37, 145
Gerald of Wales 31, 244
Gigha, Isle of 378
Gilsland 335
Gladstone, W. E.250
Glamis Castle 371

Glasgow 372–375, 397, 399
accommodation 408
airport 44
Botanic Gardens 375
Burrell Collection 11, 372
Clydebuilt 375
Gallery of Modern Art
(GoMA) 373
Glasgow Necropolis 373
Glasgow School of Art
373
Glasgow Science Centre
373
House for an Art Lover
373–374
Hunterian Museum and
Art Gallery 373, 374
Mackintosh Trail 373–5
People's Palace 375
restaurants 402–403
St. Mungo Museum of
Religious Life and Art
375
Scottish Football
Museum 375
Subway 47
Tall Ship at Glasgow
Harbour 375
Tenement House 375
Willow Tearooms 373
Glastonbury 133, 159
Glen Affric 371
Glen Coe 371
Glenfinnan 371, 390
Gloucester 133, 157
Glyndwr, Owain 32, 229, 240
Goathland 332
Goonhilly Earth Station 135
Gordale Scar 321
Gosforth 327
Gospel Pass 227, 241
Gosport 193
Gower Peninsula 232
Grasmere 326
Grassington 321, 339, 355
Great Dixter 182
Great Fire of London (1666)
96–97
Great Glen 376
Great Orme Mines 233
Great Whin Sill 336
Green Bridge of Wales 236
Greenwood Forest Park
232, 254
Grimspound 146
Grinton 338
Grizedale Forest 343
Grosmont 330
guidebooks and maps 427
Guy Fawkes Night 436

H

Haddington 371
Haddon Hall 271
Hadrian's Wall 11, 308, 335, 336–337
Halifax 310, 350
Hampton Court Palace 10, 183
Handel, George Friederic 21
Hardknott Roman Fort 327
Hardwick Hall 271
Hardy, Thomas 130
Harewood House and Bird Garden 310
Harlech Castle 232
Harlow Carr Botanical Garden 310
Harris, Isle of 380, 403, 408
Harris tweed 428
Harrogate 12, 310, 343, 347, 350, 355
Hastings 30, 184
Hatfield House 184
Haverfordwest 244, 245, 262
Hawkshead 310–311, 355
Haworth 309, 350–351, 355
Hay-on-Wye 227, 240, 255, 257, 262
Haytor 148–149
health 417–418
Hebden Bridge 311
Heights of Abraham 282, 288
Helford 135
Helmsley 317, 351, 355
Hendrix, Jimi 21
Hengistbury Head 126
Henry VIII 32, 183, 187
Heptonstall 311
Hepworth, Barbara 140
Hereford 271, 287, 294, 297
Hermitage Castle 334, 335
Hever Castle and Gardens 184
Hexham 311
Hickling Broad 176
Hidcote Manor Garden 133
High Force 319
Highclere Castle 184
Highland Folk Museum 376
Hill Top 312
history 27–42
    Act of Union (1707) 35
    English Civil War 34, 35, 280
    Industrial Revolution 36
    Magna Carta 31, 139
    medieval Britain 30–31
    Napoleonic Wars 37, 246–247
    Norman Conquest 30
    prehistoric era 28
    Roman Britain 28, 29
    Tudor Britain 32–33
    twentieth century 40–41
    twenty-first century 42
    Victorian Britain 38–39
    Wars of the Roses 32, 33, 229, 232, 319
    world wars 40, 41
Hogmanay 12
Hole of Horcum 330
Holker Hall 311
Holkham Hall 185
Holst Birthplace Museum 129
Holyhead Mountain 226
home exchange agencies 445
Honister Slate Mine 327
Horseshoe Falls 235
hospitals 417
hostels 445
hotels 445 see also individual regions
Houghton Hall 185
Housesteads Roman Fort 308
How Stean Gorge 338
Howgill Fells 321
Hoy 381
Hubberholme 339
Hull 311, 343
Hutton-le-Hole 317, 331

I

Ightham Mote 185
immunization 417
Imperial War Museum, Duxford 179
Imperial War Museum, London 79
Imperial War Museum North 315
Inner Hebrides 378
Innerleithen 386, 403, 408
insurance 414, 417
internet access 421
Inveraray 376
Inverewe Gardens 11, 376
Inverness 376, 403, 408–409
Iona 378
Ironbridge Gorge Museums 11, 272, 287
Islay, Isle of 378, 403, 409
Isle of Man 311, 347, 355–356
Isle of Wight 186, 211, 214, 219–220
Isles of Scilly 133, 163, 168

J

James, Henry 195
Jane Austen's House 185
Jarlshof Prehistoric and Norse Settlement 383
Jedburgh 377, 397, 409
Jervaulx Abbey 338, 341
Jodrell Bank Observatory and Arboretum 273
John O'Groats 377
Johnson, Amy 26, 85
Johnson, Samuel 273
Jura, Isle of 378

K

Keats, John 78
Kelso 377, 409
Kendal 312, 343
Kenilworth Castle 273
Kent's Cavern 142
Keswick 312, 347, 351, 356
Kettlewell 339
Kielder Castle 334
Kielder Forest 317, 334
Kielder Water 317, 334, 343
Killin 377
Kilnsey Crag 321, 339
Kingston Lacy 133
Kintyre 377
Kipling, Rudyard 174
Kirkcudbright 380, 397, 403–404, 409
Kirkwall 381
Knebworth House 185
Knightwood Oak 204
Knole 187
Kylerhea Otter Haven 384
Kynance Cove 135

L

Lacock Abbey 134
Ladies of Llangollen 235
Lake District National Park 312, 326–327
Lakeland Motor Museum 311
Lamphey 244
Land's End 134
Lanercost Priory 335
Langdale 326
language 7
    glossary 452
    menu reader 441
Lanhydrock House 134
laptops 421
Lastingham 331
Laugharne 232, 257
Launceston 135, 157
laundry 419
Layer Marney Tower 187

Leeds 313, 344, 351, 356
    City Art Gallery 313
    Henry Moore Institute 313
    Leeds Industrial Museum 313
    Royal Armouries Museum 313
    Temple Newsam 313
    Thackray Medical Museum 313
Leeds Castle 187
Lepe Country Park 203
Lerwick 383, 399
Levisham 330
Lewis, Isle of 380, 397
Leyburn 338
licensing laws 23, 425, 439
Lichfield 273
Liddell, Alice 202, 208
Lincoln 273, 294
Lindisfarne (Holy Island) 312
Lindisfarne Castle 312
Lindisfarne Gospels 29, 312
Lindisfarne Priory 11, 312
listed buildings 452
Little Moreton Hall 273
Liverpool 314, 344–345, 347, 351, 356
    Aintree Racecourse 344, 347
    Albert Dock 314, 344
    Anglican Liverpool Cathedral 314
    Beatles Story 314
    Maritime Museum 314
    Metropolitan Cathedral 314
    Royal Liver Building 314
    Tate Liverpool 314
    Walker Art Gallery 314
The Lizard 135, 157
Llanberis 233, 248, 254, 257, 262
Llanddwyn Island 226
Llandrindod Wells 233, 255, 262
Llandudno 233, 237, 254
Llangollen 235, 262
    Eisteddfod 235, 255
    Llangollen Railway 235
    Motor Museum and Canal Exhibition 235
    Plas Newydd 235
Llangorse Lake 242–3
Llanthony Priory 227, 241
Llechwedd Slate Caverns 249
Lleyn Peninsula 233
Llyn Idwal 248

Loch Lomond 379
Loch of the Lowes 365
Loch Ness 376
Lochaline 391
Lockton 330
Londmoor Country Park 145
London 8, 10, 12, 64–117
  accommodation 114–117
  airports 44
  Albert Memorial 79
  Big Ben 84
  British Library 73
  British Museum 10, 74–75
  Buckingham Palace 76
  Canary Wharf 73
  Cenotaph 91, 94
  Changing of the Guard 12, 107
  Charles Dickens Museum 73
  Chelsea Physic Garden 77
  Churchill Museum and Cabinet War Rooms 91
  congestion charge 48
  County Hall 77
  Courtauld Institute of Art Gallery 88
  Covent Garden 77
  Cutty Sark 78
  Dalí Universe 77
  Design Museum 77
  Diana, Princess of Wales Memorial Playground 79
  Docklands 73
  Downing Street 91
  entertainment and night life 102–104
  Fenton House 78
  festivals and events 107
  Freud Museum 78
  Globe Theatre 12
  Greenwich 78
  Ham House 81
  Hampstead 78
  Handel House Museum 21
  Harrods 12, 101
  health and beauty 106
  HMS Belfast 79
  Houses of Parliament 6–7, 16–17, 84
  Hyde Park 79
  Imperial War Museum 79
  Inns of Court 79
  Keats House 78
  Kensington 79
  Kensington Palace 79
  Kenwood House 78
  London Aquarium 77
  London Eye 12, 81

London Wetland Centre 105
Madame Tussaud's 81
National Gallery 88
National Maritime Museum 78
National Portrait Gallery 14, 88
Natural History Museum 82–83
Old Bailey 95
Old Royal Naval College 78
Palace of Westminster 84
Primrose Hill 99
public transport 46–47
Regent's Park 98, 105
restaurants 108–113
Richmond 81
Richmond Park 81
riverboats 46
Royal Academy of Arts 85
Royal Botanic Gardens, Kew 81
Royal Hospital Chelsea 77
Royal Observatory 78
Saatchi Gallery 25
St. Martin-in-the-Fields 88
St Pauls Cathedral 10
St. Paul's Cathedral 86
Science Museum 85
Serpentine Gallery 79
Shakespeare's Globe 87
shopping 100–101
Sir John Soane's Museum 85
Smithfield 95
Somerset House 88, 94
South Bank 92–93, 104
sports and activities 104–106
Stardome 81
streetmap 66–70
Tate Britain 88
Tate Modern 10, 89
taxis 60
Tower Bridge 88
Tower of London 10, 90
Trafalgar Square 88
Transport Museum 77
Underground 46, 47, 61, 62, 71
Victoria and Albert Museum 91
walks 92–99
Wallace Collection 91
Westminster Abbey 91, 94
Whitehall 91
ZSL London Zoo 98–99, 106

Long Man of Wilmington 173
Long Mynd 270
Longleat 135
Lost Gardens of Heligan 10, 135
lost property 424
Ludlow 274, 291, 294, 298
Lullingstone Castle 178
Lullingstone Roman Villa 187
Lulworth Cove 136
Lundy Island 135
Lustleigh 130
Lutyens, Sir Edwin 182, 185, 201, 312
Lydford Gorge 137
Lyme Park 274
Lyme Regis 137, 163, 168
Lymington 203
Lyndhurst 192, 202
Lynmouth 132, 153, 168
Lynton 132

M
MacArthur, Ellen 26
Macclesfield Silk Museum 274
Macgregor, Rob Roy 363
Mackintosh, Charles Rennie 373–375
McQueen, Alexander 25
Maes Howe 11, 381
Magna Science Adventure Centre 346
Maiden Castle 130
Malham Cove 321
Mallaig 390–391
Mallyan Spout 330, 332
Malvern Hills 274
Manchester 21, 315, 345, 347, 351, 356
  airport 44
  Imperial War Museum North 315
  the Lowry 17, 315, 345
  Manchester Art Gallery 315
  Metrolink 47
  Museum of Science and Industry in Manchester 315
  Salford Quays 315
  Urbis 315
Manorbier 244
Mar Lodge Estate 361
Martin Mere 312
Marwell Zoological Park 187
Mary, Queen of Scots 32, 271, 334, 339, 370, 377, 385

Matlock Bath 282
Max Gate 130
measurements 419
medical treatment 417, 418
Mellerstain House 377
Melrose 380, 398, 404, 409
Menai Suspension Bridge 226
Middleham 321, 340
Midlands 8, 11, 264–99
  accommodation 296–299
  drive 282–283
  festivals and events 291
  restaurants 292–295
  sights 266–281
  walk 284–285
  what to do 286–290
Milecastle 335
Milford Haven 236, 244
Millennium Seed Bank 23, 197
Milne, A.A. 173
Milton Abbas 137
Mithraic Temple 308
mobile phones 420–421
Moffat 386, 409
monarchy 14, 15, 450–451
money 415–416
  ATMs (cashpoints) 415
  banks and post offices 415, 425
  bureaux de change 415
  concessions 415, 425
  credit cards 415
  euro 415–416
  everyday items and prices 415
  tipping 416
  VAT refunds 416, 429
Monmouth 239
Monmouthshire and Brecon Canal 241
Montgomery 233, 258
Moors Centre 330–331
Morar 390
Moretonhampstead 146
Morris, William 39, 304
Morwenstow 137
Mount Grace Priory 317
Mousa Broch 383
Mouseman Visitor Centre 346
Mr Straw's House 274
Mull, Isle of 378, 409
Mull of Kintyre 377
Mumbles 232
Munros 12, 379
museum opening hours 425
music
  classical 430, 434

contemporary music 435
estivals 159, 211, 255,
   291, 347, 399, 436
pop music 25

N

National Botanic Garden of
   Wales 234
National Cycle Collection
   233
National Gallery 88
National Gallery of Scotland
   367
national holidays 425
National Lottery 17
National Marine Aquarium
   138
National Maritime Museum,
   Cornwall 132
National Maritime Museum,
   London 78
National Media Museum
   304
National Museum of
   Scotland 367
National Portrait Gallery
   14, 88
National Railway Museum
   325
National Slate Museum 233
National Tramway Museum
   283
National Trust 21, 425
National Wallace Monument
   385
National Waterfront
   Museum 238
National Waterways
   Museum 133
National Wetlands Centre
   Wales 234
National Wool Museum 234
The Needles 186
Neidpath Castle 386
Nelson, Lord 86, 88, 91, 177
Nether Stowey 137, 169
New Forest 192, 202–205
New Forest Reptile Centre
   205
New Lanark World Heritage
   Site 380
Newby Hall and Gardens
   312
Newcastle upon Tyne 316,
   345–346, 347, 352,
   356–357
   Baltic Centre for
      Contemporary Art 11, 316
   Bessie Surtees' House 316
   Centre for Life 316

Discovery Museum 316
Great North Museum 316
Laing Art Gallery 316
Metro 47
Newcastleton 334–335
Newport 245, 258
newspapers and
   magazines 426
Newton, Sir Isaac 35
Nine Nicks of Thirlwall
   335, 336
Norfolk Lavender 207
the North 8, 11, 300–357
   accommodation 354–357
   drives 326–327, 330–331,
      334–335, 338–339
   festivals and events 347
   restaurants 348–353
   sights 302–25
   walks 328–9, 332–3,
      336–7, 340–1
   what to do 342–346
North Bovey 130
North York Moors coast 320
North York Moors National
   Park 317, 330–331
North Yorkshire Moors
   Railway 12, 317, 330,
   332, 333
Northumberland National
   Park 317, 334–5
Norwich 192, 208, 215, 220
Nostell Priory 317
Nothe Fort 145
Notting Hill Carnival 12, 436
Nottingham 274, 288–289,
   295, 299

O

Oakwood Park 234
Offa's Dyke Path 254
Old Man of Storr 384
Old Sarum 139
opening times 425
opticians 418
Orford 192
Orford Ness 192
organic farming 20
Orkney Islands 381, 404
Osborne House 186
Oxford 12, 188–91, 208–9,
   211
   accommodation 220
   Ashmolean Museum 190
   Bodleian Library 190
   Christ Church 189–190
   colleges 189, 190
   Modern Art Oxford 191
   Museum of Oxford 191
   Oxford Castle 191

Oxford University 31
Pitt-Rivers Museum 191
Radcliffe Camera 190
restaurants 215
Sheldonian Theatre 190
Oxwich Bay 232
Oxwich Castle 232

P

packing 419
Padarn Country Park 233
Padstow 138, 164, 169
Painswick 138
Painswick Rococo Garden
   138
Pankhurst, Emmeline 40
Paradise Mill 274
Parham House and Gardens
   192
Park, Mungo 387, 388
Parracombe 150
passports and visas 414
Pateley Bridge 338
Peak District Mining
   Museum 282, 283
Peak District National Park
   11, 275, 282–3, 286
Peel Castle 311
Peel, Sir Robert 37
Pembroke 244
Pembroke Castle 35, 234,
   244, 245
Pembrokeshire Coast
   National Park
   236, 244–245
Pendennis Castle 132
Pennard Castle 232
Pennine Way 336
Penrhyn Castle 236
Penshurst Place and Gardens
   194
Pentre Ifan 245
personal security 424
Perth 382, 398, 404,
   409–410
Petworth House and Park
   194
Pevensey Castle 194
Peveril Castle 275, 282
pharmacies (chemists) 417,
   418, 425
Pickering 330, 331, 352
Pilgrim Fathers 34, 138
Pistyll Rhaeadr 236
Pitlochry 382, 398, 404–405,
   410
Pittenweem 365
place names 7
Plas yn Rhiw 233
Plymouth 138, 164

Polesden Lacey 194
police 424
Police and Prison Museum
   318
politics 6–7, 16–17
Polperro 138
Pontcysyllte Aqueduct 235
Poole's Cavern 268
population 18, 20
Port Isaac 139
Port Sunlight 317
Porthmadog 233
Portmeirion 236, 254, 258,
   263
Portsmouth 193, 209, 220
   Explosion! Museum of
      Naval Firepower 193
   Historic Dockyard 193
   HMS Victory 193
   Southsea Castle 193
post offices and postal
   services 415, 421, 425
Postbridge 146
Potter, Beatrix 310–311, 312
Potter Heigham 176
potteries 278, 428
Powderham Castle 139
Powis Castle 237
Preseli Hills 236
Princetown 147
Proms 19
property market 17
public holidays (bank
   holidays) 425
public transport
   child travellers 61
   see also air travel; buses;
      coaches; ferries; taxis;
      train services
pubs and bars 12, 23, 430
   accommodation 445
   food 440
Pwllheli 233, 258

Q

Quarry Bank Mill 275
Queen Elizabeth Forest
   Park 379
Queen Street Mill 318

R

radio 426
Ranworth Broad 176
reading list 427
Reeth 321
restaurants
   dress code 438–439
   menu reader 441
   opening hours 425
   reservations 438

smoking etiquette 439
see also individual
regions
Restormel Castle 139
Rheged 318
Rhinefield Ornamental Drive
192, 202, 204
Rhondda Heritage Park 237
Rhossili Down 232
Richborough Roman Fort 195
Richmond 318, 338, 346
Ridgeway National Trail 209
Rievaulx Abbey 11, 318
Ripon 318–319, 346
Robin Hood's Bay 317, 320
Rockbourne 202
Rockbourne Roman Villa
202, 203
Rollright Stones 194
Roman Army Museum 337
Romney, George 312
Roseberry Topping 317
Rosedale Abbey 331, 357
Rosedale Chimney Bank 331
Rosslyn Chapel 382
Rothiemurchus Estate 362,
395
Rowling, J.K. 25
Royal Botanic Gardens,
Kew 10
royal warrants 15
Rum, Isle of 378
Runswick Bay 320
rural Britain 20–1
Ruskin, John 150, 304, 328
Rydal Mount 312, 326
Rye 195, 211, 220
Ryedale Folk Museum 317,
331

S

St. Albans 195, 215, 220
St. Andrews 382, 398, 405,
410
St. David's 237, 245, 254,
258
St. David's Head 236, 245
St. Fagans National History
Museum 237
St. Ives 140, 158, 164
Barbara Hepworth
Museum and Sculpture
Gallery 140
Tate St. Ives 140
St. Just-in-Roseland 141
St. Mary's Loch 387
St. Mawes Castle 132
St. Michael's Mount 141
St. Monans 365, 405
St. Ninian's Isle 383

Sackville-West, Vita 187, 196
Saffron Walden 174
Salisbury 139, 159, 220
Saltaire 304
Sandringham 195
Sandwich 195
Savill Garden 201
Scafell Pike 327
Scapa Flow 381
Scarborough 319, 346, 357
Scotland 8, 11, 358–410
accommodation 406–410
drives 386–387, 390–391
festivals and events 399
restaurants 400–405
sights 360–385
walks 388–389, 392–393
what to do 394–398
Scott, Sir Walter 273, 282,
361, 366, 379, 387
Scottish Crannog Centre 382
Scottish Fisheries Museum
365
Scottish National Portrait
Gallery 369
The Season 12, 15, 436
Segedunum Roman Fort 308
Segontium 227
self-catering 445
Selkirk 388
Sellafield Visitor Centre 327
Selworthy 132, 151
seniors 415
Seven Sisters 174
Sgwd yr Eira 227
Shakespeare, William 12,
87, 270, 276–277, 291
Sheffield Park Garden 195
Shetland Islands 383, 410
shopping 22, 428–429
British specialities
428–429
consumer rights 429
department stores 429
markets 429
opening hours 425, 429
sales 429
shopping malls and
factory outlets 429
tax-free shopping 429
Shrewsbury 278, 289
Shropshire Hills Discovery
Centre 270
Shugborough Estate 278
Shuttleworth Collection 196
Sidney, Sir Philip 194
Sikhs 19
Simonsbath 151
Sissinghurst Castle Garden
196

Sizergh Castle 319
Skara Brae 381
Skipton 319
Skokholm 237
Skomer 237
Skye, Isle of 384, 405, 410
Slimbridge 141
smoking etiquette 418, 439
Snape Maltings 173, 206
Snibston Discovery Park 278
Snowdon Mountain Railway
233, 237, 248, 249
Snowdonia National Park 10,
237, 248–251
Snowshill Manor 141
society, British 14–15
Solva 245
South East and East Anglia
8, 10, 170–221
accommodation 218–221
drive 202–203
festivals and events 211
restaurants 212–217
sights 172–201
walk 204–205
what to do 206–210
Southampton 196, 209–210
Southsea Castle 193
Southwell 278
Southwold 196, 216, 221
spas and spa towns 12, 106,
155, 210, 282, 287, 289,
290, 310, 319, 343, 398
Speyside 382, 399
sports and activities 22–23,
431–433
angling 431
beaches 431
canoeing and kayaking
207, 225, 253, 398, 432
caving 286
for children 433
climbing 286, 371, 431
coasteering 254
cricket 23, 105, 155, 209,
253, 287, 289, 344, 431,
436
cycling 431–2
football (soccer) 22, 23,
105, 106, 345, 432, 436
golf 105, 159, 253–4, 290,
382, 398, 432
hang-gliding 288
horse racing 156, 206,
253, 290, 342, 344, 347,
432, 436
horseback riding 158,
287, 398, 432
hot-air ballooning 344, 431
ice-skating 288

kitesurfing 207
llama trekking 290
motor cycling 347
motor racing 211, 287,
289, 432
mountain biking 253, 254,
432
polo 208
powerboating 207, 225
quad biking 398
rugby 12, 106, 396, 433
sailing 158, 207, 208,
211, 225, 253, 342, 398,
433
scuba diving 433
skiing 207, 290, 362, 396,
433
surfing and windsurfing
157, 158, 207, 225, 253,
398, 433
tennis 23, 104–5, 433
walking 433
Staffa 378
Staithes 317, 320
Stamford 196, 295, 299
Standen 196–197
Stephenson, George 332
Stirling 385, 405, 410
Stoke-on-Trent 278, 289
Stokesay Castle 270
Stonehenge 143
Stoneleigh Abbey 279
Stourhead 142
Stratford-upon-Avon 11, 12,
276–7, 290, 291
accommodation 299
Anne Hathaway's Cottage
277
Hall's Croft 277
Harvard House 277
Holy Trinity Church 277
Mary Arden's House 277
New Place 277
restaurants 295
Royal Shakespeare
Company 276–7, 290
Shakespeare Countryside
Museum 277
Shakespeare's Birthplace
276
Strathspey Steam Railway
362
The Strid 321
Stromness 381
Strontian 391
Strumble Head 236,
246–247
Studley Royal Water Garden
307
Stump Cross Caverns 339

INDEX BRITAIN

Styal Country Park 275
Sudbury Hall and National
    Trust Museum of
    Childhood 279
suffragettes 40
Sugar Loaf 241
sun safety 417
Sutton Bank 317
Sutton Hoo 197
Swaledale 321
Swallow Falls 248
Swansea 238, 254, 255,
    258–9, 263

T

Talybont-on-Usk 240–241,
    259
Tarbert 377
Tarka Trail 154
Tarr Steps 151
Tatton Park 279
taxis 60
telephones 420–421
television 426
Temple Newsam 313
Tenby 238, 263
Tennyson Down 186
theatre 430, 435
Thirlmere 326
Thirlwall Castle 335, 337
Thomas, Dylan 232, 255
Thorpe Park 207
Thorpe St. Andrew 176
Threave Garden and Estate
    385
Three Peaks 321
ticket agencies and outlets
    435
Tideswell 283
time zones 413
Tintagel Castle 142
Tintern Abbey 239
tipping 416
Tissington 275
Titanic 196
toilets 419
Torosay Castle 378
Torquay 142, 165, 169
Torridon 385, 410
Totnes 142
tourist information 422–423
Townend 319
train services 44, 52–53
    child passengers 61
    concessions 53
    disabilities, visitors with
        62
    Eurostar 44
    steam railways 12, 128,
        129, 130, 182, 225, 233,
        235, 317, 330, 332, 333,
        362, 390, 396, 432
    tickets 52–3
    train information 52, 53
Traquair 385, 386
travel passes 53
Tredegar House 238
Trefriw Woollen Mills 238
Trelissick Garden 144
Trentishoe 150
Tre'r Ceiri 233
Tresco 133, 163, 168
Trossachs National Park 379
Truro 144, 159
Tyntesfield House 21, 144

U

Ullapool 385, 398
Unst 383
Upper Teesdale 319

V

Valley of the Rocks 150
VAT refunds 416, 429
Ventnor 186, 210
Verulamium Museum 195
Victoria, Queen 39, 41, 186,
    279, 361
Vindolanda Fort 308

W

Waddesdon Manor 197
Wade's Causeway 333
Wakehurst Place 23, 197
Wales 8, 10, 222–63
    accommodation 260–263
    drives 240–241, 244–245,
        248–249
    festivals and events 255
    restaurants 256–259
    sights 224–239
    walks 242–243, 246–247,
        250–251
    what to do 252–254
walks
    Caledonian Canal
        392–393
    Cave Dale and the
        Castleton caves 284–5
    Dartmoor National Park
        146–9
    Friar's Crag and
        Castlerigg Stone Circle
        328
    Hadrian's Wall and
        Thirlwall Castle 336–337
    Llangorse Lake 242–243
    London 92–99
    Mallyan Spout and Wade's
        Causeway 332–333
Middleham and Jervaulx
    Abbey 340–341
New Forest 204–205
Selkirk and Ettrck Water
    388–389
Snowdon 250–251
Strumble Head 246–247
Watersmeet and
    Lynmouth 152–153
Wall Roman Site 280
Walltown 336
Warwick 281
Warwick Castle 11, 281
Wast Water 327
Waterfall Country 227
Watersmeet 132, 152–153
Weald and Downland Open
    Air Museum 10, 197
weather reports 412, 413
websites 423
Wegwood, Josiah 36
Wellington, Duke of 37,
    86, 201
Wells 144, 165
Welsh Wildlife Centre 238
Wensleydale 321
Weobley Castle 232
West Burton 339
West Country 8, 10, 118–169
    accommodation 166–169
    drive 150–151
    festivals and events 159
    restaurants 160–165
    sights 120–145
    walks 146–149, 152–153
    what to do 154–159
West Kennet Long Barrow 121
West Linton 386
West Midlands Safari and
    Leisure Park 280
Westbury White Horse 145
Westonbirth Arboretum
    10, 145
Weymouth 145
Wharfedale 321
what to do 428–437
    see also individual regions
whisky 399, 443
Whitby 320, 353, 357
    Captain Cook Memorial
        Museum 320
    Dracula Experience 320
Whitby Abbey 320
Whitesands Bay 236, 245
Widecombe in the Moor 146
Wilberforce, William 311
Winchelsea 195
Winchester 198, 210, 217,
    221
    Hospital of St. Cross 198
King Arthur's Round Table
    198
Winchester Cathedral 198
Winchester College 198
Windermere 321, 353, 357
Windsor 200–201, 217, 221
    Guildhall 201
    Legoland Windsor 210
    Savill Garden 201
Windsor Castle 10, 200–1
Windsor Great park 201
Windy Gyle 317
Winsford 151
Wisley, RHS Garden 199
Woburn Abbey 199
Woburn Safari Park 199
women travellers 424
Wookey Hole Caves 128
Wooltack Point 236
Worcester 280, 290, 295, 299
Wordsworth, William 150,
    239, 310, 312, 326, 387
work permits 414
The Workhouse 278
Workhouse Museum 318
Worms Head 232
Wren, Sir Christopher 78,
    86,
    179, 190, 201, 448
Wroxeter Roman City 278
Wroxham 176
Wye Valley 239

Y

Yarmouth 186
Yarrowford 387
Ynyslas 238
York 12, 322–5, 346, 347
    accommodation 357
    city wall 323–4
    Jorvik Viking Centre
        324–325
    Merchant Taylors' Hall
        324
    Museum Gardens 325
    National Railway
        Museum 325
    restaurants 353
    Richard III Museum 324
    the Shambles 324
York Castle Museum 324
York Minster 323
Yorkshire Museum 325
Yorkshire Dales National
    Park 321, 338–339
Yorkshire Scultpure Park
    321

Z

ZSL Whipsnade Zoo 199

PICTURES

The Automobile Association wishes to thank the following photographers and organisations for their assistance in the preparation of this book.

Abbreviations for the picture credits are as follows –
(t) top;
(b) bottom;
(l) left;
(r) right;
(c) centre;
(dps) double page spread;
(AA) AA World Travel Library

2 AA/Tom Mackie;
3t AA/Wyn Voysey;
3ctr AA/Max Jourdan;
3cbr AA;
3b AA;
4 AA/Jim Carnie;
5 AA/Nick Jenkins;
6 AA/Eric Meacher;
7 AA/Stephen Whitehorne;
8l AA/Linda Whitwam;
8r AA/Anna Mockford and Nick Bonetti;
10 Bruce McGowan/Alamy;
11t AA/Forbes Stephenson;
11b AA/Jon Wyand;
12 AA/Max Jourdan;
13 AA/Max Jourdan;
14 Joanna McCarthy/The Image Bank/Getty Images;
15t Andrew Stuart/AP/PA Photos;
15c Sipa Press/Rex Features;
15b Jonathan Hordle/Rex Features;
16 Tim Graham/Getty Images;
17cl Nicholas Bailey/Rex Features;
17bl NDP/Alamy;
17r AA/Rick Strange;
18 LondonPhotos - Homer Sykes/Alamy;
19t AA/Max Jourdan;
19b Richard Saker/Rex Features;
20 AA/James Tims;
21tr AA/Rick Strange;
21cl AA/Neil Setchfield;
21bl Robert Harding Travel/Photolibrary.com;
22 Adam Davy/Empics Sport/PA Photos;
23r Phil Walter/Empics Sport/PA Photosports Photo Agency;

23cl Sean Dempsey/PA Wire/PA Photos;
23bl AA/Jackie Ranken;
24 AA/Neil Setchfield;
25cl AA/Richard Turpin;
25bl AA/Roger Coulam;
25r AA/Neil Setchfield;
26l Tim Ockenden/PA Archive/PA Photos;
26r Roslin Institute/PA Photos;
27 AA;
28l AA/Tony Souter;
28r British Library Board. All Rights Reserved/The Bridgeman Art Library;
29tl AA/Rupert Tenison;
29cl Mary Evans Picture Library;
29r eye35.com/Alamy;
30l Mary Evans Picture Library;
30r AA/Caroline Jones;
31tr Mary Evans Picture Library/Mary Evans ILN Pictures;
31cl Mary Evans Picture Library;
31bl AA/Steve Day;
32 AA;
33l Mary Evans Picture Library;
33cr AA;
33br AA/Jeff Beazley;
34 Mary Evans Picture Library;
35tr AA;
35cr Science Photo Library;
35bl AA/Rick Strange;
36 AA/Jonathon Welsh;
37tl Mary Evans Picture Library;
37cl Mary Evans Picture Library;
37br AA;
38 AA/John Wood;
39bl Bradford Art Galleries and Museums, West Yorkshire, UK/The Bridgeman Art Library;
39br Illustrated London News;
40 Mary Evans Picture Library 2005;
41l Illustrated London News;
41r Keystone/Getty Images;
42 Stan Kujawa/Alamy;
43 AA/James Tims;
46 AA/James Tims;
50 AA/Caroline Jones;
51 AA/James Tims;
54 AA/Kenya Doran;
56 AA/Wyn Voysey;
57 AA/Jonathan Smith;
58 Digitalvision;
59 AA/Max Jourdan;
60 AA/Max Jourdan;
61 AA/John Miller;
63 AA/Jonathan Smith;
64 Jon Arnold Travel /

Photolibrary.com;
72 AA/James Tims;
73t AA/Neil Setchfield;
73b AA/Richard Turpin;
74 AA/Max Jourdan;
75 AA/Neil Setchfield;
76 AA/Martin Trelawny;
77 AA/Max Jourdan;
78l AA/Neil Setchfield;
78r AA/Simon McBride;
79 AA/Neil Setchfield;
80 AA/Clive Sawyer;
81 AA/Neil Setchfield;
82 AA/Neil Setchfield;
83 AA/Tim Woodcock;
84 AA/Wyn Voysey;
85 AA/James Tims;
86 AA/Rick Strange;
87 AA/Richard Turpin;
89 AA/Max Jourdan;
90 AA/Simon McBride;
91l AA/Neil Setchfield;
91r AA/Neil Setchfield;
92 AA/Max Jourdan;
94 AA/Max Jourdan;
96 Mary Evans Picture Library;
98 AA/Simon McBride;
99 AA/Neil Setchfield;
100 AA/Neil Setchfield;
102 Brand X Pics;
105 Alex Livesey/Getty Images;
106 AA/Neil Setchfield;
107 AA/Simon McBride;
108 AA/Max Jourdan;
111 AA/Neil Setchfield;
112 AA/Neil Setchfield;
114 AA/Wyn Voysey;
117 AA/James Tims;
118 AA/John Wood;
120 AA/Max Jourdan;
121 AA;
122 AA/Caroline Jones;
123 AA/Steve Day;
124 AA/Malcolm Birkitt;
125t AA/Eric Meacher;
125cr AA/Steve Day;
125br AA/Caroline Jones;
126 AA;
127 AA/Steve Day;
128 AA/James Tims;
130l AA/Guy Edwardes;
130r AA/Nigel Hicks;
131 AA/John Wood;
132 AA/Nigel Hicks;
133 AA/Steve Day;
134 AA/Caroline Jones;
135 AA/Richard Ireland;

BRITAIN

ACKNOWLEDGMENTS

136 AA/Max Jourdan;
137l AA/Caroline Jones;
137r AA/Max Jourdan;
138 AA/Roger Moss;
139 AA/James Tims;
140 AA/John Wood;
141 AA/Caroline Jones;
142 AA/John Wood;
143 AA/Steve Day;
144 NTPL/Stephen Robson;
145 AA/Caroline Jones;
146 AA/Guy Edwardes;
147l AA/Peter Baker;
147r AA/Guy Edwardes;
148 AA/Caroline Jones;
149 AA/Nigel Hicks;
150 AA/Caroline Jones;
151 AA/Nigel Hicks;
152 AA/Nigel Hicks;
153 AA/Nigel Hicks;
154 AA/Caroline Jones;
156 AA/Wyn Voysey;
157 AA/Caroline Jones;
158 AA/Rupert Tenison;
160t AA/Andrew Lawson;
160b AA/Neil Setchfield;
162 AA/Caroline Jones;
163 Michael Caines at The Royal Clarence;
165 AA/Nigel Hicks;
166 AA/Caroline Jones;
169 AA/Caroline Jones;
170 AA/Derek Forss;
172 AA/John Miller;
173 AA/John Miller;
174 AA/Wyn Voysey;
175 AA/Wyn Voysey;
176 AA/Tom Mackie;
178 AA/Malcolm Birkitt;
179 AA/Chris Coe;
180l Skyscan Balloon Photography/ English Heritage Photo Library;
180r AA/Martin Trelawny;
182l AA/Wyn Voysey;
182r AA/John Miller;
183 AA/Robert Mort;
184l AA/Michael Busselle;
184r AA/John Miller;
185 AA/Michael Moody;
186 AA/Simon McBride;
187 AA/Derek Forss;
188 AA;
190 AA/Caroline Jones;
192 AA/Richard Ireland;
193 AA/Wyn Voysey;
194 AA/John Miller;
195 NTPL/Andrew Butler;

196 AA/Tom Mackie;
197 Robert Bird/Alamy;
198 AA/Michael Moody;
199 AA/Malcolm Birkitt;
200 AA/Wyn Voysey;
202 AA/Adam Burton;
203l AA/Wyn Voysey;
203r AA/Adam Burton;
204 AA/Tony Souter;
205 AA/Adam Burton;
206 AA/John Miller;
208 AA/Tom Mackie;
209 AA/James Tims;
210 AA/Wyn Voysey;
211 AA/John Miller;
212 AA/John Miller;
215 AA/Richard Ireland;
216 AA/John Miller;
218 AA/Tom Mackie;
221 AA/Wyn Voysey;
222 AA/Stephen Lewis;
224 PulpFoto/Alamy;
225 AA/Caroline Jones;
226 AA/Derek Croucher;
227t AA/Dan Santillo;
227b AA/Pat Aithie;
228 AA/Nick Jenkins;
229 AA/Ian Burgum;
230 AA/Martyn Adelman;
231 AA/Nick Jenkins;
232 AA/Steve Watkins;
233 AA/Stephen Lewis;
234 Simon Burns/WWT National Wetland Centre Wales;
235 AA/Caroline Jones;
236 AA/Roger Coulam;
238 AA;
239 AA/Harry Williams;
240 AA/Dan Santillo;
242 AA/Nick Jenkins;
243l AA/Nick Jenkins;
243r AA/Nick Jenkins;
244 AA/Chris Warren;
246 AA/Nick Jenkins;
247 AA/Nick Jenkins;
248 AA/Stephen Lewis;
250 AA/Stephen Lewis;
251 AA/Stephen Lewis;
252 AA/Chris Warren;
255 AA/Dan Santillo;
256 AA/Dan Santillo;
259 AA/Nick Jenkins;
260 AA/Michael Moody;
263 AA/Michael Moody;
264 AA/Tom Mackie;
266 AA/Van Greaves;
268l AA/Tom Mackie;

268r NTPL/Christopher Hurst;
269 AA/Andy Midgley;
270 AA/Hugh Palmer;
271 NTPL/Andreas von Einsiedel;
272 AA/Mike Haywood;
273 AA/Hugh Palmer;
275 AA/Tom Mackie;
276 AA/Jonathon Welsh;
278 www.britainonview.com;
279 AA;
280 AA/Michael Moody;
281 AA/Van Greaves;
282 AA/Tom Mackie;
284 AA/Malcolm Birkitt;
285 AA/Malcolm Birkitt;
286 AA/Tom Mackie;
289 AA/Andy Midgley;
290 AA/Hugh Palmer;
291 AA/A J Hopkins;
292 AA/Andy Midgley;
293 ImageState;
294 AA/Caroline Jones;
296 AA/Tom Mackie;
297 AA/Andy Midgley;
298 AA/Michael Moody;
299 AA/Michael Moody;
300 AA/Steve Gregory;
302 britainonview/Lee Beel;
303 AA/Jeff Beazley;
305 AA/Jeff Beazley;
307 AA/David Tarn;
308 AA/Jeff Beazley;
309 Darryl Gill/Alamy;
310 AA/Roger Coulam;
313 AA/Steve Day;
314 AA/Steve Day;
315 FAN travelstock/Alamy;
316 AA/Roger Coulam;
318 English Heritage Photo Library;
320 AA/Mike Kipling;
321 AA/Anna Mockford and Nick Bonetti;
322 AA;
324tl AA/Pete Bennett;
324tr AA/Pete Bennett;
324b AA/Pete Bennett;
326 AA/Anna Mockford and Nick Bonetti;
328 AA/Tom Mackie;
330 AA/Mike Kipling;
332 AA/Steve Gregory;
334 AA/Roger Coulam;
336 AA/Cameron Lees;
338 AA/Tom Mackie;
340 AA/David Tarn;
341 AA/Linda Whitwam;
342 AA/Jon Sparks;

484

347 Digitalvision;
348 AA/Roger Coulam;
350 AA/Terry Marsh;
353 AA/Mike Kipling;
354 AA/Anna Mockford and
Nick Bonetti;
358 AA/Sue Anderson;
360 P Tomkins/VisitScotland/
Scottish Viewpoint;
362 AA/Mark Hamblin;
364l AA/Jonathan Smith;
364r AA/Sue Anderson;
365 AA/Jonathan Smith;
366 AA;
367 AA/Jonathan Smith;
368 AA/Ken Paterson;
369 AA/Ken Paterson;
370 AA/Jim Henderson;
371 AA/Jim Henderson;
372 AA/Stephen Whitehorne;
373t AA/Stephen Whitehorne;
373b AA/Stephen Whitehorne;
374 AA/Stephen Whitehorne;
375t Clyde Maritime Trust;
375b AA;
376 AA/Stephen Whitehorne;
377 AA/Sue Anderson;
378 AA/Stephen Whitehorne;
379 AA/David W Robertson;
380l AA/Stephen Gibson;
380r AA/Sue Anderson;
381 AA/Stephen Whitehorne;
382 AA/Richard Elliot;
383 Imagebroker/Alamy;
384t AA/Stephen Whitehorne;
384b AA/Ronnie Weir;
385 AA/Stephen Whitehorne;
386 AA/Cameron Lees;
387 AA/Harry Williams;
388 AA/Cameron Lees;
389l AA/Cameron Lees;
389r AA/Cameron Lees;
390 AA/Steve Day;
391 AA/Sue Anderson;
392 AA/Stephen Whitehorne;
393 AA/Stephen Whitehorne;
394 AA/Ken Paterson;
396 AA;
399 AA/Jim Carnie;
400 AA/Eric Ellington;
402 AA/Sue Anderson;
404 Imagestate;
406 AA;
407 Edinburgh Inspiring Capital
www.edinburgh-inspiringcapital.
com;
410 AA/Jonathan Smith;

411 AA/Max Jourdan;
416 AA/Anna Mockford and
Nick Bonetti;
418 AA/James Tims;
419 AA/Simon McBride;
420 AA/Max Jourdan;
428 AA/Rick Strange;
429 AA/Paul Kenward;
430 Digitalvision;
431 AA/Jon Sparks;
432 AA/Michael Moody;
433 AA/Nigel Hicks;
434 AA/Caroline Jones;
435 AA;
437 AA/Wyn Voysey;
438 AA/Clive Sawyer;
439 AA/Clive Sawyer;
440 AA/Sarah Montgomery;
441 AA/Neil Setchfield;
442 AA/John Freeman;
443 AA/Jonathan Smith;
444 AA/Peter Baker;
446 AA/Jeff Beazley;
447 AA/Derek Forss;
448 AA/Caroline Jones;
449l AA/Max Jourdan;
449r AA/Rick Strange;
450t AA;
451tl AA/James Tims;
451tr AA;
451bl AA;
451br AA;
455 David W Robertson.

Every effort has been made to
trace the copyright holders, and
we apologise in advance for any
unintentional omissions or errors.
We would be pleased to apply any
corrections in any following edition
of this publication.

CREDITS

Managing editor
Sheila Hawkins

Design
Drew Jones, pentacorbig, Nick Otway

Cover design
Chie Ushio

Picture research
Alice Earle

Image retouching and repro
Mike Moody

Mapping
Maps produced by the Mapping Services
Department of AA Publishing

Main contributors
Chris Bagshaw, Judith Bamber, Oliver Bennett,
Colin Follett, Mike Gerrard, Tim Locke, Penny Phenix,
Jackie Staddon, Hilary Weston, Jenny White,
Nia Williams, David Winpenny

Updater
Chris Bagshaw, Penny Phenix

Indexer
Marie Lorimer

Production
Karen Gibson, Lyn Kirby

See It Britain
ISBN 978-1-4000-0770-7
Third Edition

Color separation by Keenes, Andover, UK
Printed and bound by Leo Paper Products, China
10 9 8 7 6 5 4 3 2 1

A03307

This product includes mapping data licensed from Ordnance Survey® with the permission of the Controller of Her Majesty's Stationery Office. © Crown copyright 2008.
All rights reserved. Licence number 100021153.
Traffic signs © Crown copyright. Reproduced with the permission of the Controller of Her Majesty's Stationery Office.
Weather chart statistics © Copyright 2004 Canty and Associates, LLC.

Dear Traveler,

From buying a plane ticket to booking a
room and seeing the sights, a trip goes much
more smoothly when you have a good travel
guide. Dozens of writers, editors, designers,
and cartographers have worked hard to
make the book you hold in your hands a
good one. Was it everything you expected?
Were our descriptions accurate? Were our
recommendations on target? And did you find
our tips and practical advice helpful? Your
ideas and experiences matter to us. If we have
missed or misstated something, we'd love
to hear about it. Fill out our survey at www.
fodors.com/books/feedback/, or e-mail us at
seeit@fodors.com. Or you can snail mail to the
See It Editor at Fodor's, 1745 Broadway, New
York, New York 10019. We'll look forward to
hearing from you.

Tim Jarrell
Publisher